1249 Eighth Street, Berkeley, California 94710
An Imprint of Peachpit, A Division of Pearson Education

Inside 3ds max 7

Copyright © 2005 by New Riders Publishing

New Riders
1249 Eighth Street
Berkeley, CA 94710
510/524-2178
800/283-9444
510/524-2221 (fax)

Find us on the World Wide Web at: www.peachpit.com
To report errors, please send a note to errata@peachpit.com

Peachpit Press is a division of Pearson Education

Project Editor
Cheryl England

Development Editor
Steve Anzovin

Production Editor
Becky Winter

Copyeditor
Janet Podell

Tech Editor
Jon McFarland

Media Editor
Eric Geoffroy

Compositor
*Happenstance
Type-O-Rama*

Indexer
Rebecca Plunkett

Cover design
Aren Howell

Cover Illustrators
*Sami Sorjonen
Sean Bonney
Sean Feely*

Notice of Rights

Notice of Liability

Trademarks

ISBN 0-7357-1387-1

9 8 7 6 5 4 3 2 1

Printed and bound in the United States of America

Contents at a Glance

Table of Contents

To: _____ CW37 BARUW_____

From: Book Bug Books
8899 Paseo de Valencia Street
Fort Myers, FL 33908

Re: _____ INSIDE 3ds MxT_____

Total: $30.72

Thank you for your purchase! Now that you have received your order, please look it over to make sure you are happy with your order. If you are satisfied, we would appreciate it if you would take a moment to go on Amazon and rate our service. If you are not satisfied, please contact me first so that I can assist you further.

To leave feedback: http://www.amazon.com/feedback

Thank you for allowing us to do business with you….we hope you enjoy your purchase.

Sincerely,
Book Bug Books

864-884-4534

Part VIII   Rendering and Compositing

19   Rendering Basics   795

20   Advanced Rendering   839

About the Authors

Doug Barnard has been using and writing about 3ds max since the days of 3D Studio DOS. Currently, he uses the software to freelance in the field of architectural visualization and set design, and to further his dreams of land development and furniture design. He lives in Key West, Florida with his wife and ill-tempered cat, where he also teaches aikido.

Jon A. Bell is a writer, 3D artist, and software consultant. After working 10 years as an editor and writer in the computer magazine industry, Jon changed careers in 1991 to concentrate on the computer graphics industry, and has produced CGI for television, films, computer games, multimedia, and print. His hobbies include 3D computer graphics, scuba diving, hiking, and travel to exotic places. Jon and his wife Joan love to travel around the world and are the parents of the world's most spoiled cat, Greystone.

Sean Bonney (www.anvil-studio.com) is a 3D artist with a BFA in Illustration and Design from Virginia Commonwealth University. He has worked as lead designer for a top-rated regional library system, as freelance designer for several game development studios, and contributed to three previous New Riders titles: *3D Studio Max 4 Magic*, *3D Studio Max 3 Magic*, and *3D Studio Max 3 Professional Animation*. Sean lives in historic Fredericksburg, VA, with his beautiful librarian wife and three kinetic sons.

Mark Gerhard was hired in 1990 to test the original 3D Studio release 1 and train dealers, educators, and students in 3D modeling and animation. Mark served as lead technical writer at discreet for the 3ds max tutorials. He has also been an instructor of computer graphics since the late 1980s and currently teaches 3D animation at Santa Rosa Junior College in Petaluma, CA. Mark also acknowledges **David Duberman** and **Michael McCarthy**, who wrote sections of Chapter 15. David, a technical writer specializing in 3D graphics, wrote the Motion Mixer and Crowd sections; Mike, a fine artist and computer animator, wrote about Physique, Biped Animation, and Motion Capture.

Ryan Greene began his 3D career as an artist for various video/television productions studios. He then moved on to work in game development at Microsoft Game Studios. Ryan now works for Valkyrie Entertainment (www.valent.us) doing third party game development as well as video and game cinematics. He is a certified 3ds max instructor. When he is not working, he trains in Filipino martial arts, spends time with his wife Stephenie, and enjoys the fine pubs of Seattle, WA.

A.J. Jefferies (www.moonjam.com) has been modeling 3D characters and creations since he was 14. A 3ds max user for the last 5 years, he currently works in the UK for Digital Progression, creating high resolution artwork for videogames and advertising.

Daniel Manahan (www.danielmanahan.com) is a vegetarian, professor, artist, musician, singer, dancer, athlete, master of Chess and Go, father, and husband. He started working with 3ds over ten years ago. Currently Daniel offers extremely low-cost training in 3ds max at AFOC, Los Angeles, and Rio Hondo College, Whittier, CA. Nothing makes Daniel happier than seeing the success of his students pay off with a career at the end of their long journey.

Jon McFarland manages the design department for a national owner, manager and developer of retail, office and residential properties, where he spends much of the day creating mock-ups of potential facilities. He also teaches 3ds max at the Virginia Marti College of Art and Design, a small, accredited art school in Lakewood, OH. Jon lives outside of Cleveland with his wife Lucy and two sons, Zach and Jacob.

Sergio Muciño has been using discreet products since the release of 3D Studio DOS R4. He began his career as an animator at Tecnología Gráfica Industrial, doing TV commercials, documentaries, and educational animation for clients including Kimberly-Clark, Pepsico, Sictel, Atrax Producciones, and Mercurio. Currently, he works at Digital Dimension as a Technical Director. Sergio teaches 3D at the Instituto Tecnologico y de Estudios Superiores de Monterrey and at other institutes and training centers. Aside from being an animator, he's also a professional musician.

Erin Nicholson, a 3D artist for seven years, has been involved in numerous animation productions, usually for broadcast and feature films. Erin is currently the modeling supervisor at Elliott Animation in Toronto, Ontario, where he recently oversaw the creation of characters for an upcoming feature.

Jon Seagull is a 3D artist and animator specializing in architectural illustration. His images have appeared in billboards, newspapers, magazines, books, television, and feature films. He is currently a freelance artist, and enjoys working on diverse projects with firms of every size. In addition, Jon has taught 3ds max at Parsons School of Design in New York since 2000, and provides private 3ds max training services as a discreet Certified Instructor. He is treasurer of the New York Society of Renderers, a professional organization for architectural illustrators. Jon lives in New York City with his wife Debbie.

Steve Anzovin and **Janet Podell**, the development editor and copyeditor for *Inside 3ds max 7,* own a book editing and packaging company in Amherst, MA. Steve, the author of eight books on computing and computer graphics, co-founded Anzovin Studio (www.anzovin.com) in 2000 to provide action-oriented CG character animation for films, TV, and games. Janet is the co-writer and editor of many books on U.S. and world history, including *Famous First Facts in American Politics* and *Speeches of the American Presidents, 2nd Edition.* Steve and Janet live in Amherst with their three children and two unruly German Shepherds.

Acknowledgments

For their insight and advice, I'd like to thank Allan McKay and Frederick Speers; for their patience and dedication, my co-authors; for his generosity, Sami Sorjonen; and for her professionalism and support, Cheryl England. For his help in keeping the project moving and well-coordinated, I'd also like to thank Steve Anzovin. The copyeditors, tech editors, and the production team at New Riders were also tremendously helpful in pulling this project together and creating a truly high-quality book.

And most of all, to my three sons—Jack, Cable, and Quinn, without whose exciting presence in my life this book would have been released on time.

About the Cover

The humanoid model was modeled by Sami Sorjonen (s-s@sci.fi, www.cgmill.com/ss) using 3ds max 7 and ZBrush. Sami textured the figure using a Shadow/Light Falloff material. The model was blended into the lava, particles added, and rendered by Sean Bonney. Sean Feely provided the background vines.

This Book Is Safari Enabled

The Safari® Enabled icon on the cover of your favorite technology book means the book is available through Safari Bookshelf. When you buy this book, you get free access to the online edition for 45 days.

Safari Bookshelf is an electronic reference library that lets you easily search thousands of technical books, find code samples, download chapters, and access technical information whenever and wherever you need it.

To gain 45-day Safari Enabled access to this book:

- Go to http://www.peachpit.com/safarienabled
- Complete the brief registration form
- Enter the coupon code PMCQ-L04D-KX0N-CJDE-4HY6

If you have difficulty registering on Safari Bookshelf or accessing the online edition, please e-mail customer-service@safaribooksonline.com.

Introduction

Welcome, fellow artists, to the latest installment of the Inside series. Our goal in writing *Inside 3ds max 7* is to take you beyond the shipping tutorials, to show you how to take advantage of each tool's strengths (while avoiding any weaknesses), and to bring you up to speed on the latest tricks, tips, and battle-tested techniques in use by CG artists today. We assume that you have some familiarity with 3ds max; this is not a beginner's book. An effort has been made, however, to present tutorials clearly and completely, so if you are learning about a new tool, only an occasional side trip to the online help docs may be necessary.

This book does not follow a single production process throughout; our artists have each been given the freedom to choose the very best exercises to illuminate their subject matter. You will find a wide variety of subject matter, from architecture to volcanoes, from alien invasions to splashing dolphins. This menagerie of subject matter is used here to demonstrate workflows familiar to many in CG filmmaking and game development. Our intent is to provide techniques that can be of use no matter what your job is—an exercise on blasting an airplane with a lightning bolt could just as easily show you how to make your giant spider target it's lunch. Our aim is to teach you what 3ds max is capable of; how to apply those lessons is up to you.

The latest version of 3ds max continues the expansion of max as a serious game development tool. max has long been a favorite tool of game artists, and in adding tools specifically targeting game development, as well as making game-friendly enhancements to existing tools, discreet has made clear their intentions to maintain their domination as the 3D tool of choice for game developers. In this book, actual production game artists have shared their most successful workflow techniques and shortcuts to give help make 3ds max an even more essential tool for game development.

The visual sophistication of games have improved by enormous bounds during the past few years, narrowing the visual gap between are created for games as opposed to broadcast. Even 3D models intended for real-time deformation, such as characters, are beginning to rival the complexity and texture depth of their pre-rendered counterparts. This allows us to present detailed analyses of the most powerful and useful 3ds max tools, in a manner that will be useful for both disciplines. In cases where the uses of max for film or broadcast are distinct from game creation, we have treated these two branches of CG art separately, so that hopefully this book will be useful for artists interested in real-time graphics, pre-rendered animation, or both.

I have been a user of 3ds max since Release 1, and have gotten excited with each new version of max, and the production improvements and incredible new features introduced each time. The last few releases have seen some amazing advances in sophisticated particle systems, powerful modeling, custom scripting tools, lighting and rendering, character rigging and even the inclusion of Character Studio. In this book, our talented artists examine these powerful features and more, taking you inside their processes as professional CG artists.

Enough introduction—the first tutorial awaits!

—*Sean Bonney*

NOTE:

Just as this book went to press, Autodesk, the parent company of discreet, has announced a name change for both discreet and 3ds max 7. Discreet's new name is Autodesk Media and Entertainment. 3ds max 7's new name is Autodesk 3ds Max® 7.

Part I

What's New

Chapter 1

What's New in the Interface and Tools

By Daniel Manahan

The interface in 3ds max 7 can be compared to everything you see in front of you when you're driving a car. Think of the 3ds max cursor as your steering wheel and the viewports as your windshield. So adjust your seat, fasten your seatbelt, and let's take a spin through the changes to the 3ds max 7 interface.

Later on this chapter, we'll turn from max 7's interface improvements and take a look at the new tools that will speed your workflow. There are some significant new features that you won't want to miss.

Interface: Same Overall Look

If you've used an earlier version of 3ds max, you'll be happy to know that you will not have to learn a new set of interface functions and keyboard shortcuts for 3ds max 7. The interface for 3ds max 7 provides the same basic layout and functionality as 3ds max 4, 5, and 6. There are only two visible changes: The home grid has been cleaned up and some minor items have been added to the menus. These additions make it easier for you to access common functions. The interface has become slightly more intuitive and some functions are more available in the menus and quads. The overall look, however, is the same.

The home grid now appears in a lighter, less prominent color. It is now slightly harder to see, but it is less distracting and less likely to interfere with your viewport when you are modeling.

Flat Shaded Mode

3ds max 7 does not accurately render the true effects and complicated calculations of lighting in a scene within the viewport. This is a deliberate performance tradeoff so that the viewport can maintain fast screen redraw. Therefore, shading and textures that display in the viewport may be over-lit or under-lit, with inaccurate highlights and shadows that make it harder to visualize and work with a scene (**Figure 1.1**). The problem can be particularly severe when modeling a glossy object, and sub-object level selections can be difficult to see. As the view is rotated, the highlight from this glossiness can cause distracting light and dark shifts on the polygons.

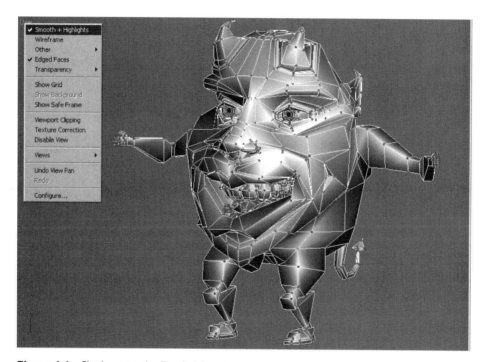

Figure 1.1   Shadows on the Deviled Egg character.

3ds max 7's new Flat Shaded mode addresses this problem, making it easier to view objects when lighting is too light or dark (**Figure 1.2**).

In Flat Shaded mode, you are viewing geometry as though on an overcast day. The lighting is even all around, with no distracting contrast, and you can see surface maps more easily. An evenly lit viewport makes it easier for you to perform such standard modeling operations as aligning geometry, moving vertices, and manipulating a camera. Likewise,

Flat Shaded mode aids precise positioning when walking a camera through a scene that has bitmaps on the walls; if the walls are too dark from the shading mode, it can be difficult to judge where the camera is located.

To access the Flat Shaded mode, right-click on the top left corner of the viewport, and choose it from within the Other submenu. It is easy to turn on and off, so that you can opt to use it only when working with geometry that needs flat shading. Unfortunately, there is no keyboard shortcut for this control. As with the other shaded modes, actual rendering is not affected by this choice.

Tip

When modeling in sub-object levels with Flat Shaded mode on, you should activate the toggle for Edged Faces.

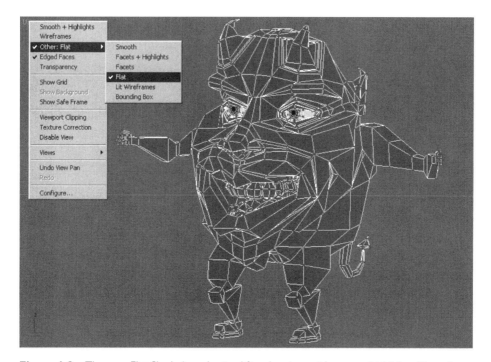

Figure 1.2   The new Flat Shaded mode simplifies the view, without any highlights. Note that the deviled egg character has no shadows.

Walkthrough Mode

Controlling the viewport is probably one of the most common and repetitive tasks in 3ds max. The processes of navigating a camera through a scene have been simplified with a Camera or Perspective view in walkthrough mode.

Using Walkthrough mode is much like traveling through many video games. It allows you to use keyboard shortcuts in combination with the mouse to fly through scenes in real time. The quickest way to access Walkthrough mode is to press the Up arrow while the Perspective or Camera viewport is active. Alternatively, go to the viewport controls, click the Pan View or Truck Camera button, and choose Walkthrough mode from the fly-out menu.

Here's a quick list of the Walkthrough mode controls:

- To travel forward, hold down either the W key or the Up arrow.

- To travel backward, hold down either the S key or the Down arrow.

- To travel left, hold down the A key or the Left arrow.

- To travel right, hold down the D key or the Right arrow.

- To travel up, hold down the E key or hold down Shift plus the Up arrow key.

- To travel down, hold down the C key or hold down Shift plus the Down arrow key.

- Holding down both the Up and Left arrow keys while dragging with the mouse in Walkthrough mode moves you both forward and to the left. The same will happen if you hold down the A and W keys. You can move along other diagonal vectors by holding down the appropriate combinations of keys.

- The spacebar toggles between two different modes: the Camera constrained to looking left and right only, or unconstrained and able to freely look all around. The spacebar only works with mouse movement, not key constraints, and does not affect vertical movement using the keys.

- To change the acceleration for Walkthrough mode, use the [key (left square bracket) to go slower and the] key (right square bracket) to go faster. Hold these keys down or press them repeatedly to effectively adjust acceleration. Pressing the Q key will toggle between a fast mode and a normal mode, and pressing the Z key will toggle between a slow mode and a normal mode.

There are a few idiosyncrasies to be aware of when navigating in Walkthrough mode with a camera that has its Orthographic Projection option checked. Traveling forward and backward will appear to have no effect. And objects that are close to the camera will appear to be the same size as the same object further away. This is because an orthographic view has no perspective. In fact, the Camera is still physically moving forward or backward through the scene.

Note

Unfortunately, Walkthrough mode will not work with any of the Light viewports, even though a Light viewport is similar to the Perspective and Camera views.

Taking a Walk with Walkthrough

You should practice working with the Walkthrough mode commands before using them on your scene files. Also, while Walkthrough mode is active, all actions will be recorded for one undo. So if you make several movements, then choose Undo, all of the movements will be undone instead of just one.

Note

If you drag the cursor up or down but the camera only pans to the right or left, it means that the Walkthrough mode is locked from any vertical rotation. You can toggle this restriction off and on by hitting the Space bar.

Let's practice using Walkthrough mode in the following prepared scene:

1. Open the file entitled Walkthrough mode start.max from the DVD (**Figure 1.3**).

2. Select the camera, activate, and maximize the Camera viewport. Use the Select By Name dialog if the camera accidentally becomes deselected.

3. Turn Auto Key to On, and change to frame 20.

4. Activate the Walkthrough mode button by pressing the Up arrow. You may need to drag on the Truck Camera button flyout to access this feature.

5. Within the Camera viewport, drag the mouse until the triangle is in the middle of the viewport (**Figure 1.4**). You may need to toggle the spacebar to allow vertical movement.

   Keys will be produced on frames 0 and 20, but you're not done. The camera needs to travel forward in the next step to its destination. This process will be repeated for each sequence.

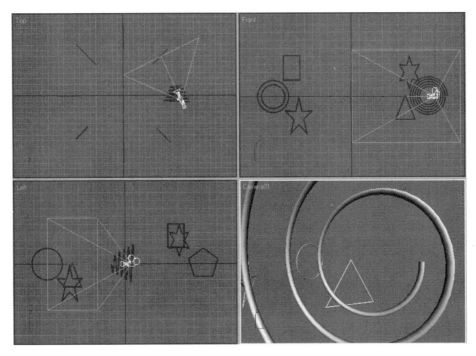

Figure 1.3 The Walkthrough scene opens with many objects to travel through.

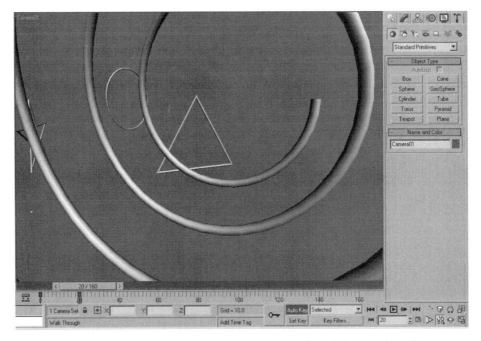

Figure 1.4 Walkthrough mode is activated when the Walkthrough button, Auto Key, is on, the Time Slider is on frame 20, and the camera is looking at the Triangle shape.

6. Hold down the W or Up arrow key to travel forward until the triangle is covering the entire camera view (**Figure 1.5**). Holding the S or Down arrow key will move the camera backward. Dragging the cursor will also help adjust the view.

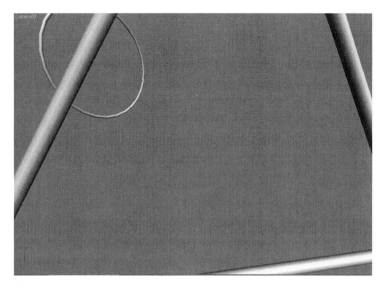

Figure 1.5   We are approaching the triangle and ready to go through.

7. Change to frame 40. Drag the cursor until the circle is in the middle of the camera view (**Figure 1.6**).

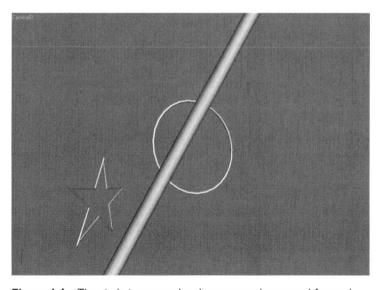

Figure 1.6   The circle is centered and we are ready to travel forward.

8. Travel forward until the circle is covering the entire camera view (**Figure 1.7**).

Figure 1.7   The Time Slider is at frame 40, a key is generated, and we are ready to go through the circle.

For each following step, we'll continue to repeat this process of first centering the destination in the Camera viewport and then traveling forward until we reach the new location. In each sequence, this process is performed after the Time Slider is changed every 20 frames.

9. Use the Next Key button to step through each key until you get to frame 60. You will see the star filling the Camera viewport. Drag the cursor until the star is in the center of the Camera viewport. Use the techniques you learned in the previous steps to continue on.

10. At frame 80, walk through to the donut.

11. At frame 100, walk through to the square.

12. At frame 120, walk through to the five-sided NGon.

13. At frame 140, walk through to the six-pointed star.

14. And finally, go to frame 160, and walk through to the helix.

15. Play the animation. The camera should accurately walk through each shape.

Tweaking the Walkthrough

Let's assume that you made a few positional mistakes when walking through some of the destinations and that you also made errors in setting the animation keys on those frames. If the camera failed to accurately go through some of the shapes, you can go to those keyframes and, using the Walkthrough tools, make the appropriate changes. Here's how:

1. Activate the Key Mode toggle when editing keyframes, to make changing the Time Slider to the keyframes easier, and perform the necessary adjustments to the camera. The Key Mode toggle is within the viewport controls on the bottom right of the interface, and to the left of the frame number.

2. With Auto Key still active, also activate the Key Mode Toggle button and use the Next Key button to step through each key until you get to frame 60. You will see the star filling the camera view. Drag the cursor until the star is in the center of the camera view.

3. Make similar adjustments to the keyframes as needed, and make sure that the shapes on those frames are centered.

4. Turn the Auto Key off and deactivate the Walkthrough mode when you've completed your changes, so that no animation will be accidentally created.

Toggling Dialogs and Editors

A new feature of 3ds max 7 is the ability to close some of the dialogs and editors using keyboard shortcuts—the same shortcuts that open them. For example, in previous versions of 3ds max, you've been able to open the Material Editor by pressing the M key. Now you can also close the Material Editor by pressing the M key.

Here's a complete list of dialogs and editors that now close with the same keyboard shortcuts that are used to open them:

- ActiveShade Floater
- Asset Browser
- Bone Tools
- Channel Info Editor
- Clone and Align Tool
- Display Floater
- Environment and Effects dialog (keyboard shortcut 8)
- Grid and Snap Settings dialog

- Layer Manager
- Light Lister
- Material Editor (keyboard shortcut M)
- Material/Map Browser
- MAXScript Listener (keyboard shortcut F11)
- mental ray Messages Window
- Parameter Collector (keyboard shortcut Alt-2)
- Parameter Editor (keyboard shortcut Alt-1)
- RAM Player
- Rename Objects
- Render Scene dialog (keyboard shortcut F10)
- Render To Texture (keyboard shortcut 0)
- Rigid Body Property Editor
- Selection Floater
- Spacing Tool (keyboard shortcut Shift I)
- Transform Type-In (keyboard shortcut F12)
- Video Post

 Tip

If a keyboard shortcut is not used to open a dialog, or you can't remember the keyboard shortcut, pressing Control-~ (tilde) should close these as well.

New Toolbar Items

The Main toolbar has a couple of new items: Paint Selection Region and Render Shortcuts (**Figure 1.8**).

Press Q multiple times to watch 3ds max 7 cycle through the Region Selection options: Rectangular Selection Region, Circular Selection Region, Fence Selection Region, Lasso Selection Region, and the new Paint Selection Region. The Paint Selection Region allows you to make a selection by dragging the mouse over an area, instead of by creating a marquee window.

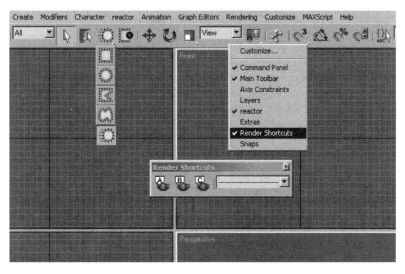

Figure 1.8   Paint Selection Region and Render Shortcuts are new to the Main toolbar.

Render Shortcuts are presets that make it easier and more convenient to change multiple settings in the Render Scene dialog. They can also define how you want the Quick Render to respond. Define a few Render Shortcut settings and Quick Render will automatically use those settings. Render Shortcuts are accessed by right-clicking in any gray portion of the Main toolbar and choosing Render Shortcuts from the menu.

Here are a few other new toolbar items:

- The Snaps Use Axis Constraints toggle in the Axis Constraints toolbar
- The Clone and Align tool in the Extras toolbar
- The Snaps toolbar

Menu Changes

A number of changes and additions have been made to the 3ds max 7 menus. Some menu items are now more logically placed; others have been renamed; a few are brand new. There's nothing revolutionary here, but the new and revised menu items will certainly speed and streamline your workflow.

File Menu

3ds max 7 now includes a File Link Manager utility, which ensures that drawings (.dwg files) created in AutoCAD, Mechanical Desktop, and Architectural Desktop will be updated in 3ds max 7 when they are modified in the original program. Access the File Link Manager from the File menu.

Note

> You must install the appropriate Object Enablers (available from the Autodesk web-site) for the Autodesk products mentioned above to see the objects in the .dwg files after they've been linked.

Tools Menu

Also new are the Quick Align and the Clone and Align tools. Both of these new features are used to accurately place objects in the scene and are accessed from the Tools menu. Shift A is the keyboard shortcut for Quick Align. The Clone and Align tool has an extra function that creates a copy of the source object in multiple target locations.

Views Menu

Object Display Culling has been added to the Views menu and its keyboard shortcut is Alt-O. Its settings can be adjusted from the Utilities panel. Use Object Display Culling to make the viewport display large scenes faster. Distant objects will be hidden or displayed as a bounding box. You define how fast the viewport will respond, and Object Display Culling decides how many objects will be culled in order to achieve the desired speed. Object Display Culling does not have any effect on a single object that contains a lot of polygons.

Animation Menu

Parameter Editor, Parameter Collector, Reaction Manager, and Delete Selected Animation have been added to the Animation menu. The Parameter Editor is not a new feature; it used to be called Add Custom Attribute, and Alt-1 is its keyboard shortcut. The Parameter Collector is used to combine useful parameters into a single interface to be animated, and Alt-2 is its keyboard shortcut. The Reaction Manager manages the Reaction Controller features and is used to allow one object to control the animation of other objects. Delete Selected Animation will delete all animation keys of a selected object.

Help Menu

License Borrowing has been added to the Help menu. It is only available in 3ds max 7 network installations and its submenu will be grayed out for stand-alone installs. License Borrowing makes it much easier to manage a pool of authorized copies of 3ds max 7 on a network when those copies also need to be available for borrowing by computers not on the network. You can now borrow a license from the pool to put on your laptop for offline work, such as a business presentation or telecommuting arrangement. Then, when you're done, you simply return the license to the network pool. Normally, you would need to purchase an extra copy of 3ds max for that laptop, so License Borrowing is definitely a money-saver.

The Quads: Right-Click Menus

Right-clicking brings up one of the Quad menus; these menus are used to quickly access functions that would normally be buried within the interface. By holding down combinations of Control, Shift, and Alt, right-clicking will bring up additional Quad menus.

Select and Dope Sheet have been added to the standard Quad menu.

In the Alt-right-click Quad menu, the new Reaction Manager and Delete Selected Animation have been added. Delete Selected Animation will remove all the animation keys assigned to the selected objects. Dope Sheet provides another way of editing animation keys that lets you see all of the animation ranges of multiple objects and how they relate.

In the Shift-right-click Quad menu, 3ds max 7 adds the Grid and Snap Settings and the following Snap toggles: Grid Points, Pivot, Vertex, Midpoint, Edge/Segment, and Face.

Tools: Workflow Timesavers

Time is the one thing we can never make more of, but we sure can waste what we already have. Any time a 3D program saves us time and speeds our work, it's cause for gratitude, because all too often, 3D workflows (the processes of getting a job done or achieving a particular effect) force you to take many more steps than you really should need.

Luckily, 3ds max 7 has added some small but significant improvements in workflow that will give you back a measure of your precious time. These include:

- Paint Selection Region
- Object Display Culling
- Array Preview
- Quick Align
- Clone and Align Tool
- Snaps Improvements

Paint Selection Region

Paint Selection Region is a new method for selection similar to the Lasso Selection Region method. Instead of clicking in or creating a marquee window around objects to make a selection, the mouse is dragged (maybe *stroked* is a better word) over the objects, as if painting with a brush. This is a good tool to use when you want to select an irregular but well-defined area.

As with the other selection methods, the Alt key is used to subtract from the selection and the Control key to add to it. The default size for the Paint Selection Region brush is 20; that can be changed from the General tab within the Preferences Settings dialog. There is a way to interactively increase or decrease the size of the brush tool, but we need to customize a keyboard shortcut for Paint Selection Size Down and Paint Selection Size Up actions from the Customize User Interface dialog.

Working with Paint Selection Region

We'll start by making our own keyboard shortcuts to make the Paint Selection Region brush larger and smaller, and then do some experimenting with how to use this new feature.

1. From the Customize menu, choose Customize User Interface.

2. Within the Action list, scroll down to highlight Paint Selection Size Down.

3. Place the cursor in the Hotkey box, press both the Shift and the minus key on the keyboard, and click the Assign button. In the Action list, to the right of Paint Selection Region, the combination Shift– (Shift together with the minus sign) is listed as the keyboard shortcut (**Figure 1.9**).

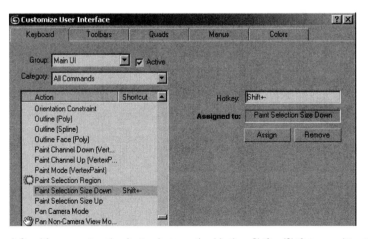

Figure 1.9   After pressing the Assign button, the Hotkey Shift– (Shift in combination with the minus sign) is assigned to Paint Selection Size Down.

4. Repeat the previous steps to assign Shift= (Shift together with the equal sign) to the Paint Selection Size Up action.

To better understand Paint Selection Region, let's try the following:

1. Open the scene entitled Paint Selection Region start.max. Switch from the Top viewport to the Perspective viewport to see vertices that form a letter S raised from a Plane primitive. We want to create another selection of vertices that form a skinnier S shape, and then lower that selection.

2. In the Top viewport, select the Plane object. Zoom in close enough to see the Plane completely fill up the view. If it does not, press the Z key to zoom to the extent of the selected object.

3. Activate Vertex mode and press the Q key until the Paint Selection Region button is active in the Main toolbar. Then Paint the selection of vertices in the middle of the S shape (**Figure 1.10**).

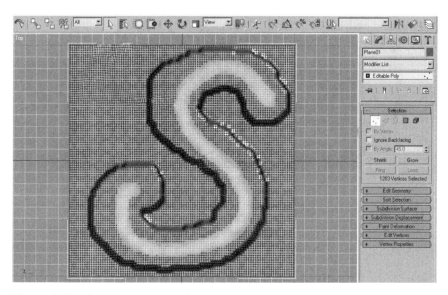

Figure 1.10   An S-shape vertex selection is painted with the selection tool and Paint Selection Region.

4. Change to the Perspective viewport and activate the Select and Move tool. Within the Transform Type-In field at the bottom of the user interface, enter for Z the value 0.0 (**Figure 1.11**).

5. Open the file entitled Paint Selection Region finish.max to see the finished example.

Of course, the same vertices could have been selected by using either the Fence or Lasso Selection Region, but these tools would have required numerous clicks of the mouse. By painting the selection, only a single curvy stroke is needed.

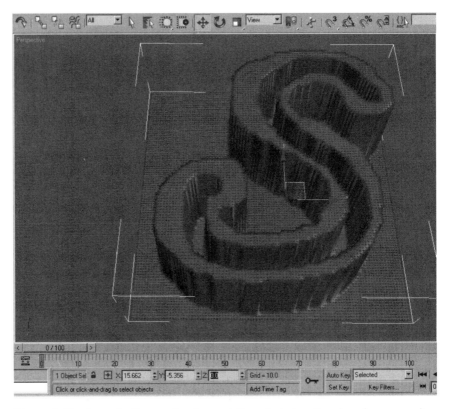

Figure 1.11   From the Perspective viewport, the selected vertices have been moved down to Z = 0.0.

Object Display Culling

Want more speed in your screen redraw (and who doesn't)? Object Display Culling allows you to quickly hide and unhide objects to maximize the available display memory—and therefore screen performance. Basically, Object Display Culling makes decisions on whether or not to display objects onscreen in full resolution or as bounding boxes according to rules such as how far the objects are from the camera, how many polygons they have, and what the viewport framerate is. When screen memory and graphic card performance are limiting factors, as they often are for big scenes with many complex objects, you can really save time, or in some cases work with a scene that you otherwise could not (**Figure 1.12**).

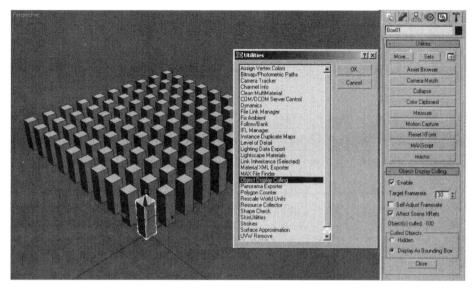

Figure 1.12   Access Object Display Culling from the Utilities Panel: Alt-O toggles Object Display Culling on and off.

Culling Boxes

To better understand how Object Display Culling works, complete the following steps. You'll find that the next exercises are sensitive to the current speed of your computer; you may have to use higher settings on a faster machine to see culling in action, while lower settings on a slower one will help prevent a stall.

1. Open the file entitled Object Display culling start.max. The scene opens in the Perspective viewport with an array of 100 Instances of a box made of editable polys (not a Box primitive).

2. Pan and zoom the scene. With a reasonably fast computer, 100 boxes at six polygons per box should not cause any significant problems for your viewport performance. Difficulties start when each object is more complex.

3. From the Utilities panel, click the More button and choose Object Display and Culling.

4. Check the Enable box, uncheck Self-Adjust Framerate, and set the Target Framerate to 30.

    By disabling Self-Adjust Framerate, we guarantee that the viewport performance will remain at 30 frames per second. This Target Framerate is high and will cause many of the objects to be culled and displayed as bounding box instead.

5. Objects will also be culled according to their number of polygons. Select one of the boxes, activate the Modify panel, drop down the Modifier list, choose the new TurboSmooth modifier, and set the Iterations at 4.

   The new TurboSmooth modifier is closely related to the MeshSmooth modifier, but is optimized for viewport performance. Assigning four Iterations to TurboSmooth will cause all 100 boxes, each with six sides, to be subdivided four times, resulting in hundreds of thousands of polygons added to your scene—a big advance in complexity over the 600 polygons in the scene we had before. If your computer is really fast, you may still not notice much difference in performance, so go ahead and try adding more Iterations and run the TurboSmooth modifier again. (Go too far, however, and you risk a stall or crash.)

6. Now try panning, zooming, and arc-rotating the viewport. Notice that many of the more distant boxes will disappear as the viewport changes (**Figure 1.13**).

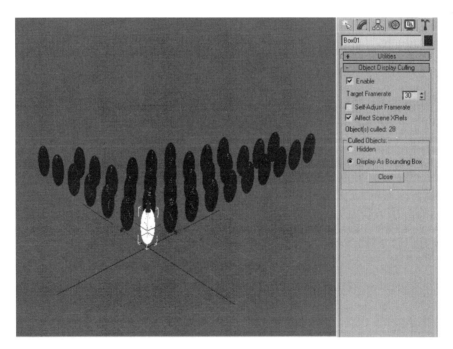

Figure 1.13   The front box is selected. The boxes further away in the back have been culled. The Target Framerate is set to 30.

7. Now set the Target Framerate to 15, and try panning as we did before. Notice that more of the boxes will display, but the viewport performance is slower (**Figure 1.14**).

Figure 1.14   Some of the boxes in the back have returned with the Framerate set lower to 15.

The finished project, Object Display Culling finish.max, can be loaded from the DVD.

Array Preview

Use the Array Preview, new to 3ds max 7, when you want to copy objects and space them out precisely. In prior versions, this task required you to go back and forth to the Array dialog to input new values and see the results, which were visible only after accepting changes. Now you can see what the results will be interactively, and make changes much more quickly. It's another great 3ds max 7 timesaver.

Array Preview also has an option to preview the scene as bounding boxes instead of fully rendered geometry. Use this for larger scenes where creating an array of many objects would slow down the viewport interaction.

 Note

The Array dialog cannot be resized and will not allow you to pan or zoom the scene while it is open. It can be difficult to see the preview of new objects if the viewport Is already panned or zoomed in the wrong position, so prior to opening the Array dialog, make sure the scene is fully visible.

Create a Spiral Staircase

Let's test the new Array Preview's powers by creating a spiral staircase.

1. Open the file entitled array start.max on the DVD. Note that the viewport is panned and zoomed, with a single Stair object sitting at the bottom left corner of the view. This will leave room for the Array dialog to be present with enough screen room available for previewing the copies. Select the Stair object and note that its pivot point is away from the object and is in the origin of the World coordinate space (**Figure 1.15**).

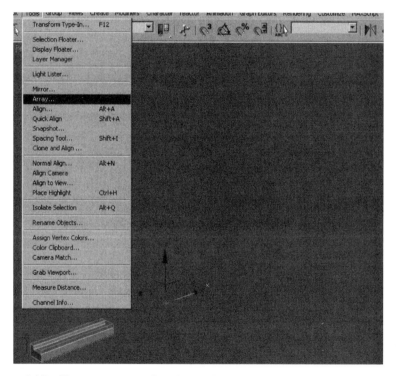

Figure 1.15   The scene is panned so that we have enough room to preview the arrayed objects as well as the Array dialog. The pivot point is away from the object.

2. Select the Stair object and open the Array tool from the Tools menu. The Array dialog pops up. Choose Instance from this dialog so that changes made to the selected Stair object will apply to ones we create in the following steps.

3. Place the Array dialog box as far to the bottom right-hand corner of the 3ds max 7 window as possible, so that we can see the preview later.

4. Set Z Move to 15, Z Rotate to −10, and Count to 20, and press the Preview button. In this example, we can leave the option for Display as Box unchecked, since

this scene is low in Polygon count. We should see the stairs arcing one by one as they climb (**Figure 1.16**). Note that the Array tool copies objects based on the location of their pivot points, so the stairs are copied in an arc as wide as the distance between the pivot point and the stair.

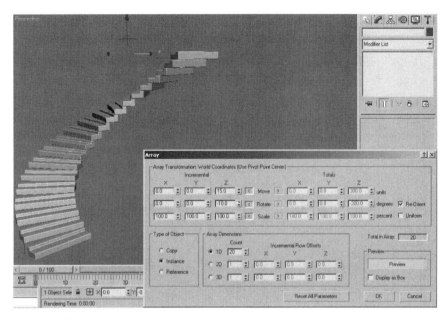

Figure 1.16   Previewing the spiral stairs.

New Align Tools

Normally, in 3ds max, you would use the Align tool to accurately place an object to the position and orientation of another object. Within the Align Selection dialog, you can choose which part of the selected object will become aligned with which part of the target object. Other controls determine which axis gets aligned, as well as deriving the orientation and scale of the target object.

Quick Align Tool

These features are essential when you need absolute control over many aspects of alignment. However, often all you need is to move one single object to the pivot point of another single object. For this simple task, it's quicker and easier to use the new Quick Align tool (**Figure 1.17**). Find the new Quick Align feature by dragging down on the Align tool from the Tools menu and the Main toolbar, or by pressing Shift-A.

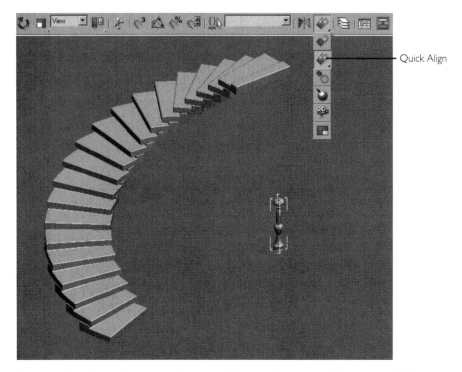

Quick Align

Figure 1.17   Quick Align is a subfeature of 3ds max 7's standard Align tool. With the Post object selected, Quick Align will move to a target object.

Quick Align operates instantly. You do not need to make choices inside a dialog. With the Quick Align tool, an object or selection of objects will move to a single target object.

Clone and Align Tool

Often, you need to copy an object or selection of objects to the location of several objects. For this, use the new Clone and Align tool. Clone and Align is similar to the Quick Align tool, except that it gives us the choice of picking which objects in the scene will be the destinations of the selected object or objects. The Clone and Align dialog also gives us the choice of offsetting, orienting, and scaling the copied object(s) based on any XYZ coordinates you specify.

To demonstrate the Clone and Align tool, let's create copies of a post for each stair.

1. Open the file entitled clone and align start.max. The project opens in the User viewport. The objects are the same as the stairs in the last example, but we have added a Post object we want to copy.

2. With the post selected, choose Clone and Align from the Tools menu (**Figure 1.18**).

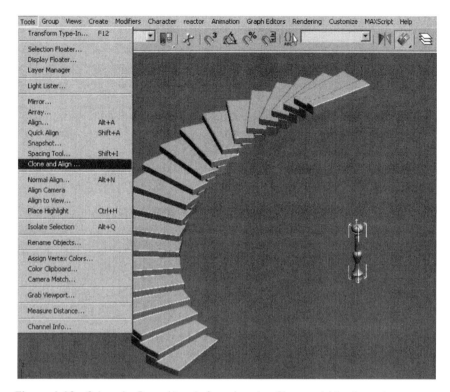

Figure 1.18   Select the Post object before choosing Clone and Align from the Tools menu.

The Clone and Align dialog pops up (**Figure 1.19**). Fortunately, this dialog does allow us to pan and zoom our scene so that we can see what is going on within the preview.

3. Click the Pick List button, and select all of the Stair objects. Note that the new posts overlap and are stacked on the stairs' pivot points.

4. Arc-Rotate the User viewport so we can clearly see each post. Set Align Offset (Local) X to –185 and Y to –10; click the Apply button and close the dialog box. A Post object will be copied and placed on each Stair object (**Figure 1.20**).

You can see the finished project in the clone and align finish.max file on the DVD.

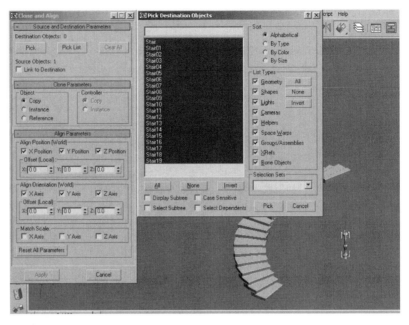

Figure 1.19 A Post object will be copied and placed on each Stair object that is picked from the list in Pick Destination Objects.

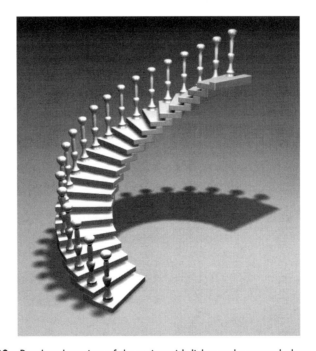

Figure 1.20 Rendered version of the stairs with lights and a ground plane added.

Snaps Improvements

Sometimes accuracy is much more important than flexibility, even when you're artistically modeling and designing a scene. You often really need exact precision, and in those cases the Snaps tools have always been your friend. However, when you are in a hurry, you may not have the time to get things just so, even with the help of Snaps. That's where 3ds max 7's new Snaps improvements come in.

Now, for example, when creating a line, snapping to grid points ensures that the vertices are plotted exactly on the intersections of the home grid. In past versions of 3ds max, you would have had to set the Grid to an appropriate spacing first.

Snaps previewing is another big assist for accurate object placement. In the past, if you placed the cursor next to a grid point and clicked the mouse, the object would snap, but not always where you expected, and you'd have to go back and move it again. 3ds max 7 now includes the ability to preview where the snaps will place the object before you actually move it there. If your cursor is within 30 pixels of the grid, a preview will let you know where the cursor will snap. If your cursor is within 20 pixels of the grid, the snap will take place. Seeing the snap before it takes place allows you to make proper adjustments with the mouse to ensure that the snap occurs where you want it.

Snap Radius is the distance where the object will snap, and the Snap Preview Radius is the distance where the Snap function will anticipate the snap without actually committing the object's position. For the Snap Preview Radius to work properly, make sure that the Snap Preview Radius is set higher than the Snap Radius. If the Snap Preview Radius and the Snap Radius are too close in value, you will not see any preview.

Playing with Snaps

Here is an example of how to use the new Snaps features. We will move a rectangle so that its corner is positioned to a specific grid point.

1. In the Perspective viewport, create a rectangle. Set the length at 50 and the width at 50.

2. Right-click any gray area of the toolbar and choose Snaps (**Figure 1.21**). Right-clicking beneath the word View in the Toolbar also opens the Snaps toolbar. Both the Snap to Grid Points toggle and the Snap to Endpoint toggle are active. The Snaps toolbar can be docked to the top for convenience.

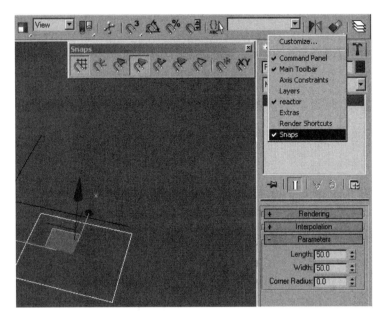

Figure 1.21   Create a rectangle in the Perspective viewport.

3. In the Main toolbar, right-click the Snaps Toggle button. The Grid and Snap Settings dialog will pop up. Make sure that only Snap to Grid Points and Snap to Endpoint have a check mark.

4. Press the S key to toggle the Snaps on. Use the Select and Move tool to drag the rectangle by its upper left corner to the coordinates (0,0,0). A new feature of 3ds max 7 is a blue rubber-band line that will show where the rectangle was and where it is going as it is moved to the middle of the coordinate system (**Figure 1.22**).

The Transform settings indicate that the pivot point of the rectangle is now located at (-25,-25,0). This is because the upper left corner is now located at (0,0,0), and the object has a length of 50 and a width of 50.

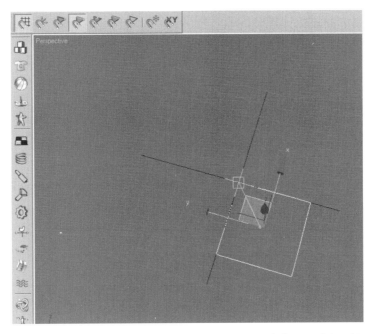

Figure 1.22   A blue rubber-band line indicates the positional change of the object while it is being snapped. Note that the Snaps toolbar is docked to the top.

Summing Up

The overall look of 3ds max 7 has changed little, but the subtle interface changes are well worth learning. The interface menus and toolbars are just a bit more intuitive when you're searching for a function. Flat Shaded mode gives you another way of viewing models to avoid distracting highlights and dark spots. Walkthrough mode offers the same freedom of navigating and animating a camera as we would have traveling through a videogame—it's now much easier to make architectural flythroughs, too. Quicker toggling of the dialog boxes may seem trivial, but the time saved will add up; you may bop in and out of a dialog dozens or hundreds of times a day and not notice the little extra incremental wasted moments that nonetheless impact on your productivity.

Likewise, your workflow will be simpler and faster with 3ds max 7's new tools. Paint Selection Region makes selecting objects and sub-objects quicker, Object Display Culling speeds up the viewport redraw, Array Preview is now more intuitive, the new Alignment tools are faster and more robust, and Snapping is more predictable.

You'll quickly master these new features as you progress through the chapters to come. Have fun!

Chapter 2

What's New in Modeling

By Daniel Manahan

Modeling in 3ds max 7, one of the program's core strengths, has been improved through the addition of new modifiers and significant new functions within the Editable Poly modifier. In this chapter, we'll take a look at the following modeling features that are specific to version 7:

- Edit Poly Modifier
- Select Poly by Angle
- Paint Soft Selection
- Make Planar
- Bridge
- Cut Tool
- Turn Edges
- Paint Deformation and Relax
- TurboSmooth Modifier

Edit Poly Modifier

The new Edit Poly modifier is similar to the Edit Mesh modifier, but the Edit Poly modifier is much more powerful. For example, within Edit Mesh, there are no Edge selection functions for Ring and Loop, nor can you animate functions or the position of the vertices. The Edit Poly modifier allows us to work with most of the modeling features that are available within Editable Poly.

There's an important workflow advantage to having a modifier for editing the model: All your changes are contained in a single modifier. This allows you to remove the modifier as if it were a layer and revert to what you had before you applied the modifier settings. In effect, it's like having one super-undo operation that brings you back to a clean model.

Of course, there's also an important exception to this advantage. Removing the Edit Poly modifier causes any objects that might be attached to your modifier to be deleted from the scene—and they will be lost from the scene for good (unless you reload it). So I recommend the following: If an object is to be attached to an Edit Poly modifier, copy it first, just in case the modifier needs to be removed. Or detach its element from the original object before removing the Edit Poly modifier.

 Note

> Here's a useful application of the Edit Poly modifier: If you use it to create a sub-object selection, any modifiers applied above it will be restricted to the selected area. This is the same workflow as with the Edit Mesh modifier.

One of the nice features of the Edit Poly modifier is its ability to animate functions with the use of a Model or Animate toggle. Only one sub-object selection can be animated per Edit Poly modifier. Animation should be done last within Edit Poly and before you go back to Model mode, or the keyframes will be lost.

You can only Commit keyframes when the toggle is on Animate. All the animation keys will be lost, but changes will be permanent. Clicking the Commit button produces the same result as if you collapsed the stack and created a new Edit Poly modifier (**Figure 2.1**).

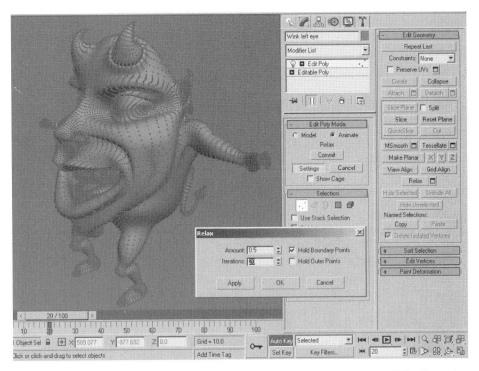

Figure 2.1   In this example, the new Relax function has its Iterations animated. The Commit button will collapse the changes and remove any animation.

Select Poly by Angle

New to both Editable Poly and Edit Poly is the ability to select polygons based on their angle relative to the currently selected polygon. Once you select a polygon, all adjacent polygons whose difference in angle lies within a defined threshold will be selected. Polygons that are adjacent to the automatically selected polygons will also be evaluated and added to the selection if they fall within the threshold. In this way, you can grow your selection using Select Poly by Angle until the change in angle becomes greater than the threshold you have set.

What can you use Select Polygon by Angle for? For one thing, it's useful when texturing terrains; you can use it to select polys at a certain "slope" and apply a slope-specific terrain. It takes a little experimentation to see how this works For example, all the polygons on a six-sided cube will be selected if a single polygon is clicked while the threshold is set to 90 degrees. The polygon at the opposite side of the cube will be selected even though its angle difference is 180 degrees. All adjacent polygons are evaluated, and then the next set of adjacent polygons, until no adjacent polygons lie within the angle threshold from the increased selection. If you press the Alt key to remove polygons from the selection while clicking a selected polygon, and the angular threshold is set to 90 degrees, the entire cube will deselect.

Setting the correct By Angle value is crucial. Set it too high and you get unpredictable results, with unwanted polygons selected. You are best off using a low By Angle threshold to quickly make a selection of polygons that are almost coplanar (**Figure 2.2**). A By Angle value of 0.0 will select only coplanar polygons.

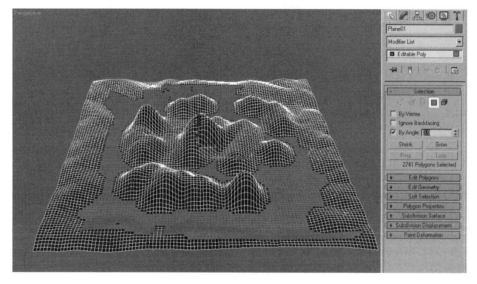

Figure 2.2   The By Angle value is set to 3 degrees. A single polygon was selected and all other polygons within an angle of 3 degrees are added to the selection set.

Paint Soft Selection

Soft Selection, available in Editable Poly and Edit Poly modes only, is a way of creating a mask for other modifiers above it. Normally, you must make a regular selection for Soft Selection to appear. The Soft Selection appears as a colorful area around a selected sub-object. The regular selection is red, surrounded by a rainbow of colors that indicate the strength of the Soft Selection. The strongest influence is Orange, then Yellow, Green, and finally Blue, the weakest.

In 3ds max 7, a Soft Selection can now be painted, instead of just being an area radiating from the selection, even if a regular selection is not made. This is a more artistic and controllable way of creating selection sets. Click the new Paint button in the Soft Selection rollout to access this feature (**Figure 2.3**). You can pass this selection up the stack to other modifiers.

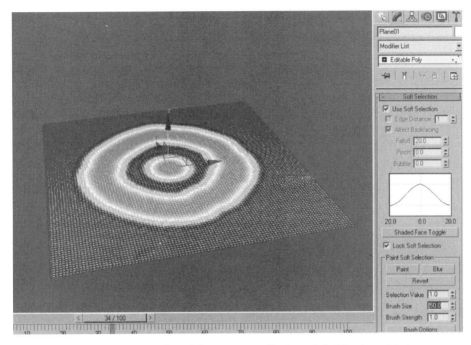

Figure 2.3   No vertices are selected, but you can still paint a Soft Selection with the new Paint button in the Soft Selection rollout.

A modifier applied to a Soft Selection produces a partial effect based on the weights of sub-objects (this weighting is indicated by the color of the Soft Selection area). A Bend modifier applied to a Soft Selection will bend just where the selection is made, and in the Soft Selection region it will only bend partially, according to the degree of the selection. Modifications such as Relax or Make Planar made within the Editable Poly also respect the Soft Selection.

A normal Soft Selection, which is based on a radius from a selected vertex, will change its influence colors if the vertex is transformed. This is because, as the vertices deform and move to a new position, the selected vertex changes its distance from each Soft Selected vertex. New to 3ds max 7 is the ability to Paint and Lock Soft Selection; when this feature is turned on, the Soft Selection can be modified and transformed without changing the colored influence of the selection.

Make Planar

Need to flatten some polys? Make Planar takes any Sub-Object Selection or Soft Selection and flattens the selection to the average angle of its parts. With an Edit Poly modifier, Make Planar ignores the Soft Selection and applies itself only to the regular selection.

A new set of X, Y, and Z buttons allows you to flatten the selection and/or the Soft Selection to the object's local axis (**Figure 2.4**). For example, if you paint a Soft Selection and then click the Z button, the Soft Selection will flatten to the object's local Z axis.

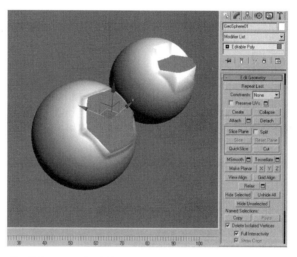

Figure 2.4   The GeoSphere on the left has its polygons flattened with Make Planar and remains at an angle based on the average of the selection. The same polygonal selection of the GeoSphere on the right is flattened based on the Z axis.

The Soft Selection color indicates how much influence Make Planar has on the selection. The selection flattens more with each successive click on one of the Make Planar axis buttons.

Bridge

The Bridge feature, available from the Edit Borders rollout, allows you to create a joined extrusion from two border selections. Bridge will create a smoother transition if the two border selections share the same edge count and have a similar shape, even if the number of edges on each border is not the same. Make a bridge between two borders that do not share the same number of edges, however, and Bridge creates three-sided polygons to make up the difference; the results can be unpredictable.

How can you use Bridge? Here's an example: You can model a hand separate from the upper arm and extrude a bridge to form the forearm. Add segments to the length to taper the bridge (**Figures 2.5** and **2.6**). The Taper function sets the degree to which the bridge cross-section becomes narrower or wider.

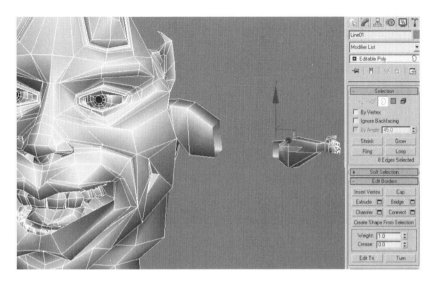

Figure 2.5   The gap between the forearm and upper arm is an ideal place to use Bridge.

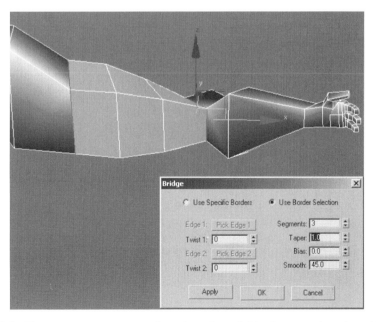

Figure 2.6   Three segments are created on the polygon bridge between the selected borders. Taper controls the width of the bridge.

Tip

Unfortunately, the Smooth control for the bridge will not automatically blend with the original model on the border. To manually smooth the border with the bridge, make an Edge selection, convert it to a Polygon selection, and smooth those polygons. Holding the Control key and clicking the Polygon button within the Selection rollout will convert the Edge selection to a Polygon selection.

Building a Bridge

Let's explore how to construct a bridge. In this example, we'll create a bridge through the interior of a box.

1. Open the file named Bridge interior start.max from this book's companion DVD. The scene opens with an object with two holes in it. Since a border is a selection of open edges, this object has two borders, which you will bridge through the middle.

Note

When you open a tutorial file, you might get a warning if the Unit Scale does not match. You should always choose to adopt the file's Unit Scale just in case the units are an important factor within any particular tutorial.

2. Select the object, then access the Modify panel.
3. Press Control-A to select all borders.
4. Within the Edit Borders rollout, click the Settings box for Bridge. Within the Bridge dialog, select Use Border Selection, and set Segments to 4 and Taper to −2.0 (**Figure 2.7**).

The more segments used for the bridge, the more round the curve of the taper will be. The negative Taper value causes the bridge to form a convex curve as it extrudes into the hole.

Open the file Bridge interior finish.max to check the result.

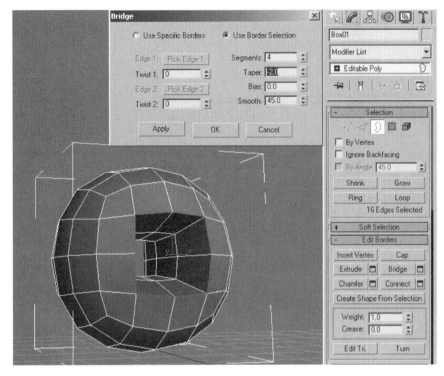

Figure 2.7   An interior bridge is created between the two borders.

Cut Tool

Cutting an edge is one way to add vertices to existing edges and divide polygons into more pieces. When you need your model to curve, cutting more segments in the opposite direction of the curve will make a rounder transition.

In prior releases of 3ds max, cutting into a polygon usually produced unwanted extra edges and required unwanted labor—selecting the edge and using the Backspace key—to remove them (**Figure 2.8**).

The Cut tool has been improved in 3ds max 7 to create new edges only where you click. Extra edges will not be created (**Figure 2.9**).

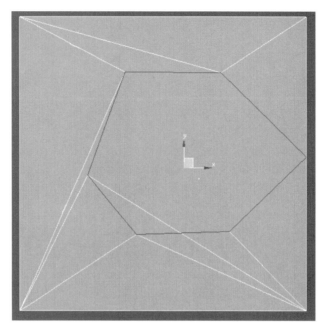

Figure 2.8   The extra white lines are unwanted edges created when the Cut tool was used in 3ds max 6 and prior releases.

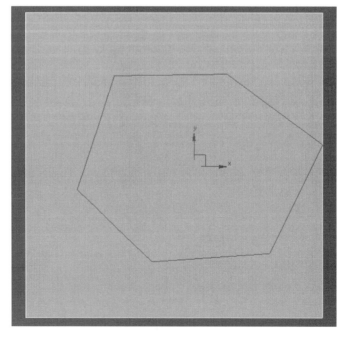

Figure 2.9   In 3ds max 7, the Cut tool no longer creates unwanted edges.

Turn Edges

The ability to turn edges is a function of Edit Mesh that was left out of Editable Poly in previous versions of 3ds max—but it's in version 7. Now you can select an edge in Editable Poly and turn it in the other direction. This affects only invisible edges, which show as dotted lines instead of solid lines.

Functionally, Turn Edges works the same in Editable Poly as it does in Edit Mesh. You turn edges by first clicking the Turn button, then clicking an invisible edge (the thin dotted line). This causes the invisible edge to be drawn diagonally from the opposite corners (**Figure 2.10**).

If the invisible edges are in the opposite direction of a model's curvature, a distracting zigzag pattern will appear. This zigzag can also appear as spikiness in an area of the model that is expected to be a smooth and curvy deformation. This usually happens in areas of a model where the deformation goes against the natural contour of the edges (**Figures 2.11** and **2.12**).

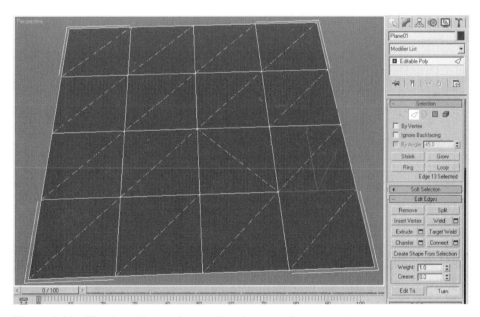

Figure 2.10   The dotted line is the invisible edge; it has been turned.

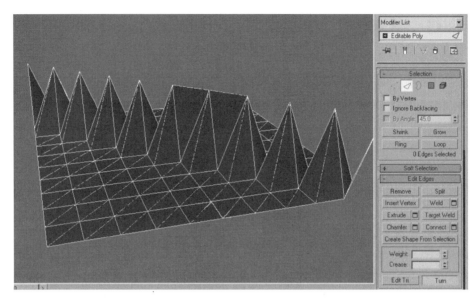

Figure 2.11   The vertices have been moved up and the spikiness is caused by the edges not following this contour. Two edges are turned in the direction of the curvature.

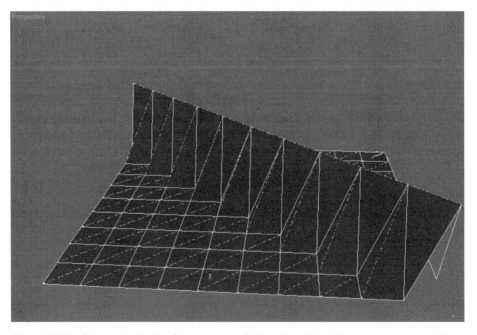

Figure 2.12   Same as in the last figure, except all the edges along this contour are turned with the contour. The model appears less spiky with this raised diagonal vertex selection.

Paint Deformation and Relax

Modeling can be a pain if you need to pick and pull, vertex by vertex, to sculpt an object. New to 3ds max 7 is Paint Deformation, available from the Paint Deformation rollout under Editable Poly. Paint Deformation offers the ability to drag the mouse (or a stylus— pressure-sensitivity is supported for tablet users) over an area to deform it. Each stroke of the cursor over the mesh surface pushes or pulls the vertices in the direction of each polygon's normals or the object's local X, Y, or Z axis (**Figures 2.13** and **2.14**). (Normals are vectors that are perpendicular to the plane of the poly.)

In Figure 2.13, the direction of deformation of the model will be along its local Z axis. When it's in Paint Deformation mode, the cursor changes to a circle with a Brush Size value of 10. The short line coming out of the brush indicates a Strength value of 5.

Figure 2.14 demonstrates the result after Paint Deformation. Use the Relax brush to smooth the mesh if there are any sharp spikes as a result of Paint Deformation.

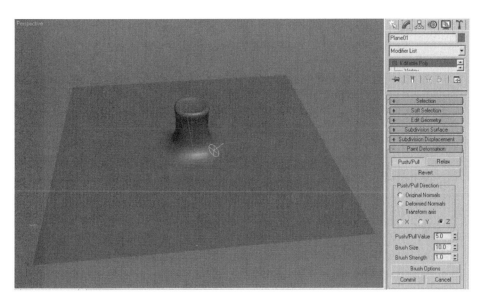

Figure 2.13   Paint Deformation is a new approach to applying poly deformations.

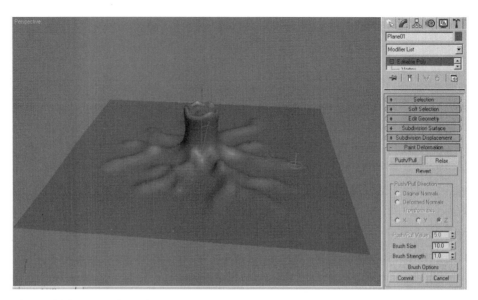

Figure 2.14   Using the Relax brush to smooth a Paint Deformation.

 Tip

> Paint Deformation uses the same painting interface as Vertex Paint and Skin. You can also mirror your work to the other side of the model.

The new Relax function found in the Edit Geometry rollout (it is different from the Relax discussed in the previous paragraph) is in some ways a complement to Paint Deformation. It blends sharp areas of a model where the surface appears to wrinkle or turn too sharply. This can be a real boon for artists creating characters and other organic objects. Relax moves each poly vertex in the brush's area of influence toward an average position relative to its neighbors. It's as if the wrinkles in the model were being ironed smoother or hard edges melted slightly.

The Relax function has been added to Editable Poly and Edit Poly; you only need to create a selection or Soft Selection and then open the Relax dialog to change values. Because there is no modifier to collapse, you can immediately make a new selection and perform the Relax function again (**Figures 2.15** and **2.16**).

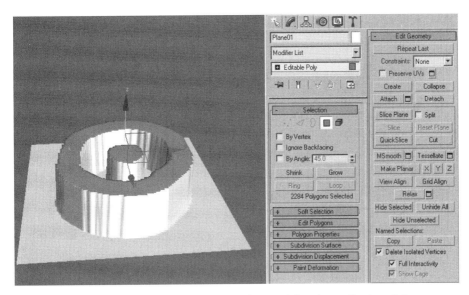

Figure 2.15   These sharp, jagged polys are a perfect candidate for application of the new Relax function.

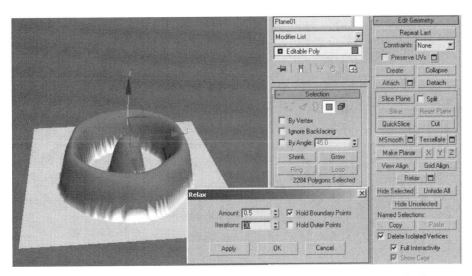

Figure 2.16   The Relax function is set to 30 iterations and applied to the selected polygons. The overall look of the selection is now much smoother.

TurboSmooth Modifier

You already are familiar with the MeshSmooth modifier and how it subdivides your mesh to smooth it. TurboSmooth is similar to MeshSmooth in the way it works, but it consumes less memory and performs much faster.

TurboSmooth helps speed up the standard subdivision surface box-modeling technique. As you know, sub-D modeling allows you to make an object with only a few polygons and turn it into a model four times smoother with each iteration (**Figures 2.17** and **2.18**). For example, a single iteration subdivides a cube into a 24-sided object (6 sides times 4). Every subsequent iteration subdivides four more times. It only takes a couple of iterations for a cube to look like a sphere.

In the box-modeling process, you typically start with an Editable Poly box, then extrude polygons and move the new vertices to deform the surface. Then you apply either a MeshSmooth modifier or the NURMS function within Editable Poly to create the subdivisions to smooth the model's surface.

Figure 2.17   The Deviled Egg prior to application of the TurboSmooth modifier has very angular polygons.

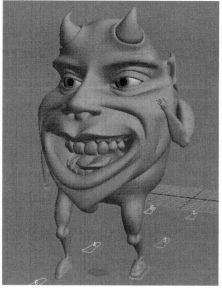

Figure 2.18   After applying the TurboSmooth modifier, the Deviled Egg is much smoother, especially around the eyes and knees.

TurboSmooth speeds the smoothing step, which can take increasing amounts of time under MeshSmooth as you apply more iterations. An advantage to the TurboSmooth modifier is its option for using explicit normals; this method computes faster than one using the normals from the mesh object's original smoothing groups. However, this option should be turned on only if no modifiers are going to be applied in the stack above TurboSmooth. When another modifier is applied above TurboSmooth, the normals will be lost and performance might drop.

TurboSmooth does have a few downsides: It does not allow you to isolate polygons, work with sub-objects, or choose from different methods of subdivision.

TurboSmooth is best used on the top of the stack and above animation modifiers such as Skin. If you are going to collapse the stack, turn off Isoline Display, or the model will lose its interior edges. Failing to turn off Isoline Display will produce unwanted vertices with no cross edges to support them, and the model might look mangled and uncontrolled.

Summing Up

As in the last few releases of 3ds max, Editable Poly continues to be the dominant area of new modeling features. With the new Edit Poly modifier expanding the capabilities of those tools, your modeling workflow will be more flexible and efficient. Being able to deform polygons with Paint Deformation offers a new and more intuitive approach to modeling. Although the Cut tool is not a new feature, its improved accuracy makes it more useful. The new Bridge tool is a quicker way of generating polygons from one border to another. And the TurboSmooth modifier saves processing time as viewport performance gets a boost from having a leaner and simpler smoothing tool. Overall, you can expect greater modeling productivity with these new tools.

In the next chapter, we will explore 3ds max 7's new texturing features.

Chapter 3

What's New in Texturing

By Daniel Manahan

3ds max 7 has a number of significant and quite useful improvements for handling textures. New features enhance your ability to visualize, apply textures to models, and render more realistic objects. In this chapter, we'll cover the following new tools:

- Highlight Seams
- Unwrap UVW Improvements
- Projection Modifier
- MPEG Files for Input
- Copying Texture Values
- VertexPaint Modifier Improvements
- Preserve UVs
- Subsurface Scattering

Highlight Seams

Highlight Seams, available through the Unwrap UVW and UVW Map modifiers, can be more easily understood if you think of how a tailor-made dress is assembled. Two-dimensional fabric is laid flat on a table, cut according to a pattern, and then decorated with appliques, embroidery, or other embellishments. This fabric is then positioned and wrapped around a three-dimensional object (a dressmaker's dummy) to fit a person or mannequin. The fabric pieces are stitched together where one piece meets another.

In the 3D world, objects that are assembled for texturing are also "stitched" together. In 3ds max 7, this stitch is called the texture seam. Highlight Seams is a tool for making this task easier.

Let's take a look at an example of how to use Highlight Seams for a 3D sleeve. Since the sleeve is in the shape of a cylinder, when texturing it you should use Cylindrical mapping (**Figure 3.1**).

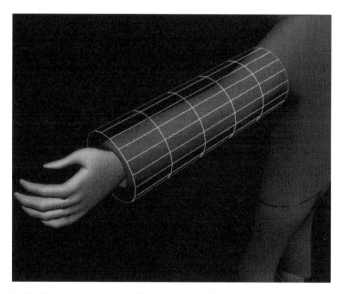

Figure 3.1   Cylindrical mapping is used for an object that resembles a cylinder.

A typical sleeve is stitched from the armpit to the hand on the inner side, toward the body. This is to make the stitched seam less noticeable, and to hide the fact that the fabric pattern may not join perfectly along the seam. By the same token, in 3ds max 7 you can rotate the seam to the inside of the sleeve, making the seam line of the texture less noticeable. During the modeling stage of production, planning the texture seam to be placed where the camera does not see it will minimize visible distortions when the object is rendered.

Highlight Seams displays the texture seam in bright green on a Plane object with the Unwrap UVW modifier (**Figure 3.2**). Both Unwrap UVW and UVW Map allow you to see this texture seam.

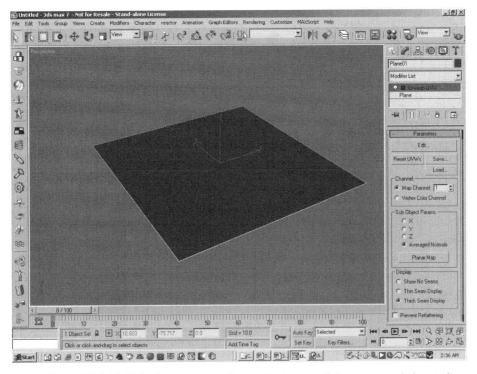

Figure 3.2   With Highlight Seams, a green line on the border of the unwrapped plane indicates the texture seam.

What about other types of objects? Unlike a plane, which is an open object, a sphere is closed because it has no border edges. By default, its mapping type is Spherical, and its texture seam is a single straight line that runs from its north pole to its south pole, like line of longitude. If you create a sphere that has its default Spherical mapping coordinates and then apply the Unwrap UVW modifier to it, the texture seam is visible running from pole to pole. Any texture that sits on the top or bottom of the Sphere will be severely distorted (**Figure 3.3**).

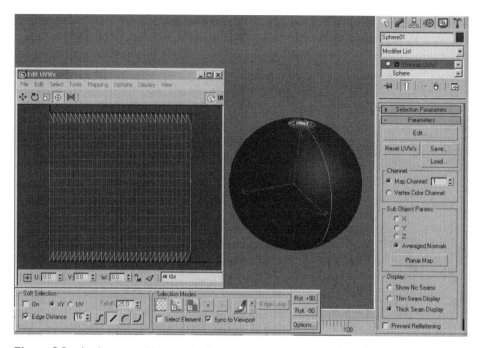

Figure 3.3   At the top and bottom of the sphere, the seam is condensed into a small point. The vertical line that runs from the top to the bottom indicates the texture seam.

This texture seam on the sphere will cause any 2D map to start and stop along the texture edge. When rendering, the edge of a texture will appear as an unnatural rip or tear in the texture, and therefore should be covered or placed where the rendering will not show it.

Unfortunately, Highlight Seams has its limitations. The highlighted seam cannot be manipulated in the viewport. Using the UVW Map Gizmo or editing in Unwrap UVW are the only ways to determine which edges of your model lie on the texture seam.

In the UVW Map modifier, the seam will follow any sub-object Gizmo transformation. In the Unwrap UVW modifier, the seam can be manipulated with precision only within the Edit UVWs window. But you can use tools for selecting, transforming, and welding UVW seam edges. Those changes are immediately demonstrated on the model, both in the visible texture and the seam. And with new improvements in the Unwrap UVW modifier, discussed next, editing the seam is easier.

Unwrap UVW Improvements

In addition to the ability to display the texture seam within the Edit window of the Unwrap UVW modifier, there are a few more new improvements to help you work with UVW mapping. Let's touch on them briefly.

Absolute/Offset Mode

The Absolute/Offset Mode toggle works like the one in the standard interface when moving objects or sub-objects. When it is toggled off, values typed into the U, V, and W fields position the selection exactly at the number specified in relation to the map. When it is toggled on, the selection moves Offset to its previous position according to the offset amounts that you enter into the U, V, and W fields (**Figure 3.4**).

Paint Select Mode

Paint Select mode, which is similar to painting a selection in the standard interface, lets you paint a sub-object selection in the Edit UVWs window. Use the plus and minus buttons to the right of the Paint Select Mode button (which looks like a paintbrush) to change the size of the selection brush. To exit the Paint Select mode, right-click in the Edit UVWs window, or activate the Move, Rotate, or Scale tool (Figure 3.4).

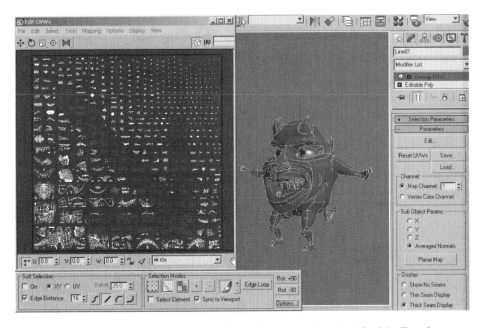

Figure 3.4   The new Absolute/Offset Mode toggle is located to the left of the Transform Type-In. The new Paint Selection mode is located to the right. Green Texture Seam lines display on the Deviled Egg after the mapping has been flattened.

Edge Loop

With Edge Loop, you can now get a loop selection in the Edit UVWs window (**Figure 3.5**). This is similar to expanding an Edge loop in Editable Poly.

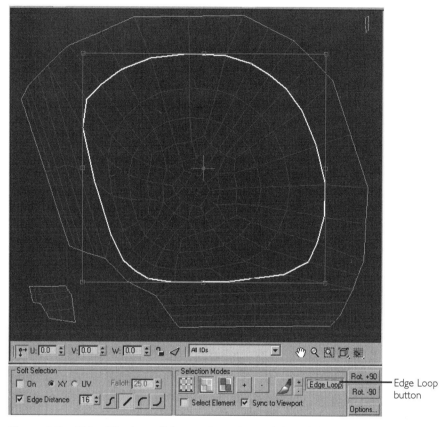

Edge Loop button

Figure 3.5   Using Edge Loop: Select a white edge, and then click the Edge Loop button. This works like Edge Loop from Editable Poly.

 Tip

> An edge loop from a green seam edge will not produce predictable results. For best results, use only the white edges for making a selection loop.

All of the texture features discussed above will help you set up good texture coordinates. This is important for a new feature called Projection, a new modifier accessible from a new area in Render To Texture.

Projection Modifier

The Projection modifier offers new ways of sending existing texture coordinates from one model to another. Specifically, some of the Vertex Channel data that exists within the geometry of an object can now be projected onto another object. The result is not always predictable—under certain conditions the transferred data will be distorted—but you will nonetheless find the Projection modifier a timesaver in appropriate situations.

To better understand how this new feature works, let's project the texture coordinates from one Plane object to another Plane object.

1. Open the project UV start.max file from this book's companion DVD. Note that the polygons on the top plane are deformed into a swirling pattern. You want to project this deformation to the bottom plane, which has polygons that are not deformed.

2. Select the Project From Plane object, apply a Projection modifier, and uncheck Cage (**Figure 3.6**).

   The Cage does not need to display, and can be distracting, as it is in this example. The Cage display is more useful with curvy and organic objects; it enables you to verify that the projection completely surrounds the target object. (We'll use the Cage in the tutorial that follows this one.)

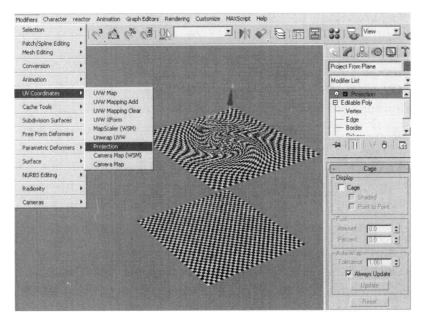

Figure 3.6   The Projection modifier is applied to the Project From Plane object, and Cage is not checked.

3. With the Pick button in the Geometry Selection rollout, click the Project To Plane object.

4. Click the Add button in the Projection rollout.

5. Click the Project button (**Figure 3.7**).

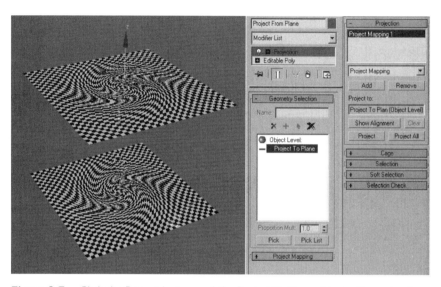

Figure 3.7   Click the Project button, and the Project To Plane object will acquire the swirly texture coordinates from the Project From Plane object.

Projecting a Normal Map

Also new to the Projection feature is the ability to generate a Normal map in the Bump map of a material directly from the geometry of other objects in the scene. A Normal map—also referred to as a Normals map in parts of the interface—is an RGB image that contains information about the curvature of the Bump map. A Normal map contains more information (256 levels for each color channel) than a grayscale image (which has only 256 levels total), and therefore is more accurate. The red channel determines the left and right influence, the green channel affects the up and down, and the blue channel affects towards and away within the bump.

Let's digress for a moment and consider why you would want to use Normal mapping with Projection. The basic aim is to project a complex high-resolution object to a simple angular low-resolution object. As you know, simple objects with fewer polygons calculate faster and are more efficient for dynamic simulations, scene management, and ultimately rendering. In particular, real-time game engines perform best with models that are lower in polygon count. But the low-polygon object must look as close as possible like its high-poly counterpart; its Bump map must display the same curvatures. Normal maps, with their higher resolution, provide better results than the grayscale maps usually used for Bump mapping, and are mainly used for game engines that perform better with models that are lower in polygon count. Many of these games typically need to render in real time, which requires the scenes to have as few polygons as possible. The highly detailed textures in the Diffuse Color and Bump maps that are made possible by Normal mapping in large part make up for the loss of polygonal detail in the model.

Let's use Normal mapping to texture a simple Plane object with a higher-resolution Plane object.

1. Open the file Project Normal to Bump start.max on the DVD. Select the Project To Plane object. Press the keyboard shortcut 0 to open the Render To Texture dialog.

2. Within the Objects To Bake rollout, check Enabled for Projection Mapping. Click the Pick button and add the Project From Plane object. Make sure that Use Existing Channel is selected for both Object and Sub-Object and that you are using channel number 1 (**Figure 3.8**).

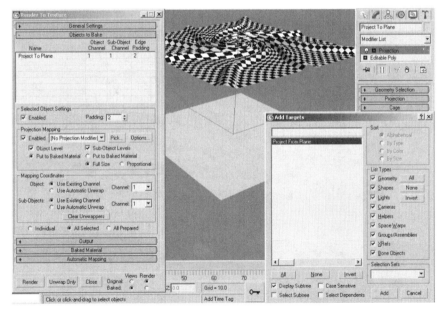

Figure 3.8   To begin the process of Normal mapping, pick the Project From Plane object and check Use Existing Channel.

A Projection modifier will automatically be applied to the Project To Plane object. Since the Project To Plane object already has mapping coordinates, you do not need Render To Texture to flatten a map, so uncheck Use Existing Channel.

 Note

> In order to maintain control, prior to choosing Render To Texture you should make your own mapping coordinates and keep Use Existing Channel selected.

3. Within the Cage rollout, check both Shaded and Point To Point. Change the Amount value to 130.

Checking both Shade and Point To Point allows you to visualize the area the Cage will use to project the Normal map. After the Amount value is typed in, the value will return to 0.0.

If for any reason you need to get the blue Cage back to its original location, press the Reset button and retype the Amount you want to push the Cage. If the Cage does not completely surround the source object, then the resulting image will clip out the misaligned areas (**Figure 3.9**).

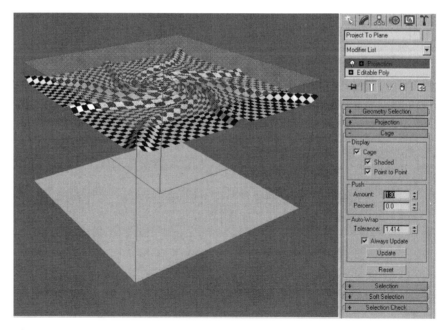

Figure 3.9   The Cage completely surrounds the Project From Plane object.

4. Press the Add button in the Output rollout of the Render To Texture dialog and choose NormalsMap from the list. Make sure that the Target Map slot shows Bump (if needed, select Bump from the Target Map Slot drop-down to show it in the Output window). Change the Size to 1024 by pressing the 1024 button. Change the Render from Original to Baked, and press the Render button (**Figure 3.10**).

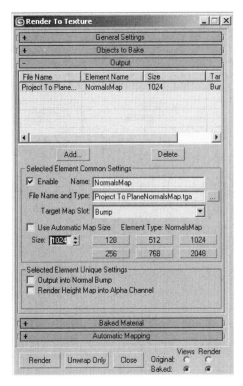

Figure 3.10   A NormalsMap is rendered and applied to the Bump slot. This figure shows the dialog's final state.

Changing the Size to 1024 gives you extra mapping pixels that make the rendered image look cleaner and more detailed. The rendered image goes into the Bump slot of a Shell material. This Shell material is automatically assigned to the Project To Plane object, but is not automatically visible in the Material Editor. You will need to put this material into one of the Material Editor slots so it can be edited.

5. Activate the third Material slot. Click the Pick Material from Object button (the eyedropper) and the Project To Plane object (**Figure 3.11**).

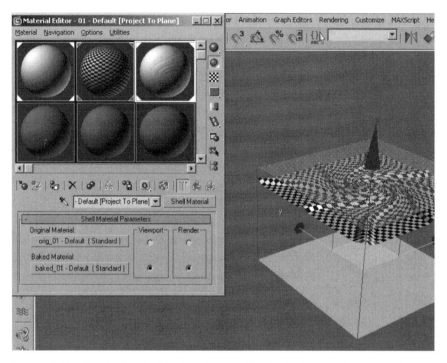

Figure 3.11   The Shell material, which is applied to the Project To Plane object, is placed into the third slot.

A Shell material is made from two materials: the Original and the Baked. You can choose to have either the Original or the Baked material used in the viewport and/or the rendering. If you render at this point, the Baked material will show the bump raised like the Project From Plane object. In the next step, you will increase this bump to exaggerate how much it lifts.

6. Click on the Baked Material button to edit it. Change the Specular Level to 50. Change the Bump Amount to 300 (**Figure 3.12**).

7. Render the Perspective viewport (**Figure 3.13**).

 Tip

Typically, when creating a Normal map, you would use two different models, one high-resolution and one low-resolution. However, the Projection technique is not limited to using separate models. A source model with a Projection modifier applied to it can be its own target.

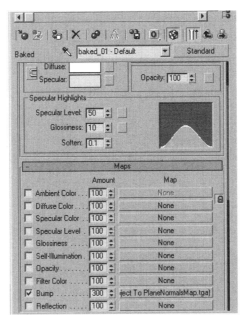

Figure 3.12   The bump has been exaggerated and will show better in the final rendering.

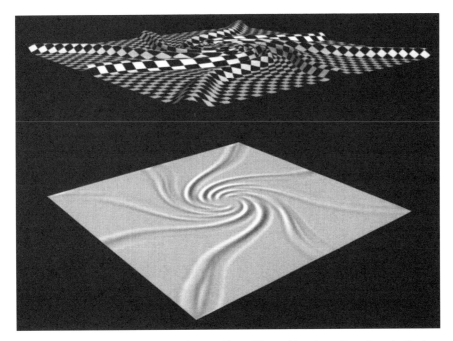

Figure 3.13   The bump from the Project From Plane object is projected to the Project To Plane object.

Compare your results with the file project Normal to Bump finish.max on the DVD. The image file Project to PlaneNormalsMap.tga found on the DVD should also now be in your 3ds max 7 Images folder; you need it to render the scene.

Note

New in 3ds max 7, you can now use mental ray as the renderer for all Render To Texture applications, such as Normal mapping projection.

MPEG Files for Input

3ds max 7 does not have the ability to output a rendering to an MPEG movie. However, you can now import MPEG files and use them anywhere in 3ds max 7 where a bitmap can be input: in texture maps, projected from lights, as viewport or environment background images, in Video Post Input Events, and so on. This convenient new function gives you one more choice for inputting images into your scenes (**Figure 3.14**).

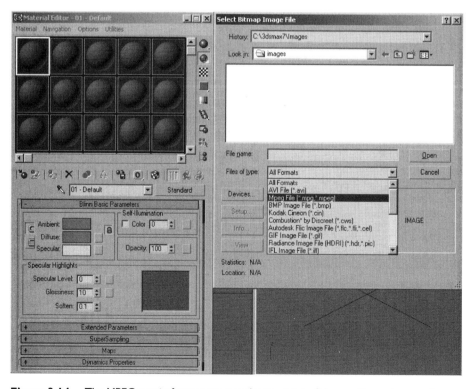

Figure 3.14   The MPEG movie format can now be input into 3ds max 7 anywhere an image file is acceptable, such as the Diffuse Color slot in the Material Editor.

Copying Texture Values

Tired of having to jot down RGB values for colors, or drag them to the right material slot? New right-click menus for copying and pasting colors, materials, and bitmaps will also save you time and trouble. In the past, if you needed to copy a color to another parameter, you would drag and drop it to the desired location; for example, you'd drag the color from a light onto a material's Specular Color swatch, so that the colors would be identical. Now you can right-click on a color swatch, map, or material and choose Copy or Paste (**Figure 3.15**). It's a little improvement, but you'll probably use it all the time.

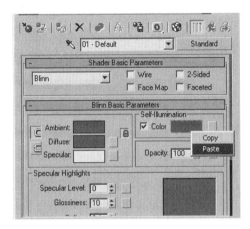

Figure 3.15 The color for Diffuse is copied and pasted into the color for Self-Illumination.

When copying and pasting a material or map, you have the option of pasting as a Copy or pasting as an Instance. The Instance option keeps the changes to the copied material or map linked, so that a change to one will change the other (**Figures 3.16** and **3.17**).

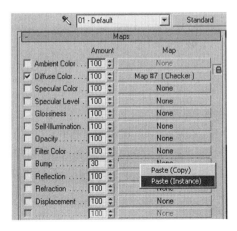

Figure 3.16 The map in the Diffuse Color slot will be pasted as an Instance into the Bump slot.

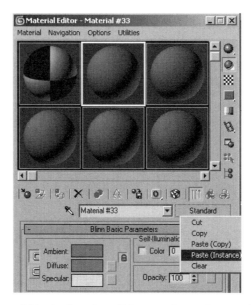

Figure 3.17   The material in the first slot will be pasted as an Instance into the second slot.

Copying and pasting items like colors can be used throughout 3ds max 7, such as in Lights, the Environment and Effects dialog, and the VertexPaint modifier.

VertexPaint Modifier Improvements

The VertexPaint modifier has improved its Adjust Color dialog and added a new Color Palette feature. Let's briefly look at these.

Adjust Color Dialog

The Adjust Color dialog is for adjusting the Hue, Saturation, Value, Red, Green, and Blue attributes of any color. You can now adjust the Contrast and Shadow, Gamma, and Highlight levels from a histogram, which gives you interactive control and a better grasp of the overall states of these color aspects.

The histogram shows how the colors in the vertex selection are distributed based on their Shadow, Gamma (mid-tone), and Highlight input levels. The spinners control the arrows to the left and right (**Figures 3.18**, **3.19**, and **3.20**).

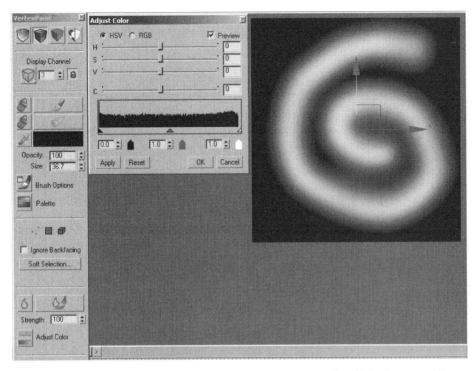

Figure 3.18   A Plane object with the Adjust Color dialog, adjusted with the histogram. The Gamma is set to 1.0. Compare the midtones on the swirly pattern with those in Figure 3.19 and Figure 3.20.

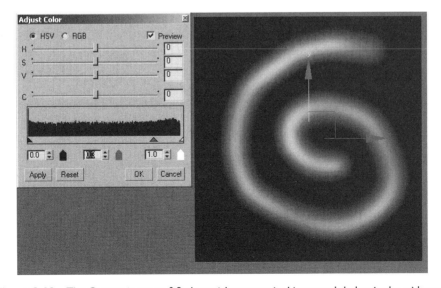

Figure 3.19   The Gamma is set to 0.3; the swirly pattern is thinner and darker in the midtones.

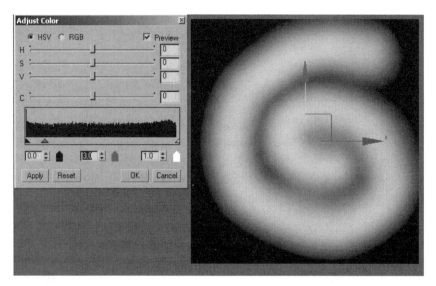

Figure 3.20   The Gamma is set to 3.0; the swirly pattern is thicker and lighter in the mid-tones.

Color Palette

Also in the VertexPaint modifier, a new Color Palette allows you to create and edit colors. The Palette can be saved and loaded as a Color Clipboard (CCB) file. You can drag and drop colors from anywhere to a Color Clipboard floater and save it to be loaded into the Vertex Color Palette. The new Copy and Paste features (right-click) are available for editing colors (**Figure 3.21**).

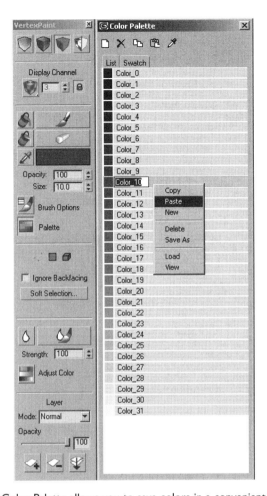

Figure 3.21   The Color Palette allows you to save colors in a convenient location.

Preserve UVs

Preserve Map Channels is a convenient way of making corrections to your UV coordinates within the viewport, instead of needing to use the Unwrap UVW modifier. When tweaking a model after its texture map has been altered, you can more conveniently make minor changes to the vertices of your model so the texture fits better.

The Preserve UVs check box (**Figure 3.22**) is new to Editable Poly and Edit Poly. When this check box is enabled, a vertex or other sub-object will "swim" through the UV coordinates, as if the texture were being held in place while the model is further deformed.

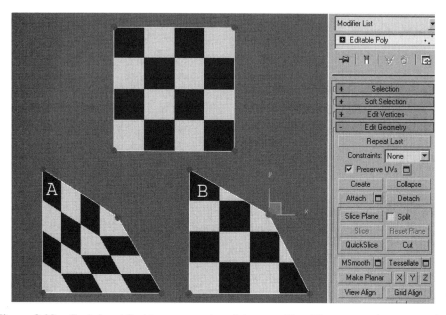

Figure 3.22 Both A and B objects are copies of the top object. The texture distortion in A is what normally happens when a vertex is moved. There's no texture distortion in B because Preserve Map Channels is applied.

Save your work prior to using this method! If vertices are moved too far, you can cause damage to the texture coordinates. For example, if a vertex of a four-sided polygon is placed within a triangle shape, further movements will damage the mapping coordinates (**Figure 3.23**).

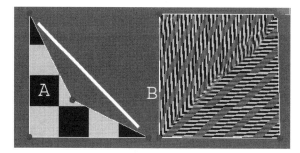

Figure 3.23 In A, the upper-right-corner vertex is moved within a triangle shape. In B, when it is moved back to its original location, the texture becomes unpredictable and unusable.

If you have several mapping channels on your model, you can pick which ones are preserved with the Preserve Map Channels dialog, accessed by clicking on the Settings button (**Figure 3.24**).

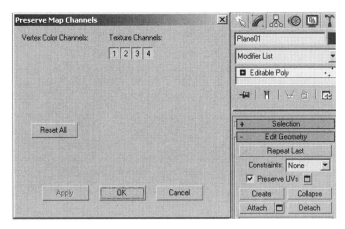

Figure 3.24   From the Preserve Map Channels dialog, you can pick which texture channels to be preserved when vertices are moved.

Subsurface Scattering (SSS)

Subsurface Scattering (SSS) is one of the hottest recent developments in texturing. Some materials, such as flesh, wax, or alabaster, allow light to pass partially though them before it bounces back. The effect is a kind of shallow translucence that is characteristic of many organic materials. Especially in the case of skin, the lack of SSS gives an opaque look that destroys any pretense of realism and warmth.

With normal rendering techniques, even objects you might expect to be translucent, like paper, can render as completely opaque, with no light passing through them. Four new SSS shaders, available only with the mental ray renderer, address this shortcoming (**Figure 3.25**). Two are especially customized for skin.

Figure 3.25 The Deviled Egg rendered with one of the new SSS shaders in mental ray. The light from behind shows through the thin areas of the model, such as the arms and ears.

An important limitation of these SSS shaders is that they will not coordinate with Blend, Composite, Shellac, Top/Bottom, and Double Sided materials. To overcome this limitation and allow a single model to appear to have multiple materials, you must use bitmap images to represent shading.

Note

When learning how to control the SSS shaders, first exaggerate the translucent lighting effect. Then make minor adjustments to achieve a more realistic rendering.

Playing with SSS

In the following exercise, we will explore some of the parameters that enable an exaggerated SSS effect.

1. Open the file sss start.max from the DVD. The scene opens with a Torus object in the Camera01 viewport. An omni light in the center of the torus provides lighting that will scatter through the surface of the object. Within the Material Editor, the first slot is assigned to the torus.

2. Render the Scene from the Camera viewport (**Figure 3.26**).

Figure 3.26   With Standard as the Material type, the scene renders the object dark where the light does not hit the surface in front of the torus.

3. You will need to assign an SSS shader to the torus. In the Material Editor, change the Material from Standard to SSS Fast Material (mi) and render the scene.

   Hmmm, you can't see much difference in the rendering. At these default values, it can be difficult to tell which parameters will exaggerate the scattering effect.

4. Within the Diffuse Subsurface Scattering rollout, change both the Front surface scatter color and the Back surface scatter color to white.

5. Change both the Front and Back surface scatter weight to 1.0.

   The color of the scattering is now white. Increasing the weight makes the effect brighter and more obvious (**Figure 3.27**).

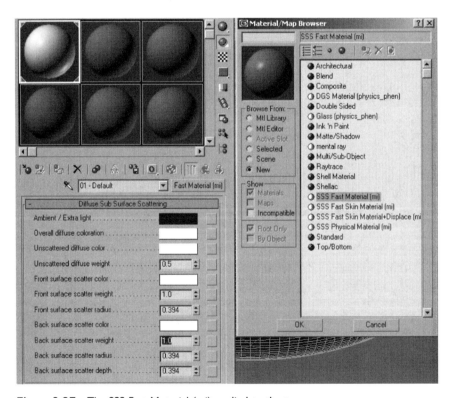

Figure 3.27   The SSS Fast Material (mi) applied to the torus.

6. In the SSS Fast Material (mi) Parameters rollout, set the Number of Samples to 1000. This will increase rendering time, but not by much. The higher the Number of Samples, the less grainy the image will render.

7. In the Advanced Options rollout, set the Scale conversion factor to 0.002 (**Figure 3.28**).

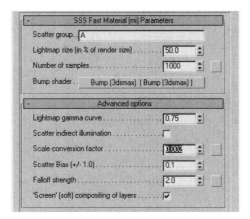

Figure 3.28   The Number of Samples affects graininess. The Scale conversion factor connects the size relationship of the translucence effect to the size of the model.

The Scale conversion factor, set to 0.002, is 500 times smaller than its original value of 1.0. If this value is set too small, then the scattering effect will be evenly spread all over the image, and the surface will appear flat instead of 3D.

Lowering the Scale conversion factor forces the model to calculate smaller. It is as if you had modeled the torus 500 times smaller! The Scale conversion factor is also highly dependent on the units you've chosen to use in 3ds max 7. You will need to first adjust the Scale conversion factor to see what works best in each individual scene.

Setting the Scale conversion factor to 0.002 is not too realistic for rendering skin. But it does work well for backlit, fresh-cut juicy fruit like grapes. Once you become proficient with the parameters, try setting up different colored lights to see a colorful scattering effect.

 Tip

If an object is modeled larger, the Scale conversion factor will need to be lowered even more to achieve the same exaggerated scattering effect. If the value needs to go below 0.001, set the Spinner Precision higher than three decimal places. The Spinner Precision is set within the Preference Settings dialog under the General tab.

8. Render the scene to see the new changes (**Figure 3.29**). To compare the final results, open the file sss finish.max from the DVD.

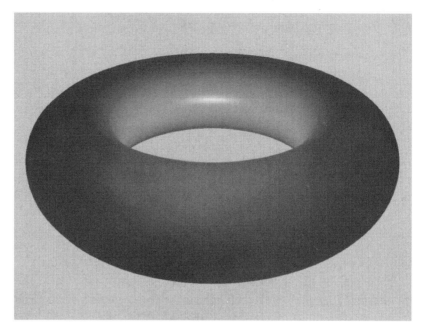

Figure 3.29   The light is traveling through the front area of the torus object as it would through a backlit grape or other translucent fruit.

Summing Up

These new texturing features should help you get your texturing done faster and increase the realism in your rendering. Highlight Seams allows you to visualize the texture seam and better predict the results that will render. Paint Selection mode makes selecting texture coordinates easier. The Projection modifier gives you a way of transferring data from one object to another. Copying and pasting texture values is a much faster and more intuitive way of getting texture information from one material slot to another. Preserve Map Channels helps us better predict the mapping coordinates and make adjustments during the modeling stage. The Subsurface Scattering materials are a quick way of simulating light passing through an object. Later chapters will demonstrate some of the techniques introduced in this chapter. As with many of these new features, you should start off with simple explorations until you understand the basics, then play with exaggerated effects, and finally apply them to more elaborate scenes. These new tools can also be explored as you review the later chapters that cover aspects of rendering.

Chapter 4

What's New in Animation

By Daniel Manahan

3ds max 7 offers significant new tools to help you animate. Animation info gathering and workflow are more flexible than ever with the addition of the following features:

- Expose Transform Helper
- Parameter Collector
- Reaction Manager
- Skin Wrap Modifier
- Skin Morph Modifier
- Bone Tools Mirror

character studio, 3ds max 7's procedural character animation environment, now ships as part of 3ds max 7. We'll look at its powerful animation modes, including several new ones:

- Figure Mode
- Footstep Mode
- Motion Flow Mode
- Mixer Mode and Motion Mixer
- Biped Animation Mode

We'll cover each of these new tools in this chapter.

Expose Transform Helper

With the new Expose Transform helper, you can now immediately expose the position, rotation, and scale values of a child object in relationship to its parent. This has important implications for the scripting of custom rigging tools and procedural animation. For example, information on how the rotation of the forearm relates to the upper arm can now be delivered to a script or wired to drive animation of the character's shoulder, without the need to jump through hoops to gather the necessary rotational, positional, and scalar values—they are all immediately available through the Expose Transform helper.

To use the Expose Transform helper, first pick a child node; Expose Transform then automatically relates the child node to its parent node. If you uncheck the Parent button, you can choose any other object in the scene and retrieve values for its relationship to the original child node.

Each exposed parameter has an M button next to it; click it to copy the correct transform name to the Windows clipboard. For example, if you press the M button to the right of the Z value for Local Euler Angles, then the string `$ExposeTransform01.localEulerZ` will be stored in the Windows clipboard. Type Control-V to paste this value into any active Windows text application or the MAXScript editor (**Figure 4.1**). In this example, the Pin Stack button is used so that transformations to bone 3 allows us to see the resulting changes to Bone 2 in the Expose Transform helper object. Even though Bone 3 is selected, the pinned modifier stack displays the parameters of the Expose Transform Helper. Using the Expose Transform helper. Bone02 can be seen to be a child of Bone01 with an angular relationship to it. The M button is used to copy the appropriate MAXScript name to the windows clipboard. That name can then be pasted into a MAXScript document, where it might be useful.

The script code `$ExposeTransform01.localEulerZ` will constantly track and return the current value in the Local Euler Z axis for the object named ExposeTransform01. Other objects in the scene can call this information to perform any number of actions as long as the current value meets certain requirements or falls into a designated range.

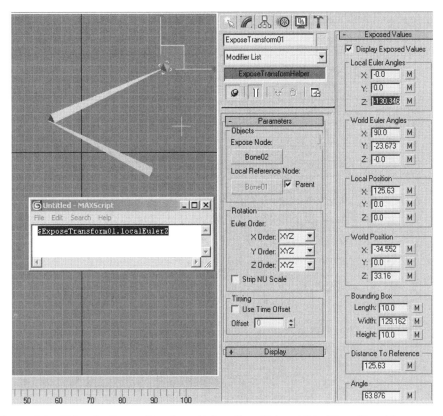

Figure 4.1   Using the Expose Transform Helper. Bone02 is a child of Bone01 and has an angular relationship to it.

Using Expose Transform

To see how the Expose Transform helper works, we'll show how to use transform data to drive an animation. The scene in the following tutorial contains three objects: a plane, a box, and a cylinder. We'll expose the distance between the plane and the box and use this value to drive an animation of the cylinder. The further the box is from the plane, the more the cylinder will bend.

1. Go to the DVD that accompanies this book and open the file entitled expose transform start.max.

2. Select the Expose Transform object, click the Expose Node button in the Modify panel, and pick the box. The Local Reference Node button is gray because the Parent box is checked (that is, with Parent on you can see only info from a parent of the chosen object).

3. Uncheck the Parent check box, click the Local Reference Node button, and pick the plane (**Figure 4.2**).

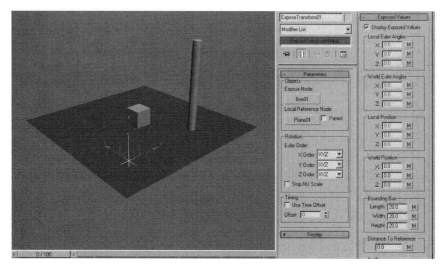

Figure 4.2   Parent is unchecked so that the plane can be assigned as the Local Reference Node. The box has a Distance To Reference relationship of 0.0 to the plane.

Note that the Distance To Reference value is 0.0 because the pivot points for the box and the plane are in the same place. Next, we'll wire the bending of the cylinder based on the distance from the plane's pivot point to the Distance To Reference value in the Expose Transform object (the pivot point of the box).

4. Click the cylinder and right-click-select Wire Parameters from the menu. Then choose Modified Object > Bend > Angle from the menu (**Figure 4.3**).

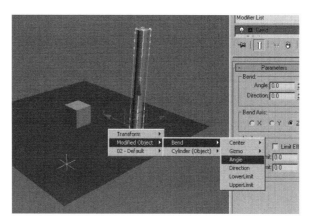

Figure 4.3   Choosing the cylinder's Bend Angle.

5. With the dotted line coming from the cylinder, click the Expose Transform helper and choose Object (ExposeTransformHelper) and Distance from the menu (**Figure 4.4**).

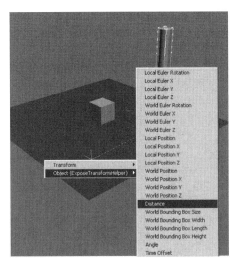

Figure 4.4   Setting the Expose Transform helper's Distance.

6. The Parameter Wiring dialog pops up. Click the One Way Connection button pointing to the left and then click the Connect button (**Figure 4.5**).

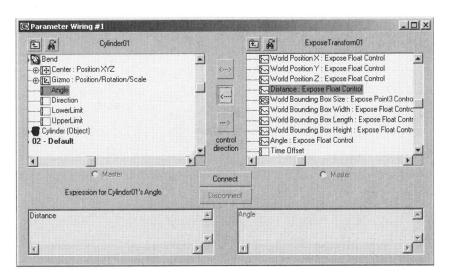

Figure 4.5   A connection is made between the cylinder's Bend Angle and the Expose Transform helper's Distance parameter.

7. Select and move the box up, down, left, and right. Then select and move the plane up, down, left, and right.

No matter which direction the box moves or the plane moves, the further they are from one another, the more the cylinder will bend. Open the file labeled expose transform finish.max to see the results.

Parameter Collector

The Parameter Collector allows you to display parameters from several objects or areas of a scene in an organized and consolidated area. Collecting important parameters in one area saves you time you'd otherwise waste in hunting through the program for each parameter when you need it for animation (**Figure 4.6**).

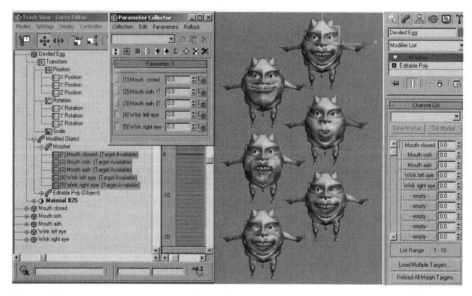

Figure 4.6   Morph targets from the Deviled Egg character are collected and can be animated from the Parameter Collector.

 Tip

If the Parameter Collector closes, it can be opened from the Animation menu or by pressing Alt-2 on the keyboard.

Be aware that if an object that has had its parameters collected is deleted in the scene, the parameters themselves are not automatically deleted. To remove those parameters, highlight them and click the Delete Selected button.

Taking Notes

Another helpful workflow enhancement available from the Parameter Collector is the ability to record Notes on each parameter. One obvious use is to pass important tips along a production pipeline—for example, from character rigger to animator.

The Notes dialog is available from the Parameter Collector's Edit menu. Highlighting the parameter's yellow button lets you add a note. Within the Notes dialog, you can give important information about that parameter. A single note can be attached to several parameters.

Here's how to collect a parameter in the Parameter Collector:

1. Create a Box primitive.

2. Open the Mini Curve Editor and highlight the Box Height Parameter.

3. Right-click to choose Collect Parameters (**Figure 4.7**).

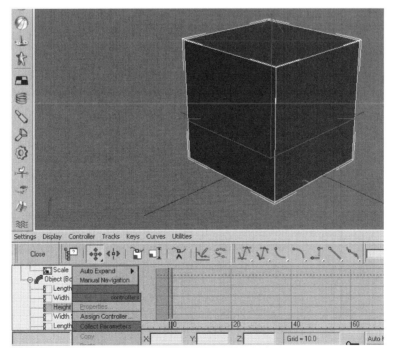

Figure 4.7   Collecting the box's Height with the Parameter Collector.

4. Parameters appear in the Parameter Collector. Use the Multiple Edits button to drag one spinner to change several of them at the same time. This is useful if you have two similar parameters, such as right and left eyes winking, and you want the character to do both actions (blink with both eyes) simultaneously.

The Absolute/Relative toggle works the same as in the standard interface. Enter Absolute values to change the original parameter to those values. Enter Relative values to offset the values by the amount typed in. If, for example, you want to change the relative radius of a teapot from 10.03 to 25.0, enter 14.97 as a Relative value (10.03 + 14.97 = 25.0). But, and this is somewhat counterintuitive, if you had offset a value by 5 units and now you want to offset by another 5 units, you need to first reset the Relative value to 0.0 and then enter 5 units again.

Reaction Manager

In event-driven animation, one object controls the animation of another. Say you want to rotate a Teapot object based on the orientation of another teapot. The two simplest ways to create a one-to-one relationship between the teapots are either to use an Orientation constraint or to wire the parameters of one teapot to the other.

The new Reaction Manager simplifies the wiring process and allows you to use a function curve to effect the change. An object that is animating at a steady pace can control the animation of another object based on this curve. The Reaction Manager provides accurate one-slider control over complex animations and rigs; for example, with it you can control the rotation of each bone in a long dinosaur neck using just a single slider.

Such setups are called Reaction controllers, logically enough. There are five different types of Reaction controllers: Position Reaction, Rotation Reaction, Point3 Reaction, Scale Reaction, and Float Reaction. Most of the setup of a Reaction controller is done within the Reaction Manager dialog, available from the Animation menu or by choosing it from the Alt-right-click Quad menu. The process is straightforward: you set up a master node to control any number of slave objects.

 Note

> The Reaction controllers replace the Reactor controllers from earlier versions of 3ds max. Any existing Reactor controller will be converted to a Reaction controller in 3ds max 7.

Getting a Reaction

Let's work through the steps needed to get one object to react to another.

1. From the DVD, open the file entitled reaction manager start.max. The 3ds max file opens with two Cylinder primitives. We'll use the height of the first cylinder to animate the height of the second cylinder. We'll also put limits on how much the movement of the second cylinder will be affected.

2. Select the left cylinder and open the Reaction Manager (**Figure 4.8**).

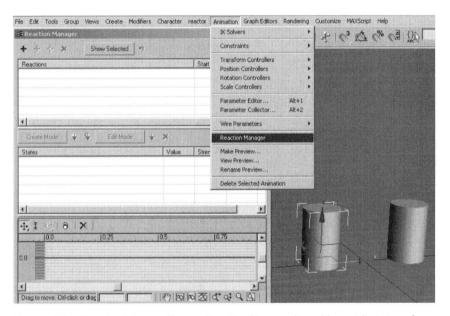

Figure 4.8   Opening 3ds max 7's new Reaction Manager. It enables quick rigging of an animation relationship between two objects.

3. Set the master object: Click the Add Master button, click the left cylinder, and choose Object (Cylinder) > Height from the menu.

4. Now set the slave object: Click the Add Slave button, click the right cylinder, and choose Object (Cylinder) > Height from the menu (**Figure 4.9**).

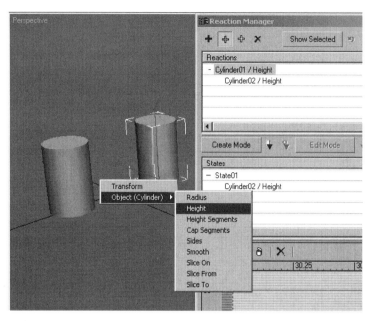

Figure 4.9 The left cylinder is the slave; its height will react to that of the right cylinder. The first State is added to the States list.

5. Click the Create State button. Double-click to highlight each value and enter the following: State01 = 50; Cylinder02/Height = 50; State02 = 100; Cylinder02/ Height = 100 (**Figure 4.10**).

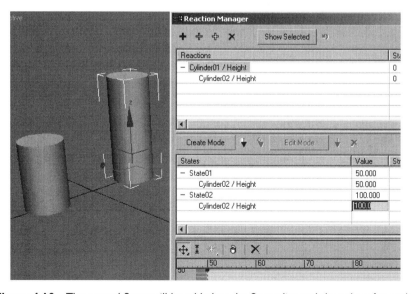

Figure 4.10 The second State will be added to the States list, and the values for each State and Height need to be changed.

The height of the right cylinder will have a range from 50 to 100. The height of the right cylinder will change when the height of the left cylinder is between 50 and 100.

6. In the graph, right-click each node and change both of them to Bézier Corner. Move the left node Bézier point up, and the right node Bézier point down (**Figure 4.11**). If necessary, do a Zoom Extents in the Reaction Manager to see the graph. The function curve graph determines how the right cylinder height will react to the left cylinder height when the height values are between 50 and 100.

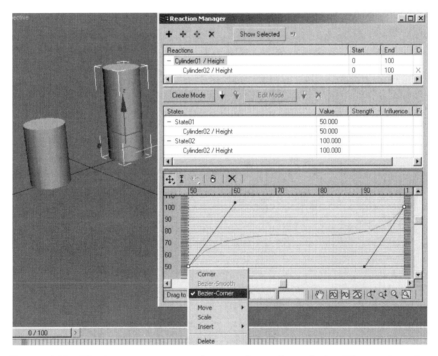

Figure 4.11   The function curve is no longer a diagonal straight line. The reaction of the right cylinder height will follow the influence of this curve.

7. Turn on Auto Key and go to frame 100. In the Modify panel, change the left cylinder's height to 150. Play the animation (**Figure 4.12**).

   At values below 50 and above 100, the left cylinder's height does not affect the right cylinder's height. Between 50 and 100, however, the right cylinder's height does change. Movement of the right cylinder's height varies according to the curve of the Reaction graph.

Open the file entitled reaction manager finish.max from the DVD and check your results.

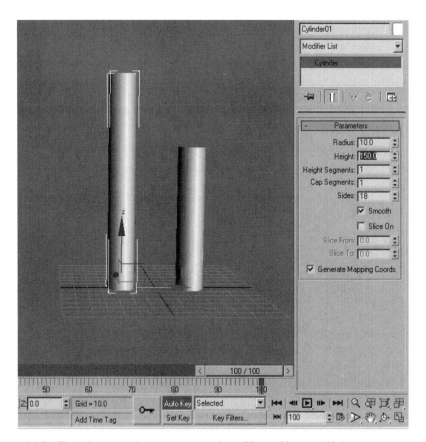

Figure 4.12 The left cylinder's height changes from 30 to 150 over 100 frames.

Skin Wrap Modifier

A character is often modeled body first, with clothing added later as separate geometry. You may want to reuse that model with different clothing, so you need a flexible workflow that lets you animate one character with several choices of clothing, without the hassle of setting up new Envelopes and Weights within the Skin Modifier for each piece of clothing. 3ds max 7's new Skin Wrap modifier simplifies the usual animation workflow for objects that wrap a character.

With Skin Wrap, you can animate a character (or any other object), remodel or clothe it, and use the original character as a proxy to control the remodeled one. This is great in a studio production situation because the animators no longer need to wait for the modelers to finish modifying a model for which an original exists—animation can move right along using the original model, or a low-polygon version, as a proxy. The modified model is swapped in for the proxy at a later time.

The Skin Wrap modifier is applied to the character (or any other objects that you want to control) with the motions of the original model. For example, let's say you want to add a hat and gloves to a character that has already been animated; from the Modifier's list, you would apply a Skin Wrap modifier to both the hat and the gloves and link the Skin Wrap to the original character model. Both the hat and the gloves would need to be properly positioned relative to the positions of the head and hands that they cover. This can be demonstrated simply by positioning some primitives on a plane.

The Skin Wrap modifier has a sub-object level called Control Vertices. Each control vertex is derived from the vertices of the animated control object and has a spherical influence, similar to an envelope from the Skin modifier. The vertices of the Skin Wrap object are influenced according to this envelope. The size of the envelope is determined by the Distance Influence parameter of the Skin Wrap modifier (**Figure 4.13**).

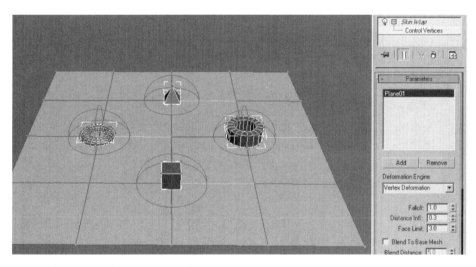

Figure 4.13   The Skin Wrap modifier is applied to each object that sits on this plane. The plane is added to the list. The Distance Influence setting determines the radius of the Skin Wrap spherical envelope of influence.

Set the Distance Influence too low, or position the Skin Wrap object too far away from the control vertices, and the animated control object will not have any influence. Set the Distance Influence too high, and the animation of each control vertex will bleed over to unwanted vertices of the Skin Wrap object. Multiple control vertices may influence individual vertices of the Skin Wrap object, producing unexpected and probably unusable results.

The value of the Distance Influence is globally assigned to all the control vertices, even though each control vertex is likely to need its own Distance. Use the Local Scale

Multiplier parameter to affect individual control vertices and avoid influence bleed-over. At the same time, you have to make sure that each control vertex envelope is large enough to influence the desired vertices of the Skin Wrap object. Some trial and error may be required to find the right values.

Once envelopes are properly sized, the original object can be deformed; this causes the Skin Wrapped object to deform also (**Figure 4.14**).

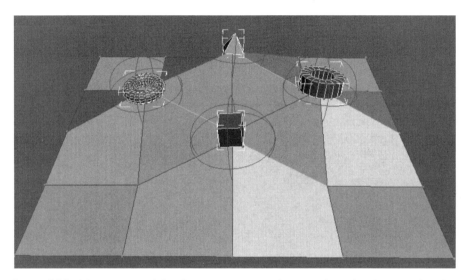

Figure 4.14   Moving some of the plane vertices upward carries along the objects within the Skin Wrap spherical influence envelopes.

 Note

> Be sure that the scale of the original object is set to 100 percent for X, Y, and Z. Otherwise, the shape of the area that is influenced by the object's control vertices will not be spherical and the vertices will influence the Skin Wrap model unpredictably. Use the Reset XForm modifier from the Utilities panel to fix the improper scale of a model.

Skin Morph Modifier

When a realistic character bends its arm, the deformation is complex. The overall volume stays the same, but the biceps bulges, the triceps stretches out, and the skin creases and flattens at the inner elbow. Getting just the right creases, and eliminating unwanted ones, has always been a time-consuming process in 3ds max, because the program does not have a native muscle deformation system that could handle this automatically. Creating good-looking deformations therefore has required much complicated interaction with the Skin Modifier.

This process has been simplified with the new Skin Morph modifier. With it, you can fine-tune your animations using bones to drive corrective morphs around problem creases and bulges. In essence, the Skin Morph modifier allows you to quickly build simple versions of a muscle system. For example, in the case of our bending, bulging arm, you would set the model to deform when a child bone (the forearm) is at a specified angle to its parent (the upper arm bone). The arm's mesh will deform back and forth every time this angular relationship is animated with the Skin Morph modifier applied over the Skin modifier.

Let's take a closer look at Skin Morph, available from the Modifier's list. Start by applying the Skin Morph modifier to your object or character. (We are using the Deviled Egg character for this discussion.) Check Beginner mode and create a morph on the desired angle change of the bones (**Figure 4.15**). Note that bones must be added in the Parameters rollout to see them in the list.

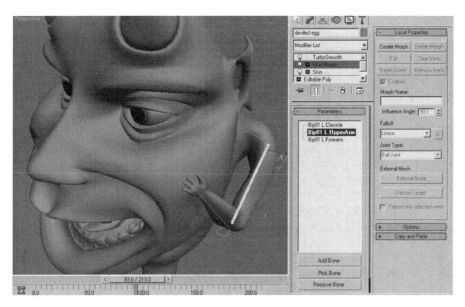

Figure 4.15   The Skin Modifier is applied to the Deviled Egg after the Skin and before the TurboSmooth modifiers. Then a morph is created at the desired bone angle change.

The Skin Morph modifier has a sub-object level for editing points. Changes made to the points are recorded based on the bone angle change. Every time the bone is at its recorded angle, it causes those points to deform. The Influence Angle parameter is set for each morph. Use as small an Influence Angle as possible to prevent multiple morphs from influencing one another (**Figure 4.16**).

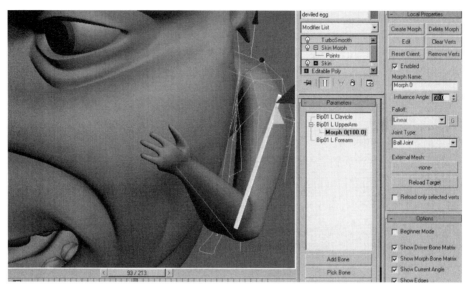

Figure 4.16   The upper arm bone's angle determines when the morph deforms the points. The Influence Angle prevents other morphs from overlapping their effect.

Note that when Beginner mode is unchecked, 3ds max 7 creates morphs automatically and without requiring you to click the Create Morph button.

Animate the forearm vertices of the Deviled Egg, and they deform according to where you moved the points (**Figure 4.17**).

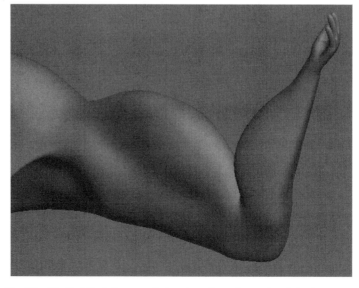

Figure 4.17   The Deviled Egg's forearm bulges based on the angle of the bones.

Bone Tools Mirror

It doesn't make sense to rig all the bones of a bilaterally symmetrical character—that's a waste of time. What you really want is to rig just one side and have the software mirror the bones to create the other side. 3ds max 7 now adds this ability with Bone Tools Mirror (Bone Tools > Bone Editing Tools > Mirror). This is accessed with a new Mirror button added to the Bone Tools dialog. You select the bones to be mirrored; the mirrored bones will be named similarly to their original bones, but with the word "mirrored" added in parentheses (**Figure 4.18**).

The old method was to use the Mirror tool from the toolbar, which caused the Scale value of the mirrored bones to be flipped to a negative 100 percent on the mirrored axis. Bones that have their scale flipped to a negative do not rotate consistently on their local axes. The new Mirror tool in the Bone Tools dialog keeps the mirrored bones at plus 100 percent, where they belong.

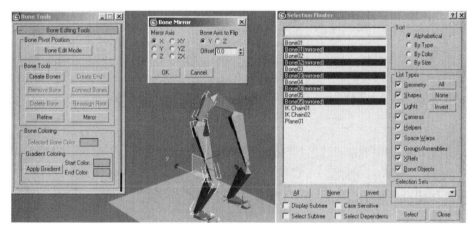

Figure 4.18   The new Mirror button, located in the Bone Tools modifier, opens a dialog to select the axis. The new bones are named according to the original, with the word "mirrored" in parenthesis.

 Tip

> The mirrored bones are not Instances, so you should only mirror the selected bones when all adjustments have been made to one side of the rig.

character studio

Happy days—character studio (cs), formerly a separate program, is now included with and fully integrated into 3ds max 7. character studio works with 3ds max 7's standard bones, weighted controllers, keyframing tools, and skinning options. cs is covered in much more depth in a later chapter, but we will take a brief look at its new features here.

character studio offers a variety of tools for maintaining accuracy and troubleshooting character animation with a set of specially linked objects collectively called a Biped. This Biped is color-coded green on its right side and blue on its left to simplify the display of its rigging and animation features (**Figure 4.19**).

Figure 4.19   character studio Biped posed as a boxer.

With Biped you can quickly create ready-made character rigs and make adjustments to the creation parameters. Most of the parameters for using the Biped are within the Motion panel. Let's examine the Biped's animation modes.

Figure Mode

Figure mode (in the Structure rollout) helps you create the Biped's internal structure—it's basically an automated rigging system. You can make the following assignments: Arms, Neck Links, Spine Links, Leg Links, Tail Links, Ponytail1 Links, Ponytail2 Links, Fingers, Finger Links, Toes, Toe Links, Props, Ankle Attach, Height, Triangle Pelvis, Forearm Twist, Forearm Links, and Body Type (**Figure 4.20**).

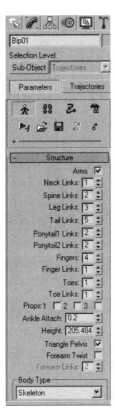

Figure 4.20   character studio's Figure Mode Structure rollout, showing the many parameters to customize the Biped.

Use Figure mode to align, scale, and rotate parts of the Biped structure to fit your modeled characters. Biped also saves you time when creating a character rig by enabling copy-and-paste bones mirroring (**Figure 4.21**) using Copy and Paste Opposite to duplicate the posture or pose of a portion of the Biped. You can rig one side of the Biped and have Figure mode rig the other.

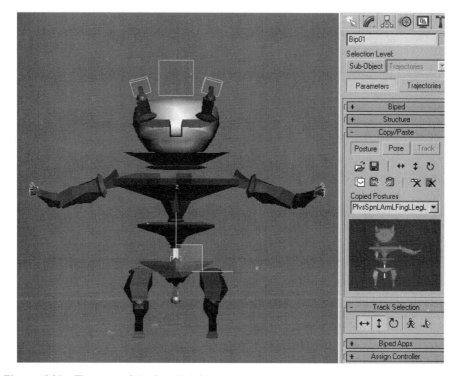

Figure 4.21   The pose of the Biped's left arm is copied and mirrored.

Proper alignment in Figure mode saves time you would otherwise spend making corrective adjustments to Skin modifier animation (**Figure 4.22**).

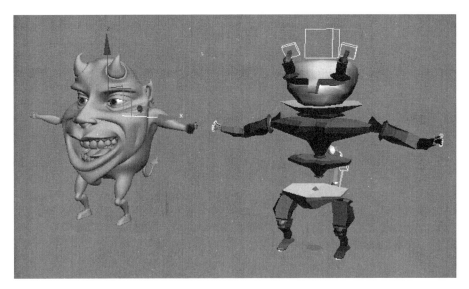

Figure 4.22 The Biped parts are scaled and rotated to fit the Deviled Egg. The next step is to align and position the Biped inside the character geometry.

Footstep Mode

character studio offers a variety of useful procedural animation tools and aids. Footstep mode allows you animate the walking path of a Biped-rigged character throughout a scene. The method is fairly simple: Footstep mode can be activated from the Biped roll-out from the Motion Panel and when any part of the Biped is selected. After activating the Create Footsteps button from the Footstep Creation rollout, you click in the Perspective viewport to place positional markers called Footsteps that indicate where and when the Biped will walk, run, or jump. Left and right Footstep sub-objects set the path for the Biped's corresponding feet. These Footsteps keep the Biped's feet locked to the ground on their designated frames.

When Footstep mode is active, you can only select, delete, position, rotate, and change the duration of the Biped's footsteps. Editing the timing of the Footsteps is done from the Curve Editor in the Dope Sheet mode (**Figure 4.23**). The Biped's body instantly reacts to changes in the curve.

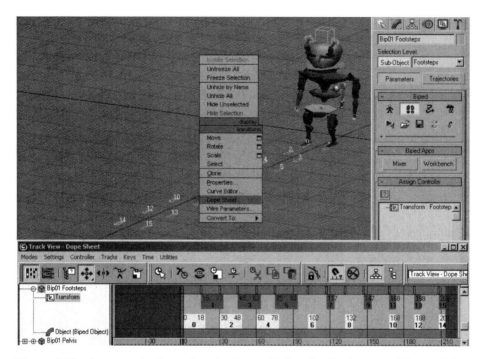

Figure 4.23 Access to the Dope Sheet has been added to the Quad menu in 3ds max 7. It displays the footsteps as blue and green tracks, which correspond to the Biped's blue and green feet.

Leg functions include Plant, Move, Touch, and Lift. When a leg is planted, it sticks to the ground. When a leg moves, it travels from one Footstep to another. If both Biped legs are moving at the same time, then the Biped is jumping, running, or performing some other motion with both feet in the air.

Footsteps cause other parts of the Biped to automatically generate keys. For example, if the Biped has a tail, it will automatically sway back and forth in sync with each step. You can assign a "freeform area" between Footsteps to accommodate Biped animation that does not involve a relationship between foot and ground, such as swimming or reclining in a chair.

Once you are finished animating a Biped, you can save the animation for use in other areas of character studio such as Motion Flow mode, Mixer mode, and the Motion Mixer. Or you can apply the animation to a Crowd of other Bipeds.

Note

Footsteps should be created *before* any extra animation is applied to any Biped parts. If you fail to create Footsteps first, and instead animate some of the Biped parts, you will commit the Biped to Freeform animation and you will not be allowed to add Footsteps later.

Motion Flow Mode

Motion Flow mode is activated from within the Biped rollout. From Motion Flow mode, you can take saved Biped animations, including motion-capture (mocap) files, and create a transition between them. For example, you can load an animation of a Biped performing a ballet and transition this into another animation of the Biped slipping on a banana peel, producing a comical animation of the Biped dancing a few steps, then slipping and falling down (**Figure 4.24**).

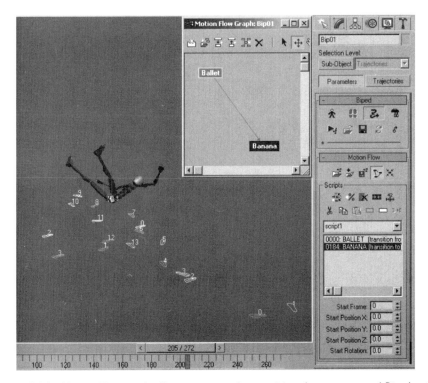

Figure 4.24 Motion Flow mode allows you to make transitions between several Biped animations. In the middle of this animation, the Biped dances, then slips and falls.

This sort of procedural animation assemblage can be very useful, but be aware that the animation clips may not work perfectly together. character studio does not necessarily know how cartoony you want that ballerina's fall to be, or just how hard she should hit the ground. Some good old manual keyframing may still be necessary.

Mixer Mode and Motion Mixer

Mixer mode is activated from the Biped rollout and the Motion Mixer is opened from the Biped Apps rollout. Mixer mode and the Motion Mixer work together. When Mixer mode is active, the Biped responds in the viewports to changes made to it in the Motion Mixer, and the Save File button is available. The Motion Mixer is used to mix together different Biped animations and filter different areas of the Biped. For example, you can take the upper-body animation of one Biped and the lower-body animation of another and mix them into one animation (**Figure 4.25**). The effect can be a timesaver when you need to quickly move a lot of characters with a few motions. A curve editor controls how much of the upper body will animate and when.

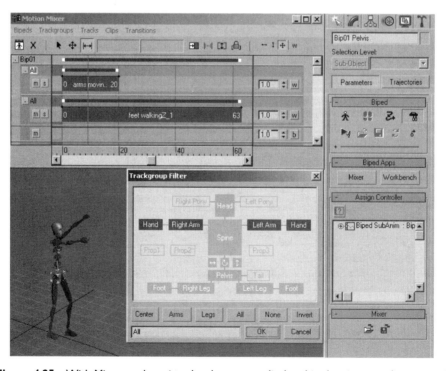

Figure 4.25   With Mixer mode active, the changes are displayed in the viewport. An animated track of upper-body arms is filtered and mixed with lower-body walking. The result: a Biped that walks and waves his arms.

In the Motion Mixer, you can also graphically edit and warp the time range of the animation files. For example, you can make the Biped move in slow motion during designated frames, then speed it up to normal again. The completed mix can be consolidated into a single animation file for the final animation.

Biped Animation Mode

Once the Biped has been created, Footsteps added, and Motions mixed, you will probably want to tweak the animation. You may have positioned the Footsteps in the correct locations and times, but the Biped's head and pelvis might need to be animated differently. For this you need to exit all previously mentioned modes and enter Biped Animation mode.

Once in Biped Animation mode, you can select and animate the Biped's individual parts, such as the arms and head, using standard keyframing and kinematics. You can also change between forward kinematics (FK) and inverse kinematics (IK) using the IK blend slider (Key Info > IK Blend).

With FK, you animate down the bone hierarchy chain from parent to child. In FK, moving the upper arm moves the hand. Since the Biped hand is a child of the forearm, it will follow. IK works in the opposite way, up the bone chain—you use the child to move the parent, the hand to move the upper arm. For example, if you temporarily constrain the Biped hand to an object, when that object moves, the Biped hand and entire arm will follow, to the limits of the rig's extensibility. (Note that under IK, rotation of the upper arm does not have a blended effect based on a Blend value for the keyframe.)

Many animators prefer to animate parts of the body using mainly one system or the other, but you really need both systems to animate characters effectively. Switching back and forth between FK and IK allows you to animate with the greatest degree of control, as well as to take advantage of special capabilities such as having the hands and feet controlled by moving objects in the scene. IK/FK blending makes it easier to throw and catch objects or pass an object from one hand to the other, simple actions that can be surprisingly hard to animate with only one form of kinematics.

The technique is not difficult. To pass an object such as a football from hand to hand, you first create a key with the Set Key button, pick the football as the object, and set IK Blend (in the Key Info modifier) to 1.0. This allows the animated football to be passed from the right Biped hand to the left (**Figure 4.26**).

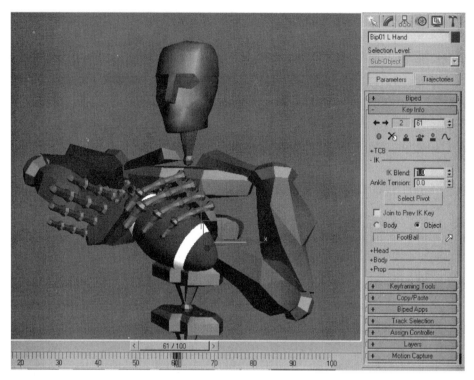

Figure 4.26   Passing a football with IK blending.

Another trick new to 3ds max 7 is the ability to set when the Biped's head will look at and follow the animation of other objects in a scene. A Biped head can track and look at one object passing, then turn to track another object traveling in a different direction. You only need to animate the objects and the Biped's head will follow.

1. Select the Biped head object. From the Key Info rollout, expand the Head section, and use the Select LookAt Target button to pick an animated object in the scene (**Figure 4.27**).

   The object can be animated after it is set as the LookAt object for the head. Keys need to be set so that the Target Blend value can be changed. A Target Blend value of 0.0 will cause the Biped head to do nothing as the designated object animates. A Target Blend value of 1.0 will force the Biped head to look at the designated object. And Target Blend values that are between 0.0 and 1.0 will cause the head to partially look at the animated object. In this example, an animated Teapot object was picked for the head to look at in frame 30. Other Target Blend keys could be set so that the animated Teapot no longer influences the Biped head.

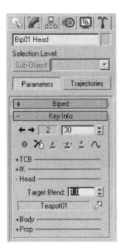

Figure 4.27   The Key Info rollout allows you to create a key, pick a LookAt object, and animate the Target Blend value.

2. Click the Set Key button, which is found within the Key Info rollout, on the frames where you want the Biped head to follow the animated object.

3. The Target Blend value on the keyframes can be set between 0.0 and 1.0, depending on how much influence you want the animated object to have on the Biped's head.

The designated LookAt object can be animated either before or after the Target Blend values are entered.

 Note

Only one LookAt object may be picked for the Biped head. It is best to pick a non-renderable Helper that is using a Link Constraint to each animated object at the various frames.

Following is a quick mention of other new character studio Biped features. The character studio Help Reference in the 3ds max 7 User Reference is the place to go to learn more about these Biped abilities.

• The location of the foot pivot point can change from the back to the front of the foot at different frames of the animation. When you animate the location of the foot's pivot, the weight of the walking Biped will appear to transfer more realistically through the feet.

• Biped has a built-in system to animate rotations and do its best to avoid unwanted limb flipping (a common problem with character rigs caused mainly by the limitations of current IK solvers and the use of Euler rather than quaternion rotational data). This allows you to animate the rotation of Biped joints without having to add keys just to fix rig problems.

- In many cases, you need to play with several types of animation ideas until you know what you want. For this, Biped offers you the same flexibility that a photo-editing program offers with layers. By adding layers, you can turn parts of the animation on and off and flatten the animation to a single track when satisfied.

- A Visual Clipboard is available to manage animation tracks and character poses. You can easily find and substitute pose data between characters.

- A set of tools within a Biped application called the Workbench is available to clean up and correct rig-based animation problems, such as unwanted jerking. You can use Workbench tools to smooth the keyframes for a more natural motion.

- Import, manage, and edit mocap data for use with the Biped. character studio has tools to aid you in tweaking mocap files from a real performer that do not calibrate with your 3ds max 7 scene.

- Use layers to test out variations in your animation, and turn these variations off and on. For example, you can put Biped spine animation on its own layer. When that layer is applied, the character will sway differently when it walks. Changes to this layer can then be removed or turned off if you aren't satisfied, returning the animation to its previous motion. Layers can be stacked to see the effects of multiple motions, and then collapsed into a single animation.

- Use Crowds to combine many different saved Biped animations into a flock of characters with various behaviors. Biped characters can be set to act as if they were attracted to or repelled by other objects or characters in the scene.

Summing Up

In all, 3ds max 7 has added impressive new animation tools. Including character studio as a standard part of the max package is certainly a champion move that positions 3ds max 7 as the leader in procedural character animation. character studio's Biped is a great way for you to quickly create simple animation that would take much longer with traditional methods. The new deformation features will help you craft more believable characters. Some of the new tools are complex, and their power (as with the Motion mixing and layering tools) has barely been tapped, but your animation production pipeline will definitely benefit from them.

These new animation tools will be useful for preparing your scene for rendering—so let's explore 3ds max 7's new render features in the next chapter.

Chapter 5
What's New in Rendering

By Daniel Manahan

The last few years have seen major advances in rendering techniques, driven by the need for ever more detailed CG images that can't be distinguished from reality. 3ds max 7 now has improved versions of the mental ray and scanline radiosity rendering engines, with particular advances in the areas of precision lighting and accurate shadows, so essential to realistic rendering.

In this chapter, you will explore 3ds max 7 rendering and speed enhancements that make setting up final scenes more efficient, including:

- Photometric Lights: Preset Lights
- mental ray Shadow Map Rollout
- Render Shortcuts Toolbar
- Renderable Spline Modifier
- Motion Blur for Lights and Cameras
- Assign Vertex Colors Utility

Photometric Lights: Preset Lights

Setting up good lighting is immensely important and is usually done in the final stages before a scene is rendered, although in some pipelines light kits are applied in the previz or layout stage. In either case, you need to make sure that lighting is accurately placed and that the intensity and color complement the scene. New light presets called Photometric Lights take a lot of the effort out of this.

If you want to light your scene with, say, a realistic 60-watt light bulb, you can choose it from the new Photometric lights available through the Create > Lights menu. These lights are the same as in previous 3ds max versions, except now the presets have been configured for you (**Figure 5.1**).

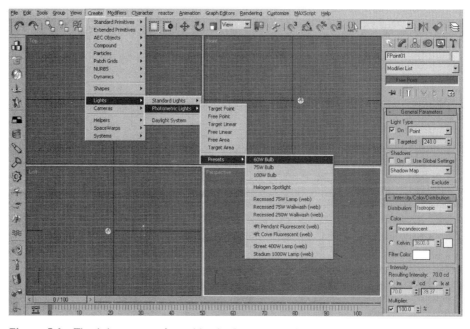

Figure 5.1 This light, auto-configured by the Photometric Light presets, realistically emulates the illumination of a standard 60-watt incandescent bulb.

One of the Photometric light types is free point lighting. As with omni lights, free point lighting emanates from a point that is infinitely small. As with a standard free spotlight, a free point light has no target to control its angle. To aim a free light, you must manually select and rotate it.

The Distribution type of the light determines how strong the light is (in other words, it determines the intensity of the light cast relative to the distance and direction from the source). The Distribution parameter can be set to Isotropic, Spotlight, or Web light types. An Isotropic distribution is even in all directions. A Spotlight distribution has a focused beam; Hotspot/Beam and Falloff/Field parameters control where the brightest point is and how the light intensity fades on the edges of the beam. A Web distribution is more complicated and requires a file to determine the surrounding intensity in 3D space. Web files can be in the IES (Illuminating Engineering Society), CIBSE (Chartered Institution of Building Services Engineers), or LTLI standard photometric profile formats. If a profile is not provided in the 3ds max 7 maps folder, it might be available through the light manufacturer and downloadable from the Internet (**Figure 5.2**).

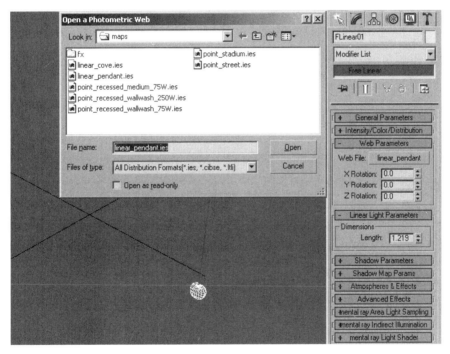

Figure 5.2   A Web lighting profile file can be in the IES, LTLI, or CIBSE photometric formats. Linear Pendant is an IES light type.

mental ray Shadow Map Rollout

In previous versions of 3ds max, you could obtain shadows with translucency (as cast by transparent or translucent objects) only if Ray Traced Shadows was chosen as the shadow type from the General Parameters rollout. Standard shadow mapping produced only solid shadows in a solid color.

The enhanced mental ray Shadow Map parameters rollout (**Figure 5.3**) in 3ds max 7 now lets you render a shadow-mapped shadow with transparency. With this new option, objects that are transparent will cast a shadow with transparency from a light that has this property checked (**Figure 5.4**). The Filter Color of the object's material determines the color of the shadow.

Figure 5.3   Within the General Parameters rollout, Shadows On is checked, mental ray Shadow Map is chosen, and Transparent Shadows Enabled is checked.

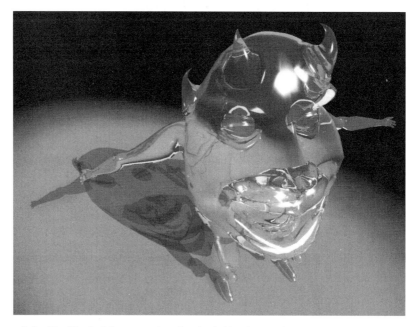

Figure 5.4   The Deviled Egg is rendered to look like glass and casts a shadow with transparency using mental ray Shadow Map.

Render Shortcuts Toolbar

The Render shortcuts allow you to quickly assign all of the settings in the Render Scene dialog to three different presets: A, B, and C.

To access the Render Shortcuts toolbar, right-click in a blank area of the Main toolbar and choose Render Shortcuts from the menu. This will expose a floating toolbar. Drag the Render Shortcuts toolbar to the top to dock it under the Main toolbar (**Figure 5.5**).

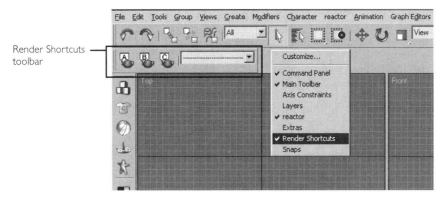

Figure 5.5   The Render Shortcuts toolbar is dragged and docked to the top.

   Tip

> If you use the right-click method to dock a toolbar to the top, it will hide itself behind the Main toolbar instead of docking below. This is probably not what you want, in which case use the drag method instead.

Let's use the Render Shortcuts feature to assign the Default Scanline Renderer to the A, B, and C buttons. Complete the following steps:

1. Make sure that Default Scanline Renderer is the current renderer, as specified in the Common tab of the Render Scene dialog. In the Assign Renderer rollout, click the "…" button next to Production and choose Scanline from the list. This only needs to be done if the Default Scanline Renderer is not the current renderer (**Figure 5.6**).

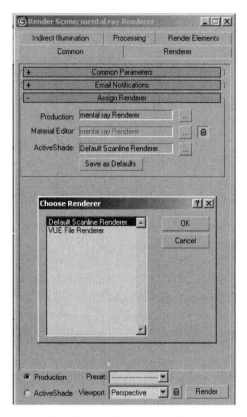

Figure 5.6   Setting the Default Scanline Renderer as the current renderer. If mental ray is the current renderer, switch to Scanline.

2. While holding the Shift key, click the shortcut button labeled A on the Render Shortcuts toolbar (**Figure 5.7**).

Figure 5.7   Holding the Shift key and clicking the A button will assign the shortcut.

The letter "a" appears in the drop-down box, indicating that the preset for A has been set to the Scanline Renderer.

Using the same technique, assign the "b" shortcut to mental ray, as follows.

3. Change the renderer to the mental ray renderer from the Assign Renderer rollout.

4. While holding the Shift key, click the B shortcut button. The letter "b" will appear in the drop-down box, indicating that the B shortcut button has been set to the mental ray renderer.

5. In both of these rendering options, 640 by 480 is the default size. Test rendering at smaller sizes saves time, so you might want the letter C to be assigned to a smaller image size. To do this, change the Output Size to 320 by 240 in the Render Scene dialog by clicking the "320x240" button (**Figure 5.8**), then click the "c" shortcut. Setting this shortcut makes it easier to switch back and forth between the preview settings and the final rendering settings.

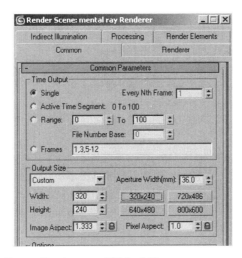

Figure 5.8   The Output Size is set to 320 by 240.

6. We can test to see if the buttons render with the proper presets. Create a Teapot object in the Perspective viewport, click the "a" preset from the list, click the Load button from the dialog that opens, and type Shift-Q. Another approach is to click the A preset button and type Shift-Q. Either technique will perform a Quick Render in the Perspective viewport using the Default Scanline Renderer.

7. Click the "b" shortcut and Quick Render again. This chooses the mental ray renderer at a window size of 640 by 480.

8. Click the "c" shortcut and Quick Render again. This time the mental ray renderer renders at 320 by 240.

These shortcuts have a few other properties. When a shortcut preset is loaded from the drop-down, you can choose which specific categories belonging to that preset to load (**Figure 5.9**).

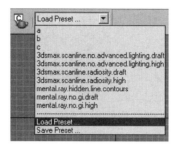

Figure 5.9   Loading a Render Shortcut preset.

This is the way to quickly access and mix rendering aspects of one preset with another. For example, with "c" as the current preset, you can load the rendering size from "a" by choosing the category called Common (**Figure 5.10**).

Figure 5.10   Choosing the Common category from the "a" Render Shortcuts preset to load into the "c" preset.

If you have set up your presets as described above, the result would set mental ray as the renderer with an output image size of 640 by 480. This is the same as if you had chosen the "b" preset. You can also reassign new render settings to presets by making new settings and Shift-clicking the A, B, or C preset buttons.

Renderable Spline Modifier

In 3ds max, you can only render objects that are composed of polygonal geometry. Lights, cameras, helpers, and space warps never render because they do not contain polygons. Splines only render if Renderable is checked from the Rendering rollout. Renderable converts splines to geometry (polys) and also gives you the option of setting the thickness of the spline and the number of sides. This arrangement has its limitations, however. For example, a circle with a large thickness renders similarly to a Torus primitive (**Figure 5.11**).

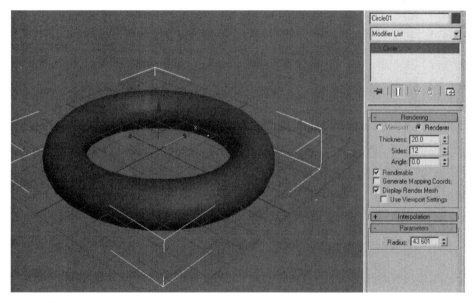

Figure 5.11   A circle with a thickness of 20; Renderable is checked. This object looks like a torus.

Using the File Link Manager, you can attach spline objects to a scene and make them all renderable by setting their Renderable parameter in the Rendering tab (**Figure 5.12**).

However, all splines brought in with the File Link Manager will render the same size.

The new Renderable Spline modifier now allows you to pick and choose which splines will and will not be renderable, providing greater render flexibility. Pick and choose which linked splines will or will not render by checking or unchecking Renderable in the Render Spline modifier that has been applied to those splines. The Renderable Spline modifier gives you more specific control than does the File Link Manager (**Figure 5.13**).

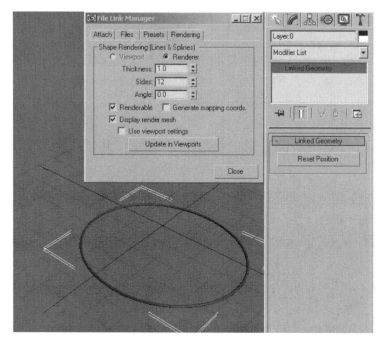

Figure 5.12   In this linked geometry, within the File Link Manager, within the Rendering tab, Renderable and Display Render Mesh are checked.

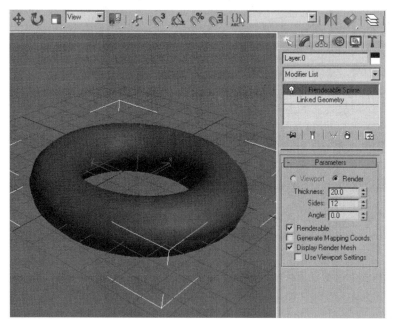

Figure 5.13   Renderable is checked and the thickness is chosen for this spline using the new Renderable Spline modifier.

You can also instance the Renderable Spline modifier to many splines, even those that are not linked files. This way, changes you make to the Renderable property of one spline will affect all the others.

Motion Blur for Lights and Cameras

Motion blur is now available in 3ds max 7 for lights and cameras in the mental ray Renderer. Animate the position or rotation of a camera or light and the moving image blurs. The blur from a light is seen in the shadows cast by the objects in the scene.

To properly render moving shadows, follow these steps:

1. First, make sure to uncheck (disable) Enable for Shadow Maps (Render Scene > Shadows & Displacement > Shadow Maps), or you will get unusable results. Without motion blur, a moving light illuminating an object generates a crisp, hard-edged shadow (**Figure 5.14**).

Figure 5.14   The Deviled Egg rendered with Shadow Maps disabled. The resulting shadow is crisp, not blocky.

2. Now add motion blur. In the Render Scene dialog, under the Render tab, open the Camera Effects rollout and check Motion Blur.

3. Enable the new Blur All Objects option under Motion Blur. This automatically affects the blur property of all objects, including lights and cameras. By checking Blur All Objects, you avoid having to manually set the property of each object, so you save time—potentially a whole lot of time, depending on the complexity of your scene (**Figure 5.15**).

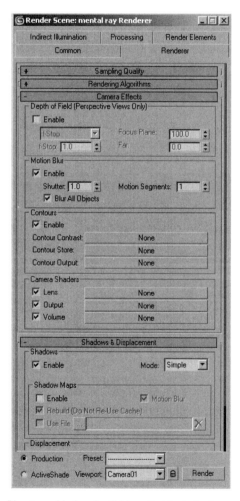

Figure 5.15   Motion Blur is enabled and will blur all objects in the scene.

With these settings, when you animate a light, its shadow will blur. That blur will be greater the further the shadow is from the source light (**Figure 5.16**).

Figure 5.16   The shadow cast from the character's feet is sharper than the shadow cast from higher up on its body. Since the motion blur of the shadow is moving horizontally with the movement of the light, the arms blur horizontally as well.

Assign Vertex Colors Utility

The Radiosity renderer realistically imitates the way lights interact with an environment. For example, if a white object is in a room with blue walls and an orange ceiling, then the white object will appear somewhat orange on top and blue on its sides, as a result of light bouncing off the colored walls and ceiling. But radiosity, though very desirable, has always come with its own set of problems and limitations.

Rendering with radiosity is relatively quick per rendered frame—but before any frame is rendered, a radiosity solution has to be calculated for the entire scene, and that can take quite a long time, depending on the complexity of the scene. Also, using radiosity requires you to keep your objects strictly in place—no animation—after a radiosity solution is generated; if you don't, you will get chaotic, unusable textures. You can get around this by enabling Regather Indirect Illumination from the Rendering Parameters rollout, but as this generates a new radiosity solution for each frame, the entire scene will take much longer to render.

Using Assign Vertex Colors, you have the flexibility to animate after the fact without causing rendering problems or taking a huge render hit. Unfortunately, since mental ray does not work with Vertex Color assignment, your only option is the Default Scanline Renderer.

Note

Vertex Colors can be assigned to either the faces or the vertices. Using the Color by Face method is less accurate but calculates faster. Using the Color by Vertex method uses each vertex of the faces, so it is more accurate and slower to calculate.

The basic workflow is as follows:

1. Light the scene.
2. Generate a radiosity solution.
3. Bake the vertex colors using Assign Vertex Colors.
4. Do additional animation as desired.
5. Do a final render.

Radiosity is generated from the Render Scene dialog, within the Advanced Lighting tab. The Start button calculates the lighting in the scene and generates a solution. The time needed for the calculation will vary based on the size of the scene, the number of lights, and the level of accuracy you specify in the Initial Quality parameter.

After the radiosity solution has been generated, the next step is to access the Assign Vertex Colors utility from the Tools menu > Utility panel.

In the previous version of 3ds max, final gathering would automatically be calculated into the vertex colors and the option to omit this was unavailable. New to 3ds max 7 is the option Radiosity, Reuse Direct Illumination from Solution, which will calculate faster but omit the final gathering. (You will need to select the option Radiosity, Render Direct Illumination, if final gathering was used to generate the solution and you want it to be calculated into the vertex colors.) By omitting the final gathering, you will get lower quality but faster calculation. Clicking the Assign to Selected button bakes the radiosity solution to the vertex colors of the selected object (**Figure 5.17**).

Figure 5.17   In the Utilities panel, enable Radiosity, Reuse Direct Illumination from Solution, to assign vertex colors to the selected object.

After vertex colors are assigned, a VertexPaint modifier appears in the modifier stack of your selected object. This allows you to edit the vertex colors. Once you are satisfied with the vertex colors, add a Vertex Color Map in the Diffuse Color slot of your object's material and render the scene.

You can also now assign vertex colors from the VertexPaint modifier using the same methods as in the Assign Vertex Colors utility (**Figure 5.18**).

Figure 5.18   New to 3ds max 7 within the Assign Vertex Colors rollout of the VertexPaint modifier: The rendering options have been changed to be consistent with the Assign Vertex Colors utility.

Blurring the vertex colors is possible from the Vertex Colors modifiers. Blurring colors may smooth out some unwanted banding or over-sharp color edges, but too much blur will cause unwanted smearing in areas that need to be sharp. Blur only once or twice in areas that need to be smoother (**Figure 5.19**).

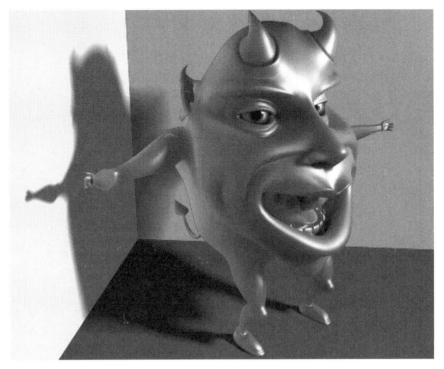

Figure 5.19   The Deviled Egg rendered with vertex colors that were blurred with the Vertex Color modifier. No radiosity solution was required for the final render, even though radiosity was used to generate the vertex colors.

Summing Up

With the new features and enhancements, you will save time setting up and rendering your scenes. Photometric lighting has presets to make choosing a light easier. mental ray shadows can now work with transparency. Render presets make switching between rendering modes and Common settings quicker. Spline rendering is organized more efficiently in the File Link Manager. mental ray motion blur works better with shadows and an animated camera. And Radiosity has greatly improved its interaction with assigning vertex colors.

Part II
Managing max

Chapter 6
Scripting

by Jon Seagull

We 3D artists hate repetitive tasks. After all, we were led to believe when we signed on for this gig that the computer was going to be doing all the grunt work. While this idea is at its core true, a few late nights troubleshooting scenes under a looming deadline have beaten the naive luster off of it for most of us. (If they haven't, bookmark this chapter. You'll be wanting to reread it in a couple of months.)

We love our tools, but there are times when it seems that they don't quite work exactly the way we want at the moment, or that if some incredibly esoteric feature existed, we'd be able to get to bed a few hours earlier. Wouldn't it be great if in those moments you could magically conjure up the exact tool you needed?

Well, you can. Seriously. That's what MAXScript (sometimes referred to as MXS) is for. If you're lucky enough to:

(a) do this for a living

(b) work at a studio with the resources to hire a technical director,

then you most likely already know the power of MAXScript. The thought of writing code yourself may still make you nervous, however.

Many artists seem to tense up when the subject of MAXScript arises. They feel that it's unpleasantly technical, worry that they won't be able to learn it for lack of programming experience, or just don't see a practical use short of total expertise, which they don't really want.

Much of the intimidation stems from the fact that there are really two faces of MAXScript: the polished tools written by technical directors or downloaded from the Internet, containing dozens, hundreds, or thousands of lines of code; and the interactive Listener, into which you can type commands to manipulate your scenes. Most people think of MAXScript exclusively in terms of the former aspect—it's what you have contact with as a nonscripter, and if you peek at the code for a substantial script, it can be intimidating. The other face of MAXScript, though, the quick and interactive one, is where the true power lies for the average production artist.

I used to be intimidated by MAXScript, too. But then I had a production problem: A client wanted me to model a structure that was covered with tens of thousands of semi-randomly oriented panels. A particle system would have been too random, and modeling the panels by hand would have blown the deadline and driven me nuts. My hand was forced; I dove into the MAXScript Reference and tutorials, asked a lot of questions on the discreet MAXScript forum, and, after a couple of days and a lot of wrong turns, had a block of code that did what I needed.

The experience opened my eyes to how many repetitive tasks I was doing every day that could be automated with MAXScript. At first I spent as much or more time coding as I saved on tedium, but I soon found opening the Listener and typing a line or two of code as natural as reaching for a modifier or utility, and as essential.

Learning MAXScript is really about streamlining your interaction with the program. Knowing a little MXS means being able to communicate with 3ds max in its own language. And, as with any foreign language, knowing even a single phrase at the right time can save you from disaster *("Où se trouve le WC?")*.

We're going to enter the world of MAXScript from both angles: learning how to use interactive MAXScript commands for common tasks, and building a couple of simple utilities to get a taste of what goes into a scripted tool. The chapter is thus divided into two main sections:

- "**Making Life Interesting**"—learning a basic MAXScript vocabulary to automate common boring tasks. This section is a primer for those with no MAXScript experience at all, focused on single-line script commands entered in the Listener.

- "**Getting Your Way**"—creating custom UI elements and tools that fit your workflow. This section explores the basics of creating longer scripts, and the use of the Visual MAXScript Editor (VMXS for short) to build interfaces for them.

  We will build two time-saving scripted utilities in this section—a draft render settings manager and a replacement for the Color Clipboard utility that docks as a toolbar.

The emphasis in this chapter is on understanding the thought process that goes into planning and writing MAXScript code. The point of this chapter is not to make you a technical director (there are a number of excellent MXS-only training materials available), but rather to put a few simple tools in your hands to help with daily problem solving and workflow trimming.

Getting into the Mindset

Turning MAXScript into an effective part of your workflow may require you to pick up some new habits. This section contains a number of tips about how to *approach* writing code before we get into the specifics of actually *writing* any.

Start with Pseudocode

Pseudocode is code that is not specific to any programming language. It is the set of instructions for a script. Pseudocode is probably more important than the code itself; if you can see logically what you want a script to do, the rest is just translating that into the syntax that MAXScript understands. Think of it in artistic terms: After you've decided on the overall composition of a piece, you can then worry about filling in the details.

Use the MAXScript Reference

I cannot recommend enough using the online help. When I'm scripting, I refer to that document every few minutes. The MAXScript Reference is a bit like a foreign language dictionary. You use it to translate your pseudocode into valid MAXScript.

The help is less helpful when it comes to questions of overall grammar or program structure, although a number of excellent how-to examples have been added to the MAXScript online Reference for this version.

You can also use the MAXScript online Reference to determine what can and can't be done. Not everything in 3ds max is scriptable, particularly in parts of the program that have changed little since before MAXScript entered the picture in version 2 of the application. In these cases, the online Reference will let you know, which can potentially save you a lot of fruitless work. For example, the entry for *loft* states, "Loft compound objects are not constructible by MAXScript."

Steal

If you don't know how to do something, find someone else's script that does something similar and then adapt it until it does what you want it to do. This practice is common, and it will save you from rewriting a lot of code that doesn't need to be reinvented. Looking at someone else's program structure can also teach you new ways of approaching problems or streamlining your code. Remember, if a substantial part of your code (or even just a function or two) belongs to someone else, it's good manners to credit that person somewhere in your script. Check the licensing agreement that comes with any script you're editing to make sure the author doesn't mind, or email the person and ask. Who knows, maybe the author can be even more help. For a good place to get scripts written by other users, try www.scriptspot.com.

Use the Macro Recorder,
but Don't Rely on It Completely

In the MAXScript menu you'll find the Macro Recorder, which echoes commands you perform in the interface. For example, if you want to write a script that makes spheres, turn on the Macro Recorder and make a sphere in your interface; a command like the following appears in the Macro Recorder (you may have to open the MAXScript Listener window to see the whole command):

```
Sphere radius:6.57503 smooth:on segs:32 chop:0 slice:off sliceFrom:0
sliceTo:0 mapCoords:on recenter:off pos:[-2.50576,-0.672316,0]
isSelected:on
```

If you want to create a sphere in your script, you now have an example of how to approach the task. For simple scripts, you can record a series of events in this manner and then just drag the text from the Macro Recorder to a toolbar. A button will appear, and anytime you press that button, it will repeat the actions.

Note

> The Macro Recorder does not echo everything that's scriptable, nor does it always generate correct code. Something in max might be scriptable but not appear in the Macro Recorder. In some instances the Macro Recorder will give you false information, and frequently the commands it outputs will include many optional parameters. Use it for what it's worth, and if your action doesn't appear in the Macro Recorder or doesn't work when pasted into your script, search the Reference file—it's probably still possible to write your script.

Try to Generalize Code When You Feel It's Worth It

In a production environment, often you make custom software to work only with the current situation. For example, suppose an animator has ten objects she wants to move along a surface in a specific fashion. You could hard-code your script to work only with those ten objects. This can be faster because you don't need to make a fancy interface and you can make certain time-saving assumptions on how these objects will react to your script. It also means, however, that your code is now throwaway, useful only in this one instance; if another job comes up where you're doing something similar, you have to rewrite a whole lot of code. Learn when to generalize and when to be more specific.

One technique I use when I'm not sure if I'll be reusing a piece of code is to write a lot of comments in the script and then save it to a "quickies" folder in my scripts directory. If I need it again, I can generalize it later (or just plug in different hard-coded values) without investing a lot of effort in figuring out what I did.

Get a Good Text Editor to Write Longer Scripts

Although you can use the text editor that exists inside max (MAXScript menu > New Script), this editor has a major disadvantage: If your script crashes max, the script is lost, and possibly a bunch of work with it. I prefer editing my scripts in an outside text editor, such as Microsoft's Notepad or Helios Software's TextPad (www.textpad.com), which I now use exclusively. TextPad is cool for a number of reasons: It formats code better, its syntax highlighting is faster and more robust than the built-in editor's, you can search and replace in multiple documents at the same time (and with regular expressions), and it uses a tabbed interface for multiple files, which helps when you have multiple scripts that need editing at the same time.

Note

The one instance in which the built-in MAXScript Editor is indispensable is when using the Visual MAXScript (VMXS) utility to create interface elements. VMXS will only write its code to a MAXScript Editor window. You can then copy and paste the block of code out to TextPad.

An evaluation copy of TextPad, as well as the MaxScript.syn file needed for TextPad's syntax highlighting features, is included on the DVD. Keep in mind that TextPad is commercial software, so you must register it if you use it past the evaluation period.

Set Up TextPad for MAXScript

1. Run the installer.

2. Copy MaxScript.syn from the DVD to your Program Files\TextPad 4\system folder. (If you don't have the DVD handy, you can download the file from www.textpad.com/add-ons/synh2m.html.)

3. Start TextPad and then choose Configure/New Document Class.

4. In the wizard, enter MAXScript as the document class name and click Next.

5. Enter *.ms,*.mcr as the class members and click Next.

6. Check the "Enable syntax highlighting" check box, choose MaxScript.syn in the drop-down menu, and click Next.

7. Verify your choices in the summary screen and click Finish.

Making Life Interesting—
Your First Ten (or So) Words of MXS

MAXScript can take a big bite out of routine tasks. With a few simple commands at your disposal, you can frequently automate your way out of tedious clicking and even approach some problems from an entirely new angle. The goal of this section is not to make you a scripting whiz but instead to provide a few tools to help you automate tasks without involving a technical director or searching ScriptSpot.

Your tool for interacting with MAXScript is called the Listener (MAXScript > MAXScript Listener), a window into which you can type script commands that are immediately executed, and into which MAXScript writes its output (**Figure 6.1**). Your commands appear in black, while MAXScript's feedback appears in blue (for output) and red (for error messages).

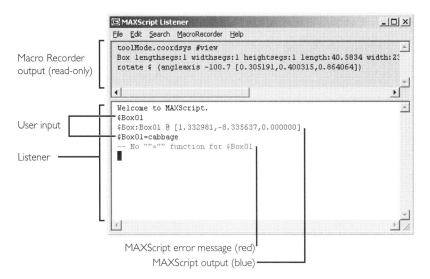

Macro Recorder output (read-only)

User input

Listener

MAXScript error message (red)
MAXScript output (blue)

Figure 6.1 The MAXScript Listener window.

Your starting vocabulary is the following:

- $
- show
- move
- rotate (eulerAngles X Y Z)
- scale
- in coordsys
- for
- where
- classOf
- random
- #() and []
- at time

Let's dig in.

The "$" Symbol

$ means the current selection. For now, it is most useful when only one object is selected, as it behaves a bit differently with multiple objects selected. Why do you need this? Well, one of the simple things MAXScript is good for is looking at and changing properties of objects in your scene. You access properties of the current object with $.*property*—for example, $.radius or $.height. Like most things in 3ds max, properties are organized into hierarchies. This means that properties can have properties of their own, and so on, all separated by dots, as in $.material.diffusemap.coords.U_Tiling, the U Tiling parameter of the Diffuse Color map of the selected object's material.

If you just type a property name into the Listener, it will tell you the value of that property. To assign a new value, use $.property = *newvalue*. For relative values, you can use the operators += , -= , *= , and /=, as in $.radius /= 2, which halves the radius of a selected object (as long as it has a radius property to change).

 Note

> Make sure to use the number pad Enter key, not the Return key, when entering MAXScript commands in the Listener. The Enter key by the number pad will always execute the code you just typed, while Return causes the Listener to wait for more input in some cases. Use Return when you want to enter multiple lines of code in the Listener before executing them all.

The value you set doesn't have to be a simple number. You can use mathematical expressions, other properties, or even math that operates on other properties.

$ has another, similar use as well: Follow it with an object name, like $Box01, and you are referring to that node, and all the access to properties described above is just as valid (for example, $Box01.height). By using the wildcards * and ?, as in $Box*, you can set properties for a whole list of objects. (We'll get to handling multiple objects in more depth later.)

 Note

> If your object names have spaces in them, you need to use single quotes around the name, as in $'my box'.

The "show" Command

How do you know if an object has a particular property? As you might guess from the examples above, there are a lot of property names—far too many to memorize. That's what the show command is for. show generates a list of an object's properties in the MAXScript Listener. For example, if you select a box and type show $, you'll get the following:

```
.height : float
.length : float
.lengthsegs : integer
.width : float
.widthsegs : integer
.mapCoords : boolean
.heightsegs : integer
false
```

The word to the left of the colon is the property name, and the word on the right describes the type of value it's expecting (The false at the end is a MAXScript hiccup, not a property name; you can safely ignore it.) If you try to set a property to the wrong kind of value, as in $Sphere01.radius = false, MAXScript will complain with an error message. The sidebar explains some of the common value types you're likely to encounter and how to format them.

Bear in mind that not all the object's properties are shown. All objects, as well as certain classes of objects, share some properties, such as name, material, and renderable, which do not appear for clarity's sake. Also, properties of the object's modifiers, materials, and other "extras" are not shown. Full listings are available in the MAXScript Reference, under "General Node Properties," as well as in the "common properties, operators, and methods" entry for that object class (see, I wasn't kidding when I said you had to use the Reference!).

  Note

Meanings of Some Common Variable Type Names

- integer: Whole number
- float: Decimal number
- string: A text value, entered with double quotes: "hello world"
- boolean: True/false value, entered as true, false, on, or off
- point2: Two-axis coordinate, entered with square brackets and a comma: [1,2]
- point3: Three-axis coordinate, also with square brackets and commas: [1,2,3]
- color: RGB values, entered with parentheses, no commas, and the word color: (color 128 128 128)

When an object's properties have properties of their own, you can use show to list those subproperties as well. For example, if you needed to find out how to view or adjust properties of the box's material, you would type show `$Box01.material`. If you then wanted to find properties of the material's Diffuse Color map, you'd find the MAXScript property name for the diffuse map in the output of the previous command and use it to write show `$Box01.material.diffusemap`, and so on.

Putting a Two-Word Vocabulary to Work

So what can you do now, with only two words of MAXScript, that you couldn't do before? You can do the following:

- Find and change any parameter of any object in your scene, even if it's hidden, frozen, or buried in a group.

- Set any parameter of any object quickly, including copying settings from one object to another and setting values using mathematical expressions.

- By using wildcards (* and ?) in object names, set a property for many objects at once.

Pretty good for just two words, huh? Armed with your amazing vocabulary, see if you can figure out what each one-line script below does:

```
$Box01.height = $Box02.height

$Box01.height = $Box01.length = $Box01.width = 10

$Sphere01.radius = $Box01.height/2

$Box*.height = 10

$Box*.isHidden = false

$Omni*.multiplier /= 2

$Box*.material = $Sphere01.material

$Spot*.on = false
```

The answers in plain English are below:

- Set Box01's Height spinner to the value of Box02's.

- Make Box01 a cube 10 units on a side.

- Set Sphere01's radius equal to half of Box01's height (in other words, make the objects the same height).

- Set the Height spinner of all objects whose name starts with *Box* to 10.

- Unhide all objects whose name starts with *Box*.

- Halve the Multiplier parameter for all objects whose name starts with *Omni*.

- Assign all objects whose name starts with *Box* the material assigned to Sphere01.

- Set the on parameter of all objects whose name starts with *Spot* to `off`. (This particular example is likely not to work as written; we will discuss why later in great detail. It is included here to get you thinking about the sorts of tasks you can automate with MAXScript.)

"move," "rotate," "scale," and "in coordsys"

Now we're going to add four more words, to give you some more verbs to use in your MAXScript sentences. You know what `move`, `rotate`, and `scale` mean already; we just need to cover syntax for those, and I'll bet you have your suspicions about `coordsys`.

For `move` commands, you provide XYZ coordinates in square brackets, separated by commas (MXS calls this kind of value a point3):

```
move $Box01 [10,0,0]
```

moves the box 10 units in the positive X direction. Note that this is a relative move. For an absolute move, you set an object's `position` property instead:

```
$Box01.position = [10,0,0]
```

moves the box to 10,0,0 in world coordinate space.

Rotation values are a little more complicated, and they require us to sneak an extra word into your vocabulary. To avoid the extremely ugly math of true 3D rotations, MXS lets you input rotation as a `eulerAngles` value: an X rotation plus a Y rotation plus a Z rotation. Like the similarly named Euler XYZ rotation controller, this method has problems with arbitrary rotation axes and with gimbal lock (the condition in which, after a lot of Euler rotation, the XYZ axes are no longer mathematically perpendicular and not all rotations are possible), but the gain in usability is well worth it.

```
rotate $Box01 (eulerAngles 90 90 0)
```

rotates the object 90 degrees in X and 90 degrees in Y.

`scale` transforms take a point3 number, just as `move` does, but considers 100% scaling to be equivalent to the number 1, so a 50% uniform scale would look like this:

```
scale $Box01 [.5,.5,.5]
```

Now, all these transforms happen in world coordinate space by default. In order to do a transform in local, parent, or any other coordinate system, you preface your transform command with `in coordSys` *some coordinate system*:

```
in coordSys local move $Box01 [10,0,0]
```

moves Box01 10 units in Local X rather than World X.

Automating with "for" Loops

Let's move on to what is arguably the most important automation tool in MAXScript—the `for` loop. As pseudocode:

```
for variable in a list of things do something
```

In other words, perform a task (or sequence of tasks—*something* can mean a whole list of commands, including other loops) on each member of a list. This is where the "automating repetitive tasks" aspect we keep talking about really takes off.

```
for i in selection do (i.wirecolor = color 0 128 0)
```

In this example, the *variable* is named `i` (this is arbitrary, but using `i` as the loop counter is a programming convention), the *list of things* is the keyword `selection`, which as you may have guessed means "the currently selected objects," and the *something* is to set one of the object's properties to a specific value, in this case the wireframe color to bright green. In other words, the pseudocode reads as follows:

```
for (each object) in (the selection) do (set the wireframe color to green)
```

See how that works?

Now, one thing to keep in mind is that each time through the loop above, `i` serves as a placeholder for *the object itself*. So anything you know how to do to a single object (transform it, query a property, change a property, or any combination) you can now do to a whole list of objects automatically, by putting the command after `do`, and substituting `i` for $ or *$objectName*.

The example above uses `selection` as the set to work on, but there are many other possibilities. These include predefined keywords (`objects`, `geometry`, `lights`, `cameras`, `helpers`, `shapes`, `systems`, `sceneMaterials`, `meditMaterials`, and `spacewarps`), wildcarded names (`for i in $Box* do i.height = 10`), numbers, or explicitly defined lists of objects called arrays (more on those later). Now that you have for in your arsenal, you can really start automating tedious tasks:

```
for i in $*Omni* do (i.multiplier = i.multiplier*0.5)
```

means "Dim all lights with Omni in their name by half."

```
for i in selection do i.material = $Box01.material
```

means "Set the material of all selected objects to Box01's material."

You can also enter multiple commands on a single line in the do statement; surround it with parentheses and use a semicolon to separate the commands:

```
for i in geometry do (i.motionblur = #image;i.motionBlurOn = true)
```

means "Turn motion blur on and set the type to image motion blur for all scene geometry."

 Note

> One of the most common errors the Macro Recorder introduces to MXS code is its use of $ to refer to the currently selected object. Since $ stands for an actual object if a single object is selected, but for the selection keyword when multiple objects are selected, it is good coding practice to purge code you are going to reuse of references to $. One way to do this that works in many cases is to put the commands from the Macro Recorder inside for i in selection loops, and substitute i for $ in the Macro Recorder code within the loop.

"where" and "classOf"

Now let's try a for loop that doesn't work. Try a one-liner to turn off all the lights in your scene:

```
for i in lights do i.on = false
```

If your scene contains any targeted lights, you'll get an error similar to the following:

```
-- Error occurred in i loop
--   Frame:
--     i: $Target:Spot01.Target @ [-11.212518,-15.219044,0.000000]
-- Unknown property: "on" in $Target:Spot01.Target @ [-11.212518,
-15.219044,0.000000]
```

What the error message means, line by line, is the following:

—The code in the for loop using the variable i had a problem.

—If this had been an animation problem, the frame number would go here.

—When the problem occurred, i represented the target object `Spot01.Target` at these coordinates.

—The problem was that there was no `"on"` property to set on the object.

In other words, our problem is that by using the keyword `lights`, we included the light target objects as well, and MAXScript complained and gave up because targets don't have an on/off switch. To do what we want, we need to exclude the target objects from processing. That's where `where` and `classOf` come in.

`where` lets you filter a `for` loop's actions by inserting a true/false statement that is checked each time through the loop. If the statement is true for that iteration of the loop, the code in the loop executes. If false, that iteration is skipped. In its purest form,

```
for i in selection where (false) do something
```

does nothing, while:

```
for i in selection where (true) do something
```

acts on everything in the selection.

To make this useful, though, we want to put an expression after the `where` that *evaluates* to a true/false, or Boolean, value. And for that we need some operators that test truth. There are several ways to compare two values (**Tables 6.1** and **6.2**).

Table 6.1   Numeric Comparison Operators

Symbol	Means	Example	Example Output
==	Is equal to	1 == 2	false
		1 == 1	true
!=	Is not equal to	1 != 2	true
		1 != 1	false
>	Is greater than	1 > 2	false
		2 > 1	true
<	Is less than	1 < 2	true
		2 < 1	false
>=	Is greater than or equal to	1 >= 2	false
		1 >= 1	true
		2 >= 1	true
<=	Is less than or equal to	1 <= 2	true
		1 <= 1	true
		2 <= 1	false

Table 6.2 Boolean (Truth) Operators

Operator	True If	Example	Example Output
and	Both are true	false and false	false
		true and false	false
		true and true	true
or	Either or both are true	false or false	false
		true or false	true
		true or true	true
not	Changes true to false and vice versa	not true	false
		not false	true

Let's try some examples:

```
for i in $Box* where (i.height > 10) do i.height = 10
```

means "Set all objects whose names start with *Box* that are taller than 10 units to a height of 10."

```
for i in $Box* where((i.height > 9) and (i.height < 11)) do i.height = 10
```

means "Set all objects whose names start with *Box* that are between 9 and 11 units tall to a height of 10."

```
for i in geometry where (i.material == undefined) do i.isHidden = false
```

means "Unhide all geometry that doesn't have a material assigned."

```
for i in shapes where (i.baseobject.renderable == true) do i.name =
"RS_" + i.name
```

means "Add *RS_* to the start of the name of all renderable splines (to make selection by name easier)."

 Note

> Spline objects' renderable property is accessed with object.baseobject.ren-derable to distinguish it from the renderable object property shared by all objects. The same goes for lights' duplicate-named castShadows property.

But what about our broken code from the start of this section? We need a way to test what kind of object something is, so that we can plug it into our where clause: classOf.

Every object in max belongs to a *class*, a category whose members share identical parameters and behave in the same way. Boxes are a class, as are spheres, and both classes are distinct from the editable mesh class. Take our beloved `Box01`, for example:

```
classOf $Box01
```

returns

```
Box
```

Like `show`, `classOf` can be used as a reference tool, except for class names rather than property names. Unlike `show`, the value it returns can also be used in a truth test expression:

```
classOf $Box01 == Box
```

returns `true`. To use it in a `where` clause, just add parentheses:

```
for i in geometry where (classOf i == Box) do i.height *= 2
```

which means, "Double the height parameter of all box primitives, regardless of name."

One more thing about `classOf` before we debug our lighting script. If you add a modifier to the box, such as Bend:

```
classOf $Box01
```

returns `Editable_mesh` instead of `Box`. The class name reflects the *current* state of the object, not the one it was born with (if you deactivate the modifier, for example, `classOf` `$Box01` will return `Box` once again). If you want to ignore all modifiers when checking class, use:

```
classOf $Box01.baseobject
```

which looks only at the bottom entry in the modifier stack and returns `Box` as before.

Turning Off the Lights

Let's debug our previous failed turn-off-all-lights script command using `where` and `classOf`. Previously we tried:

```
for i in lights do i.on = false
```

which bailed because it couldn't set the on property for target objects. To get around this error, we want to change the command so that it skips over targets. This technique turns out to be essential when doing anything that batch-processes lights or cameras.

1. Reset 3ds max.

2. Create a few lights in the scene, including at least one Target Spot or Target Direct light.

3. Select one of the light targets in the viewport, and type *classOf* $ in the Listener. Max responds with a class name of `Targetobject`.

4. Now that we know the class name, let's try a truth test just to be sure:

```
classOf $ == Targetobject
```

returns true. Now we know what to put inside our where statement to filter out targets.

5. Type in the Listener:

```
for i in lights where (classOf i != targetobject) do i.on = false
```

All the lights turn off, and MAXScript doesn't complain a bit.

Now the power of `for` is really unleashed for scene management. You can conditionally change properties for thousands of objects at a time, if needed. Here are a few highly useful sentences to get you started:

```
for i in cameras where (classOf i != targetObject) do i.mpassenabled = true
```

means "Turn Multi-Pass Effects on for all cameras."

```
for i in geometry where (i.material == $Box01.material) do i.isHidden = false
```

means "Unhide all objects sharing Box01's material." This gets around the limitations of the Material Editor's Select by Material button, which only considers visible objects.

```
for i in geometry where i.material == undefined do print i.name
```

means "Output the names of all objects with no material assigned."

```
for i in lights where (classOf i != targetobject) do i.multiplier *= 1.05
```

means "5% brightness increase on all lights in the scene."

```
for i in lights where (classOf i == targetSpot) do (i.showCone =
i.showNearAtten = i.showFarAtten = off)
```

means "Turn off Show Cone and Show Attenuation Ranges for all targeted spotlights."

```
for i in shapes where (i.baseobject.renderable == true) do (i.isHidden =
false;selectMore i)
```

means "Unhide and select all renderable splines."

Doubtless you have a number of least-favorite chores of your own—start using that `show` command to add your own.

"random" Numbers

Producing high-quality 3D imagery often means overcoming the tendency of the computer to make things look too perfect and orderly. Scenes that are too regular, ordered, or idealized break the illusion, and many of our most effective techniques involve "dirtying up" our scenes in some way. Disorder added by hand has a way of not looking random enough, however. If you've ever done any particle work, you know that particle systems' controls for adding randomness are the key to making a believable effect. The MXS command random is a fantastic tool for adding chaos to other parts of your scene (in a carefully controlled manner, of course!). You use it with the expression:

```
random value1 value2
```

where the two values are of the same type, and they define the upper and lower limits of the range of possible values.

We're now going to use your burgeoning MXS vocabulary to add some chaotic believability to a scene.

Adding Chaos to a Scene with "for" and "random"

1. On the DVD, open the file cafe_start.max. It's a scene of some instanced café tables and chairs, arranged with robotic precision.

Note

This scene has been set up so that the Listener is docked to a viewport. To do this in your own scenes, right-click the viewport label to open the Viewport Right-Click menu and choose Views > Extended > MAXScript Listener.

2. Render the camera view as is (**Figure 6.2**), then load the render into channel A of the RAM Player using the button with a teapot icon. The changes we're making are going to be subtle, and we'll want to be able to do a close comparison of the before and after.

3. First, let's make sure the tables don't all have their feet aligned. Activate the Listener viewport and type the following:

```
for i in $*Table* do rotate i (eulerAngles 0 0 (random -180 180))
```

The pseudo-code for the line above is this:

```
for every object with 'table' in its name, rotate the object a
random amount in Z.
```

Figure 6.2 The cafe looks nice, but it's too orderly. (Furniture models courtesy of Scott Onstott at www.scottonstott.com.)

Let's take a closer look at that part at the end of the line. MAXScript treats every line of code as an expression. This means that every line ends up evaluating to a value. It also means that any component part of a line can be its own expression, which, as long as it evaluates to the kind of value MXS is expecting, works the same as if a simple value were there.

When MAXScript gets to the random statement, it simply fills in the resulting value in that spot in the code. The parentheses help guide the interpreter as to what gets evaluated first, just like in a code-free mathematical expression: 2 + 3 * 2 = 8, but (2 + 3) * 2 = 10.

Now let's shift each group of tables around on the floor a little. In order for the chairs to stay properly positioned relative to the tables, they'll have to travel together. It's possible, with a larger vocabulary and more code, to do this with MAXScript directly, but we're sticking to quick and dirty in this exercise, and trying to spend less time coding than we would have spent clicking.

4. Select each group of four chairs, and link them to the nearest table with max's Select and Link tool.

5. Once the chairs are linked to the tables, type into the Listener:

```
for i in $*Table* do move i [(random -5 5),(random -5 5),0]
```

The tables are now a little less excruciatingly organized. As in the previous line of code, we're using expressions for part of the coordinates—the X and Y components in this case (Z stays 0 because we want everything to remain on the floor).

It's also worth examining why we're using a `for` loop instead of simply typing the following:

```
move $*Table* [(random -5 5),(random -5 5),0]
```

If you run the above piece of code, the `random` expressions are only evaluated once, and the same random X and Y values are applied to all the objects in unison. By generating the random number within the `for` loop, on the other hand, a different random number is used each time through the loop, and the objects move different amounts relative to each other. There are times when you might want to have a random effect work either way, however, so keep in mind that you have the option.

Now let's scramble the chairs a bit. We need to think a little bit harder about how we want them to move. On average, they'd probably be pulled out or pushed in more than they'd be displaced horizontally, but with four chairs surrounding each table, we need to use a `move` in local space for that to happen.

6. As we saw previously, putting in `coordsys local` before a transform makes it occur in local space rather than world space. And so we type the following:

```
for i in $*chair* do in coordSys local move i [(random -6 3),
(random -1 1),0]
```

and get exactly what we want. Local X is the push-pull direction of the chair, so we're adding a larger push-pull jitter that favors pulling the chairs out in local X, and a small, symmetrical side-to-side jitter in local Y. Z, as before, stays at 0.

7. One last twiddle of the chairs, just like we did with the tables at the outset, and we're set:

```
for i in $*chair* do rotate i (eulerAngles 0 0 (random -5 5))
```

8. Render the camera view and load it into channel B of the RAM Player (**Figure 6.3**).

Figure 6.3   The subtle chaos added to the scene makes it look more real.

See the difference? That little bit of chaos has given the scene a lot more life, without altering the narrative truth of "four tables, each with four chairs, pushed in." It's just that now employees, rather than robots, did the organizing. Viewers don't see the difference, but they do feel it. And all it cost you was the time to type four sentences of MAXScript!

The scene in its final state is on the DVD as cafe_01.max. If you were developing this scene further, you could take a similar approach to positioning the place settings on the tables, rotations and scale of flowers on the tables, and so on.

Just a couple more words for your MAXScript vocabulary, and you'll find yourself using it like a Swiss army knife.

#( ) and [ ]—Working with Arrays

An array is a list of data. Arrays are indicated by parentheses preceded by a number sign, and commas separate each element:

```
myArray = #($Box01,$Box02,$Box03)
```

The above code defines a variable named `myArray` as a placeholder for the list of three boxes. To access a member of the array, you type the array's name followed by an *index* number in square brackets. The number indicates the position in the array of the object you that want to access:

```
myArray[2]
```

returns something like:

```
$Box:Box02 @ [6.800152,13.702519,0.000000]
```

and:

```
myArray[2].height
```

accesses Box02's `height` parameter.

A lot of built-in data structures are stored as arrays, and being able to access them by index number in this way makes them accessible to `for` loop processing. Instead of processing the array itself, though, it is often preferable to have the `for` loop iterate over a series of numbers like so:

```
for i in 1 to 3 do myArray[i].height = i*10
```

Each time through the loop, the value of `i` increases by 1, and so Box01's height is set to 10, Box02's to 20, and Box03's to 30. In other words, we just built a simple staircase generator in two lines of code.

Using `random` and the built-in `meditMaterials` array, you can use this technique to randomly assign materials to a group of objects. Say you have a crowd shot to finish that uses textured planes for the individual people. You load your 12 people materials into the first 12 slots of the Material Editor, select the planes, and type the following:

```
for i in selection do i.material = meditMaterials[(random 1 12)]
```

Since (`random 1 12`) evaluates to a number, a random index is being generated each time through the loop, and thus a random material from the first 12 Material Editor slots is assigned to each plane in the selection.

An object's modifier stack is an array as well, with `modifiers[1]` being the top modifier in the stack. When you don't know how long your array is going to be, you can use the array's `count` property to find out.

```
for i in 1 to $.modifiers.count do $.modifiers[i].Enabled = true
```

turns on all of a selected object's modifiers.

When processing modifier stacks for multiple objects, it becomes necessary to go beyond a single line of code (actually it is possible in a single line, but it's harder to read and debug). To create multiline scripts, you need to open the MAXScript Editor rather than the Listener (MAXScript menu > New Script). To execute the Editor code, use the window's File menu > Evaluate All.

```
for i in geometry where (i.modifiers.count > 0) do
   (
   for j in i.modifiers where ((classOf j == meshsmooth) or (classOf j
== TurboSmooth)) do
      (
      j.useRenderIterations = true
      j.renderIterations = 3
      j.iterations = 1
      )
   )
```

Can you see what's going on in the above code? The parentheses and line breaks are mostly for clarity's sake. They help you visually separate sections of your code. The first `for` loop is exactly what we've been using in our examples so far—`for i in selection do` *something*. The *something* in this case, though, is a second `for` loop, using `j` instead of `i` as the index variable. `j` is used because `i` already has a meaning within the loop, so we need to pick another variable name to avoid conflicts.

In pseudo-code, our script reads like the following:

```
for all geometry with at least 1 modifier do
(
   for each of this object's modifiers that's a meshsmooth or
turbosmooth do
      (
      turn on the modifier's render iterations
      set the modifier's render iterations to 3
      set the modifier's view iterations to 1
      )
   )
```

The `j` loop looks at each object (represented by `i`) and puts each modifier into the value `j`. It then checks whether that modifier is a MeshSmooth or TurboSmooth, and if so, it performs a series of tasks: It checks the Render Iterations check box, sets the Render Iterations to 3, and sets the Viewport Iterations to 1.

Note the two parentheses at the end as well. All parentheses have to balance out in order for code to execute properly. The practice of indenting your code at each parenthesis helps you keep track visually of whether your parentheses are properly closed.

Note

Pressing Ctrl-B in the MAXScript Editor will select all the text within the nearest set of parentheses or brackets, and pressing Ctrl-M in Text Pad will move the cursor to the nearest matching brackets. These can be valuable tools for fixing unclosed parenthesis bugs.

"at time"—Animating with MAXScript

We've reached the last term you need for your basic vocabulary—congratulations! With at time, you can use MAXScript to animate, as well as to change static parameters. The usage is the following:

```
at time frame
```

followed by any valid MAXScript. If (and only if) you have Auto Key turned on, this will cause your code's actions to set a keyframe.

Note

at time is equivalent to moving the time slider to a frame and then performing an action. If you don't have Auto Key turned on in the interface, your code *will not set keyframes*.

In the following exercise, we'll use the power of at time and some MAXScript you already know to animate 20 objects in a hurry. When the specifics of the animation aren't critical (such as for background objects or for a large number of objects at once), animating with MAXScript can be a huge time-saver.

Haunting the Cafe with "at time"

1. Open the file `cafe_haunted_start.max` from the DVD. This is the same cafe you modified in the earlier exercise, but with a slight change—it's haunted.

Note

The glow that appears when the scene is rendered was created using a render effect.

2. The script calls for the cafe's furniture to levitate spookily in the air, but there isn't time to keyframe all the animation. Choose MAXScript > Open Script and

load `haunted_furniture.ms` from the DVD, or copy the listing below into a
MAXScript Editor window:

```
for i in $*table* do
for i in $*table* do
   (
   for j in 1 to 3 do
      (
      at time ((j*30) + random -10 10) i.position.z = (random 5 30)
      at time ((j*30) + random -10 10) rotate i (eulerangles
(random -2 2) (random -2 2) (random -30 30))
      )
   )

for i in $*chair* do
   (
   for j in 1 to 3 do
      (
      at time ((j*30) + random -10 10) in coordsys local move i
[(random -2 2),(random -2 2),(random -6 6)]
      at time ((j*30) + random -10 10) rotate i (eulerangles
(random -2 2) (random -2 2) (random -5 5))
      )
   )
```

3. Make sure that Auto Key is turned on.

4. Execute the script using the MAXScript Editor's File > Evaluate All.

5. Turn off Auto Key and play the animation. If you don't like the results, you can
"Undo" twice and re-run the script to get different randomization.

The script is really just an extended version of what we did to move the chairs
and tables around in the previous exercise (nested `for` loops and random transforms), but extended into all three dimensions and across time. In pseudocode it
reads as follows:

```
for all objects with "table" in the name
   (
   at about frames 30, 60, and 90 set a key for a Z position
between 5 and 30
   at about frames 30, 60, and 90, set a rotation key up to 2
degrees in X and Y, and up to 30 degrees in Z
   )
for all objects with "chair" in the name
   (
   at about frames 30, 60, and 90, set a key for a local move up to
2 units in x and Y, and up to 6 units in Z.
   at about frames 30, 60, and 90, set a key for a local rotation
up to 2 degrees in X and Y, and up to 5 degrees in Z
   )
```

Obviously, the choice of actual numbers to plug in is an aesthetic decision. The basic program structure above, however, is extremely flexible.

Bear in mind, also, that unlike particle- or modifier-driven animation, this approach can serve as a starting point for manual keyframing. If you like the motion of three of the tables but not the last one, simply adjust the keys by hand. You'd be doing a lot more manual work if you hadn't used a script—you've saved work even if the output isn't perfect.

With only a few words of MAXScript, we've managed to batch-process objects, randomize aspects of your scene, and even generate animation! Even if you don't go any deeper into scripting than this, it's still a versatile and powerful tool to have.

Getting Your Way—
Building Custom UI Elements

It may be, however, that you are interested in going further and building your own tools with interfaces. This section will go through the process of creating a simple tool and making it work both as a floater and as a dockable toolbar. To do this, we'll explore writing proof-of-concept code, prototyping the UI in the Visual MAXScript editor, and then putting code and interface together to make a fully-working tool.

quickDraft: A Render Settings Manager

3ds max's render presets, introduced with max 6, are good for managing multiple output formats or render element passes on larger projects, but I find that they slow down the workflow I actually use most of the time: turning off a few settings to speed up test renders. With the tabbed Render Scene dialog, introduced in the same release, I also find it easier to miss turning a needed setting back on before committing to a long render, which adds to my stress level.

So, do I grumble to myself and hope the designers change their minds for max 8? No! With MAXScript, it's easy to write custom UI tools. The script we'll be writing in this section is called quickDraft, and the aim is to address these problems and force fewer trips to the Render Scene dialog.

Designing the Script

The first step is to write out some design goals. This is analogous to storyboarding an animation—it keeps you focused on the goal while you're immersed in the details. My design goals are as follows:

- To control the on/off state of various speedups for the scanline renderer.
- To have a quick, one-stop way to preflight production render settings.
- To take up very little room in the interface—screen space is always precious.

It's clear from looking at this list that the first two goals need a little elaboration. We want to know specifically what settings this tool is going to let us adjust, so let's create another list:

- Render Hidden Geometry
- Rendered Frame Window
- Save File toggle
- Elements Active
- Antialiasing
- Disable All Samplers
- Shadows
- Area Lights/Shadows as Points
- Enable Raytracing
- Atmospherics
- ~~Render Effects~~
- Displacement
- ~~Video Color Check~~
- ~~Auto-Reflect/Refract and Mirrors~~

The list was a little long, so I got rid of some of the features that I initially thought I wanted but really don't use much. After all, this is *my* custom tool, and I want absolutely no clutter. *Your* custom tool might need different controls (for example, you might find a motion blur toggle essential, or want to build your tool to work with mental ray or a third-party rendering plug-in). Remember, it's all about workflow.

Proof-of-Concept Code

Before investing the time in writing a script, it's a good idea to make sure the overall functionality is workable in MAXScript and to sketch out the script's core functions. The best place to start with this is the MAXScript Reference file.

1. Open the Listener and the MAXScript Reference (Help > MAXScript Reference).

2. Since we'll be controlling the renderer, go to the Search tab of the Reference file, input *renderer,* and then click List Topics. Double-click Renderers, the first topic in the list.

 Note

> By default, all instances of the word you searched for will be highlighted in the Reference page. While this is useful when looking for a specific command within a long list, it can be distracting when the word appears many times on a page. Use Options > Search Highlight Off and reload the page if you want to get rid of the highlighting.

3. The first property listed on the Reference page is `renderers.current`. Enter it in the Listener, and note that MAXScript returns `Default_Scanline_Renderer:Default_Scanline_Renderer` (as long as that *is* the current renderer!).

4. Scroll down to the bottom of the Reference page and click the link to Default_Scanline_Renderer : RenderClass.

   You are now on a page that shows the properties of the Default Scanline Renderer that can be set through MAXScript. Some of these properties are ones we want to be able to set with quickDraft, like `.shadows`, the second entry.

5. Open the Render Scene dialog, click the Renderer tab, scroll it so that you can see the Shadows check box, then input the following in the Listener and press Enter:

   `renderers.current.shadows = false`

   The Shadows check box in the Render Scene dialog cleared when you pressed Enter (and will become checked again if you input code to set the property to `true`). In other words, you have now verified that this is the code you want to have executed when your tool's Shadows check box is unchecked.

6. Look up the parameter names for the other functions described in your design document. A few are listed on this page of the Reference (`.antiAliasing`, `.enablePixelSampler`), but you will need to search other topics to find them

all—"Render Scene Dialog" in particular. Some of the parameters will need to be changed using a different approach because they are not subproperties of `renderers.current`. Space does not permit a full explanation here, but refer to the comments and working code in quickDraft_proof_of_concept.ms on the DVD to learn more.

Sketching the Interface

Now that we know what we want to do and know that it's possible, it's time to lay out the interface. While it is possible to code a UI by hand, and many experienced scripters prefer to do so, a utility called Visual MAXScript (VMXS) enables us to create an interface using drag-and-drop methods (**Figure 6.4**).

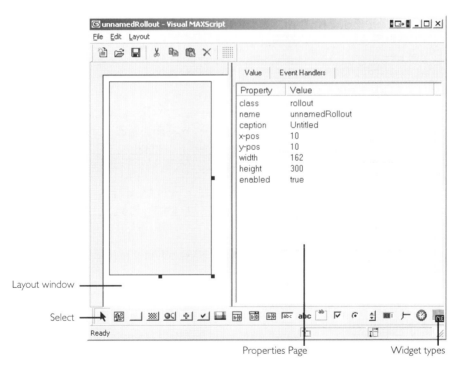

Figure 6.4   The Visual MAXScript Editor is a drag-and-drop tool for designing scripted interfaces.

1. From the MAXScript menu choose New Script.

2. In the MAXScript Editor window choose Edit > New Rollout. Notice that the script window becomes grayed out and inaccessible; until Visual MAXScript is closed, the rest of the script will be locked.

Note

There are two ways to access Visual MAXScript, and the way you choose affects the behavior of the editor: MAXScript menu > Visual MAXScript Editor in the main interface, or Edit > New Rollout or Edit > Edit Rollout from within a MAXScript Editor window.

If you open Visual MAXScript from the main interface, you will need to save the UI code you create to an .ms file, and then open the file and copy and paste the code into your script in order to use it.

Opening Visual MAXScript from an editor window will connect VMXS to the script you are writing. When you choose File > Save, UI code will be written directly into your script. This is usually an easier way to work.

3. The right side of the editor is the Properties Page, which displays the properties of the rollout you're editing. Change the `name` property to `quickDraft_rollout`, and `caption` to `quickDraft`. The `name` is how you'll refer to the rollout in your code, while `caption` is the title of your tool window in the interface.

4. Continuing down the Properties Page, set `width` to 111 and `height` to 216. This makes our rollout more compact—just big enough to hold a column of check boxes and their captions.

5. Click the icon for the check box widget at the bottom of the VMXS window, and then drag a box in the gray area on the left. A check box named Checkbox will appear, and the Properties Page on the right will show the check box's properties instead of the rollout's (**Figure 6.5**).

6. Change the `name` property to `hidden`, and the `caption` property to Render Hidden.

Tip

A UI element's `name` property cannot contain spaces, nor can it have a digit as the first character.

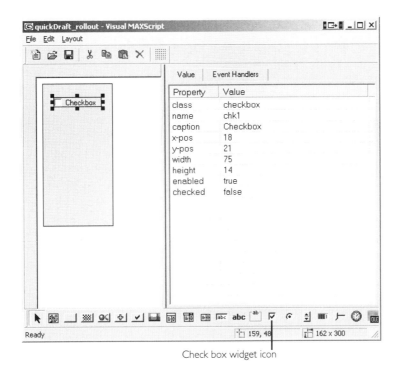

Check box widget icon

Figure 6.5   Click the widget's icon, and then drag in the Layout window to create a check box.

7. If the caption looks cut off, drag the check box's sizing handle to make it wide enough for the entire caption.

8. Set the check box's `height` property to 14 using the Properties Page. This is the "normal" height of most UI elements.

9. Choose File > Save in the VMXS window. Rollout code is written to the MAXScript Editor window, although it remains grayed out.

Tip

> The Visual MAXScript Editor has no undo. Be sure to save your UI code frequently, so that you can close and reopen the editor to revert to an earlier version of your layout if you make a mistake.

10. Create a new check box widget by clicking the Selection tool icon, selecting the Render Hidden check box, and pressing Ctrl-C to copy followed by Ctrl-V to paste. Drag the new check box to approximately the right position, and change

its name and `caption` properties to `rfw` and RFW, respectively. Don't worry about getting the position exactly right; Visual MAXScript has alignment tools to help clean up the layout.

11. Repeat the paste-move-rename operation nine more times, to create a total of 11 check boxes. Use the following names and captions (**Table 6.3**):

Table 6.3   quickDraft Check Box Properties

Name	Caption
hidden	Render Hidden
rfw	RFW
save	Save File
elements	Elements Active
aa	Antialiasing
samp	Disable Samp.
shad	Shadows
area	Area as Point
raytrace	Raytracing
atmo	Atmospherics
displace	Displacement

Now that all your check boxes are built and named, it's time to align them.

12. Choose File > Save to write out code to the MAXScript Editor. This will give you a revert point if you don't like the results of the next step.

13. With the Selection tool active, drag-select all the check boxes and choose Layout > Align > Left, then Layout > Space Evenly > Down. If you don't like the layout, you can revert, move your check boxes around manually, and repeat the alignment commands.

If you want to revert, close the Visual MAXScript Editor without saving, then choose Edit > Edit Rollout in the MAXScript Editor. Keep adjusting the UI elements until you like the layout. In my version, I decided to indent Area as Point as a subproperty of Shadows, since it's meaningless if shadows are turned off altogether (**Figure 6.6**).

 Note

You can nudge elements by using the arrow keys, and constrain mouse drags to a straight line by holding down Shift.

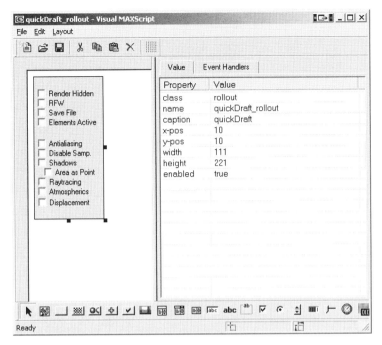

Figure 6.6   The Align and Space Evenly commands help you make a clean-looking interface.

14. When you're satisfied with the layout, choose File > Save in the Visual MAXScript Editor, close Visual MAXScript, and save your script as quickDraft_interface01.ms. Reopen Visual MAXScript by pressing F2. The layout shown in Figure 6.6 is saved on the DVD as quickDraft_interface01.ms.

Conceptually, there are two types of controls in quickDraft: controls related to file saving, whose proper settings will vary with the project; and render speed-ups that will almost always be set the same way for production renders. In the layout shown in Figure 6.6 I've put some space between the two groups, but it would be nice if there were a more definite visual cue for the difference.

15. Click the Group Box widget icon (it's immediately to the left of the Check Box widget icon you used before), and drag a frame around each of the two groups of check boxes.

16. Use the Group Boxes' size handles to adjust the border to your liking, and change their `caption` properties to Render Controls and Speed-Ups (**Figure 6.7**). This layout is saved on the DVD as quickDraft_interface02.ms.

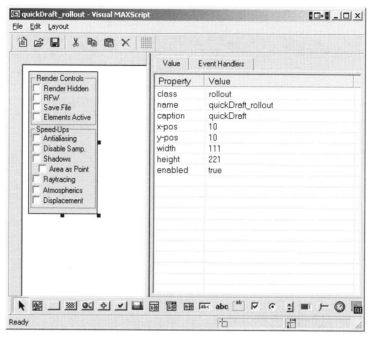

Figure 6.7 The completed quickDraft UI.

17. Use Visual MAXScript's Save command to write your finished interface code into the MAXScript Editor, close VMXS, and save your script as quickDraft_interface02.ms.

Congratulations! You've built a complete and polished UI using Visual MAXScript. Now it's time to hook up the proof-of-concept code to the interface code, and to make it launchable as a tool from within 3ds max.

Building a Fully Operational Utility

1. Relaunch Visual MAXScript from the MAXScript Editor window (open quickdraft_interface02.ms first if you are not continuing from the previous exercise).

2. In the main menu, choose MAXScript > Open Script... and open quickDraft_proof_of_concept.ms from the DVD.

3. Select the Render Hidden check box in the Visual MAXScript Editor, and click the Event Handlers tab at the top of the Properties Page.

Event handlers are blocks of code whose execution is triggered by certain events. One such event is when a check box is turned on or off. When the user clicks a MAXScript check box, the code in the check box's `changed` handler is triggered, or called, and the current on/off state of the check box is given to the event handler code as a variable named `state`.

4. Click the `changed` event handler. An Edit Event Handler window opens in which we can enter the code we want to associate with the Render Hidden check box's state change.

5. Find the Render Hidden entry in the proof-of-concept code, copy and paste it to the Edit Event Handler window (**Figure 6.8**), and click OK. Repeat for each of the other UI elements.

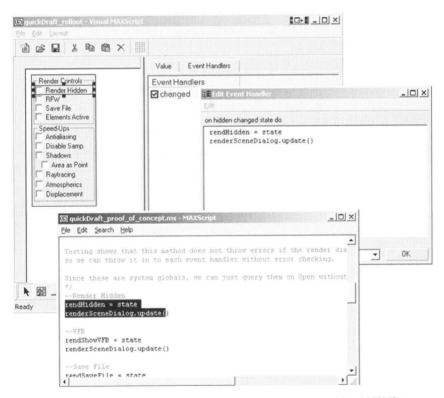

Figure 6.8   Copying proof-of-concept code into event handlers in Visual MAXScript.

> **Note**
>
> There are two entries for the Render Elements check box in the proof-of-concept file. The code for the event handler is the first entry; the second is an example and is not used in the script.

6. Choose File > Save to write the code out to the MAXScript Editor, close Visual MAXScript, and save your script as quickDraft_interface03.ms.

   We're almost ready to test our utility. We just need to add a line of code to the end of the script that launches our rollout as a dialog, a floater containing our UI elements.

7. To the very end of the script, after the last closing parenthesis, add a new line:

```
createDialog quickDraft_rollout width:111 height:216
escapeEnable:false
```

8. Choose File > Evaluate All in the MAXScript Editor. Your UI code appears as a fully functional floater in the interface. Open the Render Scene dialog and test each of the check boxes in quickDraft, watching the state of the equivalent controls in the Render Scene dialog to make sure that they work.

   If you don't have any typos in your script, all the controls should work properly, but it may take a couple of clicks to synchronize their state with the state of their counterparts in the Render Scene dialog.

   To fix this, we need to add event handler code to our script that sets the check boxes to reflect the current state of the scene when quickDraft first opens. This event handler will not belong to any particular UI widget, but rather to the rollout itself.

9. Launch Visual MAXScript again, select the rollout itself, and go to the Event Handlers tab.

   The rollout has an open handler, which is called when the floater is first launched. We want to add code to the open handler that sets the state of each MAXScript check box to match the equivalent setting in the Render Scene dialog. UI elements are objects with properties, just like everything else in MAXScript, so setting the check box state is just a matter of reading the state of each parameter from the scene and assigning those values to our check box's .state property.

   By modifying the proof-of-concept code to read from, rather than write to, the values in the Render Scene dialog, we can create our open handler without much extra work.

10. Click the open handler, and then enter the following code in the Edit Event Handler dialog (the code is also on the DVD as quickDraft_open_handler.ms if you wish to cut and paste):

```
hidden.state = rendHidden
rfw.state = rendShowVFB
save.state = rendSaveFile
re = maxops.getCurRenderElementMgr()
elements.state = re.getElementsActive()
aa.state = renderers.current.antiAliasing
samp.state = not renderers.current.enablePixelSampler
shad.state = renderers.current.shadows
area.state = rendSimplifyAreaLights
rt = rayTraceGlobalSettings()
raytrace.state = rt.enable_raytracing
atmo.state = rendAtmosphere
displace.state = renderDisplacements
```

11. Use File > Save to write the code out to the script editor again, close Visual MAXScript, and save the script as quickDraft_interface04.ms. Pick File > Evaluate All to launch your current version.

    The utility should now reflect the current state of the render controls when first opened. zIf a previous iteration of the tool was open, you may have noticed that it stayed onscreen.

12. Ideally, we'd like the script to be smart enough to close an existing dialog when it's run again. We do this with a `destroyDialog` command at the very beginning of the script, on a blank line before the rollout definition:

```
try(destroyDialog quickDraft_rollout)catch()
```

    `try()` and `catch()` are extremely useful for all kinds of scripting tasks. When code is located inside a `try()` statement, any errors encountered will cause the code inside the `catch()` to be executed instead of MAXSscript halting with an error message. Since the `catch()` is empty in the above code, we are telling MAXScript to ignore any errors (such as there being no `quickDraft_rollout` dialog bar to destroy).

    Without the `try()catch()`, the entire script would fail if there weren't a `quickdraft_rollout` in the interface to remove. With it, the script will work, and work properly, regardless of whether we're opening a new floater or replacing an existing one.

13. Run quickDraft with and without a dialog bar already onscreen to make sure that the old dialog bar is removed properly. You may have to move the old one to see it disappear.

There's just one more step. We need to add a few lines to turn our code into a macroScript. MacroScripts contain extra information that allows them to be assigned to keystrokes, toolbar buttons, and quad menus, and they carry the file extension .mcr instead of .ms.

When you run a macroScript, the script code is not executed immediately. Instead, a slightly modified copy of it is created in your UI/MacroScripts directory, and the scripted tool becomes available in the Customize User Interface dialog so that you can make it a regular part of the UI. In fact, a great many of 3ds max's built-in tools are actually macroScripts.

 Note

If you want to alter a macroScript that already exists in your UI/MacroScripts folder, edit a copy of the .mcr file in another directory and then run it from the MAXScript menu in order to update the "live" definition. This will ensure that UI elements based on the original macroScript maintain their connection after the update.

14. Add the following code to the very beginning of the script:

```
macroScript quickDraft Category:"Render" Tooltip:"quickDraft"
(
```

This means that the script will appear as a new tool, labeled quickDraft, in the Render category of the Customize User Interface dialog.

Since we added an open parenthesis to the beginning of the script, we have to close it at the end to make MAXScript happy. To the very end of the script add the following:

```
)
```

15. Save your macroScript as quickdraft_final.mcr.

16. Choose MAXScript > Run Script, browse to your saved quickdraft_final.mcr, and click Open. Nothing appears to happen, but this step makes quickDraft available as a command in the Customize User Interface dialog. A finished version of the script is also on the DVD as quickdraft_final.mcr.

17. Choose Customize > Customize User Interface, go to the Quads tab, and choose Render in the Category menu. Find quickDraft in the Action menu, and drag it to a comfortable spot in your default Viewport Quad Menu.

18. Close the Customize User Interface dialog, and right-click in a viewport. Choose quickDraft in your quad menu to launch your script.

Congratulations! You've just designed, proofed, written, tested, debugged, and installed your very own MAXScript utility. The principles and techniques you used to create it are applicable to almost anything in the interface that you find yourself reaching for on a regular basis.

colorClip—Creating a Dockable Toolbar

There are times when even the tiniest floater is too much clutter in the interface. Since max 5, scripters have been able to create dockable toolbars from their rollouts. These can contain any of the UI elements available in MAXScript but fit neatly into the interface like a regular max toolbar.

In the next few pages, we'll create a simple replacement for the stock Color Clipboard utility that's buried in the Utilities panel, creating a modeless one that fits neatly next to max's main toolbar instead. As with quickDraft, the impetus for creating this script is to save trips to out-of-the-way parts of the interface and to speed up workflow.

Design Considerations

In order to fit our UI widgets into a toolbar, we're going to have to pay close attention to size, so that the toolbar's height matches that of the toolbars it will be docked with. We also don't want to have too many controls, as there might not be much extra room in the UI to dock in, especially at lower resolutions.

Let's build our toolbar with six color swatches—a good compromise between size and utility.

One easy part of this script is that drag-and-drop functionality is hardwired into colorPicker UI elements; the color swatches need no event handler code, so there's no proof-of-concept work to do.

Writing the Script

Without any proofing to do, we can dive right in. Finding the right values for a clean layout can be a lengthy process of trial and error, so they are provided for you.

Note

Toolbars' size requirements vary depending on your Use Large Toolbar Buttons setting (found in the General tab of Customize > Preferences). The values used in this exercise will fit small toolbars.

If you use large buttons, use four color swatches instead of six, a rollout height of 39, a rollout width of 152, an X spacing of 32 between swatches, and a colorPicker width and height of 32 instead of the values given below.

A completed version of the script written for large icons is included on the DVD as colorClip_large.mcr.

1. Open a new MAXScript Editor, and choose Edit > New Rollout to start Visual MAXScript.

2. Enter the following parameters in the rollout's properties sheet:

   name: `colorClip`

   caption: `Color Clipboard`

   width: `160`

   height: `30`

3. Create a colorPicker UI element in the rollout. Size and placement aren't important, since we'll be setting those by hand.

4. Set the following properties on the colorPicker's Properties Page:

   caption: *delete the default caption, leaving the property blank*

   x-pos: `2`

   y-pos: `3`

   width: `20`

   height: `20`

   color: `(color 128 128 128)`

5. Copy and paste the colorPicker five times, manually setting the x-pos property to the following each time: 26,50,74,98,122. Make sure to keep the y-pos property at 3 for all the swatches. Your layout should look like that shown in **Figure 6.9**. The extra horizontal space is to accommodate the toolbar handle that will appear when you dock the script floater.

6. Write your UI code to the Script Editor with File> Save, then close Visual MAXScript.

7. Save your script as colorClip_layout.ms.

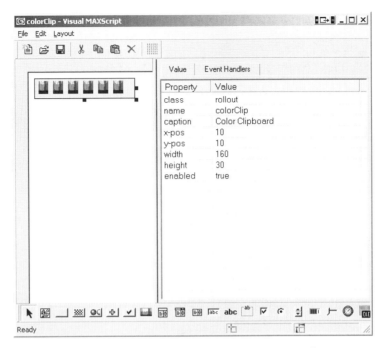

Figure 6.9   Laying out the Color Clipboard toolbar in Visual MAXScript.

8. Now let's add the macroScript header, closer, and dialog declaration as we did for quickDraft. To the beginning, add:

```
macroScript ColorClip Category:"Color Clipboard" Tooltip:"Toolbar
Color Clipboard"
(
try(destroydialog colorClip)catch()
```

and to the end add:

```
createDialog colorClip width:160 height:30
style:#(#style_toolwindow) escapeEnable:false
)
```

9. In order to make the dialog dockable, we need two more lines of code. At the end, between the `createDialog` line and the last parenthesis, add as a single line the following:

```
cui.registerdialogbar ColorClip style: #(#cui_dock_horz,#cui_
floatable,#cui_handles) minsize:[160,30] maxsize:[160,30]
```

This line of code tells max to treat our dialog floater as a dockable toolbar.

10. At the beginning, between the first open parenthesis and the `destroyDialog` line, add:

```
try(cui.unregisterdialogbar ColorClip)catch()
```

This code is necessary because in order to get rid of a dockable dialog bar, it must first be turned back into a regular dialog bar with `cui.unRegisterDialogBar` so that `destroyDialog` can act on it. Just one of those things.

11. Save your script as colorClip_complete.mcr.

12. Register the macroScript by choosing MAXScript > Run Script and browsing to the location of your saved script (or colorClip_complete.mcr on the DVD).

13. Open the Customize User Interface dialog and assign the newly minted command to launch the Color Clipboard to a toolbar or quad (**Figure 6.10**).

14. Launch the Color Clipboard toolbar and test it out (**Figure 6.11**).

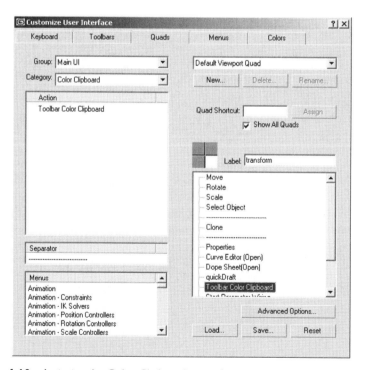

Figure 6.10   Assigning the Color Clipboard macroScript to a quad menu.

Figure 6.11   The Color Clipboard toolbar in action.

Going Further with MAXScript

Well, here we are, a ten-word vocabulary and two tools later. Hopefully this chapter has opened your eyes to the possibilities of MAXScript and made it seem more accessible. To sum up the main points:

- **A few words of MAXScript go a long way.** You learned that with a small vocabulary and a little help from the show command and for loops, you can batch-process almost anything in your scene with a line or two of code in the Listener. Judicious use of the random command can help you create more believable scenes and animation with minimal effort.

- **Everyone needs help.** Using the Reference file is mandatory, even for full-time technical directors. Refer to it constantly, and get comfortable with the various search functions. There are a lot of friendly and helpful scripters online, too, so don't be afraid to post questions (using your real name) in Discreet's MAXScript forum.

- **Create interfaces quickly with Visual MAXScript.** You learned that the Visual MAXScript utility can be used to sketch out the interface for a custom tool, separate from the code that actually does the work. Building a complete tool is then just a matter of adding proof-of-concept code to the event handlers of each UI element to make it do what you want, and debugging any problems that pop up along the way.

- **Dockable dialogs let you use MAXScript widgets in custom toolbars.** You learned that dialog bars, first introduced in 3ds max 5, are an efficient way to turn your UI code into a tool floater. Additionally, dialogs can be made dockable, so that they function as toolbars in your interface.

Taken together, these skills represent a formidable arsenal of time-saving tools. The key to developing your skills is to look for situations where a script could be useful and to force yourself to use scripted solutions, even if it's slower going at first.

Some signs that a problem may be amenable to scripting include the following:

- **Boredom.** Repetitive tasks, like adjusting the same setting on dozens of objects or performing the same series of actions on dozens of files, can often be scripted with a `for` loop.

- **Aching wrists.** 3ds max is a huge program, and its user interface is designed to be all things to all artists out of the box. If you find yourself clicking deep into an obscure dialog all day long because your workflow requires it, consider building a custom dialog to make those functions more accessible.

Once you've identified the task you want to script, use the principles from this chapter to design, proof, test, and implement your solution. Now go forth, and shorten your workday!

Part III

Modeling

Precision Modeling

By A.J. Jefferies

Architects visualize a sprawling metropolis before a shovel has touched soil. Designers market an mp3 player months before production. Engineers test prototype cars from the comfort of their desks. 3D makes all these things possible.

The representation of real-world objects by means of 3D modeling requires meticulous planning and attention to detail. To most people, the words "precision" and "computer" go hand in hand; however, the words "human" and "error" share the same association!

How can we be accurate when by our very nature we make mistakes? The fact is, to achieve precision in 3D modeling we don't need a degree in mathematics, thick-rimmed spectacles, or even an unhealthy obsession with lab coats. Instead, 3ds max allows us to be as precise as we want or need, even for basic modeling operations. In this chapter, we are going use a multitude of techniques to construct a kitchen scene; at the same time, we will look at some modeling fundamentals.

Primitives

The primitives in 3ds max are a collection of Euclidean solids and other premade objects that can serve as the starting place for almost any creation. A client might ask to see a quick visualization of 20 cars screaming down a track, or maybe you just want to block out some scenery for an animation. Either way, the fastest solution would be to use primitives to very quickly and efficiently lay out the scene. Not only that, but many objects can be created from default primitives: a lamp from a cylinder and tube, or a dining table from five boxes.

Developing Primitives

In the following exercise, we're going to start laying out the basic structure of a kitchen, then move on to create some specific furnishings and fittings, all from primitives.

I. Open the file 7_Kitchen_Start.max from the DVD.

You can see that the scene currently consists of an empty room with a few pieces (**Figure 7.1**). This is going to be the framework for the kitchen. The first step is to tile the floor.

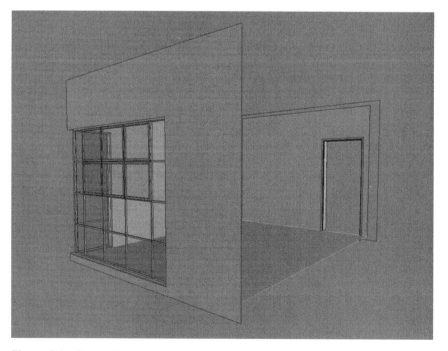

Figure 7.1 Empty kitchen scene.

Note

> The walls that are missing from the kitchen model are only temporarily removed by use of the Mesh Select and DeleteMesh modifiers. The kitchen can be made whole at the end of the exercise by disabling these.

2. To make things easier, you're going to hide most of the scene, saving only what you need to work with. The kitchen objects themselves are currently frozen, so from the Display panel, check Hide Frozen Objects in the Hide rollout.

3. The rectangle that remains represents the area of the floor. From the Modify panel, you can see that the floor is 400 units in length and 300 in width. You'll use this information to place the tiles properly. Right-click the Snaps Toggle button on the Main toolbar to bring up the Grid and Snap Settings dialog. Check the box labeled Grid Points.

   Snapping (covered in more detail in an earlier chapter) is a quick and accurate way to determine the placement of objects in a scene. Our current scene has been constructed using the grid, so you'll continue to use the grid as a guide for your objects.

4. From the Create > Geometry > Extended Primitives panel, choose ChamferBox. Maximize the Top viewport and drag out a box in the top left corner of the floor. Make the dimensions of the box 20 by 20 by snapping to the grid (**Figure 7.2**), then click twice more to finish the creation.

5. Once the box is created, manually enter the following settings:
   - Height = 1.0
   - Fillet = 0.2
   - Fillet Segments = 1
   - Smooth = Unchecked

   By turning down the Fillet Segments, you will have less geometry in your scene while retaining a defining edge for the tiles. Disabling Smooth helps to enhance this effect.

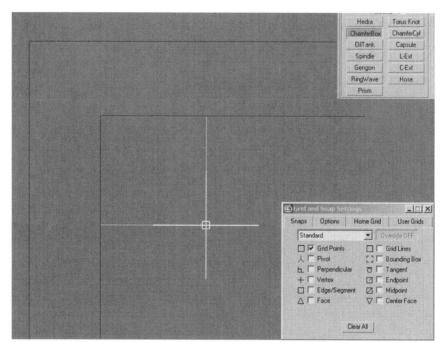

Figure 7.2 Creating a ChamferBox by snapping to the grid.

Working with Arrays

An array is nothing more than a number of similar objects arranged in a regular pattern. Although it can seem a little daunting at first, max's Array tool is invaluable for laying out many copies of identical objects such as tiles. You know that your tile is 20 units on each side and that the floor is 300 units wide, so some simple math (300 divided by 20) reveals that you need 15 copies in the X axis. Let's create these.

1. Now that you have a solitary tile, let's duplicate it to cover the floor. Right-click in a blank area of the Main toolbar to bring up a list of available toolbars, and choose Extras from the list. With the ChamferBox still selected, choose Array from the Extras toolbar to bring up the Array dialog.

2. Enter 15 as the 1D Count value in the Array Dimensions area and 20 as the value in the Incremental X axis. Set the Type of Object to Instance and click Preview to see the results (**Figure 7.3**).

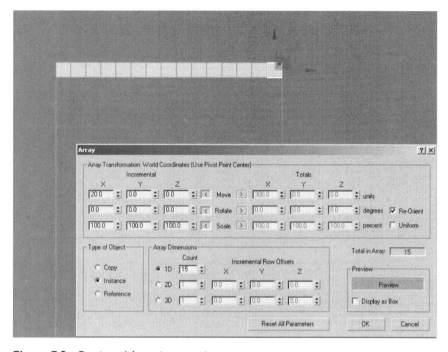

Figure 7.3 Previewed Array in one axis.

 Tip

Pressing Control-N when the cursor is in a spinner or value box will bring up the Numerical Expression Evaluator. You can use this to perform calculations like the one above and the result will be pasted as the new value.

3. You can also tell the Array to duplicate the tiles in the Y axis. Turn on the 2D button and set the Y Incremental Rows Offset to –20. Now, when you increase the value of the 2D Count, you can see the rows moving down. Set the 2D Count to 20 and hit OK to complete the tiled floor (**Figure 7.4**).

4. Since you have used Instances for the floor, you can alter the scale of all tiles simply by changing the values for one tile. To see this in effect, select any one of the tiles and change the Height value to 3.0 and the Fillet value to 0.5 (**Figure 7.5**).

   You're now going to create the basis for your kitchen's cupboards.

5. Each cupboard is going to be 60 by 60 units in dimension, and you'll need to clear some space. In the Top viewport, select and delete three rows of 15 tiles from the left down and three rows of six tiles across (**Figure 7.6**).

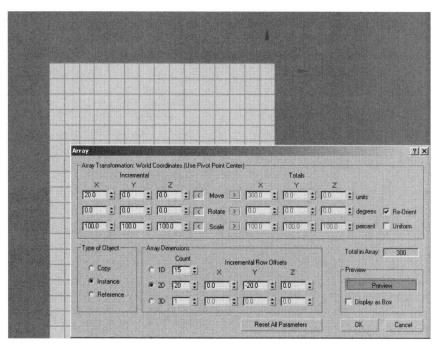

Figure 7.4   Creating an Array in two axes.

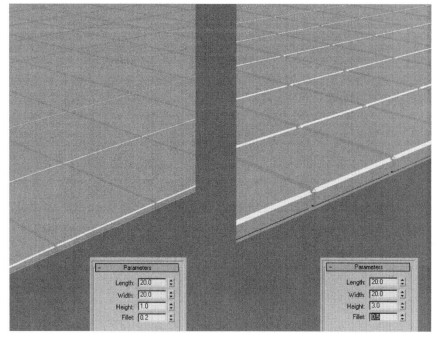

Figure 7.5   Altering the tiles via Instancing.

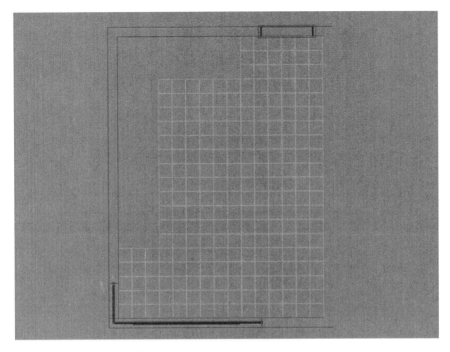

Figure 7.6   Top view of the deleted tiles.

6. Remaining in the Top viewport, create a Box primitive anywhere in the scene, entering the Length, Width, and Height values as 60. Name it Unit01.

7. Bring up the Grid and Snap Settings dialog and set the snapping to Grid Points and Endpoint. In the Perspective viewport, select the corner of the box and drag and snap it to the grid point (**Figure 7.7**).

8. Use the Array tool again to create five Instanced duplicates of the cupboard in the Y axis, incrementing by 60. Then create three duplicates in the X axis by the same amount (**Figure 7.8**).

To see my version of the scene so far, open the file 7_Kitchen_Primitives.max on the DVD.

You now have the basis for your kitchen. It might not look like much, but you can use what you have created in this exercise as the basis for all the other detail you're going to add. In the next section, you'll use splines to add a countertop to the kitchen and model an appliance.

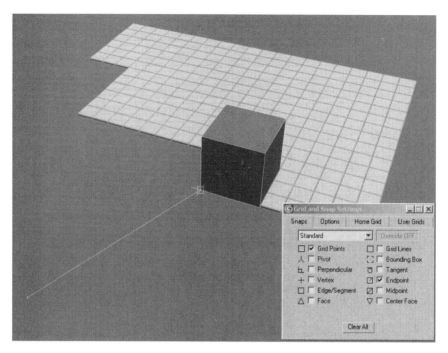

Figure 7.7 Snapping the box to the grid.

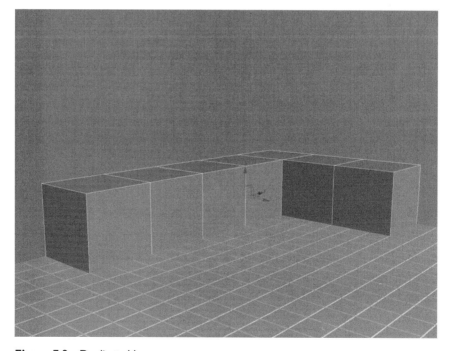

Figure 7.8 Duplicated boxes.

Shapes and Splines

We have dealt with primitives and seen the benefits of parametric control (in other words, specification by numerical parameter) over an object's shape. However, this control can also present limitations. How far can we manipulate an object while retaining the versatility to alter its structure? Here is where we can turn to max's shapes (2D forms) for our creations. Like the polygonal primitives, shapes have a series of default forms in which they can be created (circle, rectangle, and so on).

Adding Precision with Shapes

You're now going to create a work surface (countertop) for the kitchen scene using a rectangle spline as the basis for its shape. You'll also be using the primitives from the previous exercise as a guide to help you be accurate.

1. Continue with the previous exercise's file, or open 7_Kitchen_Primitives.max from the DVD.

2. Select the box named Unit01, and from the Display panel, select Hide Unselected.

 Tip

> Hiding and unhiding objects can be essential to a productive workflow. By removing unnecessary objects from your view, not only can you focus more easily on your work, but you can also get a faster response from max while you're doing it.

3. Raise the height of the cupboards by changing the Height value of the box from 60 to 80.

4. Choose Rectangle from the Create > Shapes menu, and in the Front viewport, create one with a length of 7.0 and a width of 60 (again, these can be entered manually after creation).

   This shape is going to be the basis for the countertop. It's a bit sharp at the moment, so let's smooth it off.

5. Enable Midpoint snapping and drag the bottom of the rectangle so that it meets the top edge of Unit01 (**Figure 7.9**).

6. Now apply an Edit Spline modifier to the rectangle, and in Vertex sub-object mode, move the two vertices on the right-hand side outward from the edge of the cupboard (**Figure 7.10**).

7. Still in the Front viewport, select the vertex at the top right of the rectangle, and from the Geometry rollout in the spline Modify panel, enter a Fillet amount of 3.0 (**Figure 7.11**). From the Display panel, choose Unhide All so you can see the rest of the scene.

8. Now that you've rounded the corner, apply an Extrude modifier and set the amount to −300 (**Figure 7.12**).

9. Apply the countertop material in the Material Editor to the object.

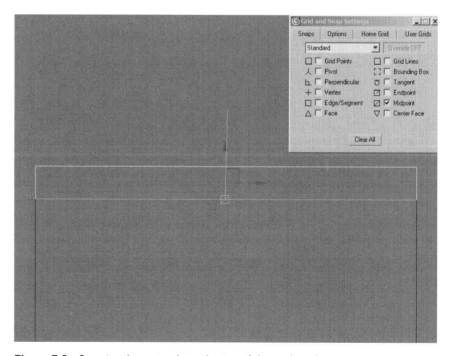

Figure 7.9   Snapping the rectangle to the top of the cupboard.

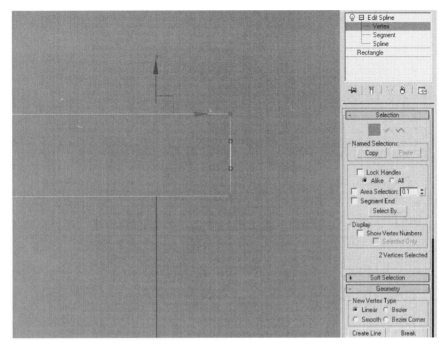

Figure 7.10 Extending the rectangle with an Edit Spline modifier.

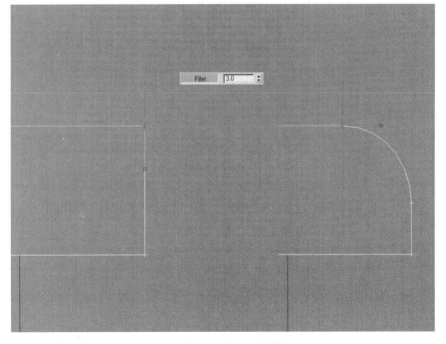

Figure 7.11 Rounding the edge of the surface with Fillet.

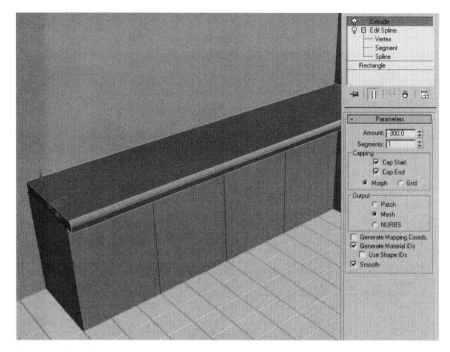

Figure 7.12   The countertop extruded.

Cutting and Fitting

By keeping the changes you've made to the shape in an Edit Spline modifier, you can go in and easily add detail to the surface or remove it. Try turning the modifier off to see the effect it has on the shape of the extruded surface, remembering to turn it back on before you proceed.

Just as real tilers do when laying a tile floor, we'll do some cutting and fitting to get our tiles to fit precisely.

1. Where the surface runs into the corner, you are going to cut it at a 45-degree angle. To do this, apply a Slice modifier to the object, and in the Top viewport, rotate its Slice Plane sub-object –45 degrees in the Z axis (**Figure 7.13**).

2. Set the Slice Type to Remove Bottom. Select the Slice Plane sub-object and move it upward until you reach the top. Snap to the Endpoint to align the Slice Plane accurately with the corner of the cupboards (**Figure 7.14**).

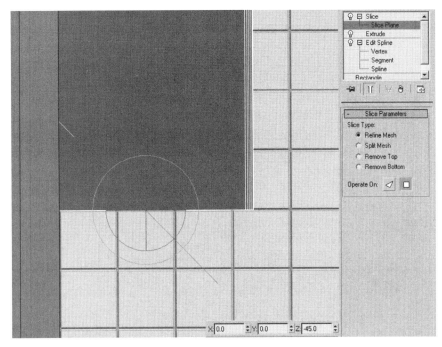

Figure 7.13   Rotating the Slice Plane through –45 degrees.

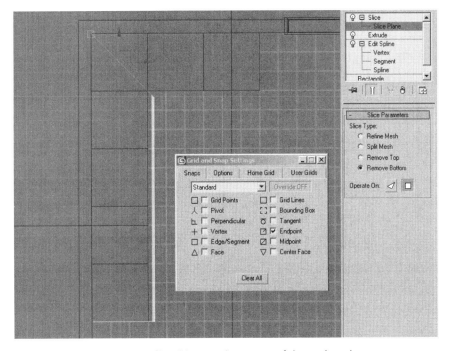

Figure 7.14   Snapping the Slice Plane to the corner of the cupboards.

3. Still in the Top viewport, use the Mirror tool to flip the countertop in its X axis and set the Clone Selection to Copy.

4. Activate Angle Snap on the Main toolbar, and rotate the duplicate countertop you've just created by 90 degrees in the Z axis.

5. With Snaps still enabled and set to Endpoint, move the countertop into place, snapping onto the corner of the right-hand cupboard (**Figure 7.15**).

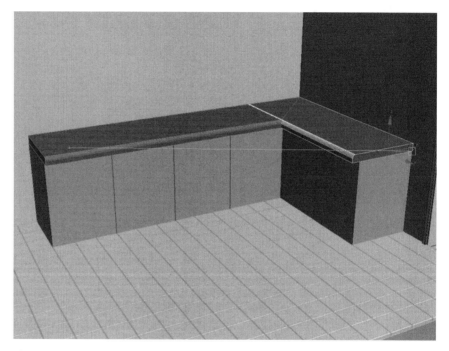

Figure 7.15   Moving the other countertop into place.

6. All that remains now is to move the Slice Plane of this countertop's Slice modifier into the same place as the other for a flush fit. Do this by again snapping to the Endpoint of the corner cupboard (**Figure 7.16**).

7. Save the file as 7_Kitchen_Worktop.max.

To see my version of the scene so far, open the file 7_Kitchen_Worktop.max on the DVD.

You've not only created a countertop for your kitchen, you've also gained the ability to easily change an object's structure.

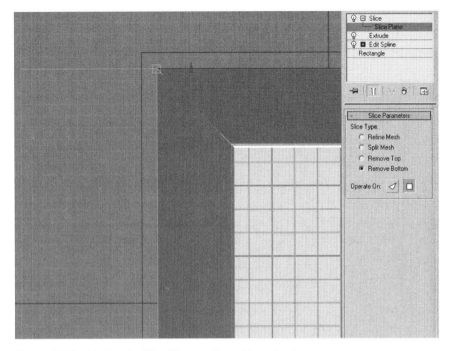

Figure 7.16 Moving the Slice Planes in line with each other.

Profiles and Shapes

Now let's move on to another application for splines—namely, the use of profiles and shapes to create custom geometry. In the following exercise, you're going to create a gas cooktop to merge into the kitchen scene.

1. Open the file 7_Kitchen_Cooktop_Start.max. The scene consists of a few Chamfer Cylinder primitives, a set of predrawn spline shapes, and some profile curves. You're going to use these splines to construct the cooktop's details and furnishings.

2. In the viewport or from the Select Objects dialog, select the spline named hob_main_panels (**Figure 7.17**). (A hob is a cooktop burner.)

3. From the Modify panel, apply a Bevel Profile modifier. Click the Pick Profile button, and in the Top viewport, pick the spline labeled Hob_curve_profile. Turn off the Capping for the End section of the modifier.

4. max will run the profile around the panels, but it's currently in the wrong direction, so we'll fix this. In the sub-object under the Bevel Profile modifier, select the Profile gizmo, and in the Perspective viewport, rotate the profile 180 degrees in the Z axis (**Figure 7.18**).

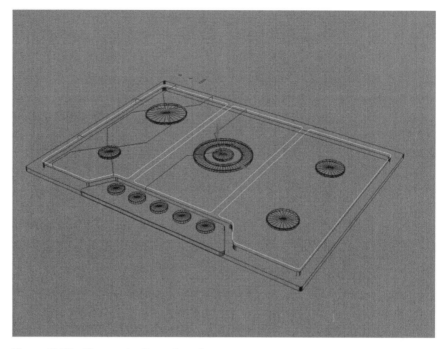

Figure 7.17   The panel spline selected.

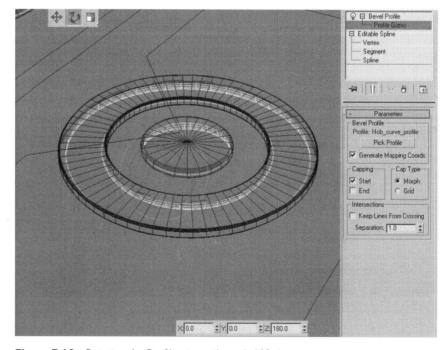

Figure 7.18   Rotating the Profile gizmo through 180 degrees.

5. If you render the cooktop, you can see through the surface you've made. This is because the faces are in the right place but facing the wrong direction. To rectify this, you must flip the direction of the object's normals. Apply a Normal modifier and ensure that Flip Normals is checked **(Figure 7.19).**

6. In the Top viewport, first select the shape named hob_bar01, and then, from the Create panel, navigate to Compound Objects and choose Loft.

7. You need to pick a shape for the loft object to use along the path (hob_bar01). Within the loft object's parameters, under the Creation Method rollout, click Get Shape. From the Top viewport, pick the rectangle labeled Hob_bar_profile **(Figure 7.20).**

8. Now that you have the basis for your metal bars, you'll need to tweak some of the default settings to make things simpler. From the Skin Parameters rollout for the loft object, check the box marked Optimize Shapes. This will result in the loft object using only as many steps as your chosen shape object, and in this case, fewer polygons as well **(Figure 7.21).**

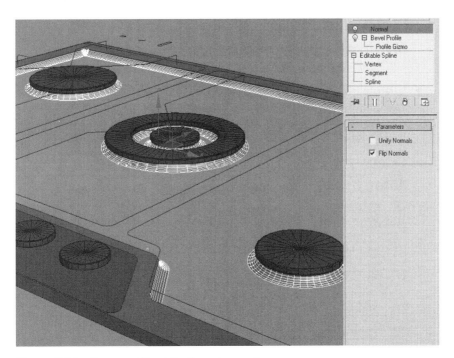

Figure 7.19   Corrected Bevel Profile and normals.

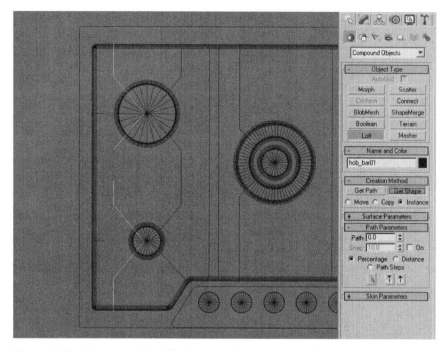

Figure 7.20   Creating a loft object from a spline.

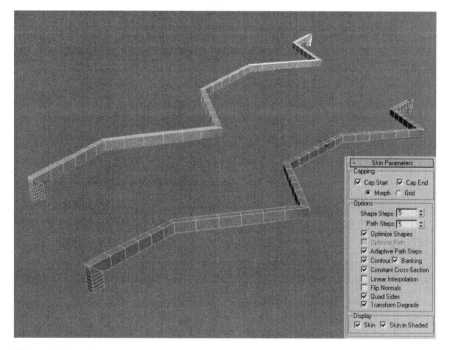

Figure 7.21   Optimized shape providing a cleaner, lighter mesh.

Note

Compound objects require two or more elements for their creation. In the case of a loft object, this is a path and a shape. Both of these must be spline-based objects. Once added to a Loft object, the shape is "run" along the direction of the path to create a mesh.

Adding Detail

Nothing in real life has a perfectly sharp edge. By rounding edges and filleting corners, you can create highlights and definition that will prevent your models from looking computer-generated. Obviously, the tradeoff is that more detail means more complex geometry. So assess how your model is going to be used: Is it going to be seen close up? Will it be directly compared to a real-world object? It's your choice as an artist to decide when an object requires that extra level of precision detail.

As a start, we'll look at some techniques for adding those all-important small details by continuing to refine the loft. The essential thing to remember about lofts is that their structure is governed by the two splines picked for the path and shape. Therefore, any changes you make to these base splines will alter the outcome of the loft. You're going to use this to your advantage in the following steps by adding some subtle detail quickly and easily.

1. Once again, select the shape named hob_bar01, and from the Modify panel, apply an Edit Spline modifier to the top of the stack.

2. Enter the Vertex sub-object mode in the Edit Spline modifier, and select all the vertices in the spline. In the Fillet field, enter the value 0.3 and press Enter (**Figure 7.22**).

   By using an Edit Spline modifier instead of directly altering the base object, you can simply and quickly undo or alter any changes you make. This is extremely useful when you're working on designs that aren't finalized, or when fleshing out ideas.

3. Move to the Perspective viewport. You can see that the fillets have affected the loft and resulted in much smoother corners (**Figure 7.23**).

4. Repeat the previous steps on the two remaining splines that represent the cook-top's bars, and apply the dark metal material to the loft objects (**Figure 7.24**).

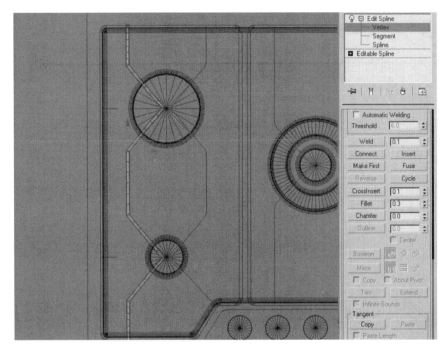

Figure 7.22   Filleting vertices with an Edit Spline modifier.

Figure 7.23   Rounded corners on the loft object.

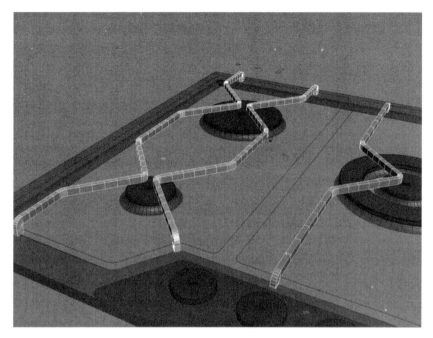

Figure 7.24   Lofted bars.

5. Using the same shape for each of these three lofts means that you can now change the cross-section of all three simultaneously. Select the rectangle named Hob_bar_profile again, and from the Parameters rollout, change the Corner Radius value to 0.05 (**Figure 7.25**).

You can see the effect this has straightaway. The bars are all equally rounded at the edges and no longer have a harsh, unnatural edge.

6. Now create the rest of the bars' support. Select the shape named hob_bars and apply a Bevel Profile modifier, picking the same Hob_bar_profile (**Figure 7.26**).

7. You need to duplicate the bars you've created for the other side of the cooktop's surface. In the Top viewport, select the three main bars; group, mirror, and position them accordingly (**Figure 7.27**).

8. All that remains now is to group and name all the elements for the object as hob_complete (**Figure 7.28**).

9. Save the file as 7_Kitchen_Cooktop_Finish.max.

To see my version of the scene, open the file 7_Kitchen_Cooktop_Finish.max on the DVD.

Now that you've created the complete gas cooktop, you're going to fit it into the kitchen scene.

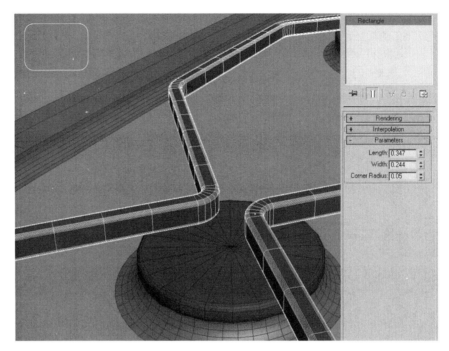

Figure 7.25 Rounding the edges of the bars using Corner Radius.

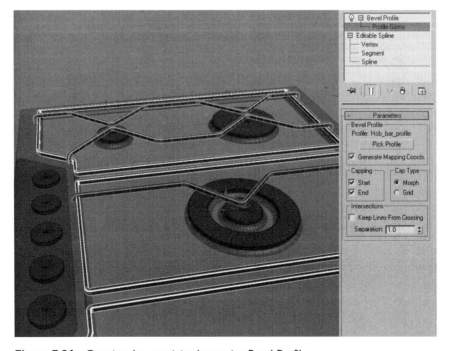

Figure 7.26 Creating the remaining bars using Bevel Profile.

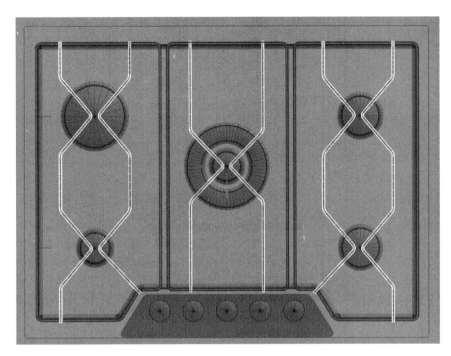

Figure 7.27   Mirroring the bars for the other side of the cooktop.

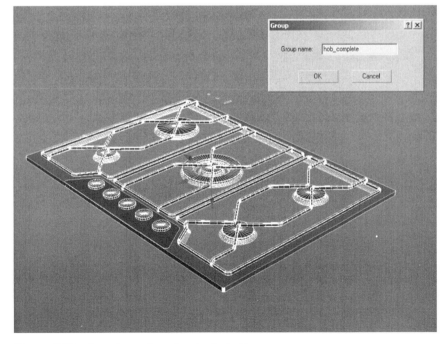

Figure 7.28   Grouping and naming the final object.

Final Assembly

In a reasonably complex scene like this, there's always a point where the separate pieces need to be assembled into the whole. At the same time, there are always additions, tweaks, and improvements to make as you see the scene coming together. These finishing touches can be accomplished using many of the same precision techniques you've already learned, plus one or two new ones.

Now you're going to merge some objects into the scene and finish dressing the kitchen. First of all, let's fit the cooktop into the countertop surface.

1. Open the file 7_Kitchen_Worktop.max, either on the DVD or from the countertop exercise above.

2. From the File menu, select Merge and navigate to the file 7_Kitchen_Cooktop_Finish.max, either on the DVD or from the previous exercise. Select the group hob_complete in the Merge dialog, then click OK.

   You can see that although the cooktop is in the right place, it is currently intersecting with the countertop. You are going to cut a hole into the countertop so that it fits properly.

3. In the Top viewport, get a clear view of the cooktop, then create a Box primitive that fits inside the boundary of the cooktop's perimeter. There's no need to be too accurate here as you are only using the box to define the hole you want to make (**Figure 7.29**).

4. Select the box you've just created and the countertop that you're going to cut; then choose Hide Unselected from the Quad menu.

5. With just the countertop selected, select Boolean from the Create > Geometry > Compound Objects menu.

   Like lofts, Boolean objects require you to create or use more than one element—for example, one to do the cutting and one to be cut. Both elements must be geometry. The Boolean operation can use one element to alter the structure of another. In this case, you're going to subtract the box from the countertop.

6. Go to the Pick Boolean rollout, click Pick Operand B, and in the viewport, select the box. You should now see a hole through the countertop where the box was (**Figure 7.30**).

7. Unhide all the objects in the scene to see how the cooktop model now sits in the hole (**Figure 7.31**).

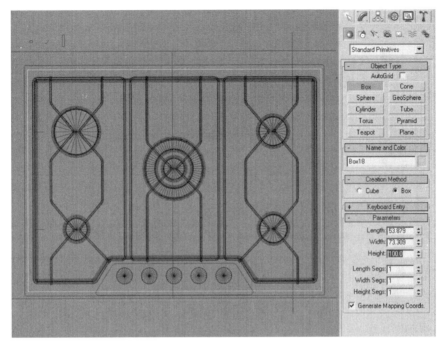

Figure 7.29   Creating a Box primitive in the Top viewport.

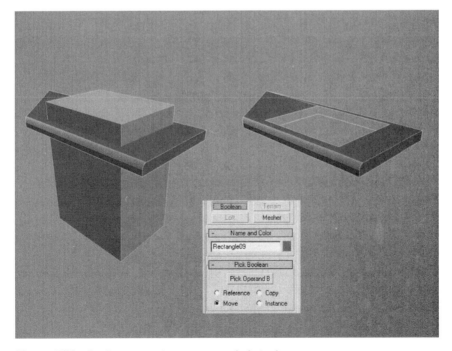

Figure 7.30   Boolean operation to create a hole in the countertop.

Figure 7.31   Newly recessed cooktop.

 Note

> Due to the complex and varied nature of Boolean operations, results can be mixed. max has to calculate the intersection between each face of the two operands. Naturally, this becomes more difficult with more complex geometry. As such, Boolean operations are often best applied to subtractions and unions between simpler objects, as these will yield more accurate results.

Finishing Touches

We've brought in some geometry from another file and fitted it into the scene. In the next few steps, you're going to do the same again to finish the cupboards.

1. Go to File > Merge from the Main menu and navigate to the file named 7_Kitchen_Cupboard_Doors.max. Choose the group named Cupboard Doors then click Open. The scene now contains two cupboard models in one group.

2. Shift-Move a clone of the cupboards along the Y axis and set the type to Instance.

3. With the duplicate doors still selected, select the Align tool from the Main toolbar and click the box labeled Unit04 in the scene.

4. max will bring up the Align Selection dialog. Set the Current Object position to Pivot Point and the Target Objects to Maximum; this will result in the group matching the far edge of the cupboard. Since you want to move the cupboard along one axis only, limit the transform to the Y axis (**Figure 7.32**).

5. Duplicate and rotate the cupboard model to finish the kitchen components (**Figure 7.33**).

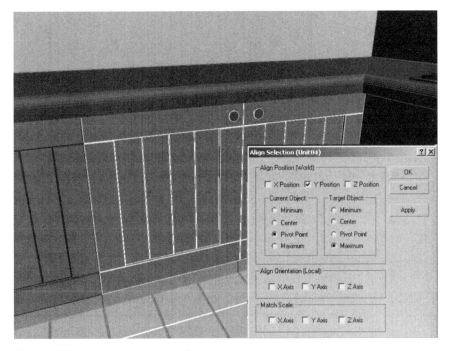

Figure 7.32   Aligning the cupboards.

Now that we've finished the basis of the kitchen, why not try the following?

- Add a set of wall-mounted cupboards.
- Create a breakfast table from primitives.
- Model and fit a sink and faucet.
- Extrude some curtains or make a set of Venetian blinds using the Array tool.

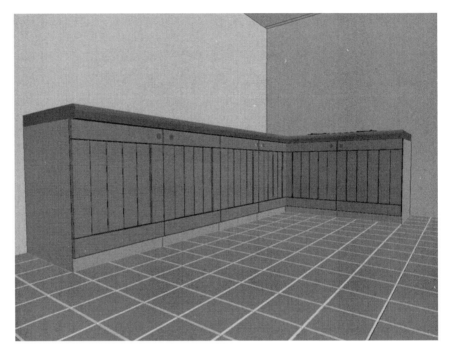

Figure 7.33   The completed components.

Summing Up

In this chapter, you've modeled a series of objects from very basic shapes. By breaking objects down into their simplest components, you can see how something complex can be described with very little actual complexity but nonetheless with considerable precision. Try taking the methods you've covered and applying them to create some of the real-world objects you see every day. Focus on the basic shapes, then observe the crucial details (rounded edges, cracks and corners), and use the precision techniques you've learned here to put them into your model. Once you have achieved this, you can turn your hand to creating the designs in your own imagination.

In the next chapters, we'll look at more involved modeling challenges—creating environments and characters.

Chapter 8

Environmental Modeling

By Erin Nicholson

An essential part of being an artist is to communicate the worlds that you imagine in your head. Many artists are somewhat at odds with reality and enjoy leaving it behind when they create their art. Thanks to the power of computer graphics, the challenging visions of fantasy artists now drive the visual style of our popular culture. From the awe-inspiring architecture of the *Lord of the Rings* films to the dark industrial designs of Id's Doom 3, the toil and visions of innumerable artists pervade our popular culture.

3ds max 7 gives you highly evolved tools for making your own virtual environments seem as nearly real as possible. Modeling an environment in 3ds max can be a liberating experience, but it can also be a dauntingly complex task if it isn't broken down into manageable steps. With a little bit of planning, the work becomes much easier.

That's how we're going to approach this chapter. First, you'll create the basic environment itself. Next, you'll populate the environment with interesting objects. Finally, you'll add atmosphere with lighting and a night sky.

To do all of this, you will need a good understanding of what's required for the scene. The easiest way to gain this understanding is to use a well-thought-out design. Whether rough or polished, a design is a great productivity tool. Designs can take the form of photographs, composites, pencil sketches, computer paint sketches, or anything else that will provide you with a visual reference for your intent.

Here is a concept that I created quickly using a pencil and paper (**Figure 8.1**). It indicates the important elements in my scene and how they are arranged, without too much detail (that will be added later).

Figure 8.1   A rough pencil sketch design.

Once you have the design, you can start to model the parts. As we go step by step through our environmental modeling project, we'll explore some of the core tools in 3ds max, as well as several cool new features in max 7.

Building Rocky Terrain

This tutorial will demonstrate the use of the Normal map and Render To Texture features with Displacement mapping in 3ds max 7. It will also cover other modeling features, both old and new. Important concepts like reuse and color choice will also be covered briefly. The goal is to teach a few of the new tools in 3ds max with an emphasis on putting together an entire project.

Roughing Out the Geometry

From our design sketch, we already have a concept of what we're going to model, so the rest becomes easier. The first thing that we're going to do is model the rock cliff in the foreground.

I. Start with a fresh scene file. First, create a plane with a length of 2000 units and a height of 3000 units. Leave the length and width segments at their default settings of 4 and 4 respectively (**Figure 8.2**).

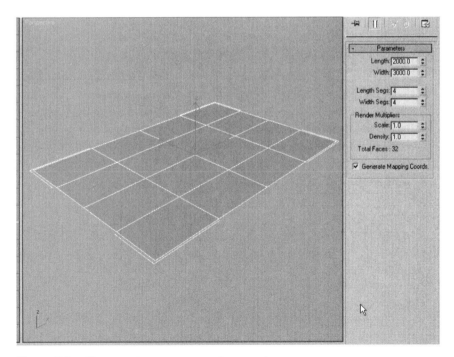

Figure 8.2 Create a plane to serve as the ground.

2. Go to the Modify Panel, hit the drop-down list of modifiers, and apply an Edit Poly modifier to the plane.

3. Look at the cliff, and imagine what the base of it would look like. We want to make this base shape before giving the cliff height. The way to obtain this shape easily is to go into Edge sub-object mode and create new polygons attached to the original plane. This is done by selecting an edge with the Move tool and then holding down the Shift key during the process of moving the edge in the desired direction. It's a very simple and easy way to make new polygons from an existing object. You can see that several edges have been selected and moved together to create new polygons connected to each other and the original plane (**Figure 8.3**).

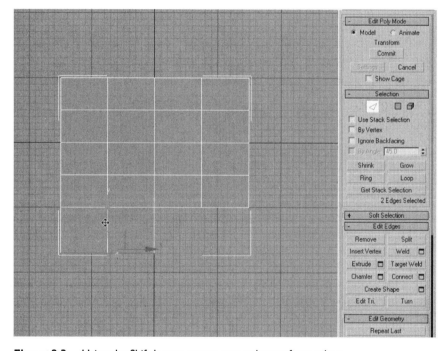

Figure 8.3   Using the Shift key to create new polygons from edges.

4. Continue to Shift-Move edges until you have the desired shape. You will also have to scale some outer edges to get the tapered edges of the cliff's border (**Figure 8.4**).

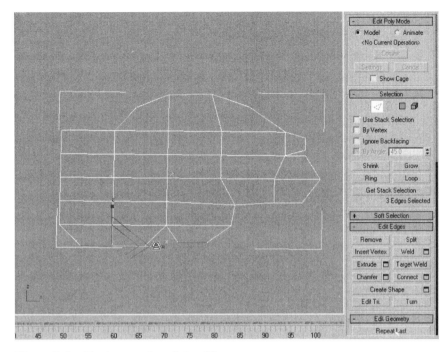

Figure 8.4   The base outline of the cliff.

We're going to give the cliff height by selecting all the polygons in the cliff object and extruding them upward. We're going to do this extrusion in four different stages so that we can create plateaus in the sides of the cliff that will break up its shape and make it more complex and interesting.

5. Select all the polygons of the cliff object, and then click the Extrude button in the Edit Polygons rollout of the Edit Poly modifier. Left-drag the polygons upward. This will create the first level or plateau (**Figure 8.5**).

6. Use the Scale transform to slightly scale the face selection so that the cliff tapers inward as it moves upward. We are using the Extrude tool with the Scale transform instead of the Bevel tool because it allows us to keep the exact border shape of the original base plane. Using the Bevel tool distorts the border shape in magnitudes relative to the bevel amount. We don't want that effect in this case.

7. Deselect the two polygons shown in Figure 8.3, and then extrude upward again to the next plateau. Scale the face selection inward once more, and deselect another face on the border (**Figure 8.6**). Repeat the extrude-upward-and-scale operation again.

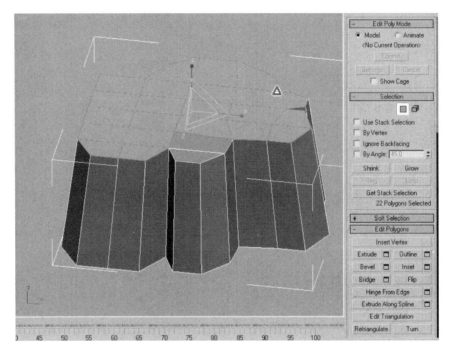

Figure 8.5 Giving the cliff some height.

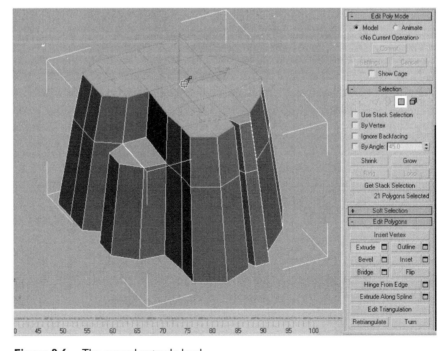

Figure 8.6 The second extrude level.

8. Deselect the two polygons shown in **Figure 8.7**, and extrude again to make another level. Scale this level slightly outward to make a small overhang. Then repeat this extrusion upward a very small amount. This small extrusion will make the top edge of the cliff stay sharp when we apply a smoothing modifier to it later.

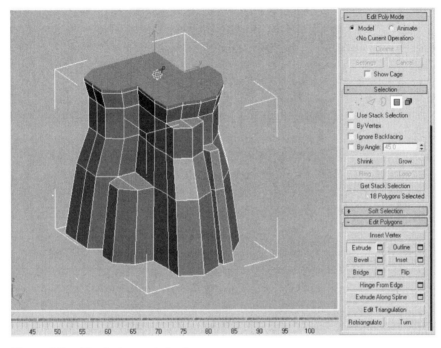

Figure 8.7   The final extrude level.

9. We're also going to put an extra loop of edges beneath each of the plateau levels to ensure that the plateaus remain flat and don't curve when the object is smoothed. We'll start creating this edge loop by selecting a vertical edge beneath each plateau and then clicking the Ring button in the Selection rollout of the Edit Poly modifier. This selects the edges adjacent to the selected edges that border on four-sided polygons. In this mesh, the edge selections will propagate around the entire object because it consists exclusively of four-sided polygons (**Figure 8.8**).

10. With these edges selected, click the Connect button in the Edit Edges rollout of the Edit Poly modifier. This will connect the adjacent edges with a continuous loop of edges (**Figure 8.9**).

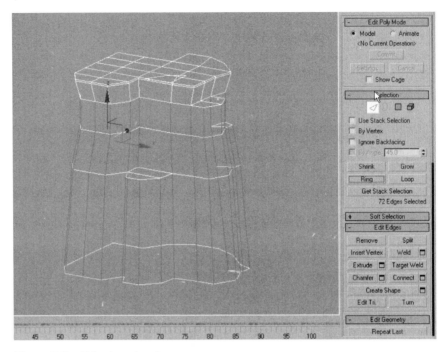

Figure 8.8 Selecting edge rings.

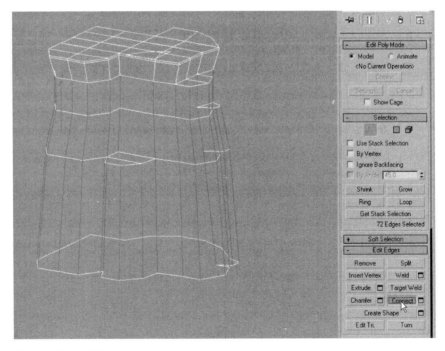

Figure 8.9 Adding edge loops.

11. In the Edit Geometry rollout of the Edit Poly modifier, select Edge from the drop-down menu of options for Constraints (**Figure 8.10**).

Figure 8.10   Selecting the Edge Constraint.

12. Deselect all these edges by left-clicking an empty space in the viewport. Select an edge on the new edge loop lowest on the model, and click the Loop button in the Selection rollout of the Edit Poly modifier. This selects the loop of edges that was just created. With the Edge constraint still active, we can slide this edge loop up along the vertical edges to just below the lowest plateau line (**Figure 8.11**).

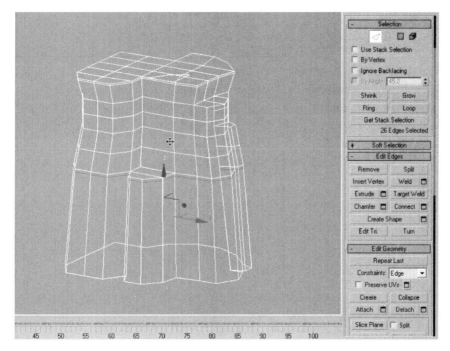

Figure 8.11   Moving an edge-constrained edge loop.

13. Repeat this procedure for the other two edge loops so that there are two edge loops near the top of each plateau level. This will ensure that the plateaus stay flat on top when you smooth them later with a MeshSmooth or TurboSmooth modifier. At this point, it is advisable to round out and fine-tune the shape of the cliff by selecting vertices or edges and moving them around until the shape is desirable (**Figure 8.12**).

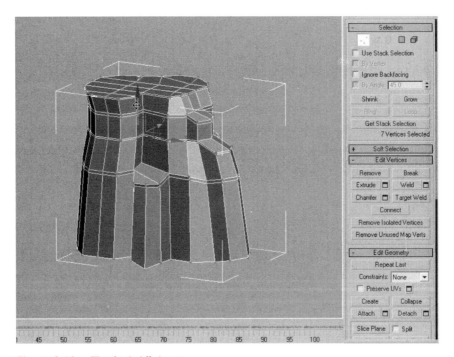

Figure 8.12   The final cliff shape.

Believe it or not, that's all the modeling we're going to do for this cliff. The rest of the detail will be added with Displacement maps. We will then derive the Normal map from the displaced mesh using the Render To Texture dialog. To have control over how the cliff is displaced with maps, we need to lay out mapping coordinates for the cliff. This leads us into the next part of the tutorial.

Mapping the Terrain

Mapping, the process of applying various surface textures and lighting effects to a 3D object, allows you to gain great control over the appearance of your models, whether rocky cliffs or rubber duckies. It's been said that textures and lighting generate at least half of the positive impact that we feel when we see a well-done 3D model. Mapping *is* that important.

In particular, the Unwrap UVW modifier is an essential tool for controlling exactly how maps will be displayed on any 3D model, and we will be using it extensively in the following tutorial. With that said, let's start unwrapping our cliff model.

1. Once the edge loops are placed under the plateaus, we need to unwrap the object. Exit sub-object mode, right-click the Edit Poly modifier in the cliff's modifier stack, and select the Collapse All option. This will convert the object to an editable polygon mesh.

2. From the Modifier drop-down list, apply an Unwrap UVW modifier to the cliff. Activate the Face sub-object mode so that the polygons of the cliff can be selected within the Unwrap UVW modifier. Make sure that the Ignore Backfacing option is enabled in the Unwrap UVW modifier's Selection Parameters rollout.

   The next step is to unwrap the object into front, back, and top sections. We will then join the edges of the front and back so that we have one long polygon strip for mapping.

3. In the Front viewport, marquee-select the polygons that are visible. Toggle the Selection mode to Window in the Main toolbar. Then deselect the top polygons of the cliff object that are perpendicular to the Front viewport. Control-left-click to add to the selection any polygons that were left out from the front of the cliff when the marquee selection was made. Also, Alt-left-click any polygons on the back of the cliff to deselect them (**Figure 8.13**).

 Note

New to 3ds max 7 is the addition of Thick Seam Display within the Unwrap UVW modifier (**Figure 8.13**). Go to the Display section of the Parameters rollout, and note that Thick Seam Display is enabled by default. In the viewport, the seams are visible as thick green lines that follow the seam edges along the model surface. It is possible to make these lines thinner by choosing Thin Seam Display or to turn them off completely by choosing Show No Seams.

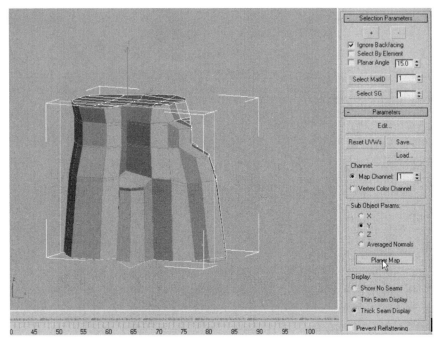

Figure 8.13 Selecting polygons for a planar projection.

4. With all the polygons on the front half of the cliff selected, align the planar map
   to the Y axis in the Sub Object Params group of the Parameter rollout and click
   the Planar Map button. Click the Edit button in the same rollout to bring up the
   Edit UVWs dialog. The planar projection of the front of the mesh is displayed in
   the dialog along with the overlapping polygons that haven't had planar projections applied to them yet. Move the selection of polygons from the front of the
   cliff away from the overlapping polygons of the rest of the cliff.

5. For the rest of the cliff we can easily separate the parts. Go to the Edit drop-down
   menu in the Main toolbar, and choose Select Invert. This will select the remaining polygons of the cliff. Click the Planar Map button. In the Edit UVWs dialog,
   and move these newly planar-mapped polygons away from the center of the
   UVW mapping area (the blue square). Then, with the Edit UVWs dialog still
   open, select the top polygons of the cliff and choose the Z axis as the axis to align
   the planar map to. Click the Planar Map button a final time while the top polygons are selected. Now the top, front, and back groups of polygons have all been
   unwrapped with planar projections (**Figure 8.14**).

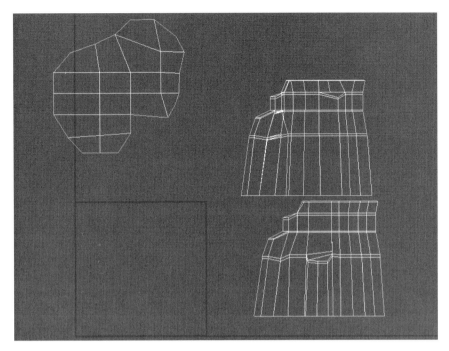

Figure 8.14 The cliff's basic planar projections laid out.

6. You'll notice that there are some overlapping edges in the back section of the cliff where there are two separate columns close to one another. The best action to take here is to manually move the vertices in the Edit UVWs dialog so that they don't overlap.

7. With the cliff's polygons now properly flattened, we can stitch the front and back polygons together. Switch to Edge sub-object mode in the Edit UVWs dialog. Select all of the edges for the cliff front, and mirror them using the Mirror Horizontal tool found on the Main toolbar of the Edit UVWs dialog.

8. Deselect the cliff front edges and then select the green edges of the front polygons that run down the center of the cliff. Once selected, they will turn red, and the corresponding edges on the back polygons will turn blue. In the Tools dropdown menu of the Edit UVWs dialog, select Stitch Selected. In the Stitch Selected tool dialog, deselect Align Clusters and Scale Clusters. Leave the bias at 0.5. Click OK to close the dialog. You will then have to move the edges around and get rid of overlaps until you come up with the result show below (**Figure 8.15**). As you can see, the objective is to unwrap the object without losing its original proportions.

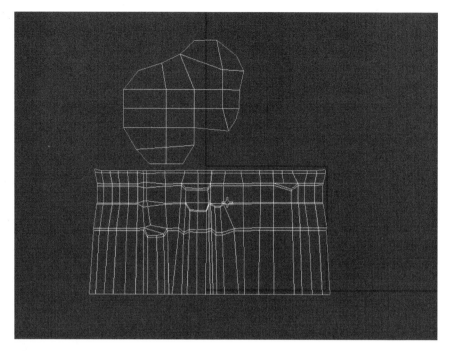

Figure 8.15   Stitching edges together.

9. The last part of unwrapping the object is to pack it into the UVW mapping area (the blue box aligned to the grid in the background). To accomplish this, we will scale the objects so that they fit into the UVW mapping area. There is a tool that does this automatically, called Pack UVs, and it can be useful. However, it doesn't size the pieces according to their actual size on the object. This is a very important point, because the proportions of the unwrapped object should remain the same as their counterparts in the 3D model. If they aren't the same proportions, it will lead to ugly stretching of textures on the object.

To do the same thing manually, select the elements and scale them down to their correct size within the UVW mapping area. After they are scaled, move them in to fit tightly—but not overlapping—in the UVW mapping area. You'll also notice that in this case I've broken this rule, and that the sides of the cliff model have been horizontally scaled to fit better in the UVW mapping area and maximize the map coverage. This horizontal scale can be offset later with horizontal map tiling in the material editor. For most cases though, try to keep the UV layouts matching in proportion to the actual polygon proportions on the model (**Figure 8.16**).

This completes the process of unwrapping the cliff object. The next step is to apply a material to the cliff object and use the Displace Mesh modifier (WSM) to displace the cliff mesh based on the material applied to it.

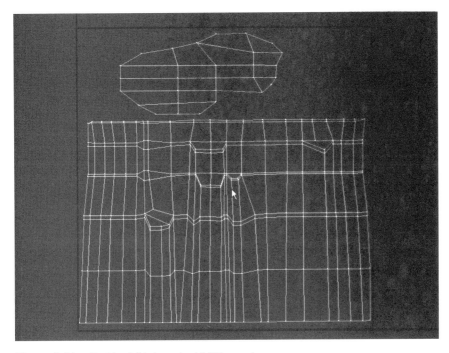

Figure 8.16   Packing UVs into the UVW mapping area.

Adding Complexity with Materials

Displacement material is a material that creates the look of surface geometry without actually adding any new polygons. For the sake of simplicity, we will be using procedural maps for the rock's Displacement map and some bitmaps for the rock's Diffuse colors. (Further information on mapping types and techniques will be found in later chapters of this book.) The procedural materials that most closely resemble the patterns of rock are the Cellular and Smoke procedural maps. There are other options within the material library, like procedural Noise and Marble, so you can always experiment to get the desired effect. It is also possible to paint Displacement maps, but this is more time-consuming and is unnecessary in this instance.

We'll be looking at Normal mapping in this section. A form of Displacement mapping, Normal mapping is a new feature of 3ds max 7 that is very useful for creating and controlling the appearance of detail without having a huge number of polygons in the scene. It uses a Color map to represent geometry data for a surface so that the surface reacts to light and shadow. Normal maps encode XYZ vector information into an RGB map, with red representing the X (horizontal) vector, green representing the Y (vertical) vector, and blue representing the Z (depth) vector. When applied to an object, these three color channels can give an object the appearance of having highly detailed geometry. Think of them as Bump maps on steroids.

Displacement-Mapping the Cliff

Now let's add some maps to your scene.

1. After saving your progress file, open the file Landscape_CliffDisplace.max. This file contains the unwrapped high- and low-resolution cliff models. You can also keep working with your own file, if you wish, by merging the contents of this sample file into your scene and applying the material and copying the modifiers onto your cliff mesh. Remember that modifiers can be copied from one object to another by right-clicking the modifier in the stack and selecting Copy. Then select the object, right-click its name in the stack, and choose either Paste or Paste Instanced in the drop-down menu that appears.

2. Take a look at the HiRes_herocliff model. After the computer thinks for bit, it will display the displaced mesh. In the Displacement Approx rollout of the Displace Mesh (WSM) modifier that has been applied to the HiRes_herocliff, Custom Settings and Subdivision Displacement are checked and the subdivision method is set to Spatial and Curvature. The Edge and Distance values are both set to 60 and the Angle value is set to 30. Without going into too much detail, the higher the numbers for all three of these values, the lower the number of polygons that will be generated by subdivision. In general, the less geometry you use to create a desired effect, the better. Also take a look at the Advanced Parameters and notice that the displacement style is set to Delaunay. This method of displacement gives the best results, but also creates very dense triangulated meshes (**Figure 8.17**).

   This is a good time to explain the term "hero" as it is used for models in computer graphics. A "hero" model is an object (or character) that is usually the visual focal point of the scene or is featured most prominently. It is also the model that will receive the most attention, so it has to look really good. Hence we are using the term "herocliff" for the cliff model that is in the foreground of the scene.

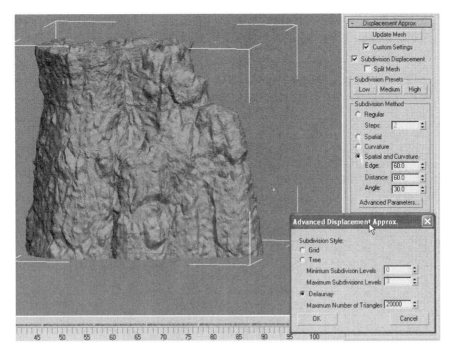

Figure 8.17   Displacement settings.

3. Open the Material Editor, and take a look at the HiRes_herocliff material applied to the HiRes_herocliff model. The Displacement slot is the most important, so focus on it first. Notice that there is a Mix material in the Displacement slot that contains a Cellular map mixed 50 percent with a Smoke material. Also notice the large sizes for the Cellular and Smoke maps, with numeric values of 3000 and 200 respectively. This is necessary because of the cliff model's large scale.

 Note

Procedural maps are different from bitmaps because they are resolution-independent. In order for them to be the right size, their values must be scaled with the object. A bitmap has a fixed number of pixels and therefore has a fixed resolution, so it will become more pixelated as the scale of the object that it is applied to increases.

Look at the Diffuse Color slot of the HiRes_herocliff material. It also contains a Mix map with Cellular and Smoke materials of the same size. The only difference is that some of the procedural colors have been changed and some bitmaps have been added to the Color slots of the Smoke map. The Displacement map has also been used in the Bump map slot because both Displacement and Bump mapping rely on the same grayscale values in maps (**Figure 8.18**).

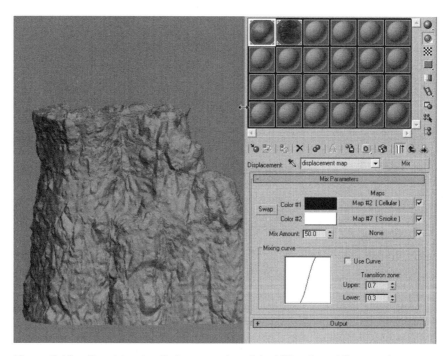

Figure 8.18   Examining the displacement slot of the HiRes_herocliff material.

4. Now disable the Displace Mesh modifier by clicking the Light Bulb icon next to it in the modifier stack. Once the displacement is no longer displayed in the view-port, hold down the Shift key while clicking the cliff model with the Move tool. A Clone dialog will appear, allowing us to create a copy of the object. Name this new cliff object LoRes_herocliff. This is the model to which we will apply Normal mapping.

Transferring Detail with Normal Mapping

In this next sequence, we are going to use Normal mapping to transfer detail from the high-resolution cliff model to apply to the low-resolution cliff model—sort of a 3D "wealth transfer" process.

1. Drag the HiRes_herocliff material to another slot in the Material Editor and rename it LoRes_herocliff. Apply the LoRes_herocliff material to the LoRes_herocliff model.

2. With the two objects still aligned and the LoRes_herocliff object selected, press 0 on the keyboard to bring up the Render To Texture dialog. In the Objects To Bake rollout, go to the Projection Mapping section and click the Enabled check box. Then, next to the Projection drop-down, click the Pick button and select HiRes_herocliff. This tells the Render To Texture tool which object's textures it will be baking. (Baking, by the way, is the process of combining several layers of textures together into one texture.) A Projection modifier appears in the stack of the LoRes_herocliff. This is what will project the textures rendered from the HiRes_herocliff onto the LoRes_herocliff object. (In essence, you are "stealing" detail from the high-resolution object to apply to the low-resolution one. Clever, no?) Deselect the Sub-Object levels check box below the Pick button in the Projection Mapping section of the Render To Texture Objects to Bake rollout (**Figure 8.19**).

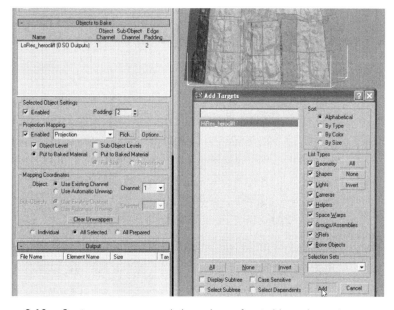

Figure 8.19   Setting up textures to bake and transfer via Normal mapping.

3. Click the Options button to see the Projection Options dialog. Choose Local XYZ as the Normal map spatial coordinate system. This will allow the map to be rendered without lighting data being baked into the Normal map. This is a good feature if you want to reuse the Normal-mapped object and rotate it into different positions in the scene—you certainly don't want the lighting baked in that case. Once this is done, close the Projection Options dialog (**Figure 8.20**).

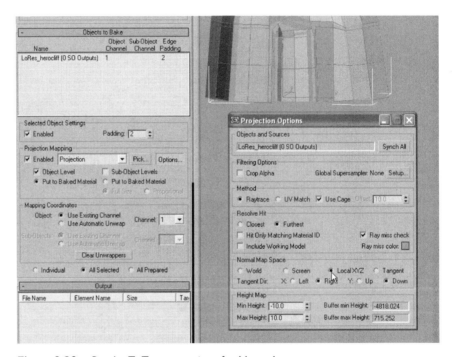

Figure 8.20   Render To Texture options for Normal maps.

4. In the Mapping Coordinates section, click the Use Existing Channel radio button. In the Output rollout, click the Add button and choose NormalsMap. Leave the size at 256 pixels for now in the Selected Element Common Settings section. In the Selected Element Unique Settings section, click the Output into Normal Bump check box. In the Baked Material rollout, click the Output into Source radio button. These last two options output the Normal map to the Bump slot of the material for the LoRes_herocliff object (**Figure 8.21**).

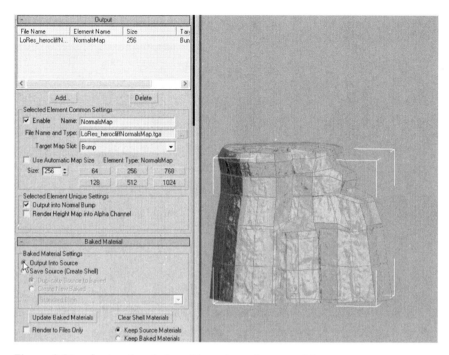

Figure 8.21 Settings for placing a Normal map in a material.

5. With the LoRes_herocliff object still selected, open the Modify panel and look at the Projection modifier that has been added to it by the Render To Texture tool.

6. Notice in the Geometry Selection rollout that the HiRes_herocliff is listed at the Object level. The projection cage that surrounds the cliff object in blue is quite messy, but it can be fixed by going to the Cage rollout and clicking the Reset button. Following this, enter a Push Amount value of 300 in the same rollout to surround the HiRes_herocliff again.

7. Now we can finally do a render. Before doing so, change the Output path in the General Settings rollout at the top of the Render To Texture dialog to a folder that you can store the maps. At the bottom of the Render To Texture dialog, click the Render button and let's see what we have (**Figure 8.22**). Check to see if it looks the same as the corresponding map include in the project files.

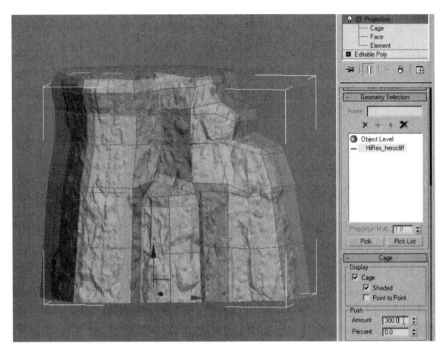

Figure 8.22 Are you Rrrready to Rrrrender?!!

Finishing the Cliff

The red areas on the cliff render show where there are holes in the mesh or (more likely) where the projection cage intersects with the HiRes_herocliff mesh (**Figure 8.23**). (The Render To Texture tool will also output an unseen render of the Normal map into the Bump slot of LoRes_herocliff material as a Normal map type.) Let's fix those now and finish up our cliff.

 Note

> The red color sometimes seen in the render signifies a ray miss. The ray miss color can be changed to another color in the Options dialog within the Projection Mapping section of the Objects To Bake rollout.

1. To get rid of the intersections, we'll manipulate the projection cage (**Figure 8.24**). In the Projection modifier, click the Cage sub-object level. Within this sub-object level, we can manipulate the vertices that make up the cage. Click the check box

for the Shaded option in the Display section of the Cage rollout. Any mesh that intersects the cage will appear to be outside the shaded surface of the cage. Once these problem areas are visible, manipulate the cage vertices so that the cage no longer intersects with them. After making these changes, rerender the image and see if there are any red spots on the render.

Figure 8.23   Checking for Render To Texture problems.

2. Change the Size of the render to 1024 in the Selected Element Common Settings section of the Output rollout. Rerender the Normal map and close the Render To Texture dialog.

3. Hide the HiRes_cliff model and render the LoRes_herocliff model. The low-resolution mode will now look as if it has been displaced, like the high-resolution object in the rendered image. We can add a TurboSmooth modifier to the LoRes_herocliff object to make it look a little less blocky around the edges. The TurboSmooth modifier, new to 3ds max 7, is just a trimmed-down version of the MeshSmooth modifier and much quicker to display its results in the viewport (**Figure 8.25**).

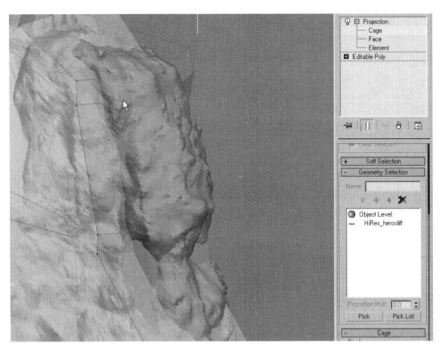

Figure 8.24 Manipulating the Projection modifier cage.

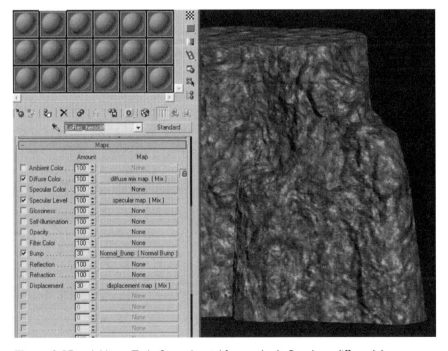

Figure 8.25 Adding a TurboSmooth modifier to the LoRes_herocliff model.

4. Open the file entitled Landscape_CliffNormalMap.max to see the final result of the Normal-mapped low-resolution cliff.

Now you've explored the basics of how displacement can be used with Normal mapping. The Displacement and Normal map workflow we used for this model will be used again when we model the ground plane. That's the next piece of the puzzle.

Modeling a Ground Plane

Now that the cliff model is done, we have something that we can alter and reuse for other cliffs and mountains in the scene. Before we do that, though, there has to be a ground plane to put these mountainous bodies on. Compared to the cliff, this will be a very quick and easy exercise, especially now that we've established a workflow for using Displacement and Normal mapping.

1. Open up a new 3ds max 7 scene, and, in the Top viewport, create a Tube primitive with the following dimensions:
   - Radius 1 = 3000
   - Radius 2 = 29000
   - Height = 5000
   - Cap Segments = 11

2. Next, apply an Edit Poly modifier to the tube. Enter Polygon sub-object mode and marquee-select the whole bottom of the tube in the Front viewport. Then click the Grow button in the Selection rollout several times, until every face is selected except for the top cap segments of the tube. Delete the selected polygons. This leaves us with only the cap segments on the top of the tube (**Figure 8.26**).

3. Rename the tube LoRes_valleyfloor. Merge in the LoRes_herocliff model from your previous file or from Landscape_CliffDisplace.max. Move the LoRes_valleyfloor object down so that it intersects just above the bottom edge of the cliff (**Figure 8.27**).

4. Quickly map the LoRes_valleyfloor object by putting a UVW Map modifier on it, with the Mapping type set to Planar and aligned with the Z axis.

5. Right-click the LoRes_valleyfloor object, and in the bottom right Quad menu, choose Convert To > Convert to Editable Poly.

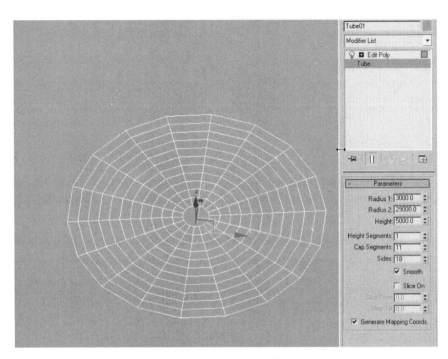

Figure 8.26   Making the valley floor with a modified Tube primitive.

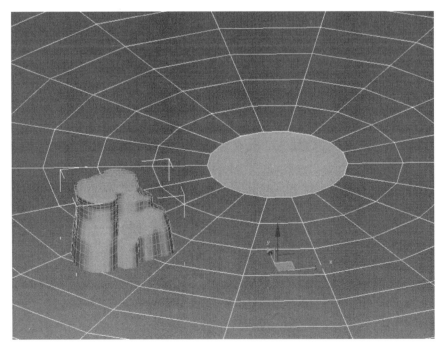

Figure 8.27   Placing the LoRes_herocliff model in the scene.

6. Right-click the LoRes_valleyfloor object again, and choose Clone from the bottom right Quad menu. Make a copy of the LoRes_valleyfloor object and rename it HiRes_valleyfloor.

7. Open the Material Editor, go to an empty Material slot, and click the Get Material button. In the Material/Map browser that appears, choose Mtl Library in Browse From and click the Open button in the File section. Find the HiRes_valleyfloor.mat file on the DVD and open it (**Figure 8.28**).

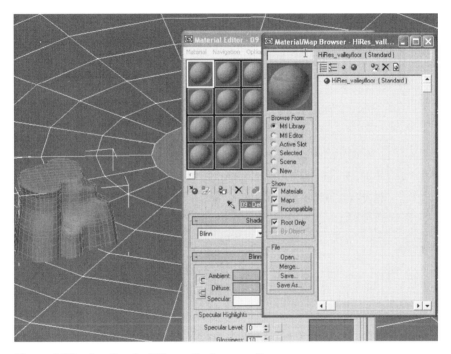

Figure 8.28   Loading the HiRes_valleyfloor.mat file.

8. Double-click the HiRes_valleyfloor material to open it in the empty material slot. Apply the HiRes_valleyfloor material to the HiRes_valleyfloor object. Then apply a Displace Mesh (WSM) modifier to the HiRes_valleyfloor object with the following settings:

- Custom Settings
- Subdivision Displacement
- Spatial and Curvature
- Edge, Distance, Angle = 30, 30, 30
- Delaunay Subdivision Style

9. Wait for the displacement to display on the HiRes_valleyfloor model. Once you can see the displacement, go back to the LoRes_valleyfloor model and add some extra edge loops with the Ring and Connect tools, as we did with the cliff. Then raise the geometry on the LoRes_valleyfloor to roughly match the raised displacements on the HiRes_valleyfloor model (**Figure 8.29**).

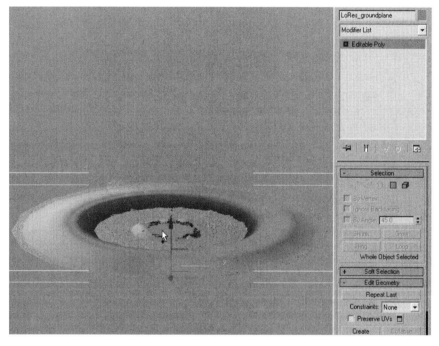

Figure 8.29   Adding geometry to the LoRes_valleyfloor model.

10. Drag the HiRes_valley floor material to an empty slot, and rename it LoRes_valleyfloor. Delete the Mix map from the Displacement map slot of this material, and then apply it to the LoRes_valleyfloor model.

11. Repeat the same Render To Texture process that we used on the herocliff models to generate Normal maps. Then hide the HiRes_valleyfloor to see how the Normal-mapped LoRes_valleyfloor looks. Open the file Landscape_ValleyFloor.max to see how it compares with your file.

12. Open Landscape_Terrain.max to see how the cliff has been modified and duplicated to populate the environment.

In this section, we've learned how a small amount of geometry can be used with Normal mapping to create impressive depth and detail in an environment. It takes a bit of time, but once it's there it can be rendered and reused with ease because the data set is so small compared to displaced geometry. We're not done yet, though, so on to the next task.

The Fiery Pit

Egad, the fiery pit! Okay, so maybe it isn't quite that scary or dramatic, but this is a different type of object than the ones that we've built so far. We're going to put a pit in the middle of our ground plane. To make it more interesting, we'll Normal-map the pit with alien inscriptions glowing red to indicate its power and evil purpose.

It's possible to create all kinds of interesting alien-style patterns with the shape and path tools in Adobe Photoshop, very much as you would with Boolean operations in 3ds max 7. For this tutorial we'll use a map that was created with these techniques.

 1. First, start with a new scene and create a Tube primitive of the following dimensions (**Figure 8.30**):

   * Radius 1 = 2900
   * Radius 2 = 3400
   * Height = 7500

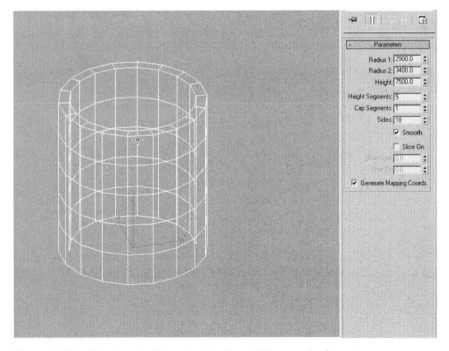

Figure 8.30   Creating the Tube primitive that will become the fiery pit.

2. Convert the Tube to an editable poly, select the polygons on the top edge of the tube, and extrude them up about 300 units (**Figure 8.31**).

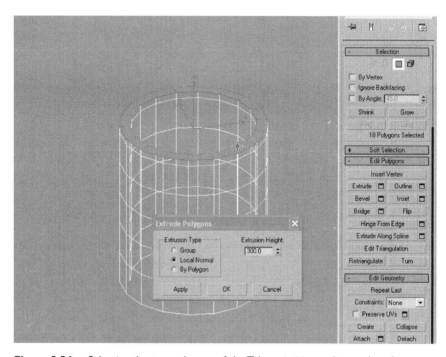

Figure 8.31   Selecting the top polygons of the Tube primitive and extruding them.

3. Select the vertical polygons just below the top edge of the tube. Extrude these polygons outward to create a lip on the top of the tube (**Figure 8.32**).

4. Select every second face along this lip, and extrude these polygons outward, first a small amount and then a longer distance, to create fins along the edge of the lip. With the polygons still selected, extrude a small distance on the ends to keep the ends of the fins sharp. Delete the outside of the tube underneath the lip so that only the inside of the tube and the lip remain. Add extra loops of edges on the inside of the lip and along the top and bottom of the fins. This will keep the edges of the lip and fins sharp when a TurboSmooth modifier is applied (**Figure 8.33**).

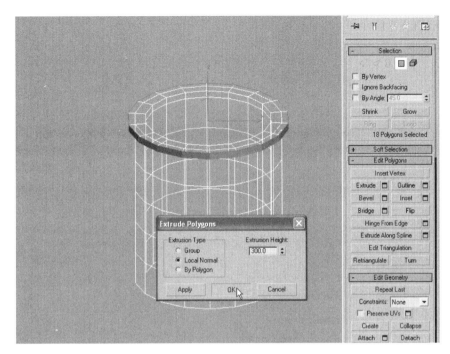

Figure 8.32   Using the Extrude tool to create a lip on the Tube.

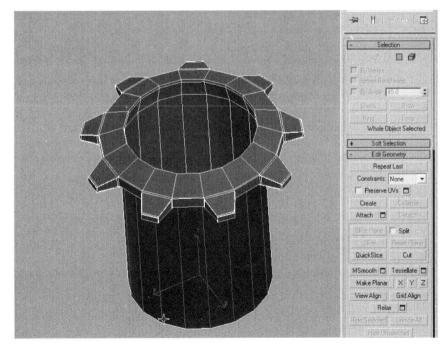

Figure 8.33   Adding fins and extra detail to the pit model (backface cull is off).

5. Apply an Unwrap UVW modifier to the Tube, and unwrap it so that the top of the lip, along with the fins, fits inside the UVW mapping area in the Edit Unwrap UVWs dialog (blue box). Unwrap the inside of the tube so that it also fits in the space within the unwrapped polygons of the lip in the Unwrap UVW dialog (**Figure 8.34**).

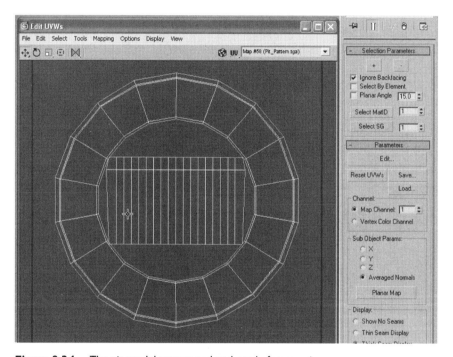

Figure 8.34   The pit model unwrapped and ready for mapping.

6. Name the tube Pit_HiRes, and apply a TurboSmooth modifier to the pit model.

7. Go to the Material Editor, and choose a blank material slot. Click Get Material, then choose Mtl Library from Browse From. Load Fierypit.mat and double-click HiRes_Pit. Apply the HiRes_Pit material to the pit model. You'll notice that the material is a Blend of a Red Lava material and a Gray Metal material with the alien design Pit_Pattern.tga in the Displacement slot (**Figure 8.35**).

8. Apply a Displace Mesh (WSM) modifier to the pit model, and enable Custom Settings and Subdivision Displacement. Use the Spatial and Curvature Subdivision Method; set the Edge and Distance values to 40 and the Angle value to 10. Click Advanced Parameters, and choose Delaunay as the Subdivision Style (**Figure 8.36**).

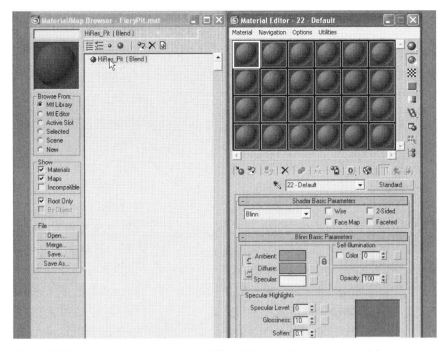

Figure 8.35   Loading and applying the HiRes_Pit material to the pit model.

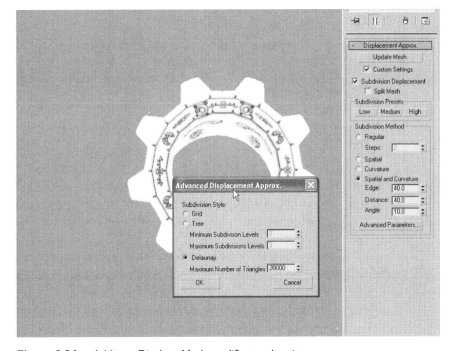

Figure 8.36   Adding a Displace Mesh modifier to the pit.

Normal-Mapping the Pit

The next thing that we're going to do is apply Normal mapping to a low-resolution version of the pit model. This should be easy for you now, but it will serve to reinforce what you've learned earlier if you still have any questions.

1. Disable the Displace Mesh modifier on the Pit_HiRes model. Shift-Copy the model without moving it, and name the copy Pit_LoRes. Delete the Displace Mesh modifier from the Pit_LoRes model.

2. Copy the Pit_HiRes material over to an empty slot, and rename it Pit_LoRes. Delete the Displacement map from the Gray Metal material, and apply the Pit_LoRes material to the Pit_LoRes model (**Figure 8.37**).

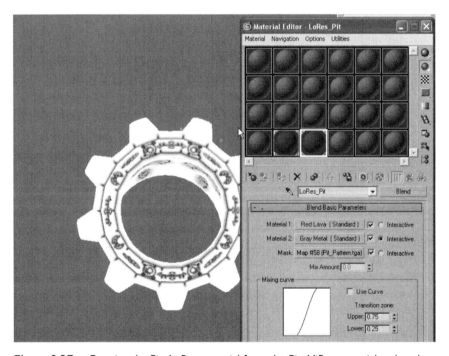

Figure 8.37   Creating the Pit_LoRes material from the Pit_HiRes material and applying it to the Pit_LoRes model.

3. With the Pit_LoRes model still selected, open the Render To Texture dialog. In the Projection Mapping group, check Enabled and click the Pick button. Choose the Pit_HiRes model as the model from which to project onto the Pit_LoRes model. Click Options and choose Local XYZ in the Normal Map Space group. In the

Mapping Coordinates group, choose Use Existing Channel and leave the Channel value at 1 (**Figure 8.38**).

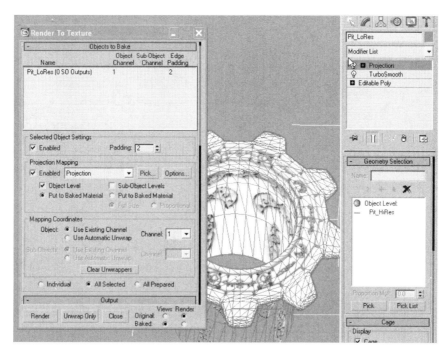

Figure 8.38   Picking the objects from which to bake out the Normal map.

4. In the Output rollout, choose Add and add a NormalsMap. In the Select Element Common Settings group, choose Bump in the Target Map slot and make the Size value 1024. In the Select Element Unique Settings, choose Output into Normal Bump. In the Baked Material rollout, choose Output Into Source (**Figure 8.39**).

5. You're now ready to render the Normal map. Before you do, make sure that you have a good projection cage around the Pit_LoRes model that also encompasses all of the Pit_HiRes model. In this case, resetting the cage and entering a Push value of 200 seems to work well. Once you've rendered the Normal map successfully, you'll see the Normal map appear as a Normal Bump map type in the Gray Metal material of the Pit_LoRes material (**Figure 8.40**).

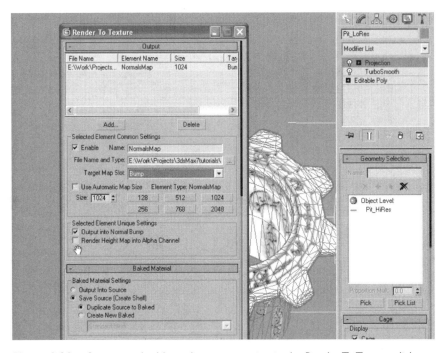

Figure 8.39 Setting up the Normal map generation in the Render To Texture dialog.

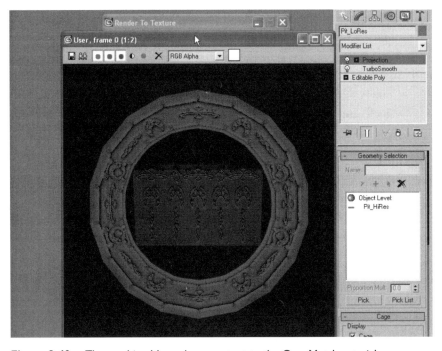

Figure 8.40 The resulting Normal map output to the Gray Metal material.

6. The only thing left to do for the pit model at this point is to merge the Pit_
LoRes model into the Landscape scene and make sure that it fits. Open the file
Landscape_FieryPit.max to see how it should look at this point (**Figure 8.41**).

Figure 8.41   The fiery pit once it is finished and merged into the environment.

That completes our coverage of modeling Normal-mapped objects. You can always add
more for your own benefit, or build onto the objects that are already there. After using
Normal maps and displacement to model our cliffs, valley floor, and fiery pit, the process
should now be almost second nature to you. Displacement is always a challenge, but
Normal maps are well worth the effort. Luckily, our next small addition to the environment will seem very easy in comparison. We're going to light up the land with some shiny
glowing crystals.

Crystals

Crystals are the final inorganic things that we're going to add to the scene. The scene is a
little dark and bare, so they will add contrasting elements to keep the viewer interested.
We're going to make the crystals glow a misty blue color to offset the overall red. The blue
will also make the scene look cold on the edges and warmer in the middle. It never hurts

to make the viewer think a little, even if your work has no deeper meaning than "Oooh, look at the pretty colors!"

1. Start with a new scene. Begin by making a Pyramid primitive with a Width and Depth of 400 units and a Height of 300 units (**Figure 8.42**).

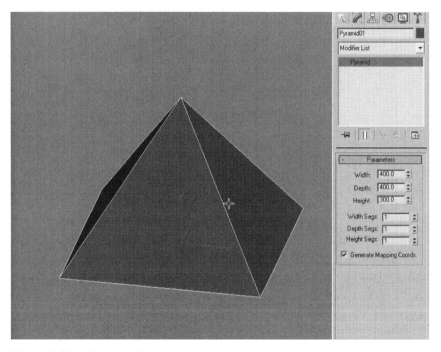

Figure 8.42 Creating a Pyramid.

2. Convert the Pyramid to an Editable Poly object. Select the bottom polygons of the pyramid, use the Bevel tool to extrude the polygons downward about 1500 units, and then scale them in to about half the size of the top section. Name the modified pyramid Crystal01. This is a very simple way to make a crystal shape.

3. Go to the Hierarchy panel and click Affect Pivot Only. Move the pivot point down to the bottom of the crystal (**Figure 8.43**).

4. Turn off Affect Pivot Only, then hold down the Shift key, and use the Rotate tool to make copies of the crystal around the original Crystal01. Once you're happy with the arrangement, select Crystal01, and in the Edit Geometry rollout, click the Attach List button to the right of the Attach button. Select all the Crystal copies in the list and attach them to Crystal01 (**Figure 8.44**).

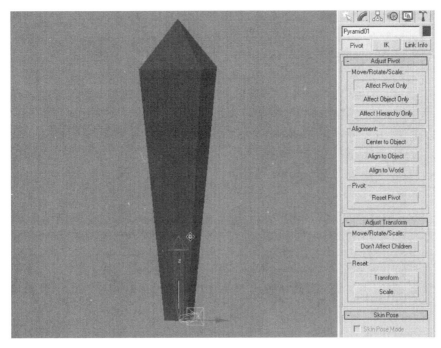

Figure 8.43   Modifying the crystal's pivot point.

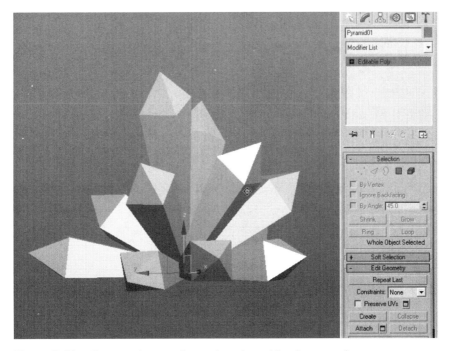

Figure 8.44   Creating clusters of crystals and attaching them together.

5. In the Material Editor, select an empty material slot and then click Get Material. Choose Mtl Library and then click Open. Click Crystals.mat, and click Open on the dialog box. Apply this material to the Crystal01 model. It's a Raytrace material with a misty blue color. Also notice that the Material Effects Channel is set to a value of 1. This will allow us to assign a glow to the crystal once we have it in the scene. Save your work as Crystal01.max.

6. Open Landscape_FieryPit.max. Merge the Crystal01 model into the Landscape_FieryPit.max file and duplicate it around the scene at the bottoms of the cliffs. You can also add lights and a glow to each of the crystals to make them really stand out. To see what you might end up with at this point, open Landscape_Crystals.max. This scene has a Lens Effects Glow added to the crystals and omni lights added to light up the cliffs close to the crystal formations. Also present is a red volume light coming up from the bottom of the pit to make the scene more dramatic. If you want to speed up the render, turn down the Sample Range for the red light that is casting the volume light in the scene. The Sample Range of the volume light is set to 20 to avoid banding (an ugly render artifact caused by a too-small Sample Range, among other things).

Now we've got the start of an interesting environment that's polygon-light and therefore relatively quick to render (**Figure 8.45**). Thanks to Normal mapping, the cliffs and the valley floor have lots of depth and detail. The pit, glowing red with alien inscriptions, is the focal point, with the crystals and moonlight illuminating the cliffs above. Fog adds a bit of mystery, and the field of stars above makes it look cold and silent.

Is it complete, though? Hardly! You can always add more to your environments to make them more rich and interesting. Perhaps our landscape needs a plant or two.

Creating Plant Life

The vast diversity of flora around us is staggering, if we stop to think about it. Recent estimates of the number of earthly plant species alone are close to 450,000, with as many as 50,000 yet unknown. While this diversity wouldn't be practical to re-create in computer graphics, we can at least try to give the illusion of it. In this section we're going to create a small sampling of plant life that can be used to populate our recently finished landscape environment. Don't limit yourself to just the landscape tutorial, though. As you continue to build trees and other plants, it is a great idea to build a library of them and reuse them in your own environments!

Figure 8.45   A rendered image of the Landscape_Crystals.max file.

Modeling a Tree

Modeling a tree can be a very daunting task because trees are so complex and have so many individual pieces. However, a tree can still be broken down into manageable parts. There is a lot of repetition in a tree, and that is what can help make it easier to model. The aim of this tutorial is to start simply and build complexity by using repetition of the different elements of a tree. If done in the right order, a fairly simple tree can be modeled quickly and efficiently.

The Trunk

1. Start with a new scene. Make a Box primitive with the following dimensions:

   - Length = 40
   - Width = 40
   - Height = 20

- Length Segments = 2
- Width Segments = 2
- Height Segments = 1

2. Add an Edit Poly modifier to the box and select an edge in the middle of two perpendicular sides. Click the Loop button in the Selection rollout so that you have selected two loops of edges meeting at the center of the box on the top and the bottom.

3. Scale these edge selections outward equally along the X and Y axes until the box takes on a more circular shape from the top down (**Figure 8.46**).

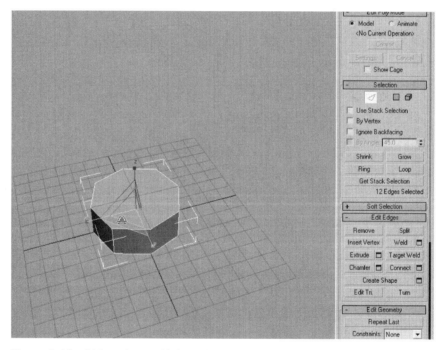

Figure 8.46   Making the trunk's base shape.

4. Draw a curved spline in the Front viewport above the box object. Once the spline is in position above the box and still selected, go to the Hierarchy panel and click the Affect Pivot Only button. Then click the Align tool in the Main toolbar, and click the box. Choose to align the pivot point of the spline with that of the box

and also align their XYZ axes. Turn off Affect Pivot Only in the Hierarchy panel
(**Figure 8.47**).

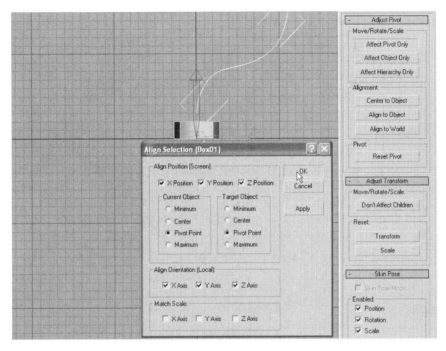

Figure 8.47   Preparing to use Extrude Along Spline.

5. Select the four polygons on the top of the box and click the Settings button next
   to the Extrude Along Spline button. This will bring up the Extrude Along Spline
   dialog. Click the Pick Spline button and select Line01 in the viewport. Check the
   Align To Face Normal box and set the Taper Amount to –0.8. Click OK to close
   the dialog. This operation has formed the trunk of the tree (**Figure 8.48**).

6. Before going on, it is best to unwrap the trunk so that it's ready for the next
   step—adding branches. Use the Unwrap UVW modifier to unwrap the trunk
   with three Planar projections. Unwrap the front of the trunk, the back, and the
   top. Stitch the front and back of the trunk together to minimize seams, and leave
   the top a separate piece (**Figure 8.49**).

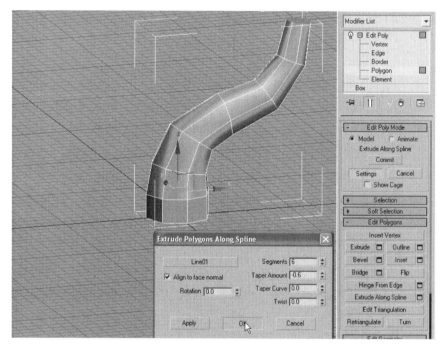

Figure 8.48 Extruding the polygon along the spline.

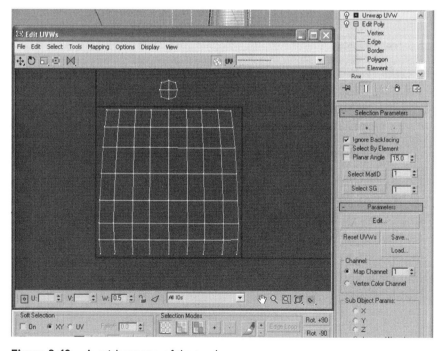

Figure 8.49 A quick unwrap of the trunk.

Branches

As in a real tree, the 3D branches are outgrowths of the trunk. Here's how to make them:

1. Add another edge loop between the top two loops so that you can make branches at the top of the trunk.

2. After adding the extra loop, select every second vertical edge on the side at the top of the trunk and scale them up. This will make the branch cross-sections round (**Figure 8.50**).

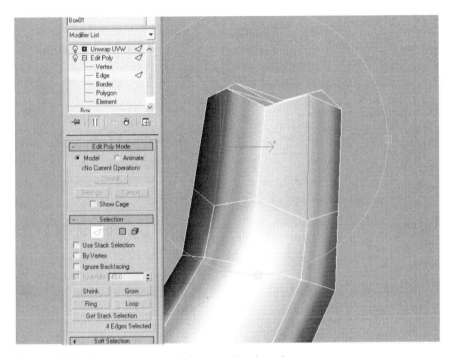

Figure 8.50   Preparing the trunk for extruding branches.

3. Create another spline to represent the curvature of a branch, and then select two polygons on the right side of the tree trunk's top row of polygons. Use the Extrude Along Spline tool and select Line02 to create the tree branch. Use all the same settings, including the Align To Face Normal and the Taper amount of –0.8 (**Figure 8.51**).

4. Unwrap the branch in the same way that the trunk was unwrapped before continuing to the next step.

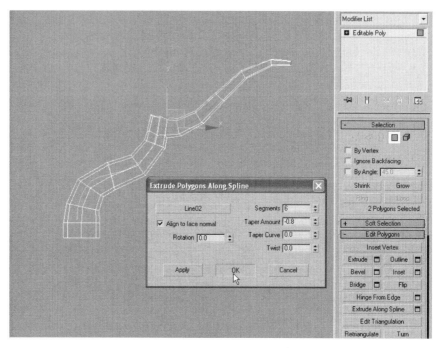

Figure 8.51   Extruding a branch from the trunk.

5. Select the end polygons of the branch, and then hit the Grow button in the Selection rollout until the entire branch is selected. Hold down the Shift key and Copy the branch polygons. Choose Clone To Element in the Clone Part Of Mesh dialog. Rotate them into place in front of the polygons where the next branch will connect to the trunk (**Figure 8.52**).

6. Repeat this for the other two branch positions. Delete the two polygons on the trunk where each branch will be connected. Right-click the Snaps Toggle button to open the Grid and Snap Settings dialog. On the Snaps tab, pick Vertex and Endpoint as the types of targets for the Snap tool. Close the Grid and Snap Settings dialog. Use the 3D Snap tool to snap the vertices of the branch to the vertices along the border of the hole in the trunk (**Figure 8.53**).

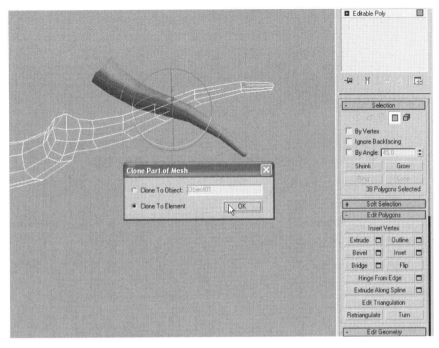

Figure 8.52   Making a copy of the branch.

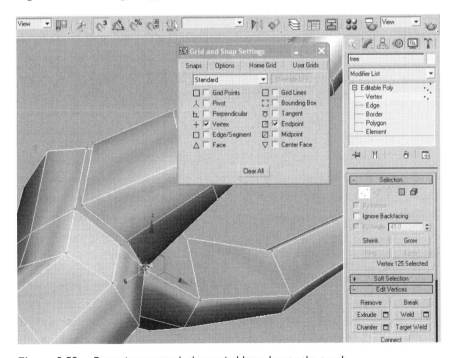

Figure 8.53   Preparing to attach the copied branches to the trunk.

7. Once this is done for each of the branches, go into Border mode, marquee-select each of the trunk/branch borders, and right-click to bring up the Quad menu. From the top left Quad menu, choose Convert to Vertex. This will convert all the border selections to the vertices along those borders. Then use the Weld tool to weld the branches together all at once. If the vertices were properly snapped into place with the 3D Snap tool, they will weld without difficulty (**Figure 8.54**).

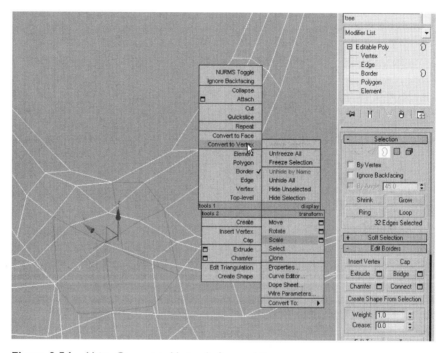

Figure 8.54 Using Convert to Vertex before welding.

Roots—Reusing Meshes and Maps

Now that the branches are done, the next thing to model is the root system. Making the tree roots is simpler than making the branches because we will use the branch geometry and maps as our starting point. This is a good example of repurposing work to save time and effort.

1. We're going to take the branches and copy them, rotate them upside down, and attach them to the bottom of the trunk in the same way the branches were attached. Since all these parts were unwrapped earlier, we don't even have to unwrap the roots again (**Figure 8.55**).

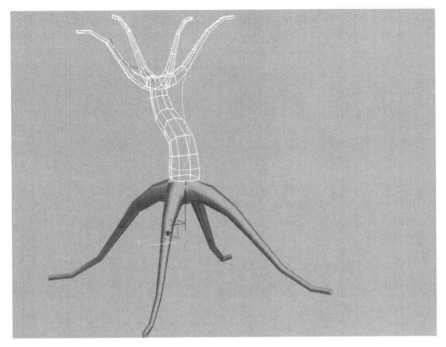

Figure 8.55   Making the roots from the branches.

2. The next step is to reconfigure the unwrap so that it has fewer seams. This will make it much easier to map the roots later on. It will take some welding of seams and repositioning of unwrapped branches and roots, but the worst of the work is over. Open the file entitled Tree_Unwrapped.max and look at the Edit UVWs dialog for an idea of how it should look once it is put together (**Figure 8.56**).

3. Now use Soft Selection to put the branches and roots in more natural and varied positions. Activate Soft Selection in the Soft Selection rollout and click the Paint button to activate Paint Selection. Paint the ends of the branches and then move them into the desired positions. Do the same for the roots. You can also use Soft Selection on its own, without Paint Selection, and set the Falloff and Edge Distance to control how much the selected vertices are affected (**Figure 8.57**).

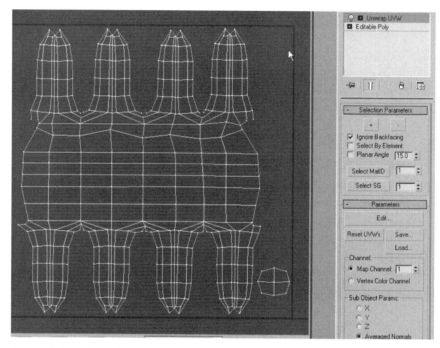

Figure 8.56   Reconfiguring the tree UVWs for mapping.

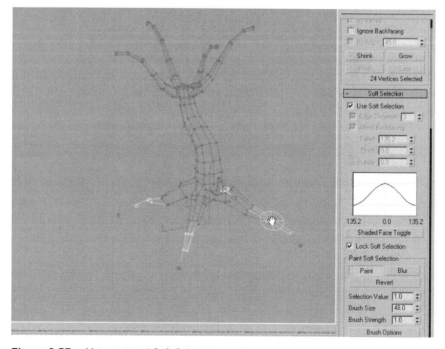

Figure 8.57   Using painted Soft Selection to select parts of the roots and change their shape.

Entwining Two Trees

Now that we have a tree that is unwrapped and ready for mapping, we're going to exercise the reuse principle again.

1. Duplicate the tree and wrap this second tree around the first tree. The easiest way to do this is to select edges and then click the Loop button to select edge loops that are cross-sections of the trunk. These cross-sections can then be moved into positions around the first trunk and rotated to follow their new path. It will also be easier to wrap around the trunk if some new cross-sections are added (**Figure 8.58**).

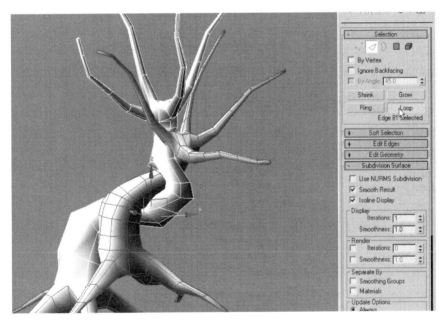

Figure 8.58   Duplicating the tree, adding edge loops, and wrapping the two trees around each other.

2. Next, add loose sheets of bark to the trees. One way to do this is to select a bunch of polygons along the trunk and Shift-Move them outward to create an Object Copy of the polygons just above the surface of the trunk. This way, they will also follow the surface of the trunk. Use the Shell modifier to give them thickness (**Figure 8.59**).

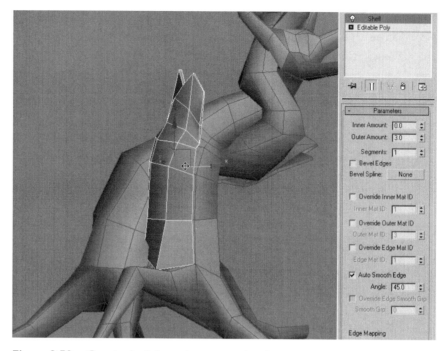

Figure 8.59 Creating bark from the tree-trunk polygons.

Leaf Canopy

It's time to add some smaller branches and leaves to the big branches. In this case, since the tree is shaping up to look like a simple version of a bristlecone pine, the best idea would be to make pine needles for leaves.

1. The best way to create the little branches is to copy one of the big branches and then scale it down in sub-object mode. Move the pivot point to the base of the small branch so that it can be duplicated by holding down the Shift key while rotating the branch. This will create arrays of small branches. Before we do additional branches, however, we must make some leaves.

2. Create a pine needle by making a small Plane object with one Length and Width segment to outline the needle's shape. Once the needle is modeled, map it with a UVW Map modifier right away and apply a material with a green Gradient

Ramp map in the Diffuse Color slot. Once it is mapped, it can be duplicated. Once the pivot point of the needle has been repositioned at the base, the needle model can also be rotated and copied into arrays very easily (**Figure 8.60**).

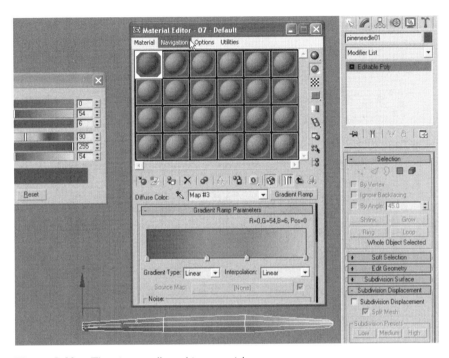

Figure 8.60   The pine needle and its material.

3. Make the arrays of needles by holding down the Shift key while rotating the needle along its Y axis. This brings up the Clone Options dialog, where we can specify the number of needle copies required to make a round cluster of eight to ten needles. Repeat this cluster assembly after rotating the needle along its Z axis and have a new cluster at a different rotation to the first. Do this a third time at yet another Z angle, and you have a fairly random-looking cluster (**Figure 8.61**).

4. Attach this needle cluster to the small tree branch you created earlier and you've got a complete branch-and-cluster unit that can be duplicated all over the larger tree branches (**Figure 8.62**).

Figure 8.61 Creating a cluster of pine needles.

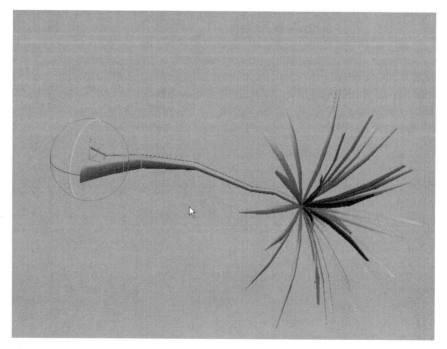

Figure 8.62 A cluster of pine needles attached to a small branch.

5. Once again, because of the pivot placement we can create arrays of these branch clusters. The result is clouds of small branches spouting clusters of pine needles. All this complexity started out with one small branch and one pine-needle model. This is a great display of the power of reusing assets when assembling a 3D model (**Figure 8.63**).

Figure 8.63   A cluster of small branches and pine needles created from one pine needle and one small branch.

The small branches and pine needles will stay separate from the trunk and main branches so that we can apply Displacement maps to the trunk and big branches. These tree models can then be used to generate Normal maps in the same way that we used the high-resolution cliff models to render textures for the low-resolution cliff models.

6. Open the file entitled Tree_Displacement.max to see the results of this work. A hand-painted map was used to displace the mesh and functioned as a Diffuse Color map.

7. Open the file entitled Tree_NormalMap.max to see the result of applying the displacement-derived Normal map to the low-resolution tree (**Figure 8.64**).

Figure 8.64   The final Normal-mapped tree.

It is important to note that the tree will need to be scaled up using an XForm modifier if it is to be used in the scene as seen in the drawing in **Figure 8.1**. It is usually better to use XForm when scaling a model or group of models because it doesn't negatively affect their transform matrices. For a more technical explanation, go to www.paulneale.com and look at his Transform Matrix tutorial. It's really just a short explanation of how the 3ds max Transform Matrix works, but it is worth the read.

Grass

The ground still looks bare, especially around the tree, so now let's model some grass to put on the herocliff in the scene.

1. Start by creating a plane with the following dimensions (**Figure 8.65**):

    - Length = 400
    - Width = 30
    - Length Segments = 4
    - Width Segments = 2

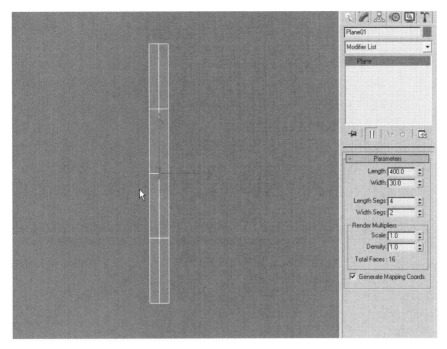

Figure 8.65   Creating the plane that will become a blade of grass.

2. Convert the plane to an editable poly. Select the top three vertices and choose Collapse in the Edit Geometry rollout. Name the plane GrassBlade01.

3. Turn on Use Soft Selection in the Soft Selection rollout. Set the Falloff value to 220. Move the top vertex back and downward, then rotate it so that the plane has a nice curvature. Finally, scale the vertex in the X axis so that the grass tapers gradually as it comes to a point. Exit sub-object mode, then apply a TurboSmooth modifier to the grass model and then a UVW Unwrap modifier to make the mapping stay in place (**Figure 8.66**).

4. Apply a Standard material to the grass model. In the Diffuse Color slot, add a Stucco map and choose to tile it 30 times in the X axis. Leave the other axis at the default value of 1. Choose two different shades of green for the two stucco colors. Name the material Grass. See Grass.max to see the grass model (**Figure 8.67**).

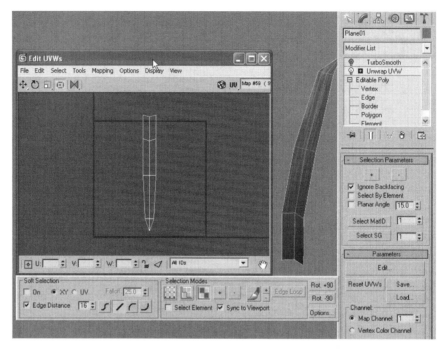

Figure 8.66   Shaping the blade of grass and getting it ready for mapping.

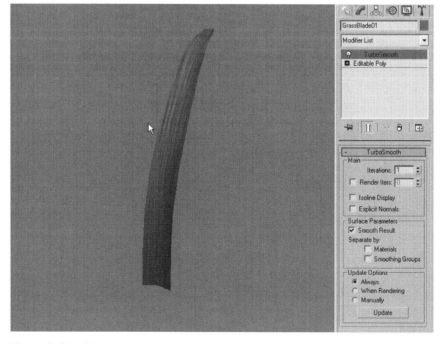

Figure 8.67   The simple GrassBlade01 model.

5. Using the same technique, create two other blades of grass that are modified copies of the original. Make one copy taller and straighter. Make another copy that curves out to the side.

6. Now use these three blades to make a lot more with the Scatter tool. Choose GrassBlade01 and go to Creation panel > Geometry > Compound Objects > Scatter. In the Scatter Objects rollout, select Use Transforms Only. In the same rollout, under Source Object Parameters, enter a value of 600 for Duplicates. This will create 600 blades of GrassBlade01.

7. In the Transforms rollout, enter a value of 90 degrees for the Y value of the Rotation group. For the Local Translation group, enter the following values: X = 900, Y = 200, Z = 900 (**Figure 8.68**).

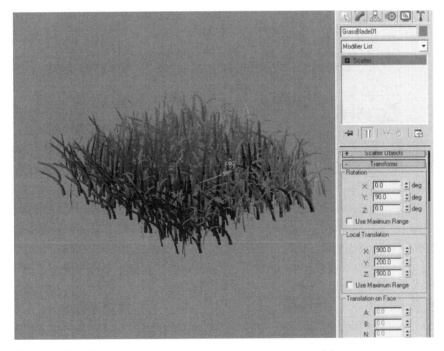

Figure 8.68   Using the Scatter tool to distribute the grass models.

8. For the GrassBlade02 model, use the same method, but this time change the Local Translation values to X = 800, Y = 200, Z = 800. For GrassBlade03, change the Local Translation values to X = 1000, Y = 200, Z = 1000.

9. We now have a small patch of grass that can be used for the top of the herocliff. Open the file entitled Landscape_Final.max. For this file, the tree was scaled up

using the XForm modifier and was added to the top of the herocliff. The grass was then added to help the tree blend in with the rock. A gradient material was also added to the herocliff to make the top of the cliff look like soil (**Figure 8.69**).

Figure 8.69   A render of the final landscape scene.

If you've made it this far, be proud of what you've accomplished! It's no small task building a 3D environment from the ground up, but it can certainly be a rewarding experience. After finishing this environment tutorial, you should be able to create your own fantasy environments. With any luck, you've understood the importance of project management—any modeling task becomes much easier when you've planned out your work in a series of stages. This really reduces the learning curve for any project. Last, always remember to reuse your modeled assets whenever possible to save time and create complexity within your scenes.

There's one last item on the agenda for this chapter. How can the words "microscopic" and "dramatic" be used in the same sentence? Read on to expose the dramatic lives of microbial organisms—and learn some more cool modeling features of 3ds max 7.

Modeling Microscopic Worlds

In this section, we will examine a battle on a microscopic scale: *the attack of the macrophage!* One of the most dramatic images seen in biology textbooks is that of a macrophage (a type of white blood cell) using its filopodia (tentacle-like arms) to reach out and grab bacteria it then devours. Macrophages are the guardians that protect our bodies from internal threats like bacteria, tiny parasites, and other foreign invaders.

Images of cells can be taken with a variety of lab instruments, such as light microscopes, scanning electron microscopes, and so on. Each type of instrument reveals unique data about a cell and also produces its own distinctive visual look. The look we will be shooting for here is that created by a scanning electron microscope (SEM). SEMs use electrons rather than light waves to create an image. Surface features too small to be detailed by light waves are easily captured by the much smaller electrons, which are beamed onto the surface of the cell and bounce off onto a collection plate.

However, in SEM images there's no reflection, refraction, or absorption of different wavelengths of light from the cell surface, so there is no transparency or color information. An original SEM image is in black and white, but it is usually artificially colored for a more exciting presentation. For example, the cell might be shown as bright red and the bacteria as bright yellow, both against a stark dark ground showcasing the power and complexity of the cellular forms. Such images can be very dramatic!

Building a Cell

Let's create our own cell wars with some of the great new tools in 3ds max 7. We'll begin with the macrophage.

1. Start with a new 3ds max scene, and in the Top viewport, create a Sphere primitive with a radius of 30 units and 18 segments.

2. Apply an FFD (box) modifier to the sphere. Activate the Control Points sub-object mode in the FFD (box) modifier, and then move the lattice to obtain the desired shape. This is going to be the macrophage cell body (**Figure 8.70**).

3. Draw a spline in the Left viewport that curves up and away as it gets further from the cell body (**Figure 8.71**). This will define the curve of the first of the filopodia.

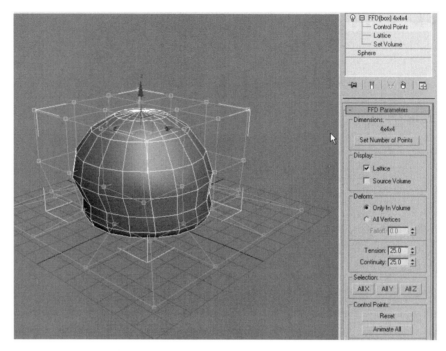

Figure 8.70 Creating the macrophage cell body from a sphere.

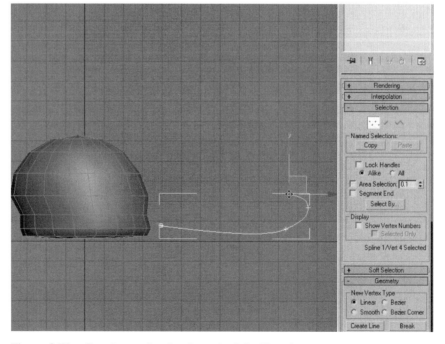

Figure 8.71 Drawing a spline for the path of the filopodia.

4. Add an Edit Poly modifier on top of the FFD (box) modifier in the Modifier Stack. Select a number of polygons and extrude them to a height of 0 units. This probably seems odd, but when these polygons are scaled in their local coordinate system, they will allow us to create a smaller polygon inside a bigger polygon. Or you could use the Inset tool which does the same thing, followed by the scale tool for adjusting the shape of the new inset polygon (**Figure 9.72**).

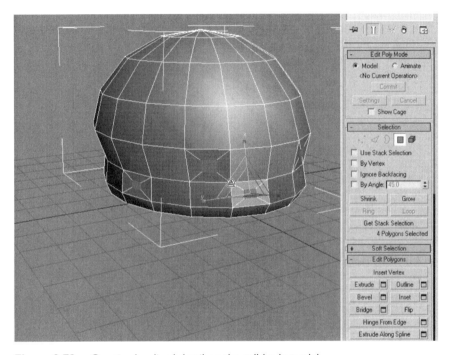

Figure 8.72   Creating localized detail on the cell-body model.

5. Use the Extrude Along Spline tool to extrude small filopodia from each of these polygon selections. If you do them one at a time, you can give each of the extrusions a different rotation so that they'll point generally upward. Use a Taper Amount of –0.8 for the filopodia (**Figure 8.73**).

6. For more variety, create another, smaller curved spline similar to the first one and add some more filopodia in other places along the base of the cell body. Also create a long, undulating spline and use the Extrude Along Spline tool to create some longer, more stretched-out filopodia with this new spline (**Figure 8.74**).

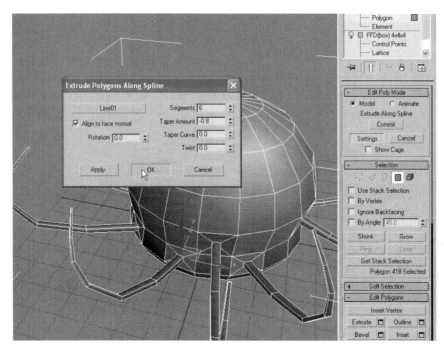

Figure 8.73 Creating filopodia with the Extrude Along Spline tool.

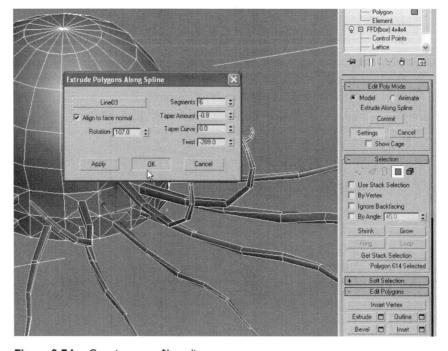

Figure 8.74 Creating more filopodia.

7. Marquee-select the end of one of these filopodia and click the Grow button in the Selection rollout until the whole filopodium is selected. Shift-Move the selected polygons to copy the filopodium. Move this unattached selection of polygons to another part of the cell body. Delete the face on the cell body where you would like to connect the filopodium polygons and select the borders on the open face in the cell body and on the end of the filopodium. In the Edit Borders rollout, click the Bridge settings button. This will connect the two borders with a "bridge" of polygons (**Figure 8.75**).

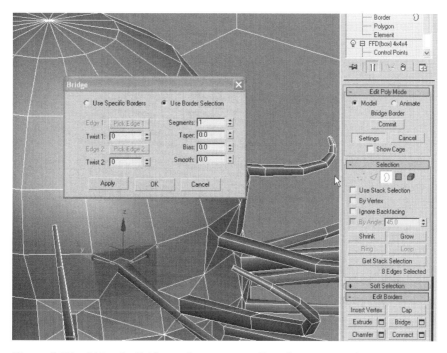

Figure 8.75 Using the Bridge tool to connect a filopodium copy to the cell body.

8. Switch to Vertex sub-object level, then use the Paint Selection Region with the Select Object tool to select the end vertices of some of the filopodia and turn on Use Soft Selection. Turn up the Falloff value and Edge Distance high enough that you can influence about half the filopodia's lengths with the vertices selected at the ends. You can also paint the soft selection with the Paint button in the Soft Selection rollout. Pull the vertices into more random positions so that they don't all look the same (**Figure 8.76**).

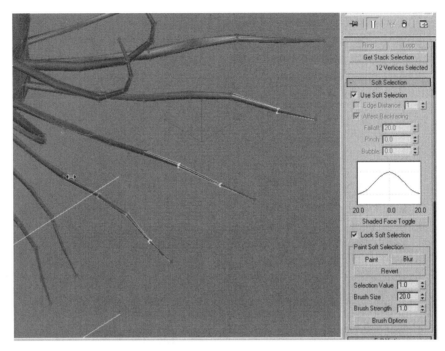

Figure 8.76 Using Soft Selection to randomize the macrophage model.

9. While we're on the topic of painting, let's take a quick look at using Paint Deformations (**Figure 8.77**). These will help you add more organic irregularitiesto the cell body and the filopodia. Exit sub-object mode, open the Paint Deformation rollout, and click the Push/Pull Value button. Click and drag with the left mouse button on the mesh and watch the mesh deform. A positive Push/Pull value pushes the mesh, while a negative value pulls it. The Brush Size is the area of the brush's influence, and the Brush Strength value determines how far the mesh is pushed or pulled. There are also brush options similar to the Paint Skin Weights brush. The Revert button in the same rollout allows location-specific undo of the mesh manipulation done by the Paint Deformation brush. It's a very useful and intuitive tool that makes modeling feel more like working with pieces of clay.

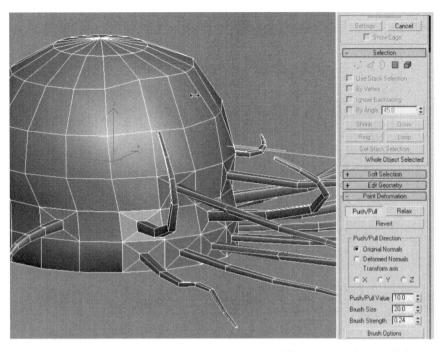

Figure 8.77   Using the Paint Deformation tool to modify the macrophage model further.

Texturing the Cell

We're now done with the polygon modeling and we're next going to add more detail to the mesh by displacing it.

1. First, right-click the macrophage model and select Convert To > Convert to Editable Poly in the lower right Quad menu.

2. In Polygon sub-object mode, select the tips of all the filopodia and click the Grow button until they're all selected. All the polygons for the filopodia have a Face ID of 2, and they can stay that way. Now go the Edit menu on the Main toolbar and choose Select Invert. The cell body also has a Face ID of 2, but we will change it to 1.

3. Do a rough unwrap of the macrophage model with the Unwrap UVW modifier, and then collapse it back to an Editable Poly (**Figure 8.78**).

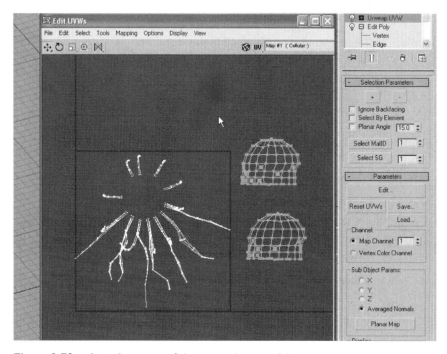

Figure 8.78   A quick unwrap of the macrophage model.

4. Take a look at the Multi/Sub-Object material in the Material Editor for the Macrophage_Material.max file. The first material is for the cell body, and the second is for the filopodia. Save this material and apply it to the model in your own scene file, or continue the exercise with this file (**Figure 8.79**).

5. Apply a TurboSmooth modifier and a Displace Mesh (WSM) modifier to the macrophage model. Enable Custom Settings and Subdivision Displacement, and choose Spatial and Curvature as the Subdivision Method. For the Edge and Distance values, enter 60, and for the Angle, enter 25. Click on the Advanced Parameters button, then in the Advanced Displacement Approx. dialog, choose Delaunay as the Subdivision Style and click OK (**Figure 8.80**).

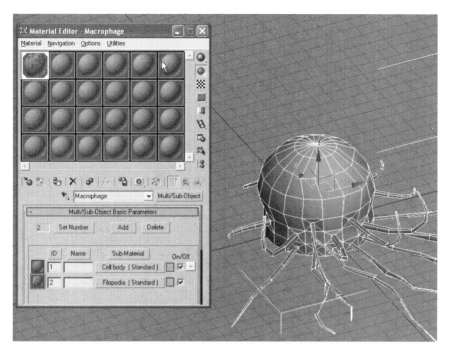

Figure 8.79   The macrophage material.

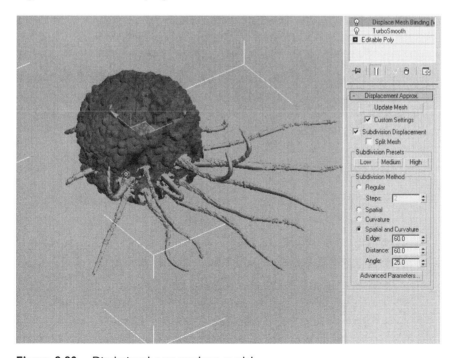

Figure 8.80   Displacing the macrophage model.

The Micro Environment

We're ready to add the final touches and put our macrophage into an appropriate environment.

1. Put a plane below the macrophage in the scene to function as a ground plane. You can also add a reflective material to the Plane if you want add extra dimension to the scene.

2. The last step is to add the bacteria in clusters around the scene. Use the Capsule primitive with the Melt modifier to give the bacteria the appearance of being saggy, flexible, and somewhat irregular (**Figure 8.81**).

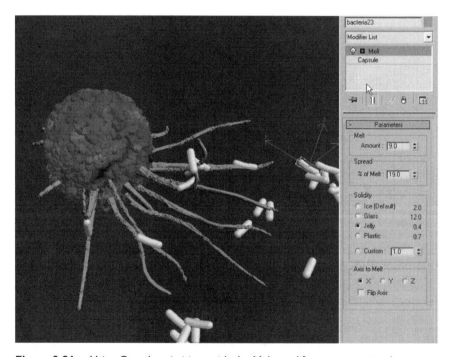

Figure 8.81   Using Capsule primitives with the Melt modifier to create simple bacteria models.

3. Open the file entitled Macrophage_Final.max to see the final look. Make the camera viewport active and render the scene. You can add depth of field, as was done here. Anything in optical microscopy is seen with an extremely shallow depth of field. Adding a shallow depth of field to this scene reinforces the small size of these organic objects, even though, strictly speaking, there is neither depth of field nor reflections in a scanning electron microscope image (**Figure 8.82**).

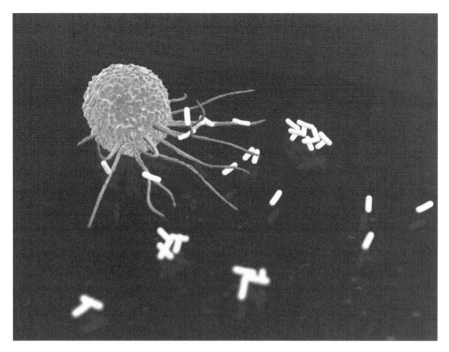

Figure 8.82   The final render of the macrophage scene.

Summing Up

This chapter outlined some of the workflows used when modeling organic and irregular objects in 3ds max 7. Feel free to continue adding more elements to our alien environment to make it more interesting, such as more rock cliffs and plants and more inorganic structures that complement the fiery pit. You could even put a moon or a big planet in the background, or a storm of fiery comets filling the night sky. Another interesting idea might be to duplicate the tree, change its textures, and add some cracks in it to make it look dead and dried out. A few of these would add drama around the fiery pit. And of course some aliens would bring it alive even more—in fact, you'll be tackling character modeling in the next chapter.

The scene that we created in these tutorials is a start, but given a little more time and effort, it could become much better. A good rule of thumb is to plan out what you can do and then prioritize what is most important to do in a specific amount of time. In this way, you'll be more likely to make your deadlines and spend your valuable time on the most important aspects of your scene. The sky is the limit, but always make sure that you're well grounded first!

Be sure to further explore the new 3ds max 7 features and examine the online help if you run into any trouble. The workflows in this chapter will serve you well, but that's not to say that a different way of doing things might not serve you better. Always be open to new ways of working. Nobody knows it all, but the person sitting next to you definitely knows something that you don't, so open up your ears and listen. The best way to learn is by doing projects that demand that you use your problem-solving abilities. And 3ds max 7 will always help you get the job done. Happy modeling!

Chapter 9

Character Modeling

By A.J. Jefferies

As technology and aspirations increase, we are seeing more and more jaw-dropping computer-generated effects in film and animation. Some the most prominent advances in this field are evident in the number of fully CG characters on the screen. It has become commonplace to see virtual stuntmen taking a fall, fantastic beasts storming a castle, or even a lead role being filled by an actor who exists entirely on a hard-drive. In fact, our culture has adapted to a point where we treat a videogame character as a celebrity, placing her on the front page of magazines and posters and even casting her in her own live-action films!

With 3D characters taking a stronger role, it's no wonder that characters are one of the most popular things to start modeling. However, they can also be one of the most daunting. With the myriad of character-modeling methods, styles, and applications, it can be hard to narrow down the best place to begin.

In this chapter, we're going learn some of the techniques used today to create characters, from the real to the surreal. First we're going to run through some of Editable Poly's useful features (while simultaneously creating a new friend). Then we'll attach severed limbs, build up some muscle without breaking a sweat, give a man the means to breathe, and create cartoon eyes.

So, nothing out of the ordinary there. Let's get started.

Modeling in Sub-Ds

Subdivision Surfaces (or Sub-Ds) is a method of modeling that was introduced by Pixar in 1998 and has rapidly become the preferred way to create organic, detailed surfaces. 3ds max 7 has three implementations of Sub-Ds: MeshSmooth, HSDS, and TurboSmooth. These, combined with the flexibility of Editable Poly and the new Edit Poly modifier, provide us with some of max's most powerful tools. (As you're working with Sub-Ds, you can also refer to an excellent source of information, the Subdivision Modeling Resource Page, at http://maxrovat.sns.hu/subdiv/.

Although we've already touched upon some of max's Editable Poly features in an earlier chapter, we are now going to focus on some of the more common functions used in modeling characters.

Every character is different, and so are the methods with which different characters can be created. That said, there are some techniques you can apply again and again. You will find yourself repeating many of the same steps on a realistic human face as you would on a talking carrot. This is especially true with subdivision modeling, which starts out much the same for every character, and tends to end the same, too.

A Pig in a Box

Let's build a pig out of a cube in what is called the box-modeling process.

1. Restart max and create a Box primitive in the Perspective viewport (**Figure 9.1**). In the Modify panel, set the Length, Width, and Height values all to 100. Right-click the Select and Move tool on the Main toolbar to open the Move Transform Type-In dialog. Right-click each of the X, Y, and Z spinners to set them to 0.

 Tip

> Right-clicking any spinner sets it to its lowest possible value, which in most cases is 0, regardless of the original or default value. It's a quick way to center things in the scene.

2. With the box selected, apply a MeshSmooth modifier. Ensure that Iterations is set to 1, right-click the MeshSmooth modifier in the modifier stack, and collapse the box to an Editable Poly object (**Figure 9.2**).

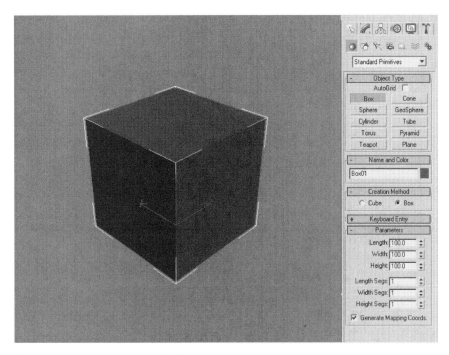

Figure 9.1   Box primitive in the Perspective viewport.

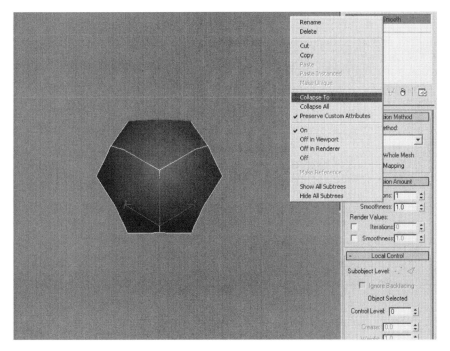

Figure 9.2   Collapsing the box to an Editable Poly object.

3. In the Modify rollout, select Polygon as the sub-object, and then in the Front viewport, drag-select the polygons on the left side of the object and hit Delete (**Figure 9.3**). You have now halved your object, so you'll apply a Symmetry modifier to give you a whole one back. You must exit sub-object mode to apply the Symmetry modifier.

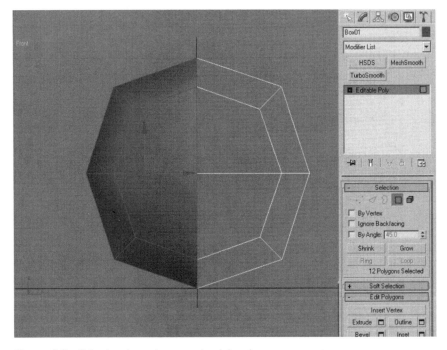

Figure 9.3   Selecting the polygons to be deleted.

 Note

Most characters are bilaterally symmetrical, and the Symmetry modifier is an essential tool for creating them. It allows you to see your object as a whole as you model while cutting your effort in half.

4. Now to start pulling a pig out of that ball. In the modifier stack, make sure you are at the Editable Poly level and that Show End Result is turned on so you can see the effects of Symmetry as you work. Also, turn off the orange Control Cage that is on by default. The Control Cage is very useful when you edit with

MeshSmooth or TurboSmooth, but you won't need it at the moment. To disable it, uncheck the box labeled Show Cage in the Edit Geometry rollout.

5. Switch to the Edge sub-object mode in the Perspective viewport, select the appropriate edges (**Figure 9.4**), and then choose Ring from the Selection rollout. Switch to Edged Faces mode if you need to see the edges. You may have to rotate your Perspective viewport to select the correct edge for the symmetry to work. With these edges still selected, choose Connect from the Edit Edges rollout to create a new loop of edges (**Figure 9.5**).

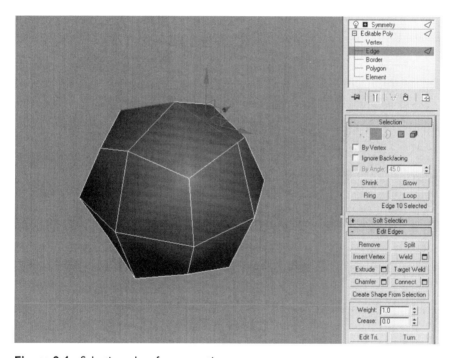

Figure 9.4   Selecting edges for connection.

6. These new edges don't quite follow the curve you want for a fat pig, so change the selection level to Vertex by Control-clicking the Vertex icon. Then, with the Scale tool, nudge them ever so slightly outward until the curve has returned.

7. Now go through the same steps to create another two Edge loops in our model (**Figure 9.6**).

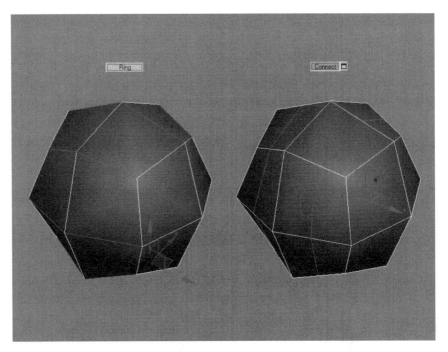

Figure 9.5 Connecting edges to create a new loop.

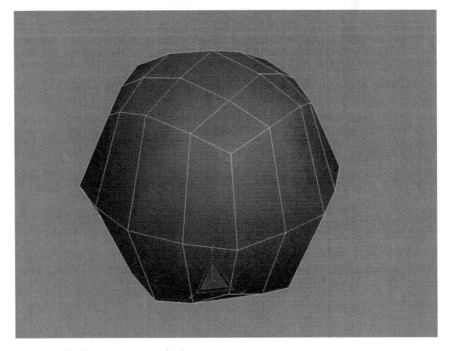

Figure 9.6 Two more rows of edges.

Pig's Feet

Time to give our pig some feet.

1. At the Polygon sub-object level, select four polygons at the base and bring up the Extrude Polygons dialog (the button next to Extrude in the Edit Polygons roll-out). Keep the Extrusion Type set to Group, and enter 20 as the Extrusion Height (**Figure 9.7**).

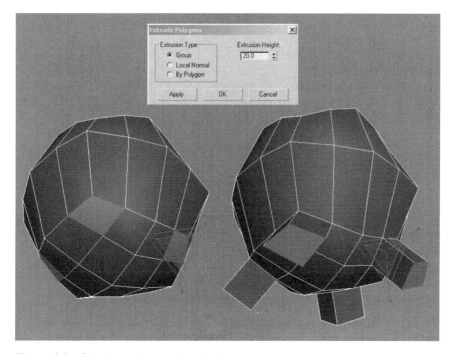

Figure 9.7   Selecting and extruding the feet.

One of the most enjoyable aspects of modeling your own character is that it isn't an exact science. No one can say your pig's feet have to be a certain size, so, if you like, you can make them any size.

2. Right now our pig would definitely wobble around on those trotters, so let's even them off. Keeping the same polygons selected, find Make Planar in the Edit Geometry rollout and press Z (**Figure 9.8**). This will force the polygons to flatten off in the Z Axis and give us some flatter feet.

To give a little more shape to them, you can also use the Outline tool to drag down the tips of the feet. There's no right or wrong answer as to how much you do this, so whatever looks good to you is fine.

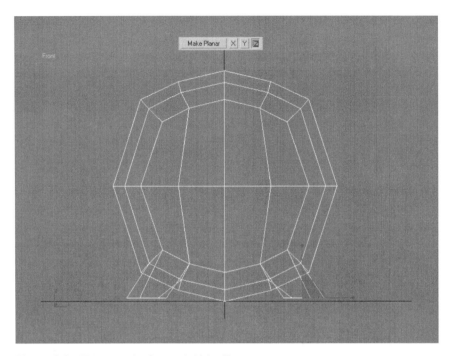

Figure 9.8   Flattening the feet with Make Planar.

The Pig's Head

All right, we now have a little ball on legs. Let's give it a head.

1. Apply an Edit Poly modifier above the Symmetry modifier in your stack. While editing inside the Edit Poly modifier, any changes that you make to the mesh will no longer be reproduced on the other side—you have, in effect, "collapsed" the model, with the added bonus that any changes you don't like can be undone by removing the modifier. Select the two rings of edges that run around the middle of the pig, and connect them to create some more detail that you can use for the head (**Figure 9.9**).

2. Select and extrude the newly divided eight polygons at the front of the pig (remember that because we're no longer using Symmetry, any operations you perform will have to include both sides of the model), and using Outline once more, pull them in slightly (**Figure 9.10**). Once you are happy with the neck shape, right-click the Edit Poly modifier and choose Collapse To.

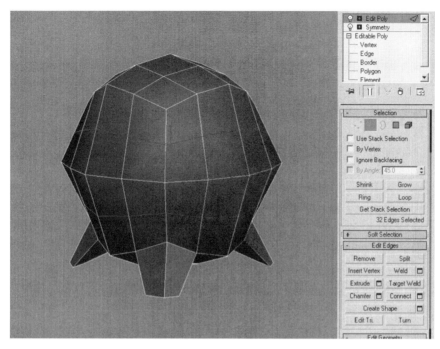

Figure 9.9   Two newly created edge loops.

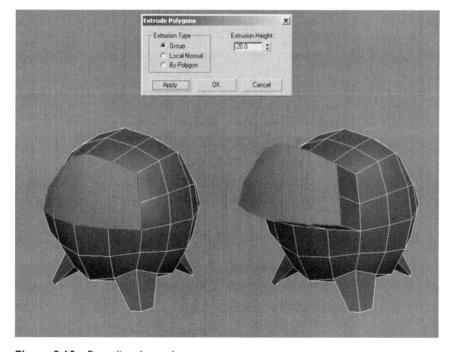

Figure 9.10   Extruding the neck.

Note

Collapsing geometry will bake the effect of any modifiers applied to your object, so it's wise to make sure that you're not going to lose anything that might be hard to change later. That said, in modeling you will often move back and forth between a collapsed and a modified object as you progress. In this case, you are going to re-apply a Symmetry modifier to reduce the amount of work and also speed up the modeling process.

3. In the Front or Top viewport, select the left-hand half of the pig's polygons and delete them. Apply a Symmetry modifier (Mirror Axis set to X) to reclaim the lost half. In Vertex sub-object mode, reshape the end of the neck to make it rounder and ready for the start of the head (**Figure 9.11**). Once you're happy, collapse the object again

4. Select the four polygons that are going to make up the snout. Use Bevel to extrude the polygons and outline them before finally moving the vertices to create a rounder shape (**Figure 9.12**).

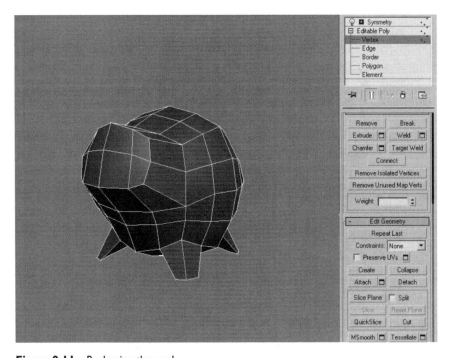

Figure 9.11   Reshaping the neck.

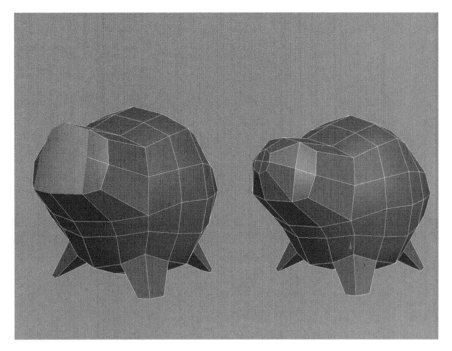

Figure 9.12   Shaping the snout.

5. Before you finish the snout, apply a MeshSmooth modifier to see how your pig is shaping up (**Figure 9.13**). You can see the effect that subdividing the mesh has—it rounds and smoothes the shapes. However, soft isn't always what you want, and we're going to sharpen things up for the snout.

6. Leave the MeshSmooth still applied, and go back down the stack to Editable Poly, making sure that Show End Result is turned on. Go to the Polygon sub-object level, select the Bevel tool, then pull out the polygons to start making the snout—just a little for the first Bevel, then one longer extrusion followed by another small step to tighten up the shape (**Figure 9.14**). At each stage, you can experiment with how much you Bevel the snout outward as you go.

 Tip

> Placing two edges close to one another will create a much more defined crease in your model. Following this practice will help you put detail and definition into your creations.

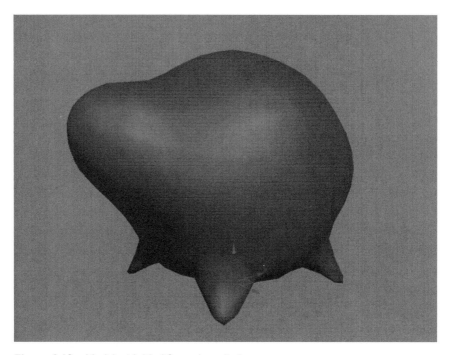

Figure 9.13 Model with MeshSmooth applied.

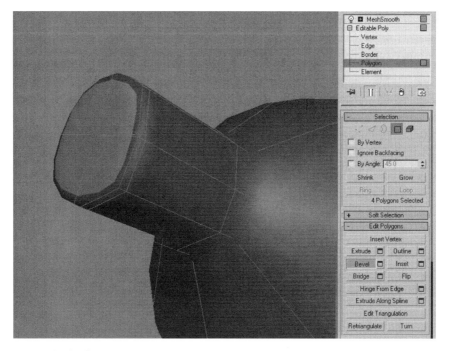

Figure 9.14 Sharpening the snout.

7. Delete the MeshSmooth modifier from the stack and once again delete one half of the pig and re-apply a Symmetry modifier. Select the two polygons on either side of the snout and extrude them outward to create the ears (**Figure 9.15**).

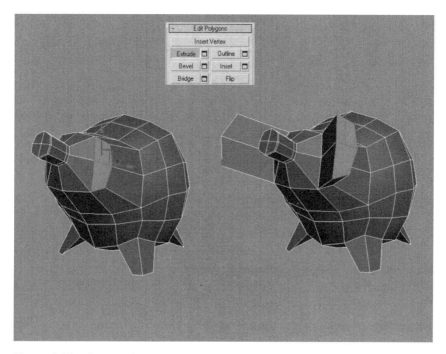

Figure 9.15   Creating the ears.

8. Using the Scale tool, size the polygons down to bring the ears to a point, and then use the Move tool to bring the tips of the ears forward so that they point in the right direction.

9. We're going to give them a bit more curve now. In Edge mode, use Ring and Connect to give us some more points to play with, and then pull the new edges out (**Figure 9.16**).

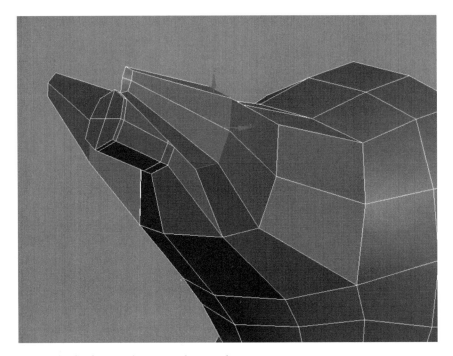

Figure 9.16   Shaping the ears with new edges.

Polishing the Pig

OK, you now have the basic shape of our pig. He could do with a few extra details, so apply an Edit Poly modifier, below Symmetry in the stack, and let's see what you can do.

 Note

> The Edit modifiers (Poly, Mesh, and Spline) are fantastic for making alterations to an object while retaining the underlying structure. So if you want to see what horns look like on your character but don't want to have to live with them if you don't like them, you can keep your edits in an Edit Poly modifier and protect your original mesh.

1. Apply a MeshSmooth modifier at the top of the stack. With the Edit Poly modifier selected, enter Polygon sub-object mode. Select the polygons at the end of the snout for nostrils and the polygon at the base of the snout near the top of the head for eyes. By pressing F2, you can toggle Shade Selected Faces, which can make it easier to see which faces you are editing.

2. Inset the polygons inward and then extrude them down (**Figure 9.17**). You can edit the eyes or nostrils as you see fit, perhaps adding some more edges to change their shape or size.

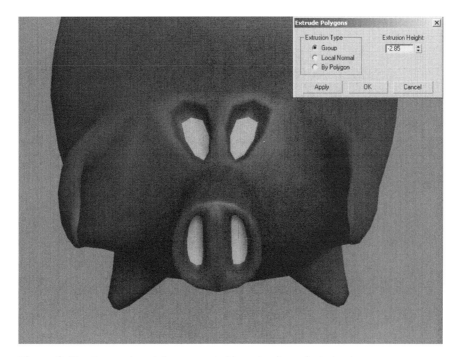

Figure 9.17   Eyes and nostrils are created by extruding selected polygons.

Adding the Tail

There's still something missing: Our pig needs a tail.

1. If you're happy with the eye and nostril edits you've made, collapse the model to an Editable Poly again and venture to the Create panel, where you'll choose Splines and then Helix. In any viewport, drag out a Helix, clicking three times to set Radius 1, Height, and finally Radius 2. In the Modify panel, set these values:

   • Radius 1 = 2

   • Radius 2 = 2

   • Height = 15

   • Turns = 2

   • Bias = 0

Leave the orientation as CW (clockwise). This is going to be the basis of our tail (**Figure 9.18**).

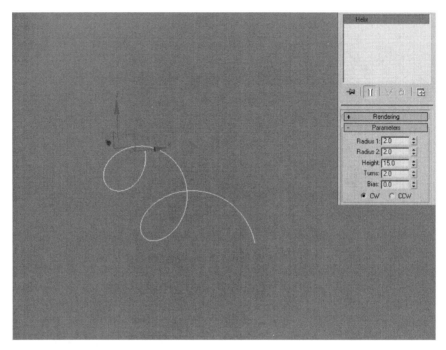

Figure 9.18 Helix for the tail.

2. With the pig selected again, apply an Edit Poly modifier and enter Vertex sub-object mode. Choose where you would like the tail to start and select that vertex, then use the Chamfer tool to create a new polygon from it.

3. Select the new polygon, and open the Extrude Polygons Along Spline dialog (the small box to the right of the Extrude Along Spline button of the Edit Polygons rollout). Ensure that Align to Face Normal is checked, then click Pick Spline and choose the helix (**Figure 9.19**).

4. 3ds max 7 has now created a tail for you, but it still needs some tweaking. Set the Segments value all the way up to 20 to bring out the twist, and decrease the Taper Amount to bring the tail's size down at the end. Experiment with the Rotation as well for a perky pig or a droopy hog (**Figure 9.20**).

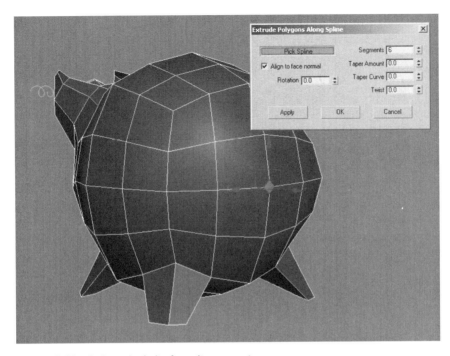

Figure 9.19   Picking the helix for spline extrusion.

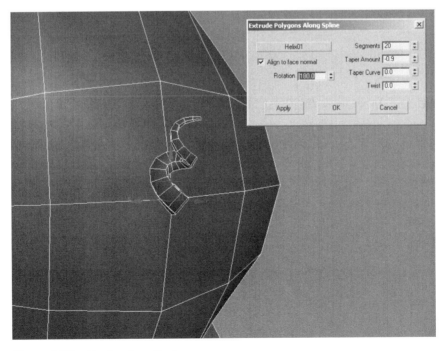

Figure 9.20   Altering the tail's shape.

5. Apply a MeshSmooth modifier to see what the new tail looks like (**Figure 9.21**)! If you're happy with it, then you can move on. If not, then you can just delete the Edit Poly modifier and try something else.

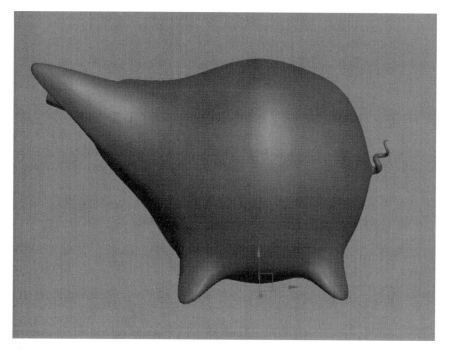

Figure 9.21   MeshSmoothed pig from the side.

Adding the Eyeballs

One last step for our little pig is to give him some eyeballs. You've created the sockets, so let's put something in them.

1. With MeshSmooth still applied to the pig, go to the Create panel and choose Sphere under Standard Primitives; also, turn on AutoGrid. This will align our sphere to the surface of any object in the scene, so it saves us having to manually move and rotate the eye in place.

2. In the sphere's Creation settings, check Base To Pivot (this just means that you are creating the sphere from its base instead of its center). Now pan and rotate in the Perspective viewport so you can see the head and eyes clearly. Move the

mouse until you see the transform gizmo in the place where you want the eye, then drag out a sphere until it's the size you want (**Figure 9.22**).

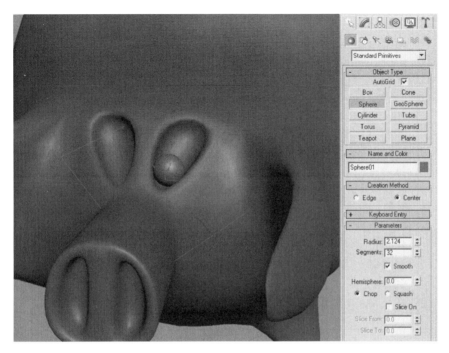

Figure 9.22   Using AutoGrid to create an eye.

You can do the same for the other socket, but to keep things flexible we're going to make an instance of the one you have just created.

3. Select the newly created eye, click the Select and Move tool, change the Reference Coordinate System from View to Pick, and click the pig. You are now "borrowing" the pig's coordinate system, which means that if you set the Use Pivot Center flyout to Use Transform Coordinate Center, you will have the exact center point of the pig.

4. Use the Mirror tool (on the Main toolbar), and from the Mirror dialog, choose X as the Mirror Axis and set the Clone Selection to Instance (**Figure 9.23**). Now you have two eyes for the price of one, and because they are instances, any changes made to one of them in the Modify panel (such as UV Mapping) will apply to the other.

One pig, made to order (**Figure 9.24**).

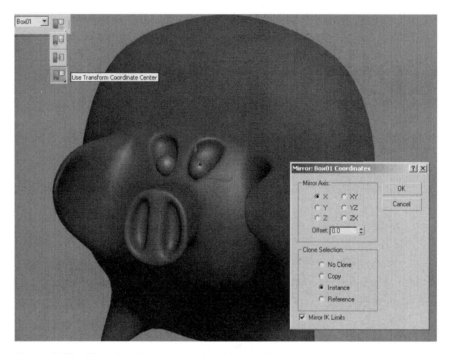

Figure 9.23 Mirroring the eye using the pig's coordinate center.

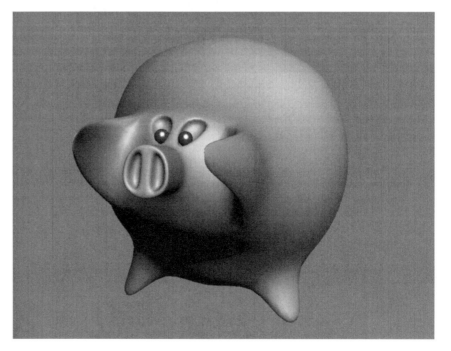

Figure 9.24 Completed pig.

To check out my version of the pig, open the file 9_pig_complete.max on the accompanying DVD.

There's no denying that this isn't the most complicated character, but the steps we've followed and methods we've used to create a simple pig from a box can be applied to far more complex creations. In the following sections, we're going to look at just such a case and, using some new features in max 7's modeling arsenal, assemble a body.

Attaching Limbs

From ogre to octopus, characters can have any structure that the artist desires. However, more often than not characters have arms and legs of some description. In this section, we're going to take separate parts of a polygon body, created using the same box-modeling method used to build our pig, and assemble them into a fully joined torso. This modular approach to modeling is not only fast and efficient, it also makes it possible to reuse elements of one model when building another. By attaching previously created limbs (with some modification), you can construct an entirely different character in much less time—a great advantage when deadlines loom.

Assembling a Hand

We'll demonstrate this approach by adding fingers to a partially modeled hand. 3ds max's new Bridge tool is what really makes this easy, as you'll see.

1. Open the file 9_body_start.max (**Figure 9.25**).

2. This hand model is missing a couple of fingers. Select the finger in the Top viewport. With the Shift key held down, move a copy of the finger up until it's roughly in the right place (**Figure 9.26**).

3. Now, in the Perspective viewport, you can rotate and move the finger until it's in a more natural position compared to the rest of the hand. Once this is done, select the hand itself, and from the Edit Geometry rollout, open the Attach List dialog (the small button next to Attach). Choose both of the fingers before clicking Attach (**Figure 9.27**).

4. The fingers are now part of the same geometry—max will treat them as one object. However, they're still not fully attached, so let's fill in the gaps. In the Border sub-object level, select both the open ends of the fingers and the holes in the hand (**Figure 9.28**).

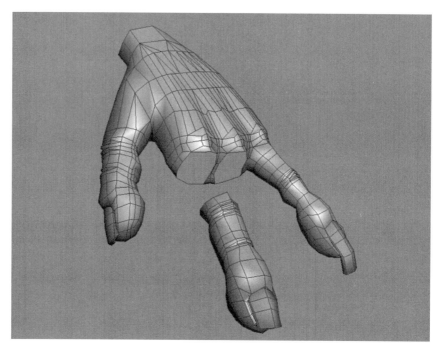

Figure 9.25 Hand model and detached finger.

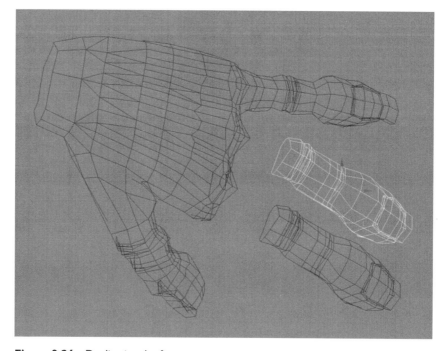

Figure 9.26 Duplicating the finger.

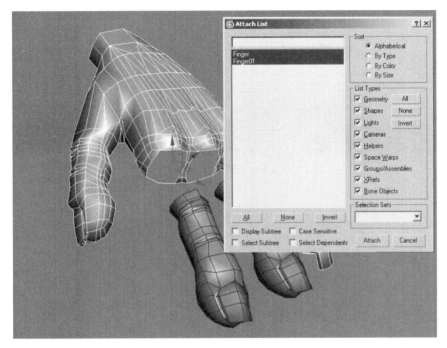

Figure 9.27   Attaching the finger objects to the hand.

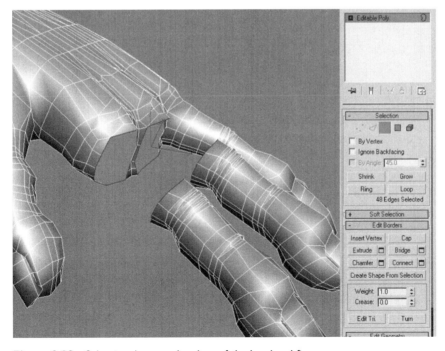

Figure 9.28   Selecting the open borders of the hand and fingers.

5. From the Edit Borders rollout, open the Bridge dialog (the button next to Bridge) and note that the gaps from the fingers have been closed over (**Figure 9.29**).

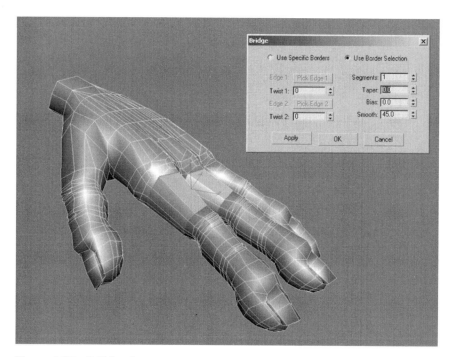

Figure 9.29 Bridging the gap.

 Note

The Bridge tool is a new addition to max 7 and can be used to connect polygons or borders of an Editable Poly, or an object with the Edit Poly modifier applied, with a set of parameters defined by the user. It is perfect for when you need to fill in gaps or join objects together.

6. These new polygons are great, but since you need to match the structure of the finger that's already attached, you'll want to change some parameters. Set the Segments value to 3, which gives us more edges to play with later. Apply a little Taper to make the join more natural—around –0.16 should be enough. You can also set the Smooth angle of the newly created polygons; it's not essential for what we're doing right now, but if you want the faces to "fit in" with the smoothing of the model, you can set this value to 180.

Completing the Torso

You now have a hand complete with fingers freshly attached. So give yourself a hand! (Yes, that was inexcusable.) Disembodied hands tend to look a little lost when they don't have an arm to belong to, so let's see what you can do to address this problem.

1. If there are no objects visible in the scene, right-click in any viewport and choose Unhide All from the Display Quad menu. Otherwise, you'll see a floating torso and biceps in the scene. First things first—let's heal the join between the two. With the Torso object selected, choose Attach from the Edit geometry rollout and then select the Biceps object (**Figure 9.30**).

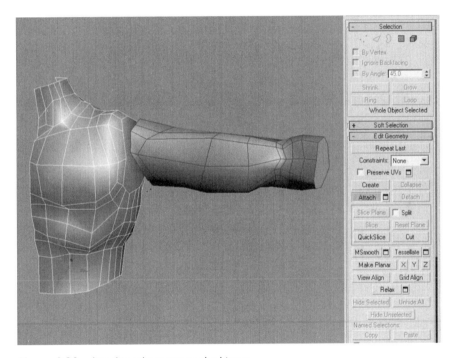

Figure 9.30 Attaching the torso to the biceps.

2. Now you'll apply an Edit Poly modifier and enter the Polygon sub-object mode. Select the two large polygons opposite each other between the torso and the biceps, then use the Bridge tool to fix the gap (**Figure 9.31**).

3. You might notice that our biceps and our torso don't quite fit. Let's go back down to the base of the modifier stack, and with Show End Result enabled, edit the vertices on either side of the newly bridged gap to smooth things out.

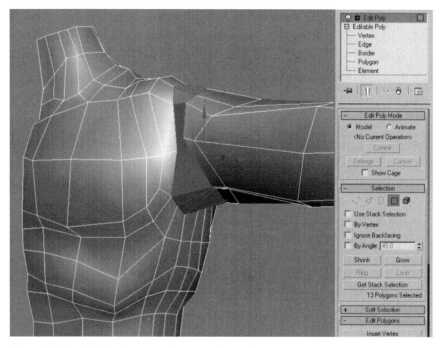

Figure 9.31   Bridging between the two polygons.

With Show End Result enabled, you can see how the changes you make will affect the Bridge operation in the Edit Poly modifier above. If you add a MeshSmooth modifier at the top of the stack, you can get an even clearer idea of how the arm looks (**Figure 9.32**).

4. Once you're happy with the edits you've made, remove the MeshSmooth modifier and collapse the object back down to an Editable Poly. Use Attach to make the hand part of the same object so you can finish off the arm.

5. Select the open borders of the biceps and the hand and Bridge across, setting the Segments value to 3 or more (**Figure 9.33**).

 Note

Increasing the number of segments is important: Not only will it provide you with more geometry to control the shape of the arm, but it will also help when the character is rigged. Too few polys in key areas like the forearm will result in the object flattening when the wrist turns or the elbow bends. So the more divisions, the more "support" that area will have when it deforms.

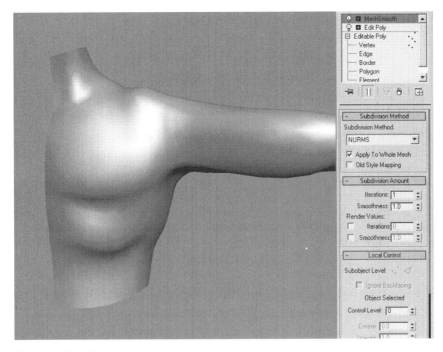

Figure 9.32   MeshSmoothed model.

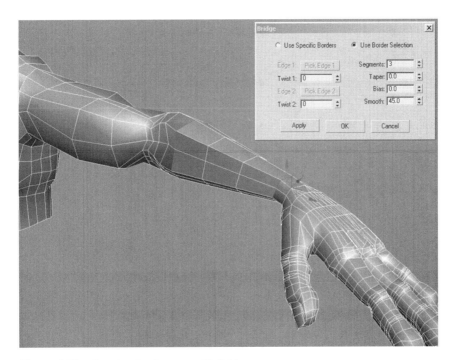

Figure 9.33   Creating the forearm with Bridge.

6. If you apply a TurboSmooth modifier to the body, you'll see that the forearm is a bit rigid and overly straight along the edges and surfaces. This can be a problem when creating organic characters in Editable Poly. As character artists, we have to make sure that the shape is as natural as possible. So a bit of manual vertex-pushing is needed to round off the surface. With the TurboSmooth still at the top of the stack, go back down to the Editable Poly level, and with Show End Result turned on, move the new vertices to smooth things over.

 Note

> TurboSmooth operates much faster than MeshSmooth when editing complex geometry. It lacks a few of MeshSmooth's classic features, but TurboSmooth's speed increase more than makes up for this if you have to make alterations to an object and want fast visual feedback.

7. All that's left now is to take one half of the model and make it a whole, so apply a Symmetry modifier to the body (under the TurboSmooth modifier in the stack) and set the Mirror Axis to X if it hasn't been set already.

Ta-da! One upper body, stitched and assembled (**Figure 9.34**).

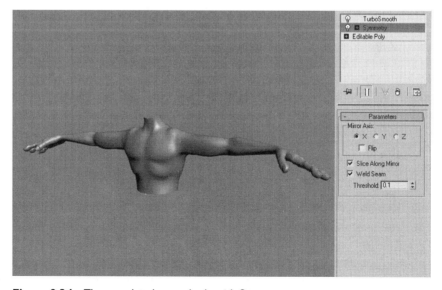

Figure 9.34   The completed upper body with Symmetry.

To check out my version of this exercise, open the file 9_body_finish.max on this book's DVD.

Building Muscle

Next we'll explore another important aspect of body morphology—the muscles. Coming to our aid is a versatile new feature of Editable Poly called Paint Deformation. Paint Deformation allows us to push and pull an object's surface with a customizable brush. It's one of the closest digital equivalents to sculpting from clay and can be extremely useful in adding organic detail to a model.

In this example, we're going to take the (rather puny) upper body from the previous exercise and bulk it up.

1. Open the file 9_body_muscle_start.max (or use the model from the previous exercise).

2. Convert it to an Editable Poly object (**Figure 9.35**).

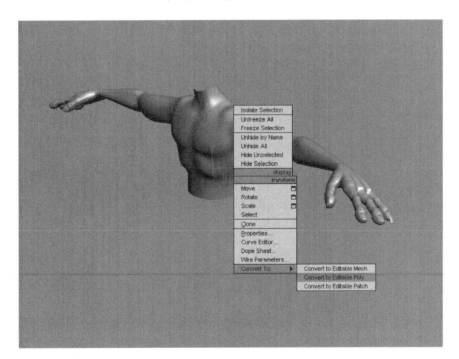

Figure 9.35   Converting the body to an Editable Poly object.

You could use an Edit Poly modifier and retain the Symmetry of the base model, but since you are going to be working on a relatively dense mesh, feedback will be quicker from a collapsed object.

3. Scroll to the Paint Deformation rollout and select Painter Options (**Figure 9.36**).

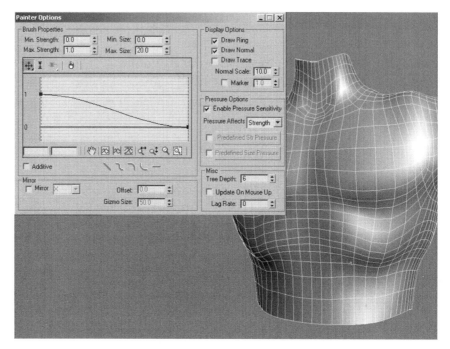

Figure 9.36   The Painter Options dialog.

4. Since you have lost the effects of the Symmetry modifier by collapsing, you can enable the Mirror function in the Painter Options dialog and set the Mirror Axis to X, if it isn't already (**Figure 9.37**). Now any deformations you make will be reproduced on the opposite side of the model.

5. In the Paint Deformation rollout, set the following values:

   - Push/Pull Value = 2.0
   - Brush Size = 20.0
   - Brush Strength = 0.7

   Turn on the Push/Pull button and start to paint on the shoulder to bring it out (**Figure 9.38**).

6. Once you have bulked up the muscles to your liking, you can move on to the chest area and beef up those pecs. You can keep your brush settings the same, but feel free to experiment with different values to see the effects. Work around the pectoral area, taking time to bring out the shoulders (**Figure 9.39**).

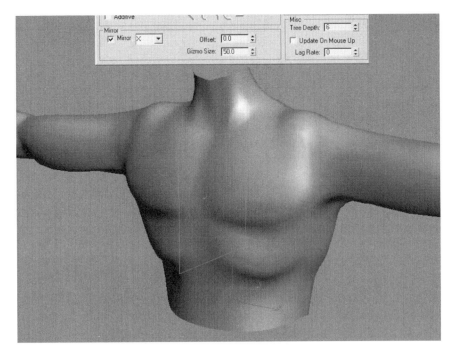

Figure 9.37   Setting the Mirror Axis for the deformation.

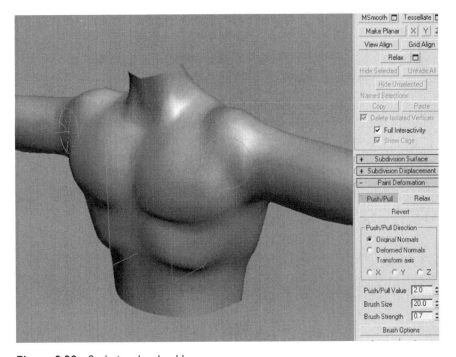

Figure 9.38   Sculpting the shoulders.

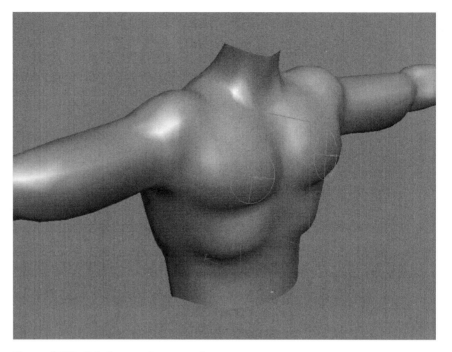

Figure 9.39   Bringing out the pectorals.

7. Arc Rotate around to the back now and let's thicken the neck a little—pull the sides and shoulder muscles to give a little more mass to our character's frame. Once you've worked up that area, set the Paint Deform from Push/Pull to Relax, and smooth over any areas that are starting to look a little too sharp or jagged.

It's always a good idea to use the Relax option when using Paint Deformation, as it keeps things from getting too distorted while retaining any changes.

8. Those forearms look pretty weak, don't they? Let's pump them up too, using Push/Pull again (**Figure 9.40**) before smoothing out with Relax.

9. Arc Rotate the viewport so that you can see into the armpit, which doesn't look very defined at the moment. Set the Push/Pull value to –2.0 and the Brush Size to 5. Get in there and shape the armpit (**Figure 9.41**).

Now step back and admire the new, more buff physique that you've created with a few brush strokes (**Figure 9.42**).

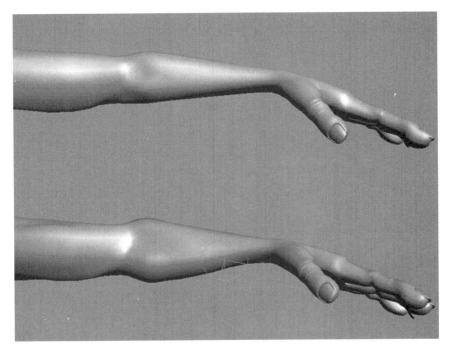

Figure 9.40   Pulling out and defining the forearm.

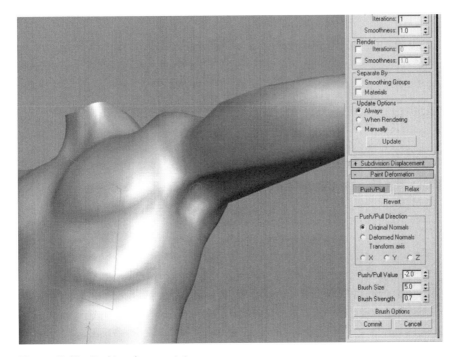

Figure 9.41   Pushing the armpit in.

Figure 9.42 The completed, more muscular body.

Paint Deformation is an extremely useful and unique tool. Its scope goes far beyond what we've covered here. For example, you can use it to add veins and skin wrinkles, as well as creases and folds in fabric.

To check out my version of this exercise, open the file 9_body_muscle_finish.max on the accompanying DVD.

Modeling the Head

Next, we'll move on the head. Here's where you'll put another 3ds max trick, edge looping, into play.

Given the flexible nature of Subdivision Surface modeling, it can be difficult to nail down exactly how an object should be structured. The current school of thought among 3D character artists is to apply the method of edge looping to control the shapes of their models. In this technique, the artist constructs deformable areas with expanding loops of edges, resulting in a much more versatile model for deforming and animating. You can visualize this by looking at your mouth in a mirror. Imagine that the outline (edge) of your lips is a flexible, expandable line like a rubber band. Changing your mouth shape deforms that rubber band. If you were to draw an ever-expanding series of these lines outwards from your mouth, you could see how the lines deform when you smile or yawn. These lines correspond to the edge loops in a 3D mesh. Your model will more accurately reflect the deforming mouth shapes if you create it with edge loops linking to the adjacent areas of the face.

Edge-Looping the Mouth

What you'll do in this exercise is to create the mouth and nose of a human character, using edge loops to define the face topology. Then you'll be able to apply these methods to any and all characters you create.

1. Begin by opening the file 9_head_start.max (**Figure 9.43**).

   The scene consists of an incomplete head model. Around the eye area, you can see edges looping out from the eyelid. It's our goal to create the mouth and nostrils using a similar layout of geometry.

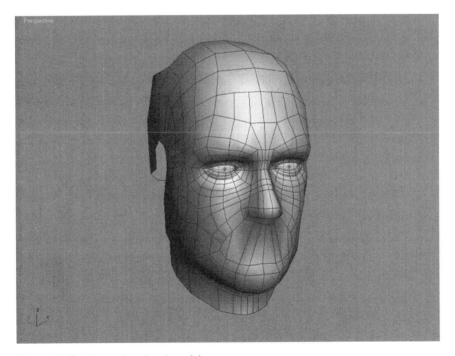

Figure 9.43 Incomplete head model.

2. In the Perspective viewport, zoom in to get a good view of the area you're working on—in this case, the mouth region (**Figure 9.44**). Select the head, and navigate to Edge sub-object mode in the object's modifier stack. Enable Show End
   Result and disable Show Cage to make things clearer.

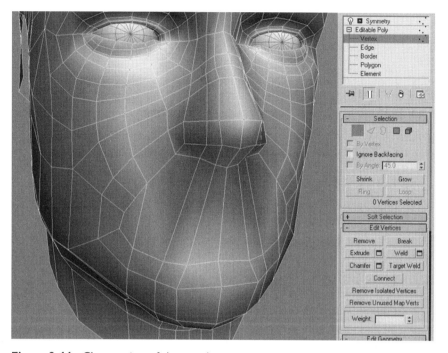

Figure 9.44   Closeup view of the mouth region.

3. From the Edit Geometry rollout, activate Cut. From the top of the place where
   the lips will begin, start to cut, clicking at each edge around the top to form the
   outline of the lips (**Figure 9.45**). At the corner of the mouth, add three cuts
   before continuing around to the bottom lip; you will need these extra points to
   connect to the existing edges.

   Think of this technique with the Cut tool as "sketching into your model."
   You're drawing the outline for the model's lips directly onto the geometry.
   You can then refine/tweak the shape to suit your needs. The benefit of this
   is very quick visual feedback about where your detail is going before you
   fully commit to it.

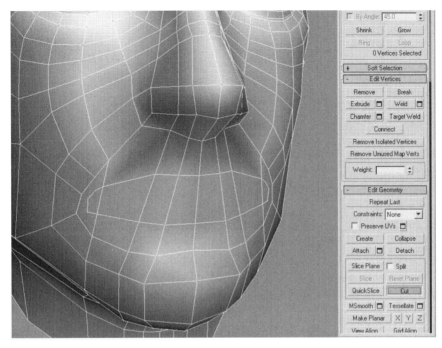

Figure 9.45   Cutting the shape of the lips.

4. In Vertex sub-object mode, select corresponding pairs of vertices, and in the Edit Vertices rollout, connect them at what will become the corners of the mouth (**Figure 9.46**).

5. Now it's time to tweak, using the Move tool to select vertices and fashion them into a more recognizable mouth shape (**Figure 9.47**). Be sure to keep Arc Rotating the viewport to see if the shape is working from all angles. If you alter the Reference Coordinate System to Local, it can be easier to move vertices while in the Perspective viewport.

Tip

Whenever you are modeling directly in the Perspective viewport, it's always a good idea to continually rotate around your object to see how shapes and forms are working. All too often, you'll see heads modeled that look wonderful from the front, but as soon as you rotate them left or right, they become flat or misshapen. By constantly checking the shape of your creations in all axes, you'll have a much better understanding of when things aren't looking right.

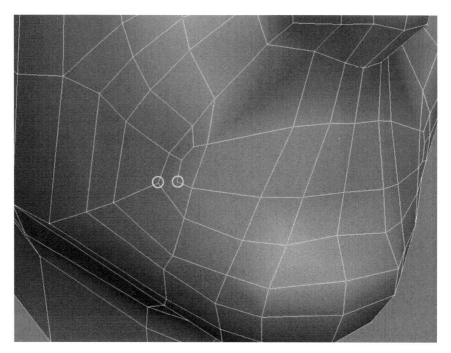

Figure 9.46 Connecting vertices at the corner of the mouth.

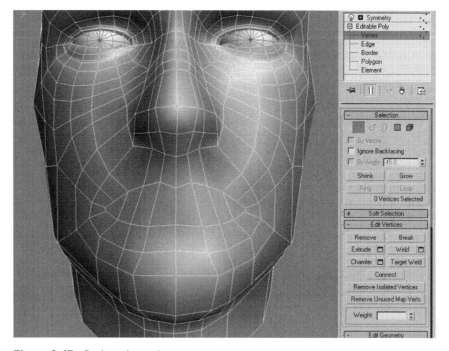

Figure 9.47 Reshaped mouth.

6. Once you're happy with the shape of the mouth, select the edges that make up the outline, and from the Edit Edges rollout of the Modify panel, chamfer them slightly, creating two edges where you had one (**Figure 9.48**).

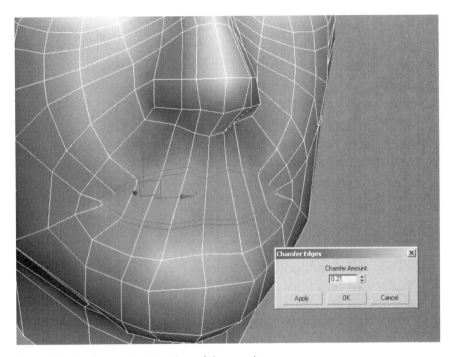

Figure 9.48   Chamfering the edges of the mouth.

7. You now have two outlines of edges. Leave the outer loop so it still represents the shape you want. We're going to treat the new inner edges as the opening of the mouth. To make this clearer, select all the polygons on the "inside" of the mouth and delete them.

8. Now reshape the vertices to form the line of the inner lips, again remembering to keep rotating around to check the shape (**Figure 9.49**).

9. You've created the two defining borders of the lips—the outer edges and the inner edges. The next step is to flesh out the lips. Select one of the vertical edges that run around the lips, use Ring to select all the adjacent edges, and then use Connect to create a new edge loop.

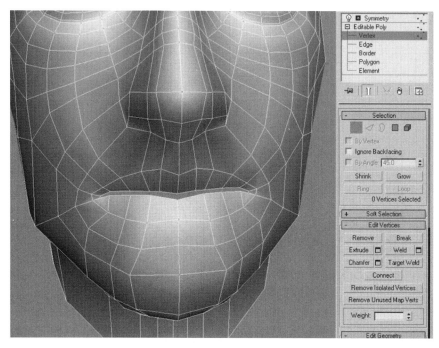

Figure 9.49   Reshaped inner lips.

 Note

> Functions such as Connect, Loop, and Ring are used extensively when modeling a
> character this way. Speed things up by using the right-click Quad menus to quickly
> access these commands. Or assign your own keyboard shortcuts from the
> Customize > Customize User Interface menu.

10. Go back to the Vertex level. This time, pull out the definition of the lips using the
    points you've just created. The bottom lip tends to be the fleshier of the two, so
    try to reflect that in the shape you give it (**Figure 9.50**).

11. Connect the edges and then, at the Vertex level, move the points so that the
    newly created edges form a more natural flow with their neighboring polygons
    (**Figure 9.51**).

 Note

> It's very common for the surfaces of models to take on a stiff or rigid appearance
> when modeled this way. Newly created vertices usually need to be manipulated to
> keep the model looking organic.

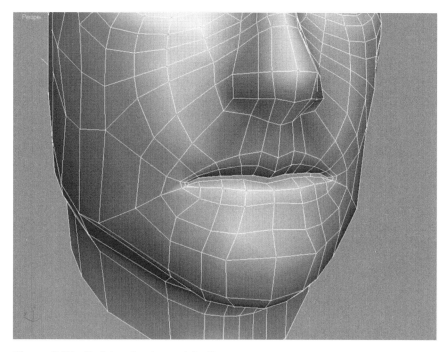

Figure 9.50   Defining the shape of the lips.

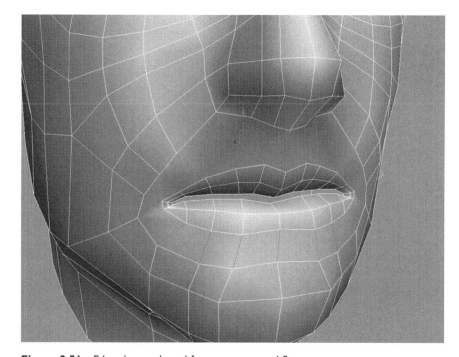

Figure 9.51   Edge shapes altered for a more natural flow.

12. Apply a TurboSmooth modifier to the head so you can see how it's shaping up. At the Editable Poly level of the stack, turn on Show Cage (if it isn't active already).

13. At the Edge sub-object level, select the loop of edges that makes up the perimeter of the mouth, and from the Edit Edges rollout, open the Chamfer Edges dialog. Set the Chamfer Amount to around 0.10 (**Figure 9.52**).

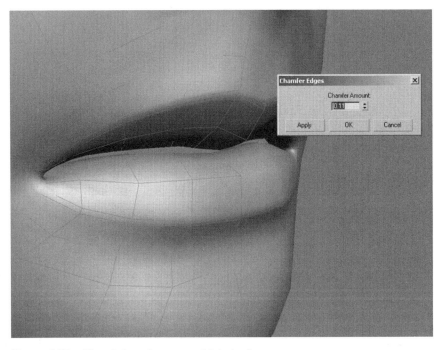

Figure 9.52   Chamfering edges to establish the lips.

Chamfering the edges around the mouth gives definition to the mouth, pulling it out from the face without the transition being unnaturally sharp or soft.

Building the Nose

We'll now try to do the same for the nose, the adjacent cheek areas, and the area above just the upper lip.

1. Remove the TurboSmooth modifier from the stack and disable Show End Result. Select the five edges shown in **Figure 9.53** and then connect them.

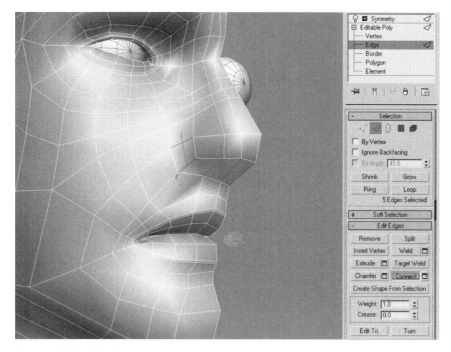

Figure 9.53   Selecting edges to be connected.

2. Switch to Vertex sub-object mode, and move the new points toward the edge of what will become the nostrils. Bunching the edges together like this will give us the desired definition from the face when it's smoothed.

3. We're going to need some more points to flesh out the shape of the nostrils further. Select and connect the edges shown in **Figure 9.54**.

4. In Vertex sub-object mode, select and connect the two vertices (**Figure 9.55**).

5. You'll need to tidy things up in this area now, as you've got a few too many polygons with more than four edges. So choose Insert Vertex from the Edit Edges rollout and click the two edges of the triangular polygons you've made.

6. Now you'll anchor these points by connecting them to their neighboring vertices. Then connect them to the vertices opposite and move them out (**Figure 9.56**).

7. Turn on Show End Result and Arc Rotate the viewport until you can see under the nose. Select the large polygon face you've left there, and from the Edit Polygons rollout, bring up the dialog for Inset. Using the Inset Amount value brings the face inward (**Figure 9.57**); this poly face will now become the nostril opening.

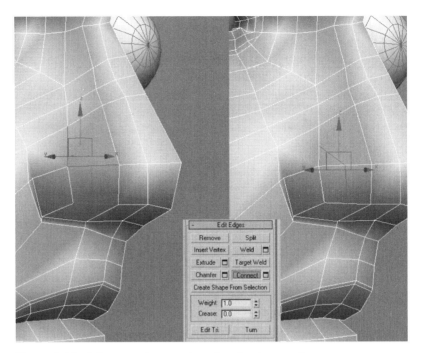

Figure 9.54 Selecting and connecting edges for the nostrils.

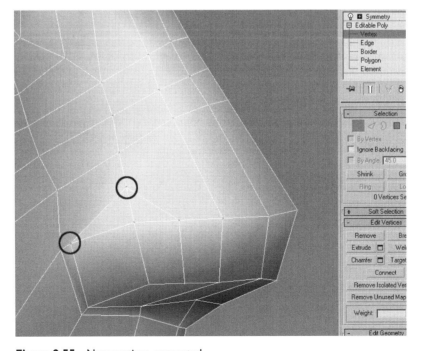

Figure 9.55 New vertices connected.

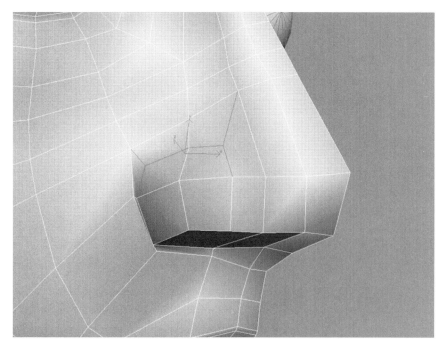

Figure 9.56   Edges after being moved and connected.

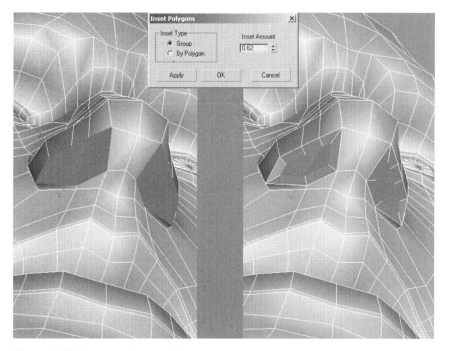

Figure 9.57   Insetting the nostrils.

8. Delete the face you've just inset to get a clearer view of what the nose will look like when you create the nostril. You can probably see that the shape of the hole isn't quite right. You'll need to add some more geometry.

9. In Edge sub-object mode, select the ring of edges that made up the septum (the bridge between the two nostrils) and connect them.

10. This is the time to be looking in the mirror! In Vertex mode, move the points around the nostril until you have defined the shape of the nostril (**Figure 9.58**).

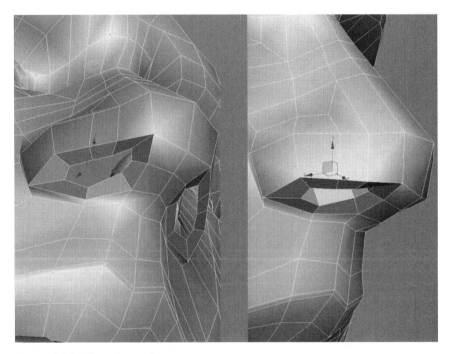

Figure 9.58   Shaped nostrils.

Completing the Head

Remember, there's no better reference for a head than your own. Turn your neck around to study your head in the mirror from as many different angles as possible while simultaneously rotating your working view in max. (See what amazing skills you have to acquire to be a character modeler?)

1. Time to bring the skin of the nostril back up into the head. Select the border of the hole and Shift-drag it back up into the nose (**Figure 9.59**).

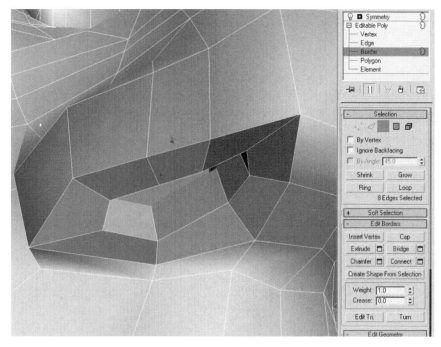

Figure 9.59   Shift-dragging the border of the nostrils upward.

2. Select the ring of edges that now make up the ridge around the nostril area and connect them to create a new edge loop. This will give us sharper detail in this area when the model is subdivided (**Figure 9.60**).

3. Apply a MeshSmooth modifier to the head model, and with Show End Result and Show Cage both enabled, tweak and pull the points until you're satisfied with the final shape of the nose (**Figure 9.61**).

    You've almost completed the mouth and nose regions of the head. The only thing left is to check the flow of the edges you've used so far.

4. If you zoom in on the region where the top lip meets the nose, you can see that you have a five-sided polygon where you would rather have a quad poly. To rectify this, first add some more points to the lip. Select and connect the edges that run from the lip upward to the five-sided polygon.

5. Connect one new vertex to the existing one at the edge of the nostrils (**Figure 9.62**).

    You can see how this has helped our model's structure by highlighting the clear set of edges that flow outward from the lips (**Figure 9.63**).

6. Finally, just in case you did not do it earlier, apply a MeshSmooth modifier to the model (**Figure 9.64**).

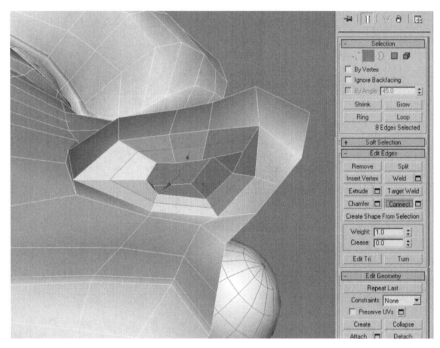

Figure 9.60   Creating a new edge loop around the nostril.

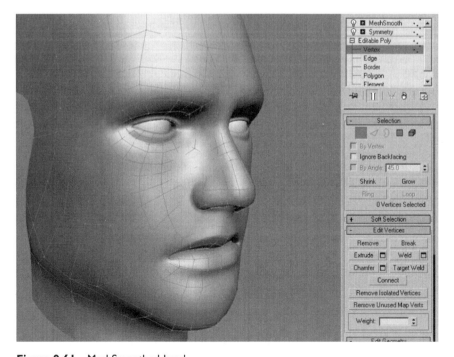

Figure 9.61   MeshSmoothed head.

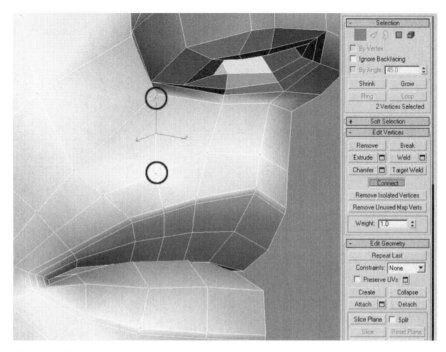

Figure 9.62   Vertices after connection.

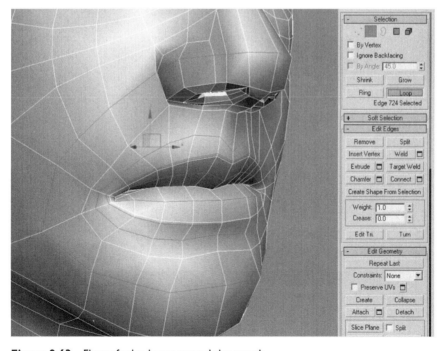

Figure 9.63   Flow of edge loops around the mouth.

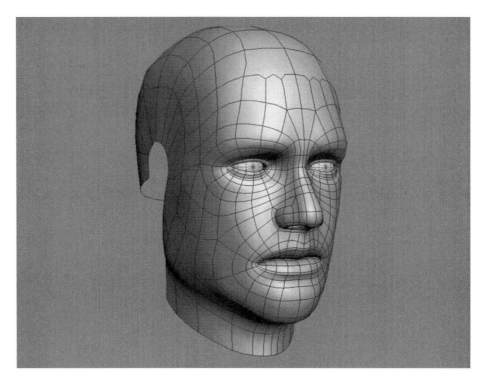

Figure 9.64   Head with MeshSmooth applied.

At the moment, our head has the essentials (eyes, nose, and mouth), but there's no rea-son to stop here. Using techniques from this and previous sections, why not try com-pleting the head model? It can be difficult at first to see how edge loops should be implemented in every case, so I strongly advise looking at the work of others for ideas on how to improve your own approach.

To check out my version of this exercise, open the file 9_head_finish.max on the DVD.

An excellent way to see the benefit of a well-ordered mesh is to create morph targets. This involves moving geometry to create different expressions or poses for animation (**Figure 9.65**). Once you start to reshape an area of your model, you can see both the potential and the limitations of the geometry you created.

So far, we've been dealing with models that use Subdivision Surface routines (MeshSmooth or TurboSmooth) to arrive at the finished result. The dividing process has two characteristics: it rounds off sharp corners and surfaces, and it increases the number of polygons in the model. It's not practical to create such "dense" or "heavy" meshes when you need to move them around onscreen quickly—for example, when using ani-mation proxies. Proxies are required when the animator needs to work with a much lighter (or low-poly) substitute model to gain faster feedback. The other main use for lower-polygon models is in videogaming. All onscreen content in a videogame has to be created with the absolute minimum of geometry consonant with the game design and available processor speed. Creating low-poly models involves employing exactly the same tools you have already used. In fact, before you applied MeshSmooth to the pig in the first exercise, it was a low-poly model.

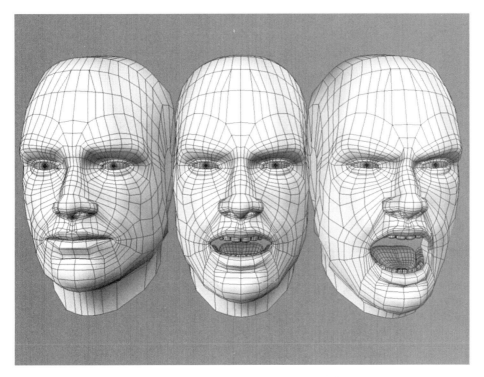

Figure 9.65   Examples of morph targets and edge loops around the mouth.

The Eyes Have It

Almost every character you create will need eyes in one form or another. Eyes provide a character with the most essential element of life (I assure you, a piercing gaze from your monitor can be quite unnerving!).

However, as with many aspects of character modeling, there are numerous styles of eyes and numerous ways to tackle them. In this section, you are going to create a very simple cartoon eye using only Sphere primitives, taking advantage of some of 3ds max's default settings.

The Cartoon Eye

The cartoon eye has certain typical characteristics. It is much larger or occasionally much smaller than a real eye in proportion to the face; it usually bulges out much more; it need not be spherical (although the ones we create will be); and the pupil and iris are often much larger in relation to the sclera (the white of the eye) than they would be in a real eye. Let's see how quickly we can make an expressive cartoony eye. In the following steps, we're going to create a character's eye from primitives that can be edited later to change the style or expression.

1. Open the file 9_robot_blind.max (**Figure 9.66**).

   In this scene, you already have a simple jointed robot character, but he needs some eyes.

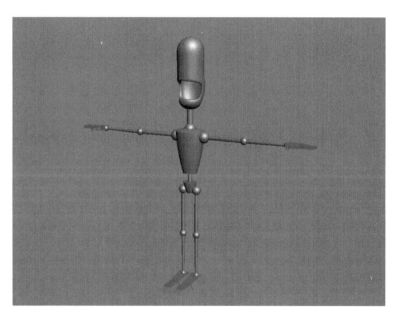

Figure 9.66   Robot model without eyes.

2. In the Left viewport, create a Sphere primitive from the Standard Primitives category. Set the Radius value to 15 and leave the Segments value set to 32. In the Front viewport, maneuver the sphere so it's roughly where you'd like the robot's left eye to be (**Figure 9.67**). (You can also apply the Eye material from the Material Editor to make the eye easier to distinguish in the next few steps.)

3. With the sphere still selected, hold down Shift and click once to bring up the Clone Options dialog. Leave the Object Type set to Copy and the Number of Copies set to 1.

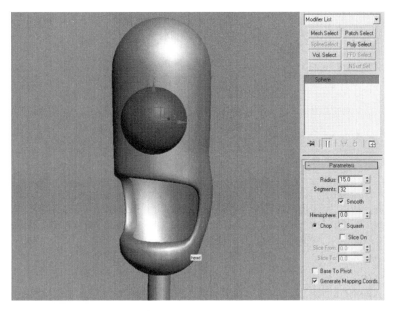

Figure 9.67   Creating a sphere for the eye.

4. With our newly cloned sphere selected, let's create some eyelids. First, apply the Metal material from the Material Editor to it. Then, in the Modify panel, set the Radius value to 16, making it just a little larger than our eyeball.

5. Check the box labeled Slice On and enter the following settings:

   - Slice From = 200
   - Slice To = 340

   This creates an upper and a lower eyelid from the larger sphere (**Figure 9.68**). What's more, you can easily adjust or animate the position of the eyelids using the values you've just set.

6. You can open and close the eye, but the robot can't quite see yet. In the Front viewport, create another sphere roughly where you would like the pupil to be. Make the radius as large or as small as you like—I'd go for around 2. Apply the Pupil material.

Note

Many aspects of a character can be conveyed by the eyes, specifically the shape and scale of the pupils. Smaller pupils tend to give a more startled or focused look, while larger pupils often make a character look cuter or more childlike. This isn't always the case, but it's a good guide. Look at some of the early Disney films to see where the artists used larger eyes for cuter creatures.

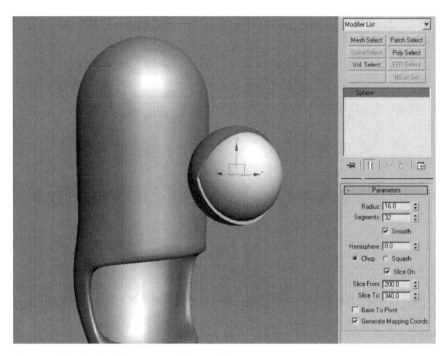

Figure 9.68   Using Slice to open the eyelids.

7. You want the pupil to sit flat on the surface of the eyeball. First, in the Left viewport, move the pupil so that it is in front of the eyeball; then, from the Create panel, go to the Geometry > Compound Objects subgroup and (with the pupil selected) choose Conform.

8. Highlight the Pick Wrap-To Object button, and in the Front viewport, select the eyeball sphere. From the Modify panel, scroll down to the Update section of the rollout and check the box Hide Wrap-To Object (**Figure 9.69**).

   If you move to the Perspective viewport, you can now see that the pupil has flattened to the surface of the eyeball. Another way to do this would be to create a separate texture map for the pupil and map it directly onto the eyeball.

9. Now to keep everything together. If we're happy with the pupil, right-click and convert to an editable mesh. With the Select and Link tool, drag from the pupil to the eyeball itself. This means that when you rotate the eyeball, the pupil will follow. Use the Select and Rotate tool on the eyeball to move the direction of the robot's gaze (**Figure 9.70**).

10. There's one more fairly obvious step, and that's duplicating the eye for the other side. Select the eyelids, eyeball, and pupil, and in the Front viewport, Shift-drag a clone onto the other side of the head.

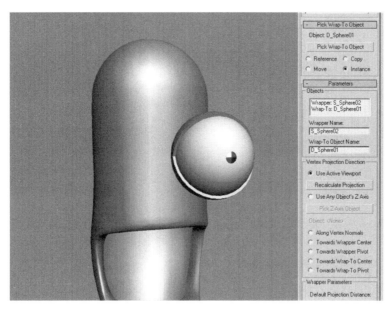

Figure 9.69   The pupil wrapped to the eyeball with Conform.

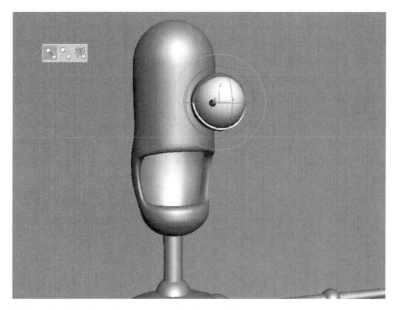

Figure 9.70   The linked pupil rotating with the eyeball.

Now that you've created a pair of eyes, try changing the setting of the Slice To/From in the eyelid spheres' parameters to give different expressions (**Figure 9.71**).

9.71 Altering the robot's expression using Slice.

To check out my version of this exercise, open the file 9_robot_final.max on the accompanying DVD.

You've created a pair of simple yet highly expressive eyes. It can be amazing how much character comes across from the eyes, so always experiment with different ways to represent them. For example, take the eyes you've created for the robot character and use an FFD (box) modifier to change the shape—after all, not all eyes are round!

Summing Up

The techniques learned in this chapter can be applied to a multitude of creations. And although we've covered some standard procedures for successful character modeling, the greatest achievements will come from your own creativity. So don't feel that every time you make a head you have to start it one way, or that every pig should start with a box. These are just the building blocks for you to adapt to your needs.

So why not tackle one of your own designs? If you're stuck for inspiration, simply look around your desk, your workplace, even your mirror—there are literally hundreds of interesting and unique characters waiting for you.

Part IV

Texturing

Chapter 10

Texture Mapping

By Jon A. Bell

In this chapter, you'll see how the 3ds max 7 Material Editor, when coupled with the wide range of available UVW mapping techniques and modifiers, provides a one-two punch to help you solve almost any texturing problem for almost any conceivable piece of geometry. Whether you're building a complex organic character for a film or video project, a low-resolution poly model for a computer game, or a "hard surface" model for an industrial or architectural visualization, 3ds max 7 gives you the tools you need to make your models look their best.

Specifically, we'll cover the following topics:

- The Material Editor and the Material/Map Browser
- Shader and Material Types
- Map Types: Bitmaps and Procedurals
- Mapping Coordinates (Procedural, Object-Space UVW, and World-Space UVW Mapping)
- Camera Mapping
- Multi/Sub-Object Mapping

 Note

For the purposes of this chapter, we'll be looking at the standard 3ds max 7 shader types, materials, and maps for the Default Scanline Renderer only.

The Material Editor

Materials, which you create and modify through the Materials Editor, control how light interacts with an object's surface. Since this chapter assumes that you've already gone through all the basic 3ds max 7 tutorials included with the program and are familiar with most 3ds max features, I'll provide only a brief overview of the Material Editor.

The Material Editor for 3ds max 7 (**Figure 10.1**) hasn't changed substantially since the release of 3D Studio MAX R1 back in the spring of 1996. This isn't necessarily a criticism, because the original design of the Material Editor was extremely advanced for its time and gave users the ability to create complex layered textures with relative ease. In short, it's aged pretty well, although there's always room for improvement.

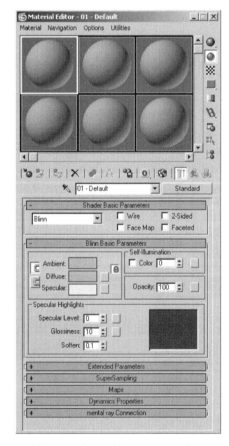

Figure 10.1   The 3ds max 7 Material Editor (default settings).

This figure shows the default settings of the Material Editor when you first open it, using the Material Editor icon on the Main toolbar. An array of buttons on the right side of the menu enables you to change the material sample sphere display options—sample type (sphere, cylinder, and box), the lighting on the sample objects (backlight on or off), the background display of the sample objects (useful when working with translucent materials), and so on.

Double-clicking a sample sphere window opens a larger, floating version of the sample for closer inspection of the texture. Right-clicking the sample sphere area also brings up a menu where you can display more texture sample windows—3 by 2, 5 by 3, or 6 by 4.

Although the maximum number of material samples you can show in the Material Editor at one time is 24, remember that you're not limited to only 24 materials in your scene! Create new materials in the Material Editor (and apply them in your scene) by clicking any sample sphere, clicking the Material Editor X icon (which resets your Map/Material to the default settings), and then checking "Affect only mtl/map in the editor slot." This clears the material slot. Name this new material whatever you like and alter its parameters and maps as needed.

Resetting your Map/Material to the default settings enables you to create new materials for your scene, even if all your Material Editor slots are currently filled. **Figure 10.2** shows the Map Reset dialog.

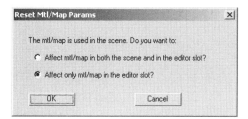

Figure 10.2   The Map Reset dialog.

Shader Types

The first materials component item we'll look at in the Material Editor is the shader type. (A shader determines global aspects of how a surface will render.) The initial shader type forms the backbone of all Standard materials you create in 3ds max 7.

At the top of the Material Editor is the Shader Basic Parameters rollout, which contains a drop-down list of different shader types. The default shader is Blinn (named after James Blinn, one of the pioneers of computer graphics rendering). Blinn works well in many situations, but if you click the drop-down list you can choose from other shader types, including these:

- **Anisotropic**—Creates custom specular highlights for metals, hair, velvet cloth, and other glossy, textured materials where the angle of incident light affects the brightness and color of the object.

- **Metal**—For metallic finishes.

- **Multi-Layer**—For complex materials with different shading components.

- **Oren-Nayar-Blinn**—Ideal for rough or matte surfaces such as a chalkboard.

- **Phong**—Provides shinier highlights than Blinn.

- **Strauss**—Similar to the Metal shader, but with only one color component and no separate specular component.

- **Translucent Shader**—Simulates translucent, "two-sided" materials. This shader, new to 3ds max 7, can help you create thin, translucent materials such as paper or frosted glass. It is not, however, a true subsurface scattering (SSS) shader that can accurately simulate materials such as marble, wax, and skin that allow a percentage of light to penetrate their surfaces.

Many third-party plug-in shaders are available for free download or purchase to supplement the core 3ds max 7 shader options.

Material Types

The second major component of 3ds max 7 Materials is the actual material type. The default material type is Standard. Clicking the Material Type button brings up the Material/Map Browser (**Figure 10.3**), which lets you pick additional types.

The core 3ds max materials (that is, materials not specific to mental ray) are these:

- **Advanced Lighting Override**—Used in conjunction with the 3ds max 7 Light Tracer and Radiosity features.

- **Architectural**—Provides features taken from the Autodesk VIZ program, an engineering/architectural offshoot of the base 3ds max program.

- **Blend**—Blends and combines multiple material types.

- **Composite**—Layers complex materials and maps.

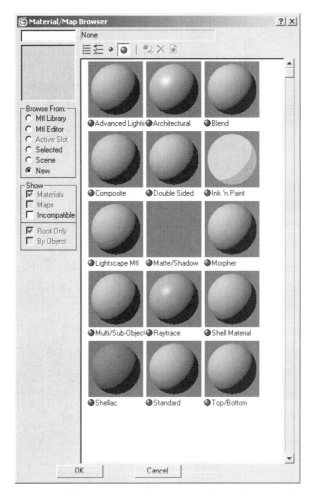

Figure 10.3   The Material/Map Browser allows you to change from your Standard 3ds max material to other custom materials.

- **Double Sided**—Creates two-sided materials, with one material showing on the front of your model's face normals while a different material shows on its back-face normals.
- **Ink 'n Paint**—A basic cartoon and cel-look shader.
- **Lightscape Mtl**—The Lightscape material enables you to set radiosity parameters for meshes that you want to export to Lightscape. Lightscape (now a discontinued product) is an Autodesk 3D rendering package, used primarily for architectural visualization where extremely high-quality radiosity rendering is required.

- **Matte/Shadow**—For special effects and compositing purposes when you need an object to reveal whatever environment background you've loaded.

- **Morpher**—Used to transition between morphing object types and their materials.

- **Multi/Sub-Object**—Allows you to more carefully organize and place specific materials on selected faces of your geometry using assigned Material ID numbers. We'll cover this material in detail later in this chapter.

- **Raytrace**—Provides a host of reflection and refraction options, offers greater Specular control than a Standard material, and includes Diffusion mapping (lacking in other 3ds max 7 materials). There's also a Raytrace map type, described below, which you can use in the map slot of any regular 3ds max 7 material.

- **Shell Material**—Works in conjunction with the Render To Texture feature to bake a complex texture hierarchy (consisting perhaps of multiple procedural texture layers) down to a single bitmap that can be saved to disk. This material can save on rendering time.

- **Shellac**—Another composite material that creates glossy surfaces.

- **Top/Bottom**—Blends different materials based on object coordinates or world coordinates or both. Top/Bottom is useful for varying textures according to the "height" of a surface—for example, creating snow on mountaintops, dust on the tops of objects, and so on.

Now that you've seen the basic shader and material types, let's take a look at 3ds max 7's huge variety of map types.

Map Types and Examples

There are two main map types in 3ds max 7 (and pretty much every other 3D program): bitmaps and procedural maps.

Bitmaps consist of single still images in typical image file formats such as .jpg, .tif, .tga, and .bmp, or image sequences applied to create animated surface effects. They can be created from scratch using a paint program such as Adobe Photoshop or Corel Painter, imported from scanned print or digital photos, digitized from video, created as a rendering from an existing 3D scene, or crafted using a combination of any of these techniques.

For the most photorealistic results, it's better to use as many real-world textures in your scene as possible. For example, if you're depicting a wooden tabletop with scratches, dings, and dents, an actual photo of a wooden tabletop (along with a separate Bump map for the surface imperfections) will invariably look better than a map you've painted from scratch (unless you're an absolutely amazing 2D artist). The inherent flaws and idiosyncrasies of real-world images are tough to duplicate in digital artwork, so going back to nature is the obvious solution. Examples of such textures are shown in **Figure 10.4.**

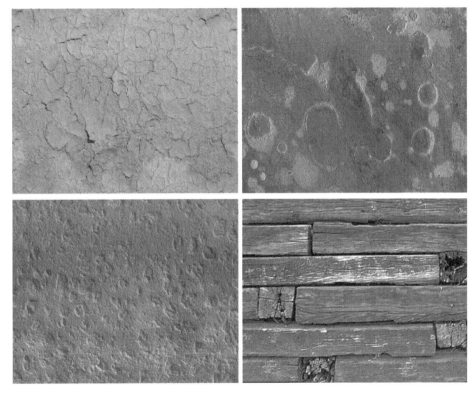

Figure 10.4   Real-world bitmap images are almost always better than hand-painted textures for producing realistic 3D surfaces.

Procedural maps are purely mathematical creations—algorithms that generate surface effects. They range from standard, bread-and-butter Noise functions that "rough up" any surface to custom effects such as electricity, water surfaces, fantasy patterns, and so on. You can often use combinations of procedural and bitmap textures to produce more varied effects in your scene. One thing to remember: Bitmaps are 2D in nature and can be thought of as paint on the surface of your 3D objects, while procedurals are 3D in nature and "permeate" the entirety of your object. Keep this essential difference in mind as you plan future experiments in texturing.

Max's Map Types

Here is the list of 3ds max 7 standard map types (**Figure 10.5**):

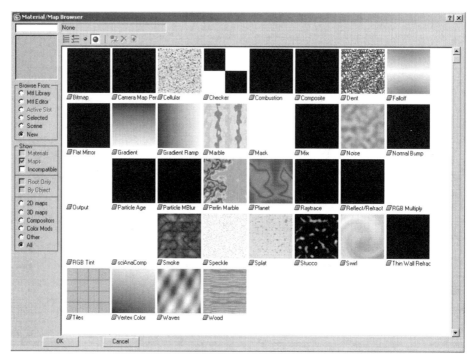

Figure 10.5   3ds max 7 offers a large variety of map types.

- **Bitmap**—For still images or image sequences.
- **Camera Map Per Pixel**—Enables you to render and save high-resolution images of 3D scenes, retouch them (if necessary), then reapply those images as Camera Projection maps onto the original geometry. This is most useful for creating high-resolution matte paintings for the backgrounds and virtual sets of visual effects shots.
- **Cellular**—Complex map useful for organic patterns such as skin cells, as well as water surfaces, electrical arcs, and other effects.
- **Checker**—Creates checkerboard patterns; squares can be customized according to number of squares, color, width, and height.
- **Combustion**—Provides a link to combustion, discreet's paint and compositing program. Use combustion to paint on the surface of a max object and see the results in the viewports.
- **Composite**—Helpful for layering additional maps.

- **Dent**—Most useful in the Bump map slot.

- **Falloff**—An extremely versatile map for iridescent and reflection effects (as you'll see in the next chapter).

- **Flat Mirror**—Makes flat reflective surfaces.

- **Gradient**—Creates either linear or radial gradients; especially useful for masking.

- **Gradient Ramp**—Similar to Gradient, but with more color and mapping controls.

- **Marble**—Imitates the veining and coloration of marble.

- **Mask**—A map put in the Mask slot will mask underlying maps.

- **Mix**—Used to blend two or more maps.

- **Noise**—A workhorse procedural texture that you can use throughout your 3D scenes.

- **Normal Bump**—Creates material Bump maps using color channel information.

- **Output**—For boosting the output of a submap that lacks the standard Output Parameter controls.

- **Particle Age**—Helps control particle color and opacity.

- **Particle Mblur**—Helps adjust particle motion blur.

- **Perlin Marble**—A modified Marble texture offering additional controls.

- **Planet**—A generic planet surface map.

- **Raytrace**—Most often used in the Reflection and Refraction slots of a Standard material to generate realistic mirror and glass surfaces.

- **Reflect/Refract**—Applies environmental reflections in your 3D scene; usually faster than a Raytrace map.

- **RGB Multiply**—Useful when you want to use a map to boost or suppress the RGB values of a submap.

- **RGB Tint**—Similar to RGB Multiply; used to color-correct an existing submap.

- **Smoke**—A softer Noise function.

- **Speckle**—Produces random speckles and blobs.

- **Splat**—Similar to Speckle, but with larger, spikier blobs.

- **Stucco**—A pattern most useful for Bump mapping.

- **Swirl**—Produces soft, swirled color transitions.

- **Thin Wall Refraction**—Used to suggest the refraction of glass panes when you don't want to use a Raytrace map.

- **Tiles**—Produces geometric tesselated patterns; replaces the Brick map in earlier versions of 3ds max.

- **Vertex Color**—Creates special color effects; used for model shading in game engines.

- **Waves**—Produces convincing water surface effects.

- **Wood**—A simple procedural wood shader.

In the next chapter, you'll learn how to make your own custom textures using a combination of bitmaps and procedural textures. We'll also discuss modifying and improving existing bitmap textures for 3D rendering.

Dancing About Architecture

There's a saying that "writing about music is like dancing about architecture." The same could be said about text descriptions of colorful CG textures—they're uninformative at best, misleading at worst. It's much better to see the images up close and personal so you can figure out what they do. Without further ado, let's look at all the shader, material, and map types, all at once.

1. Load the file All_Materials_Maps_Shaders.max (**Figure 10.6**) from this book's DVD.

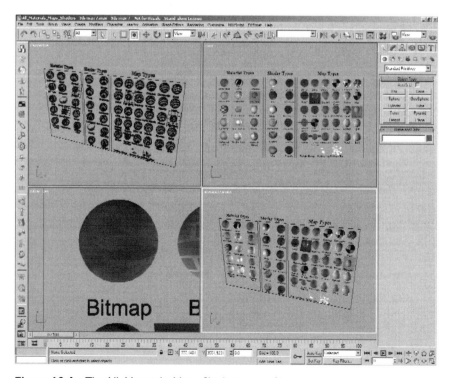

Figure 10.6   The All_Materials_Maps_Shaders scene file.

2. Activate the Front viewport in this scene, and then select Render Scene > Render (**Figure 10.7**).

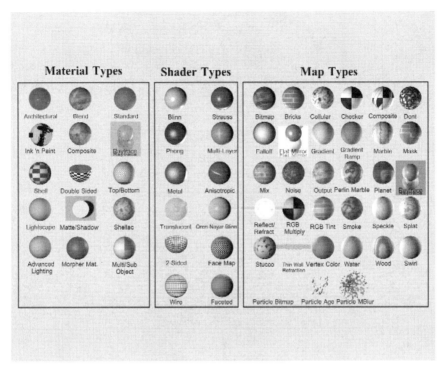

Figure 10.7   This scene file contains examples of all the standard 3ds max 7 shader types, materials, and maps for the Default Scanline Renderer.

This file, by 3D artist Peter Clay of discreet's Quality Engineering (software testing) department, includes samples of every shader, material, and map type that is not specific to mental ray. Each type is clearly labeled and accompanied by its own appropriately mapped Sphere object. If you go to the Command panel > Display tab and uncheck the Cameras box, you'll also see that there is a close-up camera for each sample sphere, as well as a moving camera that pans past every sphere during the course of 100 frames. If you're unfamiliar with what any shader, material, or map does in 3ds max 7, use this scene as a quick reference.

Texture Mapping

No doubt you are eager to delve into the basics of applying these materials in a real scene. First, we'll examine applying mapping to procedural objects.

Mapping Procedural Objects

Procedural objects such as Standard primitives, Extended primitives, and Patch Grids that are created using the path Create panel > Geometry are generated with mapping coordinates already in place—the relevant check box is selected by default (**Figure 10.8**)—so maps can render properly for them. You can also render Spline objects (lines, circles, rectangles, and so on), although their Renderable and Generate Mapping Coordinates options (under each object's Rendering rollout) are off by default. (This is so you don't have left-over construction splines and shapes rendering in your animations by mistake.)

Figure 10.8   Procedural objects in 3ds max 7 have their mapping coordinates selected by default.

Certain compound objects, notably loft objects, allow you to generate mapping coordinates upon creation (**Figure 10.9**). This is very helpful, since it can be quite difficult to apply standard UVW mapping to a complex lofted object such as a length of cable or hose snaking around a 3D car engine. Maintaining the existing mapping on procedural objects in your scene will save you time and trouble later when you begin applying materials.

 Note

Collapsing procedural objects into Editable Meshes, Patches, Poly objects, or NURBS objects preserves their original mapping coordinates, but if you apply a UVW Map on top of these objects and then collapse them again, your original Procedural mapping coordinates will be lost.

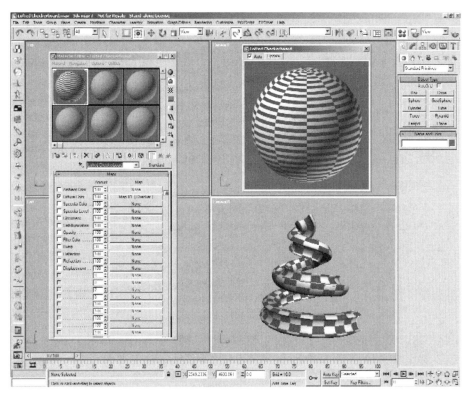

Figure 10.9   Lofted objects get mapping coordinates when they are created.

Mapping Modifiers

Now let's look at the various options for modifying the application of maps to objects.

Unless you're creating a scene consisting entirely of untouched procedural objects (which is unlikely!), you'll probably want to apply specific UVW mapping coordinates to your objects. These allow you to custom-fit your textures to almost any object or group of faces.

UVW mapping gizmos operate in both World space (global coordinates) and Object space (local coordinates.) You find both types in the Command panel > Modify tab > Modifier List menu.

These are the World-Space UVW Map modifiers in 3ds max 7:

- **Camera Map**—Projects the map from the camera's view; used for "front projection" special effects in your scene.

- **MapScaler**—Preserves a UVW-mapped object's map size in relationship to World space when you scale the underlying object.

- **Surface Mapper**—Takes a map assigned to a NURBS surface and projects it onto a modified object. Only useful if you build NURBS objects in 3ds max.

These are the Object-Space UVW Map (and Material) modifiers in 3ds max 7:

- **MapScaler**—Preserves a UVW-mapped object's map size in relationship to Object space when you scale the underlying object.

- **Material**—Assigns specific materials to objects, faces, and elements in your scene.

- **MaterialByElement**—Applies different material IDs to objects containing multiple elements, either to specific elements or randomly.

- **Unwrap UVW**—Modifies the placement of a bitmap's details on the surface of an object at the face/edge/vertex level. You can see this in action in the Unwrap UVW modifier menu (**Figure 10.10**) after you click the Edit button under this modifier's Parameters rollout.

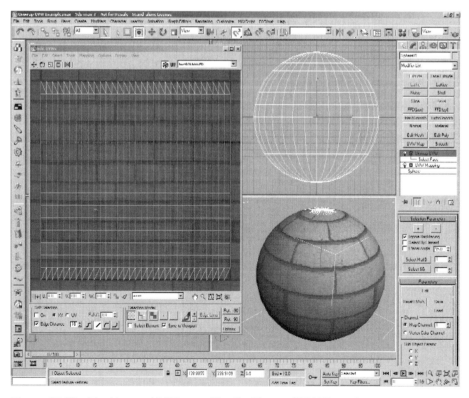

Figure 10.10 The Unwrap UVW menu. This file, Unwrap UVW Example.max, is on this book's DVD.

- **UVW Map**—The standard workhorse modifier for applying mapping coordinates to meshes, patches, and polys. The coordinate types are Planar, Cylindrical, Spherical, Shrink Wrap, Box, Face, and XYZ to UVW (converts from one coordinate system to another).

- **UVW Mapping Add**—Used in conjunction with the Channel Info Utility (Command panel > Utility tab > More > Channel Info). It's mainly for game developers who need low-level access to vertex color and mapping data of 3D objects that they'll later export to a game engine.

- **UVW Mapping Clear**—Clears the previous UVW channel information.

- **UVW Xform**—Adjusts the tiling and offset in existing UVW coordinates. Also used to tweak the default mapping coordinates of procedural objects.

- **VertexPaint**—Another game developer tool, enabling artists and programmers to modify low-poly model textures for output to game engines.

 Note

> The Shell modifier (under Object-Space Modifiers) is different from the Shell material. The former allows you to create "thickness" in the walls of your 3D geometry; the latter is used to bake procedural textures into a single bitmap.

That covers the core 3ds max 7 shaders, maps, material types, and map-related modifiers (all that are not specific to mental ray). Now let's play with a couple of fast and easy mapping tricks.

Mapping Tricks

In the following example, we'll take a quick look at the difference between Object-Space mapping and World-Space mapping and explain how you can use these differences to create some interesting texture effects.

1. From the DVD, load the file Object Space vs World Space.max (**Figure 10.11**).

2. Scroll the Time Slider bar to see two spheres that travel across the screen in front of a checkerboard background. Both spheres have UVW Map modifiers applied, with Spherical mapping coordinates.

3. Open the Material Editor, and inspect the materials in the scene. There are two different materials (one for each sphere), both using the Checker map. Another Checker map (with Screen mapping coordinates) forms the Environment Background image.

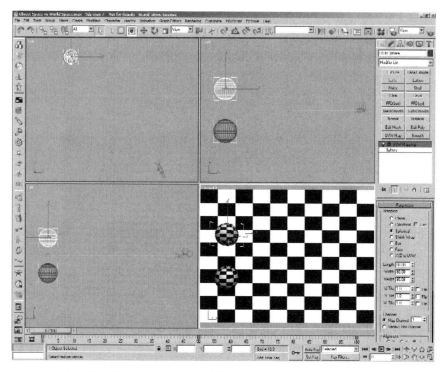

Figure 10.11 The Object Space vs World Space.max scene.

4. Select the first material (Object-Space Mapping), and open its Diffuse Color map slot, loaded with the Checker map. Under the Coordinates rollout, you'll see that the Texture radio button is checked and that the Mapping coordinates are set to Explicit Map Channel.

5. Select the second material (World-Space Mapping), and open its Diffuse Color map slot. Under its Coordinates rollout, you'll see that the Environment button is checked, with the Mapping coordinates set to Screen—the same parameters used in the background map.

6. Activate the Camera01 viewport, and render a still image of this scene on frame 0 (**Figure 10.12**). You'll see that the top sphere has a distinctive checker pattern on it that wraps around the object. However, the bottom sphere blends into the background. Its mapping coordinates match the background's coordinates, so it is virtually invisible—only its shadow helps you discern the sphere's shape.

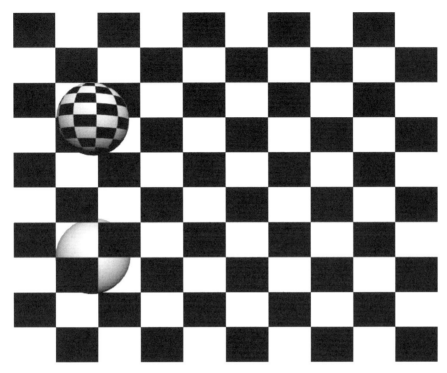

Figure 10.12   The top sphere uses explicit (object-space) mapping coordinates; the bottom sphere uses environment (world-space) mapping coordinates.

7. From the DVD, select the file OSM vs WSM 1.avi. This 320-by-240 .avi shows the spheres flying through the scene. The movement clearly shows how the object-space coordinates on the top sphere move with the sphere, while the sphere below appears to move "through" the background texture.

8. Now return to the Material Editor. Select the second (World-Space) material, and click the Go To Parent button to go to the top level of this material. Under the Blinn Basic Parameters rollout, drag the Self-Illumination slider from 0 to 100.

9. Activate your Camera01 viewport again, and render a test image. You'll notice that the bottom sphere completely disappears. It is mapped with the background image and there are no shadows on it, so it's effectively invisible.

At this point, you may well be wondering why you would want to create an invisible object in this way. Even if you needed an invisible object to, say, cast shadows on another object, you could simply apply a Matte/Shadow material to it to make it transparent to the background but still cast shadows on other objects. Or you could use a Camera Map (WSM) on the object instead.

Both of those techniques will work. However, by applying Environmental mapping coordinates to objects, you can produce a number of special effects that you can't duplicate with the Matte/Shadow material. Take the following example:

1. Return to the Material Editor, go to the WSM material, open its Checker diffuse map, and under the Checker Parameters rollout, click the Swap button to switch the black and white color swatches. Now render another test image. Result: You see that the sphere appears to invert the background image texture, but only where the sphere appears "over" the background image.

2. Return to the Material Editor again, and in the WSM material, click the Swap button to return the color swatches to their original positions. Under the Coordinates rollout, change Blur Offset from 0.0 to 0.1, then render another test image of the Camera01 viewport. Result: The bottom sphere appears to blur the background map, but again, only where the sphere appears "over" the background image.

3. Return to the Material Editor once more, go to the WSM material, turn Blur Offset back to 0.0, and click the Color #1 swatch to open the Color Selector. Change the black Color #1 swatch to RGB coordinates (0, 0, 255), bright blue; then select the Color #2 swatch and change it to RGB (255, 255, 0), bright yellow.

4. Render the Camera01 viewport. The colors that you switched on the foreground sphere (while retaining identical mapping coordinates on the background) cause the self-illuminated bottom sphere to "colorize" the background over which it passes. You can also reverse this effect: Make the background Checker pattern colorful, but have the sphere appear to turn it black and white.

You will probably use Object-Space mapping coordinates for the overwhelming majority of 3D objects in your scenes, but remember that World-Space mapping coordinates have their place as well. By slightly differentiating your WSM "foreground" object map from an existing and similar Environment Background map, you can produce an illusion of diffuse transmission such as the one that appeared in the move *Predator* (the alien Predator wore an cloaking device that slightly but characteristically distorted anything he passed in front of). This and other nifty rendering effects can be generated "in camera" and without using complex compositing tricks—a real boon if you don't have access to a compositing program such as discreet's combustion or Adobe After Effects.

Note

To properly match the anti-aliasing and texture filtering of the background image (or background plate, in VFX jargon), you should pick the Plate Match/MAX 2.5 filter from the Render tab of the Render Scene dialog and use that for your final rendering.

Multi/Sub-Objects

Multi/Sub-Object mapping is a way for 3ds max 7 users to select various components of their 3D geometry (such as groups of faces), assign different mapping ID numbers to them, and then apply one "master" material (consisting of two or more submaterials) that corresponds to each individual mapping ID number, for each group of previously selected faces.

If you think that's a convoluted definition, it's less complex than actually *doing* the process on a complex mesh. (A basic 3ds max primitive object is less of a challenge.) Regardless of the complexity, let's take a quick look at Multi/Sub-Object mapping as it pertains to one of the most common questions asked by newcomers to 3ds max: "How do I map a different texture onto every side of a box?"

Mapping the Sides of a Box

Odd as it seems, the common task of mapping the sides of a box in 3ds max 7 is actually not quite as intuitive as one might hope. The key is knowing that when you create a Box primitive in 3ds max 7, it already has Material ID numbers set on each face, and that you can change these ID assignments if you need to. Here's the process:

1. Go to Command panel > Create tab > Standard primitives and create a Box primitive in the scene of 100 units on each side.

2. Click the Modify tab, make sure the box is selected, and from the Modifiers panel, apply an Edit Mesh modifier to the box.

3. Go to the Edit Mesh modifier's Polygon sub-object level, select the top polygon of the box (in the Perspective viewport, say), and then go to the Surface Properties rollout in the Modify panel. Under Material, the Set ID number should be set to 1 (**Figure 10.13**). Click other faces on the box, and notice how the Material ID number changes. From this rollout you can also modify the ID numbers that 3ds max 7 automatically assigns to the box faces.

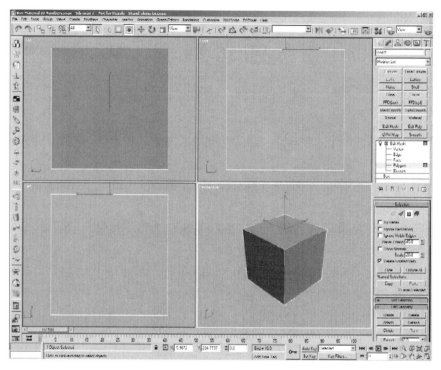

Figure 10.13   Each face of a Box primitive has Material ID numbers assigned automatically upon creation.

4. The job of assigning a different map to each face on this box is where the Multi/Sub-Object material comes in. From the DVD, load the file Box Multi-Sub Object Mapping.max. When the file loads, select the box, open the Material Editor, and take a look at the Material Settings.

   The first material slot contains the initial Multi/Sub-Object Material used on the box. It has six slots, one per box face and Material ID number (**Figure 10.14**).

5. Activate the Camera01 viewport, and render the scene (**Figure 10.15**). Each of the (self-illuminated) submaterials has one bitmap assigned to its Diffuse Color channel. These bitmaps are simply big, colorful numbers that correspond to each Material ID number.

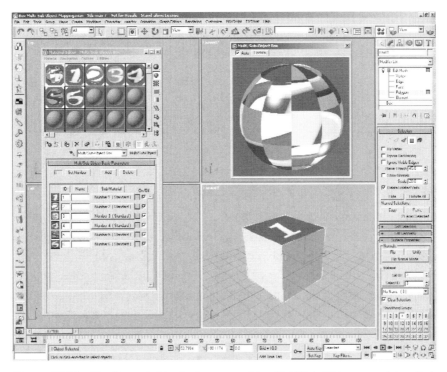

Figure 10.14   The Box primitive in the scene with a Multi/Sub-Object material applied. Each of the six Material ID numbers corresponds to one side of the box.

Figure 10.15   Each face of the box gets a different map, courtesy of the Multi/Sub-Object material.

6. To create your own Multi/Sub-Object material, click an empty Material slot, click the Standard button, and from the Material/Map Browser, pick Multi/Sub-Object. Discard the existing Standard material unless you began with a Standard material that you want to use as a submaterial in the final Multi/Sub-Object material.

Under the Multi/Sub-Object Basic Parameters rollout, you'll see a default of ten different sub-object materials. Change this number, if desired, by clicking the Set Number button. Then open each Sub-Material slot, and adjust its parameters as needed.

Mapping the Sides of Complex Objects

Suppose you would like to assign Box Multi/Sub-Object materials to more complex objects that you've built from scratch. The basic process is as follows: Apply Edit Mesh or Edit Poly modifiers to your object, select the specific faces you want to map, assign Material ID numbers to them, apply UVW mapping coordinates to each group of faces, and then repeat the process until you have the entire object mapped. If you require, say, 12 different submaterials to cover the entire object, create a new Multi/Sub-Object material, set the submaterial number to 12, and create the appropriate materials for each group of numbered faces.

Let's explore this method in detail:

1. Load the entitled Box Multi-Sub Object Map 2.max from this book's DVD. It is a tesseract-shaped object—basically, a box with each of its six faces extruded and a MeshSmooth modifier applied to chamfer the corners and sharp edges (**Figure 10.16**).

2. Activate the Camera01 or Camera02 viewport, and render the scene (**Figure 10.17**). This object has a modified version of the previous scene's Multi/Sub-Object material. (The default U and V tiling on some of the submaterial bitmaps has been changed to make them more noticeable on the different parts of the object.)

3. Select the box, then go to the Modify tab in the Command panel and look at this object's modifier stack. Yow! This object has a complex stack of Edit Mesh and UVW Map modifiers applied to create the final effect. In addition, the UVW Map modifiers are of different types—Planar, Cylindrical, and Spherical—and are oriented differently on each of their assigned groups of faces.

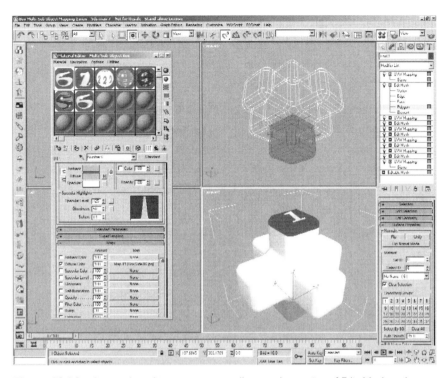

Figure 10.16   A complex object gets an equally complex series of Edit Mesh and UVW mapping coordinates assigned to its faces.

Figure 10.17   The tesseract shows the Multi/Sub-Object material assigned to its faces, using a variety of different mapping coordinates.

The Model Kit Approach

Unless you absolutely must use the above type of mapping, it may be easier to cut your model up into its component pieces like those in a plastic model kit and apply your textures to each piece. Here's how to do this:

1. Go to the Edit Geometry rollout of the Modify panel. Detach the desired group (or groups) of selected faces, and give each new object a unique name. Then apply separate Standard (not Multi/Sub-Object) materials and mapping coordinates to the individual pieces of the original object.

2. There are times when you can't do this; sometimes you must keep your geometry in one piece. However, you can still cut apart your model, apply materials and mapping coordinates to each piece in turn, and then put the pieces back together.

3. To rebuild, select one collapsed mesh piece, and from the Modify tab of the Command panel, click the Attach or Attach List button under the Edit Geometry rollout. (Or press the H key to bring up the Select By Name menu to speed up this process.) You'll be given the option of Condensing your existing Materials and ID numbers into a new Multi/Sub-Object material (**Figure 10.18**).

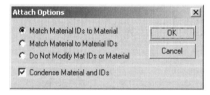

Figure 10.18 The Attach Options box allows you to pick different types of Multi/Sub-Object material "consolidation" schemes.

4. Go to your Material Editor and modify the components of this new Multi/Sub-Object material as necessary.

Decal Techniques

Here's another texture-mapping question commonly asked by newcomers to 3ds max: "How do you place a bitmap 'label'—basically, a decal—on top of another map?"

There are many ways to layer textures in 3ds max. You can use Mix maps, Masks, Blend materials, Shellac materials, Composite materials, and combinations of all these. But the simplest way to add a Decal bitmap on another map is to make sure that the decal image has an alpha (masking) channel and then use it in a Mix map in a Standard material Diffuse Color slot.

Applying a Decal

Here are the specifics of how to make decals in 3ds max 7:

1. Go to Command panel > Create tab > Create a Sphere, setting the radius to 50 units. Increase the Segments value to 60 to make it smooth, and make sure that the Generate Mapping Coordinates check box is checked (as mentioned earlier, it will be checked automatically unless you've deselected it).

2. Open the Material Editor, click the first material slot, and go down to the Maps rollout. Click the Diffuse Color map button. When the Material/Map Browser appears, double-click Mix.

3. In the Mix Parameters rollout, next to the Color #1 (black) swatch, click the Maps button, and from the Material/Map Browser, pick Noise. Leave the Noise settings as they are, then click the Go To Parent button to return to the top level of the Mix map.

4. Click the Maps button next to the Color #2 swatch. From the Material/Map Browser, pick Bitmap. When the Select Bitmap Image File menu appears, go to the DVD and select the file Decal with Alpha.tga, then click the View button. The Decal with Alpha.tga image is a 32-bit image of beveled text.

5. In the View window, click the Display Alpha Channel button to the right of the three (selected) RGB color component buttons. The text turns pure white. This is the alpha or masking channel for the color text.

6. Close the View window, and then click Open to load the bitmap image into the Mix map Color #2 slot. Under the Bitmap Parameters rollout, click the Alpha radio button under the Mono Channel Output section of the menu. Then click the Go To Parent button to return to the top level of the Mix map.

7. Left-click-drag the Color #2 Decal bitmap down to the Mix Amount map slot. When the Copy (Instance) Map menu appears, make sure Instance is selected, then click OK.

8. Finally, make sure your sphere is selected, click the Assign Material to Selection button, then activate your Perspective viewport and render the scene. Your rendering should look something like the ActiveShade Perspective viewport (**Figure 10.19**). (Note that, for this illustration, the Show Map in Viewport button of the Decal bitmap is checked so that the bitmap appears also in the Shaded Perspective viewport.)

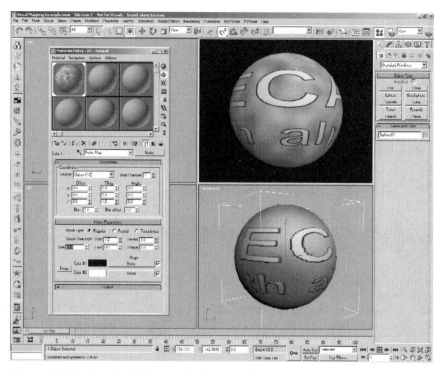

Figure 10.19   The Decal bitmap with the alpha channel appears over the Noise texture on the sphere.

Now you've got a Decal bitmap floating on top of the underlying Noise texture, but the decal is wrapped around the sphere using the default mapping coordinates. (It's also stretched horizontally, but we'll fix that in a second.) This is not the effect you would normally want—you more likely want the decal to look like a label applied to a smaller area of the sphere.

9. To do this, go back to the Material Editor, click one of the Instanced Decal with Alpha bitmap slots to open it, and under the Coordinates rollout, change both the U and the V Tiling from 1.0 to 4.0. Now rerender your scene (**Figure 10.20**).

Now the decal is smaller on the sphere, but it's also tiled across the surface, and you want it to appear only once. You also want to fix the stretch problem, which is caused by the fact that the square Decal bitmap is made to appear twice as wide by the sphere's inherent Spherical mapping coordinates. Fixing both problems is not difficult.

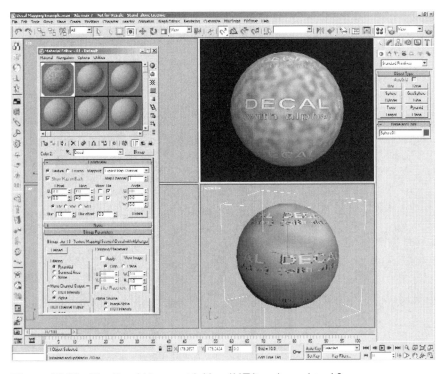

Figure 10.20   The Decal bitmap with U and V Tiling changed to 4.0.

10. Return to the Material Editor. Under Coordinates, change the U Tiling from 4.0 to 8.0 (leave the V Tiling of 4.0 unchanged), then uncheck both the U and the V Tile buttons. (Don't check the Mirror buttons, either—leave them blank as well.) Then rerender your scene (**Figure 10.21**). The Decal bitmap now appears smaller on the sphere, and the surrounding Tiled images of it disappear, since you unchecked the Tile boxes.

11. To reposition the decal on the surface of the sphere (while not affecting the underlying Noise texture), return to the Material Editor, and under Coordinates, adjust the U and V Offset values. Changing these will enable you to place the Decal bitmap anywhere you want. Experiment with these settings, and do some test renderings to see the results.

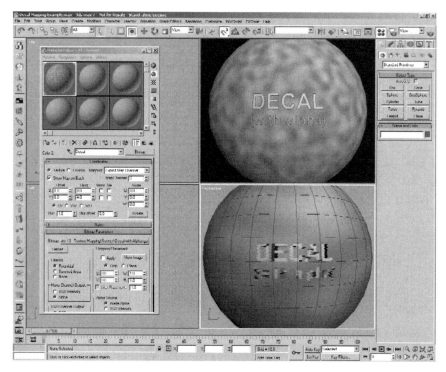

Figure 10.21 The Decal bitmap with U Tiling changed to 8.0 and the Tile boxes unchecked.

If your original "decal" bitmap does not have an alpha channel, you'll have to create one. You can load the bitmap into Adobe Photoshop, add a new channel to the image, and then either paint a new alpha mask for your bitmap or create one from your existing RGB image elements. To do this, you might paste the image into a new Photoshop file, change it to grayscale, then increase the Brightness and Contrast settings until you get a solid mask. You can then paste this image back into the alpha channel of the existing bitmap and re-save it in a file format that supports 32-bit images, such as .tif, .tga, or .png. The .gif and .jpg file formats do not support alpha channels.

Summing Up

In this chapter, we took a quick look at the core 3ds max shader, map, and material types, the difference between World-Space and Object-Space mapping, Multi/Sub-Object mapping, and simple techniques for overlaying decals.

In the next chapter, we'll tackle more complex texture-mapping techniques and combine these with various shaders and custom textures to create impressive and useful effects.

Chapter 11

Developing Textures

By Jon A. Bell

In the previous chapter, we introduced the 3ds max 7 Material Editor; discussed map, material, and shader types; and looked at basic texture-mapping techniques, including Multi/Sub-Object mapping and placing decals on objects.

In this chapter, we'll explore more complex texture-mapping techniques and learn more about texture creation. Among the topics we'll cover are the following:

- Planar mapping
- Procedural mapping
- Noise and Falloff maps
- Diffuse shading: Blinn and Oren-Nayar-Blinn
- Multi-Layer materials

This chapter, like the previous one, covers the standard 3ds max 7 shader types, materials, and maps for the 3ds max Default Scanline Renderer only.

Planar Mapping

When you apply a UVW Map modifier to an object or to selected object faces, the mapping gizmo defaults to Planar mapping coordinates, the simplest type of UVW mapping coordinates. Planar mapping simply projects a flat version of your bitmap onto your selected object or faces. (Procedural maps, such as Noise, Checker, and Smoke, don't need specific mapping coordinates.) Planar mapping works best when applied to surfaces that are mainly parallel to the mapping plane itself. If polygons on the surface slant more than 45 degrees away from parallel, then you'll probably see smearing or stretching of a bitmap texture along those areas.

Planar mapping coordinates come in handy when you wish to create custom bitmap textures that fit your geometry perfectly. The basic approach is to apply the 3ds max rendering feature Render Bounding Box/Selected. This feature allows you to render an image of a selected object to specific dimensions constrained by an orthographic "bounding box" view. You can then load the image into any image editor and use it as a template for painting a custom bitmap texture for the object. When you're finished with the painted bitmap, load it into the appropriate map slot (usually Diffuse Color) and apply it to the original object. Since the object has already been UVW-mapped, your custom-painted details will fit it exactly.

Using Planar Mapping for Texturing

In the following example, we'll see how to use Planar mapping to create a custom bitmap texture for a simple jet fighter model.

The scene shows a futuristic fighter plane model built using box modeling and MeshSmooth techniques. The model is split into two major components—the upper and lower fuselage surfaces—with a Fuselage Middle Strip piece running around the midline of the plane. The basic jet design is rather flat, so applying a Planar UVW map to the top and bottom surfaces will enable you to apply custom bitmap textures covering the majority of the plane's body. (You could then apply a separate Cylindrical UVW map to the Fuselage Middle Strip piece to finish it off.)

1. From this book's DVD, load the file Future Jet Planar Map.max (**Figure 11.1**).

2. In the Camera01 viewport, click the Fuselage Top piece to select it. (If you go to the Modify panel, you'll see that it already has Planar UVW mapping coordinates applied.) Now click the Render Type drop-down menu (on your top, Main toolbar) to bring up a list of render options. Select the Box Selected option.

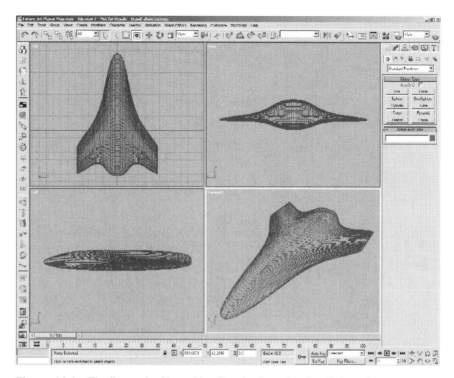

Figure 11.1   The Future Jet Planar Map (Render Bounding Box/Selected) example scene.

3. Right-click your Top viewport to activate it, then select Rendering > Render > Render. When you do, a Render Bounding Box/Selected menu will appear (**Figure 11.2**).

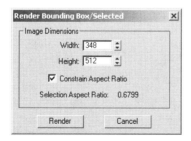

Figure 11.2   The Render Bounding Box/Selected menu.

4. The Future Jet Height and Width orthographic rendering values are constrained by the Constrain Aspect Ratio check box, below; in most cases this box should be checked. The width of the top-view bounding box is 348 pixels; the height is 512 pixels.

5. Change the Height value to 800 and hit Enter. When you do, you'll see the width "scale up" to match the new Height value.

6. Click the Render button. After a moment, the image will render (**Figure 11.3**).

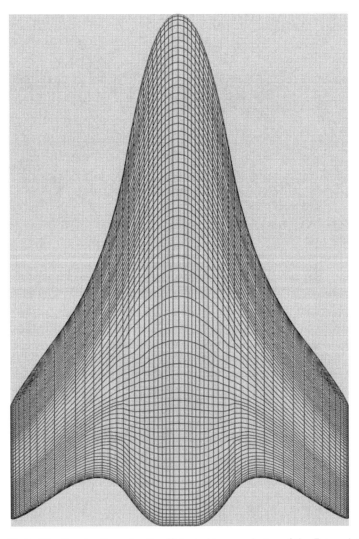

Figure 11.3   The Render Bounding Box/Selected top rendering of the Future Jet fuselage.

For this example, I've applied a black wireframe texture. This enables you to follow the actual wireframe contours of your model as a template or guide in placing painted details in your image editing program. You can also render a shaded version of the model or one with a preliminary bitmap texture already applied that you can then paint over or retouch.

7. Click the Save Bitmap button in the Rendered Frame window and save the image in whatever file format you want. You can then use this example image as a painting template in your image editor.

8. To see an example of the basic Planar maps applied to the jet, load the file Future Jet Top Texture.max from this book's DVD. When the file loads, activate the Camera01 viewport and render the scene.

9. The rendered image (**Figure 11.4**) shows this simple fighter mapped with a basic texture applied to the Fuselage Top piece. I used the Render Bounding Box/Selected top view of the fighter as a template for the details, which I created in Adobe Photoshop. You can see the texture I painted by opening the Material Editor and looking at the Top Planar Map material's Diffuse bitmap image (Future Jet Top Color.tif).

Figure 11.4 A rendered example of the Fighter Jet with a basic Planar-mapped texture on the top fuselage piece.

Note

If you want to modify or improve this texture (and finish the rest of the jet!), feel free; the files you need are on the DVD.

Procedural Mapping

Now that you've taken a quick look at Planar mapping and Render Bounding Box/Selected, let's investigate some of 3ds max 7's most useful map types: Noise and Falloff. These procedural maps are extremely versatile and can be applied in many situations to solve difficult texturing problems and to create quick and eye-catching texture effects.

Noise Mapping

Noise maps, which apply random marks to a surface, among the most widely used of procedural materials. Typically employed to reduce unwanted smoothness and add grain and grunge to a surface, Noise is also useful for creating lightning, fire, and water effects. Caustic patterns, the lighting effects caused by internal reflections and refractions in a body of water, can be made with a Noise map by loading it as a projector map in a spotlight or projector light. A Noise map employed as a Diffusion map in the 3ds max 7 Raytrace material is effective for "dirtying up" underlying textures. And Noise can break up tiled bitmap patterns that look too regular.

Falloff maps, which set 3D gradients, are also quite versatile, especially when you need unusual effects. Use Falloff maps to make reflection maps more realistic; to add iridescence and pearlescence to a surface; and to create X-ray effects and what I call the "retro computer graphics" look.

Using Noise Maps

The following steps show some quick examples of Noise maps in action:

1. Load the file Noise Tiling Mask.max from the DVD. You'll see a very simple scene: a Quad Patch object representing the ground, with a targeted camera looking at it and a spotlight shining down (**Figure 11.5**).

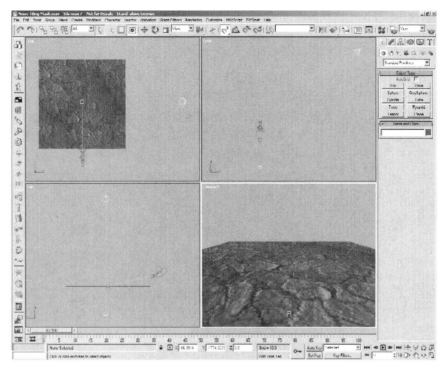

Figure 11.5   A simple test scene to demonstrate texture tiling and masking with the Noise map.

2. Activate your Camera01 viewport and render this test scene. The rendering shows a cracked mud texture on the Quad Patch object representing the ground (**Figure 11.6**). I created this texture by retouching a scanned photo of a real cracked mud surface and made it seamlessly tileable by using Adobe Photoshop's Filter: Offset > Wrap Around feature.

3. Open the Material Editor, and you'll see that the Cracked Mud material applied to the Quad Patch is in Slot #1. Click the Diffuse Color map slot to open it, and take a look at the Cracked Mud A.jpg bitmap settings. Tiling is currently set to 1.0 on both U and V, so change these settings from 1.0 to 3.0 and render the scene again.

4. With that change, the map now tiles seamlessly across the surface of the Quad Patch. In other words, you can't see obvious edges. However, the overall pattern in the mud texture noticeably repeats. There are bothersome dark areas that repeat diagonally across the surface (**Figure 11.7**).

Figure 11.6   A cracked mud bitmap texture applied to the Quad Patch object.

Figure 11.7   The cracked mud bitmap texture tiled 3 by 3 across the surface.

An excellent way to fix visible tiling artifacts like this one is to mix the existing bitmap with another bitmap, with each tiled differently, then blend them with a completely non-repeating procedural map (such as Noise!).

5. Return to the Material Editor, make sure you're in the Diffuse Color map slot, and click the Bitmap button. When the Material/Map Browser appears, make sure New is checked in the Browse From section, double-click Mix, and choose "Keep old map as sub-map" when the Replace Map dialog appears. You now have a new Mix map, with the Cracked Mud A.jpg bitmap loaded into the Color #1 (top) slot.

6. Click-hold and drag this map from the Color #1 slot to the Color #2 slot, choose Copy (*not* Instance) when the Copy Instance Map dialog appears, then click OK.

7. Open this new map slot and change both the U and the V tiling from 3.0 to 7.0. Under Angle, leave the U and V values at 0.0, but change W from 0.0 to 90.0. This will rotate the existing map 90 degrees.

8. Click the Go To Parent button to return to the Mix map level, then click the Map button next to the Mix Amount spinner. When the Material/Map Browser appears, pick Noise from the list.

9. Activate your Camera01 viewport again and render the scene (**Figure 11.8**).

Figure 11.8 Two differently tiled bitmap textures blended with a Noise map.

What you've done is to blend two differently tiled bitmap textures together with a grayscale Noise procedural map. Since the Noise procedural map is a mathematically random texture, it camouflages the appearance of unwanted repeating textures.

To take further advantage of this Noise mapping technique, try the following:

- Load different bitmaps in each Mix map slot.

- Change the Noise Threshold settings to make the transitions between the two bitmaps more distinct.

- Use other procedural maps, such as Dent, Marble, Smoke, Stucco, and so on, to blend the bitmaps.

Fun with Falloff

As mentioned earlier, the Falloff map is also one of the most useful of the 3ds max 7 procedural maps. Once you master it, you will find reasons to use it often.

Understanding the use of Falloff maps can save you time and effort in producing effects such as reflections. For example, I use Falloff frequently in the Reflection map slot of a Standard material to fix problems in the rendering of highly reflective objects.

Often, you don't need to render physically correct reflections (raytraced reflections, for example) for your scene; a simple Reflection map can suffice, and it will render much faster than a raytraced reflection. However, the default Reflection mapping often produces reflective objects that look self-illuminated, especially in 3D scenes with dim lighting. Although we tend to think of reflective objects such as chrome-plated car bumpers as "bright," they actually don't have the high ambient value of brightly colored or self-illuminated objects—they simply reflect their surroundings. So a self-illuminated appearance for such objects usually looks wrong.

One way to fix this is to knock down the levels of apparent illumination along the edges of the reflective object, reducing the strength and brightness of the reflection in those areas. The Falloff map is perfectly suited for this effect.

Modifying a Reflection with a Falloff Map

The following steps show how to use a Falloff map to tone down a reflection:

1. From the DVD, load the file Reflection Falloff Example.max. Once again you'll see a very simple scene: a Sphere primitive sitting inside a large Box

primitive, with multiple spotlights shining on the sphere (**Figure 11.9**). (Show Map in viewport should be turned off for the Reflection Map Example" material in the .max file, to make the Camera01 viewport in the scene look like the viewport in Figure 11.9.)

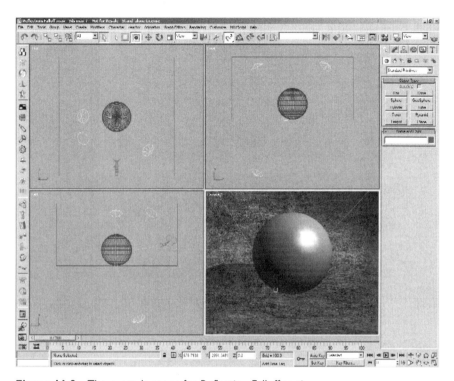

Figure 11.9   The example scene for Reflection Falloff testing.

2. Open the Material Editor, and look at the materials used in the scene. The Reflection Map Example material is applied to the sphere; it consists of a "copper" texture bitmap (Copper Sheet Scratches Dark.jpg) loaded in the Reflection map slot. Environmental: Spherical Environment mapping coordinates are used. The Room Interior texture uses the same copper image, but this time as a simple Diffuse Color and Bump map, with no reflection component.

3. Activate your Camera01 viewport and render the scene (**Figure 11.10**).

Figure 11.10   A "copper" bitmap texture applied as a Reflection map on the sphere and as a Diffuse Color and Bump map on the walls of the surrounding box.

4. Note that the sphere appears to reflect the scratchy copper texture in the room, but the sphere itself is a bit too bright—the reflection makes it look self-illuminated. We will address this problem by adjusting the look of the reflection with the Falloff map.

5. Return to the Material Editor, click the Reflection map slot of the first material to open it, and then click the Bitmap button. When the Material/Map Browser appears, make sure New is checked in the Browse From section, double-click Falloff, and choose "Keep old map as sub-map" when the Replace Map dialog appears. The copper bitmap loads into the Front (top) slot of the Perpendicular/Parallel Falloff type (the default).

6. Activate your Camera01 viewport and render the scene again.

   Hmm, this isn't very good—the white "outer" color makes the sphere look not just self-illuminated, but also translucent in the center, which isn't the effect we want. Let's fix this now.

7. Return to the Material Editor. Click-hold and drag the Black (front) color swatch down to the White (side) slot to make it black as well. Or you can choose Copy in the Copy or Swap Colors dialog. Now rerender the sphere.

8. Result: The sphere reflection shades off into a darker color along the edges of the sphere, relative to the camera (**Figure 11.11**).

Figure 11.11   The modified Perpendicular/Parallel Falloff type reflection.

9. Return to the Material Editor, click the Swap Colors/Maps button on the right-hand side of the Falloff Parameters rollout, then render the Camera01 viewport again. The sphere retains most of its Diffuse color, but the reflection now appears more along the edges of the object.

10. Return to the Material Editor. Under Falloff Type, change the type from Perpendicular/Parallel to Fresnel, then render the Camera01 viewport again. The Fresnel falloff type restricts the reflection to the very outer edges of the sphere, relative to the Camera01 viewpoint.

11. Return to the Material Editor once more. Under Falloff Type, change the type from Perpendicular/Parallel to Shadow/Light, then render the Camera01 viewport again. You can see the difference in the reflection effect (**Figure 11.12**). The "glow" is gone.

Figure 11.12   The Shadow/Light Falloff type used in the Reflection map slot.

As its name implies, the Shadow/Light Falloff type restricts whatever procedural map or bitmap type has been applied to the areas that are either illuminated by the lights in your scene or else fall into shadow. This is perhaps the most useful setting for ensuring that your reflection maps don't make your object appear to be self-illuminated.

 Note

You can also reverse this concept to impart an edge-lit look to your objects.

Using Falloff for Iridescent Effects

For the next Falloff example, we'll create some iridescent effects using the Falloff map to mix two very different material colors.

Iridescence in nature is the rainbow effect seen on the surface of a soap bubble, oil slick, or other surface with special refractive properties. Iridescence can depend on the angle at which you view the surface of an object (as with a beetle's carapace, scratched aluminum, or stainless steel) or the nature of chemical reactions occurring on the surface (as with the aforementioned soap bubble and oil slick).

First we'll create a simple iridescent material:

1. From the DVD, load the file Human Skull.max (**Figure 11.13**). This high-resolution human skull model is perfect for demonstrating some of the properties of Falloff.

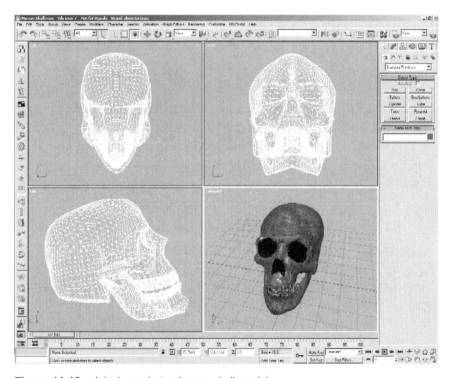

Figure 11.13   A high-resolution human skull model.

2. Activate your Camera01 viewport and render the image (**Figure 11.14**).

Figure 11.14 The skull model with its existing moldy texture.

Now let's discard the existing skull texture and create an iridescent effect.

3. Open the Material Editor, select an unused material slot, and change the Material Type from Standard to Blend. (You can discard the existing material if you want.) Click the Material 1 (the button calls it "#0") slot, and when it opens, change its Diffuse Color values to RGB coordinates (0, 0, 128), dark blue. Change the Specular color to RGB (255, 255, 255), pure white, the Specular Level to 100, and Glossiness to 25. Change the material name to Blue and click the Go To Parent button.

4. Open Material 2 and change the Diffuse Color values to RGB (0, 255, 0), pure bright green). Change the Specular color to RGB (255, 255, 255), or pure white, the Specular Level to 100, and Glossiness to 25. Change this material name to Green, click the Go To Parent icon again, and name the Blend material Iridescent Blue-Green.

5. Click the Mask button, and when the Material/Map Browser appears, make sure New is selected. Select Falloff, and when it appears in the Material Editor, you'll see the sample sphere (or box) in the Material Editor change to a dark blue with a bright green halo around its edges.

6. Next, select the skull geometry (either from your viewports or from the Select Objects dialog), and assign the Iridescent Blue-Green material to it.

7. When you're finished, activate your Camera01 viewport and render the scene (**Figure 11.15**). (The shading effects will be obviously more noticeable on your screen, in color, than in this black-and-white illustration.)

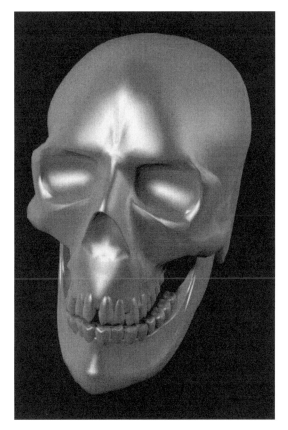

Figure 11.15   The Falloff map blends two different material colors and creates unusual shading effects across the surface of this model.

The end result looks a bit like an old 1960s blacklight poster. As you can see on your screen, the bright green material appears on the outer edges of the geometry, roughly parallel to your Camera01 viewpoint. The green material then blends into the dark blue material, which appears predominantly on the surfaces that are more perpendicular to your viewpoint. This iridescent effect can be quite striking when applied to complex geometry and enhanced with different Diffuse Color, Bump, or Reflection maps.

Again, as with the earlier Falloff Reflection map examples, you can return to the Material Editor, change the Falloff type to Fresnel or other settings, and rerender to check the results.

Creating a "Retro CG" or X-Ray Material

Continuing our exploration of Falloff map effects, here's a simple way to modify the material you've just created to produce an X-ray effect or a "retro computer graphics" look:

1. Go to the Material Editor and drag-copy the Iridescent Blue-Green Blend material to another material slot. Change this new material's name to X-Ray Green, select the Skull model (if it's not already selected), and apply the X-Ray material to it.

2. Open the existing Green material component (Material #2) of the X-Ray Green material. Make sure the Diffuse Color is RGB (0, 255, 0), bright green. Change Glossiness to 40 and Specular Level to 30, then change the Self-Illumination value to 100.

3. Open the Extended Parameters section. Verify that Falloff is set to In, set the Amount to 100, and change Falloff Type to Additive.

4. Click the Go To Parent button, drag the Green Material #2 up to the (current) Blue Material #1 slot, make it a Copy (not an Instance), and then open this new material. Change its name from Green to Inner, and then make the Diffuse Color pure black, or RGB (0, 0, 0). Change Self-Illumination to 0.

5. Now activate your Camera01 viewport, and render a test image (**Figure 11.16**).

You've undoubtedly seen this computer graphics look in older movies and TV shows, where wireframe or edge-lit computer graphics were employed to illustrate technical data. It's still a useful technique for depicting the inner workings of mechanical devices for industrial or illustrative work.

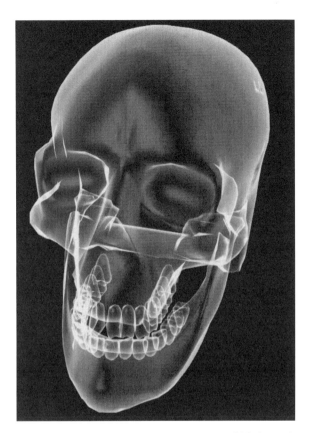

Figure 11.16 The new X-Ray Green material creates an old-fashioned computer graphics look.

So, how else can we use this material? It would be particularly effective used in medical graphics, as for example on a complex human skeleton mesh (especially if that mesh were itself inside another, properly proportioned human mesh object). By changing the green outer color to a bluish-white and adjusting the Glossiness and Specular Level values, you could simulate the Martian spaceport "full-body X-ray scanner" scene in the movie *Total Recall*.

More Falloff Map Suggestions

Here are some additional Falloff mapping tricks you can try:

- Change the Material Effects channel of Material 1 (the "outer" material) to 1 or above, and then apply a Lens Effects Glow to it. With a careful choice of material color gradients (such as blue-white or purple, shading off to black) and Glow, you can simulate an eerie ultraviolet or black-light look.

- Apply an automatic (Raytrace) Reflection map to just one of the materials. This would work best on an object surrounded by other geometry and an Environment map.

- Use a Raytrace map for one of the materials.

Diffuse Shading

Now let's take a look at how 3ds max 7's various shader types allow you to alter the appearance of light across a 3D surface. Here, we'll look at "dry rock" settings, then modify them to produce the illusion of wet, shiny rock. By animating certain material parameters, we can even simulate the appearance of water cascading down the rock face.

Diffuse shaders, which use a map to spread out (diffuse) the play of light across an object, are the key to these effects. Of 3ds max 7's available diffuse shader types (see below), the Oren-Nayar-Blinn type is especially well suited for rough, dry surfaces such as rock, stucco, brick, and the like. Such substances tend to absorb and scatter light with little falloff across their surface. For many rough, matte, or satin materials, an Oren-Nayar-Blinn look is more realistic than those created by the standard Phong- or Blinn-shaded materials, even if you've cranked down the specular highlights on the material. Overall, altering the shader types of your materials to better match their real-world physical lighting responses can dramatically improve the overall realism of your renderings.

Creating a Dry Rock Surface

Let's investigate how Oren-Nayar-Blinn diffuse shading can be made to produce a dry rock effect.

1. From the DVD, load the file Dry Rock Example.max (**Figure 11.17**).

    The Dry Rock Example.max scene consists of a high-res Quad Patch object sitting in the middle of your 3ds max 7 desktop, with several shadow-casting spotlights pointing at it. (One spotlight is off at the moment; ignore it for now.) If you click the Quad Patch object and go to the Modify panel, you'll see that the Quad Patch grid has a Displace modifier applied to it below the UVW Map modifier. A bitmap called Dry Rock.jpg is used to distort the patch geometry.

2. Open the Material Editor and take a look at the material in Slot #1. This material, called Dry Rock, consists of a Blinn-shaded material with the Dry Rock bitmap loaded in both the Diffuse Color and Bump map slots.

3. Open the Diffuse Color map slot and View the Dry Rock.jpg image (**Figure 11.18**).

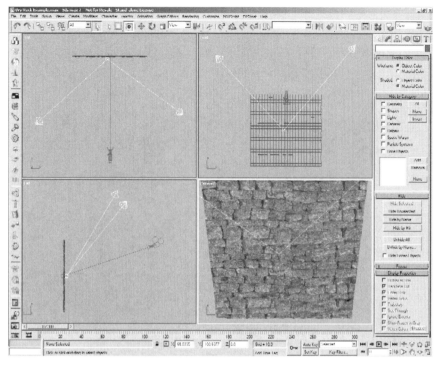

Figure 11.17   The Dry Rock Example test scene.

Figure 11.18   A mossy stone wall texture.

This seamlessly tileable bitmap is of a stone wall with light tan and brown rough-hewn rocks; the rocks are covered in various mosses and lichens, which give them a further mottled appearance.

4. Close the Diffuse Color map, choose Go to Parent, activate the Camera01 viewport, and render the scene (**Figure 11.19**).

Figure 11.19   The Dry Rock.jpg texture used on the Displaced Quad Patch objects.

As your rendering shows, the Dry Rock.jpg bitmap, coupled with the intense multiple spotlights in the scene, produces a bright rock face.

5. Return to the Material Editor, and change the shader type of the Dry Rock material from Blinn to Oren-Nayar-Blinn. (You may need to Go To Parent to see this.) As you do, you'll notice that the sample sphere in Material Slot #1 becomes darker.

6. Now render the scene again, and notice the differences between this rendering and the previous one with the Blinn shader type. I suggest using the Clone Rendered Frame Window tool to compare these.

Creating a Wet Rock Surface

Now that you've seen the differences between Blinn and Oren-Nayar-Blinn shader types for the dry rock, what about creating the illusion of wet rock? In the next example, you'll modify the textures used on this rock face to create the illusion of wet, shiny rock. You'll even see how using an animated Noise map in the Glossiness slot produces the effect of sheets of water cascading down the rock face.

To create a wet rock surface, follow these steps:

1. Return to the Material Editor, and click Material Slot #2. Change the name of this material to Wet Rock 1, and then change the Diffuse Color to RGB (137, 50, 50). Make Specular pure white, or RGB (255, 255, 255). Keep this material's shader type set to Blinn.

2. Under Specular Highlights, change the Specular Level to 200 and Glossiness to 50.

3. Go to the Maps rollout, and open the Diffuse Color slot. When the Material/Map Browser appears, double-click the RGB Multiply map to load it. In the RGB Multiply map, click the name slot for Color #1, and select Bitmap from the Material/Map Browser. Next, from the Select Bitmap Image File menu, select the image Dry Rock.jpg from the DVD. When you return to the Material Editor, change UV Tiling to U 1.0, V 2.0, then click the Go To Parent button.

4. Drag-copy the Dry Rock.jpg bitmap from the Color #1 slot down to Color #2. Make it a Copy, not an Instance. Then click the Go To Parent button again. Drag-copy the entire RGB Multiply map from the Diffuse map slot down to the Bump map slot, but make this an Instance. (You want any changes you make to the Diffuse component to be updated for the Bump map.)

5. Click the Glossiness slot, and from the Material/Map Browser, select Noise. Change the Noise type to Fractal, and under Noise Parameters, change Size from 25 to 1. Then click the Go To Parent button to return to the top-level rollout of the Material Editor.

6. Now select the Quad Patch object in your scene, apply this new Wet Rock 1 material to it, then activate the Camera01 viewport and render the scene (**Figure 11.20**).

   The rock face no longer looks completely dry, but the rock surface still needs to look wetter and more saturated.

Figure 11.20 The duplicated Dry Rock.jpg image used in both slots of an RGB Multiply material darkens the overall image.

7. Press the H key to bring up the Select Objects dialog, and select the (inactive) Spot03 spotlight. As your viewports indicate, the Spot03 spotlight is a duplicate of Spot01, which has been moved down slightly along its local Z axis. This produces a "doubled-up" light that greatly enhances the apparent illumination provided by the spotlight on the upper left side of the rock face.

   Now, you may be asking yourself, "Why duplicate the Spot01 light at all? Why not simply increase the existing Spot01 Multiplier from 1.5 to an even higher setting?" The reason you're doing this is so you have greater control over the lighting on both the Diffuse and Specular components of the Quad Patch object, as you'll see in a second.

8. With Spot03 selected, go to the Modify panel and check the Spot03 Light's On box. Then, under the Advanced Effects rollout's Affect Surfaces area, uncheck Diffuse, but leave Specular checked. Now the Spot03 light will affect only the

specular highlights of the Quad Patch object; it won't add light to the Diffuse component of the material.

9. Return to the Material Editor and make the following changes to the Wet Rock 1 material. Go to the Diffuse Color map slot and open the RGB Multiply material. Click the Color #2 slot, click the Bitmap button (under Bitmap Parameters), and from the DVD, load the file Wet Rock.jpg.

   The Wet Rock.jpg image is a darker, more saturated version of the original Dry Rock.jpg image. I created this image by loading the "dry" version into Adobe Photoshop and using the Multiply feature to layer it several times on top of itself. I then increased the brightness and contrast of the image to produce the final result.

10. Click the Go To Parent button twice to return to the top level of the Material Editor, activate your Camera01 viewport, and render another test image (**Figure 11.21**).

Figure 11.21 The darker Wet Rock.jpg image, when used in the second RGB Multiply slot, creates an even more saturated rock face.

Now we're starting to get closer to our ideal wet rock surface. The combination of multiple spotlights—including Spot03, which affects only the Rock Face's specular component—and the dark, saturated, and very shiny material creates the illusion of a wet, mossy green surface.

Animating the Water Effect

Animating the wet rock effect so that the water appears to be flowing down over the rock surface involves building on the mapping effects we've already created. You can do this in a number of different ways.

One obvious approach would be to apply a particle emitter (or several) to the rock face geometry. By adding a particle system with a high particle count, then applying Object Space Deflectors, Wind Space Warps, Gravity Space Warps, or a combination of these, you could suggest sparkling water droplets bouncing down the surface. However, if you want to produce a more subtle effect, you can still suggest flowing water without using a particle system at all. The trick is to animate the coordinates of the Noise map used in the Wet Rock 1 Glossiness slot.

To do this, select the Animate Auto Key button and go to the last frame (number 300) of the scene used in the wet rock tutorial. Then return to the Material Editor and open the Glossiness/Noise slot of the Wet Rock 1 material. Under XYZ Coordinates, change the Y Offset value from 0 to 300, turn off the Auto Key button, and drag the Time Slider back to frame 0. As you do, you'll see the specular highlight on the sample sphere in Slot #2 change as the Noise coordinates animate.

A rendered version of this sequence is available as Wet Rock.avi on the DVD. As the file plays, you'll see that the animated Noise texture, when used in the Glossiness slot, creates the impression that a thin sheet of water is flowing down the surface of the rock.

 Note

The relevant files are included on the DVD as Wet Rock Example 1.max and Wet Rock Example 2.max.

Multi-Layer Materials

Another useful type of material shading in 3ds max 7 is the Multi-Layer material. This material can be used to create shiny materials that have depth, such as lacquered paint surfaces. Although similar to a standard Phong or Blinn shader type, the Multi-Layer material gives you the ability to define multiple specular highlights. The blending between these multiple layers is additive, which produces an extremely glossy appearance.

Creating a Lacquered Surface

Here's how to create a shiny "car lacquer" surface using Multi-Layer materials:

1. From the DVD, load the file Lacquer Paint.max. You'll see a simple sphere sitting in the middle of a room with several spotlights illuminating the scene (**Figure 11.22**). An omni light provides additional illumination for the walls.

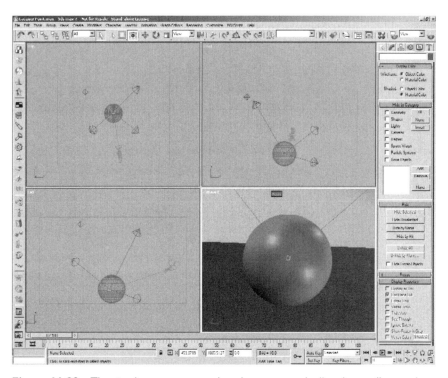

Figure 11.22 The simple test scene used to demonstrate the "car lacquer" example.

2. Open the Material Editor and select the first sample slot, or Material #1. You'll alter this material to create the "red car paint." First, change the name to Red Lacquer Paint 1, then click the Shading drop-down and change the default shader type from Blinn to Multi-Layer.

3. Next, go down to the Multi-Layer Basic Parameters rollout, and take a look at the settings. You'll see the standard color swatches for Ambient and Diffuse, but you'll also see a spinner box for Diffuse Level and separate sections for two different Specular Layer sections. You'll also see spinners for Anisotropy, which allows you to create nonuniform specular highlights on the surface of your objects.

4. If you open the Maps section of the rollout, you'll see several new map slots, including Diffuse Level and Diffuse Roughness, and separate maps for Specular Color, Specular Levels 1 and 2, Glossiness 1 and 2, Anisotropy 1 and 2, and Orientation 1 and 2 (which affect anisotropy). Each enables you to adjust the settings for the underlying "base" coat of the material and the overlaying "lacquer" coating.

5. Return to the Multi-Layer Basic Parameters rollout, and make the following changes. If the Ambient and Diffuse Color swatches are locked, unlock them, then change Ambient to RGB (0, 0, 0), pure black. Change Diffuse to RGB (128, 0, 0), dark red. Change Diffuse Level to 40—this mixes the primary red Diffuse color with the black Ambient, making it darker and more rich.

6. Change the Specular Layer 1 color to pure white, or RGB (255, 255, 255). Then change the Level value to 150 and the Glossiness value to 75. You'll see a bright, hot specular highlight appear on the sample sphere in Material Slot #1.

7. Next, go down to the Specular Layer 2 section, and change its Color to RGB (255, 0, 0), bright red. Then change the Level value to 75 and the Glossiness value to 35.

8. Select the Sphere01 object in your scene, apply the Red Lacquer Paint 1 material to it, activate your Camera01 viewport, and render a test image (**Figure 11.23**).

The effect is subtle, but noticeable. What you should see is how the second specular layer spreads out underneath the hot-white specular highlight produced by the Specular Layer 1 settings. The image looks extremely glossy—almost wet—and simulates the effect of a lacquer car paint. These types of paint finishes produce multiple specular highlights, with underlying specular highlights that are softer and more diffused; the clear gloss coating on top of the surface then provides a sharper, additive highlight on the surface.

Figure 11.23   The red lacquer paint example.

Creating a "Candy Apple" Finish

Let's dress up this effect a little more. What if we add a map to the second Glossiness slot to spread out and further diffuse the softer specular highlight? The effect we're striving for is similar to a "candy apple" or metal-flake car finish, where tiny bits of metal suspended in the paint emulsion generate iridescent sparkles on the underlying layer(s).

To create a candy apple finish, follow these steps:

1. Return to the Material Editor and go down to the Maps rollout. Double-click the Name button for Specular Level 2, and when the Material/Map Browser appears, click Noise.

2. Under Noise Parameters, change Noise Type from Regular to Fractal and then change Size from 25.0 to 0.25—you want the overall size to be fairly small. Change the name of this map to Noise Specular 2 (you're going to reuse this map in the next example).

3. Click the Go To Parent button to return to the main Material Editor level, activate your Camera01 viewport again, and render another test image (**Figure 11.24**).

Figure 11.24   A close-up of the second specular highlight on the sphere, after a Noise map is added to the Specular Level 2 slot. Note the speckled appearance.

Refining with Reflections

This Multi-Layer lacquer effect is capable of yet more development—we can add appropriate reflections.

The painted sphere is extremely shiny, so it would definitely reflect its surroundings. So let's add a Reflection map. However, instead of simply using a Reflection map alone, we will combine it with a Falloff map to better control the final effect.

1. Go back to the Material Editor, and if necessary, click the Go To Parent button to return to the top map level of the Red Lacquer Paint 1 material. Then click the Reflection map slot. When the Material/Map Browser appears, select our old friend Falloff. Leave the settings at their defaults—for example, Falloff Type set to Perpendicular/Parallel and Falloff Direction set to the Viewing Direction (Camera Z-Axis.)

2. Click the None button next to the White (Color #2) side spinner swatch, and from the Material/Map Browser, select RGB Tint. When the RGB Tint Parameters rollout appears, click the Green color swatch and set it to pure black, or RGB (0, 0, 0). Do the same for the Blue color swatch—you're going to want the final reflection map to be tinted pure red, the same base color as the overall material.

3. Next, click the Map Name button in the RGB Tint slot, and from the Material/Map Browser, select Reflect/Refract. When it loads, make the following changes. Under Source, select From File. Change Size to 256 and Blur Offset to 0.01.

4. Go down to the bottom of the rollout. Under the Render Cubic Map Files section, click the To File button, and save a file as Red_.jpg. Set Image Quality to the highest setting (100). Click the Save button, and you'll see the initial Cubic Reflection map created as Red_UP.jpg.

5. Now click the Pick Object and Render Maps buttons. Then, either click the Sphere01 model or use the Pick Object dialog to select it from the list. When you do, you'll see a small Rendered Frame window appear as 3ds max 7 renders the 256-by-256-pixel Cubic maps, one right after the other. After a few moments, all the maps will finish rendering, and you'll see the Red Lacquer Paint 1 sample sphere update with the new Reflect/Refract map tree.

6. Activate your Camera01 viewport and render another test image (**Figure 11.25**).

Figure 11.25   The Red Lacquer Paint 1 material with a tinted Reflect/Refract Cubic environment map.

By using the Falloff map to mask the Cubic environment map, you're clamping the reflection more toward the outer edges of the sphere. In addition, the RGB Tint material changes the overall color of the reflection maps to better match the existing red paint color.

7. To further see the effects of the Falloff material on this sphere, return to the Material Editor, and click the Go To Parent button twice to return to the main Falloff level of this Reflection material. Under Falloff Type, change from Perpendicular/Parallel to Fresnel, then rerender the scene. As the rendered image indicates, the Fresnel falloff setting darkens the overall Reflection map and restricts it further to the outer edges of the sphere, based on the viewing angle of the camera.

Summing Up

In this chapter, we've explored various 3ds max 7 map, shader, and material types and saw how you could create striking texture effects by blending bitmap textures with procedural maps such as Noise and Falloff. We also covered the differences between the Blinn and Oren-Nayar-Blinn shader types and discussed how to create Multi-Layer textures.

Now that you've got these solid texturing concepts well in hand, it's time to look at 3ds max 7's lighting tools.

Part V

Lighting

C h a p t e r   1 2

Lighting Basics

By Jon McFarland

Lighting in computer graphics, in its simplest terms, is the addition of illumination in a scene. This must be done with forethought and planning to ensure that the proper look and feel of the scene is communicated to the intended audience. If the scene light is too bright, the scene will be washed out and unappealing. If the scene is too dark, the subtle intricacies and fine details may be lost. If a CG character's lighting doesn't match the real-world environment into which it is being composited, the intended realism will never coalesce. Although lighting has become more powerful in recent years, its proper implementation will require practice, patience, and an ongoing desire to expand your skills.

Lighting Tells a Story

While the concept of lighting a scene in 3ds max is rather simple, the implementation takes practice and can be a bit time-consuming. The primary light, or key light, should be located and oriented in such a way that the viewer's focus is directed to the proper features. Secondary fill lights are added to lighten features that are not in the path of the key light and to simulate light that is bounced off the other objects in the scene. A backlight can be added to frame the foreground objects against the background. Then special lights can be added to represent particular lighting conditions—such as illuminated signs, flashing warning lights, or a helicopter's probing spotlight—which add to a scene's lighting scheme. Their effects must be considered. The intensity and location of all the lights must be balanced against one another to convey the proper look and feel that the artist is attempting.

Color also plays a large part in setting the mood in your scene. While a late-night bonfire's key light will cast a primarily yellow light that fills the campground, the fill lights in the scene will generally have a bluish hue to represent the ambient light provided by the moon and stars. Once that fire has burned down to its final log and embers, that same key light becomes more reddish and the light no longer penetrates as far into the darkness. Offices and homes have a lighting scheme that is closer to white; however, you should avoid using the default pure white (RGB = 255, 255, 255) of max's lights, as this tends to make them look too sterile and uninviting. The bright daylight of a vast arctic wasteland may have a very pale blue tint, while the daylight in a vast desert wasteland may be tinted with a very pale yellow. Whether you're representing sunlight transitioning through sheer, dyed drapes or a flashing red MOTEL sign outside a window, the color emitted from lights helps clarify the nature of the scene.

Finally, the shadows that lights cast can add drama or subtle clarity to your scenes by helping the viewer understand the type of light that is casting those shadows. Stark, hard-edged shadows indicate a bright, focused light source such as a searchlight or the sun, high in the sky, on a clear day. (Although the sun is not truly "focused," its distance from earth creates a condition where the light rays that it emits are nearly parallel to each other.) Softer shadows can give a sense of calmness or convey the idea that many light sources are contributing to the overall illumination. A lack of shadows altogether can result in an unnatural look to your environment and a sense that objects are floating in space rather than being tied to the ground by gravity.

Let's introduce our sample character, affectionately known as Claymore the Clown (**Figure 12.1**). It shows how a single key light that is poorly positioned and casts no shadows illuminates only one side of the character's bust, leaving the scene looking flat and less appealing than it could be. The absence of shadows doesn't give the viewer an idea of the character's location in the scene. Notice how the collar doesn't cast shadows onto the neck and how the light has passed unobstructed through the head to illuminate unintended areas at the nostrils and the corner of the mouth.

If a hard shadow is cast by the light onto a surface behind Claymore, you get an idea of his proximity to that surface (**Figure 12.2**). He's close enough to the back wall to allow light to bounce off that wall and illuminate the left side of his face.

The addition of fill lights help frames the character's face while also lightening the wall behind him (**Figure 12.3**). The key light now casts a softer shadow and has been tinted to a slightly reddish hue to help the color transition from the background to the character look less abrupt.

Figure 12.1   A single poorly positioned and non-shadow-casting key light illuminates only one side of the character and leaves the scene looking flat.

Figure 12.2.   The addition of a shadow helps locate Claymore in relation to the back wall.

Figure 12.3   Fill lights, a softer shadow, and a little color help the appeal of the scene and make it more comprehensible.

I've always felt that the cinematographers who made the old black-and-white movies put more thought into the lighting and resultant shadows than those who shoot many of today's colorful movies. This was probably due to their inability to allow color to contribute to a shot. The bad guy (or monster) was often lit from below, to make his face look more ominous (**Figure 12.4**), while the good guy's lighting was much more direct. The female lead frequently had her eyes specially lit. And if there was a hanging light in a fight scene, it would inevitably be struck and spun wildly about so that its random flickers and shadows would add the impression of confusion to the action. You should be creative with your lighting and use it to communicate or add to ideas that your modeling and texturing can't complete.

 Note

> The time required to create and adjust the lighting in any CG system is often underestimated. The lights may need to be positioned, oriented, adjusted, tweaked, added, deleted, and so on several times before the proper lighting has been achieved. If a real-world situation must be matched, research may be required to identify the orientation of the objects in the world or to locate the manufacturer and specifications of the light fixtures. A good rule of thumb is to expect to spend 20 to 25 percent of your production time lighting an indoor scene and 5 to 10 percent lighting an outdoor scene, depending on the complexity of your models.

Figure 12.4   By relocating the key light below the character and casting the light upward, he looks a bit more ominous than in the prior figures.

The Three Components of Light

Early in our primary education, we learned that when we "see" something, our brains are calculating the effect of light as it bounces off the surface of an object. While the object absorbs a portion of the color spectrum, the remainder is reflected and diffused into the surrounding environment. The light that is reflected gives us information about the object's color and texture. Compare a well-used "alley ball" from your local bowling alley to a new and recently polished counterpart. They're both spheres of the same size and weight, yet the new ball will look sleeker and harder, while the alley ball will give the impression of being slower and heavier.

Light is broken down into three distinct components, known as diffuse, ambient, and specular light. Although the parameters of these components are primarily determined in the Material Editor, it's the lights in your scene that bring them to life. **Figure 12.5** shows two standard 3ds max teapots, with slightly different materials applied, which emphasize these components. The file Light Components.max is available on the DVD if you would like to follow along.

Figure 12.5   The three components of light: diffuse, ambient, and specular.

The scene contains two lights: a key light from the right and a single fill light from the left. Both lights are positioned above the objects. The diffuse light is the illumination that shows the viewer the coloring of the objects when they're in the path of a direct light source. Diffuse lighting is what makes the red teapot appear red (left) and the blue teapot appear blue (right). As we saw in Figure 12.2, the absence of either bounced light or a fill light results in the objects' illumination falling off (fading at the edges) in an unnatural way. The left side of each teapot appears to be slightly illuminated by a low-energy bounced light from within the scene. Because a fill light is used to generate the illusion of ambience, the light isn't truly an ambient effect. The necessity of faking a real-world condition within max to accommodate a required look is a common situation.

3ds max allows a default amount of global ambient light to be automatically generated in a scene. This can be adjusted by selecting Rendering > Environment from the Main toolbar and opening the Color Selector by clicking in the Ambient swatch in the Common Parameters rollout (**Figure 12.6**). Raising the default ambient light level has its rare uses, but it often leaves a scene looking washed out and flat. Try running the Ambient Light RBG values to (255, 255, 255) to see an extreme use (or abuse) of this tool and its effect on the scene. I highly recommend retaining the default value of (0, 0, 0) and creating the ambient light manually.

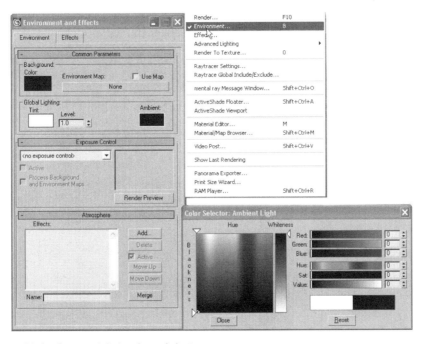

Figure 12.6   Setting global ambient light in a scene.

The specular light, also called a specular highlight or specular bloom, is the light that reflects off an object in a concentrated pattern parallel to the viewer's line of sight. This component gives the viewer more information about the texture of your object than does either the diffuse or the ambient light. The small, tight specular highlights returned by the left teapot indicates that the surface is hard and polished. The specular highlights from the right teapot are weak and spread out, giving the impression of a softer, rougher surface. Care should be taken to ensure that the specular highlight accurately reproduces the texture you are trying to simulate. Nothing will make an old, weathered brick wall look incorrect like giving it a bright and glossy highlight.

Light Types

3ds max contains an array of light types that can fulfill nearly every conceivable need. Basic Standard lights will cast illumination in specific (or all) directions, with no reference to a bounced light or special rendering conditions. There are two light types to be used specifically with the mental ray renderer and a light type that simulates an overall lighting environment. Several photometric light types are included with max's radiosity renderer to generate the effects of bounced light from real-world light fixtures, such as a 60-watt incandescent bulb or an industrial fluorescent strip. There are even systems that can tie a light into the location, date, and time of your scenes to simulate the sun's location at specific times. These are great tools for creating light-and-shadow studies.

Standard Lights

The standard light types offered in max 7 are much the same as in previous versions.

- **Omni light**—Also called point lights in some CG programs, omnis have no volume and radiate light in all directions equally.

- **Spotlight (target and free)**—A spotlight represents a conical section of an omni light and focuses that beam in a single direction. Target spotlights are composed of two parts, the light that casts the illumination and the target toward which the light will always be oriented. A free spot is controlled with the Rotate transform or by parenting it to another object.

- **Directional light (target and free)**—Like a spotlight, a directional light represents a beam of light aimed in a single direction. However, instead of emanating from a point, the beam in a directional light is cylindrical or rectangular, with parallel light rays. This results in a shadow that may elongate, depending on its angle to the objects, but won't spread out as the distance increases. Use a directional light to simulate sunlight.

- **Skylight**—Skylights represent the overall lighting in a daytime outdoor scene where the atmosphere has diffused the sun's light. A skylight's location is unimportant, as its effect will be similar to the illumination cast by a dome of lights from above your scene.

- **mr area omni** and **mr area spot**—These lights are intended to work with the mental ray renderer. Each represents light emitted from a volume of space shaped like a sphere or cylinder (mr area omni) or like a rectangle or disk (mr area spot). To learn more about the power of mental ray, please refer to the 3ds max 7 User Reference.

 Note

> Once a light is created, you're not restricted to using only that light type's parameters. With the light selected, go to the Modify panel, and in the Light Type section of the General Parameters rollout, expand the drop-down list; then choose another light, which will convert your selected light. Spot and directional lights can be switched between targeted and free versions in the same section. Be aware that the name of a light does not automatically change when you converted its type—Omni01 will still be Omni01 even after you change it into a targeted spotlight (**Figure 12.7**).

Figure 12.7   Changing a light's type in the Modify panel.

Photometric Lights

You don't have to guess at the brightness of a light as it affects your scene. Using photometric lights allows you to represent the physical effects of actual light fixtures, including color, distribution, and intensity. It's a snap to change a light source from fluorescent to incandescent or xenon, simply by picking from the Color section of the lights' Intensity/Color/Distribution rollout. An Isotropic distribution emits light in all directions equally. A Spotlight distribution projects the light in a specific direction. For architectural scenes, the true power of photometric lights resides in the Web distribution method. Web distribution allows you to point to a file (.ies, .cibse, or .ltli) that follows a photometric format specified by one of the three major lighting industry associations. These are provided for free download by most larger lighting manufacturers. A Web file for a particular fixture allows max to simulate that fixture's light dissemination exactly as the manufacturer designed it. Two sources for Web files are: http://www.gelighting .com/na/specoem/iesdownloads.htm and http://www.hadcolighting.com/ies_agree.htm

The following are the 3ds max 7 photometric light types:

- **Point light (target and free)**—Like a Standard omni light or spotlight, a point light emits its energy from a single point in space, but its distribution can be set to Isotropic (like an omni), Spot (like a spotlight), or Web (to match a real-world fixture).

- **Linear light (target and free)**—Unlike a point light, a linear light emanates illumination evenly along a line centered on the light source, using Diffuse distribution.

- **Area light (target and free)**—An area light produces light from a plane centered on the light source.

  Figure 12.8 shows the three photometric lights with either Isotropic or Diffuse distribution.

Figure 12.8   A point light (left) with Isotropic distribution; a linear light (center) and an area light (right), both with Diffuse distribution.

There are also two photometric light types for max's mental ray renderer. IES Sun and IES Sky, when used with a Skylight system (see the next section), add physically based illumination to your scenes. New to 3ds max 7, the IES Sun light no longer requires that Final Gather be enabled. IES Sky still has this restriction.

Tip

After a light is modified in max, many of that light's values (Color, Multiplier, and so forth) become the default values for the next light created. This even extends to subsequent scenes that are opened without restarting or resetting 3ds max. To ensure that your next scene's new lights are created with the max default values, set Multiplier to 1, Color to (255, 255, 255), Shadows to Off, and so on.

Light Systems

In addition to the standard and photometric lights that can be created in 3ds max, there are two lighting systems that can significantly add to the efficiency of lighting an outdoor scene or an indoor scene with a light source that originates outside. Both systems, located in the Create panel > Systems > Standard, calculate the light's location based on your model's location on earth.

Sunlight System

This system links a directional light, representing the sun, to a compass object to determine the sun's location in the sky.

1. Reset max to change the light settings to the defaults. From the Main menu, choose Customize > Units Setup. In the Units Setup dialog, make sure your units are set to US Standard Feet w/Fractional Inches (**Figure 12.9**).

2. Create several Box primitives, variously sized, to represent buildings.

3. Create a Plane object under the boxes, and apply neutral colors to all the objects. View the scene through a camera (**Figure 12.10**).

Tip

When selecting a background color for your renderings, it is best to avoid using either black or white. Black detracts from the effect of shadows and dark areas, while a white background has the same effect on specular highlights.

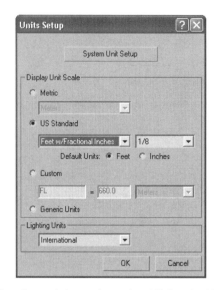

Figure 12.9   The Units Setup dialog is changed to US Standard Feet w/Fractional Inches for this exercise.

Figure 12.10   Primitive objects are used to represent buildings in a cityscape.

4. Go to the Create panel > Systems > Standard, and select Sunlight. Then, in the Top viewport, click and drag near the center of your buildings to create the compass rose. The size of the rose doesn't matter—it's just a helper object used to orient the light.

5. Once the compass rose is created, drag and click again to set the Orbital Scale—the distance from the light source to the target. Make sure that this number, also available in the Site section of the Create panel, is large enough to place the light above buildings. Once the light is deselected, then selected again, this field can be located in the Lights Control Parameters rollout under the Motion tab.

   Architectural projects are generally laid out with the sides of the structures parallel to the axis in your coordinate system. It's more convenient for the artist to create, move, or copy objects using World coordinates than the local system to which the buildings are set. The Sunlight system allows the user to orient the compass (which is the parent) and the light (which is the child) to the real-world coordinates system.

6. Select the Compass object, and rotate it until its North arrow points in the direction where you want true north to be in your scene, or where it would be in a real-world situation (**Figure 12.11**).

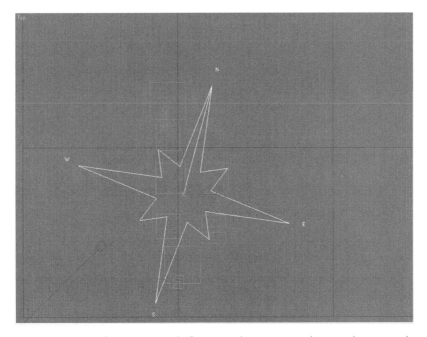

Figure 12.11   The Sunlight system's Compass object is rotated to match true north.

7. Select the Sun01 light object, and open the Motion panel. Within the Location section, click the Get Location button to open the Geographic Location dialog. Choose a region from the Map drop-down list and a city from the City list. The City list is very extensive, and you should be able to find a city at or near the location where your scene is located. You can also click directly on the map to choose the nearest city, or enter Latitude or Longitude values back in the Motion panel. **Figure 12.12** shows Cleveland, Ohio, selected as the location for the current scene.

8. Click OK to close the Geographic Location dialog. In the Motion panel, set the time and date that you want the Sunlight to reflect, and check the Daylight Saving Time box if your location observes that standard.

9. Switch to the Camera viewport and Quick Render your scene, set for Cleveland, Ohio, on June 22, 2005, at 11:00 a.m., with Daylight Saving Time being observed (**Figure 12.13**).

Daylight System

The Daylight system allows the user to combine the benefits of using a direct light to represent the sun with a skylight effect to add indirect illumination. Let's investigate how this system works.

1. Delete the compass and light from your current scene. Be aware that the relationship of the light and compass is only a parent/child link. Deleting only the compass object will leave a free directional light behind.

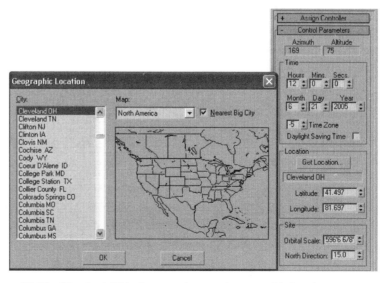

Figure 12.12   Cleveland, Ohio, is set as the scene's geographic location.

Figure 12.13   A render of the scene at the specified real-world location, date, and time.

2. From the Create panel > Systems > Standard, create a Daylight system in the same manner that you created the Sunlight system. Choose the same time, date, and location as well, and rotate the compass accordingly.

3. Render the scene (**Figure 12.14**). The rendering is much too bright and washed out. It needs exposure control added to reduce the brightness to an acceptable level.

4. Choose Rendering > Environment from the Main menu. Expand the drop-down list in the Exposure Control rollout, and choose Automatic Exposure Control. Close the Environment and Effects dialog, then render the scene again. It's much more appealing this time (**Figure 12.15**). If you want more contrast, try setting the Exposure Control to 0.5 or so.

5. Select the Daylight object and open the Modify panel, where you'll find a large number of controls for adjusting every feature of both the direct light and sky-light components of the Daylight system.

Figure 12.14   The cityscape scene without exposure control added to the rendering environment.

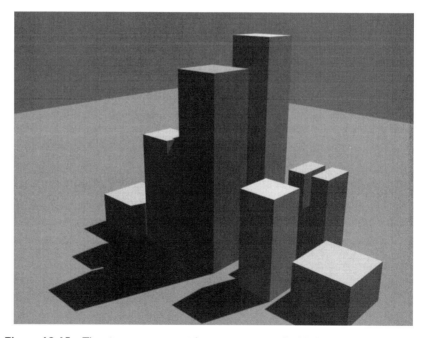

Figure 12.15   The cityscape scene with exposure control added to the rendering environment.

6. Expand the Daylight Parameters and Skylight Parameters rollouts and minimize the others. We're going to verify and adjust the values in these two rollouts to make the scene a bit more appealing.

7. In the Daylight Parameters rollout, ensure that a Standard light controls the sunlight and that a skylight (rather than a parametric IES Sky light) controls the Skylight functionality. (Your scene may show that the skylight is already the default.) In the Skylight Parameters rollout, increase the Multiplier to approximately 85. This may seem like an enormous number, but, taking into account the exposure control, smaller numbers may show no effect. In the Render section, enable Cast Shadows; then render the scene. This will take longer than your last rendering, because 3ds max is calculating the shadows generated by the skylight. Notice how the tall central building now receives shadows cast from the slightly lower building in front of it, even though the primary light source is from the rear (**Figure 12.16**).

Both the Sunlight and the Daylight systems can be animated to show the changes in sunlight and shadows over time, and they are great tools for gauging how much light may be hitting the reception area, executive's office, or studio in a future construction project.

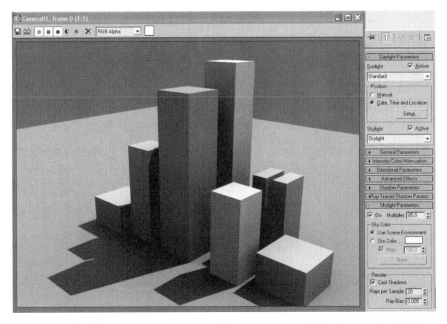

Figure 12.16   The same massing scene with a more powerful, shadow-casting skylight.

Shadow Types

Shadows help tie your geometry to the surfaces in your scene. They give the impression of density and size and help the viewer understand the positional relationships between all the objects in the scene. There are a few different types of shadows available in 3ds max, each with its own benefits and drawbacks.

- **Shadow map shadows** are images (bitmaps) that are generated by the Default Scanline Renderer prior to the actual rendering and are then applied to your scene. The renderer calculates the distance from the light to the objects on its path to determine which objects obstruct the rays of light. Any surfaces beyond the obstruction do not receive any illumination. These shadows use more RAM than the other shadow types, but they do have soft edges, are reasonably quick to render, and are the default shadow type for most lights found in max.

- **Raytraced shadows** are determined by tracing the path that each light ray follows, whether it passes through an object or not. Raytraced shadows are more accurate than shadow map shadows but take longer to calculate. Raytraced shadows have hard edges along their perimeters and are the default shadow type for the Sunlight system.

- **Advanced raytraced shadows** are similar to raytraced shadows in the method that they use to calculate the shadow area, but they also have anti-aliasing controls to manage how the shadow edges appear in the scene. This allows raytraced shadows to have softer edges, similar to shadow map shadows, while retaining the greater accuracy of raytracing.

- **mental ray shadow maps** are used with the mental ray renderer. They are not as precise as raytraced shadows but render fast, thereby decreasing the time it takes to render a scene.

- **Area shadows** give the impression that the light source is generated by a surface, such as a diffusing cover, rather than by a single point. This spreads the shadows over a larger area, with a large variance between the dark and light areas. Area shadows can provide results not achieved by the other shadow types but may greatly increase your rendering time.

Shadow Maps

Open the file entitled Shadows Start.max from the DVD. This is a simple interior corner with a potted plant and a rough opening for a window that we'll deal with later. Two lights are already placed and oriented in the scene: a directional light coming through the window and an omni light providing fill light to illuminate the inside walls, the floor, and the right side of the plant. We're going to adjust the shadows to make the scene more appealing.

1. Make sure the Camera01 viewport is active; then render the scene. The directional light washes out the right wall and does not cast any shadows from the left wall (**Figure 12.17**).

2. Select the directional light, then open the Modify panel. In the General Parameters rollout, click the On check box in the Shadows area (**Figure 12.18**). Notice that Shadow Map is the chosen shadow type. This will force the light to consider the left wall and window opening in the shadow calculations. Render the Camera01 viewport to see how this looks.

   Even these quick and basic shadows make a world of difference in the scene (**Figure 12.19**). The illumination of the right wall, except the area lit by the light through the window, now matches that of the left wall, which is lit only by the omni light. The shadows cast by the tree are much too pixelated (low in resolution) and need to be smoothed out a bit.

Figure 12.17   Our interior corner shows no shadows being generated by either light.

3. With the directional light still selected, expand the Shadow Map Params rollout (**Figure 12.20**). The Size value refers to the image size, in pixels, of the map applied to the shadowed area. Larger Size values result in finer, more detailed shadows, at the cost of higher RAM consumption. The Sample Range determines the softness of the shadow's perimeter. Higher Sample Range values will result in softer shadow edges. Set the Size value to 1024 and the Sample Range value to 5, then render the scene again (**Figure 12.21**).

Figure 12.18   Shadow Map is checked On in the General Parameters rollout.

Figure 12.19   The interior corner with a shadow map generated by the directional light.

The shadows are much finer now, especially near the top of the tree where the fronds are spread out.

4. The directional light in this scene represents sunlight. What if the light coming through the window comes from a car's headlights or a spotlight? Go back to the General Parameters rollout, and in the Light Type section, expand the drop-down and choose Spot to convert your directional light to a spotlight with the same parameters. The new shadows are more spread out than before because of the divergence of the spotlight rays (**Figure 12.22**). Notice how long the shadow from the top of the pot has become and how the area illuminated by the window is now expanded to an area outside the image.

Figure 12.20   The Shadow Map Params rollout.

Figure 12.21   The interior corner with the Shadow Map Size and Sample Range values increased to soften the shadows.

Figure 12.22   The spotlight generates shadows that are more spread out than the shadows produced by the directional light.

5. Switch the light back to a directional light.

6. Right-click in the viewport and choose Unhide by Name from the Quad menu. In the Unhide Objects dialog, choose CasementWindow01, then click Unhide to reveal the hidden window linked to the wall (**Figure 12.23**). Render the scene again.

Where have the light and shadows gone? As mentioned earlier, shadow maps are calculated by determining which objects obstruct the light rays and will not illuminate any surface beyond those objects. In the current case, the light rays encounter the window and stop projecting beyond that. Shadow maps do not consider the opacity or opacity-mapped features of an object when determining the shadowed area. One solution is to instruct max to disregard the glass panels. To do that, we'll need to detach them from the window.

1. Select the window and apply an Edit Poly modifier to the top of the modifier stack.

2. Activate the Polygon sub-object level. In the Modify panel's Polygon Properties rollout, enter 3 in the Select ID field, then click the Select ID button. This will select the 12 polygons that make up the glass panels (**Figure 12.24**). Click the Settings button next to the Detach button in the Edit Geometry rollout and name the new object Glass Panels.

Figure 12.23   The corner scene with the window revealed. No illumination is coming from the window.

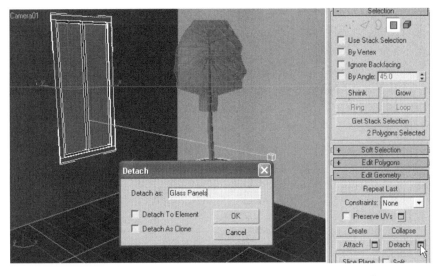

Figure 12.24   Select the two glass panels (12 polygons) and detach them from the rest of the window.

Note

The glass panels are no longer a part of the CasementWindow object. If you go lower in the stack and adjust any values (Open, Width, and so on) at the object's base level that change the layout or position of the window, the panels will not be included. If the window must be animated to open and close, consider breaking the panels into separate left and right objects and using an Attachment controller to keep them in place.

3. Exit the Polygon sub-object level. Select the directional light; then, in the General Parameters rollout, click the Exclude button to open the Exclude/Include dialog (**Figure 12.25**). The Exclude/Include dialog tells the light which objects it should or should not illuminate and which objects it can use to cast shadows. Highlight the Glass Panels entry in the left window, then click the ">>" button to move it to the right window. Make sure Exclude is selected in the top right corner, as well as Shadow Casting. The directional light will now illuminate the glass surfaces, but they will not generate shadows.

4. Render the scene one more time. You'll see that the glass panels are now ignored and the light passes through them and onto the tree and wall (**Figure 12.26**).

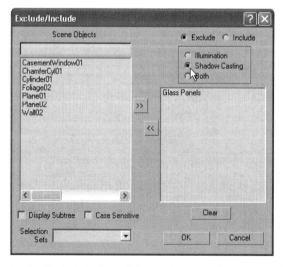

Figure 12.25 Set the Exclude/Include dialog to disregard the glass panels when generating shadows from the directional light.

Figure 12.26 With the glass panels excluded from receiving shadows, the light now properly hits the wall and tree.

Raytraced Shadows

Open the file entitled Shadows Raytraced.max from the DVD. This is the scene you were working on just prior to detaching the glass panels.

1. Select the directional light, and change its shadow type from Shadow Map to Ray Traced Shadows. Activate the Camera01 viewport, and render the scene. The shadows from the tree and the window opening are much sharper than in the previous renderings (**Figure 12.27**).

Even with a reflective floor, this corner is still too dark. The main light is coming through the window, but the left wall is blocking the majority of the illumination, causing that wall's shadows to be cast onto the right wall. Let's lighten the room up a bit.

2. In the Modify panel, open the directional light's Shadow Parameters rollout. Click the color swatch; then, in the Color Selector, choose (122, 122, 122), a medium gray. Render the scene (**Figure 12.28**). The shadows—and, as a result, the room in general—are a little lighter.

Figure 12.27   Using Ray Traced Shadows as the directional light's shadow type allows the opacity of the glass panels to be reflected in the shadows.

Figure 12.28   Lowering the shadow color to a medium gray yields lighter shadows and brighter reflections from the floor and walls.

Ray Traced Shadows can pick up the color from translucent objects and filter that color into the scene. This works with images and simple colors applied to those objects.

3. Open the Material Editor and select the Window material. In the Multi/Sub-Object Basic Parameters rollout, click the Panels button to open the parameters for sub-object 3, which controls the glass panels. In the Blinn Basic Parameters rollout, click the Diffuse color swatch and choose a pale blue color such as (176, 166, 251). Open the Extended Parameters rollout, and drag and drop the Diffuse color swatch onto the Filter color swatch. Choose Copy in the dialog that opens (**Figure 12.29**). Render the Camera01 viewport, and compare your results (**Figure 12.30**).

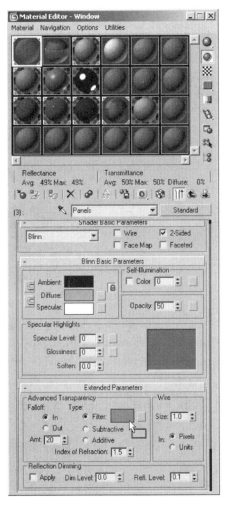

Figure 12.29   Copy the panels' diffuse color to the filter color in the Material Editor.

Figure 12.30   The Panels submaterial's filter color is passed through the window and into the scene.

 Tip

> The Reflectance and Transmittance information, shown in the Material Editor in Figure 12.29, can be activated under the Radiosity tab of the Preference Settings dialog.

4. In the Material Editor, select the Window With Color material and apply it to the CasementWindow object. This is the same as the Window material, but with a map applied to the Diffuse Color map channel. Render the scene. The map appears in the windows, but the color is not carried onto the wall because the Filter color is not yet set to accept the map.

5. Open the Maps rollout, then drag and drop the Diffuse Color map button onto the Filter Color map button and choose Instance in the Copy (Instance) Map dialog. To help bring out the stained glass borders, darken the shadow's color in the Shadow Parameters rollout. Then render the scene. **Figure 12.31** shows the scene with the mapped panels' colors being filtered onto the wall and the plant.

Figure 12.31   The window panel colors are now filtered into the scene.

Be aware that the Advanced Ray Traced Shadows feature, although faster than Ray Traced Shadows, does not consider the filter color when rendering a scene.

Area Shadows

Open the file entitled Shadows Area.max from the DVD. This is similar to the previous scene, but an omni fill light has been converted to a target spotlight with its shadows enabled. (This spotlight is still named Omni01.) We are going to use area shadows to give the impression that a diffuse light source, possibly reflected light from the opposite walls, is entering the scene and illuminating the plant and walls. The shadows cast from this light will help anchor the pot to the ground and solidify its location in the scene.

1. Render the scene to get a good reference image before we start changing the light's parameters. The spotlight casts shadows from the plant and pot onto the walls and floor. In the Rendered Frame Window, click the Clone Rendered Frame Window button to create a copy to compare with future renderings.

2. Select the spotlight (Omni01) and change its shadow type from Shadow Map to Area Shadows. Render the scene. You'll notice that your render times have increased

and that the shadows from the tree are more diffuse than before but much too pixelated to be appealing. **Figures 12.32** and **12.33** show the scene before and after area shadows were applied.

3. In the Modify panel's Area Shadows rollout, expand the drop-down list in the Basic Options section and ensure that Rectangle Light is selected. This will create the shadows as if the light source were a plane rather than a point. Increase both the Length and Width in the Area Light Dimensions section to 5 feet 0 inches.

4. The soft area around the shadow's perimeter, called the penumbra, showcases the versatility of area shadows. Controls for Area Shadow settings are located in the Antialiasing Options rollout. Set the Shadow Integrity to 10 to increase the number of rays that are cast from each shadow-casting surface to each shadow-receiving surface. Increase the Shadow Quality value to 15 to raise the number of rays cast into the penumbra; this defines its edges more accurately. Set the Sample Spread to 4 to soften the edge a bit, and set the Jitter Amount to 0.4 to change the structured initial ray locations to a more random pattern. This will cause artifacts that have been created to be converted into less noticeable noise in the shadows (**Figure 12.34**).

Figure 12.32   The corner of the scene before selecting Area Shadows.

Figure 12.33   The corner of the scene after selecting Area Shadows. The inset shows the shadows' pixelation.

Figure 12.34   The tweaked area shadows.

As you render your scene one more time, you'll notice that the render time has increased again. This is the tradeoff between the quality of area shadows and your production efficiency. Compare this rendering to the one that you saved earlier.

Lighting a Character

As artists, one of the common tasks that are required of us is to "sell" something. Whether that something is an action concept (superhero in flight, car leaping an open drawbridge), an emotion (impending doom, realization of safety), or simply a product your client wants to sell, the lighting you employ should focus the viewer's attention where you want it to be. The term "character" refers to the object that is due the most interest—be it a human, a troll, a car, or a dancing pizza—and around whom the scene is lit.

Character Key and Fill

Open the file entitled Claymore Start.max from the DVD. This is the same less-than-enthused circus worker we saw earlier, except that his facial hair has been hidden to help maintain fast viewport control. Currently, only the default 3ds max lighting exists in the scene, but this will disappear as soon as any other lights are added.

1. Open the Render Scene dialog. In the Options section of the Common Parameters rollout, check the Render Hidden Geometry check box (**Figure 12.35**). This will force the renderer to show Claymore's facial hair in the rendered image without displaying the hair in the viewports. Activate the Camera01 viewport, then render the scene (**Figure 12.36**).

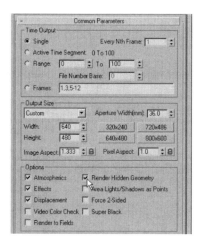

Figure 12.35 Turning on Render Hidden Geometry allows the renderer to consider objects that are currently hidden.

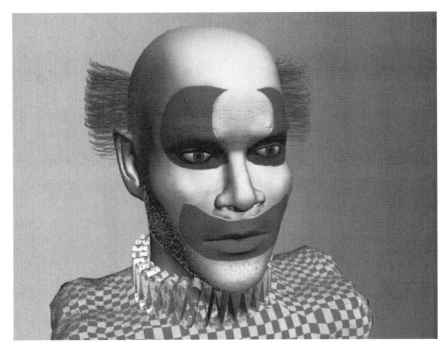

Figure 12.36 The character rendered using only 3ds max's default lighting, which does not create any shadows.

Tip

If there is an object that you do want to see in your viewport but do not want rendered, select the object, then right-click in a viewport, and choose Properties from the Quad menu. In the Rendering Control section, uncheck the Renderable check box.

The default lighting has done its job, and you can see the clown and the wall behind it, but we need to bring more life into the scene. Properly placed and controlled lighting and shadows will do the trick.

2. In the Create panel > Lights > Standard, click the Target Spot button. In the Top viewport, click at approximately (–200, -200, 0)—look at the transform type-ins at the bottom of the screen for guidance—to place the spotlight, then drag and release when the cursor is behind Claymore's left ear to create the target. This will place the light at about a 45-degree angle to the subject. Rename this light Spot Key.

3. In the Front or Top viewport, raise the spotlight, but not the target, so that the light is cast downward at about a 15-degree angle. This will be the key light in the scene. In the Modify panel's Intensity/Color/Attenuation rollout, set the Multiplier value to 1 (if it is not already), then render the Camera01 viewport.

   Our lighting still has some work to be done. There are no shadows being generated; the left side of Claymore's face is too dark; and the perimeter of the spotlight may be showing (**Figure 12.37**).

4. First we'll take care of the spotlight's perimeter. With the spotlight still selected, open the Spotlight Parameters rollout and check the Overshoot check box. Overshoot allows the illumination portion of a spot or directional light to act as if it were a non-shadow-casting omni light, while only casting shadows within its Falloff/Field cone.

5. In the General Parameters rollout, check the On check box in the Shadows section and make sure Shadow Map is the selected shadow type. In the Intensity/Color/Attenuation rollout, set the Multiplier to 0.9. Click in the color swatch and change the light's color to a very pale yellow (–255, 254, 241). A pure white light isn't realistic in most circumstances, and a little color goes a long way to add feeling to the scene. Render the scene again (**Figure 12.38**).

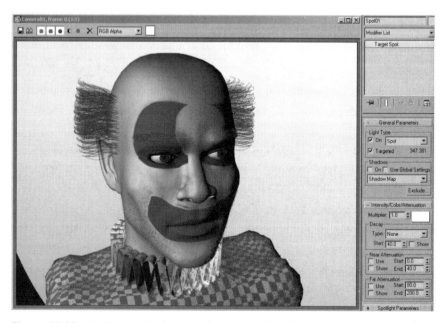

Figure 12.37 Adding a single key light did not significantly improve the lighting in the scene.

Figure 12.38   Casting shadows from our key light helps place Claymore near the wall behind him.

Hotspot and Falloff

The shadows have helped a bit, especially those inside the collar and those cast from the collar to the neck. The left side of Claymore's face is still too dark, and much of his left shoulder has disappeared, but the shadows from the hair to the head, as well as the inter-hair shadows, are very appealing. Let's continue by softening the shadows and tweaking the light itself by changing the Hotspot and Falloff values.

The Hotspot/Beam value in the Spotlight Parameters rollout controls the inner cone of the spotlight and determines where the full intensity of the light will be focused—everything within the hotspot will receive the full intensity of the light. The Falloff/Field value determines the radius of the outer cone and the limits of the spotlight's influence. Everything outside the Falloff radius will receive no light. Objects that fall between the hotspot and the falloff will receive a percentage of the light, as determined by their proximity to either the hotspot or the falloff. The separation between the hotspot and the falloff will also determine the size of the shadow's penumbra.

Note

Raytraced shadows depict the actual shape of the object being illuminated while disregarding any smoothing that is being applied. Try changing the spotlight's shadow type to Ray Traced Shadows and rendering the scene. Every facet of the perimeter of Claymore's head will appear as a straight line in the shadow against the wall, and each shadow-casting hair will be distinct. Be sure to change the shadow type back before continuing.

Hotspot and Falloff control the radii that the light influences. Far Attenuation controls the influence of the light rays as their distance from the source increases. Without using Far Attenuation, all lights will cast illumination for an infinite distance.

To explore these settings, proceed as follows:

1. In the spotlight's Spotlight Parameters rollout, increase the Falloff/Field value to 85. The Hotspot/Beam value will remain grayed out as long as Overshoot is active. In the Intensity/Color/Attenuation rollout, check the Use check box in the Far Attenuation section; then set Start to 200 and End to 650. This will cause the intensity of the light to begin decreasing 200 units from the source and completely disappear at 650 units (**Figure 12.39**).

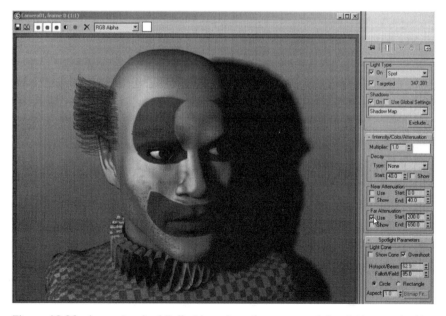

Figure 12.39   Increasing the falloff widens the soft area around the shadows and adds Far Attenuation control to the light's intensity across the scene.

2. Let's take care of the left side of Claymore's face. In the Top viewport, select Spotlight, hold down the Shift key, and then drag a clone to about X = 200, Y = −200. In the Clone Options dialog, choose Copy and rename this light Spot Fill. This will be our fill light. In the Front or Left viewport, move the spotlight below the home grid to about Z = −40. Decrease the Multiplier to 0.3; then, in the Shadow Parameters rollout, change the shadow color to a medium gray—(86, 86, 86) works well.

Lowering the position of the light in the scene will help fill in some of the dark areas created by the key light. The Multiplier was lowered so that those dark areas would not be entirely washed out, and the lighter shadow color allows the shadows to attract less attention.

3. In the Spotlight Parameters rollout, uncheck Overshoot. This feature isn't needed for the fill light. In the Advanced Effects rollout, uncheck Specular to eliminate any large specular highlight that the light may have created against the back wall (**Figure 12.40**).

The clown is standing just in front of a light-colored wall, but there is no indication of reflected light from that wall illuminating the back of Claymore's shoulders. We'll fix this by adding a light from the back. This light is called a rim light, and it is often used to give a character some separation from the background.

Figure 12.40   Claymore lit by both the key and fill lights.

4. In the Top viewport, create an omni light directly behind the character. In the Front viewport, move the light so that it is located midway between the top of the clown's head and the top of the wall (**Figure 12.41**).

5. Expand the omni light's Intensity/Color/Attenuation rollout. Open the Material Editor, select the Background material, then expand its Blinn Basic Parameters rollout. Drag the Diffuse color swatch from the Material Editor and drop it in the light's color swatch. Choose Copy in the Copy or Swap Colors dialog to match the omni's light color to the wall's diffuse color. Alternatively, taking advantage of a feature new to max 7, you can copy and paste from the right-click menu. With the cursor over the Diffuse color swatch, right-click to copy. Then, with the cursor over the omni color swatch, right-click to paste.

   Lower the Multiplier value to 0.2 so that the light is subtler.

6. Make sure that Shadow Casting is not enabled for this light. If this were a shadow-casting light, the Box03 object would need to be excluded from the omni's shadow-casting calculations. Render this scene one last time (**Figure 12.42**).

There it is: a well-lit character featured in a scene. For comparison, the file Claymore Finished.max, with all the lighting in place, is included on the DVD. You can take this scene even further by removing the back wall and replacing it with a tent or a clown's dressing room. Be sure to attenuate your lights and control which lights will affect the objects within the Exclude/Include dialog.

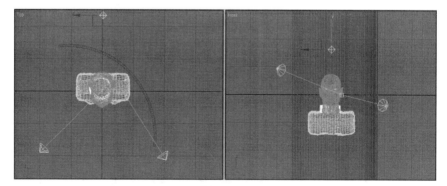

Figure 12.41   Locating the omni light.

Figure 12.42   The backlight illuminates the back of Claymore's shoulders and lightens the shadows at the back of the collar.

Summing Up

Lighting in computer graphics allows the artist to focus the viewer's attention on or away from key elements in a scene. We can change a mood or evoke an emotion by changing the lights' locations, colors, and intensities. Shadows help us tie objects together and help the viewer understand the types of lights and and their origins. Quality lighting techniques can take a lot of practice to achieve, but invest the time and you'll be rewarded with artwork that, teamed with good modeling and texturing, brings your scenes truly to life.

In the next chapter we'll take a look at CG lighting as it applies to film and video, and we'll also explore lighting in the game industry.

C h a p t e r   1 3

Lighting for Film, Video, & Games

By Jon McFarland

Lighting for a project designed for media broadcast (or even print production) differs significantly from lighting for other projects. Broadcast lighting usually entails lighting a CG model that will be composited with a background plate. This gives us the luxury, within the project's time constraints, to tweak the scene's individual components (such as shadows or specular highlights), but it also requires careful matching to the actual illumination in a real-world scene.

Video gaming, including console, PC, and online, is one of the fastest-growing entertainment sectors, and new titles and technologies push the need for qualified artists, especially lighting and technical directors who understand the particular needs of game production. Game lighting must illuminate what the designer chooses, but must also allow the scene to process quickly within the game engine. This often requires the effect of the lighting to be reflected in the objects directly—a process called "baking"—even in the absence of the lights themselves.

We'll cover several aspects of production lighting for film, video, and games, including:

- Using Light Tracer
- Rendering light elements
- Key, fill, and special lights
- VertexPaint
- Baking lighting

Combining CG and Reality

This first section will demonstrate how to render an architectural model against a background plate. The objective is to provide the compositor with the components required to join your model with an existing image to create a convincing product. We'll be rendering a model against a static image, but the same principles apply to video backgrounds. Some of the final steps of the compositing process, including masking and color correction, are beyond the scope of this chapter, but they are covered in the compositing chapter later in this book. You also may want to look into the features included in discreet's combustion composition and postproduction software.

Preparation and Research

Rendering a CG model or scene in front of a photograph of an actual location requires some knowledge and information regarding when and where the image was taken. What time of day was it and what was the date? What was the cloud cover like? Was additional lighting introduced into the scene by the lighting director or camera operator? Getting as much information as you can will help streamline your decision-making process.

Understanding the intent and context of the final image can assist in your lighting decisions. In the case of an architectural scene, is the structure a gleaming tower rising out of an area of drab urban blight, or does it need to seamlessly match the neighborhood? Should shadows be cast onto your models from objects or characters in the background plate? This may require you to create stand-in objects, with Matte/Shadow materials applied to them. Will the final scene have the same sky or foreground scenery? This can affect the reflections from your objects as well as the color bleed that creeps into them. Get a clear and complete understanding from the project manager or art director (or the client, if you are a solo shop or a subcontractor) before production begins.

Let's take a look at two typical scenes in which computer-generated models have been placed into photographs. In each one, the original photo is on the left and the composited image is on the right.

In the first situation the owner of a shop in a mall was expanding its storefront presence and was seeking approval for a new storefront design. In this scene, the signage, the large new canopy, and the left part of the wall needed to be created and lit in 3ds max (**Figure 13.1**). Since this is an outdoor scene, the main illumination comes from the sun overhead, and only a small amount of ambient light from a fill light is required. The size and shape of the shadows being cast by the sign's letters is a good indication of the location of the overhead light.

Figure 13.1   The shadows from the sign's letters help determine the location of the sun in the sky.

In the second situation, the owner of a building wanted to install an ATM inside it, in a rather secluded location. Before committing the money to install and maintain the machine and its necessary ventilation system, the building's manager wanted to see if customers would feel secure about using it, and asked for an image that would simulate the lighting (**Figure 13.2**). The chief source of light for this indoor scene is bounced light that comes into the scene from above and then fades as it travels from the left to the right. Bounced light from the floor also fades from bottom to top. In this image, the model's lighting needed to match the actual lighting at the ATM and the surrounding area. This was accomplished using an overhead directional light as the key light, a weak directional light from below as a fill light, and an omni as a second fill light off to the left. All lights were colored to match the wall or floor and attenuated to control their intensity over distance.

Figure 13.2   The more subtle indoor lighting is re-created with a key light and two fill lights.

Note

You should always consider the modeling complexity and materials that are applied to the objects in your scenes. Cars may need to be complex when they are designed for up-close viewing, but those same cars will not need that level of complexity when they are peripheral objects in a scene. Not only will they require additional memory assets, but the extra face count of a complex model can drastically increase lighting computations without any noticeable increase in scene quality.

In the following exercise, you'll be using some of the tools and techniques covered in the previous chapter, as well as some additional tools, to light a CG model in front of a background plate. We'll also see how to render the scene in separate passes so that individual features can be tweaked by the compositor.

Lighting the Scene

The image that we will be using as a background plate for our scene is a photograph taken across the street from a parking lot (**Figure 13.3**). (You can also study the image file called DCP_0220.jpg on the DVD.) We will be replacing the lot with a small condominium complex. The shadows cast by the truck in the foreground and the light posts give us an idea of the location of the sun, and the lack of leaves on the trees helps determine the time of year the photo was taken. First, let's get the basic lighting in place.

I. Open the file entitled Building_Lighting Start.max from the DVD. This consists of a building in a scene with the background plate used as both the Camera viewport's background image and the environment map (**Figure 13.4**). The background plate is a simple photograph that was taken with a digital camera.

   I've made this scene easy to work with by taking care of many of the usual details that have to be dealt with before lighting can begin. The camera is static in the scene; only the front, side, and corner facades of the building have been created. 3D objects are already in place in the same locations as the building to the front left and the car near the center-right of the image. These objects both have a Matte/Shadow material applied to them so that they will mask out the building and car. We're not going to concern ourselves with the other objects (poles, wires, trees, and so on) that will appear to be covered by the model; we'll leave the job of masking them to the compositor. The model has been camera-matched, and both the Cameras and Helpers categories have been hidden from the reader's view by checking both options in the Hide by Category rollout in the Display panel (**Figure 13.5**).

2. In the Create panel > Lights > Photometric > Object Type rollout, choose IES Sky. Click near the bottom of the Top viewport to place the Sky light, then drag and release to place the target near the front entrance to the building.

3. With Sky01 still selected, activate the Select and Move tool and use the Transform Type-Ins at the bottom of the user interface to move the light to X = 515, Y = –165, Z = 180.

Figure 13.3   The background plate onto which the model will be rendered.

Figure 13.4   The Cam Corner viewport at the start of the exercise.

Figure 13.5 Objects in the scene can be hidden by category in the Display panel.

 Note

> The IES Sky light only works properly when it is pointing downward in the World Z axis. If mental ray is used as the renderer, Final Gather must be enabled.

4. In the Modify panel, check the On check box in the IES Sky Parameters rollout and set the Coverage to Partly Cloudy (**Figure 13.6**). Leave Cast Shadows unchecked for now; then render the Camera viewport.

   The model looks extremely washed out (**Figure 13.7**). We'll enable Exposure Control to lessen this washed-out result.

5. Choose Environment from the Rendering menu. In the Exposure Control rollout, choose Automatic Exposure Control from the drop-down list. Click the Render Preview button in the same rollout to see a thumbnail image of the scene with the Exposure Control applied.

6. Rendering the scene now would result in a model that is still too bright. In the Automatic Exposure Control Parameters rollout, change the brightness value to 42 and check Desaturate Low Levels to keep your darkest areas from turning black (**Figure 13.8**). Render the scene (**Figure 13.9**).

Figure 13.6 The IES Sky light's parameters.

Figure 13.7 Without Exposure Control enabled, the scene looks extremely washed out.

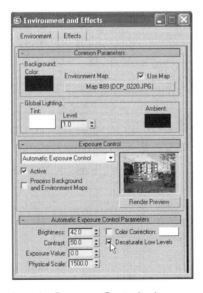

Figure 13.8 Enable and set the Exposure Control values.

Figure 13.9   With Exposure Control enabled, the scene looks much more appealing.

The scene looks much better now. It's no longer washed out, and the colors are similar to those in the photograph. But there are still areas that need to be improved, such as the dark areas under the canopies (our only light comes from above) and the lack of shadows. To address these issues, we'll turn to max's Light Tracer.

Using Light Tracer

The IES Sky light works best in a scene when it is teamed up with one of the advanced lighting plug-ins included in 3ds max. One approach is to use radiosity. Radiosity attempts to create physically accurate lighting by tracing each light ray as it bounces through a scene and loses energy with each bounce. This can create very precise shadows and color bleeding and is very useful in indoor scenes. However, the speed and accuracy of any radiosity solution is dependent on the complexity of the scene geometry; the more complex it is, the longer it takes to generate a solution.

For outdoor scenes, max's Light Tracer plug-in is often a more practical choice. Light Tracer creates a less accurate but usually faster global illumination and color bleed solution by bouncing a specified number of light rays through a scene for a limited number of bounces. This is best used in brightly lit outdoor scenes that require softer shadows.

Let's add Light Tracer to our current scene.

1. Continue with your existing scene, or open the file entitled Building_Lighting Light Tracer.max from the DVD.

2. Open the Render Scene dialog, and click the Advanced Lighting tab. Choose Light Tracer from the drop-down list to expose the Light Tracer's Parameters rollout. Leave the parameters at their defaults, and render the scene (**Figure 13.10**). This may take a while, depending on the system that you are using to render.

Tip

> When you do a standard render to the Rendered Frame Window or to a file, you'll lose the ability to continue working in max, and this can seriously interrupt your work flow. Consider investigating the Backburner feature included with 3ds max. Backburner will allow you to render in the background on your own computer or use any other systems, on a qualified network, as a render farm.

Now there's a definite improvement in the scene. The balconies really pop out against the building and the brick has lightened up, but we still need to address the dark areas and the lack of shadows.

3. First we'll speed up our renderings a bit by lowering their quality (don't worry, we'll jack the numbers back up for the final shot). In the Parameters rollout under the Render Scene dialog's Advanced Lighting tab, set the Rays/Sample value to 125 and leave the Filter Size at 0.5 (**Figure 13.11**).

The Rays/Sample value represents the number of light rays that are cast for every pixel in the scene. Lower numbers result in a blotchier rendering but at a faster speed. Filter Size refers to the smoothing of the noise that is created when the light rays impact a surface. Lower numbers result in grainer but faster renderings.

Figure 13.10   Using Light Tracer allows many of the model's features to really stand out in the image.

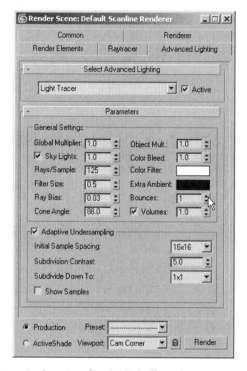

Figure 13.11   The revised settings for the Light Tracer's parameters.

4. The areas under the canopies are dark because light is not bouncing up to hit those surfaces. Increase the bounces from 0 (essentially an "off" condition for the effect) to 1. Each light ray will bounce off one surface and illuminate another. In the Rendered Frame Window, click the Clone Rendered Frame Window button so that you will have something to compare to; then render the scene.

   The scene is very blotchy, especially on the left side of the building (**Figure 13.12**). The bounced light helped the canopies, but the effect could be better. We'll help the scene by increasing the ambient light created by the Light Tracer.

5. Under the Advanced Lighting tab, click the Extra Ambient color swatch. When the Color Selector opens, change the RGB values to (15, 15, 15). This will lighten the dark areas without washing out the entire scene.

6. We need to lighten the scene and set the parameters for a better final product. Increase Bounces to 2, Rays/Sample to 250, and Filter Size to 10. Also, increase the Global Multiplier to 1.25. This should give us a nice, crisp image. Turn off Adaptive

Undersampling, since we want the light distribution to cover the model evenly. In the Environment and Effects dialog, increase the Brightness to 55. Make sure the Cam Corner viewport is still active; then render the scene (**Figure 13.13**).

Tip

> If you are using Light Tracer and not getting the expected results, try checking Show Samples in the Adaptive Undersampling section of the Render Scene dialog's Advanced Lighting tab. When used in conjunction with Adaptive Undersampling, this will render red dots at the locations where samples are taken. The red dots indicate where the light is being concentrated.

Figure 13.12   The revised parameters result in a blotchy rendering, but the effect of the bounced light is evident.

Figure 13.13   The increase in Bounces, Rays/Sample, and Filter Size as well as Exposure Control Brightness results in a better-quality rendering.

7. Finally, we need to add specular highlights to the scene (**Figure 13.14**). The IES Sky light usually produces good shadow results, but no specular highlights. We'll add a directional light to the scene to create the highlights without adding any diffuse light. In the Top viewport, create a directional light that is roughly parallel to the IES Sky light. In the Front viewport, raise it to the same level as the IES Sky light.

8. In the directional light's Modify panel, adjust the Hotspot and Falloff values so that the light is cast over the entire building model. If necessary, switch one of the viewports so that its view looks directly down the light's negative Z axis. This will give you visual feedback about the scope of the light's influence.

9. In the Advanced Effects rollout, uncheck the Diffuse check box (**Figure 13.15**). We want this light to contribute only to the specular components in this scene.

10. Render the Camera viewport one more time (**Figure 13.16**).

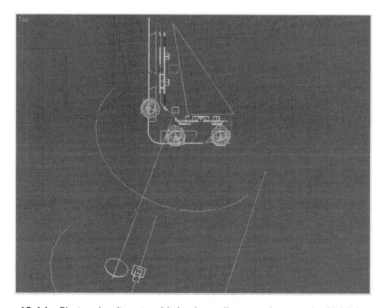

Figure 13.14   Placing the directional light that will create the specular highlights.

Figure 13.15   Unchecking Diffuse turns this component off for the directional light.

Figure 13.16   The condominium complex with the addition of shadows and specular highlights.

As this exercise has demonstrated, lighting a CG scene to match a background plate requires forethought and attention to the many aspects that real-world lights contribute to an environment. In the next section, we'll examine 3ds max's Render Elements feature, which enables you to extract lighting elements from the rendering.

Rendering Light Elements

As mentioned earlier, we need to provide the compositor with as many images as necessary to properly complete the project. This often means generating several images, each representing a different component of the rendering, rather than handing over a single well-lit image. With a variety of images, the compositing artists can edit or emphasize individual components according to the requirements of the art director, without the need to rerender the entire project. Having a distinct image of just the scene's shadows, for example, allows the compositor to lighten, darken, or tint those shadows without touching the other elements.

3ds max 7 allows you to render each element in a separate pass to generate unique images or animation files. There are several different rendering elements available:

- **Diffuse**—This element renders the diffuse aspects of the scene and is the closest to what you see in the Rendered Frame Window.

- **Specular**—This element renders only the specular highlights found in the scene. The highlights appear as white against a black background.

- **Blend**—The Blend render element is the most adaptable element. Using Blend, you can select which elements will be combined into a single image. For example, if reflections will be edited, but no other components, you can use Blend to render all the other elements into one pass, then render the reflections separately.

- **Reflection and Refraction**—Reflections and refractions in a scene can be rendered out as individual components.

- **Shadow**—One of the most common elements to detach from a scene. The ability to edit shadow elements in their own image enables the comp artist to alter the viewer's perception of the objects' location, size, density, and overall presence in the scene.

- **Atmosphere**—Atmosphere effects such as Volume Light and Fire Effect can be rendered in separate passes for later tweaking.

- **Z Depth**—The Z Depth element creates a grayscale depiction of the objects in the scene. Objects in the foreground will appear lighter, while objects that are more distant will be shown as increasingly dark. This element can be used to make objects more apparent in the scene as they approach the camera or viewport.

- **Alpha**—Often used as a tool to mask CG elements against a background plate. Opaque objects appear as white in the element; completely transparent objects, or areas where no objects exist, appear as black. Semitransparent objects are rendered as shades of gray, depending on their opacity.

- **Background**—Don't forget to provide the background as its own element, in the same context that was used to create the other elements.

- **Lighting**—The Lighting element shows where the lighting and shadows affect the scene.

Additional render elements that can be pulled from your scene include Self-Illumination, Matte, Ink, and Paint (for use with the Ink 'n Paint material). These elements do not affect the lighting of the scene and won't be covered here. Feel free to explore them on your own.

Let's create a quick render with separate elements for Alpha, Reflection, Shadow, and Specular.

1. Continuing with the previous exercise, open the Render Scene dialog, then click the Render Elements tab (**Figure 13.17**).

2. Expand the Render Elements rollout, if required, and then click the Add button.

3. Select Alpha, Reflection, Shadow, and Specular from the list (**Figures 13.18, 13.19, 13.20,** and **13.21**). Choose OK to close the dialog.

4. By default, there is no file name or output path assigned to these render passes. To save the images, select each element and enter both a file name and a location. If you are rendering a sequence of still images, max will append sequential numbers to each file name.

By pulling the individual elements out of this rendered scene, you have provided the compositor with the information needed to fine-tune the project in postproduction, so it will look its best in the final film or video version.

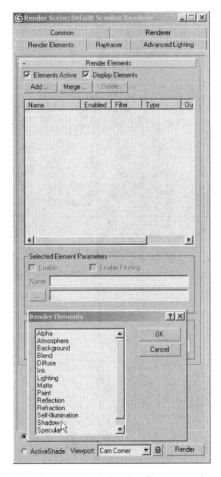

Figure 13.17   The Render Scene dialog's Render Elements tab and the Render Elements dialog showing the available render elements.

Figure 13.18   The Alpha element from the condominium scene.

Figure 13.19   The Reflection element from the condominium scene.

Figure 13.20   The Shadow element from the condominium scene.

Figure 13.21   The Specular element from the condominium scene.

Lighting for Games

We can all agree that video games have made enormous strides in their relatively short lifespan. In the old days, games like Pong, Asteroids, and Pac Man relied on a single color image restricted to an environment the size of the game's screen. There was no color, lighting, or shading, and the games were created more by programmers than by artists. As more expressive games like Donkey Kong, DigDug, and Galaga came along, they introduced color to their environments in the form of sprites. Any apparent shading or shadows were separate sprites and had nothing to do with an actual lighting model.

Today's games present an immersive, detailed 3D environment, complete with shading applied to hundreds of objects, as well as lights that interact with, or at least appear to interact with, those objects. Even the jump in visual quality from the original Doom to the new Doom3 is impressive by any standard, and much of this is due to the improvements in how lighting is handled.

When approaching a lighting project for a video game or game level, several key pieces of information must be gathered and decisions must be made. What game engine will be used and what are its lighting requirements? Can lights be animated (intensity, orientation, and so on), or should you use animated sprites or materials instead? Finally, what is the look and feel that your game is attempting to convey? In terms of lighting art direction, the game may have an established style that must be taken into account. Doom and Resident Evil, to take just two examples, have a relatively long history, and their lighting schemes have consistently been dark and foreboding. On the other hand, the veteran racing game Gran Turismo has used a variety of different lighting scenarios, so players will not come to the game with a fixed idea of what the game's lighting will look like. Having a clear goal at the beginning of the project will make sure your scene fits seamlessly into the final product.

 Tip

> New to 3ds max 7 is the ability to use the mental ray rendering option with the Render To Texture feature. In previous versions, only the Default Scanline Renderer could be used for this.

Key Lighting

As with any lighting scheme, it's best to start with the key light. Let's place the basic key, focusing on the main elements in the scene.

1. Open the file Giant_01.max from the DVD. This very nice model is available courtesy of Sami Sorjonen, s-s@sci.fi, www.cgmill.com/ss. Its face count has been reduced for this exercise.

2. There are currently no lights available in the scene and very basic materials applied. Ensure that the camera_shot1 viewport is active; then render the scene (**Figure 13.22**).

   Note that the scene renders in square patches in the Rendered Frame Window, rather than from top to bottom as you might expect from the Default Scanline Renderer. This is because mental ray is the renderer assigned to the scene, and this render pattern is a feature of mental ray called bucket rendering. Bucket rendering renders groups of nearby pixels rather than horizontal scanlines.

   Our subject, the giant, is surrounded by some type of organic structure while he remains fixated on the crystal floating overhead. With only the default lighting available, the scene looks flat and unappealing. We'll start by adding a key light to bring the focus to the giant.

3. In the Top viewport, create a target spotlight to the left of the camera. Drag and release to place the target centered on the giant (**Figure 13.23**).

4. In the Left and camera_shot1 viewports, raise the light so that it is slightly higher than the character's head and place the target even with his hips.

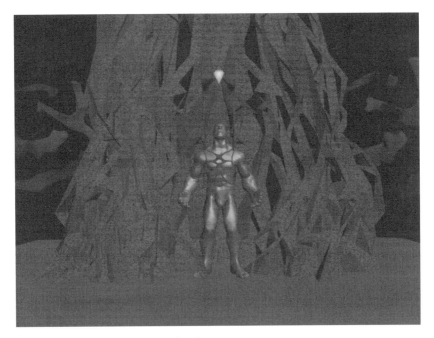

Figure 13.22 The starting point for this exercise.

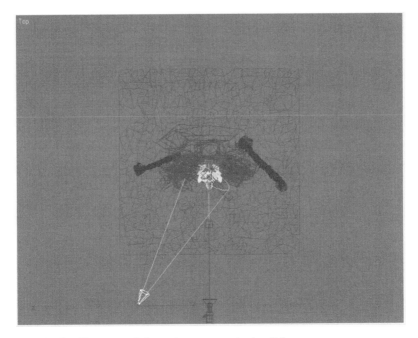

Figure 13.23 Place a spotlight in the scene as the key light.

5. Select the Spotlight. In the Modify panel's General Parameters rollout, enable Shadows and choose mental ray Shadow Map from the drop-down list. With mental ray as the renderer, we can take advantage of the speed and quality of the shadows that are specific to mental ray.

6. In the Intensity/Color/Attenuation rollout, check the Use check box for Far Attenuation. Set the Start value to 275 and the End value to 900 to force the light to decrease nicely as it passes through the scene.

7. In the Spotlight Parameters rollout, decrease the hotspot until it just barely encompasses the giant. Set the Falloff value to roughly twice the Hotspot value. The large variance between the hotspot and the falloff will give the shadows a nice soft edge (**Figure 13.24**).

8. Rename this light Light_Key; then render the scene (**Figure 13.25**).

Figure 13.24   Set the spotlight's parameters to focus on the giant and to create soft shadows.

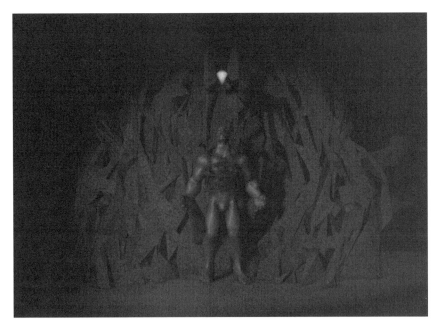

Figure 13.25   The scene after the key light has been placed and adjusted.

Fill and Special Lights

Now that the key light is in place, we need to illuminate the opposite side of our character. We'll create a new light to fill in the areas that still remain too dark. Then we'll address some special lighting needs.

1. In the Top viewport, select Light_Key. Hold down the Shift key, then drag the light to the right and slightly behind the character. In the Clone Options dialog, choose Copy and rename the light Light_Fill. The new light's placement should be similar to what you see in **Figure 13.26**.

2. In the Left viewport, move the fill light downward until it is just above the floor; then move the target until it's even with the middle of the character's chest.

3. Leave the light's parameters as they are for now. You won't be able to see the effect of the fill light from the camera_shot1 viewport, so activate the Cam Close viewport and render the scene (**Figure 13.27**).

   The two-light configuration that we currently have is easily manageable. A scene with many lights quickly becomes unwieldy as you try to select and adjust each light. Luckily, 3ds max has a tool—the Light Lister—that makes adjusting the most common light parameters a great deal easier.

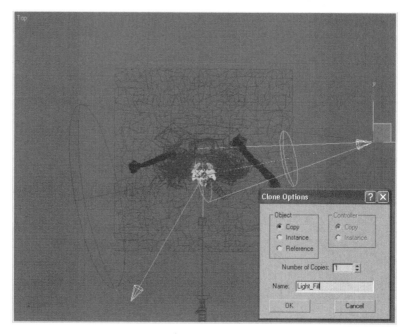

Figure 13.26   Clone the key light to create the fill light.

Figure 13.27   With the addition of the fill light, the back of the character's head gains some illumination.

4. Open the Tools menu from the menu bar, and choose Light Lister. The Light Lister dialog will open, showing a list of all the lights in the scene as well as the most commonly adjusted parameters (**Figure 13.28**).

Tip

When two or more lights are instances, only one at a time will show in the Light Lister. To see the list of instances, click the down arrow button, located next to the clone's name. This expands the list of instances.

5. Set Light_Key's Multiplier to 0.95. Select the same light's color swatch to open the Color Selector; then set the color to a very pale red. RGB values of (255, 222, 219) work well.

Tip

One of the best features of the Light Lister is that the light being adjusted does not need to be selected.

6. Select the Light_Fill's Multiplier and set it to 0.5—we'll keep it brighter than fill lights usually are because of the number of faces that are obstructing the light. Open the Color Selector, and give the light a pale gray-green color, somewhat like (216, 225, 214). This will give the impression of color bleed from the surrounding foliage.

7. Clone the Rendered Frame Window, then render the Cam Close viewport and compare the two images (**Figure 13.29**).

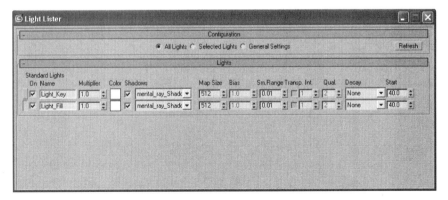

Figure 13.28   The Light Lister, showing many of the commonly adjusted parameters of a scene's lights.

Figure 13.29 The scene is a bit darker now, especially behind the giant's head and on the side of his face.

The initial lighting is almost finished. Let's add a light to represent the glowing crystal and its effect on the character's torso and the surrounding organic matter.

1. In the Top viewport, create an omni light. Its specific location is not important.

2. With the light still selected, click the Align tool in the Main toolbar. Before the Align Selection dialog opens, you need to select the object to which the light will be aligned. Press the H key to open the Pick Object dialog, then select Sphere01 from the list.

3. In the Align Selection dialog, check the X, Y, and Z Position check boxes and select Pivot Point in both the Current Object and Target Object areas. This will place the omni light at the center of the crystal (**Figure 13.30**). Click OK to execute, and close the dialog.

4. Rename the light Light_Crystal. In the Modify panel, turn Shadows on. Also, make sure mental ray Shadow Map is selected. Set the Multiplier to 1, and change the light's color to a light blue, similar to (162, 165, 225).

5. Select Sphere01, right-click in the viewport, and choose Properties from the Quad menu. In the Rendering Control area, uncheck Cast Shadows. This will prevent the crystal from obstructing the light that is cast from the omni. The crystal is also a light source in the scene and should not cast shadows from other lights.

6. Render the scene.

The omni light's shadows are definitely not what we need in the scene (**Figure 13.31**). Omni lights spread rays in all directions and often cast improper shadows onto complicated surfaces.

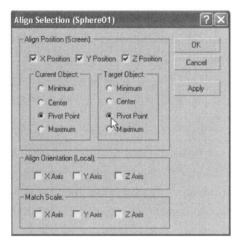

Figure 13.30 Use the Align tool to position the omni light at the center of the crystal.

Figure 13.31 The omni light's shadows are not at the level of quality that we're looking for.

7. Select the omni light, and change it into a target spotlight. Correct the orientation by moving the target behind the giant. His head should be centered in the beam of light.

8. Turn on Use for Far Attenuation, and set Start to 30 and End to 72. This will cause the light's intensity to fall off quickly from his head to the middle of his chest. In the Spotlight Parameters rollout, make sure that the hotspot is wider than the giant's spread arms; then turn on Overshoot so that the light will illuminate the area around the character.

9. In the mental ray Shadow Map rollout, increase the Map Size value to 1024 pixels, then render the scene again. **Figures 13.32** and **13.33** show the scene from both of the cameras.

That's a lot better. Replacing the omni light with a target spot gives us better control over the shadows that it casts, while Overshoot lets it illuminate the surrounding area. The larger Map Size value allows for finer detail in the shadows. Note, however, that your game engine and the general performance desired for the game may limit just how large any bitmap, including a shadow map, can be.

In the next section, we'll look at painting color and light onto specific vertices.

Figure 13.32   Replacing the omni light with a target spotlight allows better control over the light's shadows.

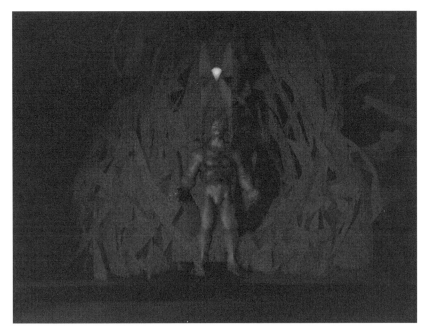

Figure 13.33 The same scene as seen from the camera_shot1 viewport.

VertexPaint

3ds max has a rich toolset for modeling, animating, and lighting in a variety of work styles and environments. One of the tools aimed squarely at the game industry is the VertexPaint modifier. In essence, this tool bakes lighting values directly into a model's geometry by means of an easy-to-use painting interface. Each vertex processed by the game engine holds data about its coordinates, color, lighting, and material. Each vertex's lighting value is determined, then blended with the lighting values of the vertices located at the opposite end of the edges that connect them. Vertex lighting is applied to each triangle that the vertex is a part of. Subdividing your scene will give you more control over the effects of VertexPaint.

1. Continue with your current scene, or open the file Giant_VertexPaint.max from the DVD.

2. Make the Cam Close viewport active. Use the Dolly Camera tool in the viewport controls to move the camera back far enough to see the giant's torso. Use the Truck Camera tool to pan the image until it looks similar to **Figure 13.34**.

Figure 13.34   Dolly the camera backward and pan to see more of the character.

 Note

> The VertexPaint modifier in 3ds max 7 is not completely compatible with the same modifier from previous versions. If a scene containing the VertexPaint modifier from a previous version of max is opened in max 7, the older version of the modifier will be loaded into the scene.

3. Maximize the Cam Close viewport so that it will be easier to work in. Then turn off Edged Faces mode.

4. Select the cage2 object; this is the green foliage that is binding the right side of the giant's body. We want to attach the two cage objects to create a single object to paint, but they are currently instances of each other. In the toolbar under the modifier stack, click the Make Unique button to change the instances into independent objects.

5. In the Modify panel's Edit Geometry rollout, click the Attach List button next to the Attach button. In the Attach List dialog, choose cage1 from the list, then click the Attach button. Rename the object "cage".

6. Expand the Modifier List and apply a VertexPaint modifier to the cage object. This will open the VertexPaint Paintbox, where you will find tools for all of your vertex painting needs.

We want to start by darkening the portions of the cage above the character's left and right shoulders that aren't receiving enough light. We'll start by adjusting the brush size and the paint color.

7. At the top of the Paintbox, click the Vertex Color Display–Unshaded button. Click the color swatch and choose a dark gray color; then set the Size value to 2.

8. Click and drag the cursor over the surfaces above the giant's left shoulder. The brush will appear as a circle with a vector pointing away from the surface. 3ds max will always keep the brush's face perpendicular to the surface normals of each triangle. Repeat the process on the areas above the right shoulder (**Figure 13.35**).

9. Select the giant, add a VertexPaint modifier, and add shadows where you feel they are best suited.

 Tip

> The VertexPaint modifier has adjustments for precise control over the brush, including using pressure data from a pen stylus to dictate variances of the brush's width. The controls can be found in the Painter Options dialog, which opens when you click the Brush Options button.

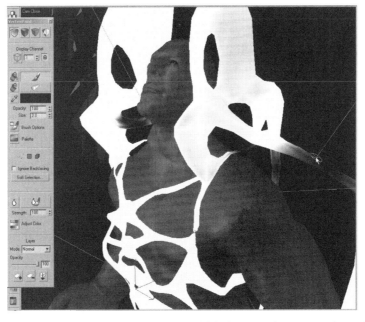

Figure 13.35 Use the VertexPaint brush to add darkness to the vertices above the giant's shoulders.

From this exercise, you can see how useful VertexPaint can be when you need to make fine adjustments to colors and lighting values without actually changing the light kit. It's a real boon for game artists who don't have the luxury of modifying the lighting scheme.

Baking Materials

Lighting calculations can significantly increase the time it takes to render a scene. A fairly simply modeled scene can take an inordinate amount of rendering time if global illumination, colored shadows, radiosity, and/or an elaborate lighting setup must be taken into account. In a game environment, this can result in poor-quality renderings, dropped frames, and slow or erratic play response. The solution is to apply the effects of the lights, shadows, and textures as materials to the objects, a process commonly known as baking.

The following tutorial shows how to bake various lighting-related elements so that they will work efficiently in a game.

1. Open the file entitled Giant_VertexPaint.max from the DVD. This is similar to the project that was completed at the end of the previous exercise, except that the model is broken into two pieces, giantHead and giantBody.

2. Select giantHead, then open the Material Editor and highlight an unused slot. Click the Get Material button in the horizontal toolbar.

3. In the Material/Map Browser, select Selected in the Browse From section, then double-click giant_skin to place that material into the selected material slot (**Figure 13.36**).

   Look at the material and you will notice that it is an uncomplicated material with a Falloff map in the Diffuse Color slot.

4. With giantHead still selected, add a UVW Map modifier and set the Mapping type to Shrink Wrap. Use the Edit UVWs dialog to stitch the appropriate edges together. (Check the texturing chapters in this book for more on UV mapping.)

5. Click Rendering > Render To Texture from the 3ds max menu bar. This opens the Render To Texture dialog (**Figure 13.37**). This dialog will determine the object to be baked, the output location for the new maps generated, what objects to consider in the rendering, and the type of map to be baked.

6. In the Output section of the General Settings rollout, click the "…" button; then assign the folder in which the new map will be placed.

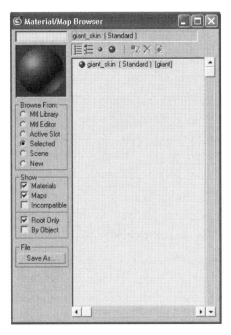

Figure 13.36 Select the giant's giant_skin material in the Material/Map Browser.

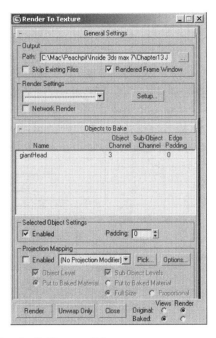

Figure 13.37 The Render To Texture dialog.

7. In the Objects to Bake rollout, check the Enabled check box in the Selected Object Settings section; then choose All Selected at the bottom of the rollout. These settings will cause max to consider the lighting effect of all the objects in the scene when generating the map for the giant's new material.

8. In the Output rollout, click the Add button to open the Add Texture Elements dialog. This dialog, similar to the Render Elements feature discussed earlier, will allow you to choose which features of the rendering will be added to the new map. Select CompleteMap from the Available Elements list (**Figure 13.38**). In the Target Map slot, select Diffuse Color from the drop-down list.

9. In the Selected Element Common Settings section of the Output rollout, select Diffuse Color from the Target Map Slot drop-down list and set the Map Size to 1024. This will allow more definition to be spread across the surface of the model.

10. Click the Render button at the bottom of the dialog. 3ds max will show several progression bars as the texture is being rendered. Once completed, a new Shell material is created and applied to the giant. The newly rendered map, including shadows, will appear in the viewport, while the original material shows during true renderings.

11. An Automatic Flatten UVs modifier is now at the top of the stack. In the Display section, choose Show No Seams to hide any bright green seam indicators that will obstruct your view. Your Cam Close viewport should look like **Figure 13.39**.

Try moving the target for the Light_Special spotlight. As you can see in the viewport, the shadows are baked into the material applied to giantHead. Open the Material Editor and get the material that is currently applied to the object; you will see that it is now a Shell material with the baked material showing in the viewports and the original material showing in the renderings. This Shell material is much more game-friendly than the scene's original lights and materials setup.

Figure 13.38   Select CompleteMap in the Add Texture Elements dialog.

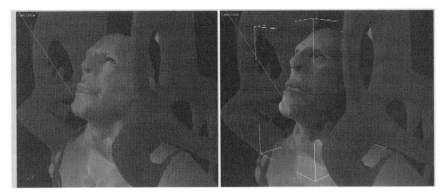

Figure 13.39   The Cam Close viewport before (left) and after (right) the Render To Texture is executed.

Summing Up

Lighting is a vital part of nearly every 3D project. A firm grasp of the principles utilized by each CG genre (film, video, games) will make each project a little easier.

This chapter covered a lot of ground in a short space, from matching the lighting of an existing scene and rendering individual elements to lighting in a game environment and baking the texture.

From lighting, we'll now move to motion. 3ds max has extensive capabilities when it comes to animating the parameters of the objects in your scene (including light parameters, of course), as you'll see in the next chapters.

Part VI
Animation

Chapter 14

Introduction to Animation

By Sean Bonney

Picture a ball—a shiny, chrome-mirrored ball. Now close your eyes and imagine doing something cool with it using 3ds max. Did your ball bounce wildly around the scene, or stretch into a crazy shape? Or perhaps explode into a thousand shards? Odds are, the first thing that came to mind involved animation.

The core of 3ds max is truly its animation system, which allows you to bring life to any alien world, crusty robot, chugging engine, or even any workaday industrial mechanism you can think up. The real trick is to plan your attack wisely, so that your swirling system of planets becomes a celestial ballet and not a tangled mess of spheres.

3ds max 7 features several commonly used animation tools, including constraints, controllers, and parameter wiring. In this chapter, we'll examine the constraints system, as well as methods of using several constraints in unison to achieve an animation goal.

Constraints are, in effect, a type of controller. You are probably already familiar with the more common 3ds max controllers, such as Bézier and Linear controllers. Animation controllers store an object's animation keyframes and, most significantly, control the manner in which the object's behavior is interpolated between keys. Anyone who has ever witnessed an animated object swing wildly between keys should be aware of the importance of using the appropriate controller. One of the most powerful, the Script controller, will be used in this chapter to give high-detail control over an object's animation.

Parameter wiring is a powerful method of controlling objects in a scene by linking animatable parameters between two objects. One object can control or otherwise relate to the other object through the Parameter Wiring dialog. This dialog supports augmenting the relationship through mathematical expressions, as we'll demonstrate.

We will also explore manipulators, which are onscreen helper objects such as sliders that can be quickly and easily wired to control nearly any parameter of any object in a scene.

Whatever tools you use to set up your animation, the real power and flexibility of max lie in the nearly open-ended ways in which max tools can be interconnected to achieve a desired effect.

Constraints

Constraints allow you to control one object's position and/or rotation with one or more other objects. For example, a boat object may be constrained to the animated surface of a body of water. Constraints are essential for most forms of keyframed animation. The constraint types offered in max 7 are these:

- **Attachment**—maintains an object on a mesh surface
- **Surface**—maintains an object on a parametric surface
- **Link**—allows the parenting of an object to change over time
- **LookAt**—forces an object to keep a specified axis oriented toward a target
- **Orientation**—rotates an object relative to the orientation of target object(s)
- **Path**—places an object along a path or a mix of multiple paths
- **Position**—positions an object relative to one or more target objects

In these next exercises, we'll work with most of these constraints, and often combine them to create automated mechanical setups.

Attachment Constraints

In this section, you will use the Attachment constraint to place a toy duck and some bubbles on the surface of a flowing body of water. You will also use the Linked XForm modifier and a loft object to attach the animated duck to a simple rope. If you wish to preview the animation you will be creating, play the rendered movie duck.mov from accompanying DVD.

1. Open the max file attachment_constraint_begin.max from the DVD. This scene contains a rubber duck and a trough filled with flowing water (**Figure 14.1**). The flowing water is created with a Plane primitive, displaced with an animated procedural map.

Note

> The Attachment constraint will only work with target objects that can be converted to meshes. Any applied modifiers must be Object Space modifiers, as World Space modifiers, such as Displace Mesh (WSM), do not translate into meshes.

2. Select the duck, open a Left viewport, and zoom in on the duck.

Before applying an Attachment constraint, always consider the pivot point of the object, as the pivot point will determine where the object will intersect the object you are attaching to. The pivot point for the duck is located in the middle of its body (**Figure 14.2**).

Figure 14.1   The scene to start with: a toy duck and some flowing water.

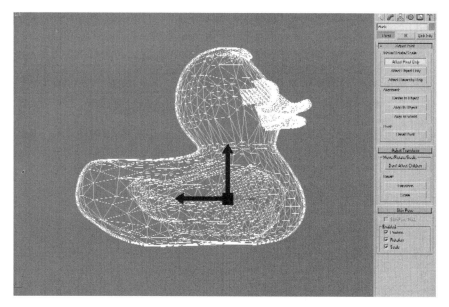

Figure 14.2   The pivot point of the duck object, shown highlighted, is in the middle of the body.

3. To move the pivot point lower in the body, giving the duck a higher placement on the water, go to Affect Pivot Only mode (Hierarchy panel > Pivot tab > Adjust Pivot rollout), and move the pivot point lower on the View Y-axis (**Figure 14.3**). Click the Affect Pivot Only button again to exit this mode.

4. To apply the Attachment constraint, go to the Camera viewport, and with the duck still selected, go to the Menu bar and click on Animation > Constraints > Attachment Constraint. In the viewport, a dotted line will appear between the duck's pivot point and the cursor (**Figure 14.4**).

5. Click on the water to select it as the surface to which you will attach the duck. Doing this in the Camera viewport will have the effect of making the duck disappear, as it has been aligned by default on Face #1 of the mesh, which is off-camera (**Figure 14.5**).

6. The Motion panel should automatically open when the constraint is assigned. If you have selected the wrong target surface, simply click the Pick Object button in the Attachment Parameters rollout and try again.

7. To set the initial position of the duck, click the Set Position button and click in the middle of the Camera viewport to place the duck (**Figure 14.6**). It may be necessary to click-and-drag to get your selection to register.

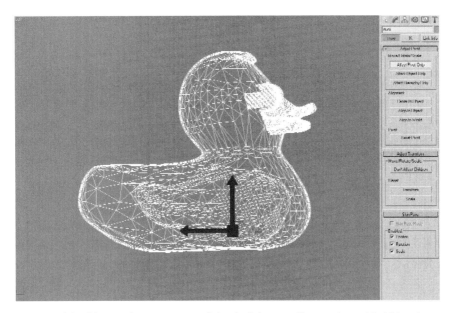

Figure 14.3   Moving the pivot point of the duck lower will cause it to ride higher in the water.

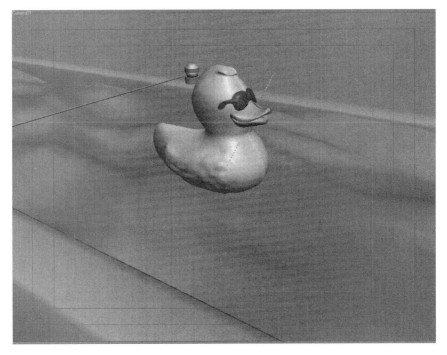

Figure 14.4   Once the Attachment constraint is applied, the dotted line indicates you can select an object to which to attach the duck.

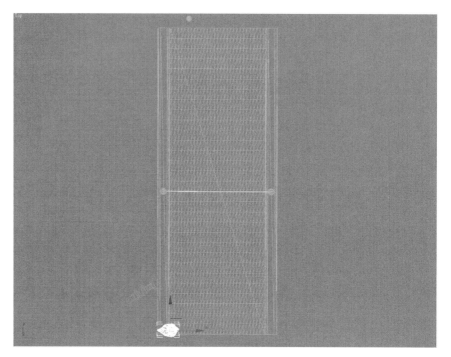

Figure 14.5   Initially, the constrained object is placed on Face #1 of the target surface.

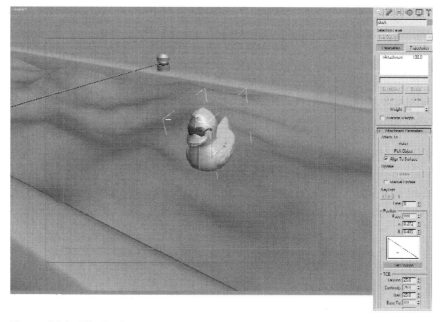

Figure 14.6   The Set Position button is used to place the constrained object on a specific part of the target surface.

Note that, by default, the duck is oriented according to the normal of the selected face, but this will be overridden later with rotational keyframes. While Align To Surface is checked, you can still rotate the duck around the target surface's normal, regardless of whether you are in Auto Key mode (previously called Animate mode) or not (**Figure 14.7**).

Figure 14.7   Attachment-constrained objects can be manually rotated with Align To Surface activated.

 Note

> Once a position has been set for the Attachment constraint, a keyframe is created at the current frame. It is possible to animate the movement of a constrained object without being in Animation mode.

8. Once you are satisfied with the initial position, turn off the Set Position button.

If you scrub the Time Slider, you'll see how the duck rides the waves and rotates to maintain its alignment with the surface. Unfortunately, this movement is lost whenever the position or rotation of the object is animated. To keep this rotational information as the Attachment constraint has calculated it, you would need to position the object at frame 0, leave Align To Surface checked, and not animate its position or rotation.

9. Turn off Align To Surface (Attachment Parameters rollout.) This will prevent the duck from rotating according to the water's changing surface, but that rotation will be lost anyway once the duck's position is animated. Later in this section, Rotation Script controllers will be used to regain this information. Turning off Align To Surface will also cause the duck to regain its initial orientation, pointing downstream.

10. To allow the duck to slide a bit on the surface of the water, go to frame 80, click the Set Position button, and move the duck to a new position a little closer to the camera. A dialog will appear, asking you to confirm the animation of the object's position. Click Yes to close it. Note that you have animated this object without necessarily being in Animation mode.

11. Go to frame 160, and check that the Set Position button is still on. Another method for animating the position is to edit the value of the Face setting in the top of the Position area of the Attachment Parameters rollout. Incrementing the Face value will move the duck laterally across the surface. Slowly change the Face value until the duck has moved to the far side of the water (**Figure 14.8**). Click Set Position again to exit that mode.

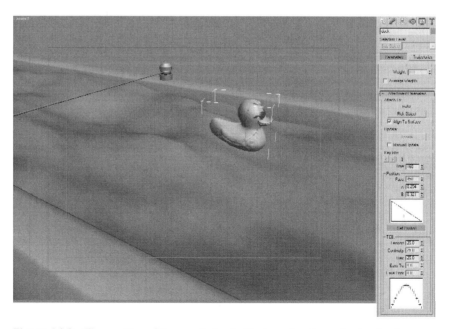

Figure 14.8   The position of the constrained object can be changed using the Face setting in the rollout.

Note

The Face value will not be editable unless Set Position is active or a position key exists at the current frame.

12. At frame 250, move the duck back to the middle of the stream, where it started, though it may now be oriented differently (as in Figure 14.6). Select the key at frame 0 displayed in the track bar and Shift-drag (hold down the Shift key and the left mouse button while dragging with the mouse) to frame 250. This will clone the frame 0 key, duplicating the attachment position. If you toggle between frames 0 and 250 (Home and End keyboard shortcuts,) you will note the duck's position is not precisely the same due to the water's changing surface.

If you scrub the Time Slider, the duck should move smoothly across the surface of the water in a rough loop. In fact, it moves too smoothly, ignoring the rippling waves. This is due to two factors. One is the way in which the Attachment constraint interpolates between keys. Constrained objects are only placed on the target surface at keys; between keys, they smoothly interpolate through space, without regard for whether they still appear to be attached to the target surface or not. This can be remedied by adding attachment keys at the points where the constrained object appears too high or too low.

The exact frames at which this occurs in your version of this scene will depend on where on the surface you have set your attachment keys, but for the version of the completed scene provided on the DVD, frame 20 represents a point where the waves have risen higher, and an attachment key is needed to correct the duck's placement.

For points along the duck's path where the attachment needs to be keyed, simply zoom in on the duck in a Top viewport, turn on Set Position, and click the duck's pivot point (**Figure 14.9**). As with the initial placement of the duck, it may be necessary to click and drag the mouse to make your selection register. Setting the new position close to the duck's pivot point will keep the new attachment keys close to the previous path.

You can add attachment keys to refine the placement of the duck and keep it riding at the same level in the water throughout the animation (**Figures 14.10** and **14.11**).

Continue through the animation, adding refinement keys whenever the duck appears to ride too high or too low.

The second factor responsible for the duck's ghost-like motion across the waves is the duck's lack of bobbing or tilting motion as it passes across the uneven surface of the waves. A limitation in the Attachment constraint makes the automatic alignment of the duck unavailable, but with some scripting, that motion can be regained.

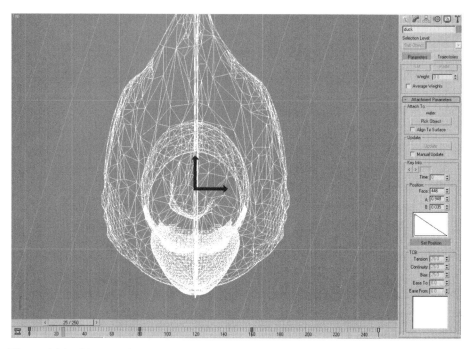

Figure 14.9   Place a refining attachment key in the Top viewport, guided by the location of the pivot point (shown enhanced in this figure).

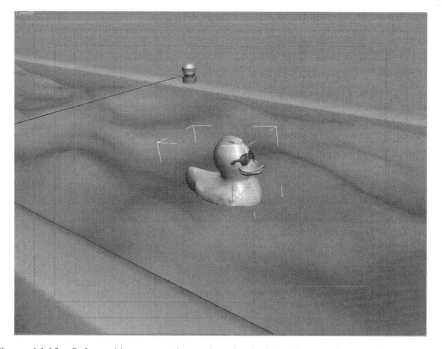

Figure 14.10   Before adding an attachment key, the duck is riding too low on the waves.

Figure 14.11   Once an attachment key has been added, the duck rides at the same level in the water.

Script Controllers

Script controllers allow all the powers of MAXScript to be used to calculate the values of other types of controllers. These values are passed to the object's rotation track, position track, scale track, or whatever track the controller has been applied to. This section will guide you through the creation of a short script designed to keep the duck aligned with the surface of the water. For more information on MAXScript, see the chapter on scripting in this book as well as the MAXScript Reference (Help > MAXScript Reference).

1. With the duck still selected, go to the top of the Motion panel, and in the Assign Controller rollout, select the Rotation controller. The Rotation controller is assigned TCB Rotation by default. Click the Assign Controller button (labeled with a question mark) to choose a new controller.

2. Highlight the Euler XYZ controller and click OK.

Note

The Euler XYZ controller lists each rotation axis separately and is useful when you wish to apply different controllers to each axis.

3. Expand the Rotation controller list to see that each axis has been assigned a Bézier Float controller (**Figure 14.12**).

Figure 14.12 The Euler XYZ rotation controller separates each axis of rotation into a separate Bézier Float controller.

4. Select the X Rotation controller and assign a Float Script controller to it (**Figure 14.13**).

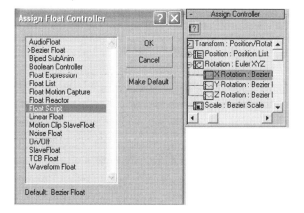

Figure 14.13 The Float Script controller allows for custom scripting of individual rotation tracks.

Working with a Script Controller

Once the script controller has been applied, a dialog opens, allowing you to enter the actual script. Initially, the dialog contains only a single value, and once the script has been entered, it must end with a single value of the correct type (float), which will be applied as the X-axis rotation.

The script you will be entering will cast a ray down toward the water's surface, which will reflect a ray back up, angled to correspond to the surface normal of the water. The X rotational value for the duck will be extracted from the angle of this reflected ray. The script is available on the DVD as rotational script.txt.

Before you start, note that a common cause of "undefined" errors in ray-casting scripts is non-intersection. If the ray were cast from under the water's surface, then it would never intersect the water, resulting in an error. A similar error would be generated if the ray were angled off to the side of the water's surface.

Tip

If you should close the Script Controller dialog and need to reopen it, select the X Rotation track in the controller list and open its Properties from the contextual menu, accessed by right-clicking.

Let's go line by line through the script. Delete the initial value and enter the following lines into the script dialog:

```
RayFromPos = [$Duck.position.x, $Duck.position.y,
  $Duck.position.z + 1000]
```

This line makes the position from which the downward ray will be cast equal to the duck's position. An increment of 1000 units has been added to the Z-axis position to ensure that the ray is not being cast from within the wave, which would result in an error.

```
RayToSurface = ray RayFromPos [0,0,-1]
```

Note

Variables set within a Script controller are not available to other scripts unless they are declared globally (see MAXScript Online Reference for more information).

This line generates the ray from the duck straight down along the World Z-axis. The three numerical values represent the ray's direction along each axis.

```
RayAtSurface = intersectRay $water RayToSurface
```

This line causes the downward-casting ray to intersect the water's surface and stores the reflecting ray in the variable RayAtSurface. Keep in mind that this second ray is not a true reflection, but corresponds to the water's surface normal at the point where it is struck.

```
EulerAtSurf = eulerangles (-RayAtSurface.dir.y*90)
  (RayAtSurface.dir.x*90) 0
```

This line converts the reflected ray's angle into X-axis and Y-axis values (the Z-axis is left at 0.) Don't be concerned if the math doesn't immediately make sense to you; just be aware that EulerAtSurf now contains a set of three Euler angles, one for each axis of rotation.

```
QuatAtSurf = EulerAtSurf as quat
```

In order to apply rotational information, the duck needs to be converted into quaternion format. This format allows for smooth interpolation between rotational keys. This line converts the Euler angles of the ray into quaternion values.

```
QuatAtSurf.x
```

This final line isolates the X-axis value of the quaternion, which will be applied to the X-axis rotation of the duck. Every Script controller needs to end with a simple declaration like this, of the correct type.

To complete and test the script, click the Evaluate button. A number should appear in the Result pane to indicate a successful script (**Figure 14.14**). If a number does not appear, check the MAXScript Listener window (F11 to open) for error messages.

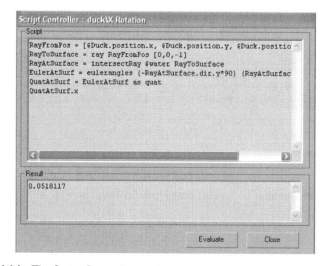

Figure 14.14   The Script Controller window showing the completed script for determining the duck's X-axis rotation.

Adding and Modifying Scripts

We can now adapt the script we've just made for another axis and apply it using a second Script controller.

1. The Script Controller window is modeless, so feel free to leave it open while you test the script's functionality. If you scrub the Time Slider, you should see that the duck now rotates along its X axis to align with the water's surface. To see what values are being set by the script, go to any frame and click the Evaluate button again.

2. Close the Script Controller editor window.

3. Select the Y Rotation controller and assign another Float Script controller to it. When the Script Controller editor window opens, it will automatically select all rotation tracks that have Float Script controllers assigned and enter the same script. In this case, this helpful feature is undesirable, so close the Script Controller window (copy the script to the clipboard for easy pasting later).

   Select only the Y Rotation track, and right-click Properties to open the Script Controller window. Replace the default value of 0 with the same script, the only difference being that the final line will refer to the Y-axis value of the quaternion:

   ```
   QuatAtSurf.y
   ```

Once both scripts have been correctly entered and evaluated and the window has been closed, the duck should accurately wobble along both its X axis (forward and back) and its Y axis (side to side) at it moves across the water's surface. An actual plastic duck wouldn't stick so tightly, though; it would overcompensate for the wave's motions. The duck's wobbling motion can be exaggerated easily by editing both scripts to multiply the final result by a factor of 1.5.

1. Edit the final line of the X-axis script to read:

   ```
   QuatAtSurf.x * 1.5
   ```

2. Edit the final line of the Y-axis script also:

   ```
   QuatAtSurf.y * 1.5
   ```

   The duck now leans in a more exaggerated fashion (**Figures 14.15** and **14.16**).

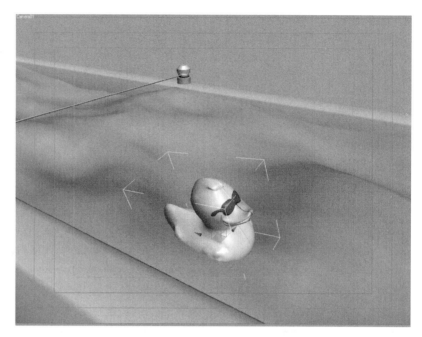

Figure 14.15   The duck at frame 59, leaning over to align with the water's surface.

Figure 14.16   The duck at frame 59 leans over farther once a multiplication factor has been applied to its rotational script controllers.

3. The duck's Z Rotation track has not had a Script controller applied to it, so you can manually key Z-axis rotations. To turn the duck toward the direction in which it moves, click the Auto Key button to activate Animate mode, go to frame 20, and rotate the duck –30 degrees on its local Z axis (**Figure 14.17**).

4. At frame 75, rotate the duck 75 degrees on its local Z axis.

5. At frame 165, rotate the duck –60 degrees on its local Z axis.

6. At frame 190, rotate the duck –30 degrees on its local Z axis.

7. At frame 250, rotate the duck 50 degrees on its local Z axis, so that it is once again pointing downstream. Exit Auto Key mode by clicking the Auto Key button again.

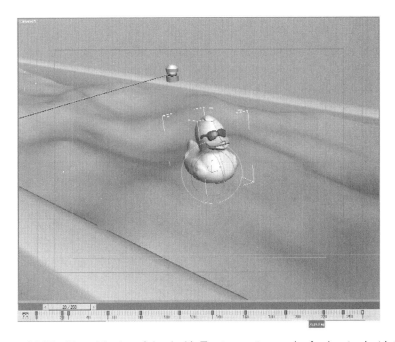

Figure 14.17   Manual keying of the duck's Z-axis rotation can be freely mixed with its scripted X-axis and Y-axis rotations.

If you scrub the Time Slider, you will see that the duck's scripted rotations are now mixed with its manual Z-axis rotations, creating a realistic sense of motion atop the waves. Now that you're familiar with the Attachment constraint, it should be a simple matter to place a few bubbles on the water's surface.

Simple Attachment

As we saw in the initial attachment of the duck, the Attachment constraint will keep an attached object aligned with the target surface, as long as positional keyframes are not applied to the attached object. Now we will place a few bubbles on the water's surface and allow the constraint to control their alignment.

1. Go to the Top viewport and look near the top end of the trough (upstream from the duck) to find four bubble meshes (**Figure 14.18**).

2. Select bubble01 and apply an Attachment constraint to the position track, choosing the water surface as the target object. Be careful not to select the trough. Use the Select Objects dialog (default shortcut H), if necessary, to select the correct target surface. As before, the mesh may disappear from the viewport as it is moved by default to Face #1.

3. Repeat step 2 for bubble02, bubble03, and bubble04. If you go to the Camera viewport, you won't see the bubbles at all, but you can place them in the scene without selecting them visually.

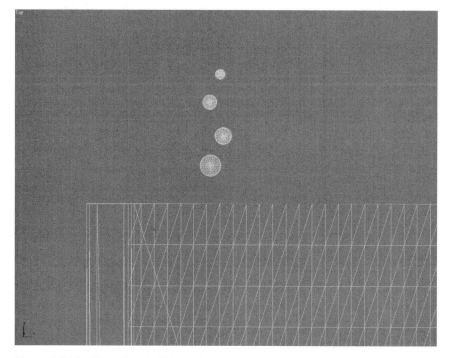

Figure 14.18   These four bubble meshes will be constrained to the water as well.

4. Bubble04 should still be selected, and the Motion panel should be open. Go to frame 0 to avoid inadvertently adding keyframes to the bubbles. Click the Set Position button and place the bubble along the far edge of the water (**Figure 14.19**).

5. Use the Select Object dialog to select each of the three remaining bubbles and set their positions near the water's edge (**Figure 14.20**).

6. If you scrub the Time Slider, you will note that the bubbles ride the water's ripples, bobbing in place. For objects that need to be attached to a surface, and to remain in place with respect to the surface, standard application of the Attachment constraint is a quick and useful tool.

As we have seen in this series of exercises, attachment can be used to keep animated objects aligned to a target surface as long as a little scripting is used, as well as to create simpler relationships with nonanimated objects. In this next exercise, we will use the Linked XForm modifier to explore another method of control.

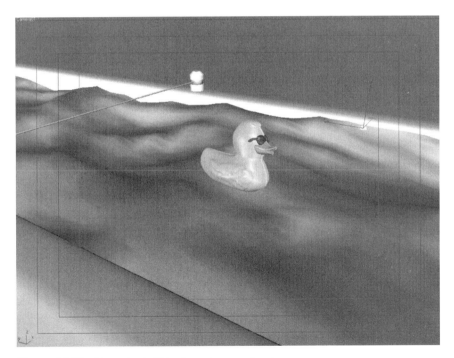

Figure 14.19   Place the bubble along the water's edge.

Figure 14.20   All four bubbles will now bob along the water's edge.

Linked XForm

Up to this point in our animation, the duck's motion looks reasonably good, except that there is no apparent reason for the duck's ability to fight the water's current. This will be taken care of by attaching the duck to the yellow string. The first step in the process is to create a helper object and use it to control the midpoint of the string.

1. The string itself is a simple loft, created from a circular shape and a path. Select string_path, activate Vertex sub-object mode, and select the middle vertex of the path (**Figure 14.21**).

2. Move the vertex around and you will see that the string itself moves as well (**Figure 14.22**). The loft object used to create the string is dependent on the path, so altering the path alters the loft. Undo your moves to return the vertex to its original location.

   In order to attach the middle of the string to the duck, we need a way to abstract the positioning of the middle vertex. The best tool for that is the Linked XForm modifier.

Figure 14.21   Select the middle vertex of the string path.

Figure 14.22   Moving vertices on the control path also changes the loft.

Linked XForm allows you to control an object, or a sub-object selection, by linking it to another object. In this case, we will control a single selected vertex with a Dummy.

3. Create a Dummy (Create panel > Helpers > Standard), and use the Align tool to align the center of the Dummy with the center of the string (or string_path) (**Figure 14.23**).

Tip

Aligning the Dummy with the object (or selection) to be controlled before linking can reduce later errors caused by offset transforms.

4. Select string_path, once again activate Vertex sub-object mode, and select the middle vertex of the path. It may already be selected, as the last sub-object selection is retained.

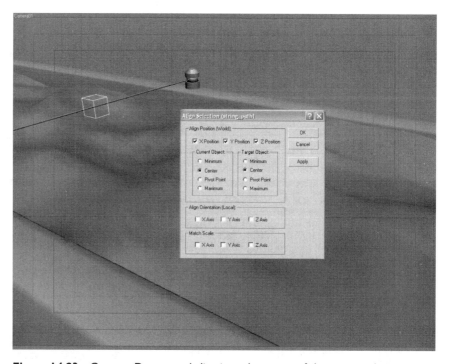

Figure 14.23   Create a Dummy and align it to the center of the string path.

5. Without exiting sub-object mode, apply a Linked XForm modifier (**Figure 14.24**). It is important not to exit sub-object mode before applying the new modifier because the selection will not be passed along the modifier stack.

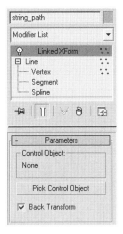

Figure 14.24   Apply a Linked XForm modifier to control the center vertex.

Note

You may find that sub-object selections are suddenly not being passed to later modifiers. This problem often results when you accidentally exit sub-object mode while editing the modifier stack. Simply return to the modifier in which the selection is made, activate sub-object mode, and go to the next modifier.

6. Click the Pick Control Object button, and choose the Dummy. If you move the Dummy around, you will see how it now controls the midpoint of the string.

The final step in this process is to attach the Dummy to the duck, so that the duck will appear to be constrained by the string, although the opposite will be true. For this level of control, we will be using a Link constraint.

Link Constraints

A Link constraint links two objects in max much the same way as the standard parenting hierarchy does, with one advantage: The link can be animated. The classic example of a situation in which you'd want to use a Link constraint is when one character hands an object to a second character. The ball needs to be linked to Person A until the moment when it is placed in the hand of Person B, at which point the link is transferred from A to B. A Link constraint allows for animated linking, as well as linking to the World (which enables the object to be freely animated, independent of any control objects).

1. Confirm that the Dummy is still selected and that the Time Slider is at frame 0. Move the Dummy to the duck's tail until the string appears to pierce the end of it. You may need to use a User viewport (keyboard shortcut U) to accurately make this placement (**Figure 14.25**).

2. The simplest way to link the string to the duck would be to use the Select and Link tool. Click the Select and Link icon and click and drag from the Dummy to the duck. The pointer will change to a pair of linked squares when it is hovering over a valid link target.

3. If you return to the Camera viewport and scrub the Time Slider, you will see that the Dummy (and the midpoint of the string) follows the duck's tail throughout the animation (**Figure 14.26**).

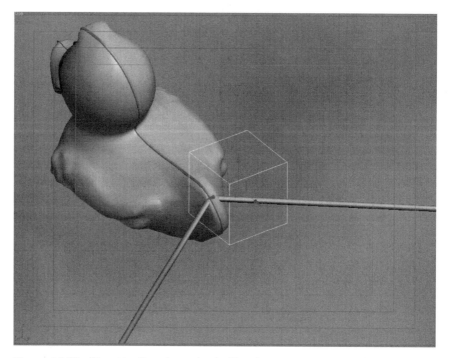

Figure 14.25 Move the Dummy to the duck's tail.

If a continuous link were all that the scene required, Select and Link would be sufficient. But if animated linking is desired, the Link constraint is the proper choice.

4. With the Dummy selected, click the Unlink Selection icon to break the link just created. The Dummy will now remain motionless and not follow the duck.

5. In the Motion panel > Assign Controller rollout, select the top-level Transform : Position/Rotation/Scale controller, and assign a Link constraint controller to the Dummy. (As with all constraints, a Link constraint can be applied either with the Animation menu item or the Assign Controller rollout.)

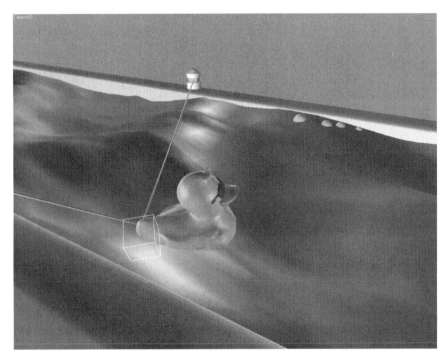

Figure 14.26 Linking the Dummy to the duck causes the midpoint of the string to follow the duck's tail.

6. The primary functions of the Link Constraint controller are handled through its Link Params rollout in the Motion panel. Link targets are listed in the Target list, with links added and deleted via the top three buttons (Add Link, Link to World, and Delete Link). The Key Mode section of the rollout pertains only to hierarchical objects, so we won't use those options in this exercise.

7. At frame 0, click the Add Link button and choose the duck. It should show up in the Target list, along with the first frame in which the link will be active.

8. Scrub the Time Slider forward to frame 180 (note that the Dummy follows the duck, just as it did with the Select and Link tool). At frame 180, click the Link to World button (**Figure 14.27**).

Figure 14.27   Choose the World as the second link target.

As long as the World is the active link target, the Dummy can be freely animated and will no longer follow the duck. At this point, we will animate the Dummy to simulate the string snapping away from the duck.

Before adding any keyframed movement to the Dummy, we need to create a key that will lock the Dummy's position as of frame 180. If we don't do this, the first positional key after frame 180 will be interpolated beginning at frame 0, which will cause the Dummy's position in relation to the duck to slowly wander when it is supposed to be linked to the duck.

At frame 180, go the PRS Parameters rollout (in the Motion panel, below the Link Params rollout) and click Position and Rotation in the Create Key area. We have now set position and rotation keys, even though Auto Key mode is not active.

1. Turn on Auto Key mode and go to a Top viewport. Go to frame 195 (note that the Dummy is no longer following the duck), and move the Dummy on the View XY plane to simulate a quick snapping motion (**Figure 14.28**).

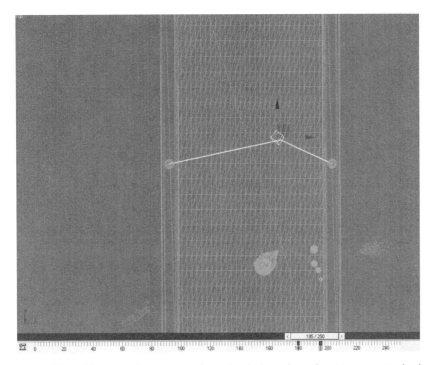

Figure 14.28   Move the Dummy away from the duck to show the string snapping back.

Over the remaining 55 frames of the animation, we will move the Dummy back and forth, ending with a position near the original center of the string. For progressive animation sequences like this, displaying an object's trajectory can be quite helpful.

2. At the top of the Motion panel, click the Trajectories button to view the Dummy's path in the viewport (**Figure 14.29**).

3. Continue moving the Dummy and setting keyframes until the Dummy returns to the original midpoint of the string at frame 250 (**Figure 14.30**). Moving objects while Trajectories is activated can be a little sluggish, because the trajectory is constantly being recalculated.

4. Turn off Auto Key mode.

   If you scrub the Time Slider, you should see the string snap away from the duck at frame 180. The final touch remaining is to allow the duck to slide downstream once its link to the string is broken.

5. Select the duck and go to frame 180. Still using the Top viewport, note the duck's position in the water. If the Motion panel is still in Trajectories mode, change it to Parameters mode to expose the Attachment Parameters rollout.

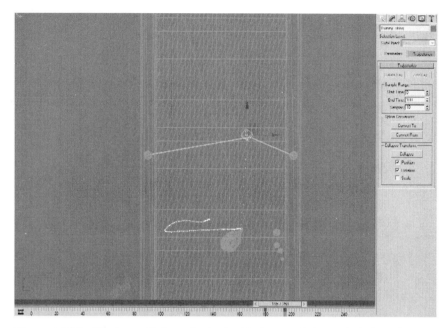

Figure 14.29 Turning on Trajectories in the Motion panel shows the selected object's path.

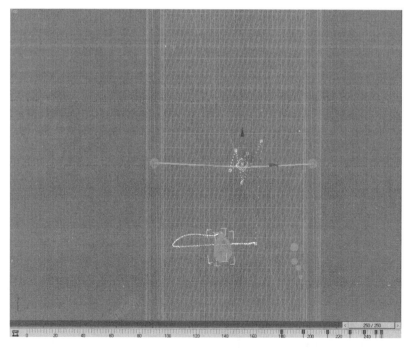

Figure 14.30 Using the displayed trajectory as your guide, animate the Dummy to bounce back to its original position.

6. Go to frame 250, click Set Position, and move the duck downstream.

   If you scrub the Time Slider between frames 180 and 250, you may see that the duck doesn't immediately head downstream. The duck's path will be affected if you set attachment keys for this time frame earlier in this exercise. In the author's version of this exercise, attachment keys were set at frames 220 and 235. In order for the duck to move directly downstream, those attachment keys need to be deleted.

7. For each key between frames 180 and 250, right-click on it in the track bar and choose Delete Key > duck: Attachment from the contextual menu. Once all the extraneous attachment keys are deleted, the duck should head downstream.

If you view this animation from the Camera viewport, or view the rendered movie duck.mov from the DVD, you will see the duck riding the waves, being constrained by the string, and finally breaking free to wander downstream. To compare your results with the author's, open the attachment_constraint_complete file on the DVD.

Next we will mix the Surface constraint with keyframes to control a wooden doll balancing on a swaying rope.

Surface and LookAt Constraints

The Surface constraint is similar to the Attachment constraint in that it constrains an object to the surface of a target object. The primary limitation of the Surface constraint is that only parametric (nonmesh) objects work as target surfaces. Eligible surfaces are the following:

- Sphere, Cone, Cylinder and Torus primitives
- Single quad patches
- NURBS objects
- Loft objects

In this exercise, we will explore the use of the Surface constraint to attach a mesh to a loft object. Lofts are one of the more commonly used compound objects, particularly for organic shapes, elaborate extrusions, and—as in this case—rope. If you wish to preview the animation you will be creating, play the rendered movie dolls.mov on the DVD.

1. Open the max file surface_constraint_begin.max from the DVD. This 300-frame scene contains a rope slung between two posts and a traditional Japanese kokeshi doll (**Figure 14.31**).

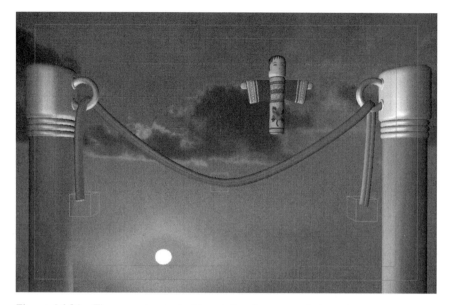

Figure 14.31   The scene to start with: a doll and a rope to balance it on.

2. Scrub the Time Slider and note how the rope sags from side to side. This effect has been set up using the same technique we used in the previous section to attach the middle of the string to the duck. In this case, three vertices in the loft's path are controlled by dummies (Dummy_left, Dummy_middle, and Dummy_right).

3. To examine how this is set up, select the rope_path spline and examine its modifier stack (**Figure 14.32**).

Figure 14.32   The rope is controlled via a series of SplineSelect and Linked XForm modifiers.

Tip

If at any time the rope starts acting strangely or fails to follow the dummies, check
that the vertex selections are being passed down the stack and that the final Linked
XForm modifier (top of the stack) is selected.

4. To attach the doll to the rope's surface, select the doll and go either to Animation >
   Constraints > Surface Constraint or to the Motion panel > Assign Position
   Controller rollout and apply the Surface constraint controller to the doll's posi-
   tion track.

5. Choose the rope as the Current Surface Object (max will not allow you to choose
   an ineligible object such as the rope's path). Surface-constrained objects are placed
   according to the target surface's UV coordinates. By default, the doll has been
   placed at (0,0) on the rope (**Figure 14.33**).

 Tip

Be very careful when you change Surface Controller UV coordinates, as inputting
negative values can crash max.

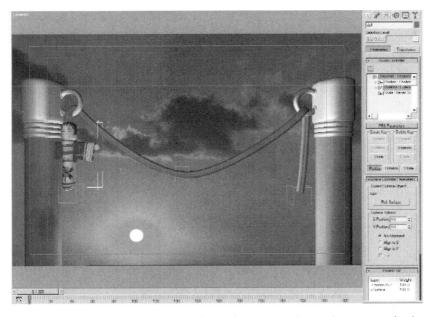

Figure 14.33   The Surface constraint places objects according to the target surface's
UV coordinates.

6. Place the doll in the center of the rope by going to the Motion panel > Position track > Surface Controller Parameters rollout and setting V Position to 50 (**Figure 14.34**).

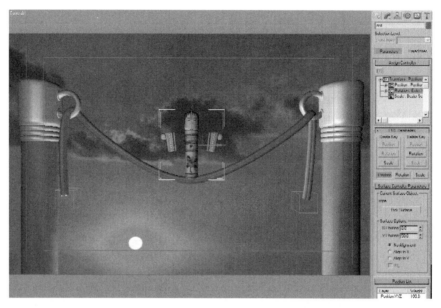

Figure 14.34 Setting V Position to 50 percent will place a Surface-constrained object in the middle (lengthwise) of a target loft.

If you use the spinners to change the U Position value, you will see the base of the doll move around the loft's circumference. Align to U should be activated so that the doll will point away from the rope's surface as it rotates. (Before continuing, confirm that U Position is set to 0 and that No Alignment is turned on.)

If you scrub the Time Slider, the doll will move to follow the rope's deformations. It may appear that the doll is moving back and forth on the rope, but that visual effect is due to the rope's stretching.

7. To slide the doll along the rope, we will animate the V Position value. Turn on Auto Key mode, go to frame 100, and set V Position to 55. The doll will move a short distance along the rope's length.

8. Go to frame 250, and set V Position to 45.

9. To return the doll to its original position, go to frame 300 and set V Position to 50. Turn off Auto Key mode. As you scrub the Time Slider, the doll will slide from side to side, following the rope's deformations.

The doll now seems to balance on the rope, but it's a bit static. How about adding a nice spin to the doll?

Mixing Keyframes with Constraints

In this section, you will rotate the doll with a manual keyframe as it follows the position track you have set up using a Surface constraint.

1. Turn on Auto Key mode and go to frame 300.

2. In the Motion panel, make sure the rotation track is active (turn it on at the bottom of the PRS Parameters rollout). Still in the same rollout, click the Rotation button under Create Key to create a key at the current frame.

3. In the Euler Parameters rollout, set Rotation Axis to Z.

4. In the Key Info (Basic) rollout, set Value to 1800. Turn off Auto Key mode.

You can now scrub the Time Slider to see the doll rotate 1800 degrees (five full rotations) over the course of the animation. Suppose we now want to add some animated objects dancing on the doll as the doll dances on the rope? The Surface constraint can help us with that as well.

Recursive Constraints

It is possible to use the Surface constraint to place new objects on already-constrained objects. The doll is a mesh, so it is not eligible to be a target surface, but by linking an eligible surface to the doll, this limitation can be overcome.

1. Unhide the objects doll_right, QuadPatch_left, and QuadPatch_right.

   The two quad patches have already been linked to the doll and placed on its shoulders. The smaller doll will be constrained to the shoulders of the original doll, using the quad patches as target surfaces.

2. Select doll_right and Surface-constrain it to QuadPatch_right (**Figure 14.35**).

   We'll have the smaller doll slide along the larger doll's shoulders during the animation, so turn on Auto Key mode, go to frame 100, and set V Position to 55 (**Figure 14.36**).

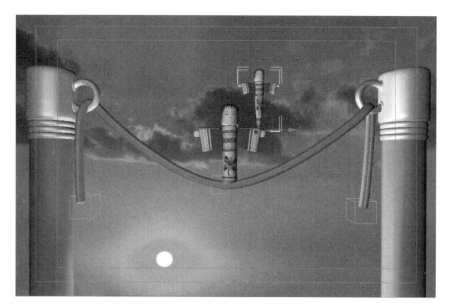

Figure 14.35 Constraining the smaller doll to the linked QuadPatch gives the appearance that it is riding on the original doll's shoulders.

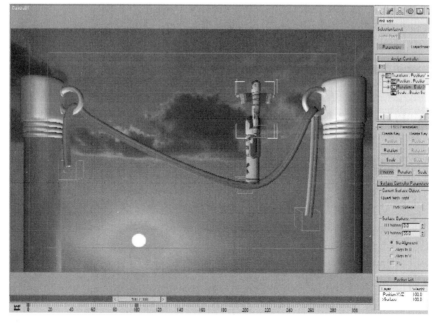

Figure 14.36 The smaller doll remains attached but does not rotate.

Note

The smaller doll does not inherit the original doll's rotation because it is not linked as a child, only constrained to follow the quad patch's surface.

3. Go to frame 250 and set V Position to 45. Turn off Auto Key mode.

4. To create a duplicate doll on the other shoulder, confirm that doll_right is still selected and Clone it, using Copy as the method. Name the clone doll_left.

5. Place the new doll on the opposite shoulder by changing its Current Surface Object (Motion Panel > Surface Controller Parameters rollout) to QuadPatch_left (**Figure 14.37**).

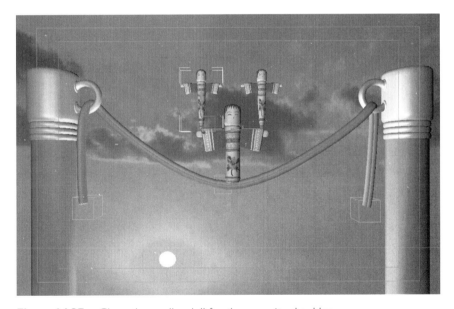

Figure 14.37   Clone the smaller doll for the opposite shoulder.

If you scrub the Time Slider, you will see that the new doll starts off on the far end of the shoulder, mirroring the position of the original. This is because the two quad patches are mirrors of each other; if they were not, you would need to change the keyframed V Position values to achieve mirrored movement.

Next we will control the leaning of the smaller dolls with a new constraint.

LookAt Constraints

The LookAt constraint gives us control over any one of an object's axes, so that it will always point toward a target object, even if the target moves.

1. Zoom out in the Front viewport, select Dummy_lookat, and in the Motion panel, turn on Trajectories mode. The path of this Dummy will be displayed (**Figure 14.38**).

   The two smaller dolls will be constrained to always point at this Dummy, giving them a nice animated lean throughout the animation.

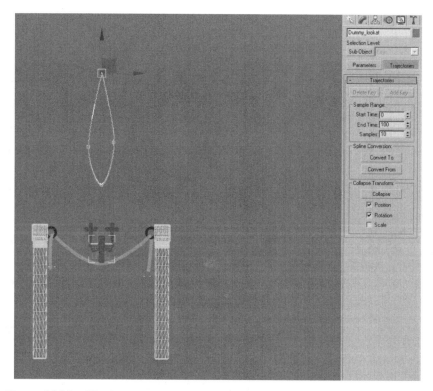

Figure 14.38   This Dummy will be used as the LookAt target.

2. Return to Parameters mode and select doll_right. Go to Animation > Constraints > LookAt Constraint and choose Dummy_lookat as the target. Turn off Add LookAt Target.

   The doll will immediately lie on its side, because the X axis is assigned, by default, as the axis to align.

3. In the LookAt Constraint rollout, set the LookAt Axis to Z to correct the doll's orientation.

4. Repeat steps 2 through 3 for doll_left, and return to the Camera viewport to more clearly see the doll's lean toward the target Dummy (**Figure 14.39**).

Figure 14.39   Both dolls are oriented using the LookAt constraint.

This lean has created a problem—the dolls will now intersect each other at several points in the animation. This can be avoided by changing their beginning rotation setting.

1. With doll_right selected, go to the Motion panel, and click the Set Orientation button. This allows you to rotate the doll free of the LookAt constraint.

2. Rotate the doll –50 degrees on the View Z Axis (**Figure 14.40**).

3. Turn off Set Orientation, and repeat the process for doll_left, except rotate it +50 degrees, so the two dolls are facing each other. This will minimize their intersection.

To compare your results with the author's, open the surface_constraint_complete.max file from the DVD. As we have seen, the Surface and LookAt constraints can be very useful in controlling aspects of an object's animation. In the next exercise, we will explore Path and Position constraints, as well as Parameter Wiring.

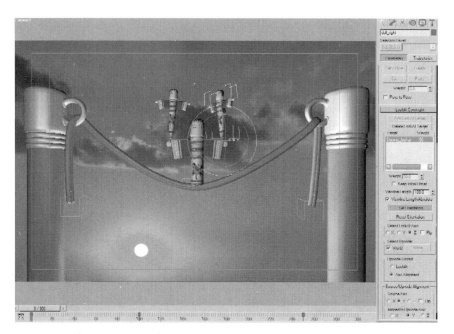

Figure 14.40   Use the Set Orientation button to change the doll's base rotation.

Path Constraints

In this section, we will use Path constraints to launch a rocket and place it into orbit around a small planetoid. A Path constraint allows an object's position to be controlled by one or more paths, with weighted influences.

1. Open the max file path_constraint_begin.max on the DVD. To preview the results of this exercise, check out launch.mov, found in the same folder. This scene contains a rotating planet, a rocket, and a small moon (**Figure 14.41**).

   Two paths have also been provided in the scene: path_launch will determine the rocket's initial course, and path_moon_orbit defines a looping path around the moon. Note that the paths have been placed so that the last node on the launch path coincides with the first node of the orbit path. When constraining an object to move directly from one path to another, it is helpful if you can align nodes in this way.

2. Select path_launch, go to the Modify panel, and enter Vertex sub-object mode. In the Top viewport, select the first vertex in the path (the one that coincides with the rocket's location) (**Figure 14.42**).

3. Without exiting sub-object mode, apply a Linked XForm modifier. Pick Dummy_launchpoint as the control object. This helper will control the first point in the launch path and thereby determine the place from which the rocket will launch.

We will want the rocket to rest on the planet's surface for the first 40 frames of this animation and then launch, so it is important that at frame 40 the rocket should be clearly visible.

Figure 14.41   A simple space scene.

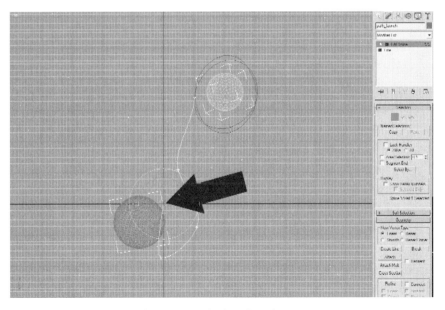

Figure 14.42   Select the first node in the launch path.

4. Go to frame 40, select the Dummy, and return to the Camera viewport. We will use the Normal Align tool to place the Dummy on the planet's surface. Activate the Normal Align tool (Toolbar > Align > Normal Align), click on the Dummy, and then click and drag on the planet's surface to place the rocket near the middle of the planet's visible surface (**Figure 14.43**). Note how the beginning of the launch path moves with the Dummy. Click OK in the Normal Align dialog when you are satisfied with your results.

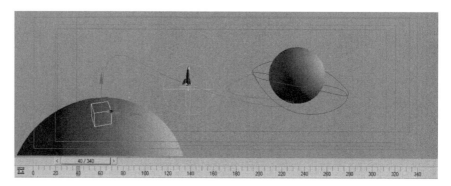

Figure 14.43   Use the Normal Align tool to place the Dummy on the planet's surface.

5. To provide an animatable link between the Dummy and the planet, assign a Link constraint to the Dummy, choosing the planet as the target. Be certain to set this constraint up at frame 40, so that the Dummy's position in the time frame will remain intact.

   If you scrub the Time Slider, you will see that the Dummy rotates along with the planet, even prior to frame 40. Beginning with frame 41, the launch path needs to be disconnected from the planet. This can be done by adding a link to the World.

6. At frame 41, go to the Motion Panel, and in the Link Params rollout, click the Link to World button. If you scrub the Time Slider, you will note that the Dummy rotates with the planet only up to frame 41.

Animating the Rocket

Now we will work on setting up the rocket and placing it on the path. To begin with, there are three objects that need to follow the rocket through the scene.

1. Select Omni_rocketflame (the source of light for the rocket's blast), PF Source 01 (a particle emitter to provide the smoke trail), and Rocket_flame (a mesh to represent the actual flame).

2. Use the Select and Link tool to link all three of these objects to the rocket. Use the Select Objects dialog, with Display Subtree checked, to check your hierarchy, if you wish (**Figure 14.44**).

3. To place the rocket on the launch path, select the rocket and apply a Path constraint to the position track, choosing path_launch as the target path. It does not matter at what frame you create the constraint.

4. Go to frame 0 and confirm that the rocket is placed on the planet's surface (**Figure 14.45**).

5. To align the rocket with the path, go to the Motion panel, and in the Path Parameters rollout, check Follow and choose the Z Axis. By default, Constant Velocity should be checked, giving the rocket a constant speed regardless of the varying distance between path vertices.

Figure 14.44   The rocket will be followed in the scene by three objects.

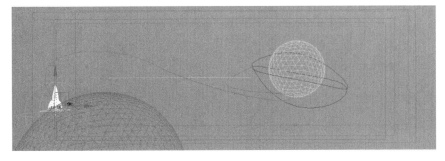

Figure 14.45   Using a Path constraint, the rocket has been placed on the launch path.

By default, Path Constraint sets keyframes at the first and last frames of the animation, animating the placement of the constrained object along the path from 0 percent to 100 percent. We will need to change these settings first to keep the rocket on the planet's surface until its launch at frame 40.

6. In the Time Bar, select the key at frame 0 and Shift-drag it to frame 40 to create a copy of the key. This key contains only the % Along Path information, so what we have done here is prolong the rocket's placement at the beginning of the path through frame 40.

7. We will need to accelerate the rocket after launch, so move the key at frame 340 to frame 75. The rocket should now reach the end of the launch path by frame 75.

Path Weighting and Percentages

Beginning with frame 76, we want the rocket to orbit the moon by following a new path.

1. In the Path Parameters rollout, click Add Path and choose path_moon_orbit.

   The rocket will now follow a rather bizarre trajectory, which is an average of the two paths, because they are weighted the same. Let's now animate their weights so that control of the rocket is handled by the launch path first and the orbit path second.

2. In the Path Parameters rollout, confirm that path_moon_orbit is still selected and set its weight to 0. This will return control to the launch path, as before.

3. Go to frame 76, turn on Auto Key mode, and set the orbit path's weight to 50. Still in the Path Parameters rollout, select path_launch and set its weight to 0.

4. These keys will transfer control of the rocket to the orbit path beginning with frame 76, but the two paths will still be averaged during frames 0 to 75. To correct this, go to frame 75 and set a Weight key of 50 for path_launch and a Weight key of 0 for path_moon_orbit.

   The two paths should now transfer control seamlessly between frames 75 and 76, as you can see in Track View (**Figure 14.46**).

   The rocket will not, however, continue along the orbit path until its % Along Path value is animated.

5. Confirm that Auto Key mode is still active, go to frame 76, and in the Path Options of the Path Parameters rollout, set % Along Path to 1. We start the rocket at 1 percent to avoid the momentary pause in its flight that would be caused if it went from 100 percent of the launch path to 0 percent of the orbit path, given that those two positions are the same.

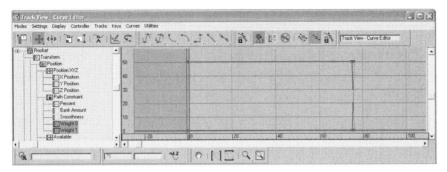

Figure 14.46   Control of the rocket will pass from one path to another.

6. We will give the rocket 2 seconds to complete its looping orbit of the moon. Go to frame 130 and set % Along Path to 100. This will cause the rocket to fly quickly around the moon twice between frames 76 and 130.

7. In order to propel the rocket along its path for another orbit, go to the next frame (frame 131) and set % Along Path to 3.5. Turn off Auto Key mode. The decrease in value from 100 percent to 3.5 percent is designed to overcome the pause we might otherwise see when the path repeats.

   We'll divide the remaining 270 frames of this animation into three more trips around the orbit path, lasting 70 frames each.

8. In the Time Bar, select the keys at frames 130 and 131, and copy them by Shift-dragging to frames 200 and 201, an offset of 70 frames.

9. Copy the keys to frames 269 and 270, and to frames 339 and 340 to complete the cycle (**Figure 14.47**).

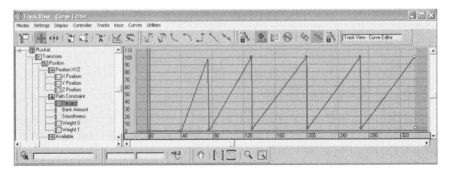

Figure 14.47   The rocket will travel along the launch path once (shown by the first ramp in the curve) and the orbital path four times (the final four ramps).

Paths Within Paths

Now that the rocket's path has been defined, suppose that we wanted to have the moon orbiting around the planet as the rocket continues to orbit around the moon. This is not difficult to achieve, so long as we preserve the relationships between the rocket and the orbit path.

1. Unhide Dummy_moonorbit and path_moon. These objects will define a path for the moon to follow.

    If you scrub the Time Slider, you will note that Dummy_moonorbit is already constrained to move along the new path. Once we have linked the moon to the Dummy, we will link the orbit path to the moon.

2. Go to frame 0, select the moon, and Link it to Dummy_moonorbit. If you scrub the Time Slider, you will see that the moon advances along its path and is well beyond the rocket at frame 76. Clearly, this is not the desired effect.

3. Return to frame 0 and Unlink the moon.

4. Go to frame 76, and once again Link the moon to the Dummy. Now the moon will be in its original position when the rocket arrives.

5. Still at frame 76, select path_moon_orbit and Link it to the moon.

If you had linked the orbit path to the moon at frame 0, a problem would crop up at frame 76, when the rocket is supposed to move from the launch path to the orbit path. Because the orbit path would have rotated from its original orientation, the paths would no longer be contiguous, causing a jump in the rocket's path between frames 75 and 76 (**Figure 14.48**).

If you scrub the Time Slider, you will note that even though the path is rotating with the planet, the rocket's transition is seamless. Next we will use the Position constraint to control the location of a satellite.

Position Constraints

The Position constraint allows you to control the location of an object using one or more other objects with weighted influences. Think of it as using magnets to pull or push an object through a scene.

1. Unhide Dummy_satellite and [Satellite]. The Dummy will be one of several objects used to control the satellite's position.

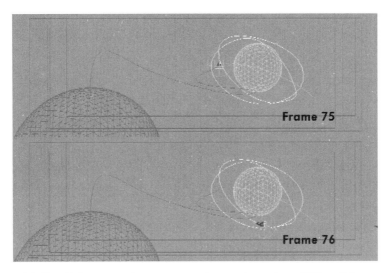

Figure 14.48   If the two paths are not contiguous, the rocket will "jump" from one to the other.

2. Select the satellite and apply a Position constraint, selecting Dummy_satellite as the target object. The satellite will immediately move to the Dummy's location, as the Dummy is the sole position target.

3. Add the planet and the moon to the Target list as well (**Figure 14.49**).

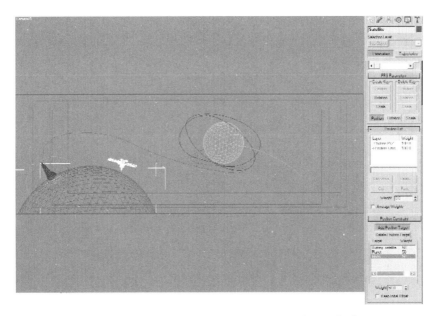

Figure 14.49   Adding two more position targets averages the satellite's position.

The influence of the position targets can be seen by scrubbing the Time Slider. The moon is the only position target with an animated position, and the satellite will be pulled slightly toward the moon as it moves.

4. To give the Dummy greater influence over the satellite's position, select Dummy_satellite in the Target list (Position Constraint rollout) and set its weight to 100.

5. Select Dummy_satellite, and turn on Auto Key mode. First, we'll use the Dummy to move the satellite close to the rocket when it goes into orbit.

6. Go to frame 75, and in the Top viewport, move the Dummy closer to the rocket's launch path (**Figure 14.50**). Note how the satellite is "pushed" along ahead of the Dummy.

7. In the Camera viewport, move the Dummy up on the View Z Axis to approximately Z = 70 to pull the satellite higher in the viewport.

8. As the scene progresses, we'll pull the satellite in tighter on the moon. Go to frame 140, and in the Top viewport, move the Dummy to approximately X = 70, Y = 10, so that the satellite follows the moon.

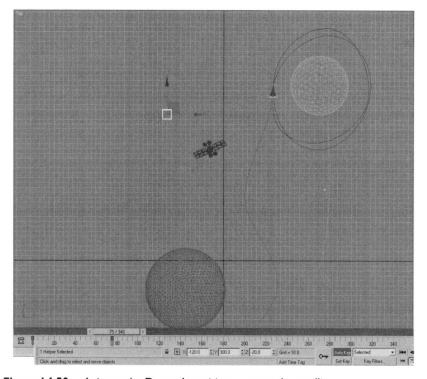

Figure 14.50   Animate the Dummy's position to move the satellite.

9. Go to frame 200, and move the Dummy to near X = 13, Y = –220.

10. Finally, go to the last frame of the animation, and move the Dummy to near X = 115, Y = –550 (**Figure 14.51**).

11. Return to the Camera viewport and scrub the Time Slider to see how the satellite swoops through the scene. Note that the satellite almost leaves the frame, but not quite. We can accelerate it out of the frame by animating the position targets' weighting.

12. Select the satellite, and in the Motion panel, set the weight of the "Planet" and "Moon" position targets to 30. Turn off Auto Key mode.

    The satellite will now follow the Dummy more closely as the scene progresses, due to the lessening influence of the other two position targets.

Something is still missing from this scene—what is a rocket launch without explosive effects? In the next section, we will add some excitement to this scene and explore the use of manipulators for rigging animations.

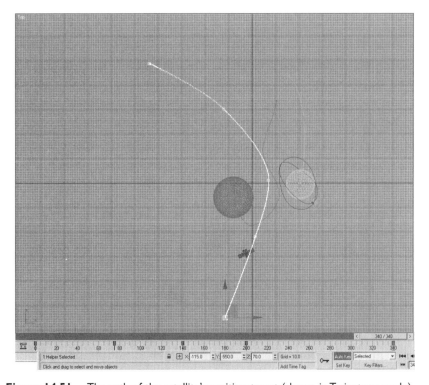

Figure 14.51   The path of the satellite's position target (shown in Trajectory mode).

Manipulators

Manipulators are onscreen helpers, such as sliders, that can be wired to specific tracks of one or more scene objects. In this section, we will create two sliders to control aspects of the rocket's launch and flight.

1. Go to Create panel > Helpers > Manipulators.

2. Go to a Front viewport (manipulators cannot be created in a Camera viewport). Click the Slider button and click in the viewport to create a slider manipulator. Name this manipulator Slider_launch_shake.

3. This slider will now appear in any active viewport. Go to the Modify panel and enter "launch shake" in the Label box to change the name of the slider as it will appear in viewports.

4. Return to the Camera viewport and move the slider, using the Select and Manipulate tool, into the upper left corner of the viewport (**Figure 14.52**). If the slider does not appear in the Camera viewport, it may be outside the cropped region, requiring you to go to the Front viewport to move the slider closer to the center of the viewport. To move the slider in an orthogonal viewport, click and drag the small box to the left of the slider. Click the Select and Manipulate button again to exit that mode.

    The primary effect of this slider will be to add a shaking motion to the rocket before it launches. In order to accomplish this, a Noise controller must be layered on the position track of the Dummy controlling the rocket's position.

5. Select Dummy_launchpoint and go to the Motion panel > Assign Controller rollout. Expand Link Params to see the individual position, rotation, and scale tracks.

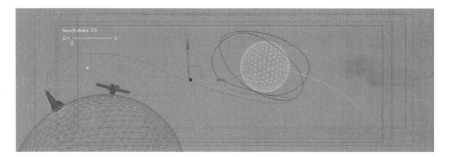

Figure 14.52   This slider will be used to control the shaking of the rocket during launch.

6. Highlight Position : Position XYZ, click the Assign Controller button, choose the Position List controller, and click OK.

7. Expand the position track, now labeled Position : Position List, to see that an empty track named Available has been added.

8. Highlight Available and assign a Noise Position controller to it. This will bring up a Properties dialog for the Noise controller.

9. We want this controller to provide a small shake on the Z axis, so set X Strength to 0, Y Strength to 0, and Z Strength to 5.

10. Close the Noise Controller dialog. Note that if you scrub the Time Slider, the Dummy will shake throughout the animation.

Wiring a Slider

Now we will wire the slider to the Weight value of the Noise controller.

1. Select the slider, and in the right-click menu, choose Wire Parameters > Object (Slider) > value. (This is the slider's output.) Choose Dummy_launchpoint as the target, going to Transform > Link Params > Position > Weights > Weight: Noise Position (**Figure 14.53**).

2. This will bring up the Parameter Wiring dialog, with the slider's value track highlighted in the top left pane and the Dummy's Weight: Noise Position track in the top right pane. Click the right arrow to establish control flowing from the slider to the Dummy. Click Connect to activate the wiring (**Figure 14.54**).

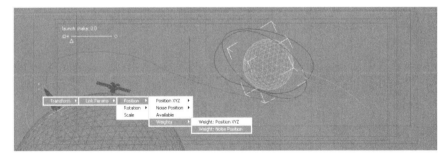

Figure 14.53   Wiring the slider to the Dummy.

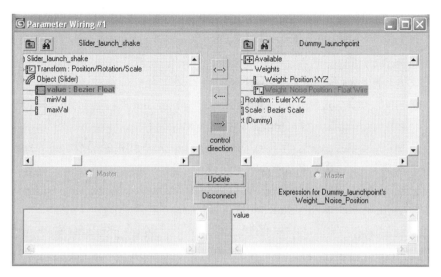

Figure 14.54 The Parameter Wiring dialog.

3. The Parameter Wiring dialog is modeless; while it is still open, you can scrub the Time Slider to evaluate the results of your wiring. The immediate result is that the shake effect is gone because the default value of the slider, which now corresponds to the weight of the Noise Controller, is 0.

4. To give a nice, subtle effect, change the code in the lower right pane (labeled Expression for Dummy_launchpoint's Weight_Noise_Position) to this:

```
value/100
```

5. Close the Parameter Wiring dialog and use the Select and Manipulate tool to drag the slider's Adjust Value indicator toward the right, to its maximum value of 100. When you scrub the Time Slider, you should now see the rocket and its parent Dummy shake slightly. Return the slider value to 0, and exit Select and Manipulate mode.

Adding Particles

It seems reasonable that this pre-launch shaking would be accompanied by some smoke. Fortunately, a particle system has been provided for just this purpose.

1. Press 6 to open Particle View (**Figure 14.55**).

    If you're unfamiliar with Particle Flow, the event-driven particle system included with 3ds max, this schematic may seem a little complicated. Basically, it represents a flow of particles from a Particle Flow source icon (which you linked to the rocket at the beginning of this exercise) to various events, which will produce a dissipating trail of smoke from the rocket. For more information on Particle Flow, including a tutorial that examines this sort of smoke effect in greater detail, see Chapter 18.

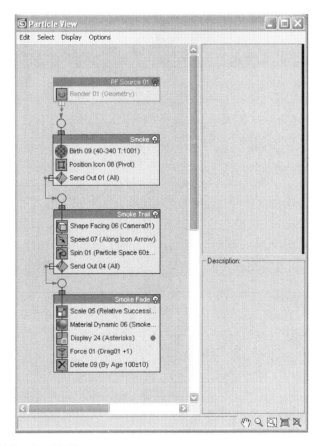

Figure 14.55   Particle View.

2. At this point, the particle flow is turned off, as evidenced by the darkened light bulb in the title bar of the first event (titled PF Source 01). Click the light bulb to turn it white and activate the particle flow. Scrub the Time Slider to see a stream of smoke particles being emitted from the rocket (**Figure 14.56**).

Let's wire the slider into a couple of parameters in this particle flow, so that, as the pre-launch shaking increases, the particles will get faster and disperse more widely.

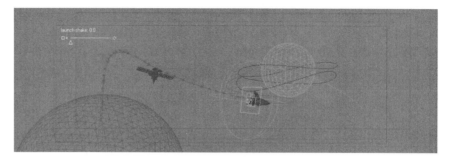

Figure 14.56   Smoke particles are emitted from the rocket.

3. Close Particle View and go to frame 0 (making particle flow edits at frame 0 increases viewport response).

4. Select the slider, and as before, in the right-click menu, choose Wire Parameters > Object (Slider) > value. Choose PF Source 01 as the target, going to Object (PF Source) > Smoke Trail > Speed 07 > Speed.

5. Set the control direction from the slider toward the PF Source, using the following code in the pane labeled "Expression for PF Source 01's Speed":

    ```
    Value/10+15
    ```

6. Click the Connect button to activate the expression. This expression will maintain the smoke particles' original speed of 15 and add a value equal to one-tenth the slider's setting, giving a top speed of 25 when the slider is at 100 percent.

 Note

> Once a Particle Flow parameter has been wired to a manipulator, it is no longer directly editable in Particle View. This holds true for any value that is controlled by a manipulator.

7. We'll also use this slider to control how widely the particles are dispersed. Wire the slider to the PF Source icon again, this time wiring to Object (PF Source) > Smoke Trail > Speed 07 > Divergence. Use the following code for the Divergence parameter:

    ```
    Value*1.8
    ```

    As the slider's value increases from 0 to 100, the angle of particle dispersion will ramp up from 0 to 180 degrees.

Animating Sliders

Now that we've set up the controls for this slider, let's get some use out of it by animating its value.

1. Go to frame 10, turn on Auto Key mode, and activate Select and Manipulate mode. Drag the triangle handle on the slider until the value reads 70.0.

2. Go to frame 40, and increase the slider value to its maximum setting of 100.0.

3. Go to frame 41 (the first frame when the rocket is no longer attached to the planet), and decrease the slider setting to 0. Turn off Auto Key mode.

    If you scrub the Time Slider, you will see that smoke particles are emitted more widely, and with greater speed, up to the moment of launch. We'll now create a second slider to control the rocket's flame.

4. Select the original slider and make a Clone of it, using Copy as the method. Rename the new slider Slider_flame_strength. In the Modify panel, change its Label to "flame strength".

5. Manipulators cannot be moved in the viewport using the standard Move tool, but the slider's viewport coordinates are available in the Modify panel. The X Position and Y Position values measure distance from the upper right corner of the viewport, so increase the Y Position value until the new slider is moved below the original (**Figure 14.57**).

6. Obviously, we don't want the same keyframes, so select all three new keys in the Time Bar, then right-click and choose Delete Selected Keys. Be sure to leave the key at frame 0 with a slider value of 0.

7. Wire this slider to the mesh used to represent the jet flame, named Rocket_flame, wiring to Transform > Scale > Z Scale (**Figure 14.58**). Be sure to indicate control direction using the correct arrow key and click the Connect button before closing the Parameter Wiring dialog.

8. If you test the flame strength slider by going to approximately frame 50 and increasing its value to 100, you will see that the length of the flame goes right out of the viewport. Let's reduce the maximum range of this slider in the Modify panel by setting Maximum to 60.

9. This slider will also be used to control the brightness and range of the light attached to the rocket's jet. Go to Animation > Wire Parameters > Parameter Wire Dialog to reopen the dialog.

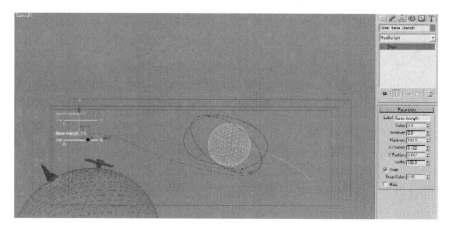

Figure 14.57   Use the new slider's Y Position value to move it in the viewport.

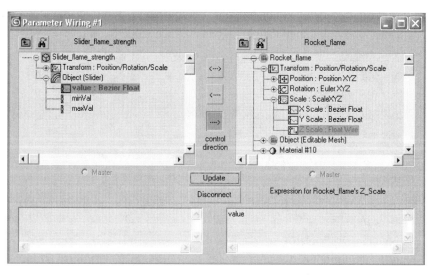

Figure 14.58   This expression will allow slider control of the flame mesh's length.

10. From the Parameter Wire dialog, select Slider_flame_strength, then go to the "value : Bezier Float" track in the left pane. Click the Find Next Parameter (binoculars) icon over the right pane to automatically bring up the parameter already wired to a slider. The first one selected will be the Weight: Noise Position parameter wired to the launch shake slider. You can use the same icon repeatedly to cycle through wired parameters.

Note

The pop-up tool tip for the Find Next Parameter icon indicates that only parameters wired to the parameter already selected in the opposite pane will be found, but in actuality the results will include any wired parameter.

11. In the right pane, go to Objects > Rocket > Omni_rocketflame > Object (Omni Light) > Multiplier.

12. Connect the slider value to the light's multiplier, using the following expression:

```
Value/60+1
```

This will give the light a minimum multiplier of 1.0, ranging up to 2.0 when the slider is at maximum. Don't forget to indicate the control direction and to connect the wire.

13. To connect the slider to the light's range, scroll down in the right pane to the Decay Falloff parameter. Wire the slider to this parameter as well, using the following expression:

```
Value/6+30
```

14. This will vary the light's range between 30 and 40 units. Close the Parameter Wiring dialog. Now let's animate the slider and see how it works.

15. Confirm that the flame strength slider is at 0. Turn on Auto Key mode, go to frame 20, and in the Modify panel, set Value to 15.

 Note

Sliders can be animated through the Modify panel without use of the Select and Manipulate tool.

16. Go to frame 43, just after the rocket launches, and increase Value to 32. Note how the rocket flame's length and the light's range increases with the slider.

17. Go to frame 47, and provide a big burst of flame by increasing the slider to its maximum of 60. Note that if you use the Modify panel to set a value greater than Maximum, the Maximum will be automatically increased.

18. Go to frame 60, as the rocket approaches the moon, and reduce the slider's value to a normal cruising value of 15.

If you like, keyframe a few more rocket bursts by bracketing a value of 60 with a pair of keys set at 15. For example, to set up a burst around frame 100, when the rocket is passing in front of the moon, set the following keys:

- Frame 100: Value = 60
- Frame 93: Value = 15
- Frame 105: Values = 15
- Turn the Auto Key button off when you're done.

If you would like to compare your results with the author's, open the max file path_constraint_complete.max from the DVD. Manipulators can be powerful tools for simplifying your animations. Consider using them whenever you have several parameters that need to be animated in unison.

Summing Up

In this chapter, you have been armed with a host of tools for taming and enhancing your animation goals. No matter what sort of creative dreams you want to bring to life in 3ds max, being smart in your approach to setting up your animation will pay huge dividends in improving production quality, saving time, and avoiding frustration. When it comes right down to it, though, sometimes the exact tool isn't found waiting for you in a menu somewhere. Then the real power of max's extensibility will become evident, when you use scripted controllers or manipulators to create custom setups on the fly.

Consider taking the exercises in this chapter even further on your own:

- Make the string used in the duck animation more realistic with the addition of more control points (more vertices on the path). Control the position of the vertices through manipulators.

- Set up a series of smaller and smaller kokeshi dolls, balanced on one another's shoulders. Use an animated Link constraint to allow them to fall or jump off their surface target quad patches.

- Use a LookAt constraint to point the satellite at the looping rocket. Use a manipulator and a Noise Position controller to shake the satellite when the rocket passes.

Now that you're adept at getting under the hood of max's animation system, apply these lessons to your next project, and see how much farther you can push the envelope.

Chapter 15

character studio

By Mark Gerhard

Everyone knew it was only a matter of time, and now, finally, it's happened. In 3ds max 7, character studio, discreet's procedural character animation plug-in, is now included as part of the base package. Every user who has 3ds max 7 will have a fully authorized copy of character studio.

So what is character studio? What's the big deal?

character studio (cs) is a powerful character animation plug-in for 3ds max developed by Unreal Pictures, now owned by discreet. 3ds max, unlike many programs, is essentially a place for plug-ins to interact, and character studio was the first plug-in to prove the power of the concept. It lets anyone create character animation instantly. (If you are interested in character rigging and animation without using character studio, see the article "Character Rigging and Animation" on the DVD.)

cs Features and Benefits

character studio is a revolutionary approach to character animation. It separates the components of the animation process into individual, interchangeable file structures that can be saved, edited, combined, reused, mixed, and matched. So the geometry of the character is independent from the animation of the character's bones. This means you could spend a week animating an ape dancing (**Figure 15.1**) and it might actually end up as a dancing alligator, or a dancing cowboy, a dancing robot, or even a dancing baby (**Figure 15.2**).

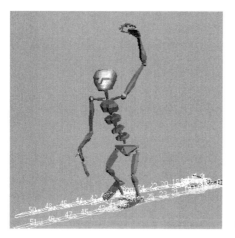

Figure 15.1   Biped skeleton of ape dancing.   **Figure 15.2**   Ape replaced by an alligator.

With character studio you can automatically generate hierarchically linked skeletons call Bipeds. These skeletons are parametrically derived—they have values that can be set at the time of creation and edited later in a Figure mode. The skeletons are already linked and rigged with inverse kinematics (IK), with joint limits that mimic a human's.

The skeletons can be animated through a variety of modes and methods including Footstep and Free Form modes, Layers, Motion Mixer, Motion Capture, Motion Scripting, and procedural Crowd systems. The animation can be saved to a .bip file (a type of motion capture file), to be reused later on the same or other characters. Using cs's Physique or Skin modifiers, or simply through hierarchical linkage, the animation of the bipedal skeleton structural can be used to drive the animation of single-skin or multi-piece characters you create yourself in 3ds max.

character studio offers unique solutions to some of the fundamental problems that face character animators. For example, it was specifically designed to address the issues of foot-to-ground contact. Animators have fought with their characters "ice-skating" instead of walking since the beginning of time (frame 0, that is), but with cs there is at last a real solution to this problem.

Character animation is by no means an easy task, even for the skilled animator, but character studio gives the novice user quick and easy tools for the creation of simple locomotion of characters. This means if you're an architect you can easily make characters walk through your environments, even if you can't hand-animate a walk cycle. On the other hand, if you are a talented 2D or 3D character animator, character studio provides a fascinating environment for making animation and does a lot of the grunt work for you.

Learning character studio might appear a daunting task at first. It does require a period of time when you can focus on tutorials. Because cs is a closed system that plays by its own rules, you can't approach it in the same way you would any other bones-and-skin-and-IK animation system. You need to spend some time to learn the cs approach. The revolutionary power comes at a price—a steep learning curve. But the time you invest in mastering character studio will definitely pay off at the other end. It's worth the effort.

Biped Rigs

Bipeds are the most common types of creatures—in the animation world, anyway. This body plan includes not only humans, but also birds, some types of dinosaurs, and any number of cartoon characters, no matter what their species. character studio has thoughtfully included a Biped body type that has much of the work done for you already. Let's take a closer look at Biped.

Creation

Biped is a 3ds max system object, so you find the tools to create the bipedal skeleton on the Create tab > Systems button. In the Object Type rollout, click the Biped button. The creation parameters are displayed in the Create Biped rollout (**Figure 15.3**).

Figure 15.3 Create Biped rollout.

There are two different Creation methods available, Drag Height or Drag Position. When you choose Drag Height, you simply press the mouse button down in the viewport where you want the feet of the standing Biped to be placed, and then move the mouse to drag out the height at that fixed position. Drag Position lets you click in the viewport and create a Biped of a specified height at the location of your mouse pointer. Moving the cursor around will reposition the Biped.

Biped skeletons come in four flavors of Body Type: Skeleton, Male, Female, and Classic (**Figures 15.4** and **15.5**).

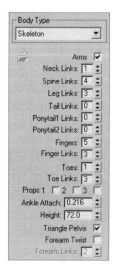

Figure 15.4 Body Type rollout.

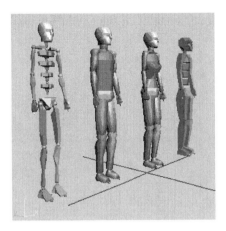

Figure 15.5   Biped Skeletons come in four choices.

The lower bottom of the rollout features a laundry list of Biped Body Parameters. These include the number of links in the neck, spine, legs, toes, and fingers. You can adjust the number of toes and fingers and specify whether you want arms, tails, ponytails, or props. These components make up the predefined Biped hierarchy and can be edited later.

These same parameters are also found in the Motion panel if you need to edit them after creating the Biped. character studio is atypical in that its parameters are all located in the Motion panel rather than the Modifier panel.

As with most 3ds max objects, upon creation you can make immediate adjustments to the control panel parameters and those changes will update automatically in the viewport.

Editing the Biped Skeleton

Once you have created a Biped rig in the viewport, you can make changes to the parts so they match the proportions of your character. The default Biped is a rather average-looking mannequin somewhat reminiscent of a crash-test dummy, but there's no reason it can't be a short squat character with a great big head instead.

The workflow that allows you to modify your Biped proportions is the following:

1. Create the Biped.

2. With the Biped selected, go to the Motion panel.

3. In the Biped rollout, click the Figure mode button. Once you are in Figure mode, you can reposition your character or change any of the structure parameters.

4. In addition to making parameter changes in the Command panel, you can use the Scale tool on the Biped bones to shorten or lengthen them. Use the Scale transform gizmo to scale along one axis to change the length of the bone. Use the other axes to make the bone wider or thicker.

 Note

Unlike the rest of 3ds max, Biped was designed to let you use the Scale tool safely on hierarchical components. Generally, you should never apply a non-uniform Scale operation to a 3ds max bone, or the effects of the scale will be passed down the hierarchy.

5. For a character with a bilaterally symmetrical body plan, click one limb in the Biped, then click the Symmetrical button in the Track Selection rollout. The opposite limb will be added to the selection of the first limb. This does not make the two limbs symmetrical, but only adds the opposite side's objects to the selection set.

6. You can reposition some of the Biped components but not others (**Figure 15.6**). For instance, you cannot move the head away from the neck, but you can move the neck away from the body. You can move the clavicles and the arms away from the body, but you cannot move the upper arm bones away from the clavicles.

7. You can further adapt the Biped bone parts by simply using Convert to Editable Mesh or Convert to Editable Poly on any Biped skeleton component. Then you can employ all the modeling techniques you are used to employing in 3ds max, such as box modeling or modifiers (**Figure 15.7**).

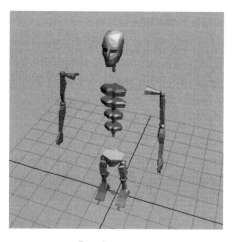

Figure 15.6   You can move some Biped parts.

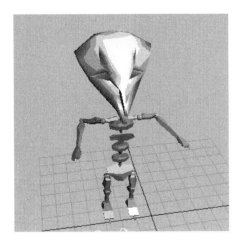

Figure 15.7   You can change any Biped body part.

Warning: You can't delete components of the Biped skeleton. If you select the head and click Delete, you will delete the entire Biped. If you don't want the Biped to have a certain part, you should hide it instead. The exceptions to this are the arms, tails, and ponytails. You can turn these off in the Structure rollout by setting the value to 0 or by unchecking the Arms check box.

Figure Mode and Figure Files

When you have finished editing your Biped skeleton, you can save the configuration as a .fig file. As long as you are in Figure mode, the Save File button will create a .fig file for you.

When you create a Biped, there is an option to use the last saved .fig file as a choice for creating new Bipeds. There is also an option to load a .fig file from that part of the UI as well.

When fitting a Biped into a mesh character, it's a good practice to make the character mesh See-Through and then freeze the character. This makes it easier to work on the Biped structure without inadvertently selecting the mesh and lets you easily see how the Biped fits within the mesh's limits (**Figure 15.8**).

 Tip

> Don't forget to turn Figure mode off after you're finished editing your Biped bones.
> When a Biped is in Figure mode, it can't be animated. If you load in a Biped file that
> doesn't animate, check and see if Figure mode is selected.

Figure 15.8   Make the mesh See-Through and freeze the character.

If you plan to use the Skin modifier, it's a good idea to make the Biped only slightly smaller than the mesh. The skin envelopes are determined by the size of the bones, so if the Biped bones are significantly smaller than the mesh, the skin envelopes may be too small to affect the mesh vertices. Unlike 3ds max bones, which were developed later, Biped bones don't have the option for front, side, or back fins.

Physique vs. Skin

First, a little history. When character studio first came out, there was no modifier in 3ds max that would let you drive the animation of a mesh using bones. So character studio included the Physique modifier as part of the product. The Physique modifier was added to the character mesh objects and then the Biped bones were added to the Physique modifier. Physique created a series of envelopes of influence that directed the relationship between the Biped bones and the mesh vertices.

Later versions of 3ds max added a default Skin modifier that could be used for the same purpose. This was included for competitive reasons, as other 3D programs came with this feature, and users were not required to pay extra for it. Since character studio was an additional plug-in that cost extra, the Skin modifier was originally designed as a "slightly lesser-than" product with simpler UI and fewer bells and whistles.

Over time, however, Skin underwent additional changes and improvements. Vertex painting and the Skin Weight table were added, as well as the ability to mirror skin weights. Meanwhile, the original developer of the Physique module left Unreal Pictures, and development more or less ceased on Physique.

So you have a choice. You can use Physique or you can use Skin.

One advantage of Physique is that it has more control over envelope editing. This can allow you to get a better handle on your mesh deformation at the envelope level before moving on to weighting vertices. Physique also has a Bulges and Tendons editor that gives you more control over deforming the mesh.

Skin has options similar to Bulge, but the toolset is not as robust. Skin is a newer option for mesh deformation. Features such as the Skin Weight table and mirroring vertex weights are better implemented. Skin is also much more exposed to MAXScript and the custom user interface. The Skin Utils feature works well with Skin.

How to decide which to use? Generally, if you like the process of painting weights, go with Skin. If you like the closer integration with cs and the Bulge editing feature, Physique is the way to go. You may have to try both on a character to make an informed choice.

Skin Your Mesh to Biped Bones

If you are creating a character that happens to be a "hard surface" character such as a robot or a mechwarrior, you can simply use the Select and Link tools to link the mesh components directly to the Biped bones. Jointed characters also fall into this category. Make sure your mesh object's pivot points coincide with the Biped bone pivots, otherwise you can get unexpected results.

Here are the general steps you use to Skin your mesh to your Biped bones:

1. Select your mesh object.

2. Add a Skin modifier to your mesh object.

 Tip

If you have multiple objects, it's a good idea to add individual Skin modifiers, rather than to use instanced Skin modifiers (one modifier added to multiple objects). Instanced Skin modifiers have reportedly been responsible for sluggish viewport performance.

3. In the Parameters rollout of the Skin modifier, click Add to add the bones you would like to deform the mesh.

4. Choose all the Biped bones except the COM object (usually Bip01).

5. Animate the Biped in different poses to see how the mesh deforms.

6. Adjust the Skin modifier's envelopes and vertex weighting so the character mesh deforms properly (**Figure 15.9**).

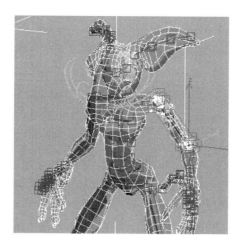

Figure 15.9   Skin envelopes.

Physique Your Mesh to Biped Bones

Here are the general steps you use to Physique your mesh to your Biped bones:

1. Select your mesh object.

2. Add a Physique modifier to your mesh object.

3. In the Physique rollout, click the Attach To Node button and click the Biped's pelvis.

4. Click Initialize in the Physique Initialization dialog. A coffee-cup icon will pop up, telling you that Physique is initializing, and then you will see orange lines running through the mesh of the character. These are the Link lines (**Figure 15.10**).

5. Adjust the Physique envelopes and vertex weighting so the character's mesh deforms properly.

Figure 15.10   Visible Physique Link lines—they would be orange in a color image.

Biped Animation Basics

Characters don't just sit or stand around—they walk, run, leap, and dance. These motions can be quite hard to get right, especial for newer animators. Luckily, character studio has special features to make locomotion much easier.

Free Form and Footstep Animation

There are two types of animation you can do with Biped: Free Form animation and Footstep animation. With Free Form animation, Biped is like a completely ready-to-animate rig. Free Form animation is done with simple keys using IK (inverse kinematics) and FK (forward kinematics) and includes very powerful pivot animation on the hands and feet. You can animate the pivot point from one position to another on the extremities to easily lock the feet down to the ground plane.

Footstep animation lets you create basic footsteps for the Biped to follow. It's a fast way to rough out animation that can then be refined. It lets almost anyone create walking characters without having to know how to animate a walk cycle.

Quaternions

character studio uses quaternion controllers to position and rotate parts of the Biped. (Quaternions are based on an alternate way of figuring rotations that takes into account a fourth, non-Cartesian axis of rotation.) Quaternions and TCB controllers have their advantages and disadvantages. Quaternions can produce smoother animation and help avoid the dreaded gimbal lock, but it can be hard to edit the interpolation between keyframes. This is because quaternions don't produce curves for editing. To edit the interpolation between quaternion keys, you must use a TCB graph.

When editing in the TCB graph, you can adjust the tension, bias, and continuity. In the most recent release of cs, you are now able to visualize and edit quaternion keys with curves in the Animation Workbench editor. The Workbench allows you to view and edit quaternion values in curve form (**Figure 15.11**).

For years there has been controversy over the issue of function curves inside character studio. Most animators adept with other software packages such as Maya or Softimage are used to using tangent handles on the curves to achieve their motion adjustments. Since character studio is built on TCB controllers, these curves were not available in earlier releases.

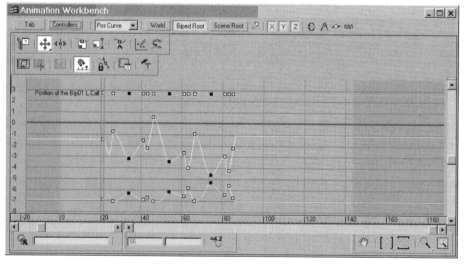

Figure 15.11 Quaternion keys displayed as curves in the Animation Workbench.

You *can* turn on tangent handles on the TCB curves by changing a setting in the BIPED.INI file in the plucfg folder. To do so, open the BIPED.INI file in Notepad, and edit it so this line appears:

AWB_ShowTangents=1

Restart max and you will have tangent handles on your TCB curves (**Figure 15.12**). Be forewarned, however, that these do not act the same as normal tangent handles on Euler curves. They are simply a device to adjust the tension, continuity, and bias. Most animators trained in 3ds max find it just as easy to right-click the keys and work with the TCB graphs.

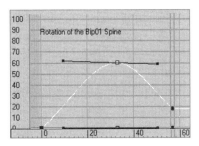

Figure 15.12   Tangent handles in Track View.

Setting Keys

There are many ways to set keys with character studio. To rough out your animation, you can use Auto Key mode to move and rotate the Biped into place. Biped switches automatically between IK and FK depending on what part of the rig you have selected and if you are moving or rotating it. When moving either the hands or the feet, you will be using IK. If you rotate the feet or part of the spine, you will be using FK. This ease of use is one of the great things about animating with character studio. When creating keys, you will want to decide whether the key is an IK or FK key. You can do this by setting two values, IK Blend and Object/Body space, in the Key Info rollout (**Figure 15.13**).

When IK Blend is set to 1 and Object is selected, the key is an IK key, and when the body is moved, the hand or foot will stay in place. When IK Blend is set to 0 and Body is selected, the key will be FK and the foot or hand will follow with the body. IK Blend can be animated from 0 to 1 to smoothly transition between IK and FK movement.

Figure 15.13 IK Blend and Object/Body space in the Key Info rollout.

One other option that is very useful when setting keys is Join to Prev IK Key. This function determines if the key should be part of (blended with) the previous key (and have the same reference position as the previous key). This option can be checked to prevent sliding of a foot or hand from one key to another.

Setting all these values for keys can be maddening, so there are shortcuts you can use. The buttons at the top of the Key Info rollout set all these values according to how you would like the key to react.

- Set Planted Key sets IK Blend to 1, turns on Join to Prev IK Key, and uses Object space. Using Set Planted Key lets you select and lock down the pivot point on the hands and feet.

- Set Sliding Key turns off Join to Prev IK Key, but IK Blend is still set to 1 and Object space is selected. Set Sliding Key lets the foot slide away from the pivot point.

- Set Free Key turns off IK Blend and Join to Prev IK Key and uses Body space.

Using these presets can save a lot of time and energy. It can make animating more about the movement. Is the foot to be locked to the ground? Use Set Planted Key. Is the foot going to be in the air? Set Free Key. It's simple, really.

When Object space is used on the hands or feet, you can select an object in the scene and lock the hand or foot to the object. Moving the object will force the rotations of the limbs between the locked object and the Biped body. Unfortunately, you must choose one object only; you cannot animate the contents of the Object space field. You can, however, animate one object between the two hands.

Tip

Never use the 3ds max Set Keys button to set character studio keys. Biped has its own key-setting system, and it doesn't like it when you use the default 3ds max Set Keys feature instead. The same caveat applies to Trajectories. In the past, using 3ds max Trajectories on Bipeds would produce a crash. Use Biped Trajectories instead.

Biped Free Form Mode

Free Form animation with Biped enables you to treat the Biped skeleton like any other rig you might animate in 3ds max. To create Free Form animation, all you need to do is turn on Auto Key and start animating. You may also use any of the cs keying shortcuts discussed above like Set Planted, Sliding, or Free Key. It is important to know that once you start making a Free Form animation by setting keys on the Biped, you cannot create Footstep animation. The Footstep mode will be grayed out, and you will not be able to make footsteps for the character. If you intend to use footsteps in your animation, it is best to set them up first and then insert Free Form animation into the footstep sequence. If you get into a situation where you have made a completely Free Form animation and need to add footsteps, you can convert the Free Form animation into Footstep and then work in Footstep mode.

To add a Free Form period within a Footstep animation, go to the Track View Dope Sheet and move the footstep keys apart. Then right-click in the space between the footsteps. Choose Edit Free Form (no physics), and then click in the Free Form period (the yellow-outlined box).

Animating Pivot Points

When animating feet and hands, character studio gives you the ability to animate pivot points for better articulation. This can be very helpful for things like toe rolls. You can animate the pivot point by choosing one of the fixed positions on the foot or hand and then setting a key (**Figure 15.14**).

It's good general practice to set a key for the pivot point, then move ahead a frame and rotate the foot about that pivot point, setting a key for the foot rotation. Working in this fashion ensures that you'll get what you expect.

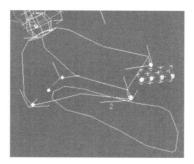

Figure 15.14 Pivot points for the foot.

A favorite former feature of character studio, Free Form animation has returned to character studio with max 7. Previously called Apply Increment and now known as Set Multiple Keys, this feature disappeared when Layers was added to cs. In response to loud and frequent whining from the user base, discreet has had the good sense to reinstate this tool to the program. Essentially Set Multiple Keys allows you to make an incremental rotation to a Biped limb, and then apply it to multiple selected keys.

Set Multiple Keys can be found in the Keyframing Tools rollout.

Biped Footstep Mode

Footsteps is a great Biped feature, but there are definitely some tricks to know to get the best-looking animation from them. We'll go over some of these below.

Footstep Creation and Editing

Creating footsteps with character studio is a great way to set up neutral movement of a character that you can then edit to refine the animation. Footsteps can be created step by step or many at a time (**Figure 15.15**).

Figure 15.15 Biped following some footsteps.

Here is the basic workflow for creating footsteps:

1. Get into Footstep mode by clicking the Footstep mode button in the Biped rollout.

2. Select the type of footsteps you would like to create from the Footstep Creation rollout. You can choose Walk, Run, or Jump.

3. Create either single footsteps with the Create Footsteps (at current frame) button or a string of footsteps by clicking Create Multiple Footsteps.

4. To get Biped to follow the footsteps you have created, click Create Keys for Inactive Footsteps.

When creating footsteps, you can have character studio use some dynamic properties to help make the base animation more realistic. Secondary animation can be applied when footsteps are initialized. On a global scale, these options can be set in the Dynamics & Adaptation rollout (**Figure 15.16**). There are options for Biped Dynamics and Spline Dynamics. Spline Dynamics is the basic interpolation of the Biped's movement, while Biped Dynamics calculates secondary motion for the body and legs.

Figure 15.16   Dynamics & Adaptation rollout.

Dynamic Steps

This can best be seen when setting a few Jump steps.

1. Create a new Biped.

2. Go to the Motion panel, enter Footstep mode, and create four Jump steps using Create Multiple Footsteps. This will create one jump.

3. Go to the Dynamics & Adaptation rollout and set Spline Dynamics to be active.

4. Initialize the footsteps by clicking Create Keys for Inactive Footsteps.

5. Scrub the Time Slider to see the result. Notice the very neutral movement of the character animation. This is a good start if you intend to key all the body animation by hand.

6. Select all the footsteps and click Deactivate Footsteps so you can reinitialize them with Biped Dynamics.

7. Choose Biped Dynamics from the Dynamics & Adaptation rollout and click Create Keys for Inactive Footsteps again.

8. Scrub the Time Slider to see the result. This time, the Biped bends its legs leading into and out of the jump (**Figure 15.17**).

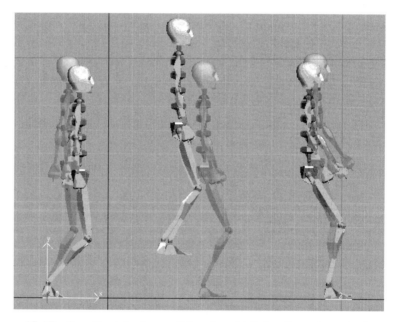

Figure 15.17   Gray Biped (background) jumping with Spline Dynamics and color Biped (foreground) using Biped Dynamics. In the foreground Biped, you can see the slight anticipation of the knee bend at the start of the jump, as well as follow-through at the end.

9. Save this scene as Dynamic_Jump_Start.max.

Try changing the GravAccel in the Dynamics & Adaptation rollout. The higher the GravAccel value, the farther off the ground the Biped will jump.

Biped Animation Tools

character studio comes with many tools to make animation easier. Making use of these tools is an important part of a good animation workflow.

Track Selection Tools

In the Track Selection rollout of the Motion panel, there are some selection tools that make it much easier to select and move the Biped. It can become difficult to select the COM (center of mass) object of a Biped as it is located inside the pelvis. The first three buttons in the Track Selection rollout select the COM and allow you to move horizontally and vertically and to rotate the Biped.

Note that Biped animation works best when there are keys placed on these three tracks. In the past, there have been bugs associated with animating Biped components without adding keys to the COM.

For this reason, some animators make a habit of doing the following:

- At frame 0, select all the Biped body parts in the viewport.
- Right-click the Time Slider and use the Create Key dialog to set a key at frame 0 for all the Biped body parts.

Tip

This process is possible when you are doing Free Form animation only. You won't be able to turn on Footstep mode if you have set these keys.

character studio behaves slightly differently from standard 3ds max when setting initial keys. In 3ds max, if you are on any frame other than 0 and you set an initial key, two keys are set (one at frame 0 and one at whatever frame you are on). character studio sets only one key at the current frame. Following the process mentioned above can help alleviate this deficiency.

Using these buttons saves a lot of selection time. If you select the left arm of the Biped and click the Symmetrical button, it will add the left arm to your selection. You can also click the Select Opposite button to deselect the right arm and select the left. These tools can really help when selecting and editing the Biped.

Layers

When doing complex character animation, you can end up creating a huge number of keyframes. Layers can organize and reduce the keys dramatically (**Figure 15.18**).

Figure 15.18   Layers rollout.

Let's say you have to animate a character's walk cycle, with its arms swinging back and forth. Later you decide that the arms need to hang away from the body more on the sides. If you have made rotation keys on the upper arm bone, you will need to adjust the upper arm on every key. If you are using layers, you can add a layer of animation and make one key to rotate the arms outward; you can also make adjustments later, to, for example, make the character slouch more or have a bit of extra head bob. This can save a lot of time. Layers do, however, have their limitations: Many of the other Biped animation tools, such as Footsteps and IK keys, don't work in any layer but the base layer. For this reason, it's a good practice to use layers as an editing tool. Make your changes, then collapse the layers into a single layer.

Head and Body Animation

Often, when animating, you need the character to look at an object. In 3ds max you can use a LookAt constraint to set this up. This sets the rotation of an object to be dependent on the position of another object in the scene. In the Head section of the Key Info rollout (**Figure 15.19**), you can choose a dummy or other object for the Biped to look at and, by adjusting the Target Blend, animate how much and when the character should look. This is an option of convenience, since you can set up a 3ds max LookAt constraint for Biped parts also using Sub Animation.

When using Footsteps or Free Form animation, you can adjust how the Biped's body reacts to motion in the Body section of the Key Info rollout (**Figure 15.20**).

Figure 15.19   Head section of the Key Info rollout.

Figure 15.20   Body section of the Key Info rollout.

Usually, this is more apparent when using Footsteps. When dealing with any type of animation, you want to be sure that the center of mass is in the right location for your character. The COM object is usually located inside the pelvis (**Figure 15.21**). The COM controls the overall transformation of the character as well as any dynamic body movement that the Biped can make.

Figure 15.21   COM inside the Pelvis.

Let's look at how you can adjust the COM to change a character's weight placement. If your character is hunched over, with a large upper body, you may want to shift its weight forward. You can move the COM object by using Rubber Band mode in Figure mode. This can create the illusion of weight for your character (**Figure 15.22**).

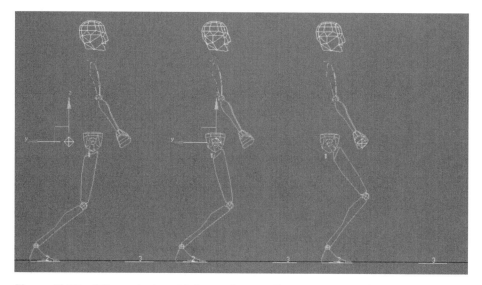

Figure 15.22   Different body weighting on the same Footstep sequence because of COM placement.

Shifting Weight

Here are the general steps you use to shift the Biped's apparent weight:

1. Select the Biped COM.

2. Go into Figure mode and click the Rubber Band Mode button in the Mode section of the Biped rollout.

3. Now you may change the position of the COM to adjust the Biped's weighting.

4. Click the Rubber Band Mode button again to exit and get out of Figure mode.

While we're talking about Rubber Band mode, it is worth mentioning that you can also use it to move the arms and legs of a character. This can be helpful if you need to relocate the placement of an elbow or knee without affecting the foot or hand positions. Remember, you must be in Figure mode to do this.

Animated IK Blend

You can animate the IK Blend by changing the IK Blend parameter between 0 and 1 when Auto Key is selected. By going to any particular frame and changing this parameter, you can control the degree to which a hand or foot is linked to an object. This has its uses when the character is going to catch a thrown object or throw a caught object. By adjusting the IK Blend, you can achieve the illusion of the hand being partially influenced by the object in flight. Another example of this is tossing a sword between two hands. During the first frames of the animation, the IK Blend on the right hand (holding the sword) is set to 1. During this period, the animation of the sword will also animate the hand. When you want to toss the sword to the alternate hand, IK Blend on the right hand is set to 0. Now the sword can be thrown to the other hand without influencing the right hand. Once the sword is in proximity to the left hand, the IK Blend can be set to 1. Here animating the sword will drive the animation of the left hand (**Figures 15.23** and **15.24**).

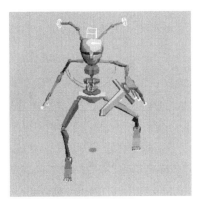

Figure 15.23   Animate the sword between the hands.

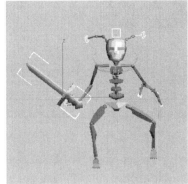

Figure 15.24   The sword has been passed from right to left.

Using List Controllers for Biped Subanimation

The Biped skeleton is ideal for creating robotic linked motion. But what do you do when you want to have cartoon bones that stretch like rubber? Fortunately, Biped allows you to use list controllers, so you can layer controllers on top of controllers. This means that you can apply scale controllers (for example) to the Biped Spine objects to add the illusion of breathing while the Biped is walking or running (**Figure 15.25**). Apply the same scale controllers to the legs or arms and you can create classic cartoon physics effects. Wile E. Coyote runs off the cliff and hangs in midair until it dawns on him that he is above the abyss. Then his feet plummet and his body stretches like a rubber band while his face, still in frame, registers his predicament.

Figure 15.25   Scale controller.

List controllers are applied in the Motion panel in the Assign Controller rollout. Go to the Assign Controllers rollout and expand the Biped Subanim. Find an Available entry, and then highlight it and click the Assign Controller button. Then assign the controller from the list.

Copy/Paste Pose/Posture/Track

character studio comes with some very useful tools in the Copy/Paste rollout. Here you can select Biped body parts and then copy the position and orientation of those body parts into a list.

Copy Pose will copy the selected objects only; Copy Posture will copy the entire Biped configuration. Once you have this in the list, you can move to another frame and repeat the pose by using Paste Pose. Even more useful is Paste Opposite, which allows you to achieve the same pose on the other side of the Biped (**Figures 15.26** and **15.27**). Best of all, you can copy poses and postures between different Bipeds! This is so fast, it's hard not to love this. The only annoying aspect of this workflow is that copying the posture doesn't automatically select the Biped parts and set keys for the posture. After pasting the posture, you need to select the corresponding Biped body parts and click the Set Key button in the Key Info rollout.

Copy Track lets you copy the entire animation track for selected Biped objects. These copied poses, postures, and tracks can be saved as .cpy files and reused in later sessions.

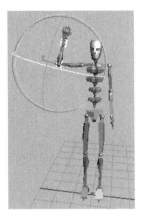
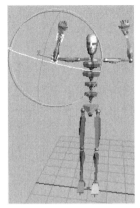

Figure 15.26 Paste Opposite.

Figure 15.27 The arm pose transferred to the other side of the Biped.

Display Tools

Biped's Display tools make it easier to control what appears in the viewport. These controls are somewhat hidden in the Biped rollout. There is a single line marked only with a plus sign just above the Track Selection rollout. Expanding the line will reveal the modes and Display tools.

If you've been following along, you've seen these tools already. The first tool on the left is a flyout that lets you quickly replace all the Biped objects with a simple line skeleton. Choose Bones to use this display mode (**Figures 15.28** and **15.29**).

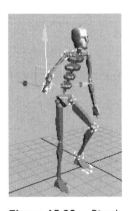
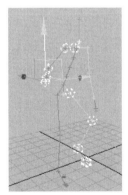

Figure 15.28 Biped posed.

Figure 15.29 Bones-only display.

Probably the most important tool in the Display group is the Biped Trajectories display (**Figure 15.30**). The Trajectory display lets you see the path through space for any selected Biped body part. Traditional animators are very familiar with the idea of motion arcs as opposed to function curves, and so they find Trajectories to be more direct for motion analysis and generally a more natural way of working.

Figure 15.30   Biped Trajectory displayed for the left hand.

Move All mode is a very handy tool found in the Biped rollout. When you load a .bip file, the action will take place with a particular start location. Wherever the animation was originally created, this will be where the action takes place. Frequently, you will want to relocate this animation sequence to another position or orientation. Move All mode is intended to be a fast method for doing just that. Simply turn on Move All mode, and then use the XYZ Position field to change the placement of the animation. You can use the Z Rotation field to reorient the animation. Collapse when finished and save the .bip file with a new name.

This is very useful when preparing animations for use with Motion Flow. It is rare that the library of .bip files you create will be exactly positioned and oriented to achieve what you want in every case.

 Tip

If you need to reorient the .bip file in a different axis than Z, you can create a dummy helper object and link the Biped COM to the dummy. Rotate the dummy on any axis and this will effectively rotate in other axes.

Motion Flow—Motion Scripting

character studio's power becomes evident when you utilize Motion Flow mode to sequence saved .bip files into a motion script. Every individual animation you create can be saved as a .bip file into a library of motions. These motions can be sequenced into a script that lets you create transitions between these motions and generate lengthy animations with amazing power. The workflow for this is quite convoluted, however, and requires a bit of practice.

character studio ships with a large library of .bip files which can be found on the Partners and Samples DVD (the second DVD that ships with max 7). The .bip files are all in a single .zip archive named Bip.zip (catchy name). Extract them and you will have access to 16 directories full of various actions. These files are nicely organized by category for your use in Motion Flow.

Here are the general steps to assemble multiple .bip files into a script:

1. In the Biped rollout, click the Motion Flow Mode button. This will display the Motion Flow rollout in the Command panel.

2. Click Show Graph. The Motion Flow graph, a floating window, appears.

3. In the Motion Flow graph, click Create Clip.

4. In the Motion Flow graph window, click multiple times, once for each .bip file you wish to sequence. Each click will result in a blue box with white text, marked clip1, clip2, and so on.

5. Click the Select Clip button on the Motion Flow toolbar, and then select the first clip.

6. Right-click the clip, then use the Browse button to select the .bip file you want. Repeat this process for all the clips you want to sequence.

7. Click the Create Transition From > To button, and drag from one clip to the next to create transitions between the clips (**Figure 15.31**).

   Now comes the tricky part. Leave the Motion Flow graph (but don't close it) and return to the Command panel.

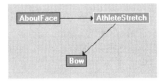

Figure 15.31   Clips with transitions in the Motion Flow graph.

8. In the Scripts group, click Define Scripts. A name will appear in the Script name field. Rename the script something you will remember.

9. Go back to the Motion Flow graph and click each of the clips in order. With each click, the name of the clip will appear in the script list (**Figure 15.32**), along with the frame number for the start of the clip.

Figure 15.32   Script list.

10. Hit the Play button, and watch the Biped in the viewport animate as per each of the .bip files.

There are all kinds of other capabilities in the Motion Flow graph. You can manipulate the transitions to adjust the exact frame where the blend from one clip to another begins and the duration of the transition. The Motion Flow graph is also used to create Shared Motion Flows for Biped crowd scenes.

Motion Capture Editing

character studio can use motion capture files in the form of .csm, .bvh, and .bip files. To load a motion capture file onto Biped, you have to go to the Motion Capture rollout and click Load Motion Capture file (**Figure 15.33**).

Figure 15.33 Motion Capture rollout.

If you want to load the motion file directly, select the file to load and click OK in the Motion Capture Conversion Parameters dialog. Now the motion file will be loaded and the Biped should animate accordingly. One great way to edit raw motion data like this is to add some layers and adjust the motion of the character to fit your needs. If you wish to edit the motion capture data as you import it, there are many options available in the Motion Capture Conversion Parameters dialog that pops up just after you select the file to use (**Figure 15.34**).

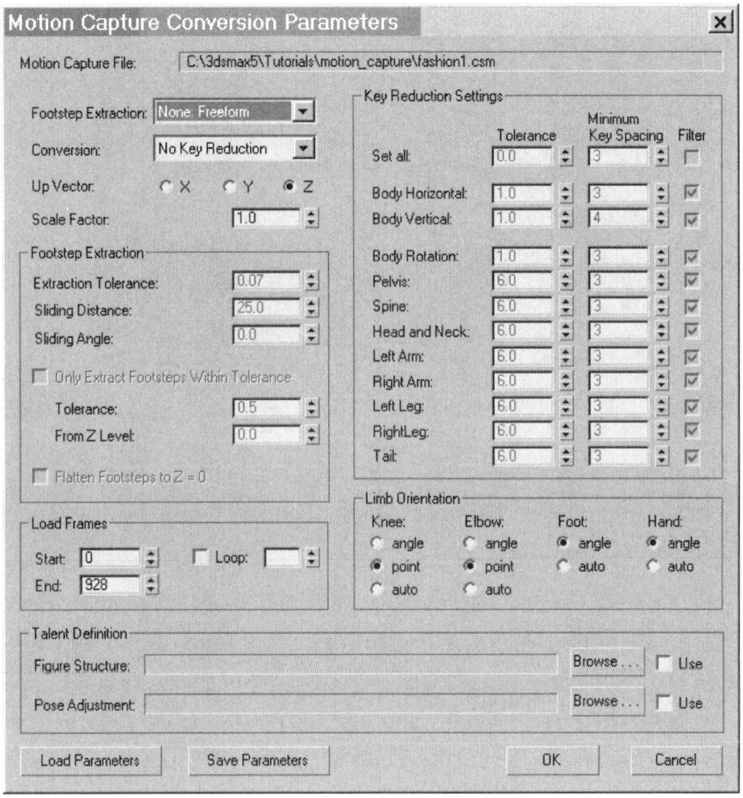

Figure 15.34   Motion Capture Conversion Parameters dialog.

The two drop-downs on the upper left of the dialog contain some powerful tools for working with mocap. The Footstep Extraction drop-down allows you to extrapolate footsteps from the data on import. This means that the keys that make up the foot place-ment and movement will be turned into footsteps that you can then edit like any other footstep in character studio. The Conversion drop-down allows you to reduce the keys of the mocap file. This can save significant amounts of time when editing the mocap data, as there will be far fewer keys to deal with. Most of the time this is a good option, but it can result in some sloppy animation that may need to be fixed later.

Sometimes, when you import a motion capture file, your Biped will collapse into a heap on the ground (**Figure 15.35**).

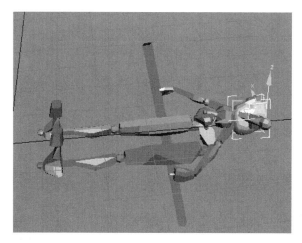

Figure 15.35   Crumpled Biped after motion capture import.

This leads us to the next issue, which is Up Vector. Usually the Z axis is a good choice for Up Vector, but when you get a crumpled Biped, changing the Up Vector to another axis will fix this problem most of the time.

The last option I'd like to talk about in the Motion Capture Conversion Parameters dialog is the Talent Definition section. Often you will spend a lot of time adjusting the figure structure of a character to fit the mesh correctly and then want to use motion capture with it. Be sure to save out the .fig file and use it here. Also make sure the check box is checked after you browse for the .fig file. This will preserve the structure of the figure and adapt the incoming data to it. Note that importing .bip files will not allow the Up Vector to be selected.

Once you have imported some motion capture data to a Biped and edited the animation to your liking, you may need to repurpose this animation to simple bones or even other packages. Using the 3ds max FBX exporter, you can export the Biped animation into .fbx (Filmbox) format and then re-import it as simple bones (**Figure 15.36**). You may also import the animation and bone setup to other applications that support .fbx.

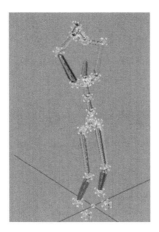

Figure 15.36   Biped exported as .fbx and re-imported as Bones.

Motion Mixer

Imagine you're animating a character in an everyday street scene. For the sake of argument, call the character Jim. Jim is walking down the street, admiring the sights, when out of the corner of his eye he notices a piece of trash on the sidewalk. He swerves to avoid the trash, then stops, backs up a step, bends down and picks it up, and then continues walking forward until he can toss the trash into a garbage can. Next, Jim spots a friend and stops to shake his hand. They start a conversation, which briefly turns intense, with both talkers waving their arms wildly in the air. Finally, Jim hails a cab and hops in.

If you've done character animation, you can imagine how much work this seemingly trivial scene might require to animate—it's quite a bit. Even after you've done the basic blocking, you'd have to spend a good deal of time fine-tuning the animation, adjusting keyframes and other settings ad infinitum until all the motions work together. But if you're using character studio, you can save yourself a lot of animation effort by exploiting the Motion Mixer feature.

Using Motion Mixer, you could animate each action separately, save it in a .bip file, and then bring all the .bips into the Motion Mixer dialog and blend them together with an array of easy-to-use tools. In a sense, Motion Mixer works similarly to compositing programs like discreet combustion and Adobe After Effects, using a layer/timeline metaphor to let you freely combine pieces of a movie or, in this case, a 3D animation. (This process is often called nonlinear animation, or NLA, by analogy with nonlinear editing, or NLE.) It's one of the most powerful new features in character studio, and by following the lessons in this section, you can become familiar with its basic functions.

Using Motion Mixer

Access Motion Mixer from the Motion panel. With any part of a Biped selected, you click the Mixer button in the Biped Apps rollout to open the Motion Mixer dialog (**Figure 15.37**).

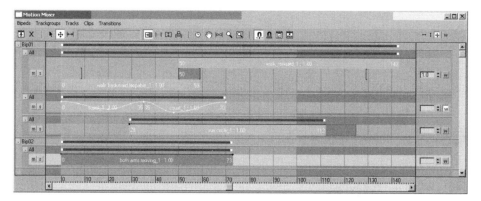

Figure 15.37   The Motion Mixer dialog.

The main part of the interface consists of a vertical array of tracks, each running horizontally across the center of the dialog. The tracks are organized on a per-Biped basis; you can control every Biped in the scene from a single Motion Mixer dialog. This central area is where you import motion clips in the form of .bip files. Once you've imported a clip, you can change the start point simply by dragging it horizontally. You can tile a clip so it repeats, and you can create and edit transitions between pairs of clips. This area also contains controls to let you mute and solo individual clips, adjust clip length either by scaling or cropping, and set Weight values that can vary over the length of the animation. But that's not all: You can also rearrange tracks and Biped groups by dragging vertically.

The transition track merits special mention here. By default, Motion Mixer tracks are linear *layer* tracks, with one clip following another. The double-height *transition* track, on the other hand, lets you overlap clips and automatically creates transitions between them. One of the lessons later in this section shows you how to use the transition function to repeat a walk motion without skipping back to the original starting point each time.

Following are brief descriptions of the remaining UI elements.

The Motion Mixer Menus

The menu bar across the top of the Motion Mixer dialog contains a number of important functions. It's arranged in hierarchical order, with the highest level of Motion Mixer elements at the left and the lowest at the right. Many of these menu functions are also available from right-click menus in other parts of the dialog.

The Biped's menu commands affect all selected Bipeds in Motion Mixer. In fact, most of the commands aren't available unless at least one Biped is selected (that is, its label is highlighted). Here you can change the track color, delete a Biped and its tracks from Motion Mixer (caution: not undoable!), and set balance parameters so the Biped doesn't appear off balance. This menu also gives you the Mixdown commands, where you can create composites of the raw clips and copy the Mixdown to the Biped.

The Trackgroups menu goes down a level in the mixer hierarchy, giving you commands that apply to selected Trackgroups. Of particular interest here is the all-important Filter command, which lets you specify which parts of a Biped the Trackgroup's clips should affect. You'll learn how to use this feature in the first lesson below.

The next level down in the hierarchy gets you to the Tracks level, where you can influence individual tracks within a Trackgroup. Here you can add layer and transition tracks, convert between track types, optimize transitions, and import clips. If you import multiple clips at once into a layer track, Motion Mixer separates them by five frames each, and if you import them into a transition track, Motion Mixer automatically creates transitions for each.

The Clips menu provides several useful functions, including the ability to replace any or all instances of a clip with another one. Even more powerful is the Time Warp function, which lets you change clip timing internally. You stretch out or compress time within a clip for the ultimate customizability in mixing motion. You'll find lots of information about using time warps in the discreet user reference and tutorials included with 3ds max 7.

Last is the Transitions menu, which lets you edit and optimize transitions as well as convert a transition to a loopable clip that you can use to repeat a motion without transitions.

The Motion Mixer Toolbar

Just below the menu bar is the toolbar, with handy buttons for a range of Motion Mixer functions. Starting at the left end, you have buttons for adding and deleting Bipeds and for selecting, moving, and sliding clips. The two numeric fields, normally blank, show relative and absolute frame positions during manipulations such as scaling a clip. Next come commands for trimming clips, editing time warps, moving tracks vertically, and locking transitions. The remaining buttons affect the viewable area, enable snapping, and provide access to preferences settings and the reservoir, which serves as a clip library.

The Mixer Mode Button

An important fact to remember regarding Motion Mixer usage is that you won't see the effects of the animation that's set up in the dialog unless the Mixer Mode button in the Motion panel > Biped rollout is on. Normally, this button comes on when you access Motion Mixer by clicking the Mixer button, but it's possible for it to be off for various reasons. If you're using Motion Mixer and you scrub the Time Slider or click the Play Animation button but nothing happens, make sure the Mixer Mode button is on.

Filtering Motion

Now we'll work through some of the Motion Mixer's capabilities. First, let's tackle motion filtering.

1. Start or reset 3ds max. In the Create panel, click Systems (**Figure 15.38**) and then Biped.

Figure 15.38   The Object Type rollout for the Systems category.

2. In the center of the Perspective viewport, drag upward to create a Biped about 72 units high (**Figure 15.39**).

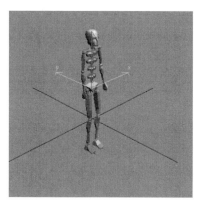

Figure 15.39   The 72-unit Biped standing in the Perspective viewport.

Note

By default (in the United States), a system unit in the 3ds max measurement system is equal to an inch, so this figure is about 6 feet tall.

3. Go the Motion panel, and in the Biped Apps rollout, click the Mixer button. This opens the Motion Mixer dialog (**Figure 15.40**). In the dialog, you can see a single track for the Biped, named Bip01. As you'll see shortly, you can do quite a bit with this one track.

Figure 15.40   The Motion Mixer dialog.

First you'll set a few options so you see the same thing as what's shown in this section. Click the Preferences button; it's the second button from the right end of the toolbar. In the Mixer Preferences dialog, in the Clips group, turn on Scales if necessary. Also, in the Other group, turn off Balance Curves if necessary. Click OK to close the dialog.

4. Position the mouse cursor over the track so it resembles a cross, and then right-click and choose New Clips > From Files.

5. You'll start with a clip of a Biped walking backwards. From the project folder for this chapter on the accompanying DVD, open the walk_backward.bip file. The clip appears in the Motion Mixer window, but it doesn't quite fit at the default zoom level.

Note

When you load a clip, Motion Mixer assigns it a random color. You can change all of a Biped's clips to another color with the Track Color command, available from the Biped menu.

6. On the Motion Mixer toolbar, click the Zoom Extents button (**Figure 15.41**).

Figure 15.41   The Zoom Extents button in Motion Mixer.

You can now see that the clip is 108 frames, a bit longer than the default 3ds max animation length of 100 frames. Unlike the standard Biped function (Load File), opening a clip in Motion Mixer doesn't automatically adjust the overall animation length. In a little while you'll repeat this clip, so you might as well make the animation a lot longer now.

7. Near the bottom right of the max window, click the Time Configuration button. In the Time Configuration dialog, set Length to 500, and then click OK to close the dialog.

8. Play the animation. The Biped walks backward for 108 frames and then stops. You needn't wait for the program to play all 500 frames to continue.

9. Click Go To Start to stop and rewind the animation.

 Note

> The instruction "play the animation" assumes that you then click Go To Start to stop and rewind the animation.

Next, let's look at the Motion Mixer filtering tool.

1. Near the top left corner of the track, right-click the word All, and from the menu that appears, choose Filter (**Figure 15.42**). This opens the Trackgroup Filter dialog, which controls which parts of the Biped the tracks in the current group control. By default, it controls all available parts. Note that parts not present in the Biped, such as the tail, appear in the dialog but can't be activated.

Figure 15.42   Right-click the All label and choose Filter.

2. Click the None button to turn off all the parts, and then click the Legs button to activate just the right and left legs and feet (**Figure 15.43**). Click OK to accept the change and close the dialog.

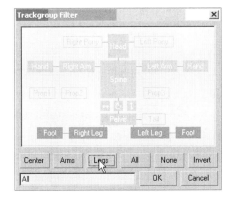

Figure 15.43   Click the Legs button in the Trackgroup Filter dialog.

  Note

The Trackgroup Filter dialog is modal, so you can't do anything else in the program while it's open.

3. Play the animation and then rewind it when the motion stops. The legs and feet move as before, but the Biped stays where it is. That's because all the movement buttons are off.

4. Reopen the Trackgroup Filter dialog. You can now see the Movement Filter buttons; they're the three arrow buttons under the big Spine button. From left to right, they filter horizontal, rotational, and vertical movement.

5. Click the Horizontal movement button to turn it on, and then click OK and play the animation (**Figure 15.44**). Now the Biped travels backward again, but there's something a little different about its motion.

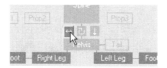

Figure 15.44   Click the Horizontal button to enable horizontal movement.

6. Play it again in the Left viewport (adjust the zoom if necessary), and watch the pelvis. The pelvis travels in a completely straight horizontal line, because the vertical motion created by the original walk animation is still filtered out.

7. Turn the vertical Movement Filter button back on and play the animation again in the Left viewport. Now the pelvis travels up and down as the Biped walks, creating a more natural-looking motion.

 Note

> The walk motion was created by using the standard Biped function Create Multiple Footsteps and then moving the footsteps behind the character. The Footsteps functionality in Biped is dismissed as a crutch by many animators, but it can be a valuable starting point for many animation tasks.

Before leaving the Filter function, you'll try one last experiment.

8. Use the Trackgroup Filter dialog to turn off the Left Leg and Foot, close the dialog, and then play the animation. The Biped walks backward using only its right leg and foot. Not too realistic, but somewhat humorous. Before continuing, reopen the Trackgroup Filter dialog and click All to turn all the body parts back on.

As you can see, Filter is a handy tool for isolating parts of a character's motion for combining with other motions. It can save you a lot of repetitive setup work. For example, if you've animated a Biped walking and waving, but want to use only the waving motion in a different animation, you can load the .bip file and then filter out everything except the waving arm and hand. You can even use filtering in Motion Mixer to combine different subanimations from the same .bip file with different timing.

Tiling a Clip

Say you want your character to continue a walk motion throughout an animation segment that might be longer than the original animation. This is relatively easy to do in Motion Mixer, as you'll see next.

1. Continuing from the previous tutorial, right-click the walk_backward_1 clip and then choose Tile Range. Click Zoom Extents on the Motion Mixer toolbar to see all the copies (**Figure 15.45**). Motion Mixer has made as many copies as it can fit within the 500-frame animation length and placed them end to end in the current track.

Figure 15.45   Tiling results in four copies of the clip.

2. Play the animation. The Biped repeats the backward walk all right, but when it gets to the end of a clip, it just jumps back to the starting point again, instead of continuing to walk backward from the current location. That's not quite what we had in mind. You'll use Motion Mixer's transition track functionality to make it right.

3. Press Control-Z to undo the Tile Range command, and then right-click the track (not the clip) and choose Convert To Transition Track. The transition track lets you sequence animation segments along the timeline and automatically creates transitions between them so that the motion continues smoothly.

   The walk_backward_1 clip now appears at the bottom of the transition track, with brackets above it. These brackets determine the amount of overlap between this clip and the one to which it transitions. In this case, the clip will transition to a copy of itself. You'll use the default transition length.

4. Right-click the track to choose New Clips > From Reservoir, and open the walk_backward.bip clip again. The Reservoir lets you easily reuse any existing

clips in Motion Mixer. Motion Mixer places the new clip in the upper part of the Trackgroup, slightly overlapping the first clip. It also creates a transition, which is the darker bar between the two clips. This is where the software changes over from the first clip to the second (**Figure 15.46**).

Figure 15.46   The walk_backward clip transitions to itself over 16 frames.

5. Play the animation; if necessary, adjust the viewport so you can see the whole thing. The first thing you'll notice is that the Biped doesn't return to its starting point before executing the second clip, which is what we wanted. You might also notice that there's a pause during the transition. You can fix this easily.

6. Right-click the transition, and then choose Optimize. In the Transition Optimization dialog, click OK to accept the default settings and perform the optimization.

Now, when you play back the animation, the pause is gone. Pretty slick! And now for an even slicker trick:

7. Right-click the transition again, and then choose Convert to Loopable Clip. A loopable clip is one that ends at a pose very close to that of the starting pose, so you can tile it without any glitches in between. It's the animation equivalent of a seamless texture.

8. The program opens the Save As dialog and prompts you for a file name. Change the file name from the default, clip00.bip, to walk_backward_loopable.bip and then click Save. The two clips are modified and the transition is deleted, creating a new, loopable clip.

9. Finally, right-click the second, upper clip and choose Tile Range.

Now, when you play the animation, the Biped walks continuously backward the whole way.

Using Track Weights

In the 3ds max List controller, you can use weighting to set the relative influences of controllers in the list. Similarly, in Motion Mixer, you can combine different tracks that control the same parts of the Biped and then set weighting to determine which track has the most influence at any given point in time. In this tutorial, you'll explore this and similar controls.

1. Reset or start 3ds max, add a Biped, then go to the Motion panel and open Motion Mixer.

2. Add the walk_backward.bip file to the available track, as before.

3. In Motion Mixer, under the Bip01 label, right-click the All label and choose Add Trackgroup Below. A new Trackgroup appears (**Figure 15.47**).

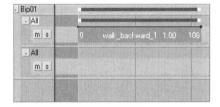

Figure 15.47   A second, empty Trackgroup appears under the first.

  Note

> You can use multiple Trackgroups to control a Biped, or combine tracks in a single Trackgroup; how you group the tracks is up to you. One difference is that you can collapse a Trackgroup by clicking the – (minus sign) button next to the Filter label ("All" by default), but you can't collapse individual tracks.

4. Into the new Trackgroup, import the walk_forward.bip file.

5. Click the Zoom Extents button on the Motion Mixer toolbar so you can see all of both clips. The walk_backward clip is a bit longer. Make sure the Scales box is checked in the Mixer Preferences dialog.

6. Drag the right ends of both clips to the 100-frame mark. Note that each track's label changes to reflect its scaling. The upper track is 93 percent of its original length, while the lower track is 8 percent longer than before.

7. Play the animation. The Biped walks backward, as if the walk_forward clip didn't exist. Given two or more tracks with a weight of 1.0 (100 percent) affecting the same body parts, the uppermost track always takes hold.

Now let's explore a couple of different quick methods to change this.

1. At the left end of the first clip, click the "m" button (**Figure 15.48**). In this case, "m" stands for "mute," which works the same way as the Mute button in an audio-editing program: It temporarily turns off the track. Now, when you play the animation, the Biped walks forward, because only the second clip is in effect.

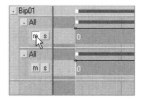

Figure 15.48   Click the "m" button to mute the track.

2. Click the "m" button again to turn it off, and then click the second track's "s" button. To continue with the audio-program metaphor, "s" (for "solo") allows only the second track to control the Biped. Try clicking the upper "s" button and then the lower one again; they turn each other off. You can mute any number of tracks, but only one can play a solo.

3. Play the animation. Again, only the forward motion takes hold.

4. Click the lower track's "s" button again to turn off Solo mode.

Setting Weights

There are several ways to affect weighting. To modify it at the beginning of the animation, change the numeric value at the right end of the track. Make sure you are at frame 0 when this is done.

1. Start by setting both weighting values to 0.5 (**Figure 15.49**).

The black line that previously ran across the top of each clip now starts at the vertical center of the left end of its clip and travels diagonally to the top of the right end. This line depicts how the Weight value changes over time (**Figure 15.50**).

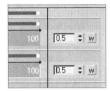

Figure 15.49   Use the spinners or keyboard to set both Weight values to 0.5.

Figure 15.50   The weighting values increase from 0.5 to 1.0.

2. Play the animation. The Biped starts walking backward slowly and then gradually accelerates to the full speed of the first clip. You'll see why this happens in a moment.

3. At the right end of the first clip, click the "w" (Edit Weight Curve) button. The weighting line turns red to show that you can now create and edit different Weight values over the course of the animation. Also, the numeric value field for Weight becomes blank, because no vertices on the line are active.

   At this point, you can edit anywhere on the line except the start point; to access the first point, you have to turn off the "w" button.

4. Position your cursor over the red dot at the right end of the red line and click. The red dot turns white, and its Weight value appears in the numeric field. You can now edit this value, either by dragging the dot vertically or by editing the numeric field.

5. Set both Weight endpoints of each track to 0.5, and then turn off the "w" buttons.

 Tip

You can toggle all tracks' Edit Weight buttons by clicking the "w" button at the right end of the Motion Mixer toolbar. To select multiple weighting vertices, drag a rectangle over them.

The black lines are now horizontal, showing that both clips' Weight values are 0.5 throughout the animation (**Figure 15.51**). Can you predict the effect this will have?

Figure 15.51   Click the weighting vertex to edit its value.

6. Play the animation. The Biped walks slowly backward, with much sliding of feet. This happens because the distances traveled in the backward and forward walk animations are mostly canceling each other out. However, because the backward walk motion contains more footsteps, it overrides the forward motion slightly. If both had the same number of steps, the Biped would walk in place.

Animating Weights

Next, you'll add vertices to animate the Weight values over the course of the animation.

1. Turn on both Edit Weight Curve buttons again, and then position the mouse cursor over the center of the weighting line in the upper clip (**Figure 15.52**). The mouse cursor image becomes a thin, downward-pointing arrow with a starburst at the end.

Figure 15.52   Ready to edit Weight values.

2. Click and then drag in any direction. When you click, a new vertex appears at the cursor location and then follows the mouse when you drag. You can move it any-where between the two existing vertices, within the limits of the clip.

3. Position the vertex at the top of the clip at about frame 33, and then click in an empty area to deselect it.

4. Add three more vertices as shown in **Figure 15.53**. Remember to deselect each vertex after adding it so you don't accidentally move it when adding another.

Figure 15.53   Animated Weight values in Motion Mixer.

Now, when you play the animation, the Biped starts walking backward, then moves quickly forward, and then resumes walking backwards.

As you can see from these few, limited exercises, character studio's Motion Mixer offers an unprecedented level of power for combining and editing character animations. There's much more to Motion Mixer; I strongly encouraged you to read the discreet documentation and work through the tutorials, and then spend lots of time experimenting to see how far you can go with mixing your own motions.

Quadrupeds and Extra Bones

Sometimes it seems that no matter what you do, it's never enough. The developers of character studio created a wonderful program for animating bipedal actors. But if two legs are good, then four legs must be better. Users immediately requested that character studio work for four-legged, six-legged, even eight-legged characters.

It is possible to use character studio to do these type of characters, but the results aren't perfect. If truth be told, cs is really a system designed mainly for bipeds. The developers have a tremendous amount of knowledge about how two-legged creatures walk, and that knowledge is the basis for cs.

That doesn't mean there are no tricks you can use to animate multiple-legged creatures. The first method for making a quadruped is to create two Bipeds and then hide the unnecessary body parts on the second Biped. You can hide the head and turn off the arms, then in Figure mode bend the spine components on the second Biped (**Figure 15.54**).

You can use Footstep animation to quickly animate each of the Bipeds. In the Create Multiple Footsteps dialog > General section, change Start Left to Start Right for the second Biped.

This method is good if you need to create creatures with large numbers of legs, like a centipede or caterpillar. But the drawback is that there is nothing to keep the two Bipeds in proximity, no linkage or constraint. You have to rely on the footstep timing to keep the rear end up with the front.

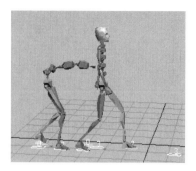

Figure 15.54   Hide the body parts on the second Biped.

Another simple method that works for four-legged creatures is to go into Figure mode and bend the Biped over, so the hands become the front legs (**Figure 15.55**). This won't work for Footstep animation; it's only really useful when you're using Free Form methodology. If you use this technique, be sure to turn off Biped Dynamics and Balance Factor, or your Biped may try to stand up when you animate it! All in all, this works quite well, since you can easily use Pivot Point animation to achieve heel-to-toe roll on the feet and the hands.

Figure 15.55   Biped hands become front legs.

The third method is to use 3ds max bones to create extra legs and other appendages (**Figure 15.56**). This method has the drawback that you cannot take advantage of Biped animation; you must animate the bones using 3ds max standard animation methods. You don't have access to the Pivot Point animation or Footstep methods.

Consider an approach within max rather than cs for tails that require more than the five links available within the Biped structure.

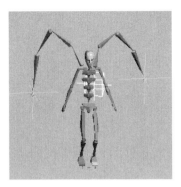

Figure 15.56   Angel wings added using max bones.

Speaking of tails, Biped includes the option for two ponytails. These Biped objects can be repositioned to be used as bones to animate jaws, ears, antennae, or any other element on the head. These have the advantage of being part of the Biped system, so you can animate them within the same context as the rest of the Biped.

Crowd

As computers and software grow faster and more powerful, it's natural to expect that 3D animation can incorporate many more characters than before. But, as in the real world, with greater power comes greater responsibility (usually) and definitely more work, and computer animation is no exception. Every character in a scene must interact in a desirable way with every other character, so the more characters in the scene, the greater the complexity of scene setup. With large numbers of moving characters, the task of keeping things straight manually can become nearly impossible.

Enter character studio's amazing Crowd feature (**Figure 15.57**).

Crowd is all about animating and managing large groups of objects; it has nothing to do with walking or gesturing or inverse kinematics or body structure or motion capture. In fact, Crowd is so different from the rest of character studio that it could almost be considered a separate program. But it's nicely integrated with the rest of cs, so that it's relatively easy to use Crowd to control a large cast of Bipeds. Demonstrating this would go a bit beyond the scope of this book, but the introductory exercises should give you a good idea of what's possible.

Figure 15.57   Biped crowd system using Delegates.

Using Crowd

Crowd uses procedural animation to produce its effects. When you animate with procedures, you use algorithms to create the motion, rather than specifying it explicitly, as in keyframing. This is roughly equivalent to particle animation, except that Crowd uses algorithms better suited to how multiple characters should behave when interacting with each other. When you use Crowd, you specify the number of characters, give each a set of behaviors, and then run the simulation to test your scene.

The basis of a Crowd simulation is the Delegate. Much as delegates at a political convention act for the voters they represent, a Crowd Delegate serves as a stand-in for the character it represents. Your simulation should contain as many Delegates as the objects the Crowd will ultimately have.

The second important element in a simulation is the Crowd object itself. The Crowd object doesn't act directly in a simulation, but it provides access to all the Crowd controls, including behaviors and cognitive controllers.

Here's the standard sequence for creating a simulation with Crowd:

1. Add one or more Delegates.
2. Assign one or more behaviors to each Delegate or group of Delegates.
3. Test and refine the simulation until the results are satisfactory.
4. Assign characters or other objects (such as birds or fish) to the Delegates, and then create the animation.

Of course, the above is a bare-bones outline; working with Crowd can become quite complex, partly because for ultimate control you need at least a nodding acquaintance with MAXScript, the scripting language included with 3ds max. Again, this introductory material won't cover that, but it's covered adequately in the program documentation.

Starting a Crowd

The best way to begin using Crowd is simply, with a single Delegate and behavior.

1. Reset or start 3ds max. In the Create panel, click the Helpers category and then the Object Type rollout > Delegate button (**Figure 15.58**).

Figure 15.58   Choose Delegate in the Helpers > Object Type rollout.

Note, in the Geometry Parameters rollout, that the default dimensions of the Delegate are 10 by 15 by 10. This really just shows the default proportions, though. You can't automatically create a Delegate of this size; you have to drag it out in the viewport.

2. In the Perspective viewport, drag out a Delegate of roughly the default dimensions (**Figure 15.59**).

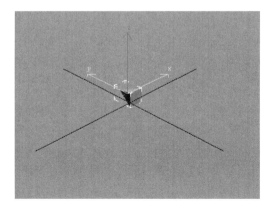

Figure 15.59   The Delegate is pyramid-shaped.

The Delegate resembles a pyramid pointed in the positive Y direction. Its simple geometry allows for fast generation of crowd simulations, and the shape makes it easy to see which direction it's heading.

3. Try rendering the scene, and you'll find that the Delegate doesn't render. In fact, if you examine its object properties, you'll see that it can't be made renderable. However, you can associate any object with a Delegate, so it's not a problem if you need to render a simple test animation.

4. In the same Object Type rollout, click the Crowd button, and then drag a Crowd object off to the side of the Perspective viewport (**Figure 15.60**).

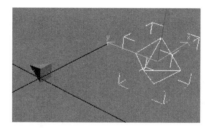

Figure 15.60 The Crowd object is a wireframe octahedron.

Like the Delegate, the Crowd object doesn't render. In fact, even in a shaded viewport it appears as a wireframe object. Also, because it's simply the control center for the simulation, its exact position in the scene is unimportant. You just need to have one there.

Next, you'll use these two objects to create a very simple animation.

5. With the Crowd object selected, go to the Modify panel. In the Setup rollout, click New, and then from the list in the Select Behavior Type dialog, choose Wander Behavior. The Wander behavior causes the Delegate to move forward continuously and change direction randomly at regular intervals.

The drop-down list in the Setup rollout now contains the single behavior Wander. You can rename it whatever you like.

6. Click the name Wander, and use the keyboard to change it to MyWander. You'll need to use another dialog to assign the MyWander behavior to the Delegate; it's a simple matter of a few clicks.

7. In the Setup rollout, click the Behavior Assignments button (**Figure 15.61**). This opens the Behavior Assignments and Teams dialog.

Figure 15.61   Click the Behavior Assignments button.

8. In the left side of the dialog, click the Delegate01 entry and then the MyWander entry to highlight both, and then click the New Assignment button; it's the tall button with the right-pointing arrows (**Figure 15.62**).

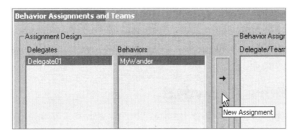

Figure 15.62   Highlight the Delegate and behavior, and then click the New Assignment button.

The new assignment appears in the Behavior Assignments list in the center of the dialog (**Figure 15.63**).

Figure 15.63   The Behavior Assignments list shows all Delegate/behavior assignments.

The entry shows the name of the Delegate, its assigned behavior, the Weight value, and its active status (the X means it's active).

That's it for the setup; easy enough, right? It remains only to generate the simulation.

1. Click the OK button at the bottom of the dialog to accept the changes and close it, and then, in the Solve rollout, click Solve.

With but a single Delegate and a simple simulation, the solution takes only a few seconds. As it progresses, you can see a blue line projecting from the

Delegate, showing the direction in which the behavior is exerting force on the Delegate from moment to moment. This diagnostic tool can be particularly helpful when you're analyzing complex simulations.

2. If you can't see where the Delegate went, zoom and/or pan the Perspective viewport until you can, and then play the animation.

That's it for this introductory lesson, but here are a few ideas for things to try so you can learn more about the process:

- Change the Wander Behavior rollout settings to modify the results of the Wander algorithm. In particular, try different Seed values.

- Click the Delegate to see its keyframes, and then reselect the Crowd object and use its Smoothing rollout to reduce the number of keyframes.

Getting More Crowded

We'll conclude this introductory look at Crowd by simulating a group of 50 Delegates wandering and avoiding each other.

1. Reset or start 3ds max, and then, as in the previous lesson, add a Delegate and a Crowd object. Also add a Wander behavior to the Crowd object.

    The Delegates tend to collide while wandering. Let's slow them down so they'll stay in a limited area. We'll also allow them to wander in three dimensions.

2. Go to the Modify panel, select the Delegate, and in the Motion Parameters rollout, turn off Constrain To XY Plane and set Average Speed to 2.0.

    Next you'll use a special facility within Crowd to create a group of Delegates.

3. Select the Crowd object, and then in the Setup rollout, click the Scatter button (**Figure 15.64**).

Figure 15.64   The Scatter button opens the Scatter Objects dialog.

Scatter makes it easy to generate multiple Delegates or other objects if you like. You can specify a surface or volume in which to scatter them, as well as give them randomized orientation and scaling values. The Scatter Objects dialog lets you experiment with different setups so you can get just the results you want. The first panel that comes up in the Scatter Objects dialog is Clone, where you can create any number of copies of a source object.

4. Click the Object To Clone button. In the Select dialog, click Delegate01 and then click the Select button. Set How Many to 49, keep the other settings at their default values, and then click Generate Clones. This generates the clones in the same location as the original, so you can't see them all yet because they are superimposed.

5. Go to the Position tab of the Scatter Objects dialog. Click In Radial Area (in the second group box, labeled Placement In Area), and change the Radius value to 50.0 (**Figure 15.65**).

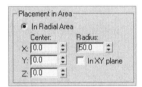

Figure 15.65   Click In Radial Area and then set the Radius value.

6. Click Generate Locations to scatter the Delegate copies within a spherical volume whose radius is 50 units (**Figure 15.66**). If you like, click it several times to see how changing the Random Seed value, which increments automatically each time you click, affects the placement of the Delegates. You might also try turning on In XY Plane to place the Delegates in a single plane parallel to the home grid. When you're satisfied, click OK to close the Scatter Objects dialog.

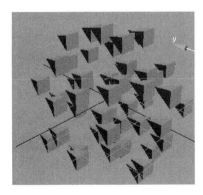

Figure 15.66   The 50 Delegates are scattered within a 50-unit sphere.

The easiest way to assign behaviors to multiple Delegates is to form a team. You'll do this next.

1. In the Setup rollout, click the Behavior Assignments button.

2. In the right side of the Behavior Assignments and Teams dialog, click New Team to open the Select Delegates dialog. In the dialog, click All, and then click OK. The Delegates appear in the Teams list under the title Team0 (**Figure 15.67**). You can change this name by editing the field at the top of the Teams group box.

Figure 15.67   The Delegates have been added to Team0.

The team name also appears in the Teams list on the left side of the Behavior Assignments and Teams dialog. You'll assign behaviors to the team, but first you'll need to add them to the list.

3. In the Assignment Design group, click New Behavior, and then from the list choose Avoid Behavior. Also, be sure the Wander behavior is added. Multiple behaviors need to be added individually in separate operations.

   Now both behaviors appear in the Behaviors list.

4. Highlight the Team0 team and the Avoid and Wander behaviors (drag or use the Control key to highlight both behaviors). Note that Team0 is highlighted in the Assignment Design section and not in the (far right) Teams section. Click the New Assignment button (**Figure 15.68**).

5. Click OK to close the dialog. At this point, the correct behaviors have been assigned, but the Avoid behavior hasn't been properly set up yet, so if you run the simulation now it'll be as if Avoid isn't working.

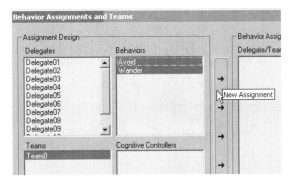

Figure 15.68   The Delegates about to be added to Team0.

6. In the Solve rollout, click the Solve button. The Delegates move more slowly than before, and they interpenetrate freely. Of course, real-world crowd members can't pass through one another, so we want to avoid this in simulations as well.

7. In the Setup rollout, click the drop-down list and choose Avoid (**Figure 15.69**). The Avoid Behavior rollout appears in the Command panel.

Figure 15.69   You can add behaviors with the dialog, but must use the Command panel to set them up.

8. In the Avoid Behavior rollout, click the Multiple Selection button, and then use the Select dialog to select all the Delegates.

9. Solve the simulation (**Figure 15.70**), and then go to various frames near the start of the animation and arc-rotate the Perspective viewport to check for interpenetrating Delegates. You probably won't find any. Even with the default settings, the Avoid behavior is very effective at preventing collisions and interpenetrations of Delegates.

This concludes our introduction to character studio's Crowd feature. Obviously, there's a great deal more to Crowd, but we'll leave it to you to explore on your own, and encourage you to do so. In addition to being an excellent, professional-level animation tool, Crowd is a great deal of fun to use.

Figure 15.70   The Delegates now wander freely without interpenetration.

Summing Up

character studio is an amazingly powerful tool with a tremendous amount of untapped potential. You can concentrate on any single portion of this package and you will find gold. Whether you're using it to take motion capture and add layers to edit the animation, or you're creating crowd simulations with cognitive controllers to create intricate behaviors, character studio will reward you.

Of course, cs is not the only amazing procedural tool in 3ds max 7. Let's now take a look at max's sophisticated dynamics systems.

Part VII

Particles
and Dynamics

Chapter 16

Physics and Dynamics

By Michael Hurwicz

You have at your fingertips an awesome weapon. It's the secret weapon used in *The Matrix Reloaded* when Neo (Keanu Reeves) sends bad guys in black suits and sunglasses flying through the air like rag dolls. (And you thought it was that stick he was swinging!) It's the same technology used for collisions, explosions, and assorted madness and mayhem in dozens of games, from *Auto Assault* to *Psi-Ops: The Mindgate Conspiracy*. It's the Havok physics simulation engine, known in its 3ds max incarnation as reactor.

The basic magic of reactor is that it creates physically accurate keyframes for you. Frank Wilczek, winner of the 2004 Nobel Prize in Physics, has been quoted as saying, "In physics, you don't have to go around making trouble for yourself—nature does it for you." In 3ds max 7, you don't necessarily have to make keyframes for yourself either—the reactor physics simulation plug-in will do it for you, faster than you could do it yourself, and (when properly applied) with far more realistic results. You create objects and provide values (or accept defaults) for properties such as mass, friction, and elasticity. The reactor plug-in calculates how objects with these properties would behave in the real world and creates keyframes to make them behave that way. reactor can also "read" keyframes that you create, to determine initial values for properties such as speed and direction of motion.

In reactor, soft bodies (objects that can squash, stretch, and bend to simulate rubber balls, insect antennas, fruit, and other flexible, deformable things) have properties like stiffness and damping. Cloth in reactor (typically used for objects like flags, curtains, and clothing) can have additional properties, such as stretch, bend, and shear. You can configure the air resistance of reactor rope (also commonly used to simulate hair). Water in reactor can have density, viscosity, and depth.

reactor also provides constraints that define how two objects move in relation to each other. For example, a Hinge Constraint can be used for a door hinge or an elbow joint. The Car-Wheel Constraint implements the motion of a wheel on an axle. The Rag Doll Constraint is designed to duplicate the motion of the human shoulder and other joints.

The Create Object option on the reactor menu on the Main toolbar shows all the different types of collections, objects, and constraints that can be created with reactor (**Figure 16.1**). All the same options are available on the reactor toolbar (**Figure 16.2**) on the left-hand side of the screen. (Figure 16.2 shows the reactor toolbar oriented horizontally in order to display all the options. You may also prefer to undock the reactor toolbar and position it horizontally, to avoid having to scroll the toolbar to get to the buttons you want.)

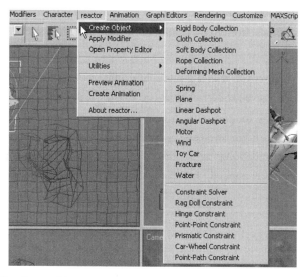

Figure 16.1   The Create Object option in the reactor menu on the Main toolbar.

Create Rigid Body Collection

Create Soft Body Collection

Create Deforming Mesh Collection

Create Spring

Create Angular Dashpot

Create Wind

Create Fracture

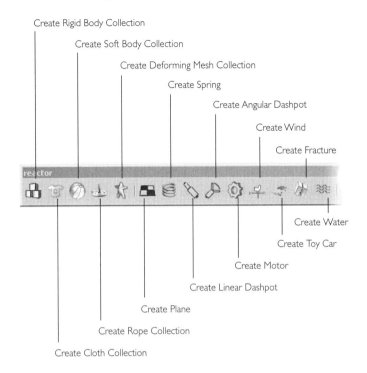

Create Water

Create Toy Car

Create Motor

Create Linear Dashpot

Create Plane

Create Rope Collection

Create Cloth Collection

Create Constraint Solver

Create Hinge Constraint

Create Prismatic Constraint

Create Point-Path Constraint

Apply Soft Body Modifier

Open Property Editor

Preview Animation

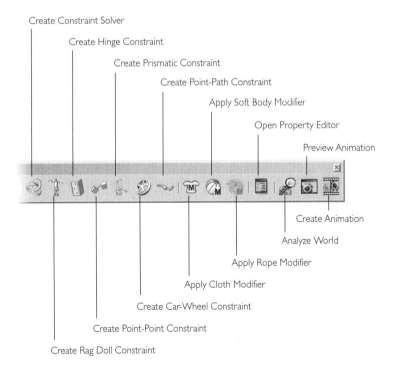

Create Animation

Analyze World

Apply Rope Modifier

Apply Cloth Modifier

Create Car-Wheel Constraint

Create Point-Point Constraint

Create Rag Doll Constraint

Figure 16.2   The reactor toolbar, positioned horizontally.

In this chapter we'll use rigid bodies, a soft body, a deforming mesh, a fracture, and water.

In the project we'll create in this chapter, a water sprite sits astride a dolphin that jumps out of the water and lands on an iceberg, shattering it. Manually keyframing the interactions of the objects in this scene (dolphin, water, ice) would be difficult. Realistically simulating the behavior of water is particularly challenging. The reactor plug-in, on the other hand, "knows" the laws of fluid dynamics and will automatically apply them to create water behavior that is much more realistic than anything you're likely to achieve manually.

That's not to say that reactor produces *perfect* water behavior. For example, reactor never creates droplets of water, so you may want to add those using other techniques, such as a Particle Flow particle system Nevertheless, reactor's water-simulation capabilities can save you a lot of time. reactor also knows about the behaviors of rigid bodies, soft bodies, cloth, rope (which can also double as hair), and lots of other hard-to-keyframe things.

reactor will seldom provide everything you need for a scene from A to Z, but if it gets you from A to M and you have to use manual techniques to get from N to Z, you're still a lot better off. Using reactor does not exclude using any other tool in 3ds max, whether related to modeling, animation, materials, or rendering. So use reactor where it's convenient and efficient, but keep your eyes open for opportunities to get the effects you want using other tools as well. You may use those other tools before creating your simulation with reactor, and you may use them after using reactor, to modify what reactor produces.

Remember, reactor's final output is keyframes that are no different from keyframes you create manually. So we can modify those keyframes to continue to enhance our reactor-produced animation, using exactly the same techniques we would use to go back and modify keyframes that we created manually. One last introductory point before we jump into the water, so to speak: reactor tends to be compute-intensive. In general, the more complex the objects in the scene, the greater the computational load. A number of the techniques in this chapter are aimed at reducing the computing load, often by allowing reactor to "pretend," for the purposes of simulation, that an object is simpler than it really is. reactor is a powerful tool, but sometimes it needs oiling. Knowing how to "lubricate" reactor so that it runs efficiently is often just as important as knowing how to apply reactor to the work at hand.

OK, let's dive in! The first task we're going to undertake is creating some ice for our water sprite and dolphin to shatter.

Breaking the Ice

We'll begin by defining some basic principles of reactor behavior. The first concerns the difference between a single object and many objects. Generally, a single cohesive object breaks apart differently than a group of separate objects that happen to be close to one another, just as a concrete wall breaks apart much differently than loose bricks stacked in the shape of a wall. In reactor, a single cohesive object destined to be broken apart is represented by a helper object called a fracture (**Figure 16.3**). This tool will be useful to you any time you need to shatter something, whether it's an eggshell, an ice cube, or an asteroid.

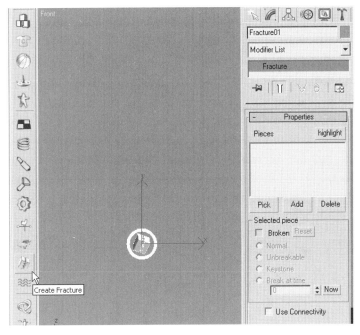

Figure 16.3   The Create Fracture button on the reactor toolbar creates a reactor fracture object.

A fracture object is basically a container, a nonrenderable object that holds a number of renderable objects. (Let's refer to the renderable objects as fragments from now on, reserving the term fracture for the nonrenderable helper object.) By grouping the fragments into a fracture, you tell reactor to apply forces to the fragments to make them behave initially as one cohesive unit. Later, if the cohesive unit is broken by some external force, the fragments may began to behave like separate objects.

In this chapter we'll create an iceberg that gets shattered by a jumping dolphin. The fracture object contains four chunks of ice that together form the iceberg. By putting the chunks in a fracture, we tell reactor to create the illusion that the iceberg is a single object breaking into pieces. In reality, it is already in pieces, but they fit together seamlessly and don't break apart until they are struck by the dolphin/sprite.

Our first job is basically to create a 3D jigsaw puzzle, something that looks like a single object but is actually made up of multiple sub-objects. There are many ways of going about this. Two related issues to consider in selecting the best approach are interpenetrations and convexity/concavity.

It is permissible in reactor for fragments to interpenetrate one another. However, for our iceberg, we want to avoid or at least minimize interpenetrations among fragments, for two reasons: First, we don't want chunks of ice visibly passing through one another, since real chunks of ice don't do that. Second, interpenetrating fragments tend to produce highly "explosive" fragmentation, as reactor by default tries to push interpenetrating objects apart very quickly, so that periods of interpenetration will be too brief to be noticeable. In the first example scene shown here (**Figure 16.4**), the lower two balls are fragments in a fracture object, with significant interpenetration. When the top ball falls on them, they are knocked far apart quickly (**Figure 16.5**). In the second example (**Figure 16.6**), the lower two balls are fragments with no interpenetration. When the top ball falls on them, they are not knocked apart nearly as fast or as far (**Figure 16.7**).

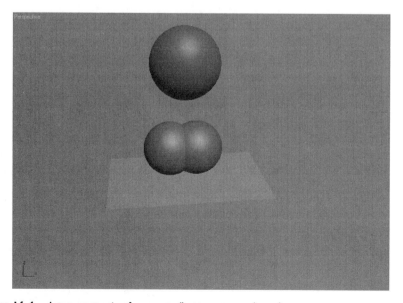

Figure 16.4   Interpenetrating fragments (bottom two spheres).

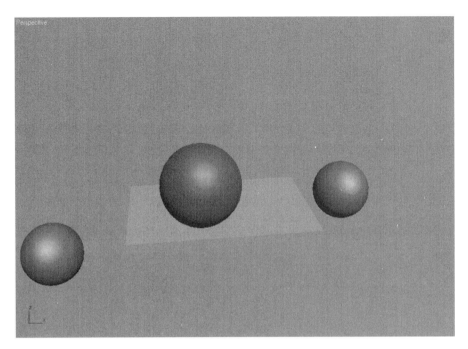

Figure 16.5   Interpenetrating fragments resulting in explosive fragmentation.

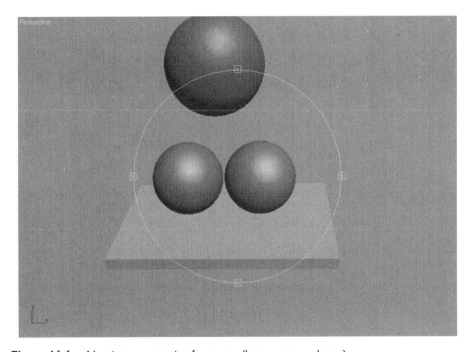

Figure 16.6   Non-interpenetrating fragments (bottom two spheres).

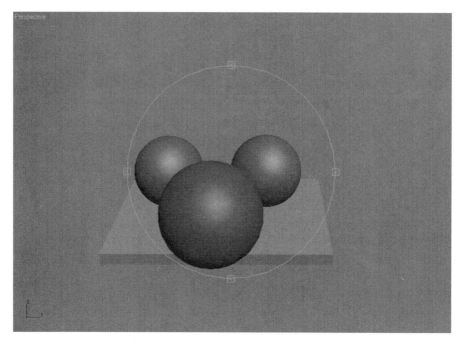

Figure 16.7 Non-interpenetrating fragments resulting in nonexplosive fragmentation.

Highly explosive fragmentation may be perfect for some situations, such as in videogame space combat. In this case, though, we don't want our ice chunks to go flying off at high velocity in all directions when struck by the dolphin, so we need to moderate the explosiveness with which the fragments separate. The most elementary precaution for moderating explosiveness is to minimize interpenetrations.

Another issue we need to take into account is the convexity or concavity of our fragments. In reactor, an object is convex if a line connecting any two points on the surface of the object will never go outside the object. Any object that is not convex is concave. For instance, in our next example (**Figure 16.8**), the egg is convex, the egg cup is concave. (The 3ds max file for this figure, egg&eggcup.max, is included on the DVD.)

 Note

To determine whether an object is convex or concave, select the object, go to Utilities > reactor > Utils > Selection, and click the Test Convexity button. You will get a message telling you whether the object is convex or concave.

Figure 16.8   The egg is convex, the egg cup is concave.

Simulating concave objects puts more stress on the processor than simulating convex ones. In many instances, the concavity really isn't important to the simulation, so by default reactor treats concave objects as if they were convex. However, if a fragment is really concave, treating it as convex can increase the explosiveness of fragmentation if another object happens to occupy the empty space created by the concavity.

For example, in **Figure 16.9**, the concave object on the left and the convex object on the right will not actually interpenetrate when brought together to form a sphere. However, if reactor doesn't know that the object on the left is concave, it will treat it as something close to a sphere, and it will consider that the two objects do interpenetrate. In such cases, reactor sees more interpenetration than really exists, so it applies a more explosive separation force than it would if it knew the truth. You can greatly reduce the explosiveness of the fragmentation by telling reactor that the fragment is in fact concave. The cost is a greater load on the processor, which can mean longer waits while reactor analyzes or creates your virtual world. (The added time, however, might not be noticeable in the case of a simple, low-poly fragment.)

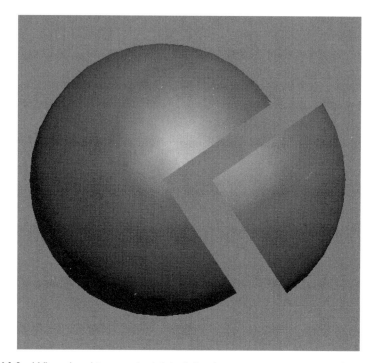

Figure 16.9   When the object on the left is defined as concave, reactor sees the two objects as non-interpenetrating.

Let's briefly explore the concavity/convexity issue in an exercise.

Convex and Concave Fragments

If you wish to examine the finished 3ds max scene implementing this exercise, open concave_convex.max on the DVD. The rendered movies are concave_convex1.avi (explosive version) and concave_convex2.avi (nonexplosive version).

1. In the Top viewport, create a sphere with a radius of 50 and position it at the origin (0,0,0).

2. In the Modify panel, apply a Squeeze modifier to Sphere01 and set the Axial Bulge Amount to –.9. This will be our concave fragment. Note that it has concavities both above and below (**Figure 16.10**).

3. In the Top viewport, create a sphere (Sphere02) with a radius of 25 and position it at (0,0,–15). This will be an interpenetrating fragment (**Figure 16.11**).

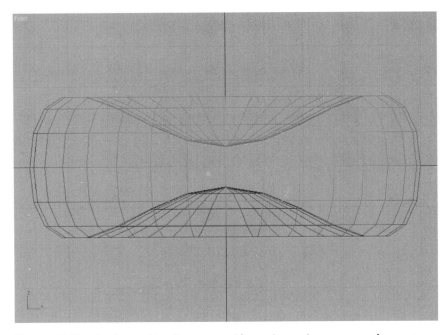

Figure 16.10 A sphere with a Squeeze modifier, to be used as a concave fragment.

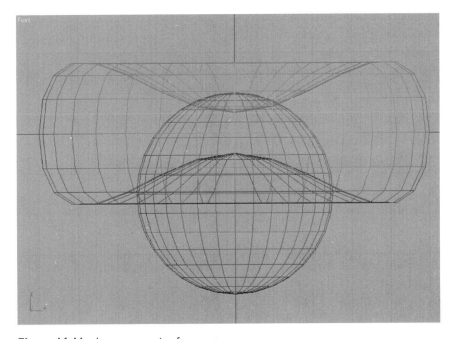

Figure 16.11 Interpenetrating fragments.

4. Select Sphere01 and Sphere02 and click the Create Fracture button on the reactor toolbar at the left-hand side of the screen. This creates a fracture object containing the two spheres.

5. Still leaving the two spheres selected, click the Open Property Editor button (**Figure 16.12**) on the reactor toolbar, and in the Rigid Body Properties dialog, set Mass to 100 (**Figure 16.13**). This sets the mass property for both fragments. The number was selected arbitrarily; it represents 100 kg. Objects with zero mass do not move in reactor, so this is an important step.

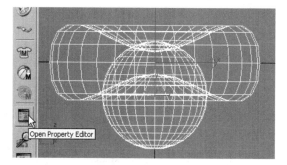

Figure 16.12   The Open Property Editor button on the reactor toolbar.

Figure 16.13   The Rigid Body Properties dialog, with Mass set to 100.

6. In the Top viewport, create a box with a length and width of 150 and a height of –10. Position it at (0,0,–75). The box is shown in the Perspective viewport in **Figure 16.14**. Note that we are not giving the box any mass, so it will not move.

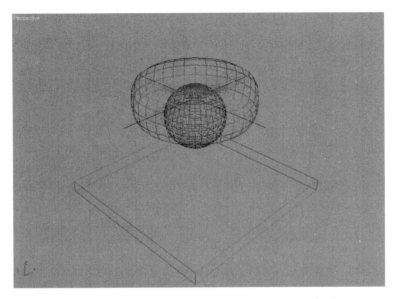

Figure 16.14   A box with a length and width of 150 and a height of –10.

7. Select everything in the scene and click the Create Rigid Body Collection button on the reactor toolbar. This creates a rigid body collection and adds both spheres and the box to it (**Figure 16.15**).

8. Click the Analyze World button on the reactor toolbar. You should get a message, "World Analysis gave no warnings".

Note

This step is not necessary if you've done everything correctly. However, it will warn you if you haven't.

9. Click Preview Animation on the reactor toolbar. When the reactor Real-Time Preview window (**Figure 16.16**) comes up, press P on the keyboard. Real-Time Preview gives us a preview of the animation without actually creating keyframes. The concave fragment bounces high in the air. It's an explosive fragmentation: We haven't yet told reactor that the Sphere01 fragment is concave, so it sees a deep interpenetration between the two fragments. Exit the reactor Real-Time Preview window by pressing Esc.

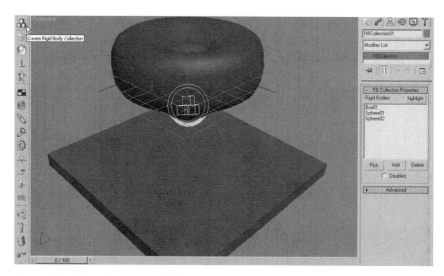

Figure 16.15 Creating a rigid body collection.

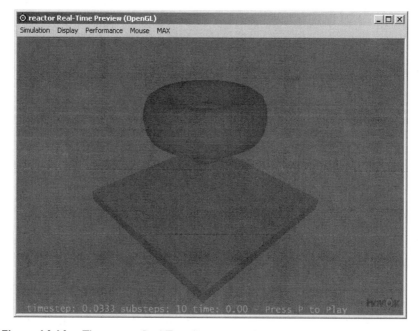

Figure 16.16 The reactor Real-Time Preview window.

10. Select Sphere01 (the concave fragment) and click the Open Property Editor button on the reactor toolbar. In the Simulation Geometry section of the Rigid Body Properties dialog, the Mesh Convex Hull radio button is selected. Select the Concave Mesh radio button instead.

11. Again, click the Preview Animation button and press P. The concave fragment hardly bounces at all this time. It's a nonexplosive fragmentation, because reactor now treats Sphere01 as concave. The scene and the objects are simple enough that the increased processing time is probably not noticeable.

The above exercise demonstrates that interpenetrations among fragments tend to cause explosive fragmentation, with a possible exception for concave fragments that reactor knows are concave. There are other configuration options that can also help moderate explosiveness. We'll look at some of them a little later. They're generally more appropriate for fine-tuning than for trying to undo the effects of massive interpenetrations.

By the way, if you want to find out whether there are interpenetrations among your fragments, there is a simple way to get that information. As long as the fragments are part of an enabled fracture object, 3ds max will not issue any warning about interpenetrations among the fragments, because interpenetrations are considered perfectly legal for fragments. However, if we disable the fracture, max will see the fragments only as members of a rigid body collection. Interpenetrations are generally considered a bad practice for rigid bodies, so we'll get warnings when there are interpenetrations. To disable the fracture, select it, go to the Modify panel, scroll down to the very bottom of the Properties rollout, and check the Disabled check box; the box should be unchecked initially for an enabled fracture, as shown in **Figure 16.17**. Now click the Analyze World button on the reactor toolbar. If there are interpenetrations, you'll get a message like "Bodies Sphere01 and Sphere02 are interpenetrating." You'll get the same message if you click Preview Animation.

Tip

If you don't get the "Bodies are interpenetrating" message, check the masses of the bodies in the Rigid Body Properties dialog by clicking the Open Property Editor button on the reactor toolbar. If both bodies have zero mass, reactor will not warn about interpenetrations.

Figure 16.17   The Properties rollout for a fracture, with the Disabled check box unchecked.

Creating Fragments

When creating fragments, it's ideal to use convex meshes, or at least meshes that can be treated as convex without causing explosive fragmentation. Using such meshes minimizes processing time without causing explosive fragmentation. That's the ideal we'll be aiming for.

Probably the easiest approach to creating fragments is to align separate objects so that they form a visually unified whole. This is easiest when all the fragments are rectangular, such as a square table with rectangular legs or a building constructed of rectangular boards.

Another simple example is a brick wall. Each brick is a member of the fracture, and they are all arranged to form the wall. The bricks are all convex, and you can easily arrange them to look like a solid wall but avoid interpenetrations. (Or you could deliberately cause them to interpenetrate to increase the strength of the explosion.) In the tutorials that are included with 3ds max 7, there is an example using bricks. (See Help > Tutorials > Using reactor and Flex for Simulation > Simulating Fractures with reactor.)

The bricks approach is not optimal for our iceberg, however. Unlike brick walls, icebergs are highly irregular in shape. There is simply no straightforward way to create separate objects that will fit together naturally, without interpenetrations, to form a nice icebergy-looking iceberg.

Another approach we *won't* pursue, though it works for some situations, is based on Booleans. Using this approach, you would create a "cutter" object, clone both cutter and iceberg, and then create a Boolean intersection of one iceberg and one cutter and a Boolean A-B of the other iceberg and cutter. You would end up with two objects: the Boolean A-B (which would essentially be the iceberg with a cutter-shaped hole in it) and the Boolean intersection (which would precisely fill that hole). You could continue cutting up either or both of these pieces by creating a new cutter object and repeating the process.

The Boolean-based technique gives maximum flexibility in defining the shapes of the fragments (which are basically determined by the shapes of the cutter objects). It also requires many keystrokes and/or mouse clicks per fragment. More significantly, if the overlapping part of your cutter is anything but perfectly flat, you'll end up creating one concave fragment and one convex fragment interpenetrating it—just what we're trying to avoid. (If the overlapping part of your cutter *is* perfectly flat, see the discussion of slicing below. It's a much easier way of doing the same thing.)

Another viable approach that we won't use here starts by creating a Connect compound object, which becomes the "quarry" from which you mine your fragments. In the simplest case, you start with two objects with holes in them, and the Connect object builds a "bridge" between the holes. More complex Connect objects can be created by bridging more than two hole-y objects. To avoid interpenetrations, make sure that the edges of each hole are coplanar (all lying in one plane). That way, at the point where they might be in danger of interpenetrating, both fragments will be perfectly flat, and there will be no interpenetrations. One way to accomplish this is to delete just one polygon per hole. Another way is to use a Slice Plane to create new edges.

The technique we will pursue in detail in this chapter is based on cutting up the iceberg object with a Slice Plane.

The Slice Approach

For this chapter, we create fragments by using a Slice Plane to cut our iceberg into elements. Then we clone those elements to create separate objects. A limitation of this approach is that the surfaces along which the "quarry" object breaks will always be perfectly planar. They can't be curved or irregular. This very limitation happens to be a strength in the case of our iceberg, though, because it eliminates interpenetrations even when reactor treats the fragments as simple convex bodies. As we've seen, non-interpenetrating convex bodies automatically moderate explosiveness without incurring any processing overhead.

The workflow for this approach is quite efficient. For example, to create the iceberg in this chapter, we create one quarry object and slice it twice, creating four chunks. Four fragments with two slices: That's efficiency! If you need more than four chunks, take any chunk and follow the same procedure to divide it into four.

The basic approach can be summarized in three steps:

1. Create a pyramid-shaped editable poly, with significant noise distortion.
2. Use Slice Planes to slice it vertically and horizontally. This creates four elements.
3. Detach those elements to clones.

If you are planning to create the main project described in this chapter, open Dolphin&Rider_start.max from the DVD. This file contains the starting scene that you will use in this project.

1. In the Top viewport, create a pyramid with four segments in each dimension (width, depth, height). Set Width and Depth to 150 and Height to 75. Position it at (120,11,–15).
2. Apply a Noise modifier. Check the Fractal box, and set Roughness to .5. Set Strength to 50 in each axis (X, Y, and Z) (**Figure 16.18**).
3. Right-click in the selected pyramid. From the Quad menu, choose Convert To > Convert to Editable Poly (**Figure 16.19**). You have completed step 1 of the basic workflow described above.
4. In the Modify panel, at the Element sub-object level, select the pyramid. It should turn red. Click Slice Plane in the Edit Geometry rollout. The Slice Plane button turns yellow, and a yellow rectangle representing the Slice Plane appears in the viewport. Check the Split box to the right of the Slice Plane button (**Figure 16.20**). The Split option creates double sets of vertices at the points where the edges are divided, resulting in a perfect snug fit between the fragments.

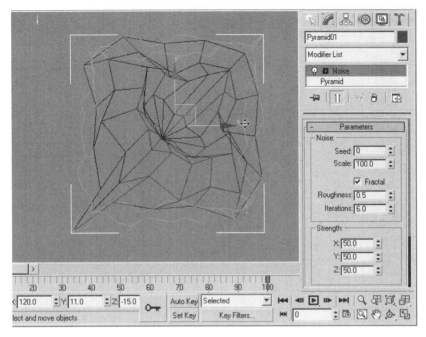

Figure 16.18   The Noise modifier.

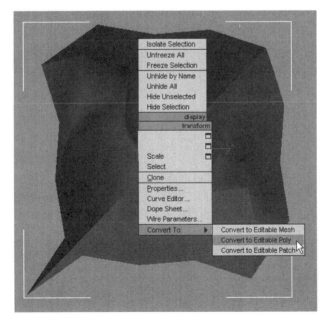

Figure 16.19   The Convert to Editable Poly option.

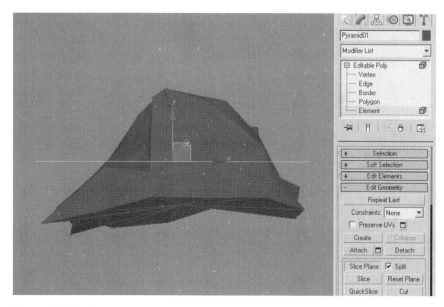

Figure 16.20   The Slice Plane option in the Edit Geometry rollout, with Split selected.

5. Position the Slice Plane horizontally about halfway through the iceberg, and click the Slice button (just below the Slice Plane button). Then rotate the Slice Plane 90 degrees to position it vertically (**Figure 16.21**) and, making sure that the whole pyramid is still selected, click the Slice button again.

6. Click the Slice Plane button to turn it off. You have completed step 2 of the basic workflow described above. You should have four elements now. To confirm, first click off the pyramid to deselect any elements. Then, staying at the Element sub-object level, select each of the elements in turn.

7. Select the lower right element and click Detach in the Edit Geometry rollout. In the Detach dialog, select Detach As Clone and click OK (**Figure 16.22**). Do this for the lower left, upper right, and upper left elements in turn. (The order is not really important, but when you do it in this order, your fragment names will match those in this chapter.) This completes step 3 of the basic workflow described above.

8. Exit the sub-object level. You can delete or hide Pyramid01, the original pyramid that you created. You don't need it any more.

9. Select Object01, Object02, Object03, and Object04, the four fragments you just created, and apply a Cap Holes modifier to them.

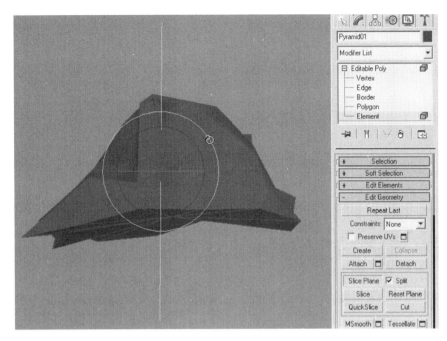

Figure 16.21 The Slice Plane.

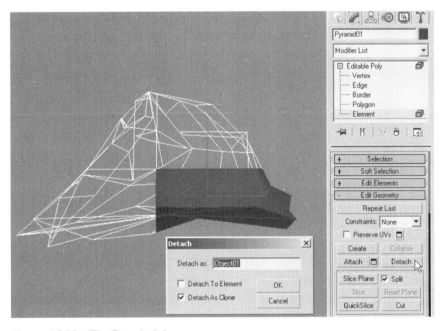

Figure 16.22 The Detach dialog.

10. Select each of the four objects in turn and assign a unique color to it. This will make it much easier to follow the trajectory of each fragment when previewing animation.

    You should now have a file resembling Dolphin&Rider_02.max in the files on the DVD.

11. Save your work as my_Dolphin&Rider_02.max.

OK, we've created our fragments! Now let's test them and make sure they start in a stable position.

Testing and Stabilizing

Open Dolphin&Rider_02.max from the DVD or continue with my_Dolphin&Rider_02.max from the previous section.

Before we can use our ice chunks in reactor, we need to give them some mass. Objects that have no mass cannot experience an impact and therefore can't be fractured or affected in any other way within the reactor virtual world.

Once the ice chunks have mass, however, reactor's gravity affects them and they immediately begin falling, rather than sitting and waiting nicely to be fractured. reactor does offer a very simple way to prevent objects from moving until they are affected by some other object or system. Here's the procedure, using our four fragments:

1. Select the four fragments.

2. Click the Open Property Editor button on the reactor toolbar (fourth from the bottom).

3. In the Rigid Body Properties dialog, check the Inactive box (**Figure 16.23**). Gravity no longer affects the fragments. They will sit still until they experience a collision, which in this case would come from the dolphin hitting them.

This technique would work fine if we just needed to immobilize the fragments in midair. In our final scene, however, this will not be sufficient, because we will be placing the ice chunks in water, with waves that will affect them just like collisions with solid objects. We want them to be affected by the water, but not so much that they start breaking apart before the dolphin hits them. For that, we need techniques that stabilize the fragments despite the presence of forces that tend to destabilize them. So let's explore what's available to accomplish that kind of stabilization.

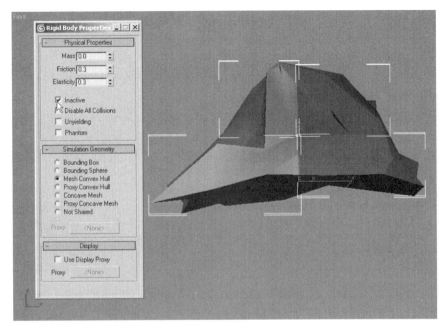

Figure 16.23   Checking the Inactive box in the Rigid Body Properties dialog.

For testing purposes, we'll create a box to act as a platform for the ice chunks to sit on. We won't give the platform any mass, so it will not fall, but it will support the ice chunks.

The techniques we use here will also work when the fragments are in water. However, stabilizing ice chunks in water can be a tricky business and hard to judge. We'll learn the ropes on dry land first.

It's not easy to position the ice chunks so that they sit stably on the platform but do not interpenetrate it. If the ice chunks start in an unstable position, they will shift slightly at the beginning of the animation and are quite likely to fragment. This is not what we want. We want the fragmentation to begin only when the dolphin hits the ice chunks.

Surprisingly, making the initial shift very small can increase the fragmentation. This may be because a fragment can start bouncing back and forth between the platform and other fragments very fast, creating multiple sequential interpenetrations with the neighboring fragments. As we saw in the earlier exercise, interpenetrations tend to cause explosive fragmentation. In some cases, initial instability can actually knock multiple fragments out of the viewport in the first instants of the animation. To the viewer, it looks as if they just disappear. reactor permits users to store and view collision data, so you can analyze situations like this in detail to determine exactly what is going on.

Luckily, it's easy to allow the ice chunks to find a stable position and then assign that position to the ice chunks in the first frame of the animation. That way, there is no initial movement and no danger of fragmentation before the dolphin hits. The key to this process is reactor's Update MAX function, which assigns the current state of the animation to the beginning of the animation.

Here are the detailed instructions. They come in three parts: initial testing of the fracture, storing and viewing of collision data, and stabilization of the fragments.

Note

Your results may vary somewhat from those described in the coming sections, depending on exactly where you positioned your Slice Planes. If you want to follow along and get exactly the same results described, open Dolphin&Rider_02.max on the DVD.

Initial Testing of the Fracture

First we'll create the fracture and test for initial instability.

1. Select Object01, Object02, Object03, and Object04, and click the Create Fracture button on the reactor toolbar. The four fragments are added to the new fracture object (**Figure 16.24**).

2. Reselect the four fragments, if they are no longer selected. Click the Open Property Editor button on the reactor toolbar, and in the Rigid Body Properties panel, set Mass to 100.

Figure 16.24   Creating a new fracture object containing four fragments.

3. In the Top viewport, create a box. Rename it "platform." Set Length to 1000, Width to 1000, and Height to –10. Position the box at (0,0,–36). One way to position the box is to click the Select and Move tool on the toolbar and then type 0, 0, and –36 into the X, Y, and Z Transform Type-In fields at the bottom of the screen (**Figure 16.25**). Make sure the fields are in Absolute mode. The button to the left of the fields should be gray, not yellow. Notice that we're not giving any mass to this box.

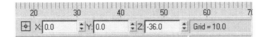

Figure 16.25   The Transform Type-In fields.

4. Select Object01, Object02, Object03, Object04, and "platform," and click the Create Rigid Body Collection button at the top of the reactor toolbar (**Figure 16.26**).

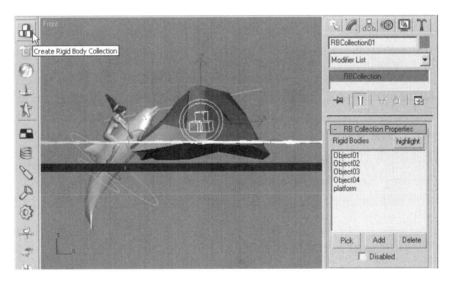

Figure 16.26   Creating a rigid body collection. (Dolphin created with Poser 5, Curious Labs.)

5. Click the Analyze World button on the reactor toolbar (it's the magnifying glass button, third from the bottom). You should get the message, "World Analysis gave no warnings."

6. Click the Preview Animation button on the reactor toolbar (second from the bottom). When the reactor Real-Time Preview window comes up, press the P key. The ice chunks fall but do not fragment. Exit Real-Time Preview by typing Esc.

7. Reposition the platform box to (0,0,–35). Click the Preview Animation button and press P again. Although the fragments now have a smaller distance to fall (since the platform has moved up a little), they do fragment this time. This is an example of a smaller initial movement causing more fragmentation. Exit Real-Time Preview.

We do have some initial instability, with more visible results when the platform is at –35 on the Z axis than when it is at –36. At this point, we could just proceed to stabilizing the fragments. Instead, let's get a more detailed view of what is going on in those first few instants of the animation. We can do this by storing and viewing collisions.

Storing and Viewing Collisions

When reactor creates keyframes, it can also optionally store data about every collision that occurs. Initially, the data is stored only in memory, not on the disk. You can view the collision data without saving it to disk, and you also have the option of saving to a text file. Since the number of collisions can be overwhelming, reactor provides a filtering capability so that you can narrow the collisions stored to make it easier to find the ones that interest you. You set the filters before storing the collisions in memory.

So far in this chapter, we haven't been creating keyframes; we've just been previewing the animation. Now we'll create keyframes and store collisions. We'll try it once with the platform at –35 and again with the platform at –36. Once you have an impression of what is going on, we'll do some filtering to make it easier to eyeball the data.

Creating Keyframed Collisions

Here's the procedure for our first test, with the platform at –35.

1. In the Utilities panel, open the reactor Utility rollouts by clicking the reactor button (**Figure 16.27**).

2. In the Collisions rollout, click the "Always store" radio button (**Figure 16.28**).

3. Click the Create Animation button at the bottom of the reactor toolbar. You'll get the message, "Are you sure you want to create an animation? This action cannot be undone."

This message is warning you that any existing keyframes for objects in the reactor simulation will be destroyed, overwritten by the keyframes that are about to be created. (Keyframes for objects not in the simulation will not be affected.) This is a concern mainly when you have manually tweaked keyframes created by reactor. If you overwrite those keyframes, your manual tweaks will be lost and you will have to redo them. In our case, we haven't created any keyframes yet, so we're perfectly safe.

Figure 16.27   The reactor Utility rollouts in the Utilities panel.

Figure 16.28   The "Always store" option on the Collisions rollout.

4. Click OK. reactor creates keyframes. In the Collisions rollout, just above the View and Clear buttons, where it previously said "No collisions stored," it now displays the number of collisions stored.

5. In the Collisions rollout, click View. The Stored Collisions window comes up. This has a spreadsheet-like format. Each row represents one collision. There are eight columns per row, representing eight pieces of information about the collision.

Stored Collisions

Here's a rundown on what each column means:

- **Ticks**—The time, in ticks (1/4800 of a second), when the collision occurred. We're using a standard video frame rate of 30 frames per second, so there are 160 ticks in each frame.

- **Frame**—The time, in frames, when the collision occurred. If the current time unit is something other than frames (such as SMPTE timecode), this column will reflect that.

- **Object A**—One of the two objects involved in the collision.

- **Object B**—The other object involved in the collision.

- **Point**—The point, expressed in world coordinates, where the objects collided. (Due to a bug in max 7, the points displayed onscreen are wrong. If you click the Save button on the Stored Collisions window to save the data as a text file, the text file contains the proper points.)

- **Normal**—This expresses the direction (but not the velocity) of the impact in terms of the XYZ coordinate system. The direction is expressed as if object A were standing still and only object B moved (even though the opposite may be the case, or both may be moving). It's expressed as three numbers, representing the X, Y, and Z axes. Imagine an arrow representing the impact. Consider the length of the arrow to be one unit. The three numbers tell you how far you need to move in the X, Y, and Z directions to get from the tail of the arrow to the point. The mathematical term for this is the unit normal vector of the collision.

- **Speed**—The relative velocity of the two objects along the unit normal vector. If you save the data to a file, this will be listed as NRV (Normal Relative Velocity).

- **Phantom**—This column indicates whether the collision involved a phantom rigid body, one that can pass freely through other bodies. Possible values are Not

Phantom (the collision didn't involve a phantom rigid body), Entering (the collision time shows when the phantom rigid body started penetrating the other rigid body), and Leaving (the collision time shows when the phantom rigid body completely exited the other rigid body).

Here are the first four collisions in the data we just created. (They are in the format produced when you click the Save button to save the data as a text file.) All four collisions involve the platform and Object02.

Time : 0
 A : Object02
 B : platform
 Point : (43.4185 –8.4282 –34.8831)
 Normal : (–4.60904e-006 –7.0279e-005 1)
 NRV : 0
 Phantom : Not Phantom

Time : 1
 A : Object02
 B : platform
 Point : (43.4185 –8.4282 –34.8831)
 Normal : (–4.60904e-006 –7.0279e-005 1)
 NRV : 0
 Phantom : Not Phantom

Time : 16
 A : Object02
 B : platform
 Point : (43.4185 –8.4282 –34.8831)
 Normal : (–4.60904e-006 –7.0279e-005 1)
 NRV : 1.20694
 Phantom : Not Phantom

Time : 18
 A : Object02
 B : platform
 Point : (43.3884 –8.44 –34.8482)
 Normal : (–3.01953e-005 –4.6361e-005 1)
 NRV : 167.956
 Phantom : Not Phantom

If the platform were moving, all four collisions would be directed straight up along the Z axis, as indicated by the final 1 in the unit normal vector. (Actually, of course, it's Object02 that's moving, and the direction of movement is down, not up.) Essentially, all the unit normal vectors are equivalent to (0,0,1), the first two numbers being extremely small in each case. (For instance, −4.60904e-006 is −.00000460904.)

The first two collisions show zero velocity (presumably a minuscule velocity rounded off), and the third shows a very low velocity (fewer than 2 units per second). The fourth, however, suddenly shows a velocity of about 168 units per second.

Close the Stored Collisions window. Select Fracture01 and go to the Modify panel. You'll see near the bottom of the Properties rollout, in the Break On section, that this fracture breaks when one of its fragments is involved in a collision with a velocity of 100 units per second or more. (This is the default setting.) So this fracture starts breaking up almost immediately, on the fourth collision between the platform and Object02, when the velocity first exceeds 100 units per second.

Move the platform to Z = −36, create animation again, and view the stored keyframes. There are 15 initial collisions between the platform and Object02:

Time : 0
 A : Object02
 B : platform
 Point : (43.4185 −8.4282 −35.3831)
 Normal : (−8.73185e-007 −1.33144e-005 1)
 NRV : 0
 Phantom : Not Phantom

Time : 8
 A : Object02
 B : platform
 Point : (43.4185 −8.4282 −35.3831)
 Normal : (−8.73185e-007 −1.33144e-005 1)
 NRV : 0
 Phantom : Not Phantom

Time : 16
  A : Oject02
  B : platform
  Point : (43.4185 −8.4282 −35.3831)
  Normal : (−8.73185e-007 −1.33144e-005 1)
  NRV : 0.643699
  Phantom : Not Phantom

Time : 23
  A : Object02
  B : platform
  Point : (43.36 −8.45117 −35.315)
  Normal : (6.10491e-006 1.37024e-005 1)
  NRV : 81.8201
  Phantom : Not Phantom

Time : 32
  A : Object02
  B : platform
  Point : (43.3017 −8.47404 −35.2468)
  Normal : (1.5911e-005 −1.16828e-005 1)
  NRV : 81.2282
  Phantom : Not Phantom

Time : 39
  A : Object02
  B : platform
  Point : (43.2435 −8.49689 −35.1791)
  Normal : (1.86716e-005 0 1)
  NRV : 81.2799
  Phantom : Not Phantom

Time : 47
  A : Object02
  B : platform
  Point : (43.1855 −8.51968 −35.1113)
  Normal : (2.42683e-006 6.6013e-006 1)
  NRV : 80.6884
  Phantom : Not Phantom

Time : 64
  A : Object02
  B : platform
  Point : (43.0698 –8.56508 –34.9767)
  Normal : (1.17392e-005 1.14664e-006 1)
  NRV : 79.5036
  Phantom : Not Phantom

Time : 80
  A : Object02
  B : platform
  Point : (42.9547 –8.61027 –34.8441)
  Normal : (8.05859e-006 –8.62837e-006 1)
  NRV : 78.3188
  Phantom : Not Phantom

Time : 96
  A : Object02
  B : platform
  Point : (42.8402 –8.65524 –34.7135)
  Normal : (7.59867e-006 –5.01621e-006 1)
  NRV : 77.1333
  Phantom : Not Phantom

Time : 112
  A : Object02
  B : platform
  Point : (42.7263 –8.70001 –34.5849)
  Normal : (1.33756e-005 2.07282e-006 1)
  NRV : 75.947
  Phantom : Not Phantom

Time : 128
  A : Object02
  B : platform
  Point : (42.6129 –8.74456 –34.4582)
  Normal : (6.45438e-006 3.80507e-006 1)
  NRV : 74.7607
  Phantom : Not Phantom

Time : 144
 A : Object02
 B : platform
 Point : (42.5001 −8.78887 −34.3335)
 Normal : (−5.95529e-006 −2.11222e-006 1)
 NRV : 73.5742
 Phantom : Not Phantom

Time : 160
 A : Object02
 B : platform
 Point : (42.3878 −8.833 −34.2108)
 Normal : (−2.73037e-006 9.18103e-006 1)
 NRV : 72.3864
 Phantom : Not Phantom

Time : 176
 A : Object02
 B : platform
 Point : (42.2762 −8.87688 −34.0901)
 Normal : (−1.14404e-005 1.22867e-006 1)
 NRV : 71.1988
 Phantom : Not Phantom

The direction of the impact is the same as before. But the highest velocity achieved is less than the 100 units per second required to break the fracture.

Filtering Collisions

Let's filter collisions to see if the trends established in the first instants of the animation continue through the rest of the animation. We'll do this by looking only at collisions with a velocity of 100 units per second or more.

1. Leaving the platform at Z = −36, go to the Collisions rollout on the Utilities panel, and in the "Filter before storing" section, check the Velocity box and enter 100 in the box to the right of it (**Figure 16.29**). Only collisions with a velocity of 100 or greater will be stored.

Figure 16.29   The Velocity settings in the "Filter before storing" section of the Collisions rollout.

2. Create animation again, and view the stored keyframes. No collisions are stored.

3. Scrub the Time Slider along the timeline. Since we created keyframes, we can now view the animation in the viewports. The fragments move as a group but never break up.

4. Move the platform to Z = −35 and create animation. Seventeen collisions are stored. View the collisions. All but one occur in frame 0.

5. Scrub the Time Slider along the timeline. The fragments begin to break up immediately.

The numerical data matches the previewed animation in the Real-Time Preview window and the keyframed animation in the viewports. They all reflect the fact that any initial instability in a reactor fracture can be magnified if the fragments start life too close to another object, particularly an immovable object like the platform. (A similar phenomenon can occur when a fragment starts life between two other fragments, particularly if there are interpenetrations. See the first paragraph in "Fracture Tips" in the 3ds max 7 user reference.)

Now that we've investigated the initial instability in some detail, let's move on to stabilizing the fragments.

Stabilizing the Fragments

We are going to be concerned here with two different kinds of stability:

- **Physical balance**

- **Nonreactivity**, which includes reduced susceptibility to fragmentation

The two are interrelated: If a group of fragments is out of balance initially, it will start moving as soon as the animation starts. That very movement may trigger fragmentation. This, in fact, is exactly what's happening to the fragments we're working with now.

Let's start with nonreactivity. reactor has a number of features aimed at taming feisty fragments that are blasting apart more easily or more enthusiastically than you'd like. For instance, there are three parameters in Utilities > reactor > World > Fracture Penetrations that are designed to make reactor less aggressive about pushing interpenetrations apart (**Figure 16.30**).

- **Separation Time** can be increased to slow down separation of fragments.

- **Velocity Cap** can be decreased to reduce the top achievable velocity.

- **Scale Tolerance** can be reduced to effectively raise reactor's standards for what constitutes a collision or an interpenetration.

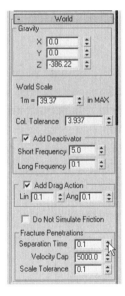

Figure 16.30   The World rollout of the reactor utility.

All three tend to result in less explosive, though possibly also less realistic, fragmentation. (Realism is decreased if visible interpenetrations occur, owing to fragments not separating fast enough.) Reducing the Scale Tolerance value, because it raises the bar for what constitutes a collision or an interpenetration, can reduce not only the intensity but also the number of collisions and interpenetrations that reactor perceives.

Of these three parameters, Scale Tolerance is generally the most powerful. Scale Tolerance changes the distance at which reactor considers that fragments have collided or interpenetrated. This distance is called the Collision Tolerance. It might seem logical that objects would have to touch in order to collide. This would be true if reactor checked for collisions continuously. In reality, reactor checks at regular, discrete intervals (called simulation time steps). A fast-moving object can move into an interpenetrating state from one simulation time step to the next. By triggering the collision reaction a little bit before the objects touch, reactor prevents some of those interpenetrations.

This does mean that objects can begin to affect each other slightly before they actually touch. However, it turns out that viewers are much less likely to see this little bit of separation than the same amount of interpenetration. Think of the standard Hollywood cowboy punch, in which Cowboy A swings his fist 3 inches from Cowboy B's chin. No contact is ever made, but Cowboy B jerks his head backward. As long as the viewers see it from the correct angle, they'll be convinced that he really was hit. Compare that with the fist's appearing to penetrate 3 inches *into* Cowboy B's head. There is no angle from which this will look right.

By default, reactor triggers nonfracture collisions when objects are 3.937 units apart. This Collision Tolerance (for the virtual world as a whole) is set at Utilities > reactor > World > World Scale > Col. Tolerance. Since by default reactor equates 39.37 max units to 1 meter (see the first parameter in the World Scale section in Figure 16.30), 3.937 units equals one-tenth of a meter, or 10 centimeters. Thus, reactor triggers collisions when nonfracture objects are the equivalent of 10 centimeters apart.

All that applies to nonfracture collisions. However, with fractures, a smaller collision tolerance is unlikely to cause visible interpenetrations: Fragments typically begin life snug against one another (so interpenetrations can't be seen), and thereafter either stay so close that interpenetrations still can't be seen, or else blast apart and never come back together so interpenetrations don't occur. There's very little opportunity for the scenario in which a fragment moves from a state of non-interpenetration to a state of interpenetration from one simulation time step to the next. In addition, fragmentation usually happens very quickly and involves multiple fragments, so that we perceive it more as an overall event, without being able to precisely follow the positions of individual fragments. For these reasons, fractures can generally accommodate a much smaller Collision Tolerance than 10 centimeters.

Scale Tolerance is a multiplier, ranging from 1 to –1, that scales the Collision Tolerance value for fractures without affecting the Collision Tolerance value for the virtual world as a whole. The default Scale Tolerance value is one-tenth (0.1), making the Collision Tolerance within fractures one-tenth of the World Collision Tolerance. Thus, by default, reactor triggers collisions when fragments are .3937 units (equivalent to 1 centimeter) apart. (Collisions between a fragment and a nonfragment use the World Collision Tolerance value. Only collisions between two fragments are affected by Scale Tolerance.)

If you set Scale Tolerance to 0, reactor doesn't detect a collision until fragments are touching. If you set a negative value for Scale Tolerance, fragments will actually interpenetrate before a collision is detected.

When fragments are fairly large in relation to Collision Tolerance, even a Scale Tolerance value of –1 may not reduce collisions as much as you want. In the project in this chapter, for instance, the bottom fragments average 75 units at the base (since the initial pyramid's base was 150 units square), so shaving approximately 4 units off the Collision Tolerance (by changing Scale Tolerance from the default of 0.1 to the maximum negative of –1) might not be expected to have a huge effect. In fact, it doesn't.

Adjusting Collision Tolerances

To attain greater stability in the overall effect, try this:

1. Leaving the platform at Z = –35, go to the Collisions rollout in the reactor section in the Utilities panel. In the "Filter before storing" section, make sure that the Velocity > box is checked and that 100 is entered in the box to the right of it. (This is how we left it in the last exercise.)

2. Set Scale Tolerance to –1.

3. Create animation again. Twelve collisions are stored. View the collisions. All but two occur in frame 0.

4. Scrub the Time Slider along the timeline. The fragments begin to break up immediately.

5. Try some other negative values for Scale Tolerance. You'll find that a Scale Tolerance of –.1 or –.9, or anything in between, results in only 11 collisions. In every case, the collisions are all between the platform and Object02, and almost all of them occur immediately. It is often the case, as it is here, that you achieve little if anything by pushing Scale Tolerance below –.1 ("below" meaning to a larger negative value).

6. When you're done experimenting, set Scale Tolerance back to the default of 0.1.

Eleven collisions are better than 17, but still not what you'd call stability.

Energy Loss and Stability

Another parameter in the nonreactivity category is Energy Loss. Select the fracture and go to the Modify panel. Energy Loss is near the bottom of the Properties rollout (**Figure 16.31**). Energy Loss determines what percentage of its energy a fragment loses when it breaks off. Increasing Energy Loss makes for less energetic fragmentation.

In the case of our project, the nonreactivity parameters, even when taken to extremes, do not prevent the initial fragmentation. So let's see what we can accomplish through physical balance.

Physical balance can be achieved through a simple, straightforward procedure that involves temporarily disabling fragmentation, allowing the fragments to settle down into a state of equilibrium, and then assigning that state to the fragments at the beginning of the animation.

Figure 16.31   The Energy Loss setting, near the bottom of the Properties rollout of the Modify panel.

Here are the details:

1. Select the fracture object, Fracture01. In the Modify panel, in the Properties roll-out, select Object01, Object02, Object03, and Object04 one at a time and click the Unbreakable radio button for each of them.

2. Click Preview Animation and press P. The ice chunks fall but do not fragment, because they are all unbreakable. When the ice chunks stop moving, select MAX > Update MAX in the Real-Time Preview window (**Figure 16.32**). Doing so assigns this stable position to the fragments in the first frame of the animation.

3. Click Simulation > Reset. Press the P key. There is no initial movement of the fragments because they now start in a stable position. We've achieved our goal—perfect initial stability—using only physical balance! Exit Real-Time Preview.

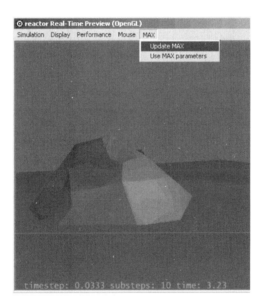

Figure 16.32 The Update MAX option in the Real-Time Preview window.

4. We don't want the fracture to be unbreakable in the final scene, so we'll make it breakable again now. With the fracture object selected, in the Modify panel, select Object01, Object02, Object03, and Object04 in turn, and click the Normal radio button for each of them so that they will no longer be unbreakable.

   You should now have a file resembling Dolphin&Rider_03.max in the files for this chapter on the DVD.

5. Save your work as my_Dolphin&Rider_03.max.

This example is typical: If you're looking for initial stability, physical balance is often the easiest way to achieve it. The nonreactive parameters are usually more appropriate for moderating the action once fragmentation begins.

Now that we've achieved a state of equilibrium, let's disturb it with a dolphin.

Animating the Dolphin

In this section, we're going to look at three basic approaches to animating the dolphin.

First, we'll just make the dolphin a rigid body, totally under reactor's control; we won't create any keyframes for it ourselves. This is very simple but doesn't happen to be capable of producing the trajectory we want for the dolphin in this scene. (It could work well, for instance, if we just wanted to simulate a ball dropping, because in that case the force of reactor's gravity alone could provide all the required movement for the ball. In this case, though, we want the dolphin to jump out of the water; there's no reactor force that's going to accomplish that.)

Then we'll move on to hand-animation of a rigid body, in which we do create keyframes for the dolphin—or, more precisely, for the dolphin's top-level control object. We'll try creating all the keyframes ourselves, as well as combining our manually created keyframes with reactor's automatically generated ones. By creating our own keyframes, we can directly determine the dolphin's initial motion, rather than leaving that entirely to reactor forces.

Hand-animation of a rigid body turns out to be a good solution for us, but it does have some limitations, the major one being that the simulation cannot take into account sub-object animation of the mesh. So we'll also look at using the dolphin as a deforming mesh, which does allow sub-object animation to be taken into account in the simulation. This results in a much more accurate simulation, but also puts an excessive load on the processor, which cannot easily handle a complex mesh like the dolphin. We'll see a technique for lightening that load, at least during the test phase.

Let Reactor Do It All

For a first simple approximation of what we want, we'll just place the dolphin above the ice chunks and let it fall under the influence of reactor's gravity, eventually hitting and shattering the ice.

Open Dolphin&Rider_03.max from the DVD or continue with my_Dolphin&Rider_03.max.

Note

In Dolphin&Rider_03.max (or my_Dolphin&Rider_03.max), the dolphin is a skinned figure, designed to be moved and animated by using its control objects (their names all start with ctrl_), not by transforming the dolphin01 mesh itself directly.

Here's the procedure:

1. Select RBCollection01, and add dolphin01 to it by clicking Add in the RB Collection Properties rollout in the Modify panel and selecting dolphin01 in the Select rigid bodies dialog (**Figure 16.33**).

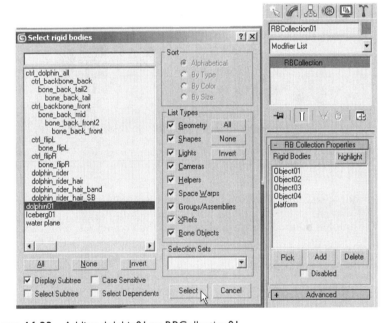

Figure 16.33   Adding dolphin01 to RBCollection01.

2. With Select Object (*not* any of the transform tools, such as Move, Rotate, or Scale) selected on the Main toolbar, choose dolphin01, click the Open Property Editor button on the reactor toolbar, and in the Rigid Body Properties dialog, set Mass to 1000. (We are suggesting that you avoid using the transform tools so that you do not accidentally transform the dolphin01 mesh.)

3. Select ctrl_dolphin_all and move it to (100,0,275).

4. Click Preview Animation and press P. The dolphin falls and the ice chunks fragment (**Figure 16.34**).

5. Save your work as my_Dolphin&Rider_04.max.

Figure 16.34   The dolphin falls and the ice chunks fragment. (Dolphin created with Poser 5, Curious Labs.)

That's encouraging, but a couple of issues are evident right away:

- The dolphin bounces off the platform and then continues to interact with the fragments. We'd get a more realistic impression of what will happen with water if the dolphin went through the platform.

- We don't want the dolphin to just drop out of the sky. The dolphin first has to jump up into the air and then come down on the ice.

There are a number of ways to address these problems. One possible approach is hand-animation of a rigid body.

Hand-Animating a Rigid Body

Now we'll create a hand-animated rigid body, entirely controlled by hand-animated keyframes. reactor-controlled rigid bodies will react to the hand-animated rigid body, but the hand-animated rigid body will not, in turn, be affected by them.

The basic workflow is simple:

1. Select the object that you want to hand-animate.

2. Click the Open Property Editor button on the reactor toolbar, and in the Rigid Body Properties dialog, check the Unyielding box. reactor does not create keyframes for an unyielding object. That's what we want in this case, because we're going to create the keyframes for the object ourselves. (There's no need to give the object any mass, since it's not involved in the simulation anyway.)

3. Add the object that you want to hand-animate to a rigid body collection.

4. Animate the object.

First, we'll do an exercise with a box, to see how hand-animation works in a simple case. Then we'll apply what we've learned to the dolphin mesh.

Hand-Animating a Box

Continue with my_Dolphin&Rider_04.max from the previous exercise, or open Dolphin&Rider_04.max in the files for this chapter on the DVD.

1. In the Top viewport, create a box with a length of 80, a width of 50, and a height of 150. Position it at (−250,0,−100). Name it dolphin_proxy.

Tip

Don't overlook the minus signs!

2. With dolphin_proxy still selected, click Open Property Editor on the reactor toolbar. In the Rigid Body Properties dialog, check the Unyielding box. Note that we are not giving the box any mass.

3. Select RBCollection01. Go to the Modify panel and click Add and select dolphin_ proxy, adding it to the rigid body collection. Also, delete dolphin01 from RBCollection01: Select dolphin01 in the list of objects in the collection, and click Delete to remove dolphin01 from the collection.

4. Turn on Auto Key Select dolphin_proxy, go to frame 25, and move the box to (0,25,250).

5. Go to frame 50 and move dolphin_proxy to (100,25,−150).

6. Turn off Auto Key.

7. Click Preview Animation and press P. The dolphin_proxy shatters the ice.

8. Save your work as my_Dolphin&Rider_05.max. To see a finished version of this exercise, open Dolphin&Rider_05.max in the files on the DVD.

That was very straightforward and worked nicely. Let's see if we can substitute dolphin01 for the dolphin_proxy box.

Hand-Animating the Dolphin Mesh

If you want to continue with the file you created in the previous exercise, clean up by removing dolphin_proxy from RBCollection01. Select RBCollection01. In the Modify panel, select dolphin_proxy in the list of objects in the collection, and click Delete to remove dolphin_proxy from the collection. Finally, hide or delete dolphin_proxy.

Alternatively, open Dolphin&Rider_06.max on the DVD.

Our goal here is to use dolphin01 to break the ice. This is a skinned and rigged mesh, so we don't want to animate the mesh directly. We want to animate control objects, which affect bones, which in turn affect the mesh.

Now, the hand-animated body must be added to RBCollection01, as in step 3 in the exercise above. So, which one do we add: the control object or dolphin01?

To try adding ctrl_dolphin_all to the rigid body collection, follow this procedure:

1. Select RBCollection01. It should contain only the four "ice chunk" objects and the platform. Click Add and select ctrl_dolphin_all. The control object is added to the rigid body collection.

2. Now let's try to assign the Unyielding property to the control object. Whoops! Everything in the Rigid Body Properties dialog is grayed out, making it impossible to assign the Unyielding property (**Figure 16.35**).

3. Click the Analyze World button on the toolbar. You get a message, "All vertices in mesh are coplanar, please use Concave Mesh." This is a fatal error, not just a warning. If you try to preview the animation, you'll find that you can't.

4. Clean up by deleting ctrl_dolphin_all from RBCollection01.

Figure 16.35   The Rigid Body Properties dialog, grayed out.

The error message in step 3 above suggests that we make the control object a Concave Mesh using the radio button in the Rigid Body Properties dialog. As we just saw in step 2, that's impossible, because the whole dialog is grayed out.

Putting this control object into a rigid body collection just doesn't seem to work. So let's try putting the dolphin mesh itself into the rigid body collection.

1. Select RBCollection01, if it isn't selected already. It should contain only the four "ice chunk" objects and the platform. Click Add and select dolphin01. The dolphin mesh is added to the rigid body collection.

2. Select dolphin01. Click Open Property Editor on the reactor toolbar, and in the Rigid Body Properties dialog, check the Unyielding box. So far so good. No need to give the dolphin any mass; it already has a mass of 1000.

3. Click the Analyze World button. You should see the message, "World Analysis gave no warnings."

4. With the Time Slider on frame 0, select ctrl_dolphin_all and position it at (−30,150,−100).

5. Turn on Auto Key. Select ctrl_dolphin_all, if necessary. Go to frame 25 and position ctrl_dolphin_all at (50,0,250). Go to frame 50 and position ctrl_dolphin_all at (100,0,–150). You will see the dolphin move as you apply the animation, and also if you scrub the Time Slider afterward.

6. In addition, at frame 50, in the Front viewport, with Auto Key still on, select the Rotate tool and use the Screen handle (the outer gray circle) to rotate ctrl_dolphin_all about 90 degrees clockwise, so that the dolphin is facing more downward (**Figure 16.36**).

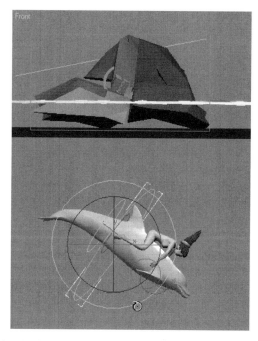

Figure 16.36 Use the Screen handle (the outer gray circle) to rotate ctrl_dolphin_all.

7. Turn Auto Key off.

8. Click Preview Animation and press P. The dolphin doesn't move because it is a deforming mesh, meaning that its vertices have been keyframed (in this case, by skinning). This differentiates it from the box in the "Hand-Animating a Box" exercise above, where the animation is applied to the whole box, not to sub-objects such as vertices. The animation of the dolphin's vertices is not taken into account in the hand-animated simulation.

9. Clean up by removing dolphin01 from RBCollection01.

10. Save your work as my_Dolphin&Rider_07.max.

Coplanar and Control Objects

We haven't obtained satisfactory results by putting either the control object or the dolphin01 mesh into the rigid body collection. This might seem like a dead end, but it's not. The "coplanar" error message gives us the clue we need to find a solution.

As we've seen, reactor will not really accept a coplanar object as a rigid body. It will put the coplanar object in the rigid body collection, but it won't allow us to give it any mass or assign the Unyielding property to it.

A circle is obviously coplanar. But what if we extruded it? It would no longer be coplanar, and perhaps we could successfully use it as a rigid body. Let's try it.

Open Dolphin&Rider_07.max from the DVD or continue with my_Dolphin&Rider_07.max.

1. Select ctrl_dolphin_all and add an Extrude modifier to it. Set Amount to 25. The circle becomes a cylinder (**Figure 16.37**).

2. Select RBCollection01. It should contain only the four "ice chunk" objects and the platform. Click Add and select ctrl_dolphin_all. The control object is added to the rigid body collection.

3. Assign the Unyielding property to the control object. (The Rigid Body Properties dialog is no longer grayed out, so there's no problem with this now.)

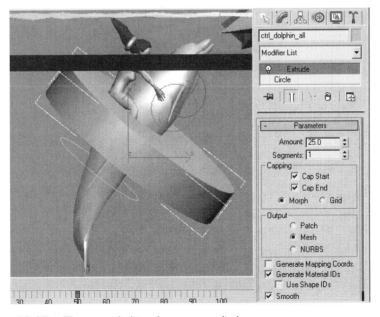

Figure 16. 37   The control object becomes a cylinder.

4. Click Preview Animation and press P. The control object moves, breaking the fracture.

5. Click the Create Animation button and scrub the Time Slider. Dolphin and rider move with ctrl_dolphin_all.

This is a rough approximation of what we want, and it indicates that this approach is workable, but we still have a problem: The fracture is affected by the control object, not by the dolphin, so the impact is all wrong. In fact, since the control object is so much wider than the dolphin, it actually hits the fragments on the way *up*, rather than on the way *down*.

This is not a showstopper, however. All we need to do is reshape the control object to conform to the shape of the dolphin. Here's one way of doing that:

1. Select ctrl_dolphin_all. Go to frame 35. Since this is close to the frame where the dolphin will hit the ice, this is where it's most important to have the control object match the dolphin mesh.

2. In the Modify panel, select Circle in the modifier stack and set the radius to 30 in the Parameters rollout (**Figure 16.38**).

Figure 16.38 Set the ctrl_dolphin_all Radius value to 30 in the Parameters rollout.

3. Select the Extrude modifier, and increase Amount to 90 in the Parameters rollout. This should just cover the dolphin's nose. If you preview the animation now, you'll see that it's already looking pretty good. Given the power of the modifier stack, however, there's no reason not to try to improve it.

4. Add a Squeeze modifier to ctrl_dolphin_all. In the Parameters rollout, in the Radial Squeeze section, set Amount to –0.11 (**Figure 16.39**). This tapers the control object a bit in front.

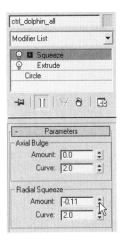

Figure 16.39 Add a Squeeze modifier to ctrl_dolphin_all to taper it.

5. Add a Mirror modifier to ctrl_dolphin_all. In the Parameters rollout, select Z for the Mirror Axis, set Offset to 2.64, and check the Copy box. This mirrors the control object front to back (**Figure 16.40**).

Figure 16.40 Add a Mirror modifier to ctrl_dolphin_all to mirror it front to back.

6. Create animation. The ice chunks react at the right time to give the illusion that it's the dolphin that's breaking them up.

Invisibility

All that remains to perfect the illusion is to make the control object invisible. Invisibility is a common requirement in reactor scenes, so you may find it convenient to keep an "invisible" material handy that you can apply to any object in one click. Here's how to create an invisible material and apply it to the control object:

1. Select ctrl_dolphin_all.

2. Press the M key to bring up the Material Editor.

3. Select an unused slot in the Material Editor, and in the Blinn Basic Parameters rollout, set Opacity to 0.

4. Click the Assign Material to Selection button (third from the left in the Material Editor) (**Figure 16.41**). The control object becomes invisible. It shows up "ghosted" in viewports (and as a gizmo, when selected) and not at all on renders. (Preview Animation still shows the control object.) The most important point is that only the dolphin is visible in the final rendered output.

 Note

If you are using the Software video driver, the control object may not be ghosted.

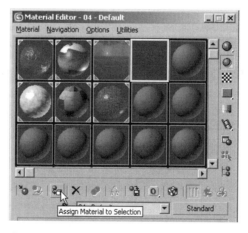

Figure 16.41   The Assign Material to Selection button in the Material Editor.

Keyframing the Dolphin

Notice that the rest of the dolphin rigging, which has not been brought into the reactor universe in any way, continues to work! Let's take advantage of this to arch the dolphin's spine and point his flippers downward when he gets to the top of his jump. Then as he dives we'll straighten him out and spread his flippers out to the side again.

Note

All dolphin controls except ctrl_dolphin_all should be manipulated using custom attributes in the Modify panel.

1. Turn on Auto Key and go to frame 25.
2. Select ctrl_backbone_back. In the Modify panel, set the arch attribute (the only attribute in the Custom Attributes rollout) to –9.2 (**Figure 16.42**).
3. Select ctrl_backbone_front. In the Modify panel, set the arch attribute to 9.2.
4. Select ctrl_flipL. In the Modify panel, set the flip attribute to 35.

Figure 16.42   The arch custom attribute for ctrl_backbone_back.

5. Select ctrl_flipR. Set the flip attribute to –35.
6. Go to frame 50.
7. Select ctrl_backbone_back. Set the arch attribute to 0.
8. Select ctrl_backbone_front. Set arch to 0.
9. Select ctrl_flipL. Set the flip attribute to 20.
10. Select ctrl_flipR. Set flip to –20.
11. Turn off Auto Key.

12. Scrub the Time Slider to see the animation you just created. It adds a subtle but important "aliveness" to the dolphin.

13. Save your work as my_Dolphin&Rider_08.max.

For a finished version of the animation described above, open Dolphin&Rider_08.max on the DVD.

For our purposes, totally hand-animating the dolphin turns out to be an excellent solution. At this point, we could well just decide to move on to adding water to our scene.

However, hand-animation does have some limitations. For instance, the hand-animated object cannot be affected by other objects. It's always a cause, never an effect. In the next section, we'll see how we can work within this limitation and still combine our own hand-animation with reactor's automatically generated keyframes.

Using Start Frame and End Frame

In any frame where reactor creates keyframes for a rigid body, any previously existing keyframes are destroyed. One common way to work within this limitation is to divide a scene into frames in which we are in control and frames in which reactor is in control. We'll do this here by manually taking the dolphin to a certain position and then "letting go" of it and allowing reactor to take over.

Open Dolphin&Rider_08.max from the files for this chapter on the DVD, or continue with my_Dolphin&Rider_08.max from the previous section.

Here's the procedure:

1. Select ctrl_dolphin_all and click the Open Property Editor button on the reactor toolbar.

2. In the Rigid Body Properties dialog, set Mass to 100. Objects that have no mass do not fall under the influence of gravity and cannot be affected by other objects.

3. Also in the Rigid Body Properties dialog, deselect Unyielding. reactor does not create keyframes for unyielding objects.

4. In Utilities > reactor > Preview & Animation, set the Start Frame parameter (the very top one) to 25 (**Figure 16.43**). reactor will start creating keyframes at frame 25, not before.

5. Preview animation. It starts at frame 25. You don't see the initial hand-animation in the preview.

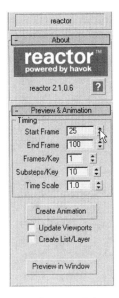

Figure 16.43 In Utilities > reactor > Preview & Animation, set Start Frame to 25.

6. Create animation. reactor creates keyframes for ctrl_dolphin_all starting at frame 25.

7. Scrub the Time Slider along the timeline from 0 to 100. In the first 25 frames, you see the hand-animation. After that, you see reactor's automatically generated animation. You see the same thing if you render the scene.

The animation of the flippers and the backbone is preserved. The control objects for flippers and backbone were never a part of the simulation, so reactor never affected them in any way.

Notice that there is also a Utilities > reactor > Preview & Animation > End Frame (100 in this case), where you can start hand-animating again. If you want to start hand-animating at frame 75, go to Utilities > reactor > Preview & Animation, and set the End Frame parameter to 75. Try this:

1. Delete the existing keyframes from frames 75 to 100. If you delete a few keyframes earlier than 75, it won't do any harm, but be sure *not* to delete keyframes preceding frame 25.

2. Create animation. reactor creates keyframes from frame 25 to 75, and the dolphin stops moving at frame 75.

3. You can start hand-animating at that point.

The dolphin no longer passes through the platform, as it did before. This can be easily corrected by disabling collisions between ctrl_dolphin_all and the platform, using reactor's Define Collision Pairs capability. Here's the procedure:

I. In Utilities > reactor > Collisions > Global Collisions, click Define Collision Pairs (**Figure 16.44**).

Figure 16.44   Define Collision Pairs in Utilities > reactor > Collisions > Global Collisions.

2. In the Define Collisions window, select ctrl_dolphin_all at the top of the Entities column on the left.

3. In the middle column, Enabled Collisions, select "platform <-> ctrl_dolphin_all" and then click the right-facing arrow between the second and third columns, at the very top. The collision pair is transferred to the Disabled Collisions column (**Figure 16.45**).

4. Click OK.

5. If you preview or create animation, the dolphin passes through the platform.

6. Save your work as my_Dolphin&Rider_09.max.

For a finished version of the animation described above, open Dolphin&Rider_09.max on the DVD.

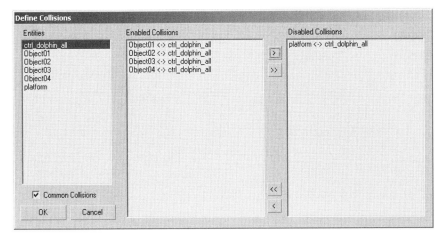

Figure 16.45   The Define Collisions window.

Reducing Keyframes

In the context of combining manual animation with reactor's automatically generated animation, we should also mention reducing keyframes. In Utilities > reactor > Utils > Key Management, the Reduce Now button deletes "unnecessary" keyframes for all the rigid bodies in the scene (**Figure 16.46**). Reduce Keys in the Selection section (Figure 16.46) does the same for any selected objects.

Figure 16.46   The Reduce Keys button deletes "unnecessary" keyframes for *selected* rigid bodies.

"Unnecessary" means that the animation won't appear to change very much if the keyframes are eliminated. The Reduction Threshold parameter determines whether the process is biased toward faithfully preserving the animation or ruthlessly getting rid of keyframes. (The lower the Reduction Threshold number, the greater the fidelity.) If you can reduce keyframes to a manageable number, you may be able to manually edit the keyframes that reactor creates. Then you will most likely want to remove the objects from the reactor simulation (by deleting the objects from any reactor collections, for instance), so that reactor will not overwrite your manually edited keyframes. This is another way of combining your animation with reactor's automatically generated animation.

In the previous sections on hand-animation, the dolphin mesh (dolphin01) was not included in the simulation, while the control object (ctrl_dolphin_all) was included. In the next section we're going to reverse that.

A Deforming Mesh

We've already seen an important limitation of working with hand-animation, namely that if you try to work directly with a deforming mesh like dolphin01, the vertex-level animation of the mesh is not taken into account in the simulation. All animation applied through skinning is vertex-level animation, even if it moves every vertex in the character, as is the case when ctrl_dolphin_all moves dolphin01. That is why, when we added dolphin01 to the rigid body collection, reactor ignored all the animation applied to dolphin01, so that dolphin01 didn't move at all. (See "Hand-Animating the Dolphin Mesh," earlier in the chapter.)

We've seen that you can work around this limitation by hand-animating the control object, which is not animated at the vertex level. You can make the control object conform to the dolphin's shape. We did this working with an existing rig, proceeding on the assumption that we wanted to be able to restore the control object to its original state. Thus, we added modifiers to the control object, which we could later remove or disable. Alternatively, you could create a new control object that would conform perfectly to the dolphin's shape, even using an optimized copy of the dolphin itself as a control object.

What you can't do with hand-animation is animate the control object at the vertex level and get reactor to take that vertex-level animation into account in the simulation. That means that as far as reactor is concerned, the control object keeps the same shape throughout the animation. So there's no way for the control object to replicate subtleties such as the arching of the spine and the flipping of the flippers.

However, there is a way to make reactor take a deforming mesh itself, with all its glorious vertex-level animation, into account in the simulation. This approach is based on the deforming mesh collection.

Creating a deforming mesh collection is very simple, as we'll see in a moment. However, before we do that, there are two tasks we need to take care of:

1. Set reactor start and end frames

2. Re-animate the control object (ctrl_dolphin_all)

Open Dolphin&Rider_09.max on the DVD, or continue with my_Dolphin&Rider_ 09.max from the previous section.

Note

We now want reactor to create keyframes throughout the animation, from frame 0 to frame 100. reactor may not be configured properly to achieve this, if you did the exercise above in "Using Start Frame and End Frame." If you are using your own file, go to Utilities > reactor > Preview & Animation, and make sure that Start Frame is 0 and End Frame is 100.

Re-animating the Control Object

In the hand-animations described above, it was the control object (ctrl_dolphin_all) that collided with the ice. In this section, the dolphin mesh (dolphin01) collides with the ice. The control object is removed from the simulation. It still has a very significant effect on the simulation, because it controls dolphin01.

In "Using Start Frame and End Frame" earlier, we let reactor create keyframes for the control object after frame 25. We could keep all the keyframes for the control object now and use them even after removing the control object from the simulation. Instead, we will delete those keyframes and re-animate the control object. (This allows you to keep working with your own file, even if you did not do the "Using Start Frame and End Frame" exercise.)

1. First, remove the control object from the simulation. Select RBCollection01. In the Modify panel, select ctrl_dolphin_all in the list of objects in the collection, and click Delete to remove it from the collection. Note that the keyframes created for ctrl_dolphin_all remain and would continue to determine the movement of dolphin01 if we didn't delete them.

2. Now delete the existing animation for the control object. Go to frame 0. Select ctrl_dolphin_all. In the main menu, choose Animation > Delete Selected Animation (the last choice on the menu). All existing animation for ctrl_dolphin_all is destroyed. The control object takes its position from the current frame, frame 0.

3. Finally, re-animate the control object. Turn on Auto Key and move ctrl_dolphin_all to the following positions:

   - Frame 0 = (−50, 150, −100)
   - Frame 25 = (−10, 0, 250)
   - Frame 50 = (40, 0, −150)

4. Turn off Auto Key.

Creating the Deforming Mesh Collection

Configuring reactor to recognize the dolphin mesh as a deforming mesh is a two-click process:

1. Select dolphin01.

2. On the reactor toolbar, click the Create Deforming Mesh Collection button (fifth from the top) (**Figure 16.47**). A deforming mesh collection is created, and dolphin01 is added to it.

Figure 16.47   Creating a deforming mesh collection.

Click the Analyze World button. You get a warning that dolphin01 and platform are interpenetrating. In this particular case, the interpenetration has no effect, because the dolphin mesh is unyielding and the platform has no mass. In this configuration, the dolphin mesh will simply pass through the platform without affecting it or being affected by it. To eliminate the warning message, disable collisions between these two objects using Define Collision Pairs, as described in the following section.

Disable Dolphin-Platform Collisions

When we hand-animated, we disabled collisions between the control object (ctrl_dolphin_all) and the platform. Now we will do the same for the dolphin mesh (dolphin01) and the platform. This will eliminate the error message encountered in the previous section. Here's the procedure:

1. In Utilities > reactor > Collisions > Global Collisions, click Define Collision Pairs.

2. In the Define Collisions window, select dolphin01.

3. In the middle column, Enabled Collisions, select "platform <-> dolphin01" and then click the right-facing arrow between the second and third columns, at the very top. The collision pair is transferred to the Disabled Collisions column.

4. Click OK.

Stuck in a Time Warp

When we put our deforming mesh (dolphin01) into a deforming mesh collection, reactor tracked vertex-level animation at each simulation time step, so we got a very accurate simulation. However, all that accuracy doesn't come free. The price you pay is in processing time. Analyzing the world, previewing animation, and creating keyframes all take longer. How much longer depends primarily on how many vertices our deforming mesh has. In the case of dolphin01, it has 8434. That's enough to slow things down to a crawl, even on a fast machine. Luckily, there is an easy way to speed things up during the testing phase. It reduces accuracy, but you can easily reverse it when you're ready for the final output.

To experience for yourself the performance degradation that can result from using a deforming mesh collection, follow the steps below. If you prefer to avoid that stuck-in-a-time-warp feeling, skip down to "Getting Unstuck."

1. Make sure no objects are selected. Having an object selected while simulating can increase simulation time. We haven't worried about this before. But now that we're using a deforming mesh, which is processor-intensive, we're going to do everything possible to decrease the processor load.

2. Click the Analyze World button. After a wait, you get the "no warnings" message.

3. Click the Preview Animation button. After a wait, the Real-Time Preview window appears.

4. Press P. The dolphin falls much more slowly than in previous previews. When the dolphin gets near the ice chunks, things get very slow and may appear to stop. If you get tired of waiting, press Esc. It may not appear to do anything for a while, but unless your computer has crashed, you will eventually exit the Real-Time Preview window. Don't be too quick to assume that your computer has crashed. Even if you go to the Windows Task Manager (Control-Alt-Delete) and it says that the application is not responding, if you wait a while, it may come around.

Getting Unstuck

To speed things up:

1. Select dolphin01.

2. In the Modify panel, select Editable Mesh in the modifier stack.

3. Add an Optimize modifier between the Editable Mesh and the Skin modifier. Set the Face Threshold parameter to 90 (**Figure 16.48**). The dolphin loses a lot of his rounded curves and becomes quite blocky.

4. Perform the steps described above in "Stuck in a Time Warp." Everything goes much faster with the radically optimized deforming mesh, though still noticeably slower than with a rigid body.

   Extreme optimization makes the dolphin look pretty weird (**Figure 16.49**). However, when it comes time for final output, just turn optimization off by clicking the lightbulb button to the left of the Optimize modifier. The lightbulb turns gray, and everything is back to normal: pretty-looking but very sl-o-ow. You can turn off optimization either before creating animation (increasing simulation accuracy but taking longer to create keyframes) or before rendering (making the mesh look pretty in the render). In this case, you would probably turn optimization off only before rendering, since the decrease in simulation accuracy due to optimization will probably not be noticed.

5. Save your work as my_Dolphin&Rider_10.max.

For a finished version of the animation described above, open Dolphin&Rider_10.max on the DVD.

Figure 16.48   The Optimize modifier between the Editable Mesh and the Skin modifier.

Figure 16.49   The radically optimized dolphin, viewed from above.

In addition to rigid bodies and deforming meshes, the other major category of reactor object is deformable bodies. In the next section we'll use a soft body to take the stiffness out of the dolphin rider's hair and allow it to react to her movements.

Attaching a Deformable Body

You may want to attach a reactor deformable body (Cloth, Rope, or Soft Body) to a deforming mesh or rigid body. (For an introduction to deformable bodies in 3ds max 7 see Help > Tutorials > Using reactor and Flex for Simulation > Deformable Bodies Tutorial.) For instance, you may want to create clothes for your character using a reactor Cloth object, hair using a reactor Rope object or Soft Body, or wobbly antennas using a reactor Soft Body. This is easy to do using an Attach to DefMesh or Attach to Rigid Body constraint. We'll try this out using the back portion of the dolphin rider's hair, dolphin_rider_hair_SB. (The "SB" stands for "Soft Body." I named it knowing that we were going to use it as a soft body eventually.)

The following procedure resets the start frame, creates a Soft Body object (the back portion of the dolphin rider's hair), and then attaches the Soft Body to the rider's hair band.

Open Dolphin&Rider_10.max on the DVD, or continue with my_Dolphin&Rider_10.max from the previous section.

1. Select RBCollection01 and add dolphin_rider_hair_band to the collection. The hair band is the rigid body to which we will attach the hair.

2. Select dolphin_rider_hair_band.

3. Click the Open Property Editor button on the reactor toolbar, and click Disable All Collisions in the Rigid Body Properties window. You are just using the hair band as an attachment point for the hair. You don't want it to participate in the simulation beyond that.

4. Also set the Unyielding property for dolphin_rider_hair_band, if it is not already checked on. Its movements are controlled by ctrl_dolphin_all. You don't want reactor to create keyframes for it.

5. Select dolphin_rider_hair_SB, and click the Apply Soft Body Modifier button on the reactor toolbar (sixth from the bottom). A reactor SoftBody modifier is added to dolphin_rider_hair_SB (**Figure 16.50**).

6. Click the Create Soft Body Collection button on the reactor toolbar (third from the top). A soft body collection is created, and dolphin_rider_hair_SB is added to it (**Figure 16.51**).

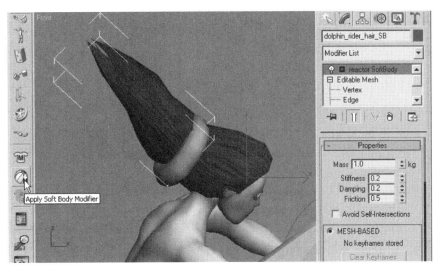

Figure 16.50   A reactor SoftBody modifier applied to dolphin_rider_hair_SB.

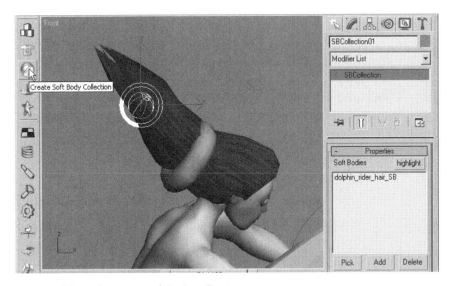

Figure 16.51   Creating a soft body collection.

7. Select the dolphin_rider_hair_SB object. In the Modify panel, go to the Vertex sub-object level in the reactor SoftBody modifier (**Figure 16.52**). This will allow you to select vertices in the Soft Body.

Figure 16.52 The Vertex sub-object level of the reactor SoftBody modifier.

8. Click Attach To Rigid Body in the Constraints rollout (**Figure 16.53**). An Attach To RigidBody constraint appears in the Constraints list, and the Attach To RigidBody rollout appears.

9. Select the Attach To RigidBody constraint in the Constraints list.

10. In the Attach To RigidBody rollout, click the Rigid Body button (which currently says None) (**Figure 16.54**). The button turns yellow.

Figure 16.53 Creating an Attach To RigidBody constraint.

Figure 16.54   Click the Rigid Body button, which currently says None.

11. Select dolphin_rider_hair_band (by clicking the hair band in the viewport or by pressing H and selecting dolphin_rider_hair_band from the Pick Object dialog).

12. Right-click in the active viewport and choose Hide Unselected. This hides everything but the hair, making it easier to select vertices of the hair. With the Front viewport active, click Zoom Extents, then select the loop of vertices closest to the hair band. This will be easier if the viewport is in Wireframe display mode (**Figure 16.55**). During simulation, dolphin_rider_hair_SB will remain attached to the hair band by these vertices.

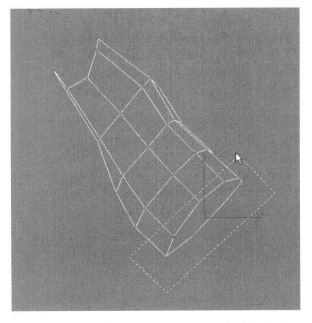

Figure 16.55   Select the loop of hair vertices closest to the hair band.

13. Click the reactor SoftBody modifier to deselect the Vertex sub-object, to make sure you don't inadvertently change your vertex selection.

14. Right-click in the active viewport and choose Unhide All.

15. Preview Animation. The hair stretches and flops around but stays attached to the hair band (**Figure 16.56**).

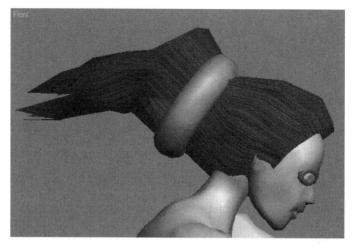

Figure 16.56   dolphin_rider_hair_SB distorts but stays attached to the hair band.

The same basic technique can be used to attach the Soft Body to a deforming mesh, using an Attach To DefMesh constraint.

16. Save your work as my_Dolphin&Rider_11.max.

For a finished version of the animation described above, open Dolphin&Rider_11.max on the DVD. Your file will only match the DVD's file if you create the animation.

All right! We have our ice, and we have experimented with several ways of animating our dolphin. Let's get into the water!

Just Add Water

In this section, we'll go back to hand-animation, add water to our simulation, stabilize the fragments in the water, and see if we can get the dolphin to break the ice in the water the way it did before on the platform.

Open Dolphin&Rider_11.max from the DVD, or continue with my_Dolphin&Rider_11.max from the previous section.

Back to Hand-Animation

Since using a deforming mesh doesn't do much for this animation except increase the processor load, let's go back to hand-animation. First, do this:

1. Select and delete DMCollection01.

2. Select dolphin01. In the Modify panel, if the lightbulb by the Optimize modifier indicates that the modifier is enabled (not grayed), click it to turn it off (grayed). We no longer need to optimize the mesh, since reactor no longer includes it in the simulation as a deforming mesh.

3. Add ctrl_dolphin_all to RBCollection01.

4. Select ctrl_dolphin_all. Click the Open Property Editor button on the reactor toolbar, and in the Rigid Body Properties dialog, check the Unyielding box.

All right! We're ready to add water!

Adding Water

Adding water to the reactor simulation is a simple click-and-drag operation, just like creating a plane. Note, however, that reactor water is a space warp: It doesn't show up in renders but can affect objects that do show up in renders. We'll use a plane ("water plane") as the renderable object.

Here's the procedure for adding water:

1. Select "platform" and delete it.

2. Click the Create Water button on the reactor toolbar (just below the Fracture button). In the Top viewport, click and drag to create the water.

3. In the Modify panel, set both Size X and Size Y to 1000 (**Figure 16.57**).

4. Position the water at (−12,−2,−10).

5. Preview Animation.

The water tosses the ice around significantly at the beginning of the animation, but the ice doesn't appear to fragment until the dolphin hits it. You can confirm this by creating animation and looking at stored collisions. The first collision is between ctrl_dolphin_all and one of the ice chunks. That indicates no breakage before the control object hits the ice.

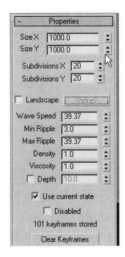

Figure 16.57   Setting properties for reactor water.

Nevertheless, the ice is tossed clear out of the water at the beginning of the animation—not the effect we're looking for. Since the ice is not breaking up of its own accord, it looks as if it might eventually find its own equilibrium if we could just prevent the control object from shattering it. Let's give it a try.

Stabilizing the Ice

To stabilize the ice in the water, we'll use Update MAX in the Real-Time Preview window, as we did to stabilize the ice on the platform. However, getting the ice to "settle down" will be a little more involved.

1. Update MAX will create new keys at frame 0 for all objects in the simulation. We want to create new keys just for the ice chunks, in a more stable position. So the first thing we'll do is temporarily remove other objects from the simulation. Start by deleting ctrl_dolphin_all and dolphin_rider_hair_band from RBCollection01. We'll put them back in again when we're through stabilizing the ice.

2. Select SBCollection01. In the Modify panel, check the Disabled box in the Properties rollout (**Figure 16.58**). We'll enable it again when we're through stabilizing the ice.

3. Preview Animation. Only the ice remains in the simulation. The ice keeps moving under the influence of the water. It never comes to rest. We can also see now that the ice is bouncing right on the surface of the water, whereas we'd like it to be somewhat submerged.

Figure 16.58 Disabling SBCollection01 in the Modify panel.

4. If we make the ice heavier, it will move less and submerge more. Exit Real-Time Preview. Select Object01 and Object02 (the bottom two ice chunks), open the Rigid Body Properties dialog, and change the Mass parameter to 300. For Object03 and Object04 (the top two ice chunks), set the Mass parameter to 250. (Increasing Mass more for the bottom two chunks makes the iceberg less likely to flip over.) Preview Animation. The ice sits lower in the water but is still tossed around forcefully and keeps moving under the influence of the water.

5. We haven't been very successful at stabilizing the ice by changing the ice. Let's try changing the water. Select the water (Water01) and go to the Modify panel. After noting their initial values so that you can reset them later, set Wave Speed, Min Ripple, and Max Ripple to 1. Set Viscosity to 100. Preview Animation again. The ice has calmed down significantly. Due to the high viscosity, the ice is now interacting with something more like sludge or heavy oil than water. The wave action is also much milder.

6. When the ice seems stable, select MAX > Update MAX in the Real-Time Preview window, assigning the more stable position to the fragments in the first frame of the animation. Exit Real-Time Preview.

7. Set the water parameters back to their initial values, and Preview Animation again. There is much less initial movement of the ice in the water.

8. Add ctrl_dolphin_all and dolphin_rider_hair_band back into RBCollection01.

9. Select SBCollection01. In the Modify panel, uncheck the Disabled box in the Properties rollout, to re-enable the soft body collection.

10. Preview Animation.

The ice is now stabilized and fracturing the way we want it to. However, the water is still not renderable. We'll take care of that in the next section.

Making the Water Renderable

Here is a procedure for completing the reactor water setup so that water will appear in renders:

1. Select Water01, and in the Modify panel, change Subdivisions X and Subdivisions Y to 30. This increases the subdivisions of the reactor water (Water01) to match the subdivisions of the plane that will provide the renderable water surface (the "water plane") In general, the more subdivisions you have, the more realistic your water will be. However, increasing the subdivisions of the reactor water beyond the subdivisions of the renderable surface is not useful. Increasing subdivisions also increases the processing load.

2. With "water plane" selected, click the Bind to Space Warp button (**Figure 16.59**) and select Water01. A reactor Water (WSM) modifier is added to "water plane" (**Figure 16.60**). (WSM stands for "world space modifier".) The plane will now provide the visible manifestation of the water.

3. Save your work as my_Dolphin&Rider_12.max.

Figure 16.59 Use Bind to Space Warp to bind "water plane" to Water01.

Figure 16.60 A reactor Water (WSM) modifier on "water plane."

For a finished version of the animation described above, open Dolphin&Rider_12.max on the DVD.

Our work with reactor is now done. However, the scene still needs two important finishing touches, which we'll take care of in the next section.

Finishing Touches

In this section we add a texture and a splash to our scene.

1. Our iceberg still looks more like a party hat than like ice. Press M to bring up the Material Editor, and find the Ice material. Apply the Ice material to Object01, Object02, Object03, and Object04.

2. To put some splash to the scene, add a SuperSpray object in the Top viewport. You'll find it in the Create panel, in the Geometry section, under Particle Systems. Just click and drag in the Perspective viewport to create the SuperSpray. Go to the frame where you want the splashing to start, and position the SuperSpray at the point where the splash should originate. Rotate the SuperSpray so that its arrow points in the direction of the splash (**Figure 16.61**). You can also animate the position and rotation of the SuperSpray.

Figure 16.61   The SuperSpray arrow points in the direction of the splash. Some additional dolphin animation has been added to this scene.

3. With the SuperSpray still selected, go to the Modify panel to set the time when the splash starts. In the Particle Generation rollout, set the Emit Start parameter to coincide with the frame where the splash should begin. Set Emit Stop to 30 or so frames after that. Set Life to 20 and Variation to 10. At the top of the rollout, set Particle Quantity > Use Rate to 100 (**Figure 16.62**).

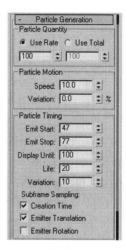

Figure 16.62   Setting SuperSpray Particle Generation parameters in the Modify panel.

4. Go to the next rollout, Particle Type, and select the Facing type in the Standard Particles section (**Figure 16.63**).

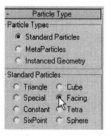

Figure 16.63   Setting SuperSpray Particle Type parameters in the Modify panel.

5. You should now see the particles appearing as ticks (plus signs) in the viewport in the appropriate frames. However, they are just coming out in a straight line. Scroll back up to the Basic Parameters rollout and play with the parameters in the Particle Formation section, to distribute the particles in a somewhat more spread-out fashion. We left Off Axis at 0, and set the first Spread to 21, Off Plane to 26, and the second Spread to 61 (**Figure 16.64**).

Figure 16.64   Setting SuperSpray Basic Parameters in the Modify panel.

All of the above represents just one possible configuration of the SuperSpray. There are many other configurations that will work fine, and you can also add more SuperSprays.

6. Save your work as my_Dolphin&Rider_13.max.

For a finished version of the animation described above, open Dolphin&Rider_13.max on the DVD.

That's it! Try rendering a few select frames, to make sure everything is to your liking, and then go ahead and render the animation. We recommend the mental ray renderer for this project.

A rendered version of this project is available as Dolphin&Rider.avi on the DVD.

Summing Up

In this chapter, you learned how to animate using reactor, replacing your own hand-animation or in addition to it. You gained insight into the strengths and weaknesses of reactor. You saw how it can save production time by automatically creating realistic animation for complex scenes, including hard-to-animate effects such as water. On the other hand, you also saw that—as Mickey Mouse discovered as the Sorcerer's Apprentice in *Fantasia*—it's often easier to get the magic going than to direct it or stop it. Once you have visualized your scene or prepared your storyboard, you have to be ready to spend time tweaking simulation parameters and experimenting in order to get reactor to produce the effects you envision.

When using a deforming mesh collection, you saw the huge benefits in efficiency that can result from simplifying the objects in your scene. At the same time, you saw that it is often possible to make objects look simpler to reactor than they really are. With reactor, you are often called upon to make a judgment about the degree of simulation accuracy required by your scene versus the processing cycles you can afford to devote to simulating it.

It can be unsettling to give your creations "minds of their own." On the other hand, there is great power in the ability to create worlds that can act intelligently according to laws you set down, without having to be told what to do at every step.

Ideas for further experimentation:

- Continue to animate ctrl_dolphin_all. For example, you may want to rotate it so that the dolphin is facing towards the water when it hits. Or you may want to work with the position of the dolphin so that it stays entirely in view during its whole trajectory. An example, Dolphin&Rider_14.max, is included on the DVD. A rendered version of this scene is available as Dolphin&Rider_14.avi.

- In the Modify panel, play with soft body properties such as Stiffness, Friction, and Damping, to change the behavior of the hair.

- Replace the hair with reactor Rope.

- Give the rider a cape of reactor Cloth.

- Add reactor Wind to the scene.

- reactor can be a good way to create natural-looking arrangements of static props. Try dropping a group of objects onto the flat iceberg. Make a snapshot of them (Tools > Snapshot) and then delete the originals, leaving only the newly created snapshot objects.

- Use a reactor Spring to keep pulling one of the lower ice chunks back to its original position.

- Use Skin Wrap to control a high-poly dolphin with a low-poly dolphin. Use the low-poly dolphin as a deforming mesh.

In the next chapter, you'll dive more deeply into the world of particles with max's Particle Flow.

Chapter 17

Introduction to Particle Flow

by Sean Bonney

Volcanic explosions, meteor swarms, falling rain, blowing snow, patchy fog, magical auras, swirling leaves—regardless of whether your scene is based in science fiction, a mythical realm, or somewhere in between, at some point you will want to add the weather elements, pyrotechnics, or special effects that particle systems excel at creating.

By definition, particles are a means of animating a large group of similar objects using procedural rules. This varies greatly from the traditional style of animating objects within 3ds max, whereby an individual object is usually animated individually. Particle systems allow the behavior of a group to be dictated by a set of rules that can vary from the general to the specific. Particle aspects such as life span, velocity, materials, and size can be applied to an entire system or to subsets of that system. What this means is that swirling leaves can be made to react to wind in your scene, or explosive debris made to adhere to gravity settings, or bouncing fruit made to change color based on the number of bounces it makes. This last example may seem absurd, but it serves to illustrate the endless applications of particles, even in situations where particle systems don't seem immediately appropriate.

The power that max gives you to animate the properties of your particle systems greatly facilitates the creation of a variety of atmospheric and expressive elements, as well as special effects, that would be impractical or less effective to create using nonprocedural methods. Anyone who has ever keyframed falling snowflakes without a particle system can certainly appreciate the effectiveness of procedural particles (**Figures 17.1** and **17.2**).

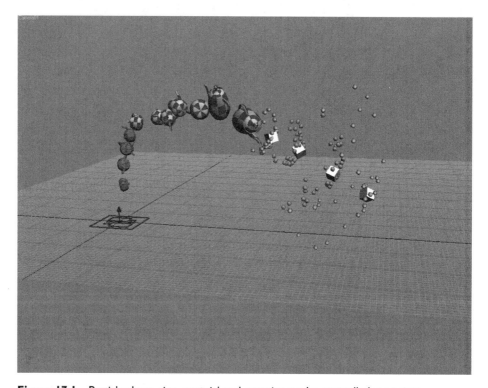

Figure 17.1   Particle shape, size, material, and quantity can be controlled over time.

A particle system consists of three basic elements—an emitter, particles, and forces. In this chapter, we will examine these specific elements and then see how they function in both non event-driven systems (such as the legacy Super Spray system) and the event-driven Particle Flow system introduced in 3ds max 6. After that, we will explore the use of Particle Flow to create a variety of environmental effects centered on an erupting volcano.

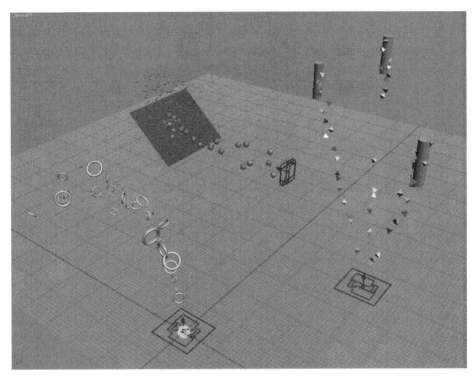

Figure 17.2   Particles can be influenced by various forces like Wind and Gravity, collide with objects, and pursue specific targets.

Elements of a Particle System

When a rocket emits a fiery trail, there is a point from which the smoke and fire spawn. In max this is the emitter. An emitter represents the location at which particles will be created, and it can occupy a single point in space, the surface of an object or helper, or a volume. Emitters can be animated, passing their movement properties to the particles they spawn (**Figure 17.3**). In the case of a rocket's trail, emitted sparks may inherit the rocket's momentum and then drift off without being further influenced. In other cases, particle movement can be influenced by emitter movement well after a particle has been created, such as with a cloud of magical sparkles surrounding a gesturing wand.

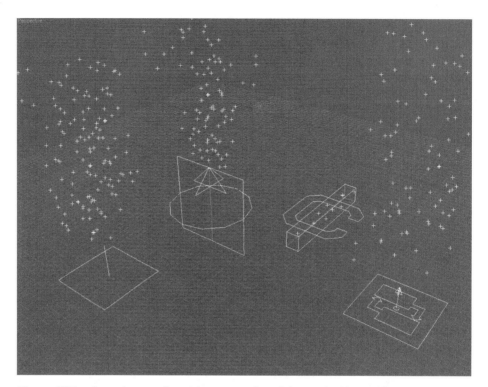

Figure 17.3   Several types of particle emitters, from left to right: Blizzard, Super Spray, PCloud, and PF Source.

The leaves, sparks, or dancing apples in your scene are, of course, the particles themselves. Particles are spawned by emitters, and they can be rendered using a variety of simple geometric shapes (spheres, tetras, or cubes) or flat polygonal shapes (sixpoint, triangles, and a hybrid shape named "Special" that consists of three intersecting polygons which together approximate a low-poly version of a geometric shape). Most often these low-poly particle representations are used when creating atmospheric or special effects, where the main visual impact will be conveyed through the materials used (**Figure 17.4**).

 Note

> When creating an effect that will depend on a large number of fine particles, such as vapor or rain, try to use the simplest appropriate particle shape to keep max from getting bogged down from calculating an excessive amount of particle geometry.

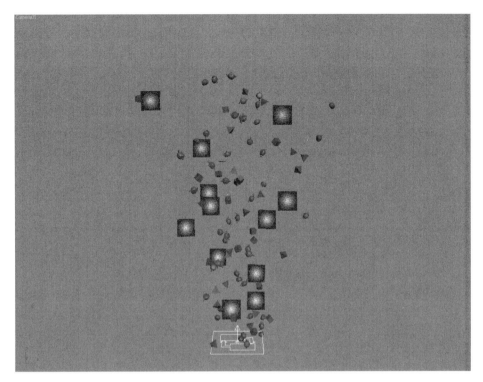

Figure 17.4 Particles can have virtually any appearance (pictured: spheres, tetras, cubes, instanced geometry, and facing planes).

One of the more visually impressive particle effects is the creation of flowing liquids, such as water, lava, or the shape-changing T-1000 in *Terminator 2: Judgment Day*. When you're creating liquid effects, the MetaParticle shape can be very effective. With this type, particles represent points within a metaball, or blob object. The coarseness and tension of the metaball effect can be varied to achieve the desired smoothness. While the MetaParticle shape is capable of creating just about any type of liquid effect that can be animated using non-event-driven particle systems, a more powerful metaball feature is available in the BlobMesh compound object (**Figure 17.5**).

BlobMesh can use geometry as well as particles to create metaball effects. Later in this chapter, you will explore the use of BlobMesh in event-driven particles.

Figure 17.5   Liquids can be easily simulated using particle systems and BlobMesh.

When your scene calls for swarms of flying bats, crawling centipedes, or diving jet fighters, the instanced geometry particle type is your best choice. Possibly the most sophisticated particle representation, the instanced geometry particle can take on nearly any modeled shape, even animated and hierarchical groups. This technique is often used for flocking creatures and large fleets of similar objects, or in situations where the other particle types are insufficient (**Figure 17.6**).

A big part of the excitement and believability of particles is in their interaction with forces of nature, such as gusting wind or explosive waves, or with unnatural forces, like tractor beams or force fields. The speed and direction of particles within a system can be influenced by several kinds of forces. Forces such as Gravity, Drag, and Wind can be used to create naturalistic particle movement. Other forces, such as Push, Motor, Vortex, and

Displace are especially appropriate for special effects and unnatural influences. The PBomb space warp is a specialized tool for applying an explosive dispersal to particles. For exacting control of particles along a spline path, the Path Follow force allows particles to converge on a path, diverge from it, or follow it throughout their life span. Using forces to influence the behavior of your particles is a handy way to add believability in an easy procedural fashion.

Figure 17.6 Particles can be used to create a flock of animated entities using instanced geometry particles.

Deflectors are another type of particle influence, and they are useful in situations where particles need to interact with scene objects. Imagine beads bouncing off and around a stack of blocks, or a laser being redirected by a lens. Deflectors can cause particles to bounce, refract, react to friction, and alter their speed or path. The shape of deflectors can be based on simple helper objects, such as planes or spheres, as well as on instanced geometry. The shape, size, and location of deflectors can also be animated to simulate moving obstacles, such as a sailing ship displacing fog.

Particle systems in max are available in two distinct types: event-driven (Particle Flow) and non-event-driven (the legacy particle systems such as Blizzard, Spray, and PArray). Each will be discussed in turn in the next two sections.

Non-Event-Driven Particle Systems

The standard particle systems that have been part of max through several revisions, such as Blizzard, Snow, Spray, Super Spray, PCloud, and PArray, are non-event-driven, meaning that their properties generally do not change over the course of an animation. These systems are adept at creating rain, for example, though if the quantity of drops needs to change in respect to an opening window, an event-driven system is more appropriate.

These systems range in complexity, with Snow and Spray being the simplest. Blizzard and Super Spray are provided as more sophisticated versions, and they make Snow and Spray basically obsolete.

Spray emits particles from a planar helper (a nonrendering plane used only to define emitter shape). Super Spray emits particles from a single point in space, typically to spread out in a fan or conical shape. SuperSpray contains all the functionality of Spray and more particle shapes, as well as controls for individual particle motion and collision. Super Spray is quite effective at producing explosive or spraying effects (**Figure 17.7**).

Snow and Blizzard emit particles from a planar helper object, with Blizzard being the more advanced version. Blizzard is quite useful for creating rain, snow, or almost any area emission effect. If your scene calls for an area of parallel-moving clouds or leaves falling over a wide area, Blizzard is probably the best choice in non-event-driven particle systems (**Figure 17.8**).

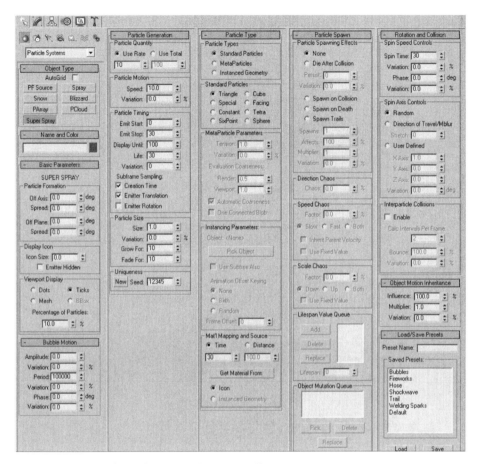

Figure 17.7   The Super Spray particle system rollouts.

The PCloud system is useful for scenes that require particles to be spawned from a volume, such as a fire, disintegration effect, or cloud. PCloud differs from other non-event-driven systems in that particles can be emitted from a geometric volume based on a cube, sphere, or cylinder helper object, or from any mesh object.

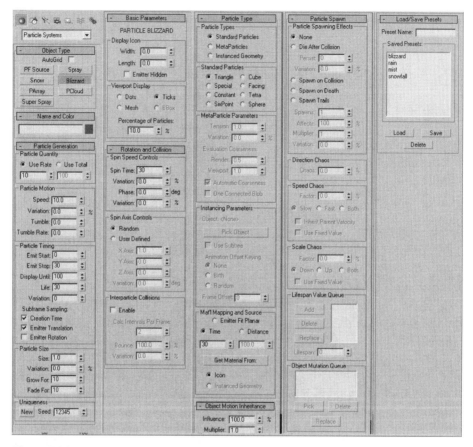

Figure 17.8   The Blizzard particle system rollouts.

What if you want to emit particles from the surface of an object, such as bubbles rising from a dissolving medicine tablet? PArray is unique in that a renderable mesh object is used as the emitter. Particles can be emitted over the entire surface, from edges or vertices, face centers, or sub-objects. A typical use for PArray is in conjunction with the PBomb space warp to blow up mesh objects. In explosive contexts, the PArray particle system would emit geometric particles matching the original exploded object, and PBomb would provide explosive momentum and dispersal to the fragments.

The particle systems we've explored in this section are certainly adequate for many needs, but max also offers event-driven systems, which allow you go much further in customizing the behavior of your particles.

Event-Driven Particles

Imagine a forest fire, in which a tall tree is burning from the top down. Chunks of flaming wood break free from the top, trailing smoke and flames, bouncing against branches on their way to the ground, sending up a shower of sparks at every collision, and finally detonating in an explosion of ash, splinters, and sparks at ground level. Such a scene could conceivably be created using non-event-driven particle systems, but it would require the coordination of several different particle systems, be fairly time-consuming, and be much more difficult and less flexible than the same effect created with an event-driven particle system like max's Particle Flow.

Particle Flow is a very flexible and powerful system for creating particle effects. Particle systems can be assembled with a building-block approach using the Particle View window to create a powerful range of custom behaviors. Particles can move from state to state as needed, so that the traditional linear path of particle birth, movement, and death is replaced with a flowchart you can endlessly customize. The flaming chunk of wood debris described above can be represented by a particle in Particle Flow (PFlow) that generates new spark particle systems on impact, with their own properties of collision, life, and appearance. No longer are particles constrained to maintain most of their properties throughout their life span. With PFlow, particles can change motion, size, appearance, or behavior based on tests you set up. The falling wood pieces, for example, can be reduced in size with each impact, or broken up into smaller chunks, while maintaining speed and material parameters, if so desired.

The primary elements of Particle Flow are events, which contain individual operators and tests. Operators are used to pass along particle properties, such as rotation, material, and scale. Tests are used to direct particles into new behaviors. A test might check a particle's speed, for example, and direct it to a new event. Particles that do not test true remain in the current event. This may seem abstract, but it's very simple. Instead of setting a particle's speed in a rollout, you can control particle speed with an operator. This allows you to introduce new speed operators whenever you like, such as after testing particle age. Smoke billowing from our battered piece of falling wood, for example, should move more quickly at the moment of impact and remain more or less in place as the debris free-falls.

PFlow systems can be initiated either with the creation of a PF Source emitter object, found in the Create panel > Geometry section under Particle Systems, or within the Particle View window, where either a Standard Flow with general settings or an Empty Flow with minimal settings can be created. Each PFlow system is represented by a PF Source viewport icon, which by default is the particle emitter as well.

PF Source Parameters

Most of the Modify panel parameters we will examine in this section for the PF Source object can also be accessed from within the Particle View interface, as will be demonstrated in the next section (**Figure 17.9**).

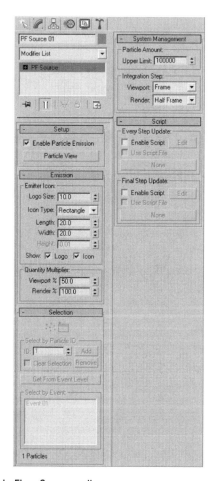

Figure 17.9   The Particle Flow Source rollouts.

Setup

If you need a quick and easy way to turn a PFlow system on or off, take note of the Enable Particle Emission check box, which controls the entire system. You can also toggle a PFlow system in Particle View.

The Particle View button opens the Particle View interface, though this can also be done with a keyboard shortcut (the default is 6).

Emission

Unlike the non-event-driven particle systems, Particle Flow can use any of the emission types. This allows you to generate your particles free of any restrictions of emission area.

The Logo Size setting only affects the logo portion of the PF Source icon, and it has absolutely no effect on particle emission. Making the logo large will give the discreet programmers an ego boost, however.

Icon Type sets the shape of the emitter. The default shape is Rectangle, but Box, Circle, and Sphere are also available (**Figure 17.10**). If one of these settings does not suit your needs, keep in mind that you can also use instanced geometry to determine emitter shape.

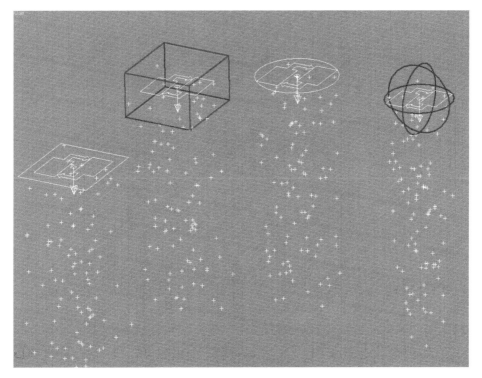

Figure 17.10   The four PF Source emitter types: Rectangle, Box, Circle, and Sphere.

Length/Diameter, Width, and Height set the dimensions of the icon. These values have a direct impact on particle emission as long as the icon is being used to generate particles.

Show Logo/Icon controls the display of these portions of the PF Source icon, and they affect only the viewport display.

The Quantity Multiplier settings allow you to change the percentage of particles that will be created in viewports or renders. These percentages are applied to the total number of generated particles, which is determined by operators and tests within PFlow, particularly the Birth operator. The utility of Quantity Multiplier settings is to quickly increase or decrease the amount of particles created across all events in a particular flow. Note that these values can be set as high as 10,000%, allowing you to increase the number of particles by a factor of 100.

 Note

Particle Flow exposes a great deal of functionality, and it consumes a lot of CPU power. If screen refresh becomes slow when scrubbing the Time Slider, consider reducing the total number of particles with the Quantity Multiplier Viewport setting.

As with the Enable Particle Emission option in the Setup rollout, the Quantity Multiplier gives you a quick control over the entirety of your PFlow system, and it can be very valuable when debugging your scene.

Selection

There are several techniques within Particle Flow to split particles into separate behaviors. Suppose you have a swarm of particle dragons, and you want to choose a few specific ones to divert from your "Soar and Menace" event to your "Dive and Flame" event. The controls within the Selection rollout will allow you to do just that.

The Selection rollout and the Sub-Object: Particle level give you access to specific particles. Click the Particle button in the Selection rollout to activate Particle Select mode. In Particle Select mode, particles can be selected in a viewport by clicking or dragging a selection marquee. Once selected, they can be affected by either the Delete operator or the Split Selected test within Particle View.

This sub-object functionality is unlike the standard operation of mesh sub-objects, where a selection is passed up the Modifier stack. The Particle sub-object level allows you to pass your selection to events within Particle View and allows only a single selection per PFlow source.

Event Select mode selects particles based on their current event in the flow. Your selection can be transferred to a Particle level selection with the Get From Event Level button, if needed. Note that you have to be in Particle Select mode for this button to be functional.

The Select by Particle ID section allows for a third method of particle selection. Particles can be selected by ID number, and added or removed from the selection.

System Management

Suppose you have set up an elaborate fountain using PFlow droplets that eject from the stone fish's mouth, fall down, and rebound from its scales and fins, spawning additional droplets with each bounce. Such a system would be easy to set up in PFlow, but consider that it is difficult to predict how many particles will wind up being emitted. If each original droplet spawns a series of smaller droplets, which in turn spawn their own child drops, your computer could easily become overloaded, or even lock up. The Particle Amount Upper Limit sets the maximum number of particles the PFlow system can have. This is useful as a fail-safe when troubleshooting flows that spawn an inordinate number of particles, allowing you to continue to tweak your particle flow without being concerned about system crashes.

The Integration Step section is fairly significant in that it determines the overall accuracy of movement and collision for the entire flow. The step settings determine how often these calculations take place, so the smaller the value, the more accurate the simulation will be, at the cost of additional time.

Viewport can be set from Frame (once per animation frame) to 1/8 Frame (eight times per frame). Render can be set from Frame to 1 Tick. A single tick is an incredibly short period, 1/160 of a frame at NTSC rates, so this level of accuracy will rarely be needed.

Note

Whenever the behavior of particles in a viewport fails to match that in a render, the cause is often differing integration steps. Try setting Viewport and Render Integration Steps to the same value to correct this.

Script

By enabling scripts at this point, you can cause a script to be run either at every integration step or after each frame's final integration step. Once either script usage has been enabled, the Edit button opens the text script editor.

While the PF Source parameters allow you to control the setup and overall operation of Particle Flow, the real power of this system is to be found in the Particle View interface, which we will examine in the next section.

Particle View

The main interface for setting up particle flows is Particle View (**Figure 17.11**). This is where you will spend the bulk of your time when creating PFlow systems. Think of Particle View as a virtual engine, where the ignition, transmission, and exhaust systems are laid out for you to drag into place and connect to suit your needs. In this section, you will explore the functionality of this interface and how elements are managed to create the desired effect.

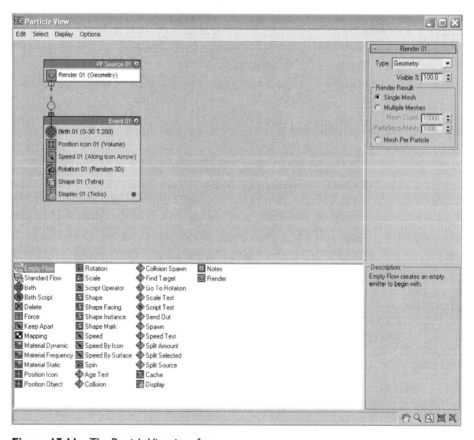

Figure 17.11   The Particle View interface.

Particle View is accessed via a button on the Modify panel of the PF Source icon or by keyboard shortcut (the default is 6). In this interface, events are wired together to control particle behavior in a visual representation of particle flow. The Particle View interface contains five main elements: a menu bar, the event display panel, the parameters panel, a depot containing the available operators and tests, and a small description panel that displays a summary of operators or tests when one of those actions is selected in the depot. A series of display tools is also located in the lower right of the interface.

 Note

> The term "actions" in the context of Particle Flow refers to the individual functions (Speed, Display, and so on) and tests (such as Age and Collision) that constitute the building blocks of this particle system.

The basic workflow of this interface is to drag operators from the depot into the event display panel, where you place them in ordered events and connect them to other events, while editing the parameters of operators in the parameters panel.

Let's examine each aspect of Particle View in turn to give you a thorough understanding of how to make PFlow fill your needs.

Menu Bar

The menu bar contains several options for adjusting and analyzing particle flow. All of these functions are available within the event display panel and are probably more intuitive to access there.

Edit Menu

The Edit menu commands allow you to add, insert, and append operators or tests (**Figure 17.12**). An action must be selected in the event display panel to make these functions available. Selected actions or all actions can be turned on and off from this menu. Instanced actions (once selected) can be made unique, tests can be wired to events, and particle flow elements can be copied and pasted. Finally, selected items can be deleted and renamed. These functions will be examined in greater detail in the "Event Display Panel" section later in this chapter.

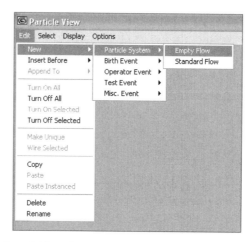

Figure 17.12   The Particle View Edit menu.

Select Menu

The Select menu offers a variety of selection options for the actions in the event display panel (**Figure 17.13**). Select Downstreams is useful for examining a highlighted event and all of the subsequent events that are derived from it. Use Save Selected to save the highlighted actions into a new .max file, including all scene objects that are explicitly referenced. This is a handy method for copying portions of your particle flow for a new scene.

Figure 17.13   The Particle View Select menu.

The Get Selection From Viewport command highlights the top-level event connected to any PF Source icons that are selected in a viewport. This function allows you to quickly locate the beginning of a particle system when you are working with multiple PF Source icons. Simply select the associated source icon in the max viewport, use the Get Selection From Viewport command, and you will be at the beginning of that system's event setup.

If you need to render only selected events in your particle flow, use the Assign Selection To Viewport command. This will create a selection in the max viewport of the type Particle Group, consisting of only the selected PFlow events. If you use the Selected Render type, only particles within the selected events will be rendered. An entire particle flow can be selectively rendered by using the Sync Source/Events Selection In Viewport command. This function differs from Get Selection From Viewport in that it selects all events associated with selected PF Source icons, not just the global ones.

The second and third Select menu commands, Select All and Select None, toggle the selection of all operators and events. The remaining Select menu commands control the selection of PFlow Actions, Operators, Tests, Sources, Events, and Wires. These PFlow elements will be described in greater detail later in this section.

Display

The Display menu contains the same view controls available in the lower right of the interface—Pan Tool, Zoom Tool, Region Zoom Tool, Zoom Extents, and No Zoom. You can also toggle the display of the Parameters, Depot, and Description panels (**Figure 17.14**).

Figure 17.14   The Particle View Display menu.

Options

The Options menu is primarily useful when debugging particle flows (**Figure 17.15**). The Default Display type determines whether Display operators are automatically added to new events. When this is set to Local, Display operators will be automatically added to newly created events, making it easier to discern in viewports when particles have moved from one event to another.

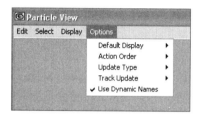

Figure 17.15   The Particle View Options menu.

The Action Order type determines whether the global event (the first and original event in a particle's flow) or local events (all of the subsequent events) are evaluated first. This decision has the most impact when identical action types are used globally and locally. If you wish to override speed settings made in local events with a global speed, for example, create a Speed operator in the global event and set the Action Order to Locals First.

Update Type determines at what point in the timeline the particle flow calculations are updated when a parameter is changed during playback. The default setting is Complete, meaning that the system is calculated from the first frame of your animation on. The Forward setting is much faster if playback is commencing well into the animation, because calculations begin at the current frame. This speed increase is at the cost of accuracy, as particle movement is usually influenced by events occurring throughout the animation.

 Note

> With Update Type set to the default value of Complete, the entire particle flow, from the first frame to the current frame, will be recalculated every time a parameter is changed within Particle View. To avoid this delay, go to the first frame of the animation whenever possible, before making parameter changes.

The Track Update options allow you to track the progress of the particle flow. Particle Count adds a counter to the global event that updates continuously to show the total number of particles in the system. In addition, a counter is added to each event displaying the number of particles local to that event. Update Progress works during playback to highlight each operator and test as it is evaluated. If the added time required for this display causes frames to be skipped during playback, you can force each frame to be displayed (though not in real time) by using the Time Configuration dialog and clearing the Real Time check box. This is an invaluable tool when troubleshooting particles to track which events are receiving particles at which time.

Use Dynamic Names is on by default; it adds a listing of an action's most significant settings to the event display panel. For example, a test for a 150% increase in size will be listed as Scale 01 with Use Dynamic Names turned off, and Scale 01 (Scale>150%) with Use Dynamic Names turned on.

Parameters Panel

In this area, you can edit the parameters for the operators in your setup, similar to the way the Modify panel allows you to edit the properties of objects selected in the max viewport (**Figure 17.16**). This panel displays available parameters for any selected operator. It can be turned on and off using the Display menu command.

Figure 17.16   The parameters panel.

Tip

If more than one action is selected in the event display panel, a separate rollout for each will be available in the Parameters Panel.

The Depot

Think of this part of the Particle View interface as a spare-parts drawer (**Figure 17.17**). This panel holds all of the available particle flow actions. Operators, such as Position, Scale, and Shape, as well as tests, such as Collision and Speed, and default particle flow templates (Empty and Standard) can be dragged from this panel into the event display panel. The display of this panel can be toggled using the Display menu command.

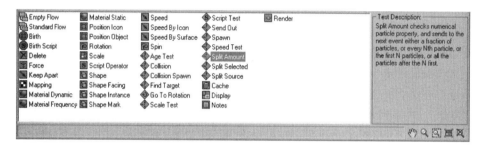

Figure 17.17   The depot and the description panel.

Tip

Once you become familiar with the available actions in Particle View, consider turning this panel off to maximize screen real estate.

Description Panel

When an action is selected in the depot, a brief text description of its functionality is displayed in the description panel.

Event Display Panel

This is where you get to the meat of Particle View, where you put all the parts together to create your particle masterpiece. The event display panel is the main element of the Particle View interface. It contains the visual representation of all particle flows in the current scene, and it diagrams their setup. The Edit menu functions are available within the event display, often by right-clicking an action.

Events

The "spare parts" you drag from the depot to assemble your particle system are grouped into collections known as events. Events are groups of actions (operators and/or tests) that are evaluated in order, top to bottom, for each particle that enters. Particles remain in an event, subject to the parameters of its constituent actions, until deleted or sent out to another event. Even when a single operator is created in the event display panel, it becomes part of an event.

There are several methods available to create an event. Right-clicking the event display background brings up a contextual menu.

Selecting New > Particle System > Empty Flow or Standard Flow creates a new PF Source global event and a corresponding PF Source icon in the viewport, at World coordinates 0, 0, 0 (**Figure 17.18**).

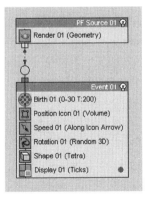

Figure 17.18   A standard Particle Flow global event and birth event.

Tip

Deleting a PF Source global event in Particle View also deletes the corresponding PF Source viewport icon.

Also available in the New submenu in the contextual menu are the entire library of Birth Events, Operator Events, Test Events, and Miscellaneous Events. Adding one of these actions to a blank area of the event display causes a new event to be created. A Display operator will be automatically added to new events if Default Display (located in the Options menu bar) is set to Local.

Tip

Using visually distinct Display types in each event is a key method for debugging particle flows in the viewport.

Editing Events

One of the simplest features of the event display panel, and one of the most useful in terms of creating a particle setup that reflects your intentions, is the freedom to move events anywhere within the panel. Once created, events can be moved by clicking their title bar and dragging them to a new area of the event display panel. Events can also be horizontally resized by dragging the right-hand border. You can also move actions by selecting and dragging them. If an action is dragged into an empty area of the event display, a new event is created, just as with using the New contextual-menu items. When an action is dragged into an existing event, a colored line shows how the action will be added. Where a blue line is indicated, the action will be inserted between existing actions. Where a red line shows, the existing action will be deleted and replaced with the action that is being moved.

Actions can be added to existing events by right-clicking the event's title bar to bring up the contextual menu (**Figures 17.19** and **17.20**). Selecting an action under Insert will insert that action at the beginning of the event. Selecting an action under Append will place the action at the end of the event. Neither option will replace any of the existing actions in the event. Moving actions can have a significant impact on the behavior of your particles, as actions are always evaluated within events in a top-down order.

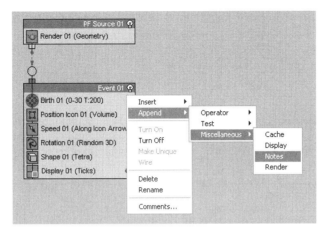

Figure 17.19 Selecting an action to append onto a Particle View event using the contextual menu.

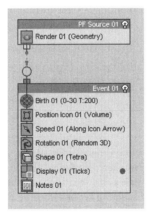

Figure 17.20 The selected action is appended to the event.

An event can be turned off via the contextual menu or by clicking the lightbulb icon on the event title bar. When an event is turned off, it does not process any particles. Particles sent to a deactivated event are deleted.

Events can also be deleted, commented, and renamed via the contextual menu. It is advisable to give meaningful names to events because event names are used in several contexts, such as when associating specific events with the BlobMesh compound object. Commented events are indicated with a small red triangle near the left end of the title bar. Click on the pointer to open the comments.

When an event is highlighted, Properties is also available as a contextual-menu option. This opens up the event's Object Properties dialog. Individual events can have differing object properties, such as Display Properties, Rendering Control, and Motion Blur.

Note

Do not make changes to the object properties of the PF Source icon; only make changes to event properties within Particle View. Changes made within the Object Properties dialog of the PF Source icon will not register properly or function as expected.

Actions

The available tests, operators, and particle sources in Particle View are known as actions. It is important to note that actions occur over different time frames. Some, like Force, Keep Apart, and Shape Facing, continuously influence particles within their events (and cease to have any influence once those particles have moved on to other events). Others, like Material Static and Shape, apply their parameters to particles one time and then are not evaluated until a new particle enters the event.

Note

One-time actions like Shape Mark can still contradict continuous actions with over-lapping influences, such as Scale (set with Scale Type Absolute or Relative). If the desired effect is to set a particle's size to a specific value and then modify that continuously, the two scale-influencing actions must be placed in separate events; otherwise the scale-initiating action will override the modifying one.

Tests

The decision-making part of Particle Flow allows you to redirect particles based on a variety of tests, by evaluating their properties (Age or Speed, for example), by evaluating their relation to other scene objects (Collision, Find Target), or arbitrarily (Split Amount). Actions that test particle or event conditions and/or direct particles to another event are known as tests. If a test is wired to another event, then particles testing True will be sent to that event. If a test is not wired to another event, then particles in effect always test False and remain in the original event.

Note

> If simple collision is required (without any derived spawning or other results), then use a Collision test without a wired target event. Particles will be bound to the collision object(s), and will be influenced by the Bounce, Friction, and other settings of the deflector, while remaining in the original event.

Tests are evaluated in the order in which they are listed in the event. If, for example, an event contains a Speed test followed by an Age Test, then particles that test True for the Speed test will be sent to that test's target event and never be evaluated for the Age Test.

Tip

> To send all particles to the next event, simply use the Send Out test.

Most tests share the same icon—a yellow diamond with a simple switch diagram. The tests available in Particle Flow are the following:

- Age Test
- Collision
- Collision Spawn
- Find Target
- Go To Rotation
- Scale
- Script
- Send Out
- Spawn
- Speed
- Split Amount
- Split Selected
- Split Source

Detailed descriptions of particle flow tests are available in the online 3ds max 7 User Reference (Help > User Reference), under Contents > Space Warps and Particle Systems > Particle Systems > Particle Flow > Actions > Tests.

Operators

Operators are particle flow actions that are used to control particle parameters such as scale, speed, rotation, and shape. Think of operators as individual components of the Modify panel properties you are accustomed to setting for scene objects, except that in the Particle View interface, you can use only the components you need.

Some operators perform functions other than controlling transformations; examples are the Birth, Birth Script, and Delete operators, which control particle life span.

In addition, there are four utility operators that serve general purposes. They are Cache (for precalculating intense particle flows), Display (determines particle appearance in viewports), Notes (stores comments), and Render (determines particle appearance when rendering).

Each operator has a unique icon, and they all share a blue background, with the exception of the two birth operators, which are green. The operators available in Particle Flow are the following:

- Birth
- Birth Script
- Delete
- Force
- Keep Apart
- Mapping
- Material Dynamic
- Material Frequency
- Material Static
- Position Icon
- Position Object
- Rotation
- Scale

- Script
- Shape
- Shape Facing
- Shape Instance
- Shape Mark
- Speed
- Speed By Icon
- Speed By Surface
- Spin
- Cache
- Display
- Notes
- Render

Detailed descriptions of particle flow operators are available in the online 3ds max 7 User Reference (Help > User Reference), under Contents > Space Warps and Particle Systems > Particle Systems > Particle Flow > Actions > Operators.

Flows

There are two available particle flows that can be used to create a new system—Empty Flow and Standard Flow.

Empty Flow creates an event with a single Render operator (and a Display operator if Options > Default Display is set to Global). This is useful for creating a new particle flow from scratch.

Standard Flow creates a more elaborate setup: The global event will be identical to that of Empty Flow, but in addition a birth event is created and wired to it. The birth event will contain a simple particle setup—Birth, Position Icon, Speed, Rotation, Shape, and Display operators. This is identical to the particle flow created when a PF Source icon is created in a viewport.

If a Camera or Perspective viewport is active when an empty or standard flow is created, the corresponding PF Source icon will be oriented on the XY plane. If an orthogonal viewport is active, the PF Source icon will be oriented parallel to the viewplane, with the icon's Z axis pointing toward the viewport.

Editing Actions

The contextual menu for actions is similar to that for events. The Insert and Append options are available for adding actions, but the placement depends on where the pointer is when opening the menu. If the pointer is placed over an action (the action name will appear as a tool tip), then Insert will replace that action with the new action. If the pointer is placed between actions (no tool tip appears), then Insert will place the new action between the two existing actions. Append will always place the new action at the end of the event, regardless of where the pointer is located.

Actions can also be turned on or off from this menu, or by clicking the action's icon. When an action is deactivated, the icon and action title are grayed.

Tests can be forced to always test True (all particles are sent to the wired destination, if any) or False (all particles are retained within the current event). For True results, click the left side of the icon (the icon will change to a green lightbulb). For False results, click the right side of the icon (the icon will change to a red lightbulb). To reset the test to normal functioning, click the icon once more.

Instanced actions can be made unique from this menu as well.

The Wire option in the contextual menu wires events and tests, or global events and birth events, together. This option is only available when eligible items are selected and when you right-click one of them. To wire an event to the outcome of a test, select the test action (not the event containing the test) and the target event (not an action within the target event), right-click on one of them, and choose Wire from the contextual menu. To wire a birth event to a global (PF Source) event, select both events (not actions within them), right-click, and choose Wire (**Figures 17.21** and **17.22**).

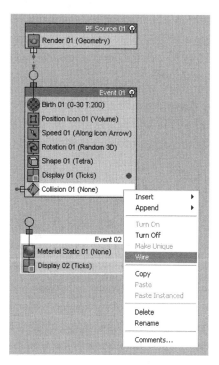

Figure 17.21   Eligible events and tests, as well as global events and birth operators, can be wired together using the right-click menu.

Copy and Paste allow actions and events to be cloned. Multiple actions can be pasted into a new event if the Paste command is applied to a blank area of the event display. If Paste is applied to an existing event, copied actions will be added to the event. Multiple events can be cloned together as well, such as when you wish to duplicate a specific particle appearance (Display, Scale [Relative Successive], and Material Static operators, for example) from one event to another in order to preserve properties that would otherwise cease to be applied once the particle left the original event.

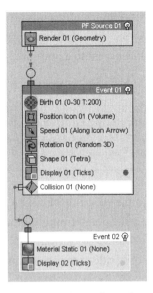

Figure 17.22   After the Wire command is chosen from the contextual menu, the eligible events are wired.

Actions and events can also be cloned by holding down the Shift key while dragging. The specific order of clicking and dragging is a bit tricky. First hold down the Shift key. Then hover the pointer over the selected items you wish to clone. Once a plus symbol has appeared on the pointer, click and drag the event(s) to clone them.

Comments can be added to actions, much as events. If you prefer, a Notes operator is available, which has no effect on event execution. The Notes operator serves as a place-holder for whatever text you wish to store within it, such as troubleshooting information, successful particle settings, or comments for other users.

Wiring Events

As noted in the "Editing Actions" section earlier in the chapter, events, tests, and birth operators can be connected via the contextual menu. A more intuitive approach is to simply drag a wire from one event to another.

When a test is added to an event, an output is created in the form of a small blue dot wired to the left side of the test. The pointer will change to a wiring icon with three arrows when you can drag a wire from this output, and to a wiring icon with four arrows when you can drop the wire into an event input. Note that this works in either direction;

wires can be dragged from events into tests. In a similar fashion, the output of a global event can be wired to a birth event (an event that begins with a Birth or Birth Script operator). You cannot wire a global event to a non-birth event.

> **Note**
>
> Multiple tests can be wired into a single event, sending particles from several tests to be influenced by the target event; however, a single test can only be wired into a single event, because particles testing True can only have one destination.

A test's output can be moved to the right side of the event listing to facilitate wiring to events placed to the right. Move the pointer onto the small square part of the output. Once the pointer has changed to a small black circle with arrows pointing to the left and right, click and drag to the opposite side of the event listing to move the output.

As we have seen in this section, there are many technical aspects to arranging particle setups within the Particle View interface, but they really just add up to an open-ended system for creating custom particles. Next, we will explore several practical techniques for using Particle Flow to simulate real-world environmental effects centered on an erupting volcano.

Particles for Environmental Effects

Consider a great CG scene that you found truly inspirational. Something evocative or exciting. Chances are that scene included atmospheric elements in the form of liquid, vapor, wind, fire, dust, or other environmental effects. While these sorts of elements aren't often the main focus of a scene, they contribute immeasurably to a scene's visual impact. After all, without a puff of dust and a spray of sparks, much of a meteor's impact would be lost. Less spectacular, yet no less essential, effects such as fog, rain, and dripping water contribute to a scene's emotional impact in ways that are more felt than logically analyzed.

A key tool in 3ds max 7 for environmental effects is the particle. The true power of particle systems is in the ability to dictate the behavior of a large group of objects with a system of controls, and Particle Flow excels at putting controls for precise particle behavior into your hands. This system allows for as little consideration for individual particles as you desire. Sweeping, general rules can easily be used to set a homogeneous group of particles in motion. If you want more precise control, you can cause smaller subsets of the group to branch off into other behaviors based on a variety of tests and conditions.

The event-driven particles in Particle Flow offer exciting capabilities for environmental effects because layers of realism can be quickly built with conditional particle behaviors. In this exercise, to create a bubbling lava effect, you will explore the following effects:

- churning, boiling liquid
- rising gas bubbles
- popping surface bubbles
- splashing liquid
- dribbling liquid
- surface smears

The lava created in this exercise will boil violently, spew into the air, collide realistically with uneven scene geometry, and trail across its surface, leaving a fading material trail. If you would like to preview the final effect, view the movie volcano_complete.avi on the DVD.

Create a Particle Source

In this next series of exercise segments, you will create several particle effects, using Particle Flow and the Particle View interface, that will culminate in a procedural and flexible volcanic eruption.

1. The first step in most particle setups is to create a source for your particle system, be it a helper object or scene geometry. In this beginning exercise, we will examine the scene, create and position the particle emitter, and modify the default Particle Flow source to form the basis of a pool of boiling lava. Open the max file volcano_begin.max, found on the DVD.

Note

If at any point in this series of exercises you wish to examine the finished max scene, open volcano_complete.max on the DVD.

This scene contains a volcano base model and a simplified version for collision purposes (**Figure 17.23**). The collision model, volcano_collision, has been set to nonrendering in its Object Properties dialog. Also included is a simple animated popping bubble, "BubblePop geometry." This mesh object uses animated Volume Select and DeleteMesh modifiers to form a sphere that disappears from the top down.

Figure 17.23   The starting point for this tutorial—a volcanic crater.

First, you will create a particle flow in conjunction with a BlobMesh compound object to simulate a bubbling pool of lava.

2. Go to the Create panel > Geometry > Particle Systems and create a PF Source icon in the Top viewport (**Figure 17.24**).

This icon will serve as the source for the lava and all the effects derived from it.

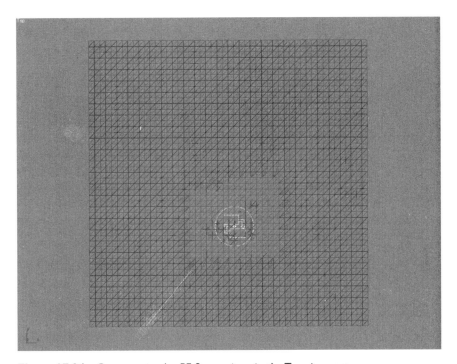

Figure 17.24   Create a circular PF Source icon in the Top viewport.

3. To better fit the icon to the volcano geometry, change its Icon Type to Circle and its Diameter to around 140 in the Emission rollout. Move the icon in the Top viewport until it's centered in the crater. Then move it along its Z axis in the Camera viewport until it appears above the volcano geometry, with the approximate coordinates X = 20, Y = –150, Z = 140 (**Figure 17.25**).

   If you scrub the Time Slider, you will see particles being released from the icon and emitted parallel to the icon's negative Z axis. This is because the default Z-axis orientation of a PF Source icon created in an orthogonal viewport is away from the user's perspective.

4. In the Camera viewport, flip the icon along its Z axis, using the Mirror tool (Tools > Mirror) (**Figure 17.26**). Now the particles should emit upward, out of the volcano (**Figure 17.27**).

Figure 17.25   Move the icon up on its Z axis until it appears in the crater.

Figure 17.26   Use the Mirror tool to flip the particle emitter.

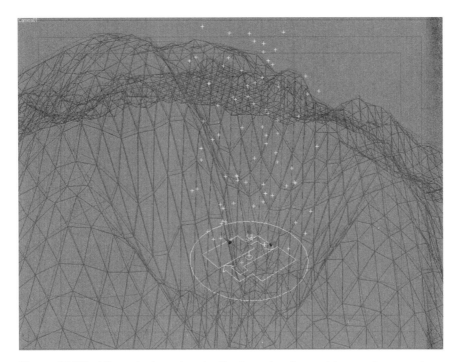

Figure 17.27   Mirror the icon along its Z axis so that the particles are shot up and out of the crater.

5. Press 6 or click the Particle View button on the source icon's Modify panel to open Particle View. A standard flow has been created to coincide with the PF Source icon.

The source event, named PF Source 01, contains only a Render operator. This operator creates renderable meshes for spawned particles. Because this action is in the global event, it will affect all particles, in all events, throughout the system. This is not desirable for the current exercise, as different sorts of particle geometry will be created at different stages of the flow.

6. To get rid of this operator, right-click the Render operator, and choose Delete from the contextual menu (**Figure 17.28**).

Examine the next event in the flow, named Event 01. This event will be used to generate the particles for the main mass of bubbling lava.

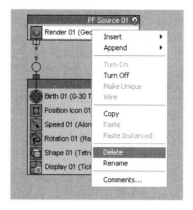

Figure 17.28   Delete the global Render operator.

7. First, right-click the event title bar, choose Rename from the contextual menu, and rename the event Bubbling Lava. This name will have significance outside of Particle View, when you're choosing particle events to be attached to other scene objects.

8. Select the Birth operator to view its properties in the Particle View Parameters panel. Change Emit Stop to 0 and Amount to 50, to create a burst of 50 particles instantly at the start of the animation. Leave Subframe Sampling on.

 Note

When Subframe Sampling is active, particle calculations occur at a higher frequency (closer interval) than rendered frames. This creates smoother effects and less bunching or puffing in particle emission.

9. Examine the Position Icon operator, which by default is set to emit particles according to the volume of the icon. This would be appropriate for a Box or Sphere icon type, but since the current icon type is set to Circle, in the Location pop-up menu choose Surface.

 Note

Just as with many other max functions, a Seed value and New seed generator button are available. Generating new seeds can drastically change the movement of particles, giving a new appearance to the system without changing any other operator parameters.

10. The Speed operator is set by default to emit particles along the icon's arrow at 300 units per second. For the desired bubbling effect, set Speed to 3 and Variation to 15.

11. Rotation control is not necessary, so delete that operator (right-click and choose Delete).

12. The Shape operator defines particle shape, and by default it creates a 10-unit-diameter tetra. Increase this to 20. This size will become significant when these particles are used in a BlobMesh object. Change the Shape type to Sphere, so that it will generate a smoother metaball effect.

13. The Display operator determines the appearance of the particles in a viewport (as opposed to the Render operator, which is used in conjunction with a Shape operator to determine appearance at render time). Change the Type to Geometry to get a feel for the volume that will be created by this particle flow.

14. Change the display color by clicking either the color-selector circle in the Display operator's Event listing or the color-selector square in the Properties panel to open the Color Selector. Set the color to a bright red to better approximate the look of lava. Your particle system should appear as shown in **Figure 17.29**.

If you scrub the Time Slider, the spawned particles, appearing instantly at the start of the animation, will flow away from the emitter. Most will flow along the emitter's positive Z axis. Some will flow in the opposite direction due to the Speed operator's Variation setting. This randomization is necessary for the desired bubbling-lava effect.

As you have seen in this exercise segment, creating and positioning a PFlow source is very similar to using non-event-driven particle systems. The difference in technique comes into play when you begin to modify particle behavior using the Particle View interface (**Figure 17.30**).

In this next portion of the exercise, we will explore the use of forces to impact particle movement, and we'll implement a simple collision solution to constrain the particles to a specific location. The result will be the addition of a quick bouncing motion to the particles in a confined space.

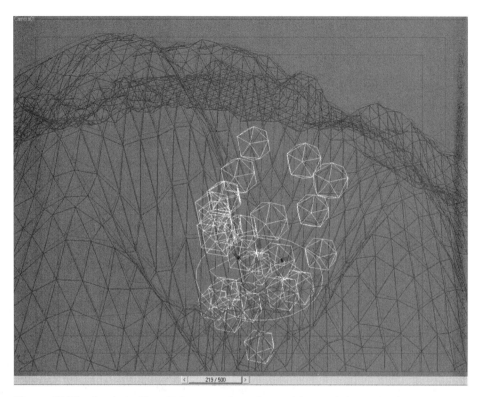

Figure 17.29 Scrub the Time Slider to see how the particles are being emitted.

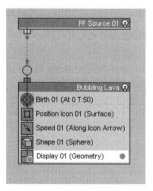

Figure 17.30 The particle system flow so far.

Force and Collision

For a bubbling movement, three elements are required: an initial speed and direction (provided in the exercise above), a motive force to pull the particles back down, and a collision force to bounce them back up. In this next segment of the exercise, the force involved will be one commonly used with particles—the Gravity space warp—and collision will be dependent on a geometry-based deflector employing the specialized volcano collision mesh.

1. Go to the Top viewport and create a Gravity space warp (Create panel > Space Warps > Forces) (**Figure 17.31**). It will be oriented by default with its Z axis pointing along the negative World Z axis. The position of the space warp is not significant, only its orientation, so long as Decay is not used.

2. Leave the Gravity Strength setting at its default setting of 1.

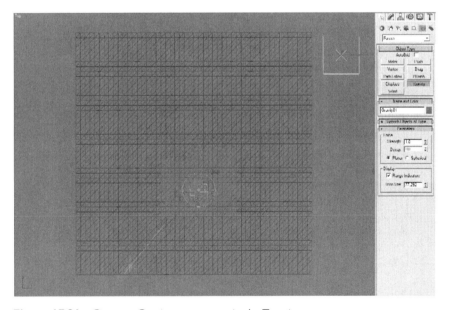

Figure 17.31   Create a Gravity space warp in the Top viewport.

3. To connect this force to the particles, go back to Particle View and append a Force operator to the Bubbling Lava event. You can do this either by right-clicking the event and choosing Append > Operator > Force, or by dragging a Force operator from the depot into the event listing and dropping it when its indicator line turns blue (**Figure 17.32**). (Dropping the action when the line is red will replace the existing action with the new one.)

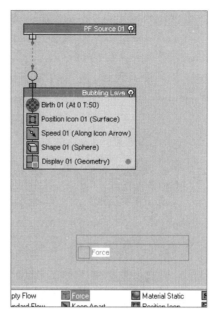

Figure 17.32   Select a Force operator from the depot and add it to the event by dragging it.

4. In the Force event Properties panel, select the Gravity01 space warp by either selecting Add and then clicking the space warp in a viewport, or by selecting By List and choosing from the Select Force Space Warps dialog.

 Note

Multiple space warps can be applied within a single Force operator, and the resulting calculations will usually be more accurate if they are applied in this way, as opposed to using individual Force operators.

5. If you scrub the Time Slider, you will note that the particles are being dragged down very quickly. To reduce this effect, set the Force operator's Influence to 15%.

   The other half of the bubbling effect is created by a collision force to bounce the particles. You will use a UDeflector space warp, which provides collision based on any mesh geometry.

6. Go to the Top viewport and create a UDeflector space warp (Create panel > Space Warps > Deflectors).

7. In the UDeflector's Modify panel, click the Pick Object button and choose the volcano_collision object. The collision mesh sits on top of the higher-resolution rendering volcano mesh, so you will have an easier time choosing the right one if you use the Select Objects dialog (keyboard shortcut H). Leave the other settings at their default values. (A Bounce setting of 1.0 means that the particles will never lose momentum or slow down as a result of collision.) Feel free to hide the volcano_collision mesh at this point to simplify the viewport.

Tip

Using proxy collision objects can be a very effective way to reduce CPU overhead when object-based collision is required.

8. To apply this collision effect to the particles, return to Particle View and append a Collision test to the event (**Figure 17.33**).

9. Add UDeflector01 to the Collision test's Deflectors list.

Scrub the Time Slider to observe the particles being repeatedly bounced back up by the collision space warp.

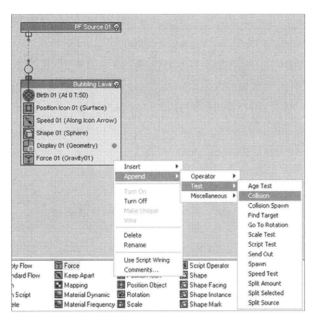

Figure 17.33   Appending a Collision test to the event using the contextual menu.

Note

A target event is not necessary with all tests—for example, the Collision test, which can provide collision functionality without directing True-testing particles to a new event.

When setting up particle systems, it's always important to keep track of where those particles might wind up, particularly if they are going to be subject to a lot of bouncing action. After all, a swarm of moths around a porch light will lose some of its believability if one of the moths flies through a solid wall. In this next section, you will add a safety guard to your scene to prevent particles from escaping.

Catching Stray Particles

If you observe the particle flow from the Front or Left viewport, you will most likely see several particles escaping from the crater and falling down the World Z axis (**Figure 17.34**). There are various methods to combat this, such as using finer collision meshes, using slower particle velocities, and increasing the PF Source icon's Integration Step. In this case, you will use one of the simplest remedies, a backup deflector.

1. Go to the Top viewport and create a POmniFlect space warp (Create panel > Space Warps > Deflectors). Make the space warp about 1000 units by 1000 units, centered on the volcano geometry, so that all of the particles will be covered.

2. Set the Time Off to 500 so that the deflector does not lose collision during the animation. Overlooking this setting is a common mistake.

3. Append a second Collision test to the Bubbling Lava event and assign POmniFlect01 to it.

Note

When multiple collision deflectors are applied with a single event, placing all of the deflectors into one Collision test will give more reliable results, unless different output events are required.

Once particles collide with this deflector, they will be deleted. Planar collisions are very reliable, so particles are not expected to escape from them.

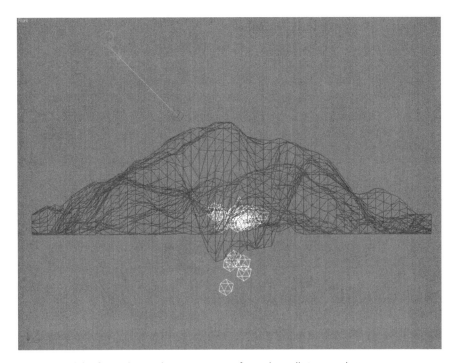

Figure 17.34   Several particles are escaping from the collision mesh.

4. In an empty area of the Event display, to the right of the event, create a new Delete operator. If it appears with a Display operator as well, feel free to delete Display. Rename this new event Bubbling Lava Delete.

5. A wire between the two events would be forced into a confusing path across the event, so move the test's output to the right of the event by dragging the square output handle to the right side of the event list (**Figure 17.35**).

6. Wire the two events by dragging from the output of the POmniFlect01 Collision test to the input of the Delete event.

If you scrub the Time Slider, you will see that particles that escape the object-based deflector are caught, and deleted, by the planar one.

 Tip

For a more sophisticated setup, try recycling these stray particles back into the main flow. Hint: Separate the Birth operator from the rest of the operators, connected with a Send Out Test, and wire the Collision test back into the Bubbling Lava event.

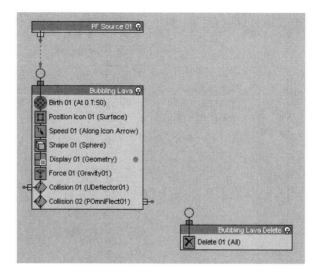

Figure 17.35   Create a new event, consisting of a Delete operator. Then drag the second Collision test's output to the right side of the event.

As we have seen here, particles in PFlow can be constrained using the same forces and collision tools used in non-event-driven particle systems, but with more specific application by being linked in Particle View to certain events. Now that the basic motion of the lava particles is set, in this next segment of the exercise you will link them to BlobMesh for rendering.

BlobMesh

BlobMesh is a compound object that is very useful for creating liquids, particularly in combination with particles. BlobMesh is a metaball geometry tool that creates a group of spheres, based on instanced geometry, helper objects, or particles. The group is then joined into a smooth mass, with close spheres blending together.

1. Go to the Top viewport and create a BlobMesh object (Create panel > Geometry > Compound Objects). The placement is not significant, as BlobMesh places its metaballs according to the position of Blob Objects.

   You can ignore the Size setting, because when using particles, metaball size is based on particle size.

2. Reduce Tension to around 0.35 for a more loosely defined surface.

   Evaluation Coarseness determines how detailed the resulting mesh will be, both in viewports and at render time. It is recommended that the Render setting be left at 3.0 or lower to ensure that the BlobMesh animates

smoothly. The Viewport setting can be set as high (as coarse) as is required
to keep screen refreshes from lagging.

3. To use the particle flow you've set up to generate metaballs, click the Add button
   in the BlobMesh's Parameters rollout and choose PF Source 01. The Pick button
   will allow you to choose directly from a viewport, which may be more difficult,
   as BlobMesh will allow you to pick nearly any screen object (**Figure 17.36**).

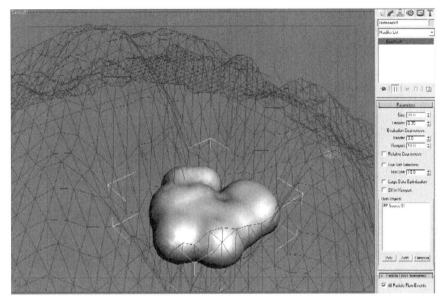

Figure 17.36   Add the PF Source 01 icon to the list of Blob Objects to form a metaball mesh around the particles.

Scrub the Time Slider to observe a blob forming around the spawned particles and bouncing in the crater. The appearance of this lava isn't quite right
yet. The bubbling geometry seems to float freely in the crater, not as part of
a viscous pool. A second blob object is called for to fill in.

4. Go to the Top viewport and create a Plane centered over the crater; set Length
   to 175 and Width to 280.

5. Go to the Camera viewport and move it up on the Z axis until it's just a little
   lower than the particle emitter, around Z = 125 (**Figure 17.37**).

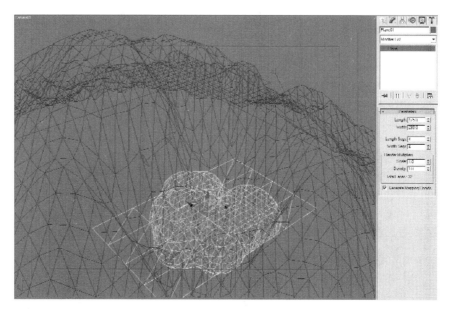

Figure 17.37 Move the Plane to a position just below the particle emitter.

Now you will create a static particle cloud along this plane to generate additional metaballs to fill in the effect.

6. In Particle View, select the Birth, Shape, and Display operators of the Bubbling Lava event and clone them, either by right-clicking a blank area and choosing Copy > Paste Instanced, or Shift-dragging and choosing Instance as the method. All three operators will appear in a new event in italics to indicate that they are instanced. Using Instance as the method allows you to make changes to the number of particles spawned, and their appearance, by editing any of the copied (original) operators.

7. Rename this new event Pool Base.

A position for these particles has not been defined. Append a Position Object operator to Pool Base.

8. In the Position Object's Parameters panel, add Plane01 to the list of Emitter Objects.

9. To prevent spawned particles from bunching up any closer than the 20-unit diameter of the metaballs, turn on Separation in the Location area and set Distance at 20.

10. Finally, wire the output of the PF Source 01 event to the input of the Pool Base event to spawn particles (**Figure 17.38**).

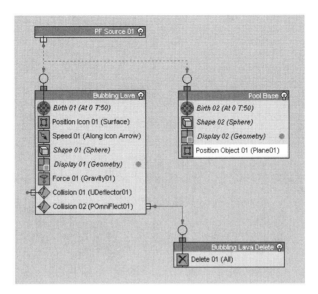

Figure 17.38   Wire the PF Source to the new event to activate the new particles.

You will immediately notice a difference in the lava's appearance, as the Plane generates a base of static particles to fill in the pool effect (**Figure 17.39**). To toggle the effect, click on the light bulb icon in the "Pool Base" title bar to turn the event on/off.

11. In a wireframe viewport, the display is becoming quite confusing, due to the overlap of spherical particles and BlobMesh. To change the viewport appearance of particles, go to either of the Display operators and change the Type to Ticks.

12. Open the Material Editor, select the Lava material, and apply the material to the BlobMesh01 object. Applying a material to the PF Source icon will have no effect, as the particles are being rendered based on the BlobMesh's geometry and materials.

13. The lava will need mapping coordinates, so apply a UVW Mapping modifier with Spherical mapping (**Figure 17.40**).

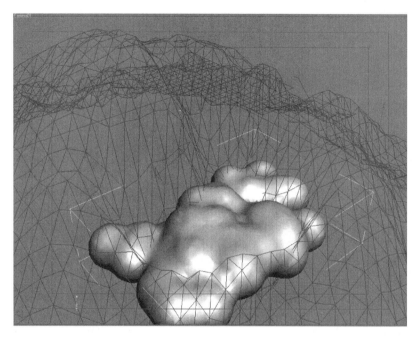

Figure 17.39   The lava is now filled in with a pool of static particles.

Figure 17.40   The BlobMesh lava, with an appropriate material.

Note

Material use with BlobMesh objects is a bit restricted given that the topography of the metaballs can change drastically. Materials cannot be "locked down" to any particular metaball, nor can different materials be applied to different metaballs, except when using standard material-blending techniques, such as Blend and Top/Bottom. For these reasons, BlobMesh objects lend themselves to general coloring materials, as opposed to materials with very distinct texture patterns.

In this section, you have created the display mesh for your lava pool using the BlobMesh compound object linked to specific events in Particle Flow. Now that the lava pool is complete, you will add some special bubbling action by birthing a new set of particles from the same source.

Rising Gas Bubbles

The main environmental cause for bubbling lava is, of course, rising areas of superheated gas. In the first part of creating bubbles for this lava, you will spawn occasional larger metaballs that will rise and swell and eventually spawn mesh bubbles.

1. Return to Particle View and select the first five Bubbling Lava operators (Birth, Position Icon, Speed, Shape, and Display), and clone them to a new event. Use Copy as the method, as you will be changing some of these operators.

2. Rename the new event Big Bubble and wire it to the PF Source event (**Figure 17.41**).

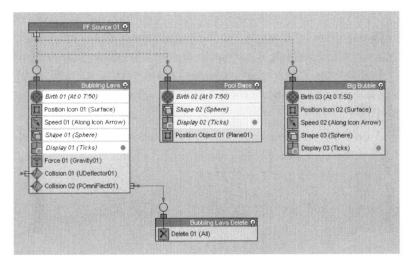

Figure 17.41   Create a new birth event by cloning operators.

3. Edit the Birth operator to emit a total amount of 5 particles, over frames 0–350.

4. Increase the Speed to 10 units per second, and set Variation to 0. Feel free to increase the speed variation later, but for debugging purposes, it is simpler to stick with a constant speed for now.

5. To keep these new particles from popping into existence, reduce the Size in the Shape operator to 10 units so that they will initially spawn at a small enough size to be concealed by the surface of the lava.

   Once these special bubbles have spawned, they need to be scaled up as they rise. This will occur in a new event, to avoid conflict with the existing Shape operator.

6. Append a Send Out test to Big Bubble. This test always yields True values; in other words, all particles are sent to the next wired event.

7. Create a new Scale operator below the Big Bubble event. Rename this event Big Bubble Grow and wire its input to the Send Out's output.

8. Change the Scale's Type to Relative Successive. This will apply scaling changes in terms of percentages, for as long as particles remain in the event.

9. You will want this rising gas bubble to expand less on the Z axis than on the X and Y axes, in order for it to blend more successfully with the other metaballs, so clear the Constrain Proportions check box.

10. Set the Scale Factors to X = 103%, Y = 103%, Z = 101%. These may seem like insignificant values, but applied continuously to particles, their effect will quickly accumulate.

11. The bubble needs to stay within this event only until it has reached a specific size, so append a Scale Test action to the event. Set the axis to be tested to Z, and the Test Value percentage to 150%, so that when a particle reaches 150% of the Z-axis scale it had when it entered the event, it will be sent out to the next event (**Figure 17.42**).

    If you slowly scrub the Time Slider, you will see the BlobMesh bulge as the big bubble increases in scale, though without a target event, the scaling will continue without end (**Figure 17.43**).

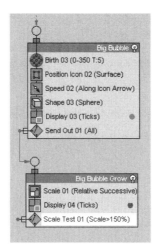

Figure 17.42   Create a small event to grow the particles over time.

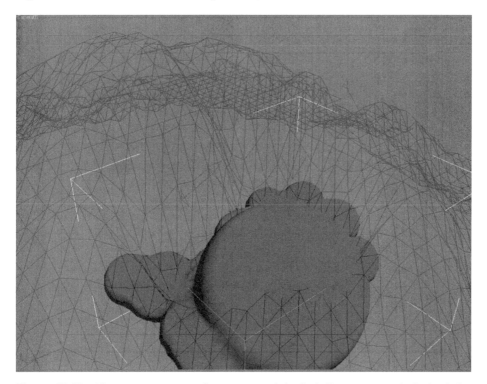

Figure 17.43   The increase in size will continue until the Scale Test action sends the big bubble to a new event.

Tip

If you scrub too far into the animation while the increasing scale of the BlobMesh is unchecked, you could consume enough CPU resources to cause max to crash.

12. Add a new Speed operator below the Big Bubble Grow event. Rename this event Big Bubble Stop and wire it to the output of the Scale test.

13. To slow this particle down dramatically, set Speed to 2. Once the particle reaches the event, it will also stop increasing in scale.

This bubble will need to shrink and die after pausing for a few frames.

14. Append an Age Test to Big Bubble Stop, and set its Test Value to 15 frames. Leave the Variation setting at its default of 5 frames.

15. Change the age type to Event Age so that particles will test True after being in this event for 15 ±5 frames. The default setting of Particle Age tests for the age of the particle since it was spawned (or had its age reset) (**Figure 17.44**).

Once a particle passes the Age Test action, it will be sent to an event that will shrink it back down.

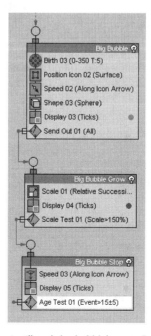

Figure 17.44   This new event will end the bubble's growth, slow it down, and retain the bubble for 15 plus or minus 5 frames.

16. Copy the Big Bubble Stop Speed operator to a new event below, and rename the new event Big Bubble Shrink.

17. Wire the Age Test output into the Big Bubble Stop event's input.

18. Set Speed to −10 to send the big bubble back down into the metaball mass.

19. Append a Scale operator with type Relative Successive.

20. Set all of the Scale operator's Scale Factors to 99%.

Scrubbing the Time Slider will reveal that the bubble grows and rises, pauses briefly, and then falls back and shrinks.

21. Again, this reduction in scale will proceed without end unless a test interrupts it, so append another Scale test, set it to test True if particle value Is Less Than Test Value, and set the Test Value percentage to 25%.

22. Wire this test to a new event containing a Delete operator, named Big Bubble Delete (**Figure 17.45**).

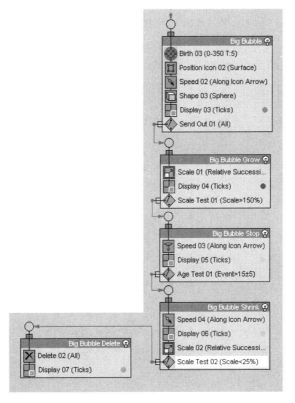

Figure 17.45   After adding a shrink event and a delete event, the "big bubble" sequence is complete.

Strictly speaking, you could just allow the particle to shrink indefinitely; at some point its size would resolve to 0 and it would stop being calculated. Alternatively, you could cause it stop (Speed = 0), but to keep the particle flow from being bogged down, it is good practice to delete unneeded particles whenever possible.

As you have seen, numerous birth events can be tied to a single Particle Source icon, each with its own animation and render appearance. This is not the conclusion of the bubble effect. An animated mesh will be spawned on top of the big bubble to represent the actual moment of escaping gas.

Spawning Animated Geometry

The "BubblePop geometry" object in the scene is a simple animated mesh that approximates a popping bubble. This mesh will be spawned in animated and nonanimated form to polish off the bubble effect (**Figures 17.46–17.48**).

   1. Insert a Spawn test into the Big Bubble Stop event. Be certain that it appears before Age Test, which should be the last action in the event.

      By default the Spawn test will generate a single particle, only once per event, with the same speed and direction as the parent particle.

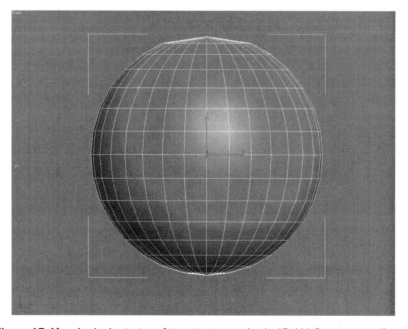

Figure 17.46   At the beginning of its animation cycle, the "BubblePop geometry" object appears as a simple sphere.

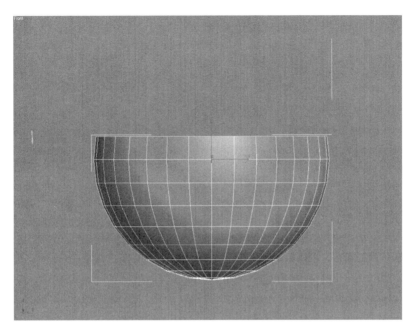

Figure 17.47   The animated bubble pops very quickly.

Figure 17.48   The bubble completely deletes itself over frames 0–15.

2. In this case, the spawned bubble needs to stop, so set Inherited to 0%.

3. Drag the Spawn test output to the right side of the event so that it can be wired to a new event.

4. Create a new Shape Instance operator event to the right of the Big Bubble event and name the new event Popping Bubble Spawn.

   The Shape Instance operator creates particle shapes based on instanced geometry, similar to the Instanced Geometry particle type in non-event-driven particle systems.

5. Wire the Spawn test to this event.

6. In the Shape Instance Properties panel, click the Particle Geometry Object button and use the Select Object dialog (keyboard shortcut H) to select the BubblePop geometry object.

7. Reduce the Scale percentage setting to 50% to start this bubble off small (**Figure 17.49**).

   At this point, step back to consider how this particle system is being rendered, specifically through BlobMesh. By default, all Particle Flow events in selected PF Source objects are used in the metaball collection. Using instanced geometry particles with metaballs can lead to undependable results, and, in this case, an incorrect visual appearance.

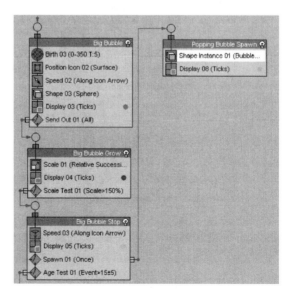

Figure 17.49   When the big bubble stops, it will spawn a popping bubble that uses instanced geometry.

8. Go to the BlobMesh's Modify panel, and in the Particle Flow Parameters rollout, clear the All Particle Flow Events check box. The BlobMesh in the viewport disappears because there are no selected objects to use.

9. Click the Add button to open the Add Particle Flow Events dialog. All events in particle flows assigned as Blob Objects are listed here. Add the following events: Bubbling Lava, Pool Base, Big Bubble Grow, Big Bubble Stop, and Big Bubble Shrink (**Figure 17.50**). The value of giving meaningful names to particle flow events should be apparent. Events that do not contribute to the metaballs, such as the Delete events, do not need to be added to the list.

   Scrub the Time Slider to observe how the lava metaballs have the same appearance as before, though the spawned geometry bubble is still not appearing in viewports.

10. Returning to the Popping Bubble Spawn event, it should be obvious why the bubble is not appearing in viewports; the Display type is set to Ticks. Change it to Geometry to see the spawned bubbles appear throughout the animation, though at this point they don't appear to pop (**Figure 17.51**).

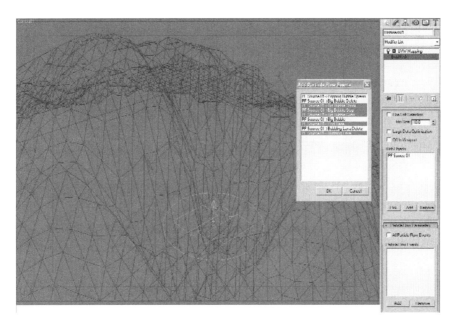

Figure 17.50   Instead of using all PFlow events, BlobMesh will use the selected ones.

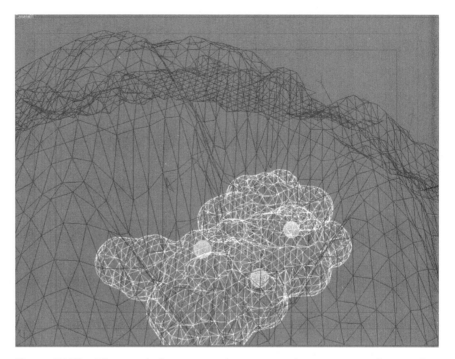

Figure 17.51   The particle flow now produces instanced geometry particles as well as metaball particles.

11. Append a Speed operator to the event and set Speed to 450. This operator will be in effect for two frames and is used to position the bubble geometry near the top of the metaball effect.

12. Append an Age Test to the event with a Test Value of 2 and a Variation of 0.

Once the bubble has been repositioned with this event, it will be passed to the next event, which will cause the instanced geometry to grow and increase in scale.

13. Select the Popping Bubble Spawn event and clone it, using Copy as the method. Rename the new event Popping Bubble Grow.

14. Wire the new event to the previous one's Age Test.

15. The bubble needs to rise at a moderate speed, so set its Speed operator to 35 units per second.

16. Insert a Scale operator (before the final Age Test), with the Type set to Relative Successive and the Scale Factors set to X = 105%, Y = 105%, Z = 102%. (The Constrain Proportions check box must be cleared.)

17. Give this bubble a little longer to grow and rise by setting the Age Test's Test Value to 10 (**Figure 17.52**).

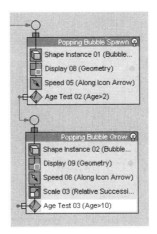

Figure 17.52 After spawning the popping bubble, the next event causes it to grow and rise for ten frames.

If you scrub the Time Slider, the spawned geometric bubble will grow (and continue to grow, at this point in the exercise), but it will not show up in renders without a Render operator.

Note

The Render operator passes along particle appearance to the renderer; without it, particles can only show up in viewports. The exception is when particles are being rendered by another max object, like BlobMesh.

18. Add a Render operator to Popping Bubble Grow. (Its position in the event list does not matter.)

Scrub to a point in the animation where the spawned geometry is obvious in viewports (**Figure 17.53**). If you render a still image, something odd occurs. The bubble appears much larger and higher in renders than in viewports (**Figure 17.54**). This is due to the Integration Step settings.

In the PF Source icon's System Management rollout, Integration Step values are given for Viewport and Render. By default, particle calculations for render time are calculated twice as often (Half Frame versus Frame) as in viewports, which results in influential operators such as Speed and Scale's having greater effect in renders.

Figure 17.53   The popping bubble appears in the expected size in the viewport.

Figure 17.54   The popping bubble appears differently in renders due to varying Integration Step settings.

19. Set the Render Integration Step to Frame. If you render another still, the render appearance should match that in the viewport (**Figure 17.55**).

Figure 17.55   The appearance of the popping bubble in renders will match that in viewports once the Integration Steps are set to the same value.

20. Select the Popping Bubble Grow event and clone it, using Copy as the method. Rename the new event Popping Bubble Pop.

21. Wire the new event to the previous one's Age Test.

22. In this event, the instanced geometry's animation is going to be used. In the Shape Instance operator, check the Animated Shape box.

23. The popping bubble's animation occurs over frames 0–15 and needs to be synced to this event, so set Sync By to Event Duration.

24. To enhance the popping animation, set the Speed to –25 units, so that the bubble will rapidly fall as it pops.

25. To cause the bubble to shrink as it pops, set all three Scale Factors to 98%.

Rather than exit this event based on age, you will exit based on scale, and then delete the particle.

26. Select the Scale Test from Big Bubble Shrink and clone it, using Copy as the method, over the Age Test at the end of Popping Bubble Pop, replacing Age Test with Scale Test. Set the Test Value percentage to 10%.

27. Add a Delete event below Popping Bubble Pop, name it Popping Bubble Delete, and wire it to the previous Scale Test (**Figure 17.56**).

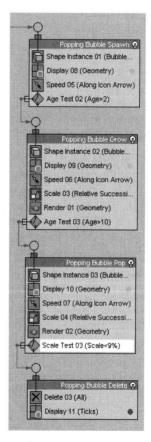

Figure 17.56   With the addition of an event to cause the bubble to pop, and a delete event to clean up, the "popping bubble" sequence is complete.

Using instanced geometry, you have created a popping bubble that will automatically spawn above the rising bulges in the lava. It's worth considering that the popping bubbles are linked to the rising bulges; changing the quantity or location of the bulges will automatically pass those changes along to the popping bubbles.

Splash Effect

When the bubble pops, it releases energy and liquid mass back into the pool. You will create this effect by spawning a ring of drops from the popping bubble. The drops will taper off as they leave the ring, an effect that you will create by spawning a ring of non-rendering "generator" particles first.

1. Insert a Spawn test into Popping Bubble Pop, just before the final Scale Test. Even though the parent particle will be in this event until it passes the Scale Test, by default the spawning will occur only once.

2. Increase the spawned Offspring # to 5, with a 20% Variation to add a random factor.

   These generator particles need to have their direction based on the position of the popping bubble. If the particle speed were not set in the Spawn operator, a later Speed operator would not be able to discern a direction away from the parent particle.

3. Under Speed, check that the Inherited % radio button is on, and set the value to –50, Variation % to 15, and Divergence to 90. This Divergence setting will spread the spawned particles over a 90-degree arc.

 Tip

Negative percentage values for inherited speed reverse the previous direction before applying the percentage velocity change.

4. Create a new Shape operator event to the right of the Popping Bubble Spawn event, and name the new event Generate Trail. This event will be used to generate a series of droplets, decreasing in size, that will trail after one another and blend together into a metaball strand.

5. Wire this event to the previously created Spawn test (move the Spawn output anchor to the right side of the event first).

6. Set the Shape operator type to Sphere and the Size to 2.

7. Append a Spawn test. Set the Spawn Rate to Per Second, and the Rate value to 25. This will generate 25 particles per second (30 frames NTSC) that the event is active.

8. Under Speed, set the type to Inherited, with a percentage value of 2000%. This large increase will "jump start" the droplets into a properly energetic dispersal.

9. Only a small amount of Variation will work here without disrupting the droplet, so set the Speed Variation to 3.

10. Set Divergence to 0, as even a small amount of randomness in the path of the particles will disrupt the stream.

11. Clear the Restart Particle Age check box. This is a very important step, as the increasing age of spawned particles will be used later to animate their scale.

12. This generator only needs to function for about 2/3 of a second, during which time it will spawn approximately 14 particles, so append an Age Test to the event. Set the Test Value to 20 and the Variation to 0.

13. When the generator particle is done, it needs to be deleted, so create a new Delete operator off to the right, name the event Delete Generator, and wire it to the Age Test (**Figures 17.57** and **17.58**).

This next event will be used to define the appearance of the droplets, and their motion while in free-fall.

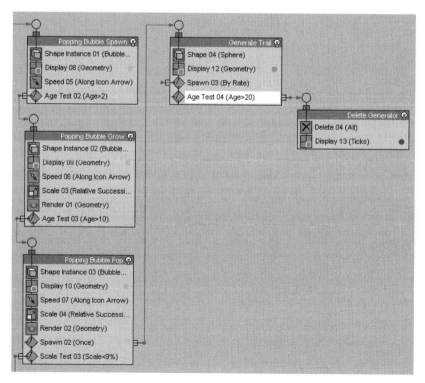

Figure 17.57 The Generate Trail event will spawn the actual droplets, after which the generator particle will be deleted.

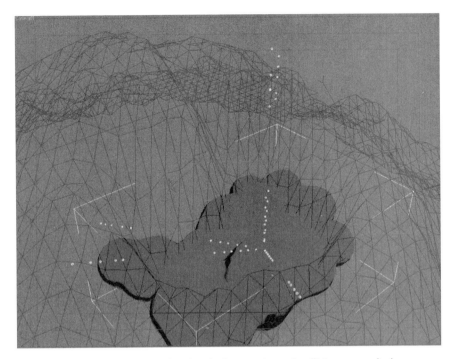

Figure 17.58   The spawned droplets, before gravity and collision are applied.

14. Create a new Scale operator event below the Generate Trail event, and name the new event Droplets Trail. Wire this event to the Spawn (By Rate) output.

You will animate the values in this Scale operator so that older particles are given a lower scale. This will create the effect of a diminishing droplet trail. It's important to note that this scale effect is difficult to apply without explicit keyframing, unless your particles are aged in a previous event.

15. Go to frame 0 and set all three Scale Factors to 190%.

16. Turn on the Auto Key button, go to frame 20, and set the Scale Factors to 10%. Turn the Auto Key button off.

17. Set the Animation Offset Keying to Particle Age. This will apply the animated scale factor to incoming particles based on their age (which in this case is based on how long the generator particle has been moving away from the parent bubble).

18. Set the Display Type to Geometry. Cloning this operator, as an instance, onto each of the successive "droplets" events to be created, will enable you to easily change the viewport preview of this effect.

19. Copy the Force operator and Collision (UDeflector01) test from the original Bubbling Lava event and paste them into the Droplets Trail event (**Figure 17.59**).

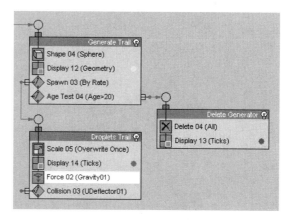

Figure 17.59   To replicate gravity and collision effects, copy operators from the original lava event.

20. The droplets need to be acted on with much more gravity to arc well, so set the Force operator's Influence percentage to 150%. The droplets should now arc nicely down toward the crater after their initial expulsion (**Figure 17.60**).

Once the droplets collide with the crater walls, they need to stick for a few ticks and then slide back down.

21. Create a new Speed operator event below the Droplets Trail event and name the new event Droplets Stick. Set the Speed to 0. Wire this event to the preceding Collision test.

22. Append an Age Test with a Test Value of 10 and Variation of 3 to provide pause for approximately 1/3 of a second.

23. Create a new Speed By Surface operator below the Droplets Stick event, and name the new event Droplets Slide. Set the Speed to 0.23. Wire this event to the preceding Age Test.

24. Under Surface Geometry, click the Add button and choose the volcano_collision mesh. (If this mesh was hidden earlier, it must be unhidden before it can be selected.) It may be simpler to select the Surface Geometry by using the By List button. Under Direction, choose Parallel To Surface. These settings will keep the particle attached to the surface object.

Figure 17.60   A strong gravity effect brings the lava droplets back down into the crater.

25. Copy the Force operator and Collision test from Droplets Trail and add it to the Droplets Slide event. The sliding droplets only need a small nudge from gravity, so set the Influence percentage to 3%.

26. Copy the Collision (POmniFlect01) test from the original Bubbling Lava event, and paste it into the bottom of the current event. This will catch any droplets that escape collision as they slide down.

27. Direct particles that test True into a delete event. Rename the new event Droplets Delete (**Figure 17.61**).

    At this point, the droplets still appear as spheres in the viewports, not meta-balls, because we have not linked them to the BlobMesh (**Figure 17.62**).

28. Before the droplets will be rendered as metaballs, they must be added to the BlobMesh. Add the following events to the BlobMesh's Particle Flow Events list: Droplets Trail, Droplets Stick, and Droplets Slide (**Figure 17.63**).

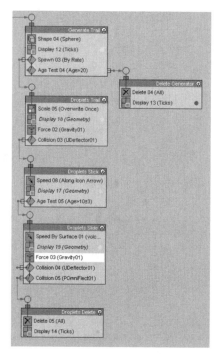

Figure 17.61   Droplets that escape collision with the crater will be deleted.

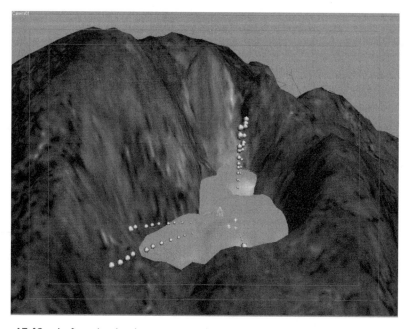

Figure 17.62   At first, the droplets appear in the viewport as spheres.

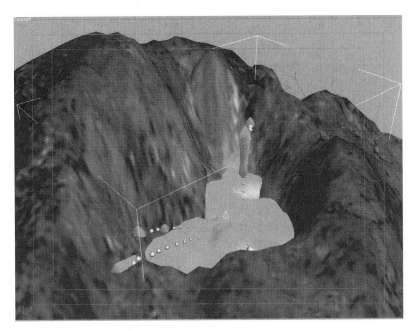

Figure 17.63   Once the droplets are linked to the BlobMesh, they appear as metaballs.

As the droplets slide down the crater walls, they will be reabsorbed into the lava mass. It is not necessary for you to add a delete event to get rid of the particles after they slide down into the metaball mass because they are not set to collide with the crater walls; just follow them until the gravity force pulls them through into the POmniFlect deflector you set up earlier, which will send them to be deleted anyway.

Smear Effect

In this section we will add an impact smear and a slide smear to the droplets, primarily through the use of the Shape Mark operator, which aligns particle shapes with a target object's surface.

1. Create a new Shape Mark operator to the right of the Droplets Stick event and name the new event Initial Smear. This event will be used to create an impact smear when the droplets first contact the crater wall.

2. In the Shape Mark's Properties panel, click the button under Contact Object and choose the Volcano mesh, as opposed to the collision mesh, which is a few units higher than the renderable volcano in order to keep more of the metaball drips visible.

Note

At this point you may be noticing some significant delays when editing the Particle Flow, particularly if the Time Slider is well into the animation. To reduce the recalculation of the flow with each change, you can go to frame 0 before applying changes to the flow or temporarily turn off the particle system.

3. Set Align To to Particle Z, which will keep the 2D particle shape flat against the surface of the volcano geometry, with its Z axis perpendicular to that surface.

4. Under Size, set the Width and Length dimensions to 45 units.

5. Surface Offset determines how far off the target object's surface the particle shape will be placed. The default setting of 0.001 is appropriate for very smooth surfaces, but for the rough volcano surface, a setting of 2 will ensure that most of the particle shape remains visible.

6. Set this event's Display operator Type to Geometry, so that the particle outlines will show up in the viewport once they have been spawned.

7. To control the spawning of this smear particle, insert a Spawn test into Droplets Stick, just before the final Age Test. The default Spawn settings will be fine—even Speed, since the droplets have been halted prior to the execution of this operator.

8. Wire the Spawn operator to the Initial Smear event (**Figure 17.64**).

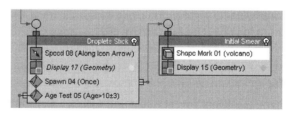

Figure 17.64 Once the droplets stick, the Spawn test will generate an impact smear particle.

If we scrub the Time Slider up to the first point that droplets impact the crater's surface, around frame 90, we will see one square particle outline appear in each frame where the droplets are sticking (**Figure 17.65**).

The smear particles will not render yet, as they have no materials and no renderable geometry.

Figure 17.65   The impact smear particles show up in viewports as 2D rectangles.

9. To add a material, append a Material Dynamic operator to Initial Smear. Material Dynamic supports animated materials, which can be timed to coincide with particle age.

10. Click the button under Assign Material and choose Mtl Editor (Material Editor) in the Browse From section of the Material/Map Browser. Select the Initial Smear material and click OK.

If we examine this material in the Material Editor, we will see that the operative portion of the material is its Opacity channel. The Gradient map which controls the material's opacity uses a Particle Age map to control the white (visible) portion of the gradient in the Color #3 slot. (The other two color slots are kept black [opaque] to keep the edges of the texture from rendering.) The Particle Age map applied to the Color #3 slot alters its output based on the age of the particle, expressed as a percentage. The first color (or assigned submaterial) is applied at birth, or 0% of total age. At a percentage of life span equal to Age #1, the output begins changing to the second color or submaterial slot. At Age #2, the output will be completely determined by the second slot. Similarly, at Age #3, the output will switch to the third slot.

The life span used by the Particle Age map is determined in the same Particle Flow event in which the Material Dynamic operator is evaluated. The most foolproof method is to use a Delete operator with the By Particle Age setting. This will inform Particle Flow as to the exact life span of the particle, and the Particle Age map will apply its age percentages to this value.

If the particle life span needs to extend beyond this event, simply use an Age Test or other test to send the particle to the next event. In this case, the Delete operator is being used to determine the life span for the Particle Age map, but it never actually deletes the particle.

 Note

Animated materials can be applied to particles using one of several methods—Particle Age maps, Particle MBlur maps, and animated textures such as .ifl (image file list) or .avi. Simply keyframing material changes in the Material Editor will not work.

11. To control the life span of the initial smear particle, append a Delete operator to the Initial Smear event.

12. Set it to delete particles By Particle Age, with a Life Span of 120 frames.

13. These particles will still not render without a Render action, so append one to the event. (This is in contrast to the metaball particles, which were rendered through BlobMesh, and so they did not require Render operators.)

If you render a frame from the Camera viewport later in the animation, around frame 240, when initial smear particles are being spawned, you should see them appear on the crater wall (**Figure 17.66**). These smears will slowly fade away, over 150 frames, according to the settings in the Particle Age map.

A second smear particle will follow the lava droplets as they slide down the crater walls.

Figure 17.66   The impact smears, rendered via 2D rectangular particles aligned to the crater's geometry.

14. Clone the Initial Smear event, as a Copy, into a new event below it, naming the new event Smear Shape.

15. Insert a Spawn test into the Droplets Slide event, before the final Collision test. Wire its output to the Smear Shape event.

16. Set this Spawn test to spawn By Travel Distance, with a Step Size of 15 (one particle emitted every 15 units of travel).

17. In the Smear Shape event's Shape Mark operator, elongate the smear particle by reducing the Width value to 20.

18. A different material is available for this effect. In the Material Dynamic operator, assign the Sliding Smear material.

19. This effect should fade out more quickly, so reduce the Life Span in the Delete operator to 100 frames.

20. A nice addition would be to shrink the smear particles, so insert a Scale operator, just before the Delete operator.

21. Set it to type Relative Successive, with all three Scale Factors set to 99%. For each integration step, the particles' scale should be reduced by 1% (**Figure 17.67**).

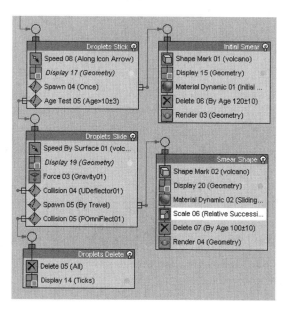

Figure 17.67   A second "smear" event is set up to create a sliding smear as the droplets move down the crater walls.

If you scrub the Time Slider, though, you will find this is not true. The smear particles are not shrinking, because the Scale operator is being overridden by the Shape Mark operator, which sets the scale as well.

22. Select the last four operators (Material Dynamic, Scale, Delete, and Render) and drag them out of the event into a new event below. Rename the new event Smear Trail.

23. Connect the two events by appending a Send Out test to Smear Shape and wiring the output to Smear Trail (**Figure 17.68**).

Scrub the Time Slider now to see the smear particles shrinking over time. Because the smear event has been split into two separate events, the conflict between the overlapping operators is resolved (**Figure 17.69**).

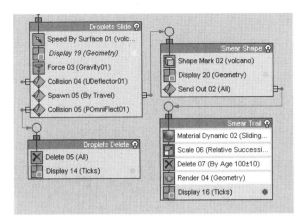

Figure 17.68   Moving the Scale operator into a new event keeps it from being overridden by the Shape Mark operator.

Figure 17.69   The droplets now leave impact smears and sliding smears.

Glow Effect

The final touch to add to this lava is a glow effect through Video Post. Because the lava is being rendered through BlobMesh, the effect will be applied to the metaball mesh, not to the individual particles.

> **Note**
>
> Particle Flow allows render effects to be applied on an event level, as opposed to the entire particle system. When assigning Object IDs for render effects, use the Object Properties dialog in Particle View (select an event, right-click its header, and choose Properties from the contextual menu), not the PF Source icon's Object Properties dialog.

1. Open Video Post (Rendering > Video Post).

2. Add a Scene Event, which by default will use the Camera viewport.

3. Add an Image Filter Event, specifically Lens Effects Glow.

4. In the Lens Effects Glow dialog, go to the Preferences tab and set the Effect Size to 20 and Color Intensity to 15.

   Note on the Properties tab that the source of this effect in the scene is selected by default by Object ID #1.

5. Click OK to close the dialog, and return to Video Post. At this point, the Video Post setup is complete for applying a glow effect, but adding an Image Output Event is required to render this scene to a movie file.

6. Add an Image Output Event to the Queue. Note that the name of the Image Output Event will reflect the filename assigned to the rendered movie. For rendering stills, clear the Enabled check box in the Edit Image Output Event dialog (**Figure 17.70**).

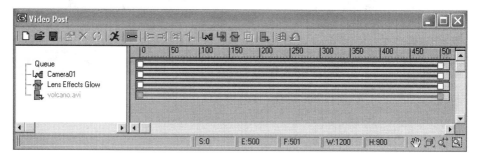

Figure 17.70 A simple Video Post sequence is used to add a glow effect.

7. Select the BlobMesh object in a viewport; right-click it and choose Object Properties. In the Object Properties dialog, set the G-Buffer Object Channel to 1.

Execute the Video Post Sequence to see a glow effect added to the lava (**Figure 17.71**).

Figure 17.71   The final lava effect.

   Tip

When rendering stills through Video Post, the actual frame rendered is determined by the Single value in the Execute Video Post dialog, not by the position of the Time Slider.

There we have it, the completed lava effect. It may seem like a complex system, but by setting it up in Particle Flow, we have complete control over each aspect: the speed of the lava's boiling, the size of swelling bubbles, the length of time each lava smear lasts, and every other property. This flexible approach to particle system setup gives us the freedom to duplicate particle emissions or just parts of the system, reuse the setup for similar effects, or expand on any segment of it.

Taking Your Exercises Further

If you wish to continue your exploration of Particle Flow in this exercise, consider the following challenges:

- When the lava droplets land on the side of the volcano, generate a lasting flame there, with a rising column of smoke.

- As each gas bubble pops, cause it to emit a rolling puff of colored steam that expands and fades from view as it rises.

- Cause the level of the lava pool to rise over time until some lava escapes over the lip of the volcanic crater.

Summing Up

The particle effects applied in this chapter have obvious uses beyond lava. Most any sort of liquid can be simulated with the combination of Particle Flow and BlobMesh. The use of Shape Mark operators would suggest itself for the creation of ink stains on linen, high-tide marks on a sea wall, or even a CG character's "milk mustache." The various sorts of colliding and bouncing behaviors could be used for any sort of constrained, viscous substance—oil in a tanker's hold, for example, or a cup of coffee in your hand.

The lessons learned should give you a fundamental basis for using Particle Flow for nearly any particle task. Creating a vast nest of hatching insects is a challenge similar to making a pool of popping gas bubbles. Spawning a spray of droplets from an expiring particle employs the same basic technique as casting chunks of flaming debris from a rocket's crash landing. If you can cause a dripping lava droplet to leave a trailing smear, you can certainly have your graffiti artist character leave an accurate spray pattern on a wall.

Particle Flow greatly expands the capability for customizing particles in 3ds max. Particles can be directed into very specific behaviors based on their own properties or scene conditions. As long as you are willing to deal with the extra CPU overhead required, extensive particle engines can be devised in the intuitive interface of the Particle View editor. Keep in mind, though, that Super Spray and Blizzard are still capable, though non-event-driven, particle systems, and when the functionality of those systems is sufficient, their lower demand on system resources makes them attractive choices. But when highly customized, behavior-driven particles are required, Particle Flow is the obvious choice.

Next, we will explore more deeply the use of Particle Flow for special effects and scripted behaviors, while employing non-event-driven particle systems when most appropriate.

Chapter 18

Particle Effects

By Sean Bonney

As we saw in the previous chapter, the particle capabilities in 3ds max 7 allow for an open-ended customization of particle behaviors. Creating a school of flying fish, for example, that trail purple smoke and explode into a cloud of tiny fish clones is simply a matter of building the proper Particle Flow setup. But what if we want those fish to change color or reverse direction when they approach a boat that has a changing path? Or if we need that boat to lower its anchor when a particle fish jumps over it? We will explore these sorts of complex relationships in this chapter.

In these exercises, you will build on your Particle Flow skills to create a more elaborate set of effects centered on a biplane navigating a stormy sky, replete with lightning and pyrotechnic elements. The event-driven nature of Particle Flow will come much more heavily into play through the use of custom particle scripting, with particle events directing scene objects and scene interaction controlling particle generation. The particle systems created in this tutorial will be fairly elaborate, and they will require several strategies to manage the CPU overhead needed for their calculation and for keeping the scene manageable.

In this tutorial, you will explore the following:

- Trail effects
- Electrical effects
- Smoke and fire effects
- Branching geometrical particles
- Event-specific Video Post effects
- Scripting for event interaction and control
- Using non-event-driven particles for simple effects
- Managing complex scenes with particle caches

Let's begin by examining the scene and applying an initial effect.

Flight Path

When animating a flying jet, diving eagle, or swinging cutlass, you can enhance the path and momentum of the moving object by adding a visible trail, which often appears as a ghostlike repetition of the original object. In the following section, we will make the swooping path of the biplane more dramatic with a striated trail.

Leaving a Trail

1. Open the max file lightning_begin.max on the accompanying DVD.

   This scene contains a grouped biplane model that has been constrained to a spline path through the scene, beginning in the distance, approaching the camera, and then looping and diving away (**Figure 18.1**). Lightning will strike near the biplane several times and then strike it directly around frame 275, resulting in an explosion of sparks and a trail of fire and smoke.

   If you scrub the Time Slider, you will note that the scene contains three lightning meshes. Two of them are placed vertically in the scene, and they animate identically. A third lightning bolt is keyed to always point to the biplane. These three objects will be used later in this chapter as helpers.

   The first effect we will create is a motion trail caused by the passage of the biplane along its path. Examine the mesh object "trail emitter," which is a child of the Plane group (**Figure 18.2**). This simple mesh will be used to emit trail particles from the biplane's wings and tail. The Renderable check box in this object's Properties dialog has been cleared to ensure that it does not appear in renders.

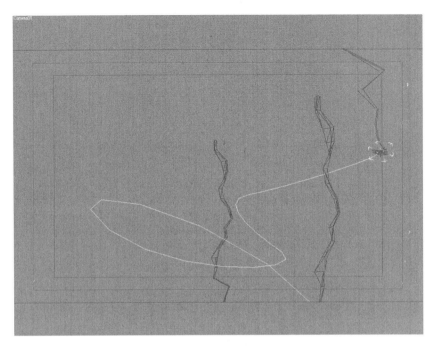

Figure 18.1   The starting point for this tutorial—a biplane constrained to a flight path, and several lightning meshes. The biplane is based on an original mesh by Chris O'Riley.

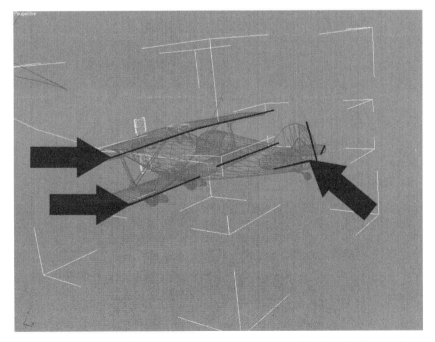

Figure 18.2   A simple mesh will be used to emit a motion-based trail effect as the biplane travels.

2. Open Particle View and create a new Standard Flow (right-click in the Event panel, and from the contextual menu, choose New > Particle System > Standard Flow). By default, the PF Source icon will be created at World coordinates (0,0,0). This is not significant, as the icon will not be used to position particles.

3. Rename the global source event Flight Path and the birth event Trail Birth.

4. The emission of particles from this source will be at high speed, so in order to avoid "puffing" from coarse frame evaluation, go to the icon's System Management rollout and set both the Viewport and Render Integration Steps to ¼ Frame. These settings will now be automatically applied to newly created source icons during the current max session.

5. A high number of particles will be necessary for this effect, so set the Birth operator to generate 10,000 particles over frames 0–300.

6. Go to frame 0 to ensure that you won't have to wait for max to update the scene as you make changes. The particles need to be generated from the biplane's trailing edges, so replace the Position Icon operator with a Position Object operator. Check the Inherit Emitter Movement box to ensure that particles are always generated from the emitter's updated position.

Note

It is a good practice to return to frame 0 whenever you're making changes to your particle flow, particularly if your setup is complex and/or deals with a high number of particles. This will reduce the lag as max recalculates the flow and will avoid possible crashes.

7. Add a trail emitter to the Emitter Objects list (**Figure 18.3**).

   If you scrub the Time Slider, you will see a continuous trail of nondecaying particles being emitted from the biplane as it flies through the scene (**Figure 18.4**).

8. Reduce the particle Speed to 130.

9. The default setting of the Rotation operator will randomly orient each particle, but that's not the effect we need. To have the trail particles aligned instead along the emitter geometry's surface normals (which will give the effect of following the flight path), set the Orientation Matrix to Speed Space.

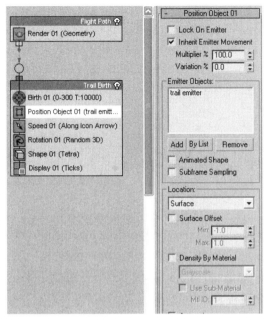

Figure 18.3   The beginnings of a particle setup to generate a motion trail.

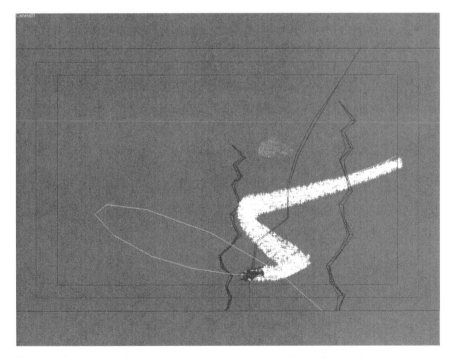

Figure 18.4   A simple nondecaying trail follows the biplane's flight path.

10. The actual particles to be emitted will use instanced geometry, so replace the Shape operator with a Shape Instance. Assign the object "trail geometry" as the Particle Geometry Object. This mesh consists of two quad polys at right angles. Once mapped with a two-sided material, it will look like a volumetric object from most angles (**Figure 18.5**).

Note

> In complex scenes utilizing large numbers of particles, use the simplest particle shape possible to keep the scene from bogging down.

To preview the effect of using this instanced shape, change the Display type to Geometry and scrub the Time Slider. It may be difficult to see the particles unless you zoom in using a Perspective viewport.

11. Initially, the particles will not be aligned properly. They seem to be perpendicular to the flight path (**Figure 18.6**).

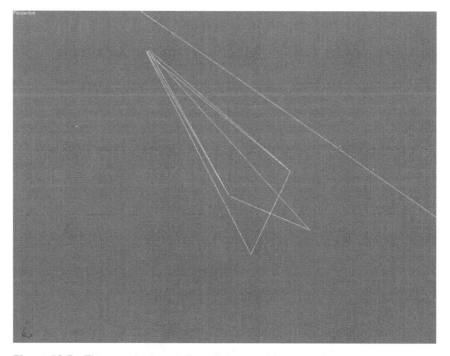

Figure 18.5 This particle shape is basically a pair of facing quad polys joined at right angles.

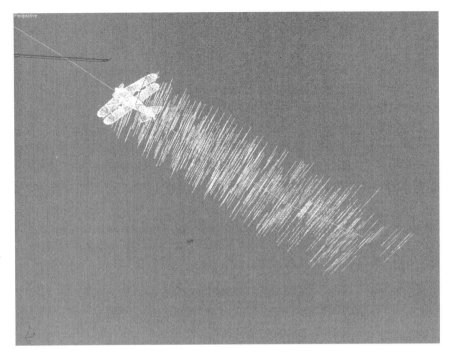

Figure 18.6   The trail particles are not following the path, due to the order of event operators.

To correct the particle orientation, move the Speed operator to a position in the event after the Rotation operator. Because the rotation of the particles is based on the vector at which particles are emitted, the rotation relationship needs to be established before the particle speed is determined (**Figure 18.7**).

12. To reduce the viewport complexity of these particles, set the Display type to Lines.

13. I've created a fading material for this effect, so append a Material Dynamic operator and assign the Trail Vapor material.

14. The opacity of this material is keyed to particle age (**Figure 18.8**), so specify a particle life span by appending a Delete operator. Select By Particle Age, with a Life Span of 50 and a Variation of 10 (**Figure 18.9**).

This quick effect shows how easy it is to underscore the motion of any object, from speeding Jeep to twirling fairy, with a properly aligned trail. In the next section we will get into the more splashy part of this scene, when we explore electrical effects.

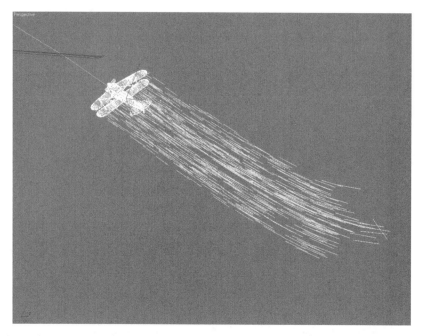

Figure 18.7   Once the operators are reordered, the particles follow the path as expected.

Figure 18.8   The trail now fades as the particles age.

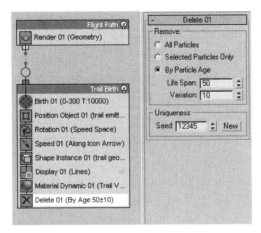

Figure 18.9   The completed particle setup for the trail effect.

Electricity

In the world of special effects, one of the most exciting tasks is simulating electricity. Whether it's in short-circuiting robots, *Matrix*-style ship propulsion, or downed power lines, electricity has a power to fascinate and induce fear, and this power can be exploited with great flexibility using Particle Flow. The primary electrical effect we will explore in this scene is a series of lightning strikes.

Triggering Lightning with Scene Objects

In this section, we will create a quick lightning strike, which will be triggered by the near-collision of objects within the scene. The technique used to trigger this lightning bolt is straightforward and could easily be expanded into any application where scene objects need to control particle effects, such as sparks flying from two colliding heavy objects.

1. Scrub the Time Slider and note that the biplane's path takes it near the two vertical lightning bolts. These meshes will serve as helper objects in this exercise, to guide the generation of particle lightning. The trigger for these two bolts of lightning will be movement within the scene, specifically the approach of the biplane. A spherical deflector will be attached to the biplane, and its collision with the particle source icons will trigger the effect.

Note

One straightforward method for triggering or influencing particles from scene objects is a collision test.

2. Go to a Top viewport and create an SDeflector space warp (found in the Create panel > Space Warps > Deflectors > SDeflector) with a diameter of 70,000 units (**Figure 18.10**). The initial location of the space warp is not important.

3. Align the deflector with the Plane group, with each of its World axis positions and Local axis orientations (**Figure 18.11**).

4. Use the Select and Link tool to link the deflector to the Plane group. Scrub the Time Slider to observe that the deflector follows the biplane's position and orientation throughout the animation.

5. In Particle View, create an Empty Flow and a birth event, renaming the source event Lightning01 and the birth event Lightning Birth01. Wire the two events together.

6. In any viewport, select the Lightning01 source icon and Align its X axis, Y axis, and Z axis pivot points to the pivot point of lightning geometry01. Do not align on any axis of orientation.

7. To make the icon more visible in the Camera viewport, go to the Modify panel and set the icon's length and width to 6000 units (**Figure 18.12**).

8. Set the Viewport Quantity Multiplier to 100%. There is not much performance gain to be had here, as the lightning effect will be produced with a relatively small number of particles.

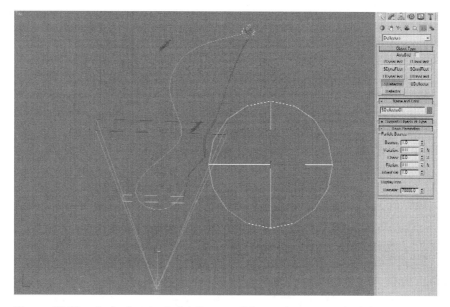

Figure 18.10   A simple spherical deflector will be used to trigger the lightning.

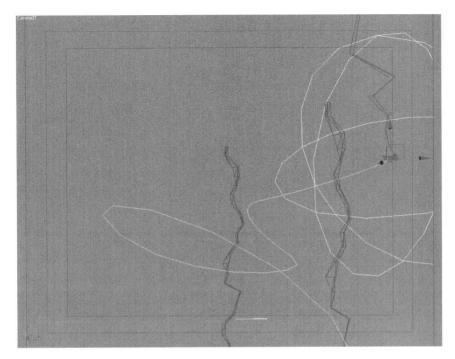

Figure 18.11   Align the deflector with the biplane.

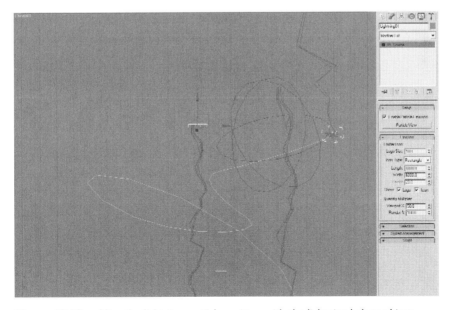

Figure 18.12   Align the lightning particle emitter with the lightning helper object.

9. In the Birth operator, set the system to generate a single particle at frame 0.

10. Append a Position Icon operator and specify Pivot as the Location. This single particle will wait to be triggered by the biplane's spherical deflector.

11. Append a Collision Spawn test, and add SDeflector01 to the Deflector list (**Figure 18.13**).

12. Create a new Shape Instance operator below the Lightning Birth01 event, renaming the new event Lightning Main Bolt01. Wire the new event to the Collision Spawn test.

13. Specify lightning geometry01 as the Particle Geometry Object, and turn on Animated Shape.

14. To preview the shape in viewports, change the Display type to Geometry.

    If you scrub the Time Slider in the Camera viewport, you will see the instanced lightning mesh spawn around frame 35 and then proceed out of the frame to the left. This is because of a speed setting in the Collision Spawn test (**Figure 18.14**).

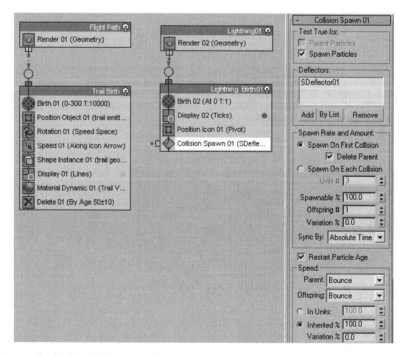

Figure 18.13   The lightning particle flow begins with a single particle, waiting for a collision to trigger the effect.

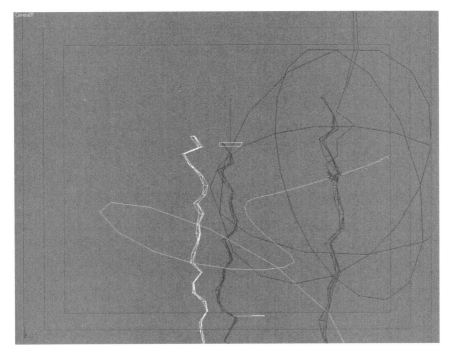

Figure 18.14   The Collision Spawn test's default settings will bounce the lightning bolt away from the deflector.

15. Under Speed, set Offspring to Continue, so that it will not be deflected by the collision. In this way, the deflector acts as a trigger without changing the particle's speed or direction.

Now when the Time Slider is scrubbed, the lightning bolt remains, and animates, at the source icon's location. The particle's animation, however, does not match the helper's. This is because the age of the spawned particle doesn't match up with the animation frame number (**Figure 18.15**).

16. To correct this problem, clear the Restart Particle Age check box in the Collision Spawn test so that the spawned particle will inherit the parent particle's age.

17. In the source icon's System Management rollout, set the Render Integration Step to 1 Tick. This will cause the particle evaluation to be updated for renders at the same rate as that of the animated helper object, at the cost of additional computational time.

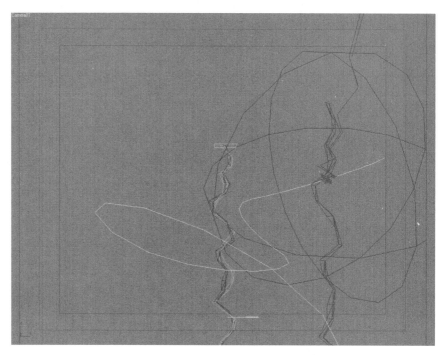

Figure 18.15   The particle lightning bolt's animation does not sync with that of the helper object.

18. This bolt only needs to be displayed for a very short time, about a third of a second, so append an Age test to the Lightning Main Bolt01 event to test Event Age against a Test Value of 10 frames, with a Variation of 0.

19. Create a new Delete event below the Lightning Main Bolt01 event, rename it Lightning Delete01, and wire it to the Age test. Delete the unneeded Display operator. Note that, in this setup, it is not possible to use a Delete By Particle Age operator because the particle's age has not been reset, and it would already be greater than the test value by the time the test was evaluated (**Figure 18.16**).

At this point in the tutorial, the main bolt of lightning has been set up to be triggered by the biplane's approach and to last for just a fraction of a second. We will continue in the next section to enhance the lightning itself.

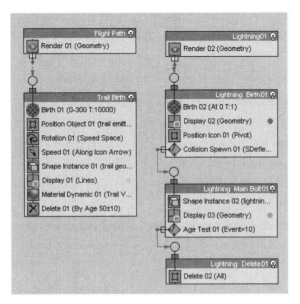

Figure 18.16   The main lightning bolt flow with Birth, Collision Trigger, and Delete By Event Age.

Branched Lightning

To make the lightning appear more complex, we need to duplicate the instanced lightning bolt along the length of the original. This will create a random branching effect. Placing particles along the surface of an instanced geometry particle is not possible in Particle Flow without heavy scripting, so the helper lightning mesh will be used again. This is why the syncing of the particle and the helper in rendering is so important—with a render integration step larger than 1 Tick, the branching bolts would not connect properly with the main bolt.

1. Insert a Spawn test just before the Age test. Set it to generate 12 Offspring, and set Variation to 20. Once again, the Restart Particle Age check box needs to be cleared to keep the animation in sync.

2. Copy the Shape Instance operator into a new event, and rename the event Lightning Branch01.

3. Reduce the Scale in the new Shape Instance operator to 30%, and set Variation to 50%.

4. To place the branching bolts along the main one, add a Position Object operator. Turn on Lock On Emitter, and add lightning geometry01 to the list of Emitter Objects.

5. Also turn on Animated Shape and Subframe Sampling.

6. To have branching bolts emitted only from the points along the main bolt where the geometry turns, change Location to Vertices.

7. Change the Display type to Geometry. If you scrub the Time Slider, you will see smaller bolts spawn along the length of the main one. They may appear to be disconnected, but keep in mind that their placement will sync up in renders (**Figure 18.17**).

8. To orient these branches randomly, add a Rotation operator. The default Orientation Matrix Random 3D will randomly point the branches away from their emitter points.

9. To cause the branches to die out when the main bolt does, clone the Age test, using Instance as the method, to the end of the Lightning01 Branch event. Making these operators instances allows the bolt duration to be changed easily from one operator.

10. Wire the Age test output to the Lightning Delete01 event (**Figure 18.18**).

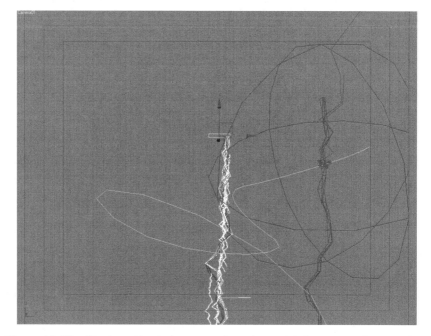

Figure 18.17   The branching bolts appear along the main bolt, spawning from random vertices.

At this point, the lightning bolt is set up to be triggered by the approaching biplane and to generate a branching electrical bolt (**Figure 18.19**). In the next section, we will add an electrical corona of sorts to simulate the charged particles that we imagine are generated by a powerful bolt of electricity.

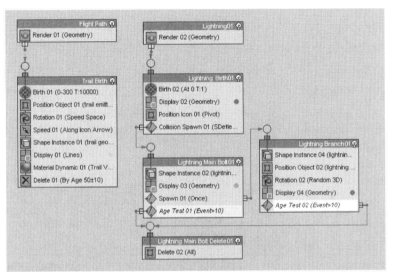

Figure 18.18   The particle setup for the lightning bolt and branching bolts.

Figure 18.19   The branching-lightning-bolt effect.

Expanding Electrical Field

Once the lightning bolt is triggered, a field of charged particles will be emitted and will rapidly disperse. While this effect is perhaps not true to the visuals of real-life lightning, we are expressing the power and style of lightning in this tutorial, and so we'll explicitly create this effect.

1. Insert another Spawn test into Lightning Main Bolt01, before the Age test. Set it to spawn 1000 offspring, and set Variation to 15%.

2. Create a new event consisting of a Shape Facing operator, and rename the event Electrical Field01. Wire the new event to the Spawn test.

3. Choose the Camera01 (not its target) as the Look At Object.

4. Set the Size/Width to In Screen Space, using a 1% Proportion and Variation set to 20%.

5. Before the particles show up, they must have a position set, so add a Position Object operator.

6. Add lightning geometry01 to the list of Emitter Objects, and turn on Animated Shape and Subframe Sampling.

7. To spawn the particles in a cloud around the bolt, turn on Surface Offset, and set the Minimum offset to 250 units and the Maximum offset to 1000 units.

8. The particles need to rapidly disperse after spawning, so add a Speed operator. Set Speed to 5000 units, Variation to 3000, and Direction to Random Horizontal (**Figure 18.20**).

   If you scrub the Time Slider, the particle field spawns in a cluster along the body of the main bolt and rapidly disperses along the World XY plane (**Figure 18.21**).

   The final aspect of the dispersing particles to create is a fade effect. The particles will shrink and become less opaque as they disperse.

9. Append a Send Out test to Electrical Field01.

10. Create a new event consisting of a Material Dynamic operator, rename the event Fade Field01, and wire it to the Send Out test.

11. Assign the material Lightning Corona. This material's opacity is keyed to particle age, becoming more transparent as the end of the particles' life span approaches.

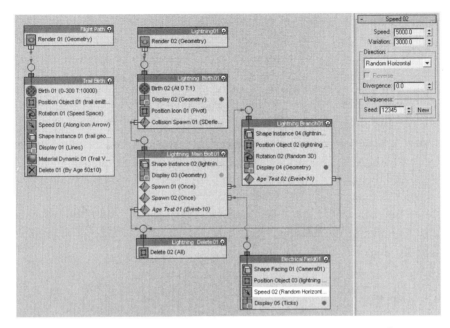

Figure 18.20   The lightning bolt will now spawn a cloud of energetic particles.

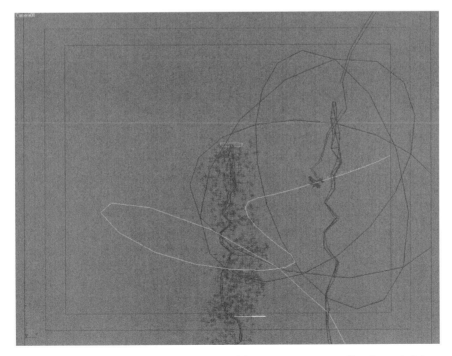

Figure 18.21   A cloud of particles is emitted from an area surrounding the main lightning bolt and rapidly disperses.

12. To shrink the particles as well, add a Scale operator, set its Type to Relative Successive, and set all three Scale Factors to 98%. This rescaling effect is the reason for separating the field fade into a separate event; otherwise, the Scale operator would conflict with the scale settings in the Shape Facing operator.

13. To specify the particle's life span, append a Delete operator, set to delete By Particle Age, with a Life Span of 15 frames and a Variation of 5 (**Figure 18.22**).

14. The lightning bolt will now display three distinct phases: the initial strike (**Figure 18.23**), the strike with electrical field (**Figure 18.24**), and the lingering electrical field (**Figure 18.25**).

In this tutorial, care has been taken to keep the particle setup controlled parametrically. The triggering of the lightning could easily be changed to another time or another deflector, and every subsequent event would follow naturally.

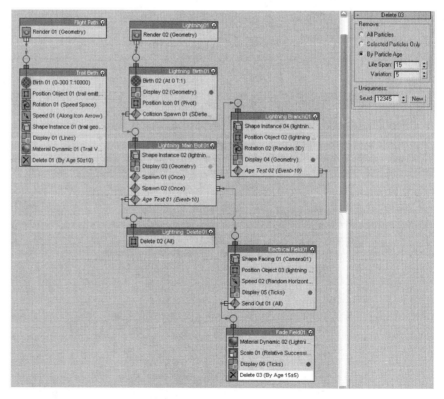

Figure 18.22   The completed lightning bolt particle setup.

Figure 18.23   The first stage of the lightning bolt.

Figure 18.24   The second stage, with electrical field.

Figure 18.25   The third stage, with lingering electrical field.

Particle Caches

If you scrub the Time Slider through the triggering of the lightning bolt, you will notice a small hitch in the refresh rate due to the particle calculations involved. While this lag may be barely noticeable at this point in the chapter, as more effects are added, the delay will rapidly increase.

There are several ways to manage this, including turning off particle flows (either through Particle View or the PF Source icon), reducing the Viewport Quantity Multiplier, reducing the percentage of particles visible through Display operators, and setting Display types to Dot or Tick wherever possible. The most effective method, however, while keeping particles active is a particle cache.

The Cache operator stores the many calculations required by Particle Flow, so that when a scene is played back (in viewports, at render, or both), the stored values are used instead of being reevaluated.

1. Return to the global Lightning01 event and append a Cache operator.

2. Set it to be used at Viewport/Render and to update manually.

3. To maintain sync with the settings in the source icon, set Sampling to Integration Step.

4. Click the Update button under Manual Update.

   The Particle View window will disappear, and the scene will play through in the viewport from beginning to end, which will take a few moments. When the process is completed, all of the particle calculations necessary for the scene will be stored in the Cache operator. This will speed up the playback of this part of the effect.

 Note

Unless Particle Caches are set to update automatically, they will not reflect future changes to the events they encompass, so be sure to update if the particle setup is changed.

Now that the first lightning bolt has been tweaked and polished, let's create an identical bolt to be associated with the second helper bolt.

Duplicating Particle Setups

Given that a second vertical lightning bolt helper exists in the scene, it seems obvious that we should duplicate the lightning particle setup from the first lightning bolt. The modular nature of Particle View makes cloning particle setups pretty easy, after considering a few minor caveats.

1. Select all seven events associated with the first bolt and clone them, using Copy as the method.

   Any of the test output handles that were repositioned from their default location will need be moved again, as this information is not conveyed with the cloning operation.

2. Any references to lightning geometry01 will need to be updated to refer to lightning geometry02, specifically two Shape Instance operators and two Position Object operators.

3. In the viewport, select the Lightning02 PF Source emitter and align its X-axis, Y-axis, and Z-axis pivot points to the pivot point of lightning geometry02 using the Align tool.

If you scrub the Time Slider, both lightning effects will be triggered at the same moment, even though the deflector has not reached the second source icon. This is due to the Cache operator, which contains information about the frame at which the deflector triggered the first source icon. When you duplicated the Cache operator, the particle information stored in it was duplicated as well, and is being applied to the duplicate bolt.

4. Select the Cache operator for the second lightning bolt and click its Update button. Once the update is complete, the second bolt should trigger around frame 130.

5. Repeat steps 1–3 to create the particle setup for the third lightning bolt. The third bolt will work a little differently, so delete its Cache operator and Collision Spawn test (**Figure 18.26**).

   It will not be necessary to update the caches again, unless changes are made to the events they cover. Note that the caches are empty when the file is reopened, unless Save Cache With File is checked. This option, however, can very quickly inflate file sizes.

In this next section, we will further explore the use of scripts in Particle Flow to control the third lightning bolt.

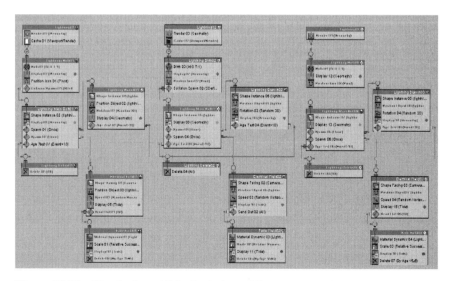

Figure 18.26 The duplicated lightning-bolt particle setups.

Triggering Lightning with Scripts

A third lightning bolt is evident in the scene, one that follows the position of the biplane throughout the scene. This bolt will actually strike the biplane and spark an explosive reaction.

Rather than using a collision trigger, we'll use a script to explicitly force the frame on which the lightning bolt fires. Particle scripting employs many of the same conventions and variables that are used in MAXScript, with the addition of parameters and controls for nearly every aspect of particles.

Particle script operators are evaluated differently from other operators in that they are immediately examined at the beginning of an animation, even if they appear to be restricted to later evaluation due to an Age test, for example. Therefore, scripts need to take into account the possibility that they will be run before any particles have even been birthed or before the particles they are intended to operate on have arrived in the proper event.

In addition, scripts are only evaluated at render time if they are located in an event that contains renderable particles, meaning at least one birthed particle with Render, Shape, and Position operators.

Particle Flow scripts have a particle-specific focus on time. Controlling particle age within a script is very straightforward; however, accessing scene time is more difficult. The usual global variable for scene time, currentTime, will only be accurate during viewport playbacks. During renders, this global is not passed to Particle Flow. A typical workaround is to birth a particle at frame 0 and use its age for scene time.

Initially, we will use a placeholder particle's age to track scene time and compare it against a specified frame for triggering the final lightning strike.

1. Create a new Standard Flow, naming the global event Script Flow and the birth event Script Holder.

2. Set this system to birth one particle at frame 0.

3. The Speed and Rotation operators are unneeded, so delete them (**Figure 18.27**).

Figure 18.27   A bare particle setup to support a particle script.

4. To ensure that the particle does not appear in the scene, select the Script Flow PF Source icon and move it –20,000 units on its Z axis.

5. Append a Script operator to Script Holder, and click the Edit Script button to open the Script Editor. The default script can appear intimidating, primarily because of the wide range of operations and variables allowed. The majority of the default script consists of commented lines, so any line beginning with "—" is not an operational portion of the script.

   - **The ChannelsUsed** section refers to properties of the particle that will need to be passed to the script. The Speed of this particle is not significant, so delete the line `pCont.useSpeed = true`.

   - **The Proceed** section contains the basis of the script's operations. Delete the sample script, leaving only the leading and trailing parentheses.

6. Replace the deleted script with the following text (**Figure 18.28**):

   ```
   persistent global StrikeFrame = 275
   ```

   This declaration creates a variable named `StrikeFrame` and assigns it the value 275. Prefacing the declaration with the terms `persistent` and `global` will make this variable persist when the scene is reopened and make it accessible to other scripts in the scene. This is the point where you can specify on which frame the third lightning bolt will strike the biplane, triggering the explosion.

Note

The completed script is available as a text file on the accompanying DVD as lightning_strike_script_final.txt.

7. To check your script for syntax errors, go to File > Evaluate All.

8. Close the window to return to Particle View. It is not necessary to save the script; it is automatically stored in the Script operator.

9. Return to the Lightning03 particle flow. Since the Collision test was deleted, there is nothing to trigger the effect at this point. Append a Script test to Lightning Birth03 and click the Edit Script button. Like the Script operator, the Script test operator contains a default test.

10. Remove the lines specifying the Time and Position channels in the ChannelsUsed section and replace them with `pCont.useAge = true` so that the particle's age channel will be available to the test.

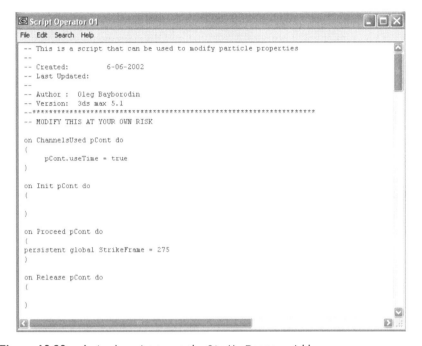

Figure 18.28   A simple script to set the `StrikeFrame` variable.

11. Replace the sample script in the Proceed section with the following:
```
if (pCont.NumParticles() > 0) AND (pCont.particleAge >
StrikeFrame ) then
(
pCont.particleTestStatus = true
)
```

Tip

Consider evaluating your script whenever you make changes, to check for simple typographical errors that might prevent your script from functioning properly.

The first line of this test script contains a Boolean test, which will allow the rest of the script to execute only if both subtests pass. The first test requires that there be at least one particle in the flow, and the second test requires that the current age of the particle (which should be equal to the scene time) is greater than the value stored in `StrikeFrame` (**Figure 18.29**).

If these subtests pass, then the test status is set to true, meaning that any particles passed to it will continue on to the event wired to the test's output. Now let's continue.

12. Wire the Script test's output to Lightning Main Bolt03.
13. If you render a still at frame 276, the third bolt can now be seen striking the biplane (**Figure 18.30**).
14. Clone the Cache operator from Lightning02 to Lightning03 and update the cache. Note that the script test results are cached as well, so if `StrikeFrame` is changed, then the cache will need to be updated or turned off before the new value is used.
15. Feel free to hide the three lightning geometry helpers now to unclutter the display.

In this section, we have used scripts and script tests to pass and evaluate a user-defined variable and control particle behavior. This is just one of many possibilities for explicitly defining event-driven particles with scripting. Any time you wish to accomplish something unusual with Particle Flow, such as particle rain clouds whose movement is synced with a shaman's dancing, consider particle scripting. In the next few tutorials, we will use the same script test to spark several explosive effects.

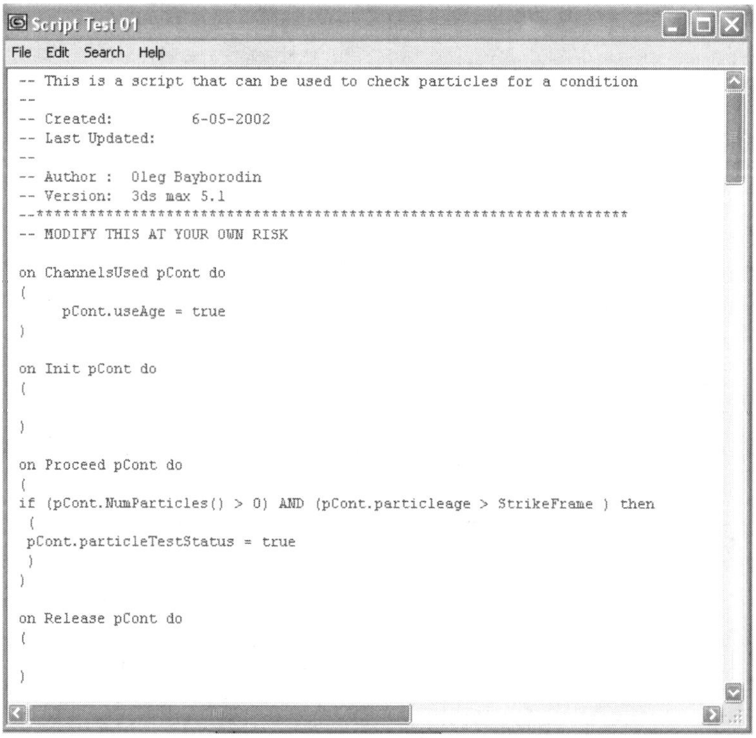


```
-- This is a script that can be used to check particles for a condition
--
-- Created:        6-05-2002
-- Last Updated:
--
-- Author :  Oleg Bayborodin
-- Version:  3ds max 5.1
--***********************************************************************
-- MODIFY THIS AT YOUR OWN RISK

on ChannelsUsed pCont do
(
    pCont.useAge = true
)

on Init pCont do
(

)

on Proceed pCont do
(
if (pCont.NumParticles() > 0) AND (pCont.particleage > StrikeFrame ) then
 (
 pCont.particleTestStatus = true
 )
)

on Release pCont do
(

)
```

Figure 18.29 A Script test to check that `StrikeFrame` has passed.

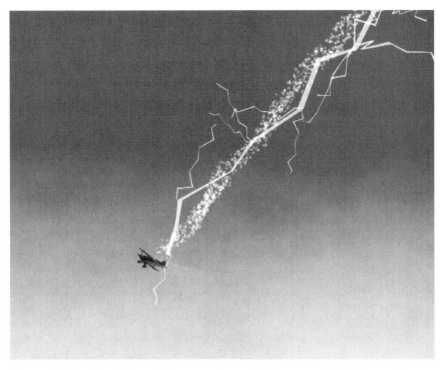

Figure 18.30   The lightning bolt now strikes at the frame specified in the particle script.

Fire

This section will appeal to your pyromaniac instincts, as we explore several techniques for creating fire effects with Particle Flow—from tiny sparks to explosive flames.

Exploding Sparks

The source for several fiery effects will be an emitter attached to the biplane itself, so we need to create and attach a properly aligned emitter.

1. Create a new Standard Flow in Particle View, renaming the global event Lightning Strike and the birth event Sparks.

2. The birth event will be separated from the rest of the flow with a Script test, so drag the Speed, Shape, and Display operators into a new event, named Sparks Fly.

3. Set the Position operator to emit from its surface, and turn on Lock On Emitter.

4. The Rotation operator is not needed, so delete it.

5. Clone the Script test from Lightning Birth03 to the end of Sparks, using Instance as the method.

6. Wire the Script test output to Sparks Fly.

7. Like the big lightning strike, the explosion of sparks will be triggered when StrikeFrame is reached.

8. Set the Birth operator to generate 100 particles, beginning and ending with frame 0.

9. Set the Speed operator to 2500 units, with a Variation of 35. For a wide dispersal of sparks, set Divergence to its maximum value of 180 degrees.

10. The default Tetra shape is fine, but increase its Size to 100 units. When viewed at short distances, the tetra particles may not appear very realistic, but at the camera's viewing range, they will stand out nicely.

11. Append a Material Dynamic operator to the Sparks Fly event. Assign Fire Sparks to the material slot, and turn on Reset Particle Age.

12. Finally, define a life span to be used in the material by appending a Delete operator, set to remove particles by age, with a Life Span of 40 and a Variation of 10 (**Figure 18.31**).

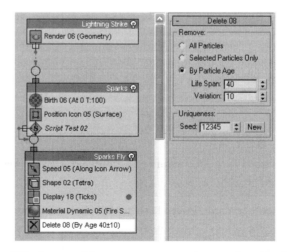

Figure 18.31   This short particle setup generates a shower of sparks when triggered.

If you scrub the Time Slider at this point, the sparks will appear near the top center of the Camera viewport because the source icon is still in its default location.

13. Select the Lightning Strike PF Source icon, and use the Align tool to align its World X, Y, and Z Center Positions, as well as X-, Y-, and Z-Axis Orientations, to "plane target."

The biplane target object is a nonrendering dummy used to specify the center of the lightning strike and ensuing fiery effects.

14. Set the source icon's Icon Type to Circle, with a diameter of 400 units.

15. Use the Select and Link tool to link the source icon to "plane target" (**Figure 18.32**).

Now when you scrub the Time Slider, the sparks should emanate just after StrikeFrame has passed (**Figure 18.33**). Since the moment of impact has been marked visually, in the next section we will add burn marks to the biplane. Typically, this effect would be achieved with an animated material, but to keep this tutorial in Particle Flow, we will use particles.

Figure 18.32   Link the source icon to the biplane as the emitter for explosive effects.

Figure 18.33   A shower of sparks is emitted at the moment of impact. (Lightning03 turned off for clarity.)

Scorch Marks

In this section, a burnt area will be created on the biplane's upper wing by virtue of the Shape Mark operator. The Shape Mark operator is a handy tool whenever you need to place stains, impact craters, or scorch marks on a target object.

1. Clone the Sparks birth event, using Copy as the method; name the new event Scorch; and wire it to the Lightning Strike global event.

2. Set the Birth Amount to 1.

3. Reclone the Script test from Sparks to Scorch, using Instance as the method this time, so that your flexibility in updating the script is retained. Note that you are overwriting the existing Script test in the Scorch event.

4. Create a new Shape Mark operator event below Scorch, naming the new event Scorch Mark. Wire it to the Script test's output.

5. Set the Size, in World Units, to a width and length of 1000 units.

6. Set the Surface Offset to 2 units.

7. Before the upper wing of the biplane can be chosen as the contact object, the Plane group must be opened. Select the Plane group and choose Group > Open.

8. In the Shape Mark operator, assign Wings as the Contact Object.

9. Close the Plane Group (Group > Close).

10. Add a Material Static operator to Scorch Mark, and choose the Fire Scorch material (**Figure 18.34**).

Now that the scorch mark is in place (**Figure 18.35**), we will use the emitter created in the Exploding Sparks tutorial to emit a trail of flames.

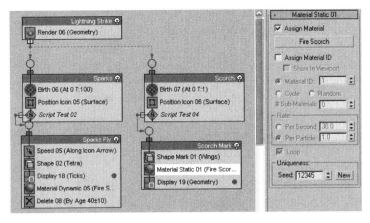

Figure 18.34   The source icon will now generate a scorch mark on the wings when triggered.

Figure 18.35   The scorch mark on the wings indicates the source of the explosive effects to come.

Going Down in Flames

In this section, we will cause a flickering fire to emanate from the source icon, using the Material Frequency operator. Material Frequency randomly applies Material ID#s to particles based on user-defined percentages. It is the ideal way to randomly apply textures based on a Multi/Sub-Object material.

1. Clone the Scorch birth event, using Copy as the method; name the new event Flames; and wire it to the Lightning Strike global event.

2. Set the Birth Amount to 4.

3. Reclone the Script test from Scorch to Flames, again using Instance as the method.

4. Create a new Material Frequency operator event below Flames, naming the new event Spawn Flames. Wire it to the Script test's output.

5. Assign Fire Sprites as the material to be used. Fire Sprites uses 27 bitmap fire textures, arranged in four different orders with IFLs.

6. The Fire Sprites material is a Multi/Sub-Object material containing four materials, so set the first four Material ID#s (Material ID #1 through Material ID #4) slots to 10. This value is not a percentage but a relative value. Using the same number for each slot will cause each submaterial to have an equal chance of being chosen. The particles will continue to be emitted from the updated location of the source icon.

7. Change the Display type to Geometry.

8. Define the shape of this particle by adding a Shape Facing operator somewhere after the Material Frequency operator, assigning Camera01 as the LookAt Object.

9. Set the particle size to 1500 units, in In World Space.

10. Set Pivot At to Bottom, so that the bottoms of the flames will be positioned on the source icon (**Figure 18.36**).

    If you scrub the Time Slider, the fire shows up as large Shape Facing particles, with their bottom edges aligned with the source icon (**Figure 18.37**).

    In addition to the flames placed on the emitter, a series of diminishing flames will trail from the biplane as it moves.

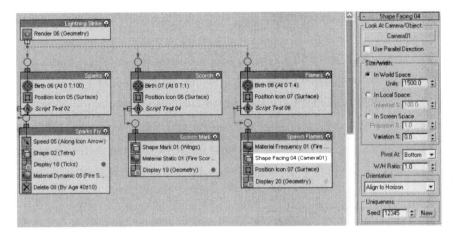

Figure 18.36   The particle setup now provides for a fire effect, grounded on the source icon.

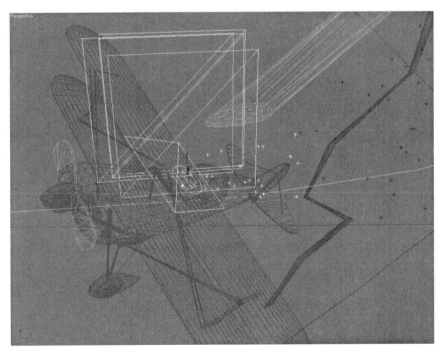

Figure 18.37   The fire effect appears in viewports as a set of four large planar particles.

11. Append a Spawn test to Spawn Flames. Set it to spawn Per Second, at a rate of 15 particles per second.

12. Make a copy of the Shape Facing operator below Spawn Flames, naming the new event Trailing Flames, and wire it to the Spawn test's output.

13. To shrink the flames as they fall behind the biplane, add a Scale operator.

14. Set the type to Relative Successive, with all three Scale Factors set to 98%.

15. Copy the Material Frequency operator from Spawn Flames to Trailing Flames.

16. To move the trailing flames away from the emitter, add a Speed operator (**Figure 18.38**).

When you render the scene with the completed fire effect, flames will now trail from the emitter (**Figure 18.39**). A flame trail will naturally diminish rapidly as it gets farther from the fuel source; a more lasting visual trail can be made with smoke effects, as we will see in the next few sections.

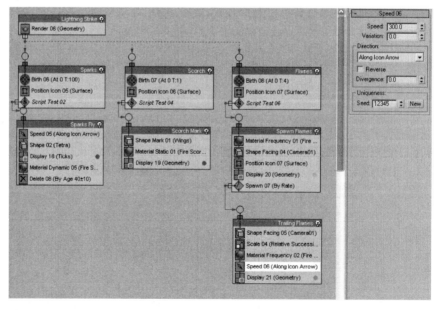

Figure 18.38   The completed Flames particle setup, with attached and trailing particle flames.

Figure 18.39   The completed fire effect.

Smoke

Creating smoke is similar to creating fire, with the differences being primarily in the animation speed of materials, the influence of outside forces on the smoke path, and the delay before the effect fades away. The first smoke effect we will create is a distinct trail to mark the biplane's demise.

Smoke Trail

One of the most important explosive effects in a doomed biplane, as anyone familiar with air battles in vintage war movies knows, is a long trail of billowing smoke. As this effect is similar to the fire effect, we will start with a copy of the fire particle setup.

1. Clone the Flames birth event, using Copy as the method; name the new event Smoke; and wire it to the Lightning Strike global event.

2. Set the Birth Amount to 1.

3. Reclone the Script test from Flames to Smoke, using Instance as the method this time, so that your flexibility in updating the script is retained.

4. Create a new Spawn test event below Smoke, naming the new event Spawn Smoke. Wire it to the Script test's output.

5. Set it to spawn according to how far the particle has traveled by turning on By Travel Distance, with a Step Size of 500 units (one particle emitted per 500 units traveled).

6. Set the Speed Variation to 20% and the Divergence to 80 degrees.

7. Copy the Position Icon operator from Smoke to maintain the particle emission from the moving source.

   We won't need any smoke particles to stick with the biplane, as we did with the fire, since smoke emanates from a source and usually doesn't contain an anchored element.

8. Create a new Shape Facing operator event below Spawn Smoke, name the new event Smoke Trail, and wire it to the Spawn test.

9. Assign the camera as the Look At Camera, and set the size to 2000 units in In World Space.

10. To give the smoke particles some momentum away from the emitter, add a Speed operator, set to a Speed of 150 units, with a Variation of 50.

11. Finally, add continuous rotation with a Spin operator. Set the Spin Rate to 180 degrees (one full rotation every 2 seconds), with a Variation of 50 degrees.

12. Set the Spin Axis to Particle Space. By default, only the Z axis is set to a non-zero value, meaning that the Shape Facing particle will only be rotated around its local Z axis. This way, its facing orientation toward the Look At Object will not change.

13. Append a Send Out test to Smoke Trail.

14. Create a new Scale operator event below Smoke Trail, name the new event Smoke Fade, and wire it to the Send Out test's output.

15. Set the scale type to Relative Successive, with all three factors set to 99.7%.

16. Add a Material Dynamic operator and assign the Smoke Trail material to it.

17. This material uses particle age to determine opacity and color, so provide a life span by appending a Delete operator to Smoke Fade.

18. Set the Delete operator to remove particles according to age by turning on By Particle Age, with a Life Span of 100 and a Variation of 10.

19. Change the Display type to Geometry (**Figure 18.40**).

The biplane will now leave a smoke trail behind it, which will shrink and change appearance over time (**Figure 18.41**). The trail will not, however, leave the flight path of the biplane. Next we will add a crosswind effect to gently blow the smoke around a bit.

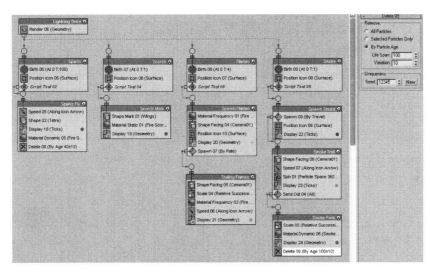

Figure 18.40   The completed smoke-trail particle setup.

Figure 18.41   The completed smoke-trail effect.

Blowing Smoke

In this section, we'll apply space warps to the smoke trail to give the appearance that it is being dispersed by a wind. Even a subtle wind effect can add a nice touch of realism, without which the smoke trail would appear starkly linear and symmetrical.

1. Go to a Top viewport and create a Drag space warp (Create panel > Space Warps > Forces) (**Figure 18.42**). The location of the space warp is not significant.

   The Drag space warp is very useful for adding a realistic element to the motion of particles that experience inertia. Particles simulating smoke, fog, dust, and expanding debris usually lose momentum over time—an effect easily created with Drag.

2. Set the Time Off to frame 400. This simple step is often overlooked.

3. Set the X-, Y-, and Z-axis Linear Damping percentages to 15%.

4. Still in the Top viewport, create a Wind space warp.

   The Wind space warp applies directional force to particles and is particularly useful when a turbulent motion is required.

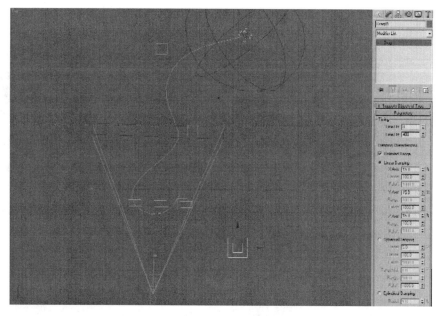

Figure 18.42   Create a Drag space warp to slow down particles over time (shown with the Modify panel open).

5. Increase its Strength to 3.

6. To give the effect greater chaos, increase Turbulence to 3 and Frequency to 15 (**Figure 18.43**).

7. Point the Wind space warp across the camera plane by rotating it, in the Top viewport, –30 degrees on its View Y axis and –40 on its View X axis (**Figure 18.44**).

8. To apply these forces to the smoke trail, go to the Smoke Fade event in Particle View and insert a Force operator before the Delete.

9. Add Wind01 and Drag01 to the Force Space Warps list.

    Before applying these two forces, the smoke trail is perfectly even (**Figure 18.45**), but with Wind and Drag turned on, a nice random element is added (**Figure 18.46**).

Even with turbulent dispersal, the smoke trail is still fairly contiguous. In the next section, we'll break up the trail even more by manually selecting particles to be removed from the effect.

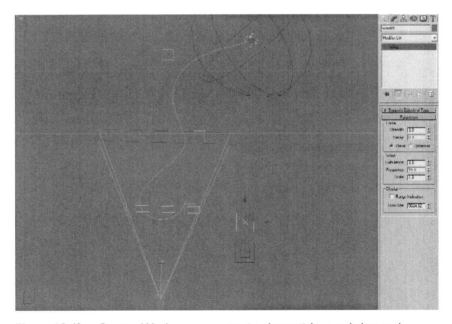

Figure 18.43   Create a Wind space warp to give the particles a turbulent push.

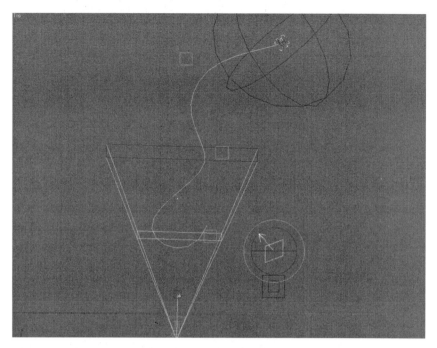

Figure 18.44   Rotate the space warp so that its push will angle across the camera's picture plane.

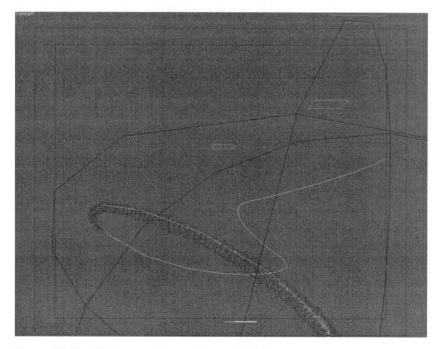

Figure 18.45   Without randomizing forces added, the smoke trail is smooth and even.

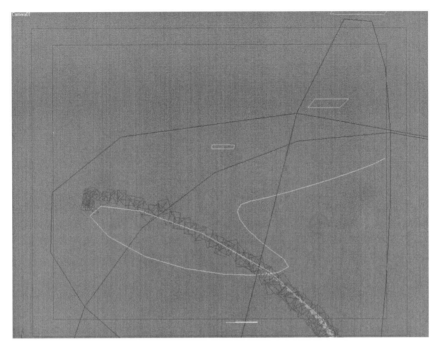

Figure 18.46   The addition of Wind and Drag forces makes the smoke trail appear more natural and broken up.

Particle Selections

One of the more interesting, albeit limited, features of Particle Flow is the ability to select particles in a viewport, either by manual selection or by event, and to pass that selection to a test operator. This allows you to interactively choose particles based on their position in a scene and have them treated specifically by Particle Flow.

1. The process of particle selection can be fairly CPU intensive, so turn off the Sparks, Scorch, and Flames birth events in Particle Flow.

2. In the Top viewport, go to frame 400 and zoom in on the smoke trail.

3. To make the particles easier to select, change their Display type (in Smoke Fade) to Asterisks.

4. Select the Lightning Strike source icon, and click the Particle button in the Selection rollout to activate selection by particle (**Figure 18.47**).

5. Use the Lasso Selection Region tool or Rectangular Selection Region tool to randomly select particles along the smoke trail. Given that the scene is at frame 400, the selection process may not be very responsive (**Figure 18.48**).

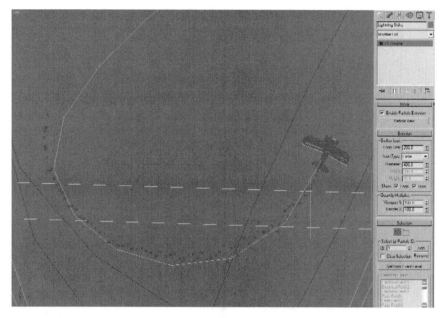

Figure 18.47   Zoom in on the smoke trail to prepare to manually select particles.

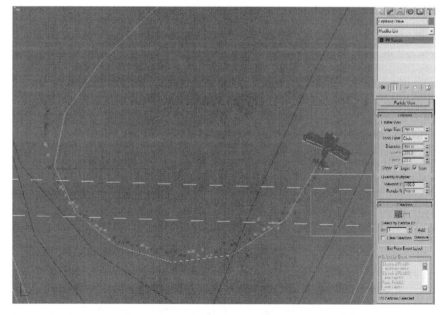

Figure 18.48   Selected particles are highlighted in the viewport, and the total number selected is reported at the bottom of the Selection rollout.

6. Return to Particle View and insert a Delete operator in Smoke Trail, just before the Send Out test.

 Tip

> Selected particles can be directed to events using the Split Selected test, which tests true only for selected particles.

7. Set it to remove Selected Particles Only. The particles selected in the viewport are deleted (**Figure 18.49**). Note that particle selection is limited to one selected per source icon; multiple selections cannot be made and passed to Particle Flow.

8. Exit Particle selection mode, change the Smoke Fade display type back to Geometry, and turn the Sparks, Scorch, and Flames birth events back on (**Figure 18.50**).

Figure 18.49   With a selection of particles deleted, the smoke trail appears more broken up, as shown in the Camera viewport.

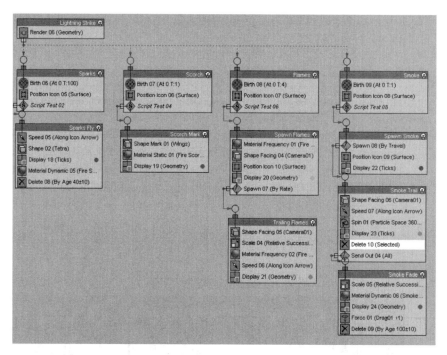

Figure 18.50   The final particle setup for the lightning strike's subsequent effects.

9. Now that the particle setup for the lightning strike is complete, this is a good time to apply a cache, so copy the Cache operator from Lightning03 to the Lightning Strike global event and update it. You may find it necessary to increase the amount of memory available to the Cache operator due to its complexity. This Memory Limit setting is available at the bottom of the Cache operator roll-out. By default, 100,000 kilobytes of memory are set aside. If you run out of memory, try increasing this value to 150,000.

The Particle Flow setup for the explosive effects triggered by the lightning strike is now complete. We have a fully parametric lightning strike, which can occur at any arbitrary keyframe; and sparks, smoke, fire, and scorch marks will be automatically generated.

Up to this point, scripting and collision have been used to control Particle Flow based on scene objects or scene time. In the next section, we will instead animate scene objects from a Particle Flow script.

More with PFlow Scripts

Earlier in this chapter, you explored how to control particle emissions from scene interaction through collision with the biplane's linked spherical deflector, as well as how to
control particles from a simple script test. In this section, the direction of control is
reversed, with scene objects controlled from a script that you will create in Particle View.

In order to gain increased flexibility in particle setup, it is important to be able to create
influences in both of these directions. For example, if you want to trigger a troll to come
out of hiding only when the last particle of a magical attack has faded, you could use a
particle script, triggered by particle speed, to move the mesh troll in the scene.

In the scene we're working with, you will use particle scripting to add a chaotic element
to the biplane's trajectory at the moment of impact.

Examine the "flight path" spline. This spline controls the path of the biplane through the
scene. A spline vertex near the impact point has been selected, and is controlled, via the
Linked XForm modifier, by a dummy object (**Figure 18.51**).

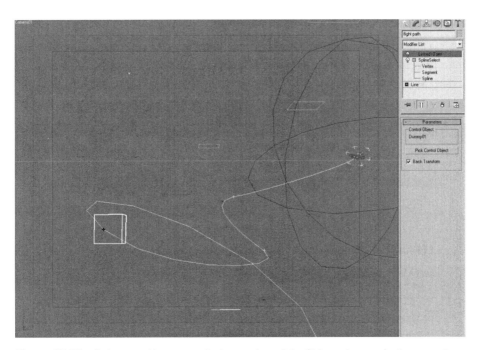

Figure 18.51   A dummy object controls the portion of the flight path near the impact point.

If you select the dummy object and go to the Motion panel > Assign Controller rollout, you will see that a Position List controller has been applied, with a Linear Position controller and a Noise Position controller.

Examining the properties of the Noise Strength track (by expanding the Noise Position controller and right-clicking on Noise Strength) reveals that the X, Y, and Z strength values are set to 0, meaning that no noise effect is created (**Figure 18.52**). It is this Strength track that will be modulated within Particle Flow to create the impact movement.

1. Return to Particle Flow, and open the script in the Script Holder event. The script to control the dummy's Noise Strength track will be inserted in the Proceed section, just after the StrikeFrame declaration line. The script is available as a text file, called lightning_strike_script_final.txt, on the accompanying DVD.

2. Enter the following lines (not the commentary) into the script. It is recommended that you copy and paste the text from the provided text file, as even a single typo can render the script nonfunctional.

```
RampUpFrames = 3
```

The variable RampUpFrames contains the number of frames over which the effect will increase from zero to full strength.

```
EffectFrames = 3
```

The variable EffectFrames indicates the duration of the full-strength effect.

```
RampDownFrames = 20
```

RampDownFrames determines the number of frames set aside for the diminishing of the effect back down to zero.

```
EffectStrength = 3000
```

EffectStrength determines the maximum Noise Strength value.

```
ProgressFrame = pCont.particleTime - StrikeFrame
```

ProgressFrame keeps track of how far into the Noise effect the script is progressing. Given the values assigned above, this value will increase from 1 to 26.

```
if pCont.particleTime < StrikeFrame then
$Dummy01.position.controller.NoisePosition.NoiseStrength =
  [0, 0, 0]
```

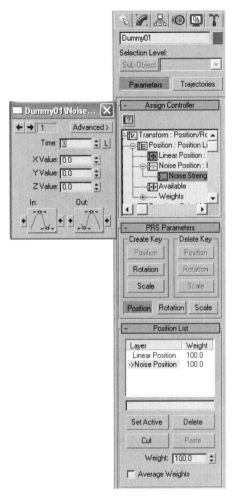

Figure 18.52   A Noise Position controller, with Strength initially set to 0, has been applied to the dummy.

If `StrikeFrame` has not yet been reached, keep the Noise Strength value at zero. To speed calculations before the lightning strike, this line could be removed (although if the Time Slider were moved directly from a frame occurring within the range of the script to the beginning, Noise Strength would not be reset, and the scene would begin playing with the strength set to a non-zero value).

```
if (pCont.particleTime >= StrikeFrame) and (pCont.particleTime <
(StrikeFrame + RampUpFrames + EffectFrames + RampDownFrames))
  then
```

If the current frame is within the duration of the effect, then continue to the next conditional test.

```
(
 if ProgressFrame <= RampUpFrames then
  (
  CurrentStrength = ((ProgressFrame + 0.1) / RampUpFrames) *
    EffectStrength
  $Dummy01.position.controller.NoisePosition.NoiseStrength =
    [CurrentStrength, CurrentStrength, CurrentStrength]
  )
```

If the frame is within the ramp-up period, then modulate the effect strength over the total number of ramp-up frames. The 0.1 value is added to avoid a zero result.

```
if (ProgressFrame > RampUpFrames) and (ProgressFrame <=
(RampUpFrames + EffectFrames)) then
  (
  CurrentStrength = EffectStrength
  $Dummy01.position.controller.NoisePosition.NoiseStrength =
    [CurrentStrength, CurrentStrength, CurrentStrength]
  )
```

If the frame is within the range of the full effect duration, then set the Noise Strength to the maximum value.

```
if ProgressFrame > (RampUpFrames + EffectFrames) then
  (
  CurrentStrength = ((RampDownFrames - (ProgressFrame -
    RampUpFrames - EffectFrames) + 0.1) / RampDownFrames) *
    EffectStrength
  $Dummy01.position.controller.NoisePosition.NoiseStrength =
    [CurrentStrength, CurrentStrength, CurrentStrength]
  )
```

If the frame is within the ramp-down period, then reduce the effect strength over the total number of ramp-down frames. The 0.1 value is added to avoid a zero result.

```
)
if pCont.particleTime > (StrikeFrame + RampUpFrames +
EffectFrames + RampDownFrames) then
  $Dummy01.position.controller.NoisePosition.NoiseStrength =
    [0, 0, 0]
```

If the current frame is after the total duration of the effect, then reset Noise Strength to zero.

With this completed script, you will cause the dummy's position to change based on the timing of the lightning strike (**Figure 18.53**).

3. Close the Script Editor. If the editor fails to close or gives an error message, recheck the script for typos, misspelled variable names, and mismatched parentheses.

If you scrub the Time Slider over the duration of the script's function, frames 275–301, the dummy will jerk at the moment of the lightning strike, moving the biplane and its emitted particles as well.

This script obviously only begins to explore the possibilities inherent in Particle Flow scripts. While the full range of scripting possibilities is beyond the scope of this chapter, more information can be found in the Scripting chapter in this book, as well as in the online MAXScript Reference (Help menu > MAXScript Reference).

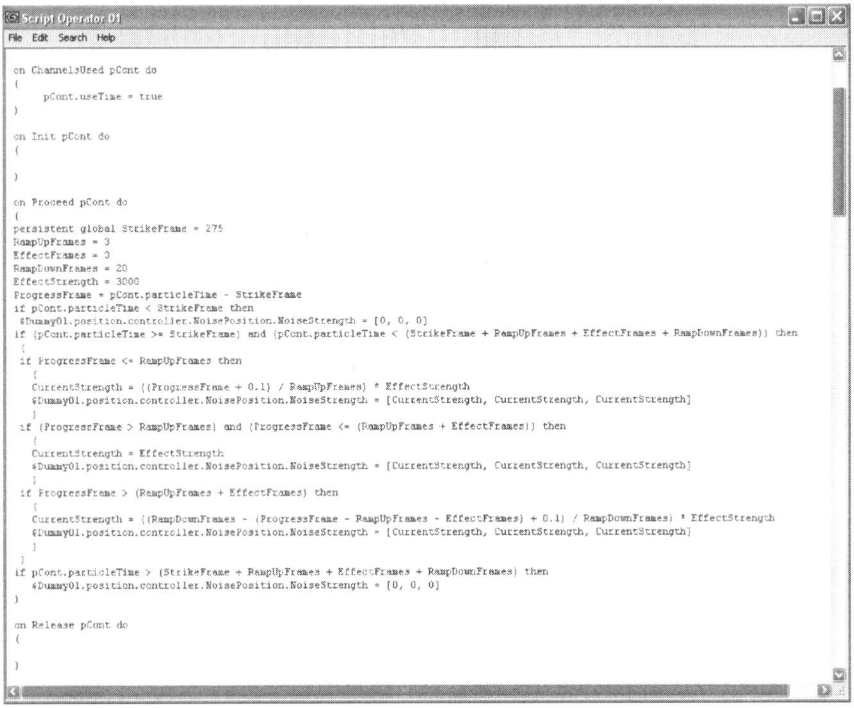

Figure 18.53   This script modulates the dummy's Noise Position Strength track according to the lightning strike's timing.

Final Touches

We're now done with Particle Flow, but our effect isn't complete. There are two remaining final touches to be created: a cloudbank above the scene, which we will create using a legacy particle system, and a glow effect for the lightning, added in Video Post.

Non-Event-Driven Particles

Visually, there is still one particle-based effect missing—clouds from which all these lightning bolts can emanate. While Particle Flow is the obvious choice for sophisticated particle effects in max, the legacy particle systems are still quite capable, calculate more quickly, and should be used whenever more advanced capabilities are not required. In this section, you will use the Blizzard particle system to create an animated cloud bank above the scene.

1. Go to a Left viewport, zoom out to show the whole scene, and create a large Blizzard particle system (found in the Create panel > Geometry > Particle Systems) with a width of 80,000 units and a length of 15,000 (**Figure 18.54**).

2. Go to a Perspective viewport. Move the Blizzard just above the camera's view of the biplane and off to the left, in the neighborhood of X = –60000, Y = 50000, Z = 20000, on the World Coordinate System (**Figure 18.55**).

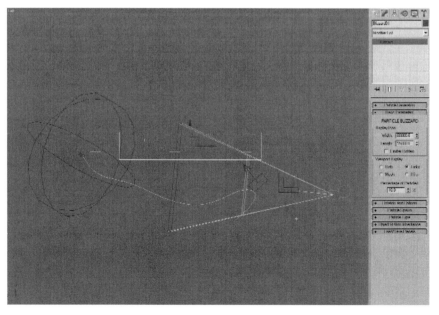

Figure 18.54   Create a large cloud bank using a Blizzard particle system, shown with the Modify panel open.

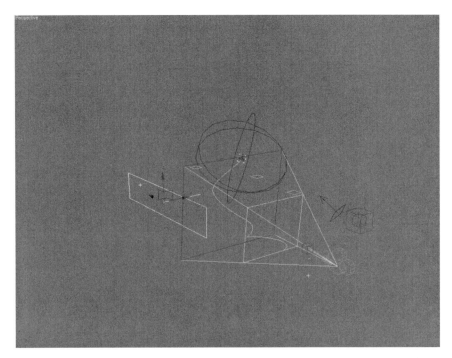

Figure 18.55   Position the particle system above the biplane and off to the side of the camera.

3. In the Basic Parameters rollout, set the Percentage of Particles to 100%.

4. In the Particle Generation rollout, set Use Rate to 1. Note that a visible percentage less than 100% will result in no visible particles at all. Each particle will represent a single cloud puff.

5. Set the particle Speed to 100 units per frame, with a Variation of 25%.

6. For a subtle tumbling effect, set Tumble to 1 and Tumble Rate to 25.

7. These particles need to start emitting before the animation begins, continue emitting throughout, and last well beyond the animation. To accomplish this, set Emit Start to –1000, Emit Stop to 350, Display Until to 400, and Life to 1400.

8. The clouds should be quite large, and should maintain their size throughout. Set Particle Size to 3500, with a 50% Variation, and both Grow For and Fade For to 0 frames.

If you go to the Camera01 viewport and scrub the Time Slider, particles will move across the scene's sky, from left to right (**Figure 18.56**).

Figure 18.56   The Blizzard particle system is now sending particles across the top of the Camera viewport.

9. To slow the rotation of the particles, go to the Rotation and Collision rollout, and set Spin Time to 1000 frames, with a 75% Variation.

10. Set the Variation to 100% so that the particles will not be rotated identically.

11. In the Particle Type rollout, leave the default setting of Standard Particles, but change the shape to Facing.

12. If you wish to preview the density and scale of the particles, change the Viewport Display setting to Mesh (found in the Basic Parameters rollout).

13. A material has been prepared for the cloud particles. Apply the material Clouds to the Blizzard particle system (**Figure 18.57**).

Certainly a more elaborate cloud formation could be created using Particle Flow or combustion effects, as opposed to this straightforward Blizzard setup (**Figure 18.58**), but when a quick particle effect is needed, you should keep in mind the capable and quick legacy particle systems still available in max 7.

Figure 18.57 A cloud bank has been created using the non-event-driven particle system Blizzard.

Video Post

The final visual effect for this scene is the addition of glow through Video Post. The glow itself will be fairly standard, but Particle Flow has the capability to apply such render effects on an event basis. This allows render effects to be applied only to selected events within a flow.

1. Open Video Post (found in the Rendering menu).

 Note

> Do not use the Object Properties dialog of a Particle Flow source icon to set its Object Channel ID. Each Particle Flow event has a separate Object Properties dialog and separate Channel ID slots.

2. Add a Scene event using the Camera01 viewport.

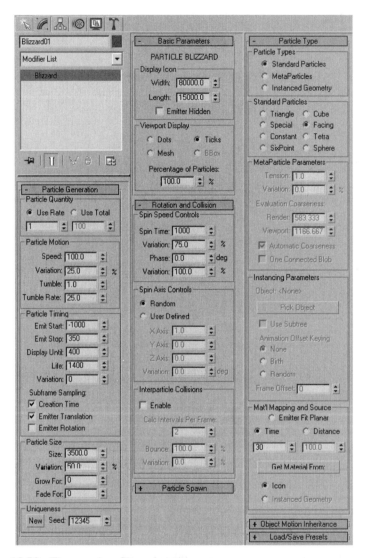

Figure 18.58 The complete Blizzard settings.

3. Add an Image Filter event, choose Lens Effects Glow, and click the Setup button to open the Lens Effect Glow dialog. Take note in the Properties tab that the effect is keyed by default to objects with an Object ID of 1.

4. In the Preferences tab, set the Effect Size to 11 and Color Intensity to 50. Click OK to close the dialog.

5. Add an Image Output event if you wish to save the animation. For single rendered frames, this event is not necessary (**Figure 18.59**).

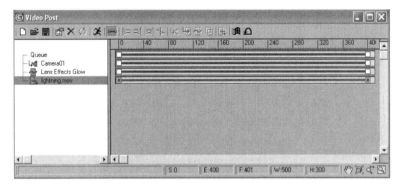

Figure 18.59   This simple Video Post queue applies a glow effect.

6. Return to Particle View. Select the events that produce renderable lightning bolts, specifically the Lightning Main Bolt and Lightning Branch events for the three lightning particle flows. Note that you must select the events (by their title bars) and not the operators they contain.

7. Right-click one of the selected events, and open the Object Properties dialog.

8. Set Object Channel to 1 to specify these events for the Video Post effect (**Figure 18.60**).

    While the lightning bolts we have created look fine without any postprocessing (**Figure 18.61**), a small amount of glow adds a nice final touch (**Figure 18.62**).

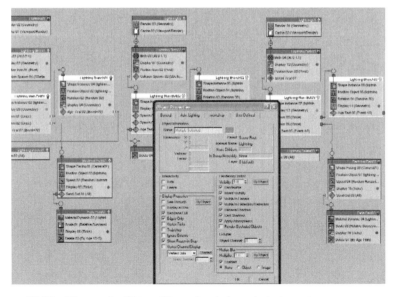

Figure 18.60   Change the Object Channel only for selected events.

Figure 18.61 The particle lightning bolt, without any Video Post effects.

Figure 18.62 The particle lightning bolt, after a glow effect is applied.

Summing Up

Particle Flow is such an open-ended system that the possibilities are limited only by the user's ambition and patience. Certain strategies are advisable to work around the CPU-intensive nature of PF calculations, but given that, particles can be made to behave in nearly any manner imaginable, moving and interacting with scene objects in realistic or fanciful ways. Particle scripting gives very fine control over most particle parameters and offers an avenue for passing control from particle systems to scene objects, as well as allowing scene objects to trigger Particle Flow events.

In this chapter, we have explored particle effects in several varieties—as trailing geometry, as instanced recursive effects, as expandable glows, and as explosive effects. Any of these techniques could easily be applied to varied situations. It is not difficult to imagine, for example, the biplane's flight path trail being modified to provide a visual "swoosh" effect for a swinging sword, or for the attached and trailing fire setup to be used for a pair of glowing, phosphorescent eyes.

If you wish to continue your exploration of Particle Flow in this exercise, consider the following challenges:

- Create an omni light to coincide with the lightning's flash. Use scripts to move it to the position of each bolt in turn, and to turn it on and off.

- Increase the Noise applied to the biplane's path, and turn on the flames and smoke from the start, increasing the size of the fire with each strike.

- Create a new version of the biplane broken into several pieces, and at the lightning's impact hide the main biplane, spawn the pieces, and send them off on separate paths.

Particle Flow is not restricted to realistic particles by any means. Consider the elaborate graphical intros played on many news and sports programs—particle systems are often used with no reference to physically accurate forces. Given the unrestricted nature of Particle Flow, using particles in max should be approached with a mind-set guided not by the default configuration of the Super Spray particle system, but instead by the user's unfettered imagination.

Part VIII

Rendering and Compositing

Chapter 19

Rendering Basics

By Doug Barnard

With the modeling, lighting, texturing, and animation completed, it's time to bring our masterpiece to the small screen. The complicated strategies that we've put into play should be manifested in all their glorious splendor—at least that's the idea. In this chapter we'll cover the basics of rendering and ways to make the process less painful.

The processing of object, material, lighting, and other data to form a picture is the formal definition of rendering. 3ds max has four primary rendering methods: ActiveShade, the Default Scanline Renderer, Radiosity, and the mental ray renderer. We are interpreting the rendering methods somewhat loosely here, so we can look at the different ways that 3ds max 7 makes pictures.

- **ActiveShade**—A fast renderer used for previewing the scene.
- **Default Scanline Renderer**—The primary method of rendering in 3ds max, a good compromise between speed, ease of use, and quality. Additional functions of the scanline renderer include raytracing, the Light Tracer, and toon shading.
- **Ray Tracing**—A rendering algorithm that traces the path of a ray of light from its source throughout the scene. This can make for excellent sharp shadows, reflections, and refractions.
- **Toon Shading**—A method of portraying geometry in a scene as if it had been hand-drawn in pen and ink. A black outline typically surrounds colored areas, for a two-dimensional look.

- **Light Tracer**—This method provides for color bleeding and soft shadows, and it works well for brightly lit settings such as outdoor scenes. Light Tracer is easier to use than Radiosity, and does not attempt to create a physically accurate model.

- **Radiosity**—A physically accurate rendering system that takes into account light reflected off objects. A favorite among architects as they design the way that buildings are lit.

- **mental ray**—A high-end renderer, formerly sold separately, that interfaces directly with 3ds max. Many Hollywood productions make use of mental ray. It delivers outstanding quality at the expense of speed and ease of use.

- **NTSC and PAL**—Various broadcast standards used throughout the world. NTSC (29.93 frames per second, or 60 fields per second) is used in North America, most of Central and South America, and Japan. PAL (25 frames per second, or 50 fields per second) is used in most European countries.

 Note

> The .vue file rendering method outputs an ASCII text file, used by other rendering systems, and will not be covered here.

ActiveShade

This first form of rendering gives us a window to preview the scene with limited interactivity. You've probably already been looking at the scene in the Camera, Perspective, or User viewports using the Smooth + Highlights shading mode. While good for modeling and overall scene arrangement, Smooth + Highlights falls short in rendering the subtle interplay between lights and materials.

ActiveShade fills the gap between straight window shading and the Production render. It is a two-stage process, the first being Initialize. All the geometry is evaluated and prepped for the next stage. The Update Shading stage finalizes the render and throws it up on the screen. When changes are made to the materials or lighting, only the Update stage needs to be processed for the changes to show.

Using ActiveShade for test renders is an excellent habit to get into, because a complex final rendering, especially one using Advanced Lighting or mental ray, can be set up in the Production settings of the Render Scene dialog. Troubleshooting can then take place in ActiveShade without disturbing the settings. Late at night, after a hurried session of fixing the scene, it's all too easy to forget to turn back on the Save File option. But don't worry, as we'll be covering proper Production rendering in the next section.

Accessing ActiveShade

There are a number of ways to access ActiveShade, but first you must decide whether you want to convert a viewport or have a separate floating window. Each method has its pluses and minuses. An ActiveShade viewport keeps the workspace uncluttered, but it allows only a single object to be selected at a time (in that viewport), and won't automatically show changes in Transforms or advanced editing. Having a floating window leaves all of your views intact, but typically it must be created and destroyed many times before a pleasing edit has been accomplished (**Figure 19.1**). Only one ActiveShade window can be present at any given time, and it is set by the Output File Size setting in the Render Scene dialog.

Note

If you convert a viewport to ActiveShade, there isn't the familiar viewport title to right-click to change views. You can use one of two methods: choose the Customize > Viewport Configuration > Layout menu selection, and click the appropriate viewport to bring up the selection floater. Or, right-click the ActiveShade viewport, and from the Quad menu, select Close from the upper-left quadrant.

Figure 19.1   An ActiveShade window.

You can summon ActiveShade in one of three ways:

- **Rendering Menu**—From the menu, select ActiveShade Floater or ActiveShade Viewport.

- **Main Toolbar**—Click the Render Scene tool, and select ActiveShade at the bottom of the Render Scene dialog. Also, the Quick Render (ActiveShade) tool is available. You might have to click and hold the Quick Render (Production) tool and select it from that flyout menu.

- **Right-Click Viewport Label**—Then choose Views > ActiveShade.

 Tip

Once you've picked ActiveShade as your rendering option, pressing the Quick Render hot key Shift-Q will update the window.

A viewport-based ActiveShade is like an ActiveShade window sitting on top of the existing viewport. So, if you close the ActiveShade viewport, it automatically reverts to the previous viewport. ActiveShade windows and viewports cannot be maximized, either. A nice feature is that Materials can be dragged and dropped onto geometry, just as they can in a regular viewport. If you select an object first, ActiveShade will update only that object and not the rest of the viewport.

Commands and Limitations in ActiveShade

The toolbar on top of the ActiveShade window allows for a few unique functions. The rendering can be saved at full size. Additional copies of the window can be made with the Clone Rendered Frame Window tool. The red, green, and blue channels can be looked at individually, as well as the alpha channel and a monochrome version.

   Tip

> If you click inside an ActiveShade viewport, then press the spacebar, the toolbar will toggle on. Pressing the spacebar again will toggle it off.

Control-clicking will zoom in the view, while Shift-clicking inside the ActiveShade window or viewport will access the Pan tool for the zoomed image. Control-right-click zooms the view out again. Of course, if you have a wheel mouse, rotating the knob zooms you in and out, and pressing the knob pans the view, just as it will any of the 3ds max viewports.

Right-clicking inside the ActiveShade window or viewport brings up the ActiveShade Quad menu (**Figure 19.2**).

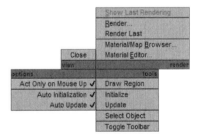

Figure 19.2   The ActiveShade Quad menu.

The upper-right area of the menu provides access to the Material/Map Browser and Material Editor, and supplies a shortcut for the Render Scene dialog and Render Last. The most commonly used selections are the View > Close in the upper-left quadrant and Initialize in the lower right. Choosing Close is the best way to dismiss an ActiveShade viewport, and Initialize is the choice you must make every time you change the scene in a way that ActiveShade can't update on its own.

Even though the ActiveShade window looks pretty good, it isn't a Production rendering. For one thing, there aren't any Atmospheric effects (fire effects, fog, or volume lights). Neither are there rendering effects or ray-traced shadows; the only shadows it can render are shadow-mapped shadows. Items like masks, reflections, and filters are degraded in the name of speedy rendering. A complete list is in the 3ds max Help system.

The Render Scene Dialog

For the real deal, you need to "Production render" your scene. To get to the Render Scene dialog (**Figure 19.3**), you can either choose Render from a Rendering menu, or click the Render Scene button.

This section may read as somewhat tedious; however, it was written to help someone troubleshoot a bad render. Even though *you* would never thrash around with unknown settings, it may become your responsibility to fix files created by colleagues complaining of malicious elves or stray cosmic rays.

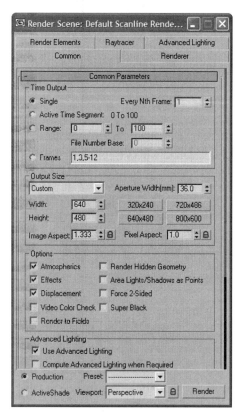

Figure 19.3   The Render Scene dialog, Common panel.

The Common Panel

In this panel, we start with the Time Output section. This is where you set up still or animation rendering. The options are pretty much self-explanatory, but there are a couple of things you should note. The Every Nth Frame parameter enables you to skip frames in your animation, a real boon when you want to test a long, complex render. The other option of note is File Number Base. This tells the renderer where to start the numbering of sequential stills, after which it will increment the frame count by one, as usual. The most common use of this is to start the rendering on frame 0001, instead of 0000. That way, if you want to render 60 frames, your last frame will be frame 0060. Otherwise, it would be frame 0059, as there is a frame 0000 at the beginning. This saves a lot of confusion when compositing or editing, as the frame counts in other software will line up properly with your rendered frames. Starting from frame 0001 may not seem like such a big deal, but having to constantly add or subtract 1 to figure out which frame is which will cause at least a few errors at some point in the production.

The Output Size section is far more than a mere designator of the pixel width and height of the finished rendering. It's also where you do the final step in matching real-world cameras, an exercise that we'll get into later in the chapter.

The output sizes are the function of a premeasured width and height (which make up the Image Aspect), the Pixel Aspect (the pixels' squareness), and the Aperture Width (the "lens" on the "projector"). By locking Image Aspect, you can quickly go from rendering a file 640 by 480 pixels to one 1280 by 960 by changing only one of the numbers; the other figure is adjusted in proportion automatically. If you have a favorite image size for your renders, you can change any of the presets by right-clicking them.

The Options section of the Render Scene Common panel contains these check boxes:

- **Atmospherics**—For using Fog, Volume Fog, Volume Lights, and Fire effects in a scene. Atmospherics will be covered in detail in the next section.

- **Effects**—Controls Lens effects, Blur, Brightness and Contrast, Color Balance, Depth of Field, File Output, Film Grain, and Motion Blur.

- **Displacement**—Turns on and off any displacement mapping in the scene. Displacement mapping creates polygons on the fly, which can have dramatic results on rendering speed.

 Note

Turning off the previous three entries can give your rendering a speed boost when you're troubleshooting a scene. Be sure to write a note to yourself, as it's easy to forget to turn them back on!

- **Video Color Check**—Flags any pixels that would be beyond the normal limits of PAL and NTSC colors (see the definitions in the beginning of the chapter). Normally, these pixels are rendered black, but this can be changed in the Rendering panel of the Preference Settings dialog. Strong, bright reds are especially prone to bleeding and can be spotted readily with this check.

- **Render to Fields**—Field renders sequential images, which helps to display animation on a non-interlaced television monitor. Only odd-numbered lines are drawn in one line, and even-numbered lines in the next. This can help to eliminate pixel popping and sizzling, but can also have undesirable dropout side effects. It's best if done from the editing or compositing program. Field order is set in the Customize > Preferences > Rendering dialog. The field order in 3ds max must match the field order in the editing program; otherwise the video will vibrate.

- **Render Hidden Geometry**—Renders all geometry in the scene, whether hidden or not. Note that if the Renderable flag is turned off in the Object Properties dialog, the geometry won't render.

- **Area Lights/Shadows as Points**—Renders all Area Lights and Area Shadows as if they were single-point light sources. This can improve rendering speeds, but will degrade cast-shadow quality.

- **Force 2-Sided**—A handy option if your objects have strange holes (especially objects imported as .dfx files), as if they were missing polygons. Force 2-Sided slows rendering time, and is a Band-Aid-type fix. Ideally, the models should have their normals unified and facing in the proper direction.

- **Super Black**—An option used primarily to help compositors to differentiate a very dark object from the background. The threshold is set in the Customize > Preferences > Rendering dialog.

Typically, Options are left at the defaults, but it never hurts to confirm the settings before a long render. The Use Advanced Lighting box is usually left checked, as the Advanced Lighting is selected in its own panel. Changing this will not affect render time if no Advanced lighting has been selected.

 Tip

> You may have to place the cursor over an unused section of the dialog to get the Hand, and scroll the dialog up to see the rest of the dialog.

The Render Output File dialog is where you specify the type and location of files to be saved. Access it by clicking the Files button. 3ds max can save in the following formats:

- **.avi**—Audio Visual Interleave, a Windows animation format. You must have the necessary codec loaded into your system.
- **.bmp**—Windows bitmap. Supports 8- and 24-bit formats.
- **.cin**—Kodak's Cineon. This 10-bit-per-channel format is a subset of the ANSI/SMPTE DPX file format. Used with high-end film-compositing systems.
- **.eps, .ps**—Encapsulated PostScript. A good format for prepress systems. The settings allow you to establish page size and resolution. See the "Print Size Wizard" section at the end of this chapter for more details.
- **.flc, .fli, .cel**—A legacy Autodesk Flic format used for limited-palette animations and stills.
- **.hdr, .pic**—Radiance formats for HDRI (High Dynamic Range Image) files. Great for background environments but difficult to use.
- **.jpg, .jpe, .jpeg**—A lossy compression scheme that produces a very small file.
- **.mov**—QuickTime animation.
- **.png**—Portable Network Graphics. Image files can have 48-bit (281 trillion) colors and built-in transparency.
- **.rgb**, **.sgi**—Silicon Graphics image file format.
- **.rla**—Wavefront raster image format. These files enable you to save additional channels of information, such as object IDs, material effects channels, and Z-depth info. Especially useful for compositing.
- **.rpf**—An extended version of .rla, with more options for channel export. A primary means of sending files to discreet's combustion compositing software.
- **.tga, .vda, .icb, .vst**—Targa image file format. The "vanilla" format that almost all software can interpret. A lossless compression is available as well as alpha channel support.

 Note

You should always leave the Pre-Multiplied Alpha option checked. This feature takes into account whatever background is in place, and anti-aliases against it. Turning it off will result in a case of the jaggies.

- **.tif**—Tagged Image File Format. Good for prepress use with assignable dot-per-inch values.

- **.dds**—Microsoft's DirectDraw Surface format. Used by game engines to display variable-resolution images (mipmaps).

 Note

> MPEG (.mpg) files can be input as textures but not output as renderings.

Carefully consider the file type of your output, as there can be serious consequences for your files down the road. A brief discussion with colleagues (and even a quickly rendered sample) can head off lengthy rerenders.

3ds max can also render to an external device, such as a film recorder. Clicking on the Devices button in the Render Output area will bring up a list of any installed drivers for these devices.

The last three features in the Common Parameters rollout are Rendered Frame Window, which allows you to display each frame as it renders; Skip Existing Images, which enables you to skip the images already rendered in a sequence; and Net Render, which turns on Network Rendering.

For those times when you can't be at your machine, you can have it e-mail your PDA with the latest render news. The Email Notifications rollout just below Common Parameters in the Render Screen dialog can be set up to let you know about failures, progress, or completion. By combining this with an email-to-pager gateway, you could get a page if your render goes down. The company Corybant offers the IVEENA Priority Voice Email, which will do same thing with a call to your cellular phone. This gives a whole new meaning to the concept of being on "render wander."

Assign Renderer, the final rollout, allows you to assign mental ray (or any other installed third-party renderers) as your default Production renderer.

Once you've taken the time to set up all of these parameters, they can be saved to a Preset file at the bottom of the dialog. This will help to maintain consistency throughout the rendering process, and make the switch from test renders to final production shots an easy one. There are a number of Rendering Presets provided for you in the dropdown menu to get you started.

The Renderer Panel

As if the Common panel didn't have enough settings, we move on to its next-door neighbor, the Renderer (**Figure 19.4**).

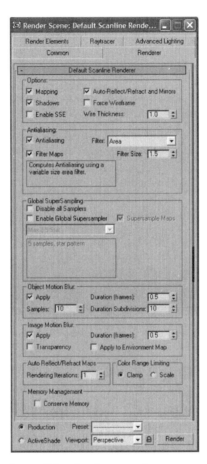

Figure 19.4   The Render Scene dialog, Renderer panel.

The top set of options is primarily used to speed up test renders, and for troubleshooting problems. As with the Options and Advanced Lighting sections in the Common panel, writing yourself a reminder of which boxes were checked can save you (or a colleague) considerable grief at that final render.

When the Enable SSE box is checked, the renderer uses streaming SIMD extensions. If you have a Pentium III or better CPU (including Celeron and AMD with 3dNow), using SSE can help speed up renderings. SSE takes advantage of the floating-point precision designed into 3ds max. The default is the unchecked box.

Anti-aliasing

Anti-aliasing removes the jagged edges from diagonal and curved edges and lines. For the most part, leaving the Filter default at Area will produce acceptable results (**Figure 19.5**). The anti-aliasing of a rendering is what establishes its "look and feel"; it can be used artistically to enhance the fantasy of a scene or bring it into hard-edged crispness. A softer method can give a dreamlike feel, whereas a harder method is better for architectural prints.

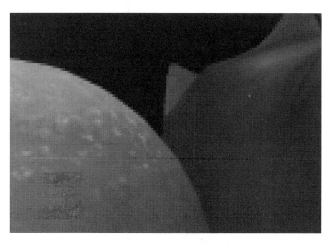

Figure 19.5   Area anti-aliasing: The default, a good overall choice.

3ds max offers a variety of anti-aliasing choices. Blackman is very crisp and can be used to mimic a Lightwave 3D rendering. The Catmull-Rom method is a nonproprietary (and scaled-down) version of the method that Pixar uses in its PhotoRealistic RenderMan product. The Video method produces a soft edge, and it's great for compositing with live video, even though it might look a bit fuzzy in your rendering. As live video is blurrier than a 3D rendering, this method can help get a better match. As with all settings in 3ds max, you should always do a test render of your scene and take it through the rest of the production process. The effects are subtle and somewhat difficult to see in the printed form. You can open the folder AAtests on the DVD to see some examples.

Supersampling

Supersampling is an additional anti-aliasing pass made on the maps assigned by the Material Editor. It's primarily used when blurry artifacts spoil a very detailed texture. Artists concerned primarily with output to video or game development need not concern themselves with supersampling, as it is a time-costly effect that will never be seen.

For a product designer or an architectural renderer, it could make or break the final illustration. Even though the master control for supersampling is located in the Renderer panel, it is best controlled on a material-by-material basis. Due to the additional time hit, you typically wouldn't want to supersample the entire scene (**Figure 19.6**). Turning it off can be useful for rendering quickie tests, but remember to turn it back on! You'll find examples of supersampling in the SS tests folder on the DVD.

 Note

> Using small texture maps negates any benefit from the supersampling due to the inherent blurring. A lossy compression format, like .jpeg, will also render supersampling useless.

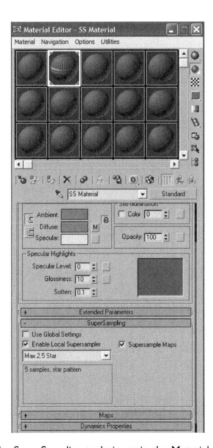

Figure 19.6   Enabling the SuperSampling techniques in the Material Editor.

The final areas of the Renderer panel deal with the Rendering Iterations of automatic reflection and refraction maps (Auto Reflect/Refract Maps); Color Range Limiting; and Memory Management. Rendering Iterations refers to the number of rendered inter-object bounces. If you have a mirror surface, the default of 1 is fine. If there is a mirror ball on this reflective surface, you would have to increase this value to 2 for both reflections to be seen.

3ds max has two methods of limiting out-of-range colors, like those in a very bright specular highlight. Clamping puts a limit on the intensity, while scaling drops the whole value of light in the scene. The Color Range Limiting default, Clamp, is usually the best.

If you find that you are consistently running out of RAM, you really should buy more. The Conserve Memory option will save only 10 to 15 percent, and it will give you a 5 percent hit on rendering time.

Note

Once 3ds max starts to page out to virtual memory, it will continue to do so until the program is restarted. This substantially slows down subsequent renderings.

The Raytracer Panel

3ds max uses a fairly elegant raytrace implementation in the Default Scanline Renderer, in that the raytracer is called into play only when necessary. Therefore, turning it off will not give you a speed increase unless you are using Raytrace Materials, Raytrace Maps, Advanced Ray Traced Shadows, or Area Shadows.

Notice in **Figure 19.7** that raytracing has its own form of anti-aliasing, and it is currently turned off. This anti-aliasing pass deals with the images presented by reflections and can substantially increase render time. In many cases, the anti-aliasing problems are dealt with adequately in the primary rendering pass or are made inconsequential by any motion blur applied. If your scene involves a close-up with a raytraced mirror reflection, at least the final hold-frame should have anti-aliasing applied to the Raytrace Material.

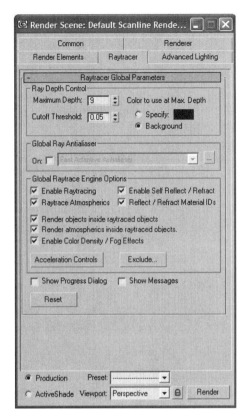

Figure 19.7   The Raytracer panel of the Render Scene dialog.

Ray Depth Control tells 3ds max how many times to bounce light rays around in the scene. In most cases, the ray comes from the light source, bounces off the object, and strikes the camera "lens." When objects reflect themselves, a practical limit needs to be placed on the number of reflections.

In **Figures 19.8** and **19.9** on the next page, the Maximum Depth has been altered to illustrate this concept. Note that when the reflections run out, the image is replaced with the background color.

 Note

> The number of reflections is strictly a function of the Raytrace Material's reflection and has nothing to do with the Flat Mirror mapping type. Flat Mirrors uses an extra rendering pass to generate the reflections.

Figure 19.8   Maximum Depth is 9, the default.

Figure 19.9   Maximum Depth is 1. The scene renders quicker, but reflections are lost.

Feel free to try your own ray bounce experiments with the raytrace.max file from the DVD.

In both Figure 19.8 and Figure 19.9, an extra anti-aliasing pass was made by turning on the Fast Adaptive Antialiaser in the Global Ray Antialiaser section. This helped to bring the reflections into sharp focus and to eliminate artifacts around the edges of the shadows.

Environment and Effects Dialog

Additions to the scene such as fire, fogs, and volume lights are specified in the Environment panel of the Environment and Effects dialog. The dialog can be chosen from the Rendering menu.

Even if you don't specifically want your outdoor scene to take place on a foggy day, adding a little bit of fog can help give a realistic distance effect. Looking at **Figure 19.10**, you can see a flat and uninteresting rendering of a city. It looks sort of like a miniature. Because of the nature of the shot, we don't really want a depth-of-field effect, either. The whole scene needs to be in focus.

Figure 19.10   The city scene, without any distance effects.

Adding Atmospheric Haze

One thing we can do is add some haze to provide a distance cue.

1. Copy the entire City directory from the DVD. Open the file called city.max from the directory. From the File menu, choose Save As, choose an appropriate subdirectory on your hard drive, and click the plus-sign button to save a new file with the name incremented to city01.max.

2. Choose Rendering > Environment and Effects. Click the Environment tab (**Figure 19.11**). In the Atmosphere rollout, click the Add button and choose Fog from the list of effects.

Figure 19.11   The Environment panel, with a Fog Environment effect enabled.

3. If you move the pointer to an unused section of the panel, it becomes a hand. Use the hand to move the panel up so that you can see the new Fog Parameters rollout.

4. Click in the Color box, and in the Color Selector, pick a very pale blue. In the example, I have used (218, 241, 252), but feel free to experiment.

5. Clear the Fog Background check box. We don't want the sky background taking on the haze.

6. In the Standard section of Fog Parameters, set Far % at 30. Close the dialog to get it out of the way.

    We're halfway set up. The way that 3ds max sets the distance to fog is through the Environment Ranges of the camera.

7. Click on the camera called Cam GROUND. In the Modify panel, click the Show check box in the Environment Ranges area. Two rectangular lines appear in the camera's field-of-view cone.

8. Set the Near Range at 0, and increase the Far Range setting until it's behind the last building. It should read about 1400 (**Figure 19.12**).

9. Activate the Cam GROUND viewport, and then click the Quick Render (Production) button to see the result (**Figure 19.13**).

You might want to look at cityNoFog.jpg and cityWithFog.jpg from the DVD to see a comparison of the scene with and without the effect. If your rendering doesn't look the way you want it to, you can check your work against CityWithHaze.max.

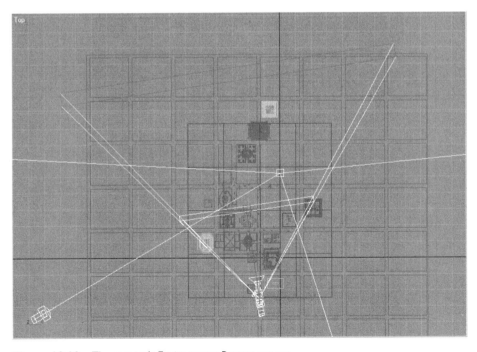

Figure 19.12   The camera's Environment Ranges are set.

Figure 19.13   A subtle use of fog conveys distance.

Standard Fog is easy to apply and should be considered for any outdoor scene. We have additional weapons in our arsenal that can slay the boring flat look of unskillfully rendered scenes.

Volume Light

When your lighting needs to appear theatrical, or it's in a smoky or dusty environment, Volume Light comes into play. Volume lighting has an added benefit in that it can increase the amount of perceived light when used with strong directional lighting.

This increase in light can be seen in **Figures 19.14** and **19.15**.

Figure 19.14   Without a Volume Light effect, the scene appears too dark.

Figure 19.15   Adding the Volume Light effect has brought out details and given the scene more character.

Volume lights are placed in the scene either from the Environment panel (choose Rendering > Environment and Effects > Environment > Add and then select Volume Light from the Effects menu) or from the Atmospheres & Effects rollout at the bottom of the light's Modify panel. Either way, you wind up at the same Volume Light Parameters rollout (**Figure 19.16**); this is very similar to the Fog Parameters rollout discussed above.

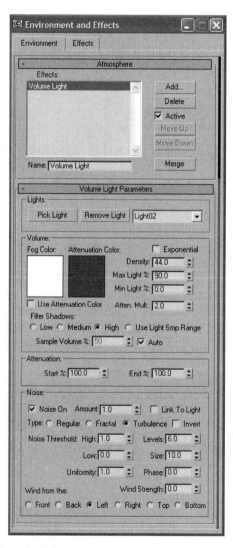

Figure 19.16   The Volume Light Parameters rollout.

In the Lights section on top, you can pick and delete lights from the scene. This is a good way to have consistent volume effects throughout the scene. Of primary interest in the dialog is the Density field. This controls the amount of glow effect; unless the scene is very foggy or smoky, less density works better than more density.

Unlike the other fog effects, the Fog Color interacts with the light's color to produce an additive color mix. A yellow fog with a red light would produce an orange volume. If you want the color of your fog to change over distance, check the Use Attenuation Color check box; choose a nice, dark Attenuation Color; and in the Attenuation Start % box, set the percentage at which you want it to appear. Playing with the End % parameter enables you to control the amount of glowing volume versus the distance that the light is illuminating. You can multiply the effect by raising the Attenuation Multiplier value. Volume Light Attenuation is used primarily in conjunction with the attenuation values that are set up in the light itself.

Adding Noise effects helps to simulate smoke in the atmosphere. It can be animated by going to the end frame of the animation, turning on Auto Key, and changing the Phase setting. Try just 2 or 3 at first, as large amounts of phase change can move smoke at an unrealistic speed. Turbulence is my favorite, as it gives a smooth and billowy effect. Play with the Size setting to get the puffs just right.

As with most effects, overuse of volume lighting can make an otherwise good scene appear hokey and amateurish. The file volumeLight.max has been included on the DVD for you to experiment with.

Volume Fog

Sometimes—as with smog, inversion layers, or the smoke after a bomb blast—you want to contain your fog within a certain area. Volume Fog works much the same way as a standard Fog, except that it's contained within an Atmospheric Apparatus (**Figure 19.17**). These items are available from the Create panel under the Helpers section.

In the next exercise, we are going to use Volume Fog to simulate puffs of smoke coming out of a locomotive's smokestack. This can be used as an alternative to, or in conjunction with, the typical way smoke is done, as a particle system.

Figure 19.17 It's a smoggy day in the city, thanks to Volume Fog.

1. Open the file called stacksmoke.max from the DVD. From the File menu, choose Save As, point to an appropriate subdirectory on your hard drive, and click the plus-sign button to save a new file with the name incremented to stacksmoke01.max.

2. Create a spherical Atmospheric Apparatus by going to the Create panel, Helpers section. Use the pulldown menu to access the Atmospheric Apparatus type, and click SphereGizmo (**Figure 19.18**).

3. Place this gizmo inside the top of the smokestack, by clicking and dragging out a Radius of about 7.

4. Drag the Time Slider to frame 30, and click the Auto Key button. With the gizmo still selected, increase the Radius to 60. Move the gizmo in the Z axis until it is almost out of the scene in the Perspective viewport.

Figure 19.18   Enabling the Atmospheric Apparatus SphereGizmo helper.

5. Click on the Auto Key button to turn it off. Make sure that the Gizmo is still selected. Under the Atmospheres & Effects rollout of the Modify panel, click Add and select Volume Fog from the list of effects. Select the entry and click the Setup button to get to the Volume Fog Parameters rollout.

6. Set Soften Gizmo Edges to 1, the Color to solid black, Step Size to 8, and the Noise type to Turbulence. Try a test render at frame 15 to make sure that you have the effect right (**Figure 19.19**).

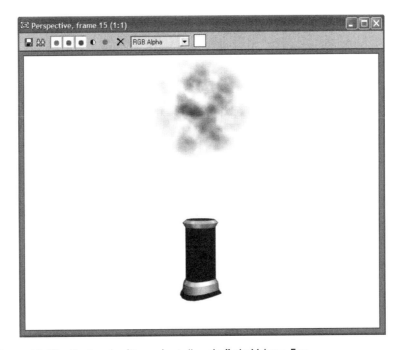

Figure 19.19   Testing the Atmospheric "smoke," aka Volume Fog.

7. Turn on the Auto Key button. Go to frame 30, and set the Density to 0.1. Set the Density at frame 0 to 30. Set the "Wind from the:" button to Bottom.

8. Render the animation, and check your work against smoketest.avi from the DVD. A puff of smoke should jet up from the smokestack, dissipating as it rises. Any problems? The file stacksmokeDone.max is on the DVD to help you troubleshoot.

Feel free to experiment with adding more puffs, to make the smokestack look like the train is ready to leave the station. Perhaps you can combine it with particles to get a great special-effects shot!

Fire Effects

This Environment effect, like Volume Fog, is controlled by the same sort of apparatus. It comes in two flavors: Tendril and Fireball. Fireball has the bonus of being able to add an explosion. This effect works well in the distance, or for a true 3D fire (**Figure 19.20**). There are video loops available of real fire that can be quickly composited in, and they look awesome, so don't drive yourself crazy looking for that *n*th-degree of perfection.

It looks like it'll be cold tonight, so let's set up a nice, warm campfire in the next exercise.

Figure 19.20   The Fire effect, Tendril type.

1. Open the file called fireStart.max on the DVD. From the File menu, choose Save As, point to an appropriate subdirectory on your hard drive, and click the plus-sign button to save a new file with the name incremented to fireStart01.max.

2. Click in the Top viewport. Use the main menu selection Create > Helper > Atmospherics, and then choosing the SphereGizmotype. The gizmo should be placed in the middle of the logs. Set the Radius to 1.7, and check the Hemisphere box.

3. In the Front viewport, use the Scale tool to set the Y axis value for the Non-Uniform Scale parameter to about 225%. You can use the readouts at the bottom of the interface to help you dial in the setting.

4. In the Rendering > Environment and Effects dialog, click the Add button and select Fire in the Atmosphere Effects area. In the resulting dialog, click the Pick Gizmo button, and select the apparatus that you just made.

5. Made sure that the Tendril type is selected, then set the Flame Size to 0.7, the Density to 500, and the Flame Detail to 10.

6. Click Auto Key, and go to frame 30. Set the Phase to 50 and the Drift to 50. Turn off Auto Key (**Figure 19.21**). Render a test frame to see how you did.

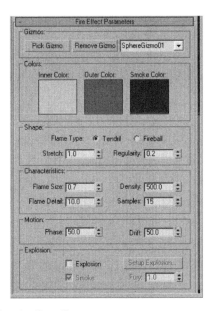

Figure 19.21   Settings for the Fire effect.

In checking out **Figure 19.22**, you can see that the flames look good, but the default lighting in the scene ruins the effect. That's because the Fire effect casts no light of its own. We'll add a suitable light source in the next steps.

Figure 19.22   The campfire, without suitable lighting.

1. Continue with the file that you've been creating. Create an Omni Light effect, and place it just above the logs. In the Light's Modify panel, turn on Shadows and choose Shadow Map as the type. Exclude the three logs and the ashes. Set the Light color to (251, 177, 49) (bright orange), and the Multiplier to 2.0.

2. In the Decay section of the Modify panel, select Inverse Square, and set Start at 2.7. This will keep the light just in the campfire area.

   The light is in place, but we need a flickering effect to fully sell the scene. A brief visit to the Dope Sheet will accomplish this.

3. With the Omni Light selected, go to Graph Editors > Track View > Dope Sheet. In the dialog, click the plus-sign button to open Omni01, then the plus-sign button to open Object (Omni Light). The second item is Multiplier; select it, then right-click it. Choose Assign Controller, and select Noise Float from the list (**Figure 19.23**).

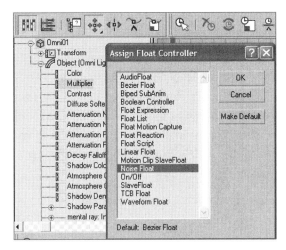

Figure 19.23   Changing the Light's Multiplier Controller type.

4. In the Noise Controller dialog that comes up, select the >0 option, set Strength to 3 and Frequency to 0.1. Be sure that Fractal Noise is selected, as well. Minimize the Dope Sheet.

That's it! Go ahead and render your animation. Compare your work to the files fire.avi and FireDone.max on the DVD.

You can continue with animating the fire on your own. Assigning a Noise Controller to the Omni Light's Position track will get the shadows to move more, as well as building a brighter yellow light like the orange one in the scene. Glowing embers can be made to shoot out.

 Note

> Functions of the Effects panel can be accessed through other parts of 3ds max. Lens Effects, File Output, and Brightness, Motion Blur, and Contrast can be done as Video Post filters.

Animation Rendering

When rendering animation files, we have to lock down a few decisions before proceeding. First, will the animation be inputted into a compositing or editing program? If the answer is yes, a numbered sequence of files is wanted. Typically, they are Targa files, but for high-end compositing, .rla and .rpc file types add additional flexibility. Size is important as well. The output sizes in the Render Scene dialog can be helpful in determining the appropriate dimensions.

The primary reasoning behind the numbered file sequence is twofold: First, you want to be able to easily break apart the sequence for editing. You know that you're exactly at whatever frame you desire. Second, you don't want to introduce any compression artifacts that you don't have to. Compressing and decompressing video will start to degrade the picture, so you want to do it the minimum number of times possible. There are additional practical reasons: numbered stills allow for network rendering and also enable a rendering to be started and stopped easily.

Why compress an animation at all? The sheer mass of data that needs to be pumped through the video card would bring even the most advanced personal computer to its knees. Compression and decompression of the animation (and sound) take place with a driver called, fittingly, a codec. Like a font, the codec has to be on the system of both the compressor and the decompressor.

Typically, you will find that whatever codec you choose, some member of your audience won't have it installed. DivX and the open-source XviD are two excellent choices in a modern MPEG-4 compression scheme. They will probably produce the highest quality with the smallest size. More info on encoding, and downloads of free drivers, are available on these Web sites:

- www.divx.com/divx/
- www.xvid.org/
- www.doom9.org/index.html?/xvid.htm

For the money, investment in a digital video camcorder (DV format) can put your animation and video projects on tape at a fairly acceptable level of quality. Suitable camcorders can be had for under $1,000; the next jump up in quality costs about an order of magnitude more. Be sure that your camcorder can accept a remote input, so that it functions just like a VCR. The camcorder can be hooked up to a standard VCR and the S-VHS quality signal will be dropped down to VHS when recorded. To produce a DVD, you'll need a DVD burner and some of the freeware listed at the Doom9 site.

As you might guess, animation comes in many forms. The 3D artist can be asked to add objects or effects to an existing scene, or on top of video. Architects and set designers use these techniques for their preliminary renderings.

Rendering to a Background

Frequently renderings are required to be composited into a scene that sits on top of a background plate. Most likely a rendering will be composited into the scene later, but the lighting and camera angle must match an existing shot. The lights are fairly straightforward, but getting the camera angle perfect can be a real pain. Fortunately, we can rely on the Camera Match utility to assist us.

This utility enables CameraPoint helpers on the scene to be married to their counterparts in the background plate. The basic rules are that you need at least six points of reference, and they cannot be all coplanar. This requires careful measurement of the physical space. Exact-scale models are built in 3ds max, and the matching process can be completed. **Figure 19.24** is an example of 3D geometry rendered over an existing background.

Figure 19.24   The crypt background plate with a door rendered over it.

To shed some light on the process, let's examine the preparations that the author undertook. First came the concept of the setting: a full moon in a cemetery, as a crypt door swings open. There happened to be a suitable cemetery nearby, so the author armed himself with tape measure, notepad, and digital camera. Shots were taken of the crypt and a pair of doors, and measurements were jotted down along with a rough sketch. After an uncomfortable interrogation by the cemetery's creepy sexton, the author adjourned to his studio to prepare the files.

Figure 19.25   The original shot of the crypt.

The original scene (**Figure 19.25**) was darkened by using Levels Adjustment in Photoshop and given a bluish tone with Hue/Saturation Adjustment. Additional darkening was spotted in with the Burn tool. Finally, the shot was cropped to 720 by 480 pixels, digital video size. The door shot (**Figure 19.26**) was dismantled and the pieces reassembled to make a single opaque door (**Figure 19.27**). A bump map was hand-built to give the door added dimension (**Figure 19.28**).

From the field dimensions, a box was built in 3ds max to match the door opening of the crypt. The texture was applied, and the door lit and animated. We are now ready to add the camera and get a match with the background plate.

Figure 19.26   The original shot of the doors to be modified.

Figure 19.27   The final texture map of the now single door.

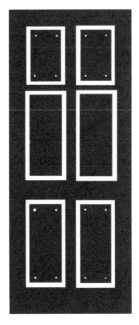

Figure 19.28   The bump map of the door.

The Door to the Crypt

Let's follow the steps needed to modify the door of the crypt.

1. Open the file called cryptStart.max from the DVD. From the File menu, choose Save As, point to an appropriate subdirectory on your hard drive, and click the plus-sign button to save a new file with the name incremented to cryptStart01.max.

2. Go to Rendering > Environment, click the Environment Map button, select Bitmap, and choose cryptBack.tga from the list. Close the window when you have completed the selection.

3. Click anywhere in the Perspective viewport to select it. Press the hot key G to remove the grid. Choose Views > Viewport Background, then click the Background Source Files button. Select the cryptBackTemp.jpg file. In the Aspect Ratio section, click the Match Rendering Output button, and make sure that Display Background is active. Click OK to close the window.

 Note

You could use the Use Environment Background check box to place your template, but as the picture is dark, a special version with notes has been prepared to make the alignment job easier.

4. Back in the Perspective viewport, right-click the window's title and change the view to Wireframe.

    As you can see in **Figure 19.29**, the door isn't anywhere near the right place in the scene. We need to mock up the main walls of the crypt to aid placement. Our field notes tell us that the main walls of the building are 9′11″ wide, 6′10″ tall, and 12′ deep. We'll next build a box to those dimensions.

5. Choose Customize > Units Setup > US Standard, Feet w/Fractional Inches. Click OK to close the dialog.

6. Draw a box whose dimensions are 12′ in length, 9′11″ in width, and 6′10″ in height. Visually align it so that it is flush with the bottom and sides of the door. See **Figure 19.30** for reference.

Figure 19.29   The door resting against the background.

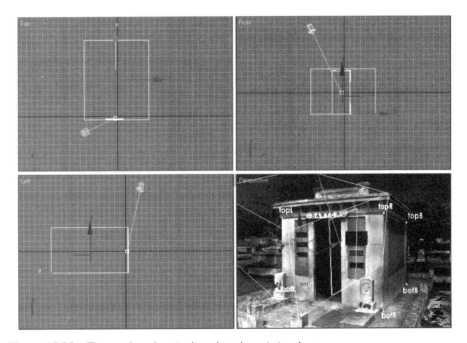

Figure 19.30   The mock-up box is aligned to the existing door.

7. In the Front viewport, draw another box that is 3´7″ in width, and whatever in the other dimensions. Still in the Front viewport, drag-clone a copy in the X axis. Move these boxes into place to align the door right in the middle of the wall (**Figure 19.31**). Once the boxes are located, a good approximation of the center of the wall can be made. Delete the boxes when you have the door placed in between them.

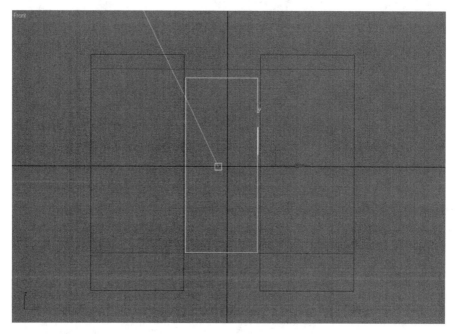

Figure 19.31   Two temporary boxes aid in door placement.

8. In the Perspective viewport, use the Arc Rotate and Zoom controls to put all of the front corners and the two back ones into view (**Figure 19.32**). Maximize the viewport for a better view.

9. Right-click the Snaps toggle, and clear the Grid Points selection. Choose Vertex as the only Snap Type. Close the dialog, and click the Snaps toggle to turn it on. Be sure that it is set to 3, the 3D position.

10. In the Render Scene dialog, set the Output Size to 720 x 480. Close the dialog. Hit the hot key M to bring up the Material Editor. Assign the yellow Wireframe material to the box.

11. Choose Create > Helpers. In the panel, open the drop-down menu and select Camera Match. Click the CamPoint button to start laying down match points.

One by one, click on the vertices of the box and give the points the corresponding names that you see in the background. The points should snap to the corner vertices. When you're done, turn off the Snaps tool.

Figure 19.32   Ready to begin Camera Match Point placement.

12. In the Utilities panel, click Camera Match. You should see all of your CameraPoints listed in the CamPoint Info rollout. Select the top point in the list, botB, and then click Assign Position. Click on the botB yellow dot in the background picture. A small red cross appears.

13. Continue with the rest of the points. Notice that the crosses go green when unselected. Click Create Camera, then press the hot key C to see the Camera01 view. The view should be fairly well aligned (**Figure 19.33**).

Try a test render. With the Wireframe material on the cube, you can see the exact placement. If you play back the animation, the door swings naturally in the scene.

Figure 19.33   The new camera is aligned to the background.

Printing and Exporting

We've got our images rendered. Now what do we do with them? Max offers several modest printing and exporting functions you may need to call upon. In this section, we will review them.

Print Size Wizard

When you get ready to print your images, a visit to an image-editing program is typically in order. 3ds max has supplied us with the Print Size Wizard, found under Rendering > Print Size Wizard, but it doesn't take the place of the other program. In fact, you can't even print from it! It's good for getting an approximate size, but the settings derived from the calculations don't take into account paper margins or printer capabilities.

Panorama Exporter

Sometimes you want to dive right into a scene and be able to interactively show how the area looks from a central vantage point. Using Panorama, with the included viewer, allows the user to look about the scene.

In **Figure 19.34**, you see a normal rendering of a jail cell.

Figure 19.34   A jail cell, rendered with radiosity.

In **Figure 19.35**, you see the 360-degree panorama created of the same scene. A free camera was placed in the middle of the cell, at about head height.

Figure 19.35   A panorama made of the same model as Figure 19.34.

To see the panorama, open the Utilities panel in 3ds max. Click the More button, and select the Panorama Exporter from the subsequent dialog. Click the Viewer button, and use the File/Open menu command to go to the DVD and select jailPano.jpg. Clicking and dragging will move the camera around, and clicking the middle mouse button will zoom in and out.

Rendering a panorama is simple: merely place a camera in a central place where you want the viewpoint to be, and click the Render button in the Utilities panel. You want to select a large size for the rendering, as there is a lot of area to display. A size of 2048 by 1024 is usually a good choice to start.

Note that the Render Scene dialog for the panorama looks very similar to the standard variety that we're used to; however, it is modal. It must be closed before you can go back to editing your scene. It also won't remember which camera is your panorama camera, so you must remember to select it every time from the bottom of the dialog.

To be able to view your work outside 3ds max, or on the Web, you need to export your render to a standard panorama format. There are a number of applications, but probably the easiest to implement is QuickTime VR. After your panorama finishes rendering, choose File > Export > Export QuickTime VR. Once the software is installed, you can view the panorama with the QuickTime viewer.

Note

You need the full "Recommended" QuickTime installation to be able to access the Export function. Go to www.apple.com/quicktime/download to get the current version.

With third-party software, virtual tours can be authored that enable the user to jump from panorama to panorama. These are very popular with real estate and tourism clients, and my architectural previsualization clients just love them. A good Web site to see all of the available software is the IQTVRA Links List, at www.360geographics.com/IQTVRA/IQTVRALinks.html. Another good site for an overview of panoramas in general is panoguide, at www.panoguide.com.

Shockwave 3D Exporter

Macromedia Shockwave 3D enables 3D animation to be viewed and manipulated on the Web; sort of a mini game engine. The reactor physics engine is supported, so games can be modeled that use real-world forces. The Macromedia Director feature Havok Xtra must be loaded; if you don't have a current version, it's available at http://oldsite.havok.com/xtra/index.html. An article on programming interactive objects can be found on the Macromedia site, at http://sdc.shockwave.com/devnet/mx/director/articles/virtual_objects.html.

If you don't have a copy of Director, be careful in that the Preview window is notoriously unreliable for an exact one-to-one depiction. Macromedia has a developer's tool that it recommends for viewing .w3d (native Shockwave 3D) files, available at www.directordev.com/tools/projectors/W3DViewer/default.htm.

The bad news in this scenario is that translation of 3ds max is limited to basic transformations: Move, Scale, and Rotate. Any animation from modifiers (Bends, Free Form Deformations, etc.) is ignored. Also ignored are animations resulting from parameter changes, such as those in the dimensions of a box. Compound Objects, like Lofts or Booleans, are ignored entirely. Cameras and lights can also be transformed, but must be attached via a group to a transforming object. Only Blinn Shader types may be exported. Oddly enough, excellent support is built in for Bones/Skin deformations, so that character animation can be accomplished.

When you have a scene ready to go, choose File > Export. Scroll down the Save As list and select Shockwave 3D Scene Export. A dialog box shows up, detailing export options.

The primary concern of artists building art and animations for Shockwave 3D output is file size. 3ds max's export function allows you to control file size by limiting quality and textures. These controls must be experimented with on individual scenes, as unpredictable outcomes can happen when files are compressed to the extreme. By far the best strategy is to build your scenes in a low-polygon fashion and to limit your texture maps and animation keyframes. Remember, it all has to be downloaded by an impatient person!

When exporting, the first thing that the 3D artist should do is to click the Author Check button. This utility examines the 3ds max file for Shockwave 3D irregularities and then displays a listing. This check should be performed repeatedly during the construction process, as work can be wasted on export failures due to the aforementioned limitations. Never consider Shockwave 3D export as an afterthought; your model must be designed and built with it in mind!

Once you get a successful export, its integration into Director for an interactive Web experience is a nontrivial task, well beyond the scope of this book. As of this writing, there aren't any plug-and-play solutions for placing a Shockwave 3D file upon the Web for an easy review. Be prepared to either custom-code one yourself or get somebody to assist. An excellent treatise that covers Shockwave 3D, and its implementation in Director, is *Shockwave 3D,* by Jason Wolf, published by New Riders (ISBN: 0735711976).

Rendering More Effectively

Here's a list of hints and tips that may help you to get the rendering that both you and your boss or client desire, hopefully under budget and on time:

- **Nothing beats raw speed.** This may seem like an obvious point, but it needs to be stated nonetheless. Try to get access to the fastest machines available, and don't let yourself get too far behind the upgrade curve. Make sure that your machine has plenty of available RAM and swap space, and that it has been defragmented recently. Check for viruses and spy bots, and don't use other memory-hungry applications (like Photoshop) during your render. See if you can use other machines on the network after hours—even the receptionist's humble workstation can give its best for the cause!

- **Render lots of tests.** The name of the game isn't how good a 3D artist you are, but how your work pushes the production forward. Spending lots of your expensive time doing the wrong thing well isn't helpful. Show your tests to any that will look at them, and keep communication lines open. This way, if the finger-pointing starts, you can make sure that the fault lies with the decision makers and doesn't undeservedly fall in your lap.

- **Render just the right length.** As a corollary to the speed issue, rendering too much "padding" on either side of a shot can put you into overtime. These days, an FX shot of 3 seconds is considered glacially long. Rendering out a quickie test animatic, using stand-in geometry and sketches, can be utilized by the editor as a proof of concept. Animatics are also helpful in working out the timing and framing of a scene and should always be used on complicated shots. Better that the scene be cut *before* you put a lot of wasted work into it!

- **Render just the right detail.** Objects in the distance don't need a high polygon face count to look good. Even if the model is "already done," using highly optimized models will make your rendering fly. Likewise, making skillful use of Render To Texture can wipe out unneeded detail and time-expensive procedural textures. Heavily motion-blurred scenes with high-speed objects and cameras can really profit from this!

- **Render with changes in mind.** Face it, no matter how good your work is, someone, probably with more importance than they deserve, will demand unreasonable changes. These usually happen right at the end in the least convenient manner possible. Having to rerender only a small piece rather than the entire thing can be the difference between going home to a nice dinner and sleeping under your desk!

And finally, the point always to remember:

- **Staring at the screen won't make it render faster!** Believe me, I've tried, and I long ago discovered that it does absolutely nothing to sit and fret. Proudly engage in the practice of "render wander"; get up and stretch, see some sunshine, check out the latest watercooler gossip. Clearing your mind with a moment or two of relaxation can keep you more focused over the long run.

Taking Your Exercises Farther

- **Environments**: Try playing around with various fogs, and see how the illusion of depth works. You can also use a Volume Fog to simulate an overcast day by placing the fog bank well above the scene.
- **Environments**: Animate a series of puffs, and then link the whole business to a master object that moves around your scene. Add some particles (a Super Spray) that use a small plane with a Falloff material mapped to it. This will simulate the smaller smoke "particles."
- **Level of Detail**: Using a fairly complicated model of your own choosing, try using the Optimize and Multi-Res modifiers to limit the polygon count. For the ultimate in low polygon counts, you can render a view of your complicated model, and map it on to an animated plane!

Summing Up

In this chapter, we've just scratched the surface of rendering possibilities with max. At first blush, the Default Scanline Renderer seems like an awesomely powerful tool, but there are many more features and techniques at our disposal. The next chapter shows some of the interesting rendering variations that can be had in 3ds max 7.

Chapter 20

Advanced Rendering

by Doug Barnard

For many jobs, the Default Scanline Renderer that you were using in the last chapter will be more than adequate. However, 3ds max has additional rendering solutions that can really put your project over the top, or provide added alternatives to the standard rendering. Be aware that with this additional power and flexibility you will have to pay the price of having to learn a more complicated set of parameters for rendering, and, in most cases, you'll have a penalty in longer rendering times.

Note

You should be familiar with standard scanline rendering before tackling this chapter.

This chapter is broken down into the following four sections:

- **Ink 'n Paint**—Technically not a renderer, but a material type, this gives your scene a 2D, hand-drawn look (**Figure 20.1**).

- **The Light Tracer**—One of the global-illumination rendering systems in 3ds max. This can give a very natural look to outdoor scenes (**Figure 20.2**).

- **Radiosity**—A physically accurate rendering solution that also takes into account the bounced light of global illumination. Radiosity can accurately simulate the light reflectance of surfaces and the properties of manufactured lighting (**Figure 20.3**).

- **mental ray**—Version 3.3 of a professional-grade rendering solution that has all of the bells and whistles. Especially good for the caustics caused by light passing through bodies of water and thick glass. Use of mental ray does require some changes in thinking and methodology from the standard scanline renderer (**Figure 20.4**).

These four sections describe the additional rendering functions available in 3ds max 7. For those who may need to match output from other software, even more rendering solutions are available from third-party vendors.

Figure 20.1   Using the Ink 'n Paint material.

Figure 20.2   Output from the Light Tracer.

Figure 20.3   A Radiosity rendering.

Figure 20.4   Rendering with mental ray.

I offer the personal caveat that I tend to use advanced rendering methods as a last resort. While all that power certainly sounds good, I find that I'll be spending a good deal of extra time to make things right. Perhaps this is because of my familiarity with the Default Scanline Renderer, and my ability to design fairly creative lighting rigs to get the look that I want. Remember that any extra effort you spend on an initial shot could multiply itself throughout the rest of the 3D production, so plan accordingly.

Ink 'n Paint

Many might think of a rendering that imitates a 2D line drawing as a giant leap backward. Now that we are in the brave new world of 3D renderings, what could the possible advantages be?

- **It's what the client wants.** There's a big tradition, especially in architectural renderings, of a nice, clean pen-and-ink sketch of a proposed design. A textured 3D rendering can portray color selections that haven't been made or materials that haven't been agreed upon. Nervous clients can think you're trying to ram an idea down their throats with a fully finished picture. A "2D" sketch (or one that imitates 2D) keeps them at a familiar comfort level.

- **It's less detail-intensive.** When toon-shading, such as with Ink 'n Paint, you only have to put the big effort into detail that you, the artist, wish to show. In a sketch of a proposed building, the rest of the city surrounding your concept only needs to be hinted at with a few lines. A detailed cartoon character can coexist with a desert background of a few lines and color masses.

- **Lighting and rendering are quick.** No need for time-intensive lighting solutions, Video Post effects, or expensive rendering packages to get as close to reality as possible. You build your scene, you add a light or two and a camera, and you're off to the races.

- **It's what the market wants.** Face it, the majority of animation sold today is 2D. There's no need to swim upstream to sell your animation—toon shading can be the best of both worlds, especially when combined with standard cel animation.

Note

An excellent example of combined 2D and 3D was the Cartoon Network show *Futurama*. Most of the background and ships were 3D, while the characters were 2D.

While not truly an alternate rendering system, Ink 'n Paint is different enough from normal scanline rendering to be considered as such. First off, don't let the seemingly simple rendering quality fool you; the computational overhead is very high, and large data sets can take quite a while to render.

Creating a toon-shaded rendering is as easy as assigning a material and rendering as you normally would. Ink 'n Paint materials are accessed by opening the Material Editor, clicking an unused material swatch, and selecting Ink 'n Paint as the material type (**Figure 20.5**).

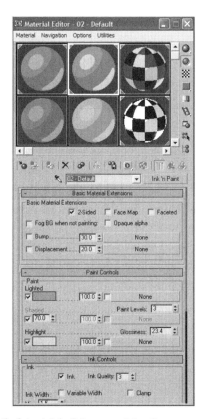

Figure 20.5   The top half of the Ink 'n Paint material rollouts.

Note

Ink 'n Paint materials will only work in Camera, User, or Perspective viewports. Trying to render in an orthographic window will lose the Ink outline and give an incorrect render.

When first using Ink 'n Paint, there is a tendency to think of the material settings in the same way as you would think of normal materials. A better way is to consider them as ways to control the color bands. Don't let existing lighting influence you too greatly when an oddly colored object jumps out at you.

In the first rollout, you can set Bump and Displacement. With Ink 'n Paint, the effects are much more subdued, and these are used primarily to add a little sloppiness to the rendering. As you can see in **Figure 20.6**, even though a high degree of both Bump and Displacement were added with a Noise map, not much has happened.

Figure 20.6   The first ball (on the left) is a standard Ink 'n Paint, while the second has a Noise Bump map and the third has a Noise Displacement map applied.

The Paint Controls rollout is where most of the action happens. The Lighted color swatch is the master color, from which the Shaded color is automatically set by the percentage spinner. A good way to get the Highlight color is to first turn it on by checking its box, and then drag-copy the Lighted color swatch onto it. Select Copy from the dialog, and then open the Highlight's Color Selector by clicking the swatch and decrease the Saturation level until it looks good.

Paint Levels controls the number of color bands—more is usually worse. The size of the highlight area is controlled by the Glossiness spinner. Maps can be applied, but the resolution differences between the toon color bands and the bitmaps make them quite problematic to use. It's best to use geometry whenever possible, even for patterns on another material.

As you scroll down in the Materials Editor, you come to the Ink Controls rollout (**Figure 20.7**). It's tough to get inking just right, especially on models with mixed interpenetrating and modeled surfaces. The Ink can be of variable width and can have a map applied (a Noise map works well) to give it a very hand-sketched look.

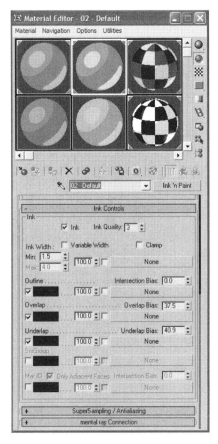

Figure 20.7   The Ink Controls rollout, in the lower half of the Ink 'n Paint material rollouts.

In its most basic usage, a pen-and-ink-style drawing can be made by setting the Lighted color to white and globally assigning this material to all objects in the scene. This is a good strategy to use when a client wants to see a "sketch" of your rendering before committing (**Figure 20.8**).

Figure 20.8   An Ink 'n Paint shader rendering at 640 by 480, with a rendering time of 9 minutes, 18 seconds.

I usually like to start with a nonvariable line, as playing with the line width can happen after a suitable set of outline characteristics is chosen. Start with just Outline, especially if you have interpenetrating objects, as in our Spaceman example. If you need to start adding more lines, experiment with the settings one at a time. If your lines seem to be doubly heavy, try adjusting the Intersection Bias value of the materials (**Figure 20.9**). Don't be afraid to duplicate materials, and tweak the Intersection Bias to get just the look that you want where you want it!

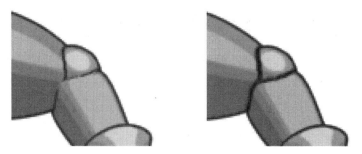

Figure 20.9   The Intersection Bias on the left has a value of 1, while the one on the right was left at 0.

When you want to add details, as on the face of the Spaceman, Smoothing Groups and Material IDs are the way to go. You can use them to outline certain portions, or use Multi/Sub-Object materials to add detailing. **Figure 20.10** is an example of this technique. To make Smoothing Groups and Material IDs easier to implement, and because the raytracer tends to choke on big scenes, it's wise to use a low-polygon style of modeling. Your models should be more exaggerated, with big differences in surface variation and lots of sharpness.

Figure 20.10   To heighten the detail, the areas under the nose and in the mouth were given separate Material IDs. The head was then assigned a Multi/Sub-Object material.

 Tip

> Sometimes the Raytrace Messages box will mysteriously turn itself on, popping up every time you render. You can tame it by going to the Render Scene dialog and selecting the Raytracer tab. Then, just clear the Show Messages box.

One thing that tends to look strange is the movement of the shadow color bands across the character's face as it moves around in the scene. A good way to eliminate this is to lock a spotlight onto the head, using the Select and Link tool. The head should be Excluded from the remaining lights in the scene and should be Included with the spotlight by using the appropriate dialogs in the light's Modify panel. Careful adjustment of the light will give a consistent look to the character's face (**Figure 20.11**).

Figure 20.11   How not to do it. Here, the head is illuminated by the direct light that also illuminates the rest of the scene. Notice how the character appears to have a five o'clock shadow, and how the rest of the shadow detail doesn't look as good as in Figure 20.1.

Great toon shading is tricky, and it takes a good bit of practice to get consistent results. Feel free to experiment with spaceman.max from the DVD. Once you get a palette of toon materials that you like, be sure to save them as a library by using the Put to Library function in the Material Editor. Character work is especially tough, as we are used to the limited views of the 2D realm. Being able to draw directly on top of our animation in 3ds max can make for the best of both worlds.

Unfortunately, since 3ds max doesn't allow for output to Macromedia Flash, you would need an add-on commercial toon renderer. Great work can be accomplished by rendering out toon-shaded files and bringing them into discreet's combustion package to have additional details hand-drawn into place.

 Note

Toon shading is also supported in the mental ray rendering system. A comparison is made later in the chapter.

Light Tracer (Global Illumination)

Global illumination takes the light bouncing off surfaces in the scene and adds it to the overall lighting solution. It is fairly easy to set up, and it can be used interchangeably with the standard Default Scanline Renderer, though it was designed to work in scenes that have a skylight placed in them. It doesn't require size accuracy (you make scenes to any scale you want) and is best used for outdoor scenes.

In the illustrations below (**Figures 20.12–20.14**), note the variations in quality in the time required to render a 1280-by-960 image on a 2.53 GHz computer with 1 GB of RAM.

Figure 20.12 Light Tracer—7 minutes, 38 seconds rendering time (buddhaLT.jpg on the DVD).

Figure 20.13 Scanline—29 minutes, 27 seconds rendering time (buddhaSL.jpg on the DVD). Not much difference in picture quality, but a huge drop in speed.

Figure 20.14 Scanline without a skylight—3 minutes, 47 seconds rendering time (buddhaSLAS.jpg on the DVD).

Notice that using the Light Tracer with a skylight actually reduced the painful rendering time of the scanline renderer. So it seems that Skylight and Advanced Lighting really go hand in hand; this is also true with the Radiosity renderer.

Skylight simulates an exterior daylight scene and can't be used "indoors." If you try to place a skylight inside a closed room, you will get nothing but a black rendering. The icon is just a placeholder, as the illumination from a skylight always comes in from the top of the scene.

Color Bleeding

A primary benefit of using the Light Tracer (or any of the GI solutions in 3ds max) is the phenomenon of color bleeding. This is infiltration of surrounding colors as light bounces around the scene. Though it sounds like a bad thing, color bleeding is a necessity for natural modeling of light properties.

Figure 20.15 shows a simple scene lit by one overhead Target Direct Light. The walls are black due to the parallel nature of the light rays.

Figure 20.15   No color bleeding in the scene. Time to render: 16 seconds. (Filename on the DVD: ballNoBleed.jpg.)

When we turn on the Light Tracer, and set Bounces to 2 and Color Bleed to 2.0, the walls are given a reddish hue by the light reflected from the floor's surface, and rendering time increases to about 13 minutes (filename on the DVD: ballWithBleed.jpg). The graduated tone would be very difficult to mimic with the Default Scanline Renderer. The shadows and overall lighting still leave much to be desired.

The Light Tracer Panel

To enable the Light Tracer, open the Render Scene dialog and go to the Advanced Lighting panel. Select Light Tracer from the drop-down menu.

The Parameters rollout in **Figure 20.16** appears in the Advanced Lighting panel.

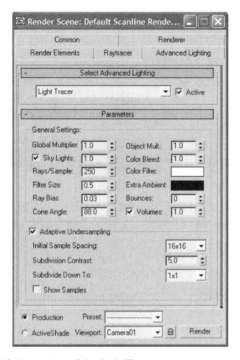

Figure 20.16   The default settings of the Light Tracer.

The General Settings break down as follows:

- **Global Multiplier**—Controls the overall amount of light in the scene; sort of an exposure control.

- **Object Multiplier**—Controls the amount of light bouncing off objects. Bounces must be set to 2 or above for this to work. Large values give a glow to the objects.

- **Sky Lights**—Controls the intensity of the skylight, or shuts it off altogether.

- **Color Bleed**—Regulates the degree to which colors infuse one another. Bounces must be set to 2 or above for this to work. A little goes a long way with this spinner!

- **Rays/Sample**—This and the Filter Size setting are the primary ways that you control the quality of the rendering. Small values in both will render faster but give a grainier appearance. Right now, 250 rays are being shot for every sample.

- **Color Filter**—An overall tint put on the scene when it's finished rendering. Anything other than white will tint the scene accordingly.

- **Filter Size**—As the Light Tracer gets close to edges, artifacts can appear. The Filter Size setting cleans this up in a specialized anti-aliasing pass. Once again, small values will speed up your render at the expense of having a grainier look.

- **Extra Ambient**—Brings up dark areas by increasing the overall light of the scene.

- **Ray Bias**—Just like the Bias in the Shadow component of lights, this spinner reduces the artifacts that happen when an object casts shadows onto itself. A small positive value is a necessity.

- **Bounces**—The number of times that light reflects in the scene and is taken into account for the lighting solution. The default zero value will cancel out the neat effects you're looking for, so increase it to at least 1. Continuing to increase this value will make for a more accurate, brighter scene with an increase in render time.

- **Cone Angle**—The angle of the ray bounce used for regathering the light. Smaller values tend to make the image more contrasty.

- **Volumes**—This has to do with light being reflected off volumetric atmospheric effects, like Volume Fog and Volume Lights. You can increase or decrease the effect, or turn it off entirely.

Adaptive Undersampling

Key to the reasonably fast production of Light Tracer renderings is the use of Adaptive Undersampling. **Figure 20.17**, below, shows how the Light Tracer can "gang up" on areas of strong contrast, and be more relaxed around areas that don't have as much going on.

 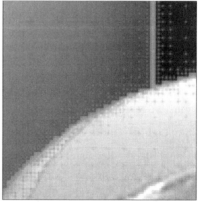

Figure 20.17   The enlargement on the left has an Adaptive Undersampling rate of 16 x 16, while the one on the right starts at 16 x 16 and then subdivides down to 1 x 1. Check the adaptive.tif file on the DVD for a clearer picture.

Clever use of Adaptive Undersampling, combined with the Rays/Sample and Filter Size settings, can really bring the rendering time down and still give acceptable quality. Notice the difference between the two figures (**Figures 20.18** and **20.19**) below:

Figure 20.18 Light Tracer with default settings; Bounces at 1: 7 minutes, 38 seconds rendering time (buddhaLT.jpg on the DVD).

Figure 20.19 Light Tracer with degraded settings; Bounces at 0: 2 minutes, 21 seconds rendering time (buddhaLTadj.jpg on the DVD).

Figure 20.19 was made with the following settings (**Figure 20.20**):

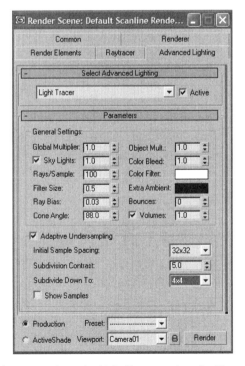

Figure 20.20 The changes made to the Light Tracer settings for Figure 20.19.

Note that Adaptive Undersampling and the Rays/Sample variables were both coarsened, and Bounces was set to zero. The shadow detail was made somewhat blotchy, but additional tweaking can get it back to an acceptable level.

Setting Up a Light Tracer Scene

By now, you should be getting the idea that using a skylight produces great shadows and a cloudy-day ambiance. Using the Direct Light with Advanced Ray Traced Shadows makes unrealistic shadows, but still leaves sunny-day specularity. So why not use both? The following exercise shows a simple setup that will work for most outdoor scenes.

Setting Up for the Light Tracer

1. Open the file called ballroom.max from the DVD. Choose File > Save As, point to an appropriate subdirectory on your hard drive, and use the plus-sign button to save a new file with the name incremented to ballroom01.max.

2. Open the Create panel and go to the Lights Type section. Click Skylight, and then click the Front viewport above the ball. A helper object appears. Note that the actual location doesn't matter, as Skylight always comes from "above."

3. From the Rendering menu select Render, and go to the Advanced Lighting panel. Light Tracer should already be selected. Make the following adjustments to the settings: Rays/Sample, 150; Color Bleed, 2; Bounces, 1; Initial Sample Spacing, 32 x 32; Subdivide Down To, 2 x 2. Click the Camera viewport and try a test render; it should be fairly fast.

   The walls have a bit of blotchiness, but that helps to sell the fact that no physical wall can be perfectly flat—there always has to be some irregularity. However, there's a bit too much here. The mirror ball has no specularity—it looks dull and flat, an impossibility with a mirrored surface. We'll fix both of those problems by adding a direct light.

4. Go back to the Create Lights panel, and put a target direct light into the scene. It should be mostly vertical but slightly offset from the ball (**Figure 20.21**). In the Directional Parameters rollout, use the spinner for Hotspot/Beam to enlarge the light's area to cover the entire scene.

5. Turn Shadows on and choose Shadow Map from the drop-down menu. Set the Intensity/Color/Attenuation Multiplier to 0.2. In the Shadow Map Params rollout, set the Size to 512 and Sample Range to 12.0. Click the Skylight button in the scene, and set its Multiplier to 0.6. Render out the file, and check the results. The 3ds max file is ballroomComplete.max, and the image file is ballShadow.jpg, both of which can be found on the DVD.

The soft direct light we added gave more character to the scene (**Figure 20.22**). We needed a shadow cast by the walls, and we got our highlight on the sphere. Setting our

Sample Range high on the shadow maps gave us a nice blurring of the edges of the cast shadow. The direct light also darkened the area right underneath the sphere, which helped to give it more weight.

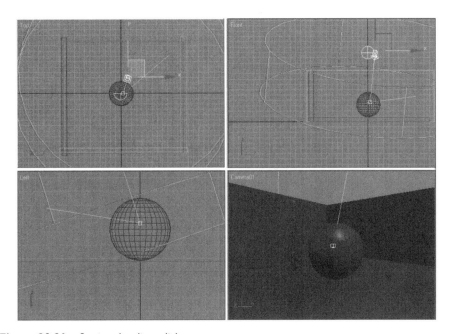

Figure 20.21   Setting the direct light.

Figure 20.22   Using a direct light and skylight combination.

Alternatives for Global Illumination

Figure 20.23   Using direct lights to imitate global illumination (buddhaFakeGI.jpg on the DVD).

In the above rendering (**Figure 20.23**), a global-illumination solution was "faked" with four direct lights casting area shadows. It made for a fairly fast rendering time (5 minutes, 35 seconds), but notice the shadowing on the face and the oversaturation on the horizontal portions of the robe. The file is available on the DVD as statueFakeGI.max if you want to see the settings used (**Figure 20.24**).

An even better way to fake global illumination is to use Ronnie Olsthoorn's (e-light@skyraider3d.com) E-Light script (E-Light_max5.ms), available at his Web site (www.skyraider3d.com) and on the DVD.

When the script runs, it places a dome and numerous lights in the scene. (The test in **Figure 20.25**, used a 900-unit-radius dome containing 91 shadow-casting lights). Once the dome is in place, the overall effect can be controlled in E-Light floater's Light Settings rollout, making for a convenient, one-stop solution (**Figure 20.26**). Even though it uses basic spotlights and shadow maps, the effect looks good, and the render is lightning-fast.

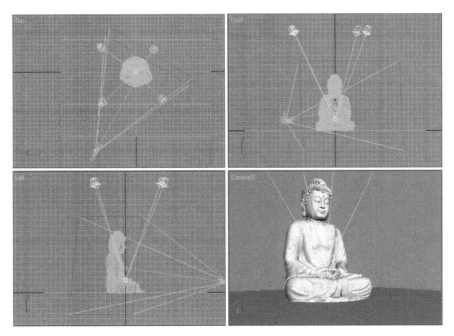

Figure 20.24   Setup of lights to imitate a global-illumination solution.

Figure 20.25   The E-Light script was used to imitate a global-illumination solution. Rendering time: 57 seconds. (see buddhaEL.jpg on the DVD.)

Figure 20.26   Settings for the rendering of Figure 20.25.

The statueEL.max file is available on the DVD for you to check out—you must place the E-Light script in your scripts directory and run the script to access the panel.

Radiosity

We've thrown together a quick solution with the Light Tracer that looks pretty good. But there are times when we need absolute accuracy, when we want real-world lights and surface reflectance. This is where radiosity rendering comes in. This entire business about light being interreflected around a scene had its start as a tool for thermal engineers. They were concerned mostly with heat reflectance from surfaces, but their equations proved valuable to graphics programmers as well. Since thermal engineers are quite concerned about the relative sizes of things (it takes a lot more energy to heat up an aircraft hangar than it does to heat up a closet), they needed a solution that was size-specific.

Enter the radiosity solution—not only a precise way to visualize bounced light, but also a means of assigning specific characteristics to lights and surfaces. The two aspects go hand in hand. Whereas the Light Tracer is a generalized solution that can be applied to most outdoor scenes regardless of scale, radiosity requires *exact* sizing of scene components to a real-world scale. Most radiosity rendering failures happen because this seemingly simple dictum wasn't heeded, so we'll put in a note for those skimming this introduction:

Note

> In order to use radiosity in 3ds max, you must work under a real-world Units Setup, such as Metric or US Standard. If you don't follow proper sizing, your interior wall could be 8 inches, 8 feet, or 8 miles tall, and radiosity errors could result.

Light Sources for Radiosity

Another important consideration is to work with photometric lights instead of the standard 3ds max lights that you're used to. These are true representations of actual lights, and they throw light in the way that their actual counterparts do. You can get away with trying to use standard lights, but as these are converted to photometric anyway, you lose the control gained from doing it the right way.

Many manufacturers will give the specs for their lights in a catalog or on their Web site. A sampling can be found at the Erco Web site (www.erco.com), though you will have to sift through lots of technical data. Look for models compatible with VIZ 4, 3ds max's cousin, written more for architectural pursuits. You will also need the companion IES files that specify how the light spreads out from the fixture. The good news here is that the lamp is already modeled, and the light is attached (it's what 3ds max calls a luminaire: a grouped object/light combination). There is even an inverse kinematic link so that the fixture points wherever the target for the light is placed.

3ds max also has a "Common Lamp Values for Photometric Lights" help item. Many different types of lights are listed, but for now, here's a list of standard bulb-type lights that you might find in your home. They are all based on a Free Point Photometric Light type:

- 60-watt bulb = 70 candelas
- 75-watt bulb = 95 candelas
- 100-watt bulb = 139 candelas

To quickly drop in standard light elements, you can access the Photometric Light presets from the Create menu > Create > Lights > Photometric Lights > Presets.

Figure 20.27 shows the setup for a 100-watt bulb.

Figure 20.27   Properties of a 100-watt bulb.

Photometric Lights are set up the same way. In addition to the method described above, they can be added to the scene by going to Create panel > Lights > Standard > Photometric. Point lights are similar to standard omnis. There are two unique light types, Area and Linear. The first, Area, simulates the light that might be given off by a glowing panel, like a fluorescent ceiling fixture. Linear lights mimic an individual fluorescent or neon tube. IES Sun is similar to a direct light and IES Sky is the radiosity version of a skylight.

Exposure Controls

Radiosity scenes tend to be too dark, and inexperienced users tend to keep bumping up the lighting power, trying to get something that they can see. This throws the lights totally out of whack. Imagine wearing dark sunglasses into a normally lit room and attempting to adjust the lights. 3ds max has Exposure Controls to rectify this situation. These controls are accessed from the Environment tab in the Environment and Effects dialog.

There are four choices available: Automatic, Linear, Logarithmic, and Pseudo Color. For most circumstances, Automatic will work fine. Linear can help scenes with not much lighting differential, while Logarithmic is better for very dynamic scenes. However, Logarithmic can give an over-saturation to files (**Figure 20.28**).

Finally, Pseudo Color is more of an analysis tool to show luminance and illuminance in the scene. A false-color rendering is made with a scale at the bottom (**Figure 20.29**).

Figure 20.28   Using Logarithmic Exposure can cause color bloom and loss of shadows in some scenes (exposureLog.jpg on the DVD).

Figure 20.29   A Pseudo Color Exposure Control rendering.

Materials Considerations

Standard 3ds max materials tend to throw off too much light and cause light blooms. Material reflectance must be monitored closely, but this is difficult because colors tend to look too dark in the interface. If you're going to be working with radiosity, it's best to turn on Reflectance & Transmittance Information. Choose Customize > Preferences, and in the Radiosity panel select Display Reflectance & Transmittance Information. Once you do that, each material will give you a readout that allows for exact control (**Figure 20.30**).

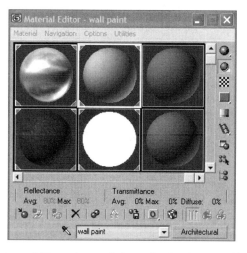

Figure 20.30   Reflectance & Transmittance Information has been enabled.

Note that the gray material in Figure 20.30 is actually the white paint on the wall. The material is toned down by adjusting the Diffuse color's Value. This is accomplished by clicking the color swatch next to Diffuse and dialing down the Value in the Color Selector.

In the case of a bitmapped material, it's done somewhat differently. You have to open up the Bitmap slot and go down to the Output rollout at the very bottom. Adjust the RGB Level to get the desired Reflectance (**Figure 20.31**).

The maximum reflectance of even the whitest of whites should be no more than 80%. A value of 100% would mean that all of the light hitting the wall would be transmitted, a physical impossibility. If your materials start to look too glowing, try turning down the Reflectance until the problem goes away.

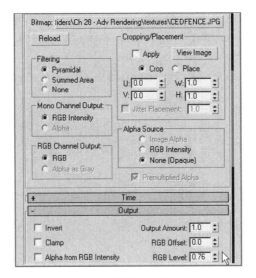

Figure 20.31   Bringing down the bitmap's RGB Level.

Transmittance has to do with clear or translucent materials; it's the amount of light that goes through. A completely opaque material has a Transmittance value of 0%.

Architectural materials have a Templates rollout that assists you in determining Reflectance and Transmittance values. You can set the material to behave like Semi-Gloss Paint, Paper, Masonry, and so on.

Note

Make sure that your geometry has lots of faces, at least one face every 2 feet. Incorrect radiosity solutions can result from not having enough vertices to hang the solution on. Also, try not to have sloppy intersections of walls—they should have connected vertices at all edges.

Using the Radiosity Renderer

The radiosity settings are activated much the same way as the Light Tracer's: You open the Render Scene dialog and click the Advanced Lighting tab, then select Radiosity from the drop-down menu. You are greeted by the settings area (**Figure 20.32**).

The major difference between Radiosity and the other renderers in 3ds max is that an additional processing step must be accomplished before rendering. The processing puts a hidden web onto the scene's geometry that stores the radiosity solution. The good news is that the entire scene is processed at once, so that any subsequent renders can use the stored information. An architectural fly-through animation would need only one pass with the processing. The bad news is that any time you make changes, the whole scene must be reprocessed. The processing is controlled by the settings in the top part of the dialog shown in Figure 20.32.

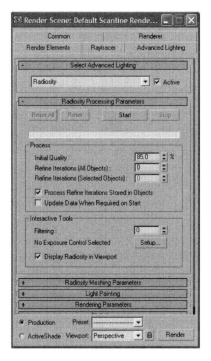

Figure 20.32   The Radiosity renderer's settings.

The Initial Quality default value of 85% is enough to see the radiosity effect, and subsequent passes may be added to bring up the light detail in the scene or on specific objects. There is a point of diminishing returns, about 90% to 95%, as there can never be a total 100% solution. If your scene looks blotchy, increasing the Initial Quality will decrease the variation of shadows on a given surface.

Filtering can also improve the look of the scene without adding the overhead of refining passes. A setting of 3 or 4 can smooth out lumpy shadows.

Note

Sometimes the radiosity solver gets overloaded with too many changes in the parameters and gives back a "Solution is invalid at current time frame" error. Memorize your settings, and flush out the settings by choosing <no lighting plug-in> from the Select Advanced Lighting rollout up at the top. Then choose Radiosity again, and re-enter your settings. Reset All will not help. This can fix many of the problems you'll encounter.

Opening two of the lower rollouts, Radiosity Meshing Parameters and Rendering Parameters, we see the controls pictured in **Figure 20.33**.

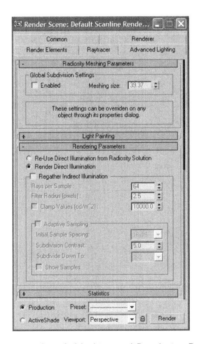

Figure 20.33   The Radiosity renderer's Meshing and Rendering Parameters.

The Radiosity renderer must break down the surfaces into smaller areas that it can map with the lighting information. The Global Subdivision Settings are used to specify the size. With good modeling, they shouldn't really need to be put into play, and can be left at a high value. If you are setting up to Regather, this also can be left at the default.

Selecting Re-Use Direct Illumination from Radiosity Solution gives the shadowing in the scene an inaccurate look. Selecting Render Direct Illumination gives a far better result (**Figures 20.34** and **20.35**).

Figure 20.34   The Rendering parameter Re-Use Direct Illumination from Radiosity Solution has been set (roomReUse.jpg on the DVD).

Figure 20.35   The Render Direct Illumination choice has been set. Regather Indirect Illumination and Adaptive Sampling have been left off. Time to render: 26 seconds. (room.jpg on the DVD.)

In the Regather Indirect Illumination option, light is re-processed for a more exact solution. Of primary interest in this section is the Filter Radius (pixels) spinner. This needs to be changed depending on the size of the finished rendering. A small rendering needs a small value, like the default value of 2.5; a large rendering will need a greater value. Rays per Sample is an overall quality control, but turning it up too high can dramatically increase your rendering times. Adaptive Sampling works much the same way as its counterpart in the Light Tracer: More effort is given to contrasting areas where objects change than to large blank areas. Turning on Regather Indirect Illumination increases rendering time, so Adaptive Sampling can help to reduce it a bit.

More Information on Radiosity

The 3ds max file room.max has been included on the DVD so that you can experiment with radiosity settings. Try importing some of your own models into the scene to see how radiosity can work for you. Those who want to delve further into radiosity and peek at some of the underlying math can find an excellent introductory paper at www.siggraph.org/education/materials/HyperGraph/radiosity/overview_1.htm. For a thorough exploration of the subject and enough math to write your own renderer, check out *Radiosity and Global Illumination,* by François X. Sillion and Claude Puech (Morgan Kaufmann, 1994).

mental ray

mental ray version 3.3 is a completely separate rendering package written by mental images (www.mentalimages.com) (**Figure 20.36**). This is industrial-grade software that has been used in movies like *The Matrix Reloaded*, *Star Wars: Episode II—Attack of the Clones*, and *Terminator 3: Rise of the Machines*. In February 2003, the Academy of Motion Picture Arts and Sciences recognized mental images for technical achievement.

Figure 20.36   mental ray's quality can be seen in this illustration, or in the stillLifeMR.jpg file on the DVD. Note the light spilling out under the crystal ball.

As you might guess, technical usage of mental ray is a vast subject, well beyond the scope of this book. We'll take a tour of the main features and get a good starting place for additional study; more information resources are provided at the end of the section.

mental ray's primary features are as follows:

- Global illumination
- Caustics (light cast onto another surface by either reflection or refraction)
- Soft shadows
- Area lights
- Vector-based motion blur
- Motion-blurred shadows
- Real-world depth of field
- Extensive shader language

mental ray is fully hyperthreaded, so having a multiprocessor setup will significantly increase rendering speeds. This translates to having four buckets working at a time with a dual-processor machine, compared with a single bucket on a single-processor machine.

One thing that 3ds max users will find tough to get used to is the limited licensing of mental ray. Each copy of 3ds max 7 ships with two licenses. A license is good for one processor. So, if you wish to implement mental ray on a multiple-machine render farm, additional licenses must be purchased from discreet.

Even though mental ray renders from within 3ds max, you can still write out a native-format .mi file to render on a non–3ds max mental ray setup. This can come in handy, as mental ray has been integrated into Softimage|XSI, Maya, Side Effects Software's Houdini 5, SolidWorks PhotoWorks 2, and Dassault Système's CATIA V4 and V5 products.

mental ray has special instances built into various parts of the 3ds max interface that need to be covered in order. First off, choose mental ray as the default Production renderer by scrolling to the bottom of the Render Scene panel. Click the Assign Renderer rollout, click the … button, then choose mental ray Renderer.

mental ray Lights

mental ray can use all 3ds max light types, but the rendering really shines when using the area lights. These lights provide for natural-looking soft shadows by causing the light to emit from a 2D plane in space rather than from a point. mr Area Omni and mr Area Spot are accessed from the bottom of the Object Type area of the Lights Create panel.

Note

If you can't see any of the mental ray Extensions in the Light parameters (or Materials), you need to enable them. Choose Customize > Preferences and select mental ray, and check the Enable mental ray Extensions box. mental ray should also be chosen as your Production renderer.

Converting 3ds max Lights to mental ray Lights

You can convert one or all of your 3ds max lights to mental ray area lights by using a scripted utility in the following manner:

1. Select one or more lights.

2. Go to the Utilities panel. Click the MAXScript button.

3. When the MAXScript rollout opens, choose Convert to mr Area Lights from the Utilities drop-down list at the bottom.

4. When the rollout comes up, click Convert Selected Lights. You have the choice whether to delete the original light. If you leave the original light, you will have double the lighting power.

Raytraced shadows are a good place to start when using area lights. Down in the Area Light Parameters rollout, of critical importance is the Height and Width (or Radius, with a Cylinder type) spinner. You should look for the blue line as you turn the spinner; this will give you an idea of the size of your light source. Bigger light sources make for greater blurring of the shadow's edge and extend rendering time (**Figure 20.37**).

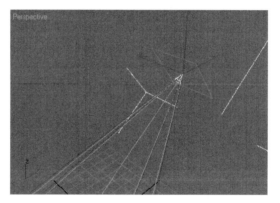

Figure 20.37 Adjusting the size of the area light.

mental ray Materials

3ds max materials can translate straight over to mental ray and then profit from some tweaking. Using the physically accurate shaders in conjunction with mental ray materials will give a more realistic look to your renderings. There is precise control over individual components, such as shadows and photon caustics. This allows you to dial in exactly the look that you're going for (**Figure 20.38**).

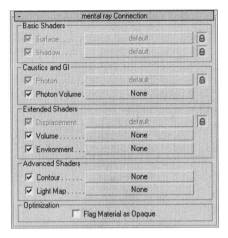

Figure 20.38 The material parameters area of a standard material, in the mental ray Connection rollout (at the bottom of the Material Editor).

3ds max comes equipped with three sets of shader libraries: the standard mental ray libraries, a specialized set for 3ds max, and the LumeTools collection. All of these try for a physically correct version of a particular surface. The term shader has a far more expanded meaning in mental ray than it does in the standard materials interface.

When you have placed a mental ray material in the slot, and you click a map button, an expanded version of the Material/Map Browser allows for access to a wide variety of mental ray effects. A good place to start is the DGS Material in the Surface slot. DGS stands for Diffuse, Glossy, Specular. This material is a mental ray phenomenon (a pre-programmed shader) that provides a physically accurate simulation of a surface. It is the "vanilla" material—one that works for most objects. If you try to put a bitmap directly in, the object won't shade properly.

 Note

> Using Displacement shading is somewhat similar to using the standard mapped material, and much more efficient in memory overhead.

mental ray also supports 3ds max's Ink 'n Paint toon shader. The results are almost indistinguishable from those of the standard Default Scanline Renderer, but mental ray is far faster (**Figure 20.39**).

Figure 20.39   Our Spaceman, rendered with mental ray. Time: 38 seconds. The same file took 4 minutes, 35 seconds to render with the scanline renderer. (Compare spaceman.jpg with mrspaceman.jpg on the DVD.)

mental ray Rendering Setup

When you are ready to render, you may notice a number of changes to the Render Scene dialog. In looking at the Indirect Illumination panel, you can see that there are quite a few references to photons. mental ray uses photons to bounce around global illumination and caustics. The overall power of the photons is controlled with the Global Energy Multiplier spinner at the bottom of the panel. Photons have nothing to do with brightness in the scene, but they can confuse neophyte mental ray users. Not setting up properly for the rendering can have frustrating consequences.

Here's the sequence of events to get good caustics and global illumination renderings:

1. Open the file called diamond01.max from the DVD. Choose File > Save As, point to an appropriate subdirectory on your hard drive, and use the plus-sign button to save a new file with the name incremented to diamond02.max.

2. Try test-rendering the Camera viewport. You should see a picture of the diamond, using the GemstoneDiamond material from the RayTraced_02.mat Material Library. A sunset environment map has been applied, as well (**Figure 20.40**).

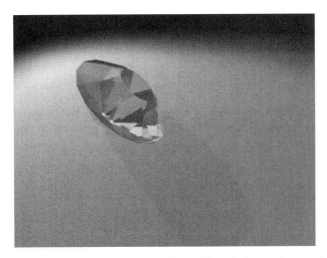

Figure 20.40   The diamond, rendered at 640 by 480 with the scanline renderer. Time: 17 seconds (diamond01.jpg on the DVD).

3. Open the Render Scene dialog and scroll to the bottom of the Common panel. Open the Assign Renderer rollout. Click the ... button next to Production, and choose mental ray Renderer from the available selections.

    Try another test render with mental ray. The picture won't change much, but the rendering time goes down. There's still more work to do to get the diamond to really sparkle.

    Next, let's change the material to something more physically accurate. We'll be using the mental ray Glass Phenomena material that ships with 3ds max 7.

4. Press the M hot key to open the Material Editor. Click the first material swatch to select it. Click the Standard button to open the Material/Map Browser. From the list, select the Glass (physics_phen) material.

Notice how the materials that are mental ray–specific have a yellow ball in front of them, as opposed to the familiar blue ball. If you had wanted to build your own mental ray material, selecting it as the material type would have presented you with the starting place.

5. In the Glass (physics_phen) Parameters rollout of the Material Editor, set the Index of Refraction to 2.5, which is the approximate value of the IOR of diamonds in the real world. Drag and drop the glass material onto the diamond. Close the Material Editor.

   Try another test render. Now the diamond looks much deeper and has internal reflections (**Figure 20.41**). Next we'll attack that stark shadow.

6. From the Utilities panel, select MAXScript. Down in the MAXScript rollout, select Convert to mr Area Lights. Select the spotlight in the scene, and click the Convert Selected Lights button. Click Yes to delete the old light.

Figure 20.41   The diamond now has a physically accurate material. Time: 7 seconds. (diamond03.jpg on the DVD.)

7. Select the light and open the Modify panel. The light's previous settings have been maintained, but we need to open the Area Light Parameters rollout. Change the type to Disc, and gradually increase the Radius spinner to about 70. Be sure to notice the blue circle around the light in one of the viewports as you work the spinner. This is a good way to eyeball the size of the area light when you build your own scenes. Set the Samples in both U and V to 10. In the Shadow Parameters rollout, set the Density spinner to 0.5.

When you test-render, you should see a big difference in the Ray Traced shadow being cast by the diamond. The area light has provided a realistic soft shadow (**Figure 20.42**). Next, we open the Render dialog to do our setup.

Note

You need to be careful where you point light sources when rendering with mental ray. If a light is pointed off into space with nothing to stop the photons, an error will result. If you absolutely have to point your light this way, the best thing to do is surround your scene with a large sphere with the normals reversed. This will catch any stray photons and also allow your scene to render faster.

Figure 20.42   The diamond casts a soft shadow. Time: 41 seconds. (diamond04.jpg on the DVD.)

8. Open the Render Scene dialog and go to the Indirect Illumination panel. Click the Enable box in the Caustics section.

If you were to try to render, you would get an error message saying that there aren't any caustic generators in the scene. The generators are assigned on an object-by-object basis.

9. Click the light, and Control-click the diamond. Right-click to bring up the Quad menus, and select Properties from the lower right.

10. Go to the mental ray panel and click on Generate Caustics; make sure that both Global Illumination check boxes are checked (**Figure 20.43**).

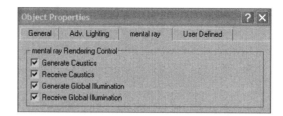

Figure 20.43 Turning on caustic generation for the diamond and the light.

11. Back in the Indirect Illumination panel, click the Enable box in the Global Illumination area. Next, scroll to the bottom of the rollout to the Light Properties area. Increase the Global Energy Multiplier value to 10, and reduce the Decay to 1.5.

Now the rendering really shines, with the generated caustics kicking the refracted light out of the diamond. mental ray did a separate photon emission pass before rendering to figure out the GI and caustics (**Figure 20.44**).

We can take this image still further. Using Final Gather will bring in some color bleed from the sunset environment and add details into the caustics.

Figure 20.44 The diamond is spectacular now, with the caustics rendering. Time: 1 minute, 24 seconds. (diamond05.jpg on the DVD.)

 Note

mental ray doesn't respect the Exclude option in lights when it comes to photons. If you try to Exclude a lightbulb from the light source inside it, no photons will be cast and an error will result. This doesn't affect the lighting in the scene at all; it can be tricky to troubleshoot.

12. In the lower half of the Indirect Illumination panel, check the Enable box in Final Gather. Reset the Samples to 100. In the Trace Depth area, set Max Reflections and Max Refractions to 12. Render out the final image.

You can look at the file diamondFinished.max from the DVD if you have had any problems with your version of the setup (**Figure 20.45**).

Figure 20.45   Additional fine details have shown up in the refractions and caustics of the diamond rendering. Time: 1 minute, 22 seconds. (diamond06.jpg on the DVD.)

Much of the power of mental ray can be unlocked through careful experimentation. We've only scratched the surface of the possibilities of this pro-grade rendering solution. The stillLifeMR.max file is on the DVD to aid in your exploration.

Additional mental ray Information

Tutorials can be found at 3dRender.com (www.3drender.com/ref/mr.htm). Many of these deal with using Maya or Softimage XSI as the genesis for mental ray, so some translation work to 3ds max is in order.

Available from Amazon.com or through special order is *Rendering with Mental Ray*, 2nd Edition, by Thomas Driemeyer (Springer Verlag, 2001). Thomas Driemeyer was the project leader for the development of mental ray, a fitting author for this general introduction to the program. He gives step-by-step tutorials for unleashing the magic of mental ray, along with tips, tricks, and solutions. The book contains a comprehensive discussion of mental ray's scene-description language and shader libraries. Be sure to specify the second edition, as it covers the additions that were included with the release of version 3.

Taking Your Exercises Farther

- **Light Tracer**: Try using the city.max scene (from the previous chapter) to work on getting the feel for outdoor lighting. If you added a Volume Fog, all the better; you can make one scene sunny and another completely overcast. Bonus points to animate between the two!

- **Ink 'n Paint**: Try a toon-shaded version of the city.max scene. You'll have to adjust the line weights, based on the distance from the camera, to avoid the line "clogging up" the painted areas.

- **mental ray**: Another area where mental ray is superior to the scanline renderer is in reflective/refractive caustics, such as light interacting with water. An excellent tutorial based on a swimming pool has been included with 3ds max 7, which will help you to understand how to use this effect.

Summing Up

In the last two chapters, we've covered a multitude of ways to get your scene out of wireframe and onto the silver screen. Yet, as they say in the infomercials, "But wait, there's more!" Adding sweet effects after the rendering process and integrating your files into the production are necessary to finish your project. We'll be covering those topics in the next chapter.

Chapter 21

Compositing

by Doug Barnard

The rendering of 3D art and animations is but a part of the larger production; sometimes a very small part. Being able to pass along elements of a rendering to a compositor is key to streamlining a workflow. Even when compositing might seem unnecessary, it can reduce the rendering time on large scenes and add flexibility at the end of the production process.

Certain effects, such as glowing lights, cannot be added during a render. They must be added to the scene in a separate pass after the main rendering is completed. There are two ways to do this: through Video Post or in the Effects panel. The Video Post utility within 3ds max can also be used for overlays, switching cameras, and many other handy functions. As the procedure is pretty much the same for the effects seen in **Figure 21.1**, they will be covered as Video Post effects only.

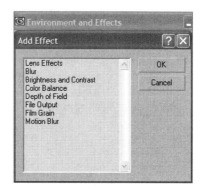

Figure 21.1   Postrendering effects that are the same in both the Effects panel and Video Post.

The Basics

Let's go over a few of the key definitions in compositing.

- **Compositing**—The assembling of various pictorial pieces to create a complete picture. The pieces can be still images or animation; they can be added or subtracted. Typically, color correction, 2D effects, and scene-transition effects are added at this time.

- **Layers**—The various pieces to be composited, and the order in which they are stacked. It's important not to think of the process as putting together pieces of a jigsaw puzzle, but as an additive process that places the layers on top of one another.

- **Alpha Channel**—An 8-bit grayscale picture that functions like a stencil. Blurring the picture will produce a soft-edged selection.

- **Matte**—Synonymous with an alpha channel, a matte can be generated on the fly in a good compositing program. This can be done with a range of pixel colors, luminance, or a variety of attributes, depending on the software. Various operations, like color correction or making the area see-through, can then be performed.

Dealing with end-game compositing requires a shift in thinking on the part of the 3D artist. We have been trained to deliver a completed picture that pleases the eye and meets the design requirements. When working with compositors, the artist must deliver an intertwined series of components that can be modified and assembled at the end of the production process.

Render Elements

The compositor's bread-and-butter production task is color correcting and balancing. For 3D art to integrate into a scene, much subtle tweaking must be done. Being able to control the final look of the rendering in 2D form is, in many cases, not enough. Even in "real life," a shot in *Star Trek* of the USS *Enterprise* in orbit over a planet would have to be shot many times, in different lighting, and the final shot would be a composite of the various camera passes.

We don't have to do anything so complex in 3ds max 7. A simple visit to the Render Elements panel in the Render Scene dialog can get us fixed up in no time (**Figure 21.2**).

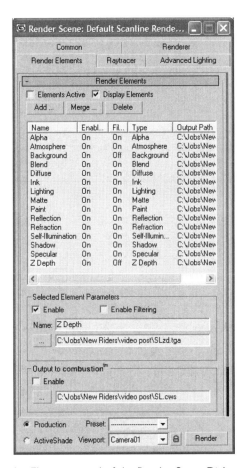

Figure 21.2   The Render Elements panel of the Render Scene Dialog.

As you can see in Figure 21.2, all the available components of the picture have been broken out into separate files. A compositor might use these to cut out the objects in the scene, to adjust the shadow color so as to fit in with the rest of the composite, and to get the specular highlights to really zing.

Next follows a brief explanation of the file types that you can render separately. First, look at **Figure 21.3**, the full rendering of the still-life. Time to render a 1280-by-960 picture using the Default Scanline Renderer: 18 minutes, 3 seconds on a 2.53 GHz machine with 1 GB of RAM.

By clicking the Add button, you can specify the additional output files that will be created when you render (**Figures 21.4** to **21.18**). Each one may be turned on and off in the Selected Element Parameters area, and the individual file location set. We have the ability to write a combustion file (see below). Finally, if there are additional parameters to be set, a rollout will appear at the bottom.

Note

You may have to scroll down in the panel to see the rollout area. It's context-sensitive, so that the appropriate info comes up when a particular Element is chosen by clicking it.

Figure 21.3   The still-life rendering. (stillLife.jpg on the DVD)

Figure 21.4   Specular: The specular element of the rendering.

Figure 21.5   Diffuse: The diffuse element of the rendering. A rollout appears at the bottom of the Render Elements panel, allowing for the addition of lighting effects.

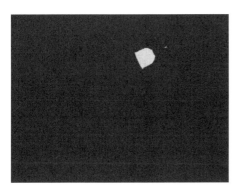

Figure 21.6   Self-Illumination: The self-illumination element of the rendering: In this case, it's the lampshade and switch.

Figure 21.7   Reflection: All the reflections in the rendering. Note that even the Ink 'n Paint material is reflected.

Figure 21.8   Refraction: All the refractions in the rendering.

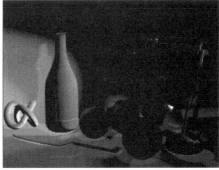

Figure 21.9   Shadow: The shadows in the rendering. Black-and-white shadows are saved only in the alpha channel.

Figure 21.10 Atmosphere: The atmospheric effects in the rendering. In this case, there were no effects, so the picture is black.

Figure 21.11 Blend: A custom combination of elements. A rollout at the bottom of the Render Elements panel allows you to choose the elements you want. In this case, Specular and Self-Illumination were chosen.

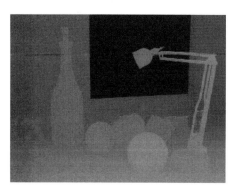

Figure 21.12 Z Depth: A grayscale representation of the depth of all objects within the scene. The nearest objects appear white or light gray, and the depth of the scene is black. It's important to set the proper Z Min and Z Max values to get the right shading. They are located in the Z Depth parameters rollout at the bottom of the Render Elements panel.

Figure 21.13 Alpha: A grayscale representation of the alpha channel, or transparency, of the scene. Transparent pixels appear black, and opaque pixels white. Translucent pixels appear gray. The darker the pixel, the more transparent it is. This would help you to composite in an object flying through the sky.

 Note

Years ago, I came up with an analogy to help me remember which color denoted transparency. Imagine a brightly lit room with white walls, and a window looking out into the darkest night. The walls are solid, of course, and the black night air is transparent. The reverse of this (black solid walls and only white light) would be almost impossible to pull off.

Figure 21.14   Background: The background of the scene. None of the Render Elements exports the Background, so this could be handy.

Figure 21.15   Ink: The Ink component (borders) of Ink 'n Paint materials. Note that this was reversed, and the alpha channel used, as the Ink was represented by black.

Figure 21.16   Paint: The Paint component (surfaces) of Ink 'n Paint materials.

Figure 21.17   Lighting: The effect of lights and shadows in the scene. Great for changing the gamma, or ratio of dark to light.

Figure 21.18   Matte: Renders a matte mask, based on Effect or Object IDs, or G-Buffer channels, or selected objects. An excellent way to cut out a mask for individual objects or materials. In the rendering, the crystal ball was given an Object ID of 2.

It's kind of a hassle to write out all those different files, then load them up individually in your compositor. Render Elements has the ability to save all of them together as a combustion .cws file, with all of the channels ready to go (**Figure 21.19**).

Figure 21.19   A full Render Elements composite as seen in discreet combustion 3.

As you might gather, rendering out every element is cumbersome. In the case of a long sequence, it's even more impractical. A good strategy would be to use an Element for a particular fix, and just render that channel. If you wanted to add a soft focus to the background, you would want a Z Depth element loaded with your main image file.

An easy way to do this is to save your rendering as a series of numbered .rla or .rpf files. The parameters are accessed when you specify the format in the Render Output File dialog. Of particular note is the .rpf format, which allows you to save Velocity and Transparency information; you must use discreet combustion to be able to take advantage of these channels.

Composition Strategies

Even when high-end compositing hasn't been specified into the production pipeline, it can sometimes be a real boon to the entire process. For simple scenes there isn't much benefit, but complex shots can make the following approach shine.

The basic idea is simple: *Render in layers according to the distance from the camera.* The background might be a layer. The midground, characters, and props could all have their own separate rendering file. Note that these groupings are different from the layers in 3ds max itself; however, layers can be a great organizational tool.

So why do this?

- **Key decisions haven't been made**—The director is waffling over whether the character should wear a hat or not. Should the jet fly overhead now, or a few scenes later? Rendering what you have right now gets you ahead of the foot-draggers in the production.

- **You don't particularly trust the decision that was made**—The script calls for a minute-long pan over the battle scene. You know that this is a dumb idea and will be cut later. A fast rendering of a simplified version of the scene can be a shortcut around hours of wasted work.

- **Maximum flexibility at the end of the project**—A few variations can be rendered separately and gracefully combined with graphics or overlays in the compositing program. Not having to render everything at once frees up the artists to experiment. In the case of large productions, end-game assembly can ensure a consistent look and feel between scenes from different artists.

- **Quicker production throughput**—Take heed of the examples of animation pioneers like Hanna-Barbera; develop a style with limited camera movement so that you can render out a static background and composite characters and midground objects on top of it. If your scene takes place in a dense forest, this tip can be a real lifesaver!

Matte Material and the Exclusion of Objects

In the next exercise, we're going to try a fast "in-camera" composite using a static background. In this scene of the fictitious production *Alien Spring Break*, space aliens looking for some fun zoom over famous Duval Street in Key West, Florida. If we were to simply render the spaceship onto the image, it wouldn't seem to emerge from behind the buildings. Also, we want to cast an ominous shadow from the saucer that tracks over the cars and buildings. To accomplish this, we'll use the Matte/Shadow material in conjunction with stand-in objects.

1. Open the file called DuvalSt.max on the DVD. From the File menu, choose Save As, point to an appropriate subdirectory on your hard drive, and click the plus-sign button to save a new file with the name incremented to DuvalSt01.max.

2. From the Rendering menu, select Environment. Click the None button under Environment Map, and in the Material/Map Browser, select Bitmap. Navigate to the same location as the 3ds max file that you just opened, and select duvalSt.tga. Once the file has loaded, close the Environment and Effects dialog (**Figure 21.20**).

Figure 21.20   Selecting an Environment Map for the background.

 Note

> You might take a minute to examine the Duval Street image. Photoshop was used to remove all the people in the shot and to add brake lights to the car. Selective cropping removed a waving flag on top of the building. One of the secrets to using static shots is to make sure there aren't any objects that would suggest movement. An alpha channel was also cut in to allow the sky to be replaced.

3. Now that we have the background for the rendering, let's use it in the viewport to aid our scene construction. Click in the Perspective viewport. From the Views menu, select Viewport Background. Click the Use Environment Background and

the Display Background check boxes, then close the dialog. The Duval Street picture appears in the viewport (**Figure 21.21**).

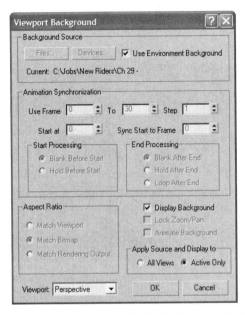

Figure 21.21   Setting up the Environment Map in the Viewport Background dialog.

Choose Render. In the Output Size section of the dialog, select "NTSC DV (video)" from the drop-down menu. The width changes to 720 by 480, in digital video format.

4. Right-click the Perspective viewport's title, and select Show Safe Frame. Right-click again and turn off Show Grid by selecting it. Our background is now lined up with the way the Environment will render. Close the Render Scene dialog.

5. Right-click inside a viewport, and from the upper-right quadrant of the menu, select Unhide by Name. You want to unhide Camera01 and its target. In the Perspective viewport, press C, the hot key to switch to the Camera view.

6. From the Create panel, select Geometry, and in the Top viewport create a plane that's about 630 pixels in length and 720 in width. The Length and Width Segs value should be set to 8. Maneuver the Plane object until the lines in the plane match the curb lines in the Camera01 viewport. You will have to move it down a bit and center the segment lines. Once you get a feel for this, you can use your plane, or unhide the ground object (Plane01). Your project should look like **Figure 21.22**.

Figure 21.22   The ground plane aligned with the camera and the background.

 Tip

> By using this prepared file, you can get a taste for how the process works. There's nothing like trying it on your own from a blank viewport, however. Don't be afraid to experiment with pushing and pulling the objects around to get the right lineup.

7. Still in the Camera01 viewport, you'll now build a box as a shadow-receiving object for the main building. Starting from behind the parked van, draw a box that approximates the size of the building. Use the Move tool to get it into position, and adjust the dimensions so that the far edge matches the building by reaching up to the same height. In this case, the dimensions are Length, 333; Width, 600; and Height, 508.

Figure 21.23 shows how the front edge of the building doesn't align with the corner of the building closest to the camera. It's difficult to get an exact match between a virtual camera and an actual one. The Camera Match utility requires exact measurements, which are almost impossible with buildings such as these. In this case, we'll cheat.

Figure 21.23 More editing needs to be done on the Box object to get a good match to the building.

8. Right-click the Box object, and from the Quad menu, use Convert To to make it into an Editable Mesh. Click the Zoom Extents All button to get all the viewports centered.

9. With the Box selected, go into Vertex mode. In the Right viewport, select the upper-left set of vertices by dragging a selection rectangle around them. Move them toward the camera in the Y axis until the vertices are parallel to the front line of the building in the Camera viewport. Select the lower set of vertices and adjust them as well, until your model matches the one in **Figure 21.24**.

You can practice on your own, building stand-ins for the buildings, trees, and cars. If you're having problems, don't worry, as these models have been provided for you, hidden in the scene. Don't bother with the large tree on the left, as it is too complex. Remember that this will be a quick two-second shot, so don't go overboard with detail.

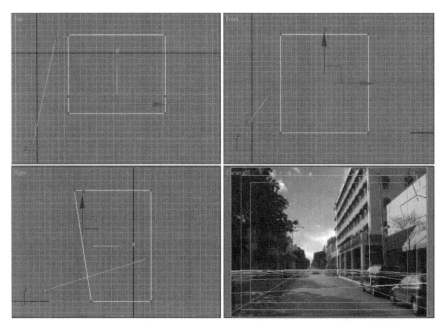

Figure 21.24   The front edge of the building now matches the background, thanks to some simple vertex editing.

10. When you are ready to continue, choose "landscape" from the Named Selection Sets (**Figure 21.25**). Click the Yes button when the dialog comes up, asking if you wish the selection to be Unhidden. Do the same for the "ship" selection in the Named Selection Sets. Now, all of the necessary geometry is in place. You can use either your creations, or the ones provided.

Figure 21.25   Using the Named Selection Set menu.

Along with the geometry, two direct lights have also been added to the scene. The settings for the upper light are at the default values, except that Shadow Map shadows have been enabled. The light was positioned with the stand-in geometry. During experimental renders, the light was moved until the cast shadows matched the ones in the background. The lower light is positioned to give only the underside of the spaceship some light.

11. If you do a test render, your scene should look something like **Figure 21.26**. The shadows cast in the street look fairly close to the ones in the background. A test rendering at frame 32 shows the saucer in place, also casting a shadow. We need to change the material so that only the shadows are visible in the scene.

Figure 21.26   The shadow-receiving geometry in place, ready for the Matte/Shadow material.

12. Press the M key to open the Material Editor. Select the first material slot, and click the Standard button. From the Material/Map Browser dialog, change the material type to Matte/Shadow (**Figure 21.27**).

13. From the Named Selection Sets drop-down menu, select "landscape." Assign the Matte/Shadow material to the entire selection.

14. If you test-render frame 32, you can see that the shadows are a bit too dark. Going into the Material Editor, in the Matte/Shadow Basic Parameters, and increasing the Shadow Brightness to 0.2 will put the shadows more in line with the existing ones in the background.

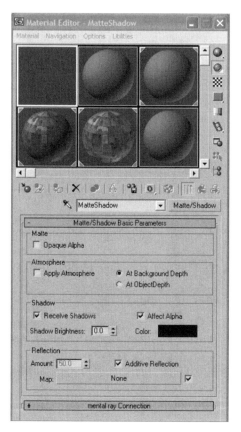

Figure 21.27 The Material Type has been changed to Matte/Shadow.

The matte part of Matte/Shadow material acts like a "hole," hiding any geometry behind it. You can see straight through to the background. By making sure that the Receive Shadows box is checked, you allow only the cast shadow component to render. If you click the small black-and-white circle in the top of the Render Frame Window, you can see that the alpha channel looks like **Figure 21.28**.

15. All that's left to do is to render the animation. In the Common panel of the Render Scene dialog, click the Active Time Segment radio button in the Time Output section. In the Output Size section, set the Width value to 360 and Height to 240. Enter a filename and location, and render an .avi file to check it against DuvalSt.avi. You can also examine the DuvalStFinished.max file if you discover any unexpected errors (**Figure 21.29**).

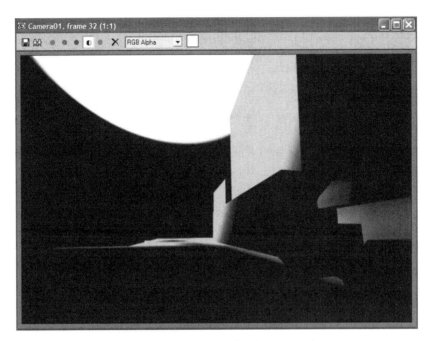

Figure 21.28   The alpha channel of the Matte/Shadow material.

Figure 21.29   Alien spacecraft composited into place.

Note

If you plan to composite 3ds max objects in another program such as discreet combustion or Adobe Photoshop, render the objects against a black background. Otherwise, a fringe of environment or background color can appear around the 3ds max objects.

This exercise shows the utility of the Matte/Shadow material. It is also nice to use with product shots that simulate a seamless background. A small ground plane can be used, just big enough to hold the cast shadow. The resulting image can then be rendered onto a background or pasted in with an image editor like Photoshop. If you save your image as a 32-bit Targa file, an excellent Pre-Multiplied alpha channel will go along with the image. Your choice of background is important; it should be either solid black or a mottled "camouflage," as rendering against light colors can leave a glowing fringe.

If you watch the DuvalSt.avi animation a few times, you can see that the shadow effect isn't particularly accurate. In the middle of a set of rapid scene cuts, it would probably be OK. A better way would be to render the elements separately and let a compositor put them together in a program like combustion or Adobe After Effects.

You would want to provide your compositor with the following files:

- **The Duval St. background plate**—This file should also have an alpha channel that has just the sky area selected, as in duvalSt.tga.

- **The saucer animation**—Only the saucer shows. The rest of the scene is hidden, except the Environment. It's a good policy to keep the Environment on to minimize any haloing that might happen on a white background through the edge of the alpha channel. The animation should be a series of numbered 32-bit Targa files, in their own directory.

- **The shadow pass on the landscape**—Also a series of 32-bit Targa files that are primarily useful for their alpha channel. By linking a Matte/Shadow plane (such as the hidden Plane02) to the saucer, and rotating it so that it hides the saucer, you can make it invisible. The animation will render so that only the shadows show. An example has been included on the DVD: the completed 3ds max file, DuvalStFinished.max. You should try unhiding this plane and experimenting on your own to get this effect (**Figure 21.30**).

Figure 21.30   A 3D view of the layers submitted to the compositor in combustion.

The compositor can stack the sets of images together and then clean up the effect. By adding a second instance of the background, and using the alpha channel provided, he can matte out the saucer as it flies by the tree to the left. As you can see in **Figure 21.31**, this will make the saucer appear to fly over the tree, increasing the perception of size.

Figure 21.31   A compositor has changed the perception of the saucer and the trees.

Video Post

With all of this discussion about compositors, don't be dismayed if you think that you don't have access to one. There's a solution right inside 3ds max itself! Video Post will not only handle postprocessing effects and composition but will manage the render for you as well. This unification allows you to skip the step of rendering the file beforehand.

That's the good news; the bad news is that these tools aren't really industrial strength when it comes to production. You shouldn't try to do the editor's or the compositor's job; concentrate on your own, which is getting the pretty pictures to come alive. Even if you are the only one involved, it's much better to use dedicated software for editing and compositing. The quality of your work will improve, as well as your peace of mind.

Video Post is accessed by selecting it from the Rendering menu. It comprises two main parts: the Queue, on the left, and the timeline, on the right (**Figure 21.32**). The timeline has range bars to specify when the Queue entry will be added into the mix. For a given frame, Video Post goes down the Queue list and, if an entry is in range, processes it.

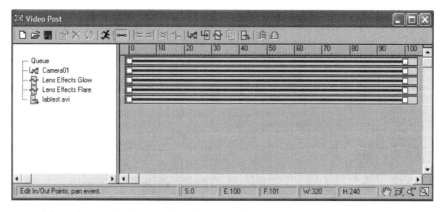

Figure 21.32   A completed Video Post Queue, ready to render.

Let's go over the Video Post components:

New Sequence—This button wipes the Queue clean and allows you to start over.

Open Sequence—This button allows you to open a saved Queue. Great for experimenting with different effects and Video Post methods.

Save Sequence—This button saves a Queue as a .vpx file. It's probably better when experimenting with different effects settings to save your scene as a separate .max file, however, as you will probably make changes to your scene in areas other than just the VP Queue.

Edit Current Event—This button accesses the Edit dialog for the selected event, allowing you to make changes to its attributes.

Delete Current Event—This button removes the entry from the Queue. There is a warning dialog to help avoid erroneous deletions.

Swap Events—This button reorders two selected Queue entries.

Execute Sequence—This button starts the Video Post rendering process.

Edit Range Bar—This switch allows for editing of the range bars; it's typically always on.

Align Selected Left—This button aligns multiple ranges from the left; each range stays the same length as it was before.

Align Selected Right—This button aligns multiple ranges to the right; each range stays the same length as it was before.

Make Selected Same Size—This button aligns multiple ranges both left and right; the ranges all change length to equal the first Queue entry.

Abut Selected—This button moves the lower range so that it starts immediately after the upper range. An excellent tool to use for switching cameras during rendering.

Add Scene Event—This button adds a rendering sequence from within the project. The rendering can be made from either a viewport or a camera, but it's best to stick with the latter, as a viewport can always change.

Add Image Input Event—This button adds an exterior file, animation, or sequence. Another way to render over an animation or to add titles to a rendering.

Add Image Filter Event—The fun part of Video Post; here's where you add all the effects.

Add Image Layer Event—This button gives you the following menu of ways to combine layers:

- **Adobe Premiere Transition Filter**—Uses the set of Premiere filters, if you have the software installed on your system.

- **Alpha Compositor**—Adds the top image to the bottom, cutting around the top's alpha channel. Note that this doesn't apply an overlay but carries out an additive process. The gain of the final image is very bright.

- **Cross Fade Transition**—Fades from one image to the next.

- **Pseudo Alpha**—Attempts to make an alpha channel composite out of the luminance of the top image.

- **Simple Additive Compositor**—Adds one image to the other in an unpredictable manner that you probably won't like.

- **Simple Wipe**—A scene transition horizontal wipe à la Premiere.

Note

You might have guessed by now that these last effects are not among the author's favorites. They are legacy code from the old 3D Studio DOS days, they can be very frustrating to use. They also don't work well with files from Photoshop, especially the alpha channels.

Add Image Output Event—This button adds the final entry in any Queue, the output to a file. Without it, the sequence renders only to RAM and the Rendered Frame Window.

Add External Event—This button adds external code to an event, executes a batch file, or copies to and from the Clipboard.

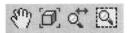 **Add Loop Event**—This button adds a loop or ping-pong action to a parent event. You could use it to cause a short animation overlay to repeat itself for the length of the render.

Standard 3ds max window tools—The controls on the bottom of the window are the standard 3ds max window controls: Pan, Zoom Extents, Zoom Time, and Zoom Region.

All these tools can be powerfully combined to get great effects for your 3ds max 7 renders. In particular, glowing effects—which are applied as image filter events—provide for rewarding eye candy.

Adding Filters

The scene is set: an exterior shot of the mad doctor's lair, on a dark and stormy night. But wait—as you can see from **Figure 21.33**, the light coming out of the windows doesn't convey unspeakably horrible experiments; it looks more like a candlelit dinner with an alluring assistant. The following exercise shows how we can use Video Post filters to give the windows an eerie glow and handle other glowing objects (**Figure 21.34**).

1. Open the file called lab01.max on the DVD. From the File menu, choose Save As, point to an appropriate subdirectory on your hard drive, and click the plus-sign button to save a new file with the name incremented to lab02.max.

2. Press the M key to bring up the Material Editor. Select "glass" from the list of materials. Click and drag down the Material Effects Channel button (the small 0 just under the material swatches). You have a choice of 16 channels; set the number to 1 (**Figure 21.35**).

 Note

At this time, all instances of the glass material will be assigned Material Effects Channel 1. That is, anytime we wish to access the same effect in Video Post, we must assign the object this material. There is a meteor streaking by in the background that we don't really want to be a glass object. We'll assign an ID in a different fashion, by Object ID, in the next step.

Figure 21.33   An exterior of the lab without the Lens Effects Glow filter.

Figure 21.34   The lab now has a menacing glow coming out of the windows.

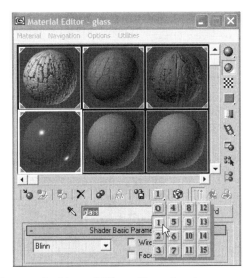

Figure 21.35   Changing the Material Effects Channel to 1.

3. Using the Select by Name tool, choose the meteor object. It's a tiny object out at the edge of the scene, and out of frame of the Camera view (**Figure 21.36**).

Figure 21.36   The meteor object has been selected.

4. From the Edit menu, select Object Properties. Another way of getting the Object Properties dialog is to right-click in the viewport and then to select Properties from the menu.

5. Change the G-Buffer Object Channel setting to 2, and click OK (**Figure 21.37**).

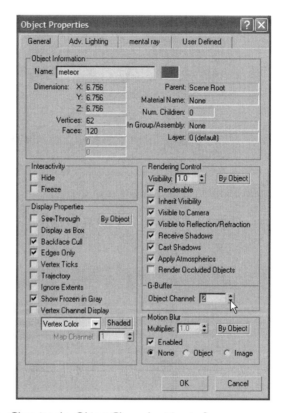

Figure 21.37   Changing the Object Channel setting to 2.

 Note

It doesn't make any difference whether you use the Material Effects channel or the object channel; the effect will be the same. Personally, I tend to use the Material Effects channel, as it is easier to find all the instances of an effect for global changes. You wouldn't want to have to individually change every firefly in a swamp scene!

6. From the Rendering menu, select Video Post. Click the Add Scene Event button (the strange cyan "teapot" icon in the Video Post's upper toolbar). Leave the settings where they are, and click OK (**Figure 21.38**).

7. We can see only the first 30 frames or so. To be able to see the entire range, click the Zoom Extents button in the Video Post's lower toolbar.

Note

Notice that the scene event (Camera01) runs for the entire 100 frames of our animation. It is of vital importance that this parameter be checked prior to the final rendering. If you increase the length of the animation, the scene event will not automatically extend with it. It will be like trying to shoot film with the camera turned off.

Add Scene Event button

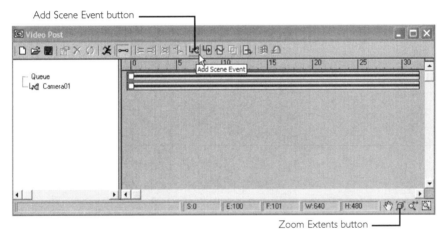

Zoom Extents button

Figure 21.38   Adding a scene event.

8. Click the Add Image Filter Event button to bring up the Add Image Filter Event dialog (**Figure 21.39**). From the Filter Plug-In drop-down menu, select Lens Effects Glow. Click OK (**Figure 21.40**).

9. Making sure that you haven't selected any of the Queue entries, click the Add Image Output Event button. In the Image File section, click the Files button. Save your file as labtest.avi in an appropriate folder on your hard drive. The default Cinepak codec will be fine for this exercise. Keep clicking OK to close the dialogs until you are back in Video Post.

10. Double-click the Lens Effects Glow entry in the Queue. Click the Setup button. The Lens Effects Glow dialog appears. Click Preview, then VP Queue. After a pause, the scene appears in the Preview window.

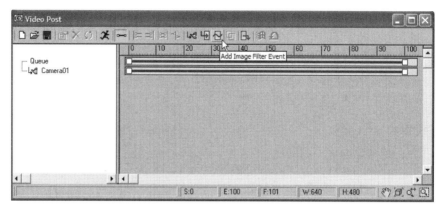

Figure 21.39   Adding an image filter event.

Figure 21.40   The Lens Effects Glow filter selected.

11. Change the Object ID setting to 2, and check the box in front of Effects ID (it should read 1). A slight glow will appear in the windows (**Figure 21.41**).

12. Click the Preferences tab. In the dialog, set the Size at 2 and press the Tab key. It may seem contradictory, but lowering the glow size makes the effect more pronounced. The windows now have a suitably evil glow.

13. Leaving the dialog open, advance to frame 37. When the scene updates, you will find that your meteor, which is now in frame, is too dim to see. Lens Effects Glow isn't powerful enough to light it properly. Click OK to close the dialog.

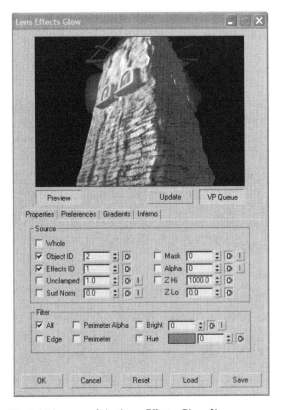

Figure 21.41 The initial setup of the Lens Effects Glow filter.

 Note

> When lens flare filters were first developed, they were overused to the point of being ridiculous. As quickly as they were adopted, they were shunned. Used properly (and tastefully), they are a powerful tool, lending a sort of "super glow." If a bright light like car headlights or a flashlight shines directly into the camera, consider the much-maligned lens flare.

14. Making sure that nothing in the Queue is selected, add another image filter event. This time, select Lens Effects Flare from the drop-down menu. Click OK, and drag the Flare up the Queue one slot, so that it is below the Glow filter.

15. Double-click the Flare filter, and click Setup to open the Lens Effects Flare dialog. Click the Preview and VP Queue buttons. Initially, the flare shows up, then disappears after the scene renders. Click Node Sources, then select "meteor" from the list. Click Update to see the changes.

16. We just want a small meteor, not Armageddon, so change Size to 22 and Intensity to 44, and clear the Streak check box in the Render column, near the bottom of the dialog. The meteor shrinks to a more appropriate size (**Figure 21.42**). Click OK to close the dialog.

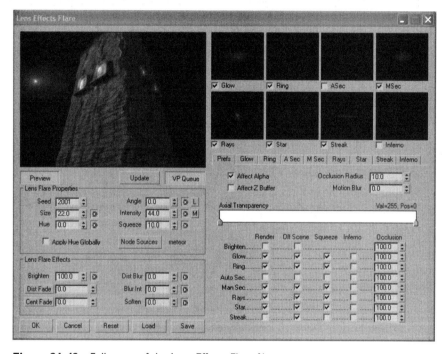

Figure 21.42   Full setup of the Lens Effects Flare filter.

17. Your Queue should look like **Figure 21.43**. Click the small running man icon to start the rendering process. Make sure that 0–100 Range is selected, and set Output Size to 320 X 240. Click the Render button, and your file should start rendering shortly.

You can check your work with the lab01finished.max file on the DVD, and view the labtest animation there, as well.

Note

> Notice that as the file renders, a separate pass is made for each filter. Sometimes, filters can interfere with one another, giving undesired results. Juggling them around in the Queue can sometimes help this problem.

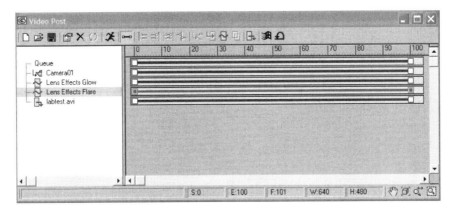

Figure 21.43   The completed Video Post Queue, ready to render.

These filters operate on the intensity of the rendered pixels, not the materials attached to the geometry. If you open labtestLightning.avi from the DVD and look at the window glow during the lightning strike, you can see that the effect is way amplified. Glow intensities, like most parameters in 3ds max, can be animated in the Dope Sheet. A resourceful animator could make the glow lessen when the lightning strikes.

Now we'll temporarily digress from Video Post to cover probably the most important form of post effect: motion blur.

Motion Blur

When objects or cameras are moving in the scene, the scanline renderer is digitally sampling their positions as each frame is rendered. As is often the case, movement takes place when the "shutter" of the virtual camera is open. This movement is compensated for by a blurring in the image. Not using motion blur with your renderings will, at best, produce an unnatural-looking crispness or a stroboscopic effect. At worst, heavily pixelated surfaces will take on a seething, boiling look. A fly-by of that granite countertop will look like millions of ants at a rave party!

Adding motion blur is not without its penalties, however. Some speed hits will be experienced, depending on the type of blur used. As these slowdowns can be quite dramatic, a careful study is necessary to get an acceptable output within the time constraints of the project.

3ds max allows for the use of four types of motion blur: Object, Image, Multi-Pass, and Scene. These effects are applied in various locations throughout 3ds max 7, so let's cover them one by one.

Note

The mental ray renderer has its own form of motion blur.

Object Motion Blur

Probably the easiest of the blurs to use is the Object Motion Blur. This is strictly for objects and not for simulating camera blurs. It's best used with a fast-moving object and a still camera. While the still rendering of the jet in **Figure 21.44** looks pretty good, you can see the jittery quality of the movie if you open up MBnone.avi from the DVD. We'll fix this in the next exercise, when we add Object Motion Blur so that an individual frame looks like **Figure 21.45**.

1. Open the motion blur-object.max file from the DVD. From the File menu, choose Save As, point to an appropriate subdirectory on your hard drive, and click the plus-sign button to save a new file with the name incremented to motion blur-object02.max.

2. Select the jet, and right-click it. From the lower-right quadrant of the menu, select Properties.

Figure 21.44   A jet with no motion blur added.

3. In the lower-right Motion Blur section of the Object Properties dialog, click the Object radio button. Make sure that the Enabled check box is checked (**Figure 21.46**). Click OK to close the dialog.

4. In the Render Scene dialog, click the Renderer tab and scroll down to the Object Motion Blur section. You can leave the default settings as shown in **Figure 21.47**.

5. Go to frame 18, and do a production render (turn on the Production radio button at the bottom of the Render Scene dialog) from the Camera01 view. The jet should be nicely blurred (**Figure 21.48**).

You can also see the results of the motion blur by watching the objectMB5.avi movie from the DVD.

The controls of Object Motion Blur are fairly easy to figure out. The Samples setting controls the number of snapshots of the object. The Duration controls how long the blur lasts, and it is "center weighted" to the middle of the frame, temporally speaking. The duration subdivisions number is usually left as equal to the number of samples.

Figure 21.45   Object Motion Blur has been applied at its default settings. Samples has been set at 10, Duration (frames) at 0.5, and Duration Subdivisions at 10.

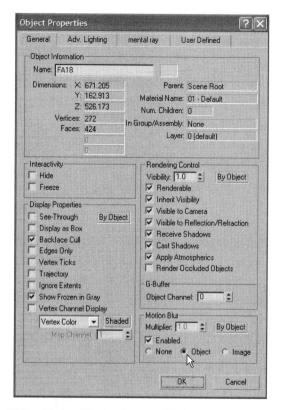

Figure 21.46 Object Motion Blur has been enabled.

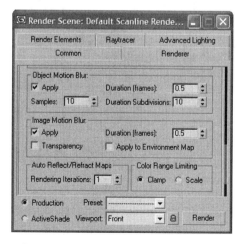

Figure 21.47 The default settings for Object Motion Blur and Image Motion Blur.

Figure 21.48   Object Motion Blur on the jet from frame 18.

The application of motion blur is much more an art than a science. Adding no blur, especially if the 3D rendering is to be composited onto live footage, won't look good at all. Adding too much can be problematic as well. If you open objectMB1.avi, you can see how increasing the duration of the blur has created a smeared effect. In some cases, this can be used to show very great speed, such as a faster-than-light superhero. With all forms of motion blurring, usually a little goes a long way.

Image Motion Blur

The real workhorse of 3ds max's motion blurs is Image Motion Blur. It's also one of discreet's favorites, as virtually the same code is used in its compositing product, combustion. You'll find that it is the blur of choice for most situations (**Figure 21.49**).

Image Motion Blur is created by applying a postrendering smearing effect, rather than by superimposing samples over one another. The blur can be applied object by object or to an entire layer. The mechanics of the process are virtually the same as with Object Motion Blur.

Figure 21.49   Image Motion Blur has been added at its default settings. Multiplier is set at 0.25, and Duration (frames) at 0.5.

Image Motion Blur has another point of superiority over its brother Object; it takes into account camera motion. Notice in **Figure 21.50** how the blur angle is quite different from the original's. This more closely resembles what would happen in real life with a camera lens. The file that created the image is motion blur-image.max, and can be set on frame 16 for a view of the jet.

The controls that operate the blur are basically Duration (found in the Renderer panel of the Render Scene dialog, the same as in Object Motion Blur) and the Multiplier (in Object Properties). The Multiplier parameter increases the smearing along the axis of combined motion. You may also choose whether the effect works through transparencies, or whether it interacts with an Environment background. If there is camera movement, you should definitely check the Apply to Environment Map box.

Multi-Pass Motion Blur

This next blur takes place by means of the camera. The entire scene is rendered multiple times, and the results composited. It, and Scene Motion Blur, are the most time-intensive solutions (**Figure 21.51**).

Figure 21.50   The Image Motion Blur settings are the same as in the previous image; however, this time the camera has been animated in an up-down move.

Figure 21.51   The Multi-Pass Motion Blur, with Total Passes at 5, Duration (frames) at 0.5, Bias at 0.5, Dither Strength at 1.0, and Tile Size at 32.

Note

Many compositing programs, including discreet's combustion, can add pixel-based motion blur in postproduction. As it has noting to do with multiple rendering passes, it is a fairly speedy process. If you get into a time crunch, this can be a good alternative to lengthy renders.

An interesting aspect of this blurring system is that the results can be seen directly in the viewport by clicking the Preview button. The attributes of the Multi-Pass Motion Blur are accessed in the individual camera's Modify panel (**Figure 21.52**). A good way to think of this process is to imagine that the camera is taking multiple exposures; when they're added up, the amount of light in the scene must be correct. The number of exposures is specified by the number of passes. The Bias number establishes temporal weighting, either early or late in the frame; 0.5 is right in the middle. Dither Strength is how much each of the passes are blended together, and Tile Size controls how much of the image is rendered at a given time; notice that as the image is coming up, it looks somewhat checkered.

Figure 21.52   The Multi-Pass Motion Blur settings for Figure 21.51, in the camera's Modify panel.

As the application of a Multi-Pass effect is fairly straightforward, there is no exercise. A file has been provided for you to experiment with: motion blur-Multipass.max. If you go to frame 16, you can see the jet in the middle of the frame.

Scene Motion Blur

Our final entry in this tour of blurs is Scene Motion Blur, accessed in Video Post. Like Multi-Pass, this blur renders the entire scene multiple times. Though time-intensive, it is typically used with large camera moves when Image Motion Blur is impractical to use on a pre-object or layer basis. Image Motion Blur has a tough time when one blurring object passes behind another object. Scene Motion Blur is also a dramatic effect, and it is best used when you want to leave speed trails behind objects.

If you open up labNoMB.avi, you can see that the animation has a near-lethal case of the sizzles. As you can see when comparing it to labtest.avi, the camera move is the culprit. Yet it helps the scene visually and could be a great bridge into the next shot, perhaps an interior of the lab.

Excessive bump mapping, as in the labNoMB.avi example, is a sure-fire cause of sizzling. In some cases, faraway objects can sometimes almost jump up and down! Turning down the amount of bump mapping can alleviate the problem before rendering time. We'll do that, and apply a combination of blurs, to get the scene right.

1. Open the motion blur-scene.max file from the DVD. From the File menu, choose Save As, point to an appropriate subdirectory on your hard drive, and click the plus-sign button to save a new file with the name incremented to motion blur-scene01.max.

2. Select the lab's walls, then right-click them and select Properties from the lower-right Quad menu. In the Object Properties dialog, click the Enabled check box and the Image radio button in the Motion Blur section.

3. From the Rendering menu, select Video Post. You might want to try a test render so that you can get a feel for the length of time that it takes—jot down the time on a piece of scratch paper. You should verify that the animation will be saved to the proper location on your hard drive.

4. Double-click the Camera01 scene event, and in the dialog click the Scene Motion Blur check box. Set Duration to 1, Duration Subdivisions to 5, and Dither % to 20 (**Figure 21.53**). Click OK to exit the dialog.

5. Double-click the last entry in the Queue, the image output event. Change the file name to labMB.avi, and make sure that it is being saved to the proper location on your hard drive. Click OK to close the dialog.

6. Press the M key to bring up the Material Editor. In the first material slot, you will notice that the Bump Amount is set to 116. Change this to 35. Close the Material Editor.

   Let's add some stars to finish off the scene.

7. Go back into Video Post from the Rendering menu, and deselect any of the entries in the Queue. Add an image filter event, and choose Starfield from the bottom of the list.

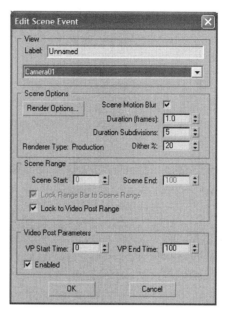

Figure 21.53   Setting up the Edit Scene Event dialog.

8. Click Setup after you have chosen Starfield. In the Stars Control dialog, leave all the settings at their defaults, or as shown in **Figure 21.54**. It's crucial that the Use check box in the Motion Blur section be selected, as without it, the Starfield will twinkle uncontrollably.

9. Drag the Starfield image filter event up in the Queue so that it is just above the labMB.avi output event. You can now render the file or open labMB.avi from the DVD to see the improved animation. Notice that a frame without motion blur took about 11 seconds to render, but now each frame takes about 32 seconds. If you're having problems, check your work against the file entitled motion blur-sceneDone.max on the DVD.

 Note

When using any motion blur, you're going to take a speed hit on your rendering times, sometimes dramatically so. This is a great opportunity to substitute simplified geometry to help get the speed back up. Because of the blurring, you'll never miss the extra detail.

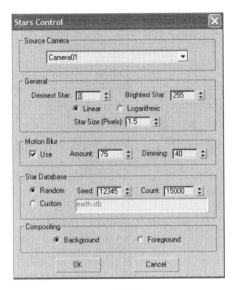

Figure 21.54   Setting up the Stars Control dialog.

There are no hard-and-fast rules about when and how to use the various motion blurs in 3ds max. The situations vary as much as the animations, and tastes vary among the many users of the software. The best way to learn is to try different blurring strategies on your own work, and find out which works the best for you.

Taking Your Exercises Farther

- **Duval Street**—You can matte out the large tree on the left to help make the saucer look bigger, as it will fly above all the trees. Import the jet fighter (used in the motion blur examples) to chase after the saucer, or animate some vehicles in the street to really sell the scene!

- **The Laboratory**—The glow effect should be lowered during the lightning strike. It will require a trip to the Dope Sheet/Curve Editor, and some drilling down through the object layers to find the Glow parameter. You would want to use a square-wave type curve so that the glow drops immediately.

- **Motion Blur**—Experiment with the settings and the frame rates of your animations to see how motion blur can be used to smooth out fast motion, or to give a dreamlike quality to a scene. Try compositing a non-motion-blurred animation on top of one that has a high degree of motion blur to see how that effect might be used. Don't hesitate to use motion blur for single-frame illustrations; it can help to convey rapid motion even in only one frame!

Summing Up

It's appropriate that this chapter concludes the book, because it's now time for you to step outside your world as a 3D artist and get involved with the rest of the production. It's easy to take a passive role and merely react to the information that the art director or your client gives you, but the quality of the production will suffer for it. By taking a proactive stance, you can head off problems and save yourself headaches down the line. Being remembered as the hero doesn't hurt when it comes time for the next hiring, either!

Here are a few suggestions:

- **Maximize your knowledge of the entire project**. Knowing what is going to be used where can bring to mind ways of streamlining that may not occur to others.

- **Become familiar with compositing software.** Even if you won't be actually touching the files in postrendering, knowing what compositors do is very helpful in figuring out how to deliver your files. The communication between 3D animation and compositing should be a two-way street.

- **Use layering on complicated renders.** If you *always* have fallback positions, your colleagues will remember you as an easy-going type who gets the job done. Pushing a production into overtime by having to rerender doesn't gain you any popularity, even if it isn't your fault.

- **Take the time to clean up your files.** Having to revisit old files to merge in a model is tougher if you're pawing through names like Object 237. Eliminating redundant tests, stand-in geometry, unrendered objects, and outdated materials (named 01-Default!) can make your life, and the lives of your colleagues, much easier.

- **Don't throw out tests and obsolete files.** There's nothing like the sinking feeling in your stomach when the art director decides that the way you did the shot last Tuesday is actually the favorite, and you have overwritten the file! Sharing tests can also help establish consistency among the artists in production.

As a final caution, always be wary of the old saying, "Don't worry, we'll fix it in post." You can help to put an end to those 11th-hour nightmare fixes that leave a bad taste in everyone's mouth by doing the best job that you can the first time around, in the most flexible manner possible.

Index

C

THIS BOOK IS SAFARI ENABLED

INCLUDES FREE 45-DAY ACCESS TO THE ONLINE EDITION

The Safari® Enabled icon on the cover of your favorite technology book means the book is available through Safari Bookshelf. When you buy this book, you get free access to the online edition for 45 days.

Safari Bookshelf is an electronic reference library that lets you easily search thousands of technical books, find code samples, download chapters, and access technical information whenever and wherever you need it.

TO GAIN 45-DAY SAFARI ENABLED ACCESS TO THIS BOOK:

- Go to **http://www.peachpit.com/safarienabled**

- Complete the brief registration form

- Enter the coupon code found in the front of this book before the Table of Contents

If you have difficulty registering on Safari Bookshelf or accessing the online edition, please e-mail customer-service@safaribooksonline.com.